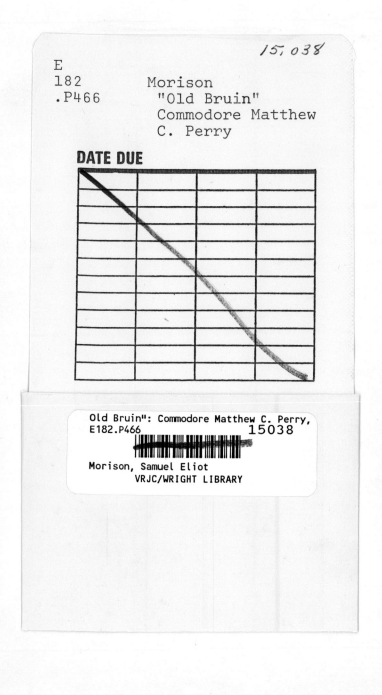

By SAMUEL ELIOT MORISON

Life and Letters of Harrison Gray Otis (1913)
The Maritime History of Massachusetts (1921, 1961)
The Oxford History of the United States (1927)
An Hour of American History (1929, 1960)
Builders of the Bay Colony (1930, 1963)
The Development of Harvard University 1868-1929 (1930)
The Founding of Harvard College (1935)
Harvard College in the Seventeenth Century (1936)
Three Centuries of Harvard (1936)
The Second Voyage of Columbus (1939)
Portuguese Voyages to America in the XV Century (1940)
Admiral of the Ocean Sea: Life of Christopher Columbus (1942)
History of United States Naval Operations in World War II,
15 vols. (1947-1962)
The Ropemakers of Plymouth (1950)
By Land and By Sea (1953)
Christopher Columbus, Mariner (1955)
The Story of the "Old Colony" of New Plymouth (1956)
The Intellectual Life of Colonial New England (1956, 1960)
Freedom in Contemporary Society (1956)
Strategy and Compromise (1958)
John Paul Jones: A Sailor's Biography (1959)
The Story of Mount Desert Island, Maine (1960)
One Boy's Boston (1962)
*The Two-Ocean War: A Short History of the United States Navy
in the Second World War* (1963)
Vistas of History (1964)
The Oxford History of the American People (1965)
Spring Tides (1965)
"Old Bruin": Commodore Matthew C. Perry 1794-1858 (1967)

(With Henry Steele Commager)
The Growth of the American Republic (Fifth Edition 1962)

(With Mauricio Obregon)
The Caribbean As Columbus Saw It (1964)

(Editor)
*Sources and Documents on the American Revolution
and Constitution* (1923, 1950)
Of Plymouth Plantation, by William Bradford (1952)
The Parkman Reader (1955)
Journals and Documents on the Voyages of Columbus (1963)

"Old Bruin"
Commodore Matthew C. Perry
1794-1858

Matthew Calbraith Perry, by William Sidney Mount, 1835

"Old Bruin"

Commodore Matthew C. Perry

1794-1858

The American Naval Officer Who Helped Found Liberia,
Hunted Pirates in the West Indies,
Practised Diplomacy with the Sultan of Turkey
And the
King of the Two Sicilies;
Commanded the Gulf Squadron in the Mexican War,
Promoted the Steam Navy and the Shell Gun,
And
Conducted the Naval Expedition Which Opened Japan

BY

SAMUEL ELIOT MORISON

An Atlantic Monthly Press Book
LITTLE, BROWN AND COMPANY · BOSTON · TORONTO

ATLANTIC–LITTLE, BROWN BOOKS
ARE PUBLISHED BY
LITTLE, BROWN AND COMPANY
IN ASSOCIATION WITH
THE ATLANTIC MONTHLY PRESS

Published simultaneously in Canada
by Little, Brown & Company (Canada) Limited

PRINTED IN THE UNITED STATES OF AMERICA

To My Beloved
Priscilla Barton Morison

Preface

ONCE more I am offering a biography of an American naval officer; but Matthew C. Perry was not one to whom the usual naval clichés apply. He was indeed courageous in battle, a taut disciplinarian, and one who conveyed his commands in so loud and gruff a voice that the sailors nicknamed him "Old Bruin." But he had a scientific rather than a salty approach to life; he was prudent rather than reckless, respectful and devout rather than irreverent and profane, even-tempered not irascible, modest not arrogant, dignified and reticent rather than hearty and outgoing, and a strong family man rather than promiscuous. Furthermore, without sacrificing any of the qualities that made him a first-rate naval tactician and strategist, he reached his greatest achievement through diplomacy rather than military force.

Perry's attitude toward the United States Navy in which he served for a few months less than half a century, may best be described by the word *commitment*. From an early age he was committed, not only to a naval career but to making the United States Navy the most efficient fighting force on the oceans, although he could never hope to see it the strongest. He was well called "father" of the steam navy, he promoted the shell gun, he worked for twenty years to establish the Naval Academy at Annapolis; and if his plans for the education and improved status of the bluejacket did not reach fruition, it was largely the fault of a tragic mutiny — the *Somers* affair. Perry's commitment to the navy did not end with internal matters. He used the navy for scientific ends — not only in the obvious fields of astronomy and hydrography, but in botany and zoölogy. Like Mahan, he regarded his chosen arm of the national defense as the first instrument of national policy, and the only one which could project his country's power abroad and enable America to achieve her "manifest destiny" to enlighten the world. He used the navy to suppress the slave trade, to advance the cause of African colonization, and promote the welfare of Liberia. To protect peaceful commerce, he helped put down piracy in the Caribbean as his father had tried to do before him. And his supreme achievement, the Japan Expedition, he conceived not as a one-sided push for trade and influence, but as the means to bring a highly civilized but rigidly secluded

people into the comity of nations. Courage of the physical type Perry did
not lack, as his gallant exploits in the Mexican War prove; but he was no
lover of fighting for its own sake. His true character shines forth in using
patience and forbearance to win a treaty from Japan without firing a shot.

In pursuance of this biography I have followed my usual method of
traveling to all parts of the world where Perry was active — with the exception (to my great regret) of the West African Coast, for lack of time
and facilities. My wife and I spent a month on the East Coast of Mexico
in 1965, examining and photographing the scenes of action of the Gulf
Squadron in 1846-1848. Similarly we spent six weeks in the Far East in
1966, visiting Hong Kong, Okinawa, the Bonin Islands, and Japanese bays,
harbors and towns where Perry had been in 1853-1854. There, with the
help of Captain Roger Pineau USNR, we turned up a rich assortment of
contemporary Japanese sources on Perry's Expedition.

I should warn the English-speaking reader that the Japanese language,
owing to its nuances, is very difficult to translate in such manner as to
convey the writer's meaning, and that no two translators will come up
with the same result; hence others may differ from the translations quoted
by me.[1] The same is true of transliterations from Japanese characters (especially the *komonjo* ancient manuscript writing and the *sosho* — grass
writing — used in the 1850's), into Roman letters. Proper names offer the
difficulty that in Japanese usage the family name comes first, the given
name second, and the title last; this has confused many Westerners — including Perry's interpreters — so that a Japanese gentleman is apt to be
referred to by his given name; and his modest title, having no precise English equivalent, has been blown up to "prince" or "lord." I have followed
Japanese usage in this respect, placing the given name, when used, in
parentheses after the family name to avoid confusion. Thus in the case of
the important personage named Ii (Naosuke) Kamon no kami, his given
name is Naosuke, his family name Ii, and Kamon no kami is his title, replaced when he became prime minister by Tairo no kami.

Deep acknowledgments are due to my beloved wife Priscilla who accompanied me on all my travels, read (or heard read to her) my successive
drafts, often supplying me with *le mot juste;* my secretary Antha E. Card
traveled all over the eastern United States on the trail of stray Perry letters, did intensive research on numerous points, and typed and retyped my
successive drafts; Captain Pineau, an accomplished Japanese scholar, now
managing editor of the Smithsonian Institution Press, interpreted for me

---

[1] Compare, for instance, Captain Pineau's translation of the old man of Shimoda's
reminiscences at head of Chapter XXIV, below, with that of Richard Lane in Oliver
Statler *The Black Ship Scroll* p. 809. They used the same text, in the *Shinri* magazine
of 2 March 1947 (also in *Izu Shimoda* for May 1965). The sense is the same, but the
words differ.

in Japan and made numerous translations; Captain Ohmae (Toshikazu), formerly of the Imperial Japanese Navy, did extensive research for me in Japanese printed books; and both captains, together with Professor Muto (Kiyoshi) of Kyushu University, translated Japanese manuscripts and extracts from printed works. And Mrs. August Belmont's Perry relationship and warm personal interest unlocked Perry manuscripts in private hands.

In the United States Navy I thank Admiral David L. McDonald, Chief of Naval Operations, who ordered Captain Pineau to active duty with me in the Far East; Rear Admiral Frank L. Johnson, Commander U. S. Naval Forces Japan, and Rear Admiral Marshall W. White, Commander Fleet Air Western Pacific, who placed aircraft at my disposition to visit Okinawa and Chichi Jima; Rear Admiral H. V. Bird, Commander Naval Forces Marianas, who cleared the way, and Lieutenant Commander D. W. Johnson, who received me at Port Lloyd; Ensign Thomas Holmes of Admiral Johnson's staff, who arranged boat trips for us in Tokyo Wan; Mr. Takemiya (Teiji) who piloted us in that Bay; Commander Philip B. Shepard, assistant naval attaché at Tokyo; Rear Admiral Ernest M. Eller and his assistants Mr. Frederick S. Hicks and Mr. Donald R. Martin, who did many things for me in Washington, and Mr. Colin J. S. Thomas of Baltimore, who took me to the old Rodgers mansion, Sion Hill. Very special thanks are due to Mr. Walter Nichols of the American Embassy for looking up private collections, arranging trips, and entertaining us in Tokyo.

Of those who lent me manuscripts, documents and prints, Mrs. August Belmont is easily first; others in this category were Mrs. Henry W. Hitzrot, the late Miss Sarah Lawrence Merrell and her executrix Mrs. Frederick Behr, Mr. and Mrs. Thaw Malin, Mrs. George Tilton, Mrs. Gouverneur Phelps, A. Perry Osborn Esq., and the Reverend DeWolf Perry, all descendants. Others, equally generous with their manuscripts, were W. Breese Welling Esq., Mrs. Ernestine Perry, Mrs. Grace Abbot Fletcher, J. Delano Hitch Esq., Mrs. Frank Lineberry, Mrs. George Warren, and Mrs. John Nicholas Brown. In Japan, Mr. Paul C. Blum and Mr. Carl H. Boehringer of Tokyo, Mr. Iwasaki (Yoshiro) of Yokosuka, and Mrs. Mori (Yoshiko) of Shimoda, private collectors, allowed me to examine and photograph their treasures.

Among others who helped us to find our way about and obtain information in Japan were William Clark Esq., U. S. Consul at Sapporo; Mr. Yoshitani (Ichiji), mayor of Hakodate; Mr. Suzuku (Saduo), former mayor of Shimoda; and Mr. L. Wesley Irwin of Okinawa; Mr. Kaneko (Shigetake) of the National Museum; Professors Kanai (Madoka) and Konishi (Shiro) of the Historiographical Institute of Tokyo; and Mr. Okta (Kenjiro) of the Yokohama Municipal Library.

In the United States, many archivists, librarians and museum directors helped me; notably, Mr. H. Bruce Fant and Mr. E. O. Parker of the National Archives, Washington; Assistant Librarian David C. Mearns, Dr. Alan M. Fern of the Prints and Photographs Division, Mr. Andrew Y. Kuroda, Head of Japanese Section, and Rear Admiral John W. McElroy of the Manuscript Division, Library of Congress; Mr. S. Dillon Ripley, Mr. Howard I. Chapelle, Dr. Philip K. Lundeberg, Mr. Samuel Suratt and Miss Anita Lonnes of the Smithsonian Institution; Miss Carolyn Jakeman of Houghton Library, Harvard; Mrs. Katharine Crane and Mr. Donald C. Gallop of Yale University Library, and Professor James F. Beard who gave me permission to use the Cooper letters there; Mrs. James Porter, Librarian of Howard University; Mr. Karl Kup of the New York Public Library; Miss Elizabeth B. Drewry of the F. D. Roosevelt Library, Hyde Park; Mr. James Heslin of the New York Historical Society; Captain Dale Mayberry of the U. S. Naval Academy Museum, Annapolis, and his assistant Mrs. Joyce L. Myers; Captain Roy C. Smith III of the Navy Yard Museum at Anacostia, Mr. R. N. Williams II, Historical Society of Pennsylvania, and Jack Pomfret of the H. E. Huntington Library; Mr. Howard P. Nash, Jr. of the Old Dartmouth Historical Society, New Bedford; Mr. John Alden of the Boston Public Library, and Mrs. Peter Bolhouse of the Newport Historical Society.

For the Mexican chapters, Mr. Albert Harkness Jr., cultural attaché of American Embassy, Mexico; vice consuls Robert Steven of Mérida and Richard T. Booth of Veracruz; Dr. Alberto Diaz Bertolini of Villahermosa; Dr. Carlos Diaz Coller of Chevy Chase, Md.; Dr. K. Jack Bauer, who allowed me to read his manuscript history of the Mexican War; Dr. Francis J. Manno of State University College at Brockport, N.Y.; Mrs. Walker E. Stewart of Carmel Valley, Calif., who allowed me to quote from Chaplain Alden's diary of U.S.S. *Delaware*. Even two of my grandsons got into the act: — Midshipman Samuel L. Morison fished up details from ships' histories in Washington, and Michael N. Morison of Hackley School visited and reported on the site of Perry's country estate in Tarrytown.

Research on Perry has not been simple because there is no *corpus* of Perry manuscripts. His widow, who became somewhat "peculiar" in her old age, started destroying all the Commodore's private letters and files; and although her daughters stopped it, they were very careless with the letters they saved. Consequently, autograph letters by and to Perry are scattered all over the United States, and it would probably have taken me another five years to run them all down. Thanks, however, to Mrs. August Belmont's valiant efforts to collect Perryana, and to the Rodgers relatives who preserved many for the Historical Society of Pennsylvania, and to hints and leads from dozens of other kind people, Miss Card and I have managed to view, copy and take notes on some two hundred letters in libraries and in private hands. Perry's official letters and reports, fortunately, are intact in the U. S. Navy division of the National Archives, Washington.

It has been a privilege, these five years past, to have lived with the surviving records of a great sailor, devoted to his country and to the cause of world fellowship.

S. E. MORISON

44 Brimmer Street, Boston
    February 1967

Contents

List of Illustrations

List of Maps, Plans and Charts

By SAMUEL HANKS BRYANT

"Old Bruin"
Commodore Matthew C. Perry
1794-1858

CHAPTER I

The Peaceful Perrys
1639 – 1775

"OLD BRUIN" the sailors nicknamed Matthew Calbraith Perry as soon as he had a command of his own, for he was a strong man who exuded authority, and (before he had a first lieutenant to do it) roared out his commands like some big mountain grizzly. He was brought up, as it were, in the United States Navy. His father, Captain Christopher Perry, fought through the War of Independence both as a soldier and a privateersman, and, though captured thrice, returned to fight again. Later he commanded a frigate in the quasi-war of 1798 with France. Matthew's eldest brother Oliver Hazard Perry, whom he adored, entered the navy well before the War of 1812 and won the Battle of Lake Erie. Matthew himself fought through that war as a midshipman. After it was over he received fascinating assignments in the Mediterranean, the Caribbean, and in African waters, suppressing pirates and the slave trade and helping the young Republic of Liberia to get on its feet. Ashore, as commandant of the Brooklyn Navy Yard, he so ardently promoted the transition from sail to steam as to be called the Father of the Steam Navy, and at the same time worked for improved lighthouses, improved naval ordnance, better methods of recruiting seamen, and an improved system of educating midshipmen. More than any other officer he was responsible for founding the Naval Academy at Annapolis. In the Mexican War he commanded the Gulf Squadron and conducted several colorful amphibious operations on the coast and up the rivers of Mexico. During all this varied service, and from the time he was thirty years old, he was ordered by his seniors to conduct diplomatic negotiations with Turks, Neapolitans and Africans, and did so with such success that when the United States government decided in 1852 to "open" Japan, it chose Matthew C. Perry to do it. That operation, conducted with finesse and firmness yet without use of force, was his crowning achievement.

But Matthew C. Perry was not merely a brave warrior and skillful diplomat. Self-educated on board ship from the age of fourteen, he became an accomplished linguist, well versed in ancient and modern literature, and a botanist and conchologist, collecting specimens of plants and rare shells wherever he sailed. His career is not without ludicrous and even comic episodes, such as sailing John Randolph of Roanoke to Russia, scuffling with a Negro chief at Little Berebee, playing off rival interpreters against each other in Okinawa, laying on spirituous banquets and minstrel shows to amuse the Japanese.

Oliver and Matthew were not the only fighting Perrys. One of their brothers commanded a ship in the Battle of Plattsburg; two others, both naval officers, died young in that service. Their sister Anna, who married Lieutenant George Washington Rodgers, had three sons who became naval officers and one an army officer, who was killed in the Mexican War. The subject of this biography had two sons who became naval officers, and a third a lieutenant in the marine corps; and his daughter, married to another Rodgers, left numerous descendants who made naval careers. No group of American families can boast such a distinguished naval record as that of the Perry-Rodgers clan.

Yet all these famous fighting Perrys are descended from peaceful Quakers. Their progenitor was Edward Perry, a Friend who emigrated from England to Sandwich, Massachusetts, about the year 1639. The utmost efforts of genealogists employed by his more affluent descendants have failed to discover who Edward's parents were or from what part of England he came, although tradition states that he was from Devonshire.

Sandwich is the mother town of Cape Cod. The Plymouth Pilgrims on their alongshore boat journeys observed a fine stand of oak indicating rich soil, and extensive salt marshes where good hay could be harvested. People moved in to farm, and their settlement became the Town of Sandwich. They organized a Congregational church, persuaded an alumnus of the University of Cambridge to be their pastor, and within a few years had created the most prosperous farming community on Cape Cod.

Edward Perry, a member of the Society of Friends, helped to organize a meeting at Sandwich. This sect began to infiltrate New England half a century before William Penn founded Pennsylvania. Despite fines, floggings, imprisonment and executions, they kept coming. It must be admitted that these early Quakers, for all their pacifist theories, were rather offensive. Edward Perry frequently appears in the records of Plymouth Colony as a troublemaker. In 1654 he was fined £5 "for unorderly proceeding, contrary to order of Court, about his marriage" with Mary Freeman. Evidently he insisted on being married by the simple Quaker ritual of clasping hands before the meeting, rather than by a magistrate, the legal New England method. The local magistrate Edmond Freeman,

Mary's father, even temporarily lost his job as councillor for "not causing Edward Perry, of Sandwidg, to bee by him orderly married." The young couple were too much for him! Nevertheless, Edward had inaugurated the Perry tradition of making an advantageous marriage. Mary Freeman belonged to one of the first families of Plymouth Colony.

Edward, given another chance to have his union with Mary made legal, declined, paid a fine of £5, and the same for every year that he remained contumacious. In 1659 he paid another twenty shillings "for using threatning speeches" to the town marshal, and "for killing a steer belonging to the countrey." Four years later he was "called to account . . . for a rayling letter which hee wrote to the Court." But the confidence of neighbors in Edward Perry is shown by his election twice as highway surveyor of Sandwich; and in 1671 the railed-at General Court named him inspector of the local "ordinary" to control drinking.

Official harassment of Quakers ceased after 1675, but two of Edward and Mary Perry's sons, who had grown up in the contentious atmosphere of Plymouth Colony, decided to remove to Rhode Island, where the Friends were officially tolerated. Benjamin, ancestor of the naval heroes, moved in 1704 to the Narragansett country on the west side of Narragansett Bay. There had already developed here a society and economy very different from those of other parts of New England. The Narragansett planters, as they were called, acquired big estates, as much as ten miles square, owned slaves (Newport then being an emporium of the African trade), and established a planter economy resembling in many respects that of tidewater Virginia. The soil on Boston Neck and Point Judith, and the lowlands bordering salt marshes, tidal rivers and ponds, proved to be excellent pasturage for horses and cattle; the upland was equally suitable for raising sheep, and sheltered coves enabled planters to ferry cattle to the thriving market town of Newport. The Narragansett planters were noted breeders of milch cows, and producers of a delicious cheddar-type cheese which they exported to other English colonies. This shore had been cleared by the Indians for a distance of eight to ten miles inland, and in their old cornfields the planters raised the maize from which white cornmeal was ground. From that meal was baked Rhode Island jonny cake, still a succulent delicacy but now almost unobtainable outside private houses.[1]

This section of Rhode Island in the eighteenth century was famous for a breed of horse known as the Narragansett pacer. In an era when there

---

[1] *Jonny* is the proper spelling; it is derived from *journey*, not John. Here is a recipe for it, from William B. Weeden *Early Rhode Island* p. 285: "The corn must be ground by fine-grained stones, which would make 'flat' meal instead of 'round.' The meal should be made into dough and spread on the middle board of a red oak barrelhead. Only walnut coals were worthy, and the crust as it browned should be basted with cream."

were few roads suitable for wheeled vehicles in the English Colonies, ladies and old gentlemen required a saddle horse with an easy gait, which the Narragansett country provided. Bred initially from the Irish hobby, a popular English pacer, they were raised on fenced-off promontories on the western shore of Narragansett Bay. Although not over 14 hands high, these horses were great "stayers," and so strong, clever, and altogether desirable as to command high prices in all English Colonies as well as in the French Antilles and Cuba. Robert Hazard raised 200 head yearly and exported them directly from South Ferry; his cousin Tom got £150 for a three-year-old in 1753 at a time when the common "plug" fetched £5 to £10. The great Edmund Burke wrote to a friend asking that he buy and ship to him in England a Narragansett pacer.

"The pleasures and pastimes of the Narragansett planters," writes their historian Miller, "were those that would be expected of men residing in the country and possessing wealth and broad acres." Horse racing, usually held on the smooth beaches adjacent to the planters' land, was the favorite sport, and Little Neck Beach was a favorite racetrack. Gentlemen who kept a few couple of hounds would combine for a meet, and chase the fox on horseback. Dr. Douglass, the crotchety Scots physician who wrote a description of the English Colonies in 1750, sneered at almost everything in New England except the Narragansett country. There, he noted, the biggest farm "milks about 110 cows, cuts about 200 load of hay, makes about 13,000 weight of cheese, besides butter; and sells off considerably in calves and fatted bullocks." As late as 1780 South Kingstown was the wealthiest township in Rhode Island, paying double the taxes of Newport and one third more than Providence. Tower Hill, from whose shore sailing ferries plied back and forth to Newport, was the "court end" of South Kingstown, with large mansions and inns. A coach passed through twice a week between the ferry terminus and New London. Guests came for dinners and dances from Newport and the neighboring plantations of Boston Neck.

Nor was this region wanting in religion. The Church of England enjoyed the greater prestige, but there was also a Quaker meeting, which the Perrys attended, especially after it moved from Tower Hill to South Kingstown in 1743. The impact of this gay, opulent, slaveholding society was unfavorable to the growth of so ascetic a sect, and the Perrys eventually moved into the Anglican communion.

This was the society to which the Perrys belonged for three generations, helping them to enhance both status and property. Benjamin Perry, after living in the Narragansett country for twenty years, lost his first wife. He then married Susanna Barber, daughter of Moses Barber, a leading citizen and large landowner of South Kingstown. Freeman Perry, third of their five children, born in 1733 and named after his Cape Cod grandfather, allied himself with another planter family by marrying in 1755 Mercy Hazard, daughter of Oliver Hazard who inherited 300 acres in North Kingstown and lived and died there. Mercy's mother was descended from Joshua Raymond, who settled at New London in 1658 and founded a family long prominent in that part of Connecticut.

Freeman Perry lived in or near the village of Matunuck on the seashore west of Point Judith. He practised medicine and surveyed lands, and during the War of Independence was appointed chief justice of the Court of Common Pleas for Washington County, which comprised the entire Narragansett country. Thereafter he was known as Judge Perry. Last of the Quaker Perrys, he continued to live at Matunuck until his death in October 1813, one month after his grandson Oliver won the Battle of Lake Erie.

CHAPTER II

Captain Christopher, the First Fighting Perry

1777–1795

THE story of the peaceful Perrys becoming one of the fightin'est families in America begins with Judge Perry's son Christopher Raymond, who not only went to war but brought in new fighting blood from Ireland. Christopher, born in 1761, broke the Quaker pattern. He himself was a young blood. At the age of fourteen or fifteen, when the War of Independence began, he defied his pacifist father by joining the Kingston Reds, an elite militia company which sported scarlet uniforms, notwithstanding the obloquy attached to redcoats. These Kingston Reds, like the Boston Cadets, the Philadelphia City Troop and other organizations more social than military, did not enlist in the Continental army en masse, but performed local guard duty and kept a keen watch on local tories and other dissidents.

Christopher became fully committed to the American cause by killing one of his father's neighbors, a Quaker farmer named Simeon Tucker, in 1777. Simeon had made no secret of his antipathy to war, especially that war; and, consistent with his religion, refused to pay war taxes or honor requisitions of food and blankets for the Continental army. The Kingston Reds decided to teach this recalcitrant citizen a lesson. A squad under Colonel Maxon marched to the Tucker farm near the village of Matunuck, dragged Simeon outdoors and presented a list of articles he was required to hand over for the army — or else. Tucker refused. Maxon then ordered his squad to level their muskets at the Quaker, and repeated the demand. The brave old farmer again refused. Maxon gave the order "Fire!" and Tucker fell dead. It was a bullet from the musket of Christopher Perry, not yet sixteen years old, that pierced his heart; all others missed. Perry then helped his fellows carry the still-warm corpse into the farmhouse and throw it at Mrs. Tucker's feet with the curt remark, "Here's your husband!"

It is understandable, as the Hazard family genealogist puts it, that Christopher "for a great many years after this was rather timid about visiting his native town."

The family theory about this deplorable affair is that Colonel Maxon, before giving the order to fire, said to his squad in a low tone, "Fire over his head!" and that Christopher did not get the word. The other theory is that young Perry heard that mitigating order but deliberately ignored it and fired to kill. This version is the more credible, as consonant with Christopher's fighting spirit and admittedly good hearing. Whatever version may be correct, the outrage stirred up the neighborhood, and not tories alone; Maxon and his men were literally run out of the Narragansett country. They were fortunate to find a boat in which they rowed to Bristol, Newport then being in British possession. Christopher, unable to return home, now walked to Boston, or perhaps to some other port still in American hands, and enlisted in a Yankee privateer, one of several called by that name. She must have made but one short and uneventful cruise, since we find Christopher in 1778 a private in the Continental army under General John Sullivan which, for want of naval coöperation, failed to recapture Newport from the enemy. His subsequent movements are difficult to untangle from the mass of later statements, rumors, and family gossip. He claimed to have been in four different British prisons during the war: at Charleston, South Carolina, Tortola in the Virgin Islands, the *Jersey* hulk at New York, and in Ireland; and to have escaped from all. But how to account for the time when he was a free fighter is a puzzle.

During the remaining four years of the war he served in two privateers and two vessels of the Continental navy. Privateering was by far the most popular war service for New Englanders. There was less discipline than in the navy, and it was much safer and more lucrative. A privateer was usually so heavily sparred that she could outsail a more powerful enemy; and capturing an unarmed or lightly armed merchantman, selling both ship and cargo in port, brought ample prize money to officers and crew. Christopher Perry, however, was not particular about the branch of service as long as it gave him a chance to fight; he shipped on the first available vessel as soon as he could escape from the prison in which his previous cruise had ended. He never received an officer's commission, not surprising in view of his youth; but whether he was a gunner, maintopman or what, in the several ships in which he served, is unknown.

His first service after his short stretch as a soldier — and as it began before General Sullivan's army was disbanded, we suspect that he deserted in order to go to sea — was in privateer *Mifflin* of Rhode Island, commanded by George Waith Babcock, one of the Perrys' neighbors in South Kingstown. Captain Babcock, a bold and enterprising man, digressed from the usual coastal and West Indies routes of privateers and, like John Paul

Jones of the Continental navy, made for the North Sea. Off Hull he preyed on the commerce of that port until the British fitted out a vessel on purpose to capture him. *Mifflin's* bottom was foul after being long at sea, and her crew had been reduced by the manning of her prizes; but she won her encounter with the Britisher by a then legitimate ruse. When the enemy ship approached and challenged him with a round shot, Captain Babcock struck his colors, then steered around the stern of the British vessel, raised his colors again and raked her fore and aft to such good purpose that he escaped. But *Mifflin* on her way home was captured by a British man-of-war and carried into Charleston, then in British possession. So this cruise ended for young Perry by imprisonment in Charleston. He escaped, made his way north, and enlisted again.

This time it was in a vessel of the Continental navy, frigate *Queen of France*, which had been purchased in Brest. She formed one of a fleet under Commodore Abraham Whipple which fitted out in Boston in the fall of 1779. Their mission was to coöperate with General Lincoln in defending Charleston from the British expeditionary force under Admiral Arbuthnot. The proud *Queen* was ignominiously scuttled in Charleston harbor in early May of 1780, to avoid being captured by the British; but Christopher Perry managed to elude the enemy. In a remarkably short time he reached New London, where the Continental frigate *Trumbull*, 28 guns, was fitting for sea under Captain James Nicholson.

Nicholson, senior captain in the Continental navy, was also its number one politician. A consistent failure as a naval officer, he organized a lobby in the Continental Congress to prevent John Paul Jones being given flag rank as a reward for his series of victories. Nicholson lost his first ship, frigate *Virginia*, with scarcely a struggle; and eventually he lost *Trumbull* too, but not until after she had fought a brisk action with British privateer *Watt* in June 1780. The two ships banged away at ranges from 80 yards down to 50 for "five glasses" — two hours and a half. At the end of that time, dismasted and disabled, they drifted apart, and under jury rig made Boston and New York respectively.

Young Christopher, too impatient to wait for the completion of *Trumbull's* repairs, signed off and took service in a privateer. We do not know the name of this ship or anything about her except that she was captured by the British off the coast of Ireland, and that Christopher found himself again a prisoner, in Newry, County Down, not far from Belfast.

Unexpectedly this proved to be pleasant and profitable, since the warden of the prison let twenty-year-old Christopher out on parole. The young Irish bucks of the neighborhood, American sympathizers, took a liking to him, and he spent most of his time in their company, hunting and drinking. Presumably anyone who had jumped horses over Narragansett stone walls was not balked by the high banks of County Down. During a drinking party at the quarters of the British military commander in Newry, two young girls burst into the room by accident and promptly retired in confusion; but not before Christopher Perry had spotted one of them — a typical Irish beauty with flashing deep blue eyes and raven-black hair — and remarked to one of his Irish pals, William B. Wallace, "There goes my future wife!" The girl, then only fourteen or fifteen years old, happened to be Wallace's cousin Sarah Wallace Alexander.

Encouraged by his Irish friends in the comfortable theory that, not being a naval officer, he was not in honor bound to respect his parole, Perry broke it. Disguised as an Irish sailor he walked all the way to Cork, and as a supposedly British subject shipped on board an English merchantman bound for St. Thomas in the neutral Danish West Indies. There he jumped ship and obtained a berth in an American vessel bound for Charleston.

By that time the war was over. Perry was now free to carry out his vow to marry Sarah Alexander. Making his way to Philadelphia, he obtained the berth of master's mate on the American ship *Favorite* bound for Dublin, Robert Alcorn master. Upon arriving at the Irish capital, he ran into a rare bit of luck. Sarah, recently left an orphan, sailed in the same vessel to Philadelphia in company with her temporary guardian, a Mr. Calbraith, and his young son Matthew. Thus Christopher Perry had a westward passage of some six weeks in which to court the girl with whom he had fallen in love at first sight. And, being a Perry, he naturally won her consent before the *Favorite* entered Philadelphia, on 2 August 1784.

But there he almost lost her. A yellow fever epidemic was raging in Philadelphia. The ship was boarded by the famous physician Dr. Benjamin Rush, bringing the sad news that a married couple named Cummings, kinsfolk of the Alexanders who had sent for Sarah to come over and live with them, were both victims of the epidemic. Before dying they had charged the Doctor to look out for the girl. She and Christopher provided the ideal solution. The young couple — Christopher not yet twenty-three years of age, and Sarah sixteen — were promptly married at Dr. Rush's house in Philadelphia. They fled from the infected city at the best speed a horse and chaise could make, and proceeded to South Kingstown, Rhode Island. There the Judge, who had not seen Christopher since the Tucker affair, welcomed him and his bride to the Perry homestead at Matunuck. Soon after, they moved into a suite in the mansion of a nearby bachelor farmer, where their eldest son Oliver Hazard Perry, named after his great-grandfather, was born in August 1785.

Christopher was not the kind of sailor who gladly went farming after a war. He had experienced "the battle and the breeze," and wanted more. No farming for him, unless as a retired gentleman of fortune; and in any case, the Narragansett planter economy, ruined by the war, never recovered. Rhode Island in the late 1780's, owing to an enormous inflation of the currency, was very depressed. There was no opening for Christopher in the mercantile line, but new ships were being built, old trade routes to the West Indies, Africa and the Mediterranean were being resumed and new ones developed to the Baltic and Far East. Perry's sea experience had been such that he had no difficulty in signing on as master of a new vessel; and as shipmasters in those days were expected to trade on the side, he accumulated a nice little property. By this time he had discarded the religion of his sires and become an Episcopalian, but the Quaker trait of shrewdness in money matters, which he inherited, stood him and his family in good stead. His descendants have followed suit. Nobody has ever heard of a really poor Perry, and the family has been consistently Episcopalian ever since.

Records of the merchant vessels that Captain Christopher commanded have not survived. It is obvious that he was long at sea, because his children's births were widely spaced. Oliver Hazard, the eldest, was born in 1785; Raymond arrived four years later; Sarah Wallace, who never married, in 1791. These were born at Wakefield in the Narragansett country. But before the next child arrived, Christopher had acquired by lease a house on "The Point," the up-and-coming residential section of Newport. There on 10 April 1794 a third son was born to Christopher and Sarah Perry. He was named Matthew Calbraith after their Irish fellow passenger, who by that time had become a prosperous merchant in Philadelphia. And he was always called Calbraith by his family and intimate friends.

On Sunday, 18 January 1795, there took place a quadruple Perry baptism in Trinity Church, Newport. Oliver, Raymond, Sarah and Matthew were christened by the rector, the Reverend William Smith.

CHAPTER III

Christopher, Oliver, and the *General Greene*

1795–1801

Newport at the Turn of the Century

"THE POINT" between Coasters Island and the main harbor was the aristocratic section of Newport in the late eighteenth century. Here the wealthy merchants built their houses; here the Marquis de Rochambeau was entertained in 1780. Christopher Raymond Perry's house, where his son Matthew Calbraith first saw the light on 10 April 1794, was on the northeast corner of Walnut and Second Streets. Freeman Perry bought it for his son's use, and deeded it to him in 1800. Even in its prime the Perry birthplace was a simple, cozy little gambrel-roofed house. It has been changed by having a new ground floor inserted in the last century to accommodate a liquor store; but a movement to restore the house to its original condition and install a Perry museum there is under way as I write.

By the time Calbraith arrived on the scene, Newport had weathered the postwar depression. He and his brothers and sisters (four more were born after him)[1] grew up in an era of burgeoning prosperity. The local merchant-shipowners were profiting from neutral trading with European belligerents, the West Indies trade, and even the African slave trade. Christopher Perry made voyages either as master or supercargo to Europe, South America and the East Indies, increasing his fortune thereby.

Newport was already the most cosmopolitan town in the United States after New York. English planters from the West Indies, including Abraham Redwood of Antigua who founded the famous Redwood Library, and others from South Carolina, began even before the Revolution to use Newport as a summer resort to escape the heats and fevers of the South. One summer before the war no fewer than three royal governors — of South Carolina, Grenada and Tobago — were rusticating there; and Newport became "Philadelphia on the Rocks" until replaced by Mount Desert

---

[1] See Appendix I.

Island. This influx brought joy to natives who had furnished houses or rooms to let, and gave rise to many little businesses. For instance, "Mary Martin, Millener and Mantua-Maker, lately arrived in NEWPORT from PARIS," advertises in the *Mercury* for 16 May 1774 that she "Makes and sells at the shop adjoining to the house of the late Capt. Teagle Taylor, ALL sorts of ladies CAPS and BONNETS. Those who will please to favor her with their custom, may depend on being served in the best manner, and have their favours gratefully acknowledged. N.B. She dresses ladies heads, for half a dollar, at the shop; if waited on, at a dollar; and washes all sorts of lace, at a reasonable rate." There were concerts of music, a dancing assembly, and visits of traveling players who were not allowed to perform in puritan Boston or other New England towns.

After the war the South Carolinians returned, and a merchant ship with the pleasant name *Rose-in-Bloom*, "fitted with elegant accommodations for passengers," plied regularly between Newport and Charleston. She brought a succession of Rutledges, Gaillards, Pinckneys, Hamiltons and Middletons who made congenial social companions for the local Federalist families. And the private schools of Newport were so good that several young sprigs of Charleston aristocracy were left there the year round, making lifelong friendships with Newport families such as Perry, Vernon, Mason and Gibbs. Oliver and Calbraith attended one of these schools, kept by a Scotsman named Frazer, who imparted to most of his pupils a sound basis in mathematics, and a taste for good literature, English and classic. But, despite the efforts of Mr. Frazer, Calbraith's spelling always remained on the salty side: a straight line, for instance, was "strait" and property about to be sold, "for sail."

Everyone who was anybody in Newport, winter or summer, voted Federalist. Only a few low fellows of the baser sort — "Jacobins" as they were called — followed Jefferson and Madison and supported revolutionary France against stable old England. So, when the depredations of French picaroons on American commerce became intolerable, and President Adams and Congress, after the insult of the X Y Z Mission, authorized a quasi-naval war against the French Republic, Rhode Island coöperated. At Warren the 124-foot frigate *General Greene*, of 32 guns, was built by contract for the United States Navy. She was appropriately named after a famous native son of the Narragansett country, General Nathanael Greene, a descendant of Edward Perry of Sandwich. The system of building and manning warships adopted during the War of Independence still prevailed; every new vessel was officered and manned by men of the region where she was built. In this instance, Christopher Perry was given complete charge of the new frigate from keel up. He not only oversaw her construction but recruited her crew, starting with the seafaring population of Narragansett Bay. Since he was well known to every shellback between Beaver Tail and Providence, that should not have been difficult; but apparently it was.

General Greene was launched 21 January 1799, Christopher Perry received his captain's commission in March, the ship was all rigged by 1 April and ready for sea but for a crew. Three weeks later she had obtained only 36 men and boys from the Bay region, and Perry was trying to get more at Boston, Salem and New London. Secretary Stoddert wrote to him, "There is the utmost necessity for your sailing without delay for the Havanna." He is immediately "to collect all his recruits, take on board 30 marines from Newport, and should then have enough to serve the ship — although her full complement is 220." Either Perry or the recruiting officers dragged their feet, for in April Stoddert sent "a peremptory order to proceed on the day you receive it, to Sea, & to the Havanna." By the end of May, Perry had 180 officers and men on board. One junior officer was his eldest son, thirteen-year-old Midshipman Oliver Hazard Perry. This cruise gave Oliver a good sample of the seamy side of naval life, as some of his fellows in the steerage were very rough characters.

Revealing as to the diet of American seamen in those days is the "estimate of provisions" for a year for a vessel of *General Greene*'s size and complement. The most expensive item is 4757 gallons of rum, at a dollar a gallon; next come 170 barrels of pork at $17, the same amount of beef at $13 a barrel, and 562 hundredweight of hardtack, at $3.33. There are fewer than 30 barrels each of wheat flour and cornmeal, and 80 hundredweight of rice. Over a thousand pounds of butter are carried at 15 cents a pound, and over eight thousand pounds of cheese, at 12 cents. The only other provisions are salt fish, potatoes (400 bushel), beans (132 bushel), vinegar (950 gallons) and molasses (670 gallons). Half these amounts, six months' supplies, were carried south by *General Greene*. One would like to know the number of different dishes that the sea cook was able to compound from these few and simple materials.

The General Greene *Gets to Sea*

Owing to a succession of head winds, it was not until 2 June 1799 that Captain Perry took the new frigate down the bay and "out South." His first instructions were to relieve U.S.S. *Delaware*, Captain Stephen Decatur, at Havana, since the terms of enlistment of her crew were about to expire, and she had many cases of yellow fever. Decatur, however, could not wait, and departed for home before *General Greene* arrived.

Captain Perry's next duty was to cruise along the north coast of Cuba in search of French armed vessels, root out a nest of French pirates who had built a fort a few miles from Matanzas, and break a blockade of American merchantmen in Nuevitas imposed by French privateers. The Secretary enjoined Perry to keep *General Greene* moving, as the best way to keep up the health and spirits of her crew, and to avoid Havana and other pestholes. Perry ignored both injunctions, to the detriment of his ship's efficiency, and his crew's health. On 18 June there broke out on board a "malignant fever" which Captain Perry ascribed to spoiled provisions and "putrid exhalations" from rotten ballast in the hold, for she had been ballasted with the shale-like rock of which stone walls are built on Aquidneck Island. No doubt the rock broke up and smelled strangely, but of course that was not the source of fever. Off the coast of Cuba more men came down with *vómito negro*, the yellow fever; ship leaked badly, and on 2 July the officers begged Captain Perry to put into Havana for relief and then return home. He did just that, embracing the opportunity to escort a convoy from Havana to Newport, where *General Greene* arrived 27 July. She had lost twenty men, and even more were treated in the hospital building which later became the nucleus of the Naval War College.

Secretary Stoddert approved Perry's prompt return, and gave orders to have the ship fumigated and to substitute iron ballast for the offensive shale. President Adams, nettled by so brief and inglorious a cruise, rightly guessed that the real cause of the epidemic was too much shore liberty in Cuba.

The Perry house at the Point having been let to summer visitors, Sarah and the children were spending the summer in a farmhouse at Tower Hill in the Narragansett country when the Captain returned. While *General Greene* refitted and sick members of her crew recovered, young Oliver joined his mother at Tower Hill. From an early biographer we have a charming picture of him and his little brothers and sisters. Raymond, now ten years old; Sarah, eight, and Matthew Calbraith, five, followed Oliver everywhere, begged for the privilege of carrying his gun or fishing rod, and rose with the dawn to pick berries with the dew still on them, for his breakfast. In turn the midshipman humored their whims, and charmed them by spinning sea yarns and playing the flute. They regarded him as the most handsome, courageous, accomplished, and altogether wonderful big brother that ever was.

Coöperating with Toussaint

On 23 September 1799 frigate *General Greene*, newly ballasted with kentledge, and with a partly fresh crew, sailed from Newport. Perry's orders were to proceed to Cape Haitien and operate under Commodore Silas Talbot in U.S.S. *Constitution*, to protect American commerce in conformity with arrangements already effected by Edward Stevens, the American consul, with the rebels of Hispaniola.

France had lost control over that richest of the Antilles. A ferocious civil war raged between Negroes and Mulattoes, while the populace starved. Toussaint L'Ouverture (Wordsworth's "most unhappy man of men"), commander of the black republican army, appealed to Philadelphia for help. President Adams's government, in agreement with that of Great Britain, decided to support Toussaint, who agreed insofar as lay in his power to suppress the French colonial privateers which were spoiling neutral commerce, and to open Cape Haitien and Port au Prince to American and British merchant ships. In return, vessels flying the tricolor, if provided with a *laissez-passer* from Toussaint, were exempted from capture by British or United States ships.

Frigates *Constitution*, *General Greene* and *Boston* operated along the north coast of Hispaniola well into the new year. Commodore Talbot on 18 January 1800 ordered Captain Perry to operate for a week in Turks Island Passage, then cruise around Hispaniola, run into the Bight of Léogane to relieve U.S.S. *Boston* on that station, and take over her duties of convoying American merchantmen to and from Port au Prince. But before *General Greene* had been operating there long, the Commodore sent him around Cape Tiburon to the south coast of Haiti to help Toussaint capture Jacmel. That was the principal port held by André Rigaud, the Mulatto leader then fighting the blacks. Rigaud had a fleet of armed barges manned by cutthroats who used the old buccaneer tactics of lying in wait close to shore for a chance to capture becalmed merchantmen. When Toussaint's army invested Jacmel, *General Greene* coöperated with the Negro liberator by blockading that port and applying naval gunfire to Rigaud's batteries. "We engaged three of Rigaud's forts warmly for 30 or 40 minutes," wrote one of Perry's officers, "in which time we obliged the enemy to evacuate the town and two of their forts, and repair to the strongest hold; this fort however soon hauled down its colours."

The correspondence between Toussaint L'Ouverture and Captain Christopher Perry has been preserved by the latter's descendants. All are copies, and Toussaint's letters are translations, made by the captain's clerk.

LIBERTY   EQUALITY
Head Quarters — Pasquet near Jackmell
3d Ventose 8th year of the french Republic [22 Feb. 1800]

Toussaint Louverture, Genl. & commander in Chief of the Island of St. Domingo

To the Commander of the United States Frigate Cruising off the South Passage.

M. the Commander:

Sir, I have the Honor to fit out a flag of truce to send you the present Letter, by which I address to you an Urgent Request and ask of your Goodness a protection that I ought to hope for against the Rebels. I have the Honor to beg of you, Sir, if it is in your power, to come so near the Bay of Jackmell that no kind of vessel whatsoever can come in without falling into your hands. I shall endeavour to acknowledge the Important Service you will render me as far as will be in my power. And I will endeavour to procure for your vessel all the fresh provision in my power either in fowels, Vegetables or any thing of that Kind. Moreover, I will give to your crew some compensation if you think it necessary. I would Even make you further offers were it not for my present Necessitous Situation, of which I am confident you are not Ignorant, and if I did not at the same time rely upon your Generosity and good will to oblige me in a Circumstance so unhappy for this Colony. I am Intirely confident of your goodness.

I will ask of you Sir another favor which is to let pass the vessels that come addressed to me. You will by that means compleat your favours & doubly oblige me. You will let them pass unmolested to come to me.

Deign to believe me thankful. If you will so far condescend as to assist my desires & Views in Blockading the Bay of Jackmell in such a manner to permit no vessel to come in, only those assigned to me.

> I have the Honor to be, Sir, with the Highest
> consideration, yr. Most obt. & Mot. Huml. Svt.
> (Signed) TOUSSAINT LOVERTURE

Captain Perry complied with the General's wishes; and, after Rigaud's garrison had cut its way out, on the night of 10-11 March, Jacmel surrendered.

The following letters, from Captain Perry to Toussaint, indicate that the *General Greene* remained in those waters for several weeks.

> United States Frigate *Gen. Greene*
> off Jackmell 11th March 1800

Sir:

I have this afternoon fell in with a french armed Schooner from St. Domingo, without the necessary passports, and as it is required, & conformably to the treaty between the United States and your Excellency, that your Commis'ers should be possessed of Passports both from your self and the American Consul General, I request you will be so good as to explain to me What this Vessel is, and by what circumstances she came here without either.

Agreably to my Instructions, she is a lawfull prise, and I shall therefore send her to Commodore Talbot off the Cape, who will Proceed with her as he may think proper, and to whom I beg leave to refer you.

It has been my intention ever since I have been upon this station to render you every Service in my power, compatible with my Instructions & the Subsisting Treaty, and it is still my Intention but at the same time, I wish Sir, to observe to you that I will not depart from the Strict principles of Honor as an officer, nor will I do any thing that might tend in the least to disgrace the Flag under which I have the honor to Command. And I doubt not but you are actuated by the same Friendly views with my self, and that you will not screen a Vessel which does not Possess the necessary Passports.

I sincerely congratulate you on the surrender of Jackmell and hope you may be equally as successful in every other attempt to suppress the Rebellion in the Colony of St. Domingo.

I have the honor to be, Sir
With the Utmost Respect
Your Obt. Servant
(Signed) CHRISTOPHER RAYMOND PERRY

The controversy over this schooner arose because she had sailed from Santo Domingo in the Spanish part of Hispaniola not under Toussaint's control, and so was not provided with his passport. Commodore Talbot ordered her to be relinquished to her owners. Perry again writes:

United States Frigate *Genl Greene*
off Jackmel 15th March 1800

Sir

This morning I send in my Boat with one of Capn. Pelot's officers to wait on you with this Letter.

I did myself the Honor of writing to you the 13th Instant stating the misrepresentations which had been made to Genl. Dessaline[1] by some of the officers of your Schooner *Department Du Nord*, which representations are gross reflections Equally on myself and my officers, and which not only tends to place my sincere endeavours to serve you in a false light, but aims a distructive blow against the peace and harmony subsisting between our two Governments, & to lessen the faith & confidence which friends ever ought to repose in each other, which I hope you never have had reason to doubt from the conduct of myself or any officers under the Government of the United States.

If I have ever been of any service to your Excellency I am highly gratified and the consciousness of having contributed in any degree to the restoration of peace and good order in the Colony of St. Domingo will be to me ample compensation. I beg leave to assure you, Sir, that I have never been actuated by any other than friendly motives, and that my Services are ever at your command, as far as is compatible with my orders from the Honbl. the Secretary of the Navy of the United States.

My Instructions make it necessary that I should leave this Station, which I shall do immediately, but Shall be succeeded by the *Boston* Frigate Commanded by George Little Esqr. to whom I shall deliver the private Signals between your Excellency, cruisers, & the United States, on the Southside of the Island. . . .

I have the Honor to be
Sir, Yr. Most Humbl/e &
Most Obt. Servt.

CHRISTOPHER R. PERRY

---

[1] Jean-Jacques Dessalines, a Negro who renewed the war against France after Toussaint had been treacherously seized, declared himself L'Empereur Jacques Ier in 1804, and was assassinated in 1806.

U. States Frigate *General Greene*
off Jacmel 16 March 1800

I am highly gratified in being honored with your two letters of the 24 and 25 of Ventose of the 8 Year of the French Republic,[1] and most cordially thank you, Sir, for the friendly and generous sentiments therein contained. I have also to offer you my most sincere Acknowledgements for the two Bullocks and other articles of refreshment, which you have been pleased to send off to me. . . .

Altho for the sake of serving you I have been upon this station untill I have very far exceeded the time allotted me by Commodore Talbot, still from a knowledge I have of his desire to assist you I will remain a few days longer and the Schooner in company with the *Gen. Greene* will act as well for the Interest of your Excellency as for the U. States.

I have the Honor to be
Sir, with much Respect & Esteem
Yr Obt. Sevt.

(Signed) C. R. PERRY

On 18 March, Toussaint wrote both to Commodore Talbot and Captain Perry, thanking them for their help, begging that it continue, and hoping to have a visit from U.S.S. *Constitution*. "I am penetrated, sir," he concludes, "with the affection and esteem that your good and generous conduct has inspired me towards you." As token of his gratitude he presented the *General Greene* with 10,000 pounds of coffee, which the Commodore thought it "improper" for Perry to have accepted. But, as the coffee bags were tossed on board the frigate just as she was departing, Perry had no way of returning them. American seamen of those days didn't like coffee (which the modern U. S. Navy can hardly believe), so Perry decided to treat this windfall as prize money. He sold the lot to a merchant at Cape Haitien for upward of $1000 and divided this according to prize regulations. He got $200 for his share, each midshipman received $30, and the enlisted men from $4 to $8 each.

After leaving Jacmel, *General Greene* silenced Rigaud's remaining forts on Cape Tiburon, patrolled around Hispaniola, and then put in at Cape Haitien. Toussaint and Dessalines repressed the Mulattoes with the utmost ferocity and cruelty, and Rigaud escaped from the island. Toussaint then carried the war into the Spanish part of Hispaniola and entered Santo Domingo in triumph on 28 January 1801. For a few brief months this miserable island enjoyed peace.

Toussaint's later capture by a French army sent to Haiti by Bonaparte, his imprisonment in an icy fortress in the Jura where he died of pneumo-

---

[1] 15 and 16 March.

nia, are outside our scope. But it is interesting that the Perrys, who grew up in an atmosphere where Negro slavery was taken for granted and even the slave trade deemed respectable, were thus early identified with efforts to help American Negroes to help themselves. Toussaint is regarded by historians of Haiti as *le premier des Noirs* — "the First of the Blacks." None of the later dictators of that unhappy republic have been his equal.

Trouble on Board

In the meantime things were pretty rough on board *General Greene*. At Newport Captain Perry had given midshipmen's warrants to four very unsavory "Long Wharf Rats," one of whom had been convicted of stealing lobsters — as serious an offense on the New England coast as horse-stealing in the West. These young ruffians pilfered ship's stores even before she sailed, brought brandy on board, slept on watch, spent much of their time quarreling and fighting, damned the ship, the officers, the navy, the secretary, and the government; even tore up a copy of the sacred Navy Regulations! Since these regulations did not allow officers to be flogged, the Captain rigged up an armchair on the quarterdeck in which warranted offenders were compelled to sit "with a board around their necks," as in an old-fashioned pillory. One, who missed his watch, was found dead drunk below, and so far gone in liquor that it was thought necessary to lay him out flat and have three or four ship's boys urinate into his mouth. The purpose of this disgusting procedure was to make the lad vomit, which he did. The court which investigated this and other doings on board the *Greene* accepted Perry's explanation that it was a therapeutic, not a correctional measure.

Commodore Talbot ordered Perry on 24 February 1800 to sail to New Orleans to pick up General Wilkinson, and, after *General Greene* reached Cape Haitien around 1 April, wrote every few days, begging him to start and asking what kept him? But Captain Perry, disregarding Secretary Stoddert's advice to keep moving (advice which his son Calbraith took to heart), could always find reasons for staying in port. He tarried at Cape Haitien until 27 April. The day before, *General Greene* received an official visit from General Toussaint, who was accorded a "federal salute" of thirteen guns. Perry paid for the delay by having to take on board seventeen sailors from *Constitution* invalided because of "old age, broken bones and long debility," to be returned to the United States; and also by having his conduct become the subject of a court of inquiry in Newport.

There was no more fighting for Captain Perry in this quasi-war, and the Wilkinson mission provided him with a pleasant interlude on the way home. The future colleague and betrayer of Aaron Burr had been sent to Louisiana, then under friendly Spanish rule, to guard against French infiltration. The following letter, written to the General from off the Passes of the Mississippi, suggests that Captain Perry was delighted to act as packet ship for him, his wife and another lady: —

> U. States Frigate *Genl. Greene*
> off the Balise May 31 1800

Sir

I was yesterday Honoured with your very Polite Letters of the 23 & 28 Instant, & beg leave to assure you that you need be under no Apprehensions of discommoding me or my Ship, for my arrangements are such that any Part will be at your command. As for Mrs. Wilkinson & her companion, my Cabin is entirely at their Service, and it shall be my study to render both your, and their, situation as agreeable, [as] a Ship of War will Admit.

The small Stores you mention, added to my Stock, I presume will be ample for the Voyage, and from your bill of good Wines, with the good Society you bring, I calculate upon an Agreeable Passage.

As you mentioned bringing down the River some Stock, from which circumstance I presume you will have a Boat appropriated entirely to that Purpose, I beg leave to suggest the conveniency of a Milch Cow [for] the use of the Ladies, as those who have been accustomed to using milk with Coffee &c cannot well relinquish it. I beg you will be pleased to purchase one on account of the Ship — she will answer to [the] Bill on our arrival at Newport. I have procured Sufficient Provender, and have now nine head of cattle on Board.

> I have the Honor to be, Sir
> With great respect,
> Your obedt. Servt.
>
> CHRIS. RAYMOND PERRY

The nine cattle mentioned in this letter were not all the livestock that *General Greene* carried. She arrived at Newport with twenty head of swine, some procured in Haiti, others at the mouth of the Mississippi, and some born at sea. In addition, Captain Perry loaded several coops full of chickens. It was not unusual for warships to carry livestock in those days; fresh beef, pork and chicken were a welcome relief from "salt horse." One midshipman testified that the Captain was generous to all hands when he slaughtered a beast, and that he furnished the sick with chicken. But the *Greene*'s spar deck must have looked and smelled like a barnyard.

With the General, Mrs. Wilkinson, her lady companion and two sons on board, Captain Perry proceeded to Havana, picked up a convoy to escort to New York, and in company with U.S.S. *Warren* sailed before the end of June. He called at Cape Henry to set the Wilkinson party ashore. The General said that he was in a hurry to reach Washington; but one suspects that the real reason was the smell, which his lady and her companion refused to stand any longer. The frigate continued to Newport, arriving 21 July 1800. She had a number of yellow fever cases on board and (reported the surgeon), "Since the arrival of the ship, three persons belonging to her have died of a fever, to which they were predisposed by excessive intemperance." Unfortunately the word got around Newport that she was a pest ship, which "excited great uneasiness in the town," made it difficult to obtain workmen for necessary repairs, and forced Captain Perry to remove her from the town dock and anchor well out in the stream.

The Navy Department was eager to send *General Greene* to sea again, but Captain Perry and his officers insisted that first she be provided with a false keel, a longer mainmast, and a new bowsprit. While these repairs were being effected, the Captain was allowed to "indulge with leave of absence" such officers as could be spared from the ship. Among them, doubtless, was Midshipman Oliver H. Perry. One can imagine the delight of six-year-old Calbraith at seeing his father and big brother again, and hearing Oliver's stories of picaroons and pirates, black generals and white.

All summer the repairing of *General Greene* dragged along. In the meantime, as a result of complaints from Commodore Talbot and the errant midshipmen, Captain Perry had to go before a naval court of inquiry convened at Newport. The first charge was his tarrying at Cape Haitien almost a month after the Commodore had ordered him to sea. Talbot himself testified that Perry's excuses were flimsy, and the court decided (13 October 1800) that *General Greene* could and should have been ready to sail in five days. The second charge related to Perry's capture off Hispaniola of Danish schooner *William and Mary*, despite the department's orders to respect neutral commerce. Perry let her go, but detained her master on board and, without a commander, she was attacked and made prize of by one of Rigaud's privateers which was hanging about. The court found that Perry should have protected the Dane against the seagoing jackal. The third charge was accepting Toussaint's coffee as a bribe. The fourth was using his ship to transport livestock to his father's farm in Narragansett. No doubt Judge Freeman Perry received any cattle that arrived alive, but the testimony that Perry shared his meat with the crew got him off that particular hook.

The most serious charge, preferred by the four rowdy midshipmen, was of "oppression and cruelty" toward them and others. Oliver Perry, naturally, did not testify; but two respectable middies, and some of the petty officers, declared that the Captain was, if anything, too lenient to the young toughs. On that count, "The Court are of opinion that Captain Perry has been very much wanting in not having proper discipline and good order kept on board his Ship. . . . But at the same time the Court are fully of opinion that the complainant Midshipmen have been very ungovernable and bad young men." Three of the four had already been put on the beach, where they belonged. The coffee bribe charge was simply laughed off.

Secretary Stoddert, after mulling over these findings for six weeks, wrote to Captain Perry that he had not paid proper attention to the Commodore's orders at Cape Haitien, and that the punishments inflicted on certain midshipmen were "without Law, & contrary to the usage of the sea service." But the President, "believing you to be a brave man & a skilful officer," decided to overlook "irregular & improper conduct." Perry was sentenced to a three-month suspension from the navy, without pay.

Before the end of the year he was relieved as commander of *General Greene;* and before she was ready for sea, the war was over. The new commander sailed her to Washington, where she was laid up in ordinary.[1] Degraded to a sheer hulk, she was burned in the British raid on Washington in 1814. On 3 April 1801 Samuel Smith, President Jefferson's temporary Secretary of the Navy, informed Christopher Perry that he had not been selected one of the nine captains to be retained in the navy. So, at the age of forty he was retired, with four months' extra pay but no pension. Young Oliver, however, as one of the "Gentlemen who are the most promising," remained under the Peace Establishment Act of 1801.

Pre-Embargo Newport

The first decade of the nineteenth century, before embargoes and nonintercourse acts ruined seaborne commerce, was long regarded as the golden age of Newport. Calbraith and the "Over to the P'int gentlemen's sons" might have to fight gangs of wharf rats — the laborers' and stevedores' sons who lived around lower Thames Street — but they had a good private school and attended Trinity Church. Nearby lay open country for hunting, shooting and skating; and in the summer, when their friends arrived from the Carolinas, there were picnics on Aquidneck, fishing excursions in catboats, sailing parties beyond Brenton's Reef; but no sea bathing yet — that was a new English fashion which had not reached America. A genial specialty in Newport's summer social life at that time was the "turtle frolic." After a ship had brought in a few big turtles from the West Indies a party was organized, usually on Goat Island. Colored citizens skilled in turtle cookery superintended the preparation of turtle flesh: — "calipash," the green meat next the upper shell, and "calipee," the yellow meat next the lower shell; each different but equally delicious. These, with plenty of Madeira wine and other accompaniments, were served at two in

---

[1] Placing a ship "in ordinary" was equivalent to modern "in mothballs." The officers and men were discharged, leaving only a skeleton caretaker crew on board, sails were unbent, yards sent down, topmasts and topgallant spars housed, gun ports closed, and sometimes a roof was built over the spar deck; but the vessel was kept afloat.

the afternoon, and the gay company lingered on into the evening, dancing, flirting and drinking.

The Perry children enjoyed long stays at old Judge Perry's place in
Matunuck, ten acres of which he had given to his son, and where Captain
Christopher maintained a hunting and shooting lodge. In those days a boy
was allowed to fire a shotgun as soon as he was big enough to hold it, and
the quantity of wildfowl in the ponds and salt marshes of South County
staggers the imagination of sportsmen today.

Captain Christopher Perry, having made a competency, settled down in
Newport, invested his prize money and savings in ships and cargoes, and
probably doubled his property before Jefferson's calamity hit the town.
His wife Sarah entered into Newport social life with great zest, especially after 1802 when, at the age of thirty-four, she bore her eighth and
last child. She was still a strikingly beautiful woman on whom all eyes
were turned at the Newport Assembly or when she entered Trinity
Church with her handsome children. During the years of the Captain's
absence at sea, she brought up Calbraith and his brothers and sisters very
strictly. An excellent family disciplinarian, she never resorted to that favorite threat of harrassed Navy wives: "Wait till your father's ship comes
in — he'll give you a good thrashing!" Her reputation was such that the
Battle of Lake Erie was first reported in Newport as, "Old lady Perry has
licked the British!" — "You must mean young Oliver, surely?" — "All
the same thing, 'twas her spirit done it!" All her sons made their careers in
the navy, and all her daughters married naval officers except Sarah junior,
who never married. We may assume that she loved a sailor who was lost at
sea.

The great local holiday in Newport during the days of Calbraith's
childhood and youth was known as Election Day. This was really an inauguration of the recently elected governor and state administration, at the
State House in April. When Commodore Perry returned to his birthplace
in 1855 for a reception and presentation of plate, he recalled half a century
earlier watching for the first glimpse of a gaily decorated packet sloop
which brought governor and suite downriver to Newport. He and the
other boys ran with the procession to the State House, and witnessed
"with childlike delight . . . the pomp, parade and festivities of Election
Day." From that same maritime town where every street led seaward, he
embarked as a fifteen-year-old midshipman "upon an element, then as always, the most congenial" to his "aspirations for honorable emprise."

CHAPTER IV

Preliminaries to the War of 1812
1809 – 1812

THE depression that struck Newport in 1809 convinced Christopher Perry that his sons, if they wanted maritime careers, must seek them in the navy. This exactly suited them. Oliver had never been out of the navy since 1798; he served in the Mediterranean Squadron during the war with Tripoli. After his father had intervened with Senator Foster of Rhode Island, Oliver was promoted acting lieutenant and detailed to the uncongenial task of superintending the construction of Jefferson's pet gunboats on the New England coast. One can imagine Oliver protesting to his father: "You know as well as I do, sir, that those gunboats will be completely useless in wartime"; to which Captain Perry would have replied, "Right, m'lad; but in the navy you obey orders!" This duty at least had the merit that Lieutenant Oliver could call frequently at Newport. His parents and brothers and sisters must have been very proud of him, in blue uniform with brass buttons and a gilt epaulette on one shoulder, when he walked up the aisle with them in Trinity Church.

As soon as a flotilla of these one-gun warships had been completed, Oliver became the commodore, with orders to enforce the embargo — an impossible task. But in 1809, at the age of twenty-four, he received a real fighting command, that of U.S. armed schooner *Revenge*. One of her midshipmen was his younger brother.

Calbraith, now almost fifteen years old, had been begging to enter the navy since the age of twelve. His father, rightly predicting that the government's policy would end in war, gave his consent and obtained for the lad a midshipman's warrant, signed by President Jefferson, on 16 January 1809. After two months' basic training on the receiving ship at the Brooklyn Navy Yard — an experience which convinced him that better training was wanted — the newly fledged reefer, as middies were then called, reported for duty to his elder brother on board *Revenge*.

The earliest letter we have found from Matthew Calbraith Perry indicates that when just past his sixteenth birthday he was becoming interested in girls, especially an unnamed "Miss Hot Cheek," apparently a blushing belle. Dated at Newport, 19 August 1810, it is directed to a boyhood friend, Thomas Breese, then in New York, who became a naval officer and a lifelong friend of the Perrys: —

Dear Breeze

I am agoing down Town directly to see if I can get a letter from you. their has nothing very meterial passed over since my last — except Mrs. Masons party which I was at; I had a charming walk last night with "hot cheek" she is as pretty as ever. Bob must [torn] not be jealous. G.M. and myself are going to walk [wi]th Miss C., "hot cheek," and Miss M. with several more tomorrow. do call on my Mother at Mrs. Purdy.

You must excuse this writing you cant expect a Sailor to write as well as a Clerk.

Yours, Sir

M. C. Perry

P.S. Anne Robinson is perfectly well Mary Ann is makeing me some Batter your sister E is going to get it for me when it is done mixing.

Duty on board U.S.S. *Revenge* in a time of nominal peace became very tedious. She patrolled between Montauk Point, Nantucket, Buzzards Bay and Newport, watching for British impressments which a 12-gun schooner was powerless to prevent, taking soundings in order to improve the charts. Calbraith thought seriously of resigning from the navy to get into the glamorous East Indies trade, when he profited by a bit of Perry luck. In mid-October 1810 he was transferred to the crack frigate *President*, flagship of Commodore[1] John Rodgers. The luck became evident early next year when *Revenge*, in the course of her hydrographic duties, was caught in a summer gale on a lee shore and wrecked on a reef off Watch Hill. Skipper Oliver survived but several lives were lost, and one of them might well have been that of his brother.

U.S.S. *President*, newest of the fleet of powerful 44-gun frigates laid down in Washington's administration, had lines almost identical with those of *Constitution*. Commissioned too late for the quasi-war with France, she had been flagship of the Mediterranean Squadron in the war with Tripoli. A favorite among officers, she was reputed to be the fastest ship in the navy, but she never enjoyed the good fortune of Old Ironsides. Commodore Rodgers commanded the "northern division of ships for the protection of the American coast."

---

[1] Commodore was not until 1862 a definite rank in the U. S. Navy. It was a courtesy rank given to any senior captain in a task force or fleet, at a time when captain was the highest naval rank authorized by Congress.

Midshipman Matthew Calbraith Perry now found himself one of a crew of four hundred officers and men, including his elder brother Raymond, a rather stolid midshipman who always did his duty but never managed to distinguish himself. The reefers lived in the steerage, a section of the berth deck, below the main deck where the principal batteries were located and below the frigate's normal waterline. Headroom measured only a few inches over five feet. The steerage lay forward of the wardroom where the officers messed, and abaft the crew's quarters. It had no lighting or ventilation except what seeped through from the main deck when the hatches were open, and light from whale-oil lanterns hanging from the beams. Along the vessel's sides were arranged the middies' personal lockers, and at night their hammocks were slung from hooks projecting from the beams. Fore and aft there was a long table to which a rating from the ship's galley brought food for the young gentlemen in a wooden "mess-kid," a small tub. The reefers then fell to, each with his individual mess-kid, clasp knife and fingers. The navy provided no forks then, or for many years to come.

Midshipmen stood watch like every other officer and had to learn not only the ancient arts of rigging, splicing and sailmaking, but gunnery and navigation. There were no shortcuts to navigation in those days; every officer had to use the old time-sight method of finding longitude from altitudes, logarithms and the chronometer, as well as the more complicated method of lunar distances. Years later, a civilian instructor with the impressive title Professor of Mathematics was attached to every big warship to "learn" the midshipmen these methods and see that they practised them on deck. But during the War of 1812 this duty fell on the chaplains. Those seagoing parsons, and their successors the professors, are the unsung heroes of our navy. They drew very little pay, and had to put up with a lot of malarkey from the young rascals to whom they sought to impart a knowledge of trigonometry, logarithms and celestial navigation; for if they failed, a valuable ship might be wrecked when a midshipman became a deck officer. The chaplain also taught French, English composition, a smattering of international law, and everything that an officer was supposed to know.

A midshipman's billet meant hard work, especially in foul weather, but there was always a good deal of scuffling and horseplay in the steerage, and during the second dog watch — 6 to 8 P.M. — the lads could skylark, chase each other over the rigging like monkeys, box and wrestle, dance hornpipes and sing sea ballads to the accompaniment of accordion or flute. They were not allowed to fraternize with the ratings or to forget that they were gentlemen. That was another thing about the navy that democrats disliked.

Nobody has left us a personal impression of Calbraith Perry at this period. We know from later portraits that he was of medium height, with thick brown hair that had a tendency to curl, and brown eyes. He had strong rather than handsome features; a powerful nose, firm mouth, cleft chin, somewhat big ears and a naturally sober expression. Humor was not his forte. Calbraith was not the dashing, hotblooded, impulsive type of naval officer like elder brother Oliver, but methodical, serious, conscientious, bent on becoming a good officer, getting on with his fellow reefers, winning the respect of the ratings and the esteem of his superiors. Commodore Rodgers seems at once to have sensed Calbraith's outstanding qualities, since he appointed him his personal aide, with the duty of keeping the official sea journal. And young Perry's first independent mission showed the Commodore's good judgment.

The *President* on 22 April 1811 anchored off Annapolis. The Commodore then took occasion to visit his estate "Sion Hill" at Havre de Grace near the head of Chesapeake Bay. On 7 May, during his absence, a peremptory dispatch from the Secretary of the Navy arrived. It stated that a British frigate, supposedly the *Guerrière*, had been holding up American merchantmen off the entrance to New York harbor and impressing American seamen. *President* was ordered to make sail immediately and do something about it. But she could not sail without the Commodore. So her fastest pulling boat was lowered, stout fellows were told off as oarsmen, and under command of Midshipman Perry they rowed up the bay to bring the Commodore back. This was a seventy-mile journey, yet faster than by land. The crew kept at it all one night and most of the next day. Midshipman Perry then ran the gig ashore near Havre de Grace and ran full-pelt uphill to the mansion with the dispatches. Rodgers promptly concluded his self-given leave, rode to the waterfront, stepped into the gig's stern sheets, and started back to his flagship off Annapolis. Happily a northerly breeze sprang up so that sail could be set and the oarsmen afforded some rest. By 3 P.M. 9 May the Commodore was being piped on board *President* in Annapolis roads; and she sailed next day after taking on stores and ammunition.

We had been on the brink of war with Great Britain for a long time. Four years had elapsed since H.M.S. *Leopard* overhauled U.S.S. *Chesapeake* off Cape Henry, forced her with a broadside to heave-to, and impressed four seamen alleged to be deserters from the Royal Navy.

All this, and still more the administration's naval policy, was very disheartening to the navy. Madison shared Jefferson's irrational prejudice against the navy, as did the Western and Southern blocs which then controlled Congress. Navies were supposed to be undemocratic, aristocratic, a danger to liberty, and a drain on the nation's economy. Nathaniel Macon of North Carolina, one of the most respected and influential members of the House, described himself frankly in debate as "an anti-navy man."

Representative James Holland of the same state observed, "If we had twenty or thirty frigates, we should soon be in war. If the United States had not had the *Chesapeake*, the nation would not have been disgraced." "What good can be derived from a navy?" inquired Representative Samuel McKee of Kentucky. "What has reduced a great portion of the British nation to a state of misery unequaled? Her navy. What has kept the British nation perpetually at war for half a century past? Her navy. . . . What enabled her to commit enormities in Hindostan, the bare relation of which would add a gloom to the regions of the dead? Her navy." John Randolph of Roanoke taunted the navy with frigate *Philadelphia's* running aground. This he declared to be the only naval exploit "for several years past."

The administration firmly believed that a flock of little gunboats (some 260 were built before the war broke) would be sufficient to defend the shores and the liberty of America. Frigates and other blue-water naval vessels were neglected; insufficient funds were appropriated for their proper upkeep, or to recruit a full complement of men, or provide reserve ammunition; and no new tonnage was authorized. Naval officers, as Mahan wrote, were "demoralized by the gunboat system, and disorganized and browbeaten by the loud-mouthed disfavor of representative congressmen."

Paul Hamilton, Madison's Secretary of the Navy and one of the most incompetent men ever to occupy that office, did nothing to remedy this state of affairs; but for rhodomontade he was second to none. In 1810, owing to the Royal Navy's resuming its unpleasant practice of impressing seamen off New York, he and the President began to get their dander up. One of Hamilton's dispatches, with which he was so pleased that he ordered every commander to read it aloud to his crew, was shot through with flamboyant eloquence about revenging "the inhuman and dastardly attack" on frigate *Chesapeake*. Our duty, he said, was to be "determined at every hazard to vindicate the injured honor of our navy and revive the drooping spirits of the nation." Naval officers would better have appreciated a few thousand more dollars appropriated for the navy. But, since words were all they got, Commodore Rodgers added a few of his own: — "Every man, woman and child in our country will be active in consigning our names to disgrace, and even the very vessels composing our little navy to the ravages of the worms, or the detestable transmigration to merchantmen should we not fulfil their expectations!" The Commodore did not despise merchantmen; he merely intended a gibe at Jefferson for having sold into the merchant marine most of the big navy built during the quasi-war with France.

As Mahan sardonically observed, "Under such reminiscences and such words the ships' guns were like to go off of themselves." Commodore

Rodgers was eager to encounter H.M.S. *Guerrière* and demand that she give up the impressed American seamen, or fight. Half an hour after noon on 16 May, *President* then being about forty-five miles northeast of Cape Henry, her lookouts raised a big ship to the east-southeast standing toward her under a press of sail. The Britisher, as it proved to be, took *President* for a Frenchman and gave chase in hope of a prize. One hour later, Commodore Rodgers decided from the cut of her sails that the pursuing vessel was a man-of-war. At 1:30 P.M. the strange ship, identifying her intended victim as an American frigate, reversed course and stood to the southward, showing no colors but setting topgallant studdingsails, obviously intending to escape. Rodgers at 1:45 (testified Midshipman Raymond Perry) raised the American ensign, broke out his broad pendant, and ordered the crew by beat of drum to their battle stations. He supposed that the strange vessel was the *Guerrière*, object of his search; actually she was British sloop-of-war *Little Belt*, Captain Bingham, with only 20 guns to *President's* 44.[1] It may seem odd that a veteran captain and his officers should identify a sloop as a frigate, but in this instance it is not surprising. *Little Belt*, a Danish warship captured by the Royal Navy in the Copenhagen campaign, had three square-rigged masts, a frigate's characteristic high poop, and painted gun ports to suggest a second gun deck; but she mounted so few guns as to be classified as a corvette or sloop-of-war. She was engaged in bringing dispatches from Jamaica to Halifax.

In a dying wind, *President* with all studdingsails set, and both ensign and pendant displayed, slowly overhauled *Little Belt*. She at 7:30 P.M. shortened sail, hove-to, loaded guns and beat to quarters. In the twilight the Americans could not make out her ensign. Rodgers now jockeyed his ship to take position to windward and within hailing distance of the Britisher, not one hundred yards away. At 8:30 he hailed, "Ahoy! What ship is that?" "Ahoy! What ship is *that*?" replied Captain Bingham. Rodgers repeated his hail; but before he could remove the speaking trumpet from his mouth the answer came in the form of a cannon shot, the ball parting a backstay and lodging in *President's* mainmast. Then, even before the Commodore could ascertain what had happened, one of his gun captains replied with a cannon shot. *Little Belt* answered this with three guns and musketry; and Rodgers, who up to that time was disposed to regard the initial shot as an accident, gave a general order to fire. The two ships banged away at each other for a period of about fifteen minutes, punctuated by a short cease-fire on both sides. *Little Belt's* fire was silenced, one yard shot down, and her colors shot away. Rodgers hailed, "Are your colors down?" meaning, "Have you surrendered?" Bingham answered,

---

[1] Both these figures are "rated" guns. *President* actually mounted 53 to 56 guns at the time, and *Little Belt* at least 23. However you count them, the British corvette was outnumbered two to one.

"No!" Rodgers nevertheless ordered Cease Fire, "to prevent further effusion of blood," hailed again, "and learnt for the first time that it was a ship of His Britannic Majesty, but owing to its blowing rather fresher than it had done, I was unable to learn her name." He now hauled off and hove-to, repairing rigging; and that was the end of the fight.

At daylight next day, 17 May, *Little Belt* was observed seven miles to leeward. *President* ran down under easy sail and sent a boat aboard her late adversary with orders to ascertain her name, to express "the Commodore's regrets at the occurrence, and to offer him assistance in repairing his ship's injuries." The boat returned with a polite message from Captain Bingham declining aid. *Little Belt* had lost thirteen men killed or died of wounds, and ten more severely wounded. *President* had none killed, one boy wounded, and damage topside from the British 32-pounders, but nothing that could not be promptly repaired at sea.

Naturally this peacetime engagement of 16 May 1811 created a furor on both sides of the Atlantic. Secretary Hamilton and the Republican press were delighted; the British government and press were horrified at the "outrage." The Secretary ordered a court of inquiry, at which some fifty officers and men testified. Captain Bingham and his officers filed depositions at Halifax, her first port of call after the fight, giving a different version. They declared that *President* fired first, and that the action lasted between 45 and 60 minutes; obviously an attempt to save face. Captain Bingham was certainly responsible for starting the fight; he disdained to show his colors until too late, and from pride or insolence refused to answer a hail from a warship which he already knew to be American. Commodore Rodgers, on the contrary, never learned what ship he was fighting until the fight was over. In the then existing system of intership communication by shouting through a speaking trumpet, there was abundant opportunity for misunderstanding. And the British shot which opened the fight was accidental, the result of a new system adopted by both navies for firing cannon. The old method of lighting off the touchhole with a burning match had been replaced by flintlocks like those on muskets, attached to a linstock or lanyard held by the gun captain. These were liable to be tripped through carelessness or jerked by the holder in excess of zeal.

Commodore Rodgers, even before exoneration by the court of inquiry, became a national hero; in England, on the contrary, he became Black Jack or Bully Rodgers. Unfortunately the incontrovertible fact that *Little Belt* threw barely half the weight of metal that *President* did, together with the false claim that she gave a good account of herself for at least 45 minutes, enhanced the feeling of contempt that the British already entertained for the United States Navy, and led to some disagreeable surprises for the Royal Navy in 1812.

Commodore John Rodgers,
by Gilbert Stuart

The *President–Little Belt* Battle 16 May 1811
Contemporary engraving by William Elmes

This brief and inglorious fight with H.M.S. *Little Belt* was the baptism of fire for both Midshipmen Perry, Calbraith and Raymond. But they had to wait more than a year before experiencing real warfare. For a good part of that interval, the winter of 1811-1812, *President* lay at Newport, and the Perry boys enjoyed leaves and liberties at home.

In the slow transatlantic communications of that era, the international crisis came very slowly to a head. President Madison wished to make one more attempt to settle impressment and neutral rights by negotiation. As to the latter, he succeeded; Britain repealed the objectionable anti-neutral decrees on 16 June 1812. The news reached Washington two weeks too late; Madison had lost patience, and on 18 June Congress declared war on Great Britain.

Three days later *President*, then in New York harbor, got the news. Young Calbraith's sea journal contains this entry for 20 June: "At 10 A.M. news arrived that war would be declared the following day against G.B. Made the signal for all officers and boats. Unmoored ship and fired a salute." Rodgers's flagship and sloop-of-war *Hornet* promptly dropped down to Sandy Hook, where they made rendezvous with Decatur's squadron, consisting of frigates *United States* and *Congress* and brig *Argus*. Rodgers, the senior naval officer on active duty, took command of the combined squadron. His orders from the department were to cruise off shore to help American merchantmen reach home safely and then return to New York; but as these never reached him before sailing, he was able to be more aggressive. He wished to employ his powerful squadron to intercept a big Jamaica convoy of 110 sail north of Bermuda, where homebound convoys commonly caught the westerly winds.

At 3 P.M. June 21, as soon as news of the actual declaration of war reached him, the Commodore made the signal to weigh. Never were anchors catted more quickly, or topsails sheeted home with more snap and zest than on that occasion.

CHAPTER V

The Second War with Great Britain
1812–1815

Midshipman Perry's War Cruises in U.S.S. President

O<small>N</small> 23 June 1812, at three in the morning, Rodgers spoke an American brig which two days earlier had sighted the big Jamaica convoy off the Bermudas. If the squadron could find it, there would be rich pickings; every sailor would have a pocketful of gold. Rodgers clapped on sail and shaped a course to intercept; but a diversion spoiled his game. Shortly after sunrise same day, at a point about one hundred miles southwest of Nantucket Shoals, a ship was discovered standing toward the squadron. It proved to be H.M.S. *Belvidera*, a 32-gun frigate commanded by Captain Richard Byron, bound for Halifax. Commodore Rodgers promptly made flag signals for his squadron to chase, upon which Byron wore ship and made best speed northeasterly, directly away, with wind on the port beam. By noon *President*, leading the American squadron, was about three miles from her intended quarry and gaining very slowly; the others were slower still. At 4:30 P.M., the flagship being within range of the Britisher, Rodgers ordered Commence Firing with his bow-chasers, hoping to cripple the enemy's top-hamper and slow her down. He himself fired the first gun of the engagement, and indeed of the war. Byron promptly returned the compliment from his stern-chasers.

At this point an Olympian observer would not have bet a copper on *Belvidera*. She resembled a very tired hare being pursued by a pack of hungry hounds, and the Byron family was notorious for bad luck. But, this time, fortune favored them. After the fight had lasted fifteen minutes and *President* had made several hits, one of her own bow-chasers burst, killing Midshipman John Taylor, wounding the gun captain, the Commodore, and Midshipman Matthew C. Perry, who was standing by his side. Rodgers, with a broken leg but supported by his men, indomitably directed the battle from his damaged forecastle. He caused *President* to yaw first to port and then to starboard in order to bring her broadsides to bear, but this maneuver lost ground, and *Belvidera's* stern-chasers in the meantime wrought considerable havoc on the American top-hamper. A dying wind gave the lighter ship the advantage, which Captain Byron enhanced by heaving overboard boats, anchors and tons of fresh water. Thus, by 6:45 P.M. *Belvidera* had forged beyond *President's* range; and shortly before midnight, when she was a good three miles in the lead, Rodgers "with more mortification than words can express" abandoned the chase. The other ships of his squadron, slower sailers than *President*, never came within gun range.

A poor beginning for a naval war. Rodgers (as Captain Byron said in his official report), having much the more powerful force, should have had the patience to withhold gunfire until he could employ his flagship's broadside on his enemy's sails and rigging; then the rest of the squadron could have closed and finished her. But Byron's almost reckless jettison of water and boats — which Rodgers at the start of a long cruise could not afford to do — might after all have enabled *Belvidera* to outsail her adversary whether or not he yawed, and even if the bow-chaser had not burst. In any case, Captain Byron deserved to escape, since he had the wit to profit by a lucky break.

After some delay to repair rigging, Commodore Rodgers, with his leg in splints, resumed searching for the Jamaica convoy. *President* at one time was hot in the convoy's wake, as evidenced by quantities of floating coconut shells and orange peel, but she then ran into a spell of thick weather and may have passed the vessels without knowing it. The squadron searched up to within a day's sail of the English Channel, then shaped a course for the Western Islands and arrived in Boston 31 August 1812. All Rodgers had to show for a seventy-day cruise were seven small prizes.

As she was entering Boston harbor through Nantasket roads, *President* spoke U.S.S. *Constitution*, Captain Isaac Hull, which had just covered herself with glory by defeating and sinking H.M.S. *Guerrière*. Both Midshipmen Perry must have felt they had been assigned to the wrong frigate. Calbraith had fully recovered from his wound made by the bursting gun, and he always entertained the greatest respect for Commodore Rodgers. His close association with the Commodore taught him many things over and above a midshipman's duty, such as handling a big ship and getting the best out of her men. He also learned to pay particular attention to the diet and health of seamen. When the Rodgers squadron arrived at Boston, frigates *United States* and *Congress* between them had three hundred men down with scurvy; the *President* had none.

The Perry boys were pleasantly surprised to find their parents living in Boston, Captain Christopher having been returned to active duty as commandant of the Boston Navy Yard. They doubtless enjoyed plenty of

U.S.S. *President* at Marseilles, by Antoine Roux, 1806

shore liberty at Charlestown during the month that the frigates refitted and obtained new recruits.

The Navy Department now divided its blue-water fleet into three divisions of three vessels each, under Commodores Rodgers, Decatur and Bainbridge. Rodgers retained *President* together with frigate *Congress* and sloop *Wasp*. The first two (*Wasp* being at Philadelphia) sailed from Boston early in October 1812 and steered eastward. H.M. frigates *Nymphe* and *Galatea* escaped them by fast sailing, but the Americans had the satisfaction of taking a British vessel with a cargo of $175,000 in specie — a nice packet of prize money for all hands. Rodgers, after entering European waters, dropped down to latitude 17° N, sailed before the trades to longitude 50° W, and then made for Bermuda. For a month he cruised to the northward of Bermuda without sighting one enemy ship — amazingly bad luck, as the squadron was astride the usual England–West Indies convoy route.

"No remarkable occurrence this day" is a frequent entry in the journal kept by Midshipman Matthew C. Perry. Foul weather provided the only change from routine; 21 December, for instance, opened "with strong gales from the north and westward and a heavy sea. Laying to. At half past 3 beat to quarters and housed the gun-deck guns. At 9 set the forestaysail. At 10 a heavy sea struck the ship abeam, carried away the starboard stantions, killed two seamen and wounded six men, broke the lower studding-sail boom, and started the launch, broke in three half-Ports & started all the others, the hatches being off for the purpose of passing shot below, took in a great quantity of water; rigged all the pumps, battened the hatches down, and soon cleared her."

Rodgers kept his squadron at sea until water and provisions were almost exhausted. Compelled then to return to port, he shaped a course for Boston. There he anchored on the last day of 1812, after a cruise of eighty-five days and nearly eleven thousand miles. He had sighted but five British vessels, and captured only two. Another very disappointing cruise.

In the meantime sloop *Wasp* which, fortunately for herself, had never caught up with Rodgers, had defeated H.M.S. *Frolic* on 17 October; frigate *United States*, Commodore Decatur's flagship, entered New London harbor on 4 December with H.M.S. *Macedonian* in tow; and on 29 December U.S.S. *Constitution* reduced H.M.S. *Java* to a useless hulk. *Macedonian*, shortly transferred to Newport where Master Commandant Oliver H. Perry was stationed prior to his Lake Erie assignment, prompted him to write to a friend, "This day has been a most gratifying sight to us — this beautiful frigate mooring as a prize in our harbor, but particularly so to one, who feels alive to everything that reflects honor on our Navy." Years later, another *Macedonian* would be his younger brother's flagship.

The moral value of these naval victories to the American people, following military disaster on the Canadian border, was vast. They even impaired democratic anti-navy prejudice, as may be read in a report of the House Committee on Naval Affairs on 27 November 1812. "It is a bright attribute to the history of the tar," it says, "that he has never destroyed the rights of the nation. Thus, aided by economy and fortified by republican principle, your committee think they ought strongly to recommend that the fostering care of the nation be extended to the Naval establishment." I doubt whether Commodores Rodgers, Decatur, Hull and Bainbridge were pleased at being called "tars" — the popular synonym for sailors, commonly used in such clichés as "honest tars," "jolly Jack-tars," etc. But they were delighted when Congress made generous appropriations to increase the navy by four ships-of-the-line and six heavy frigates. None of this new construction got to sea during the war; but after Madison had sacked Secretary Hamilton and obtained a competent successor, William Jones of Philadelphia, naval administration greatly improved.

U.S.S. *President* remained at the Boston Navy Yard for several months, effecting the extensive repairs, refitting and rerigging that these sailing frigates always seemed to require after a protracted cruise. It was an unusually cold winter, with Boston harbor frozen solid; and as frigates were regular ice chests below in winter, the Perry boys must have been grateful for frequent leaves and liberties to spend with their parents at the Charlestown Navy Yard. By the spring of 1813 the Royal Navy had clapped so tight a blockade on American seaports from Cape Cod south, that during the year only six United States warships managed to get out to sea; the *Constitution* did not break out until December. In consequence, the Navy Department decided to send ships out one by one, when and if they had a good chance of eluding the blockaders.

President accordingly put out to sea 30 April 1813 and ranged the North Atlantic looking for convoys and unescorted ships. After taking four prizes in one week of June, Commodore Rodgers shaped a course to the northward of the British Isles, with a view to intercepting the enemy's Newfoundland trade; but not until he raised the Shetlands did he sight a single sail. Having been almost two months off soundings, *President* badly needed to replenish provisions and water. So the Commodore sailed for Bergen, Norway, arriving 26 June. Upon nearing the island fringe, Midshipman Matthew C. Perry was dispatched in a cutter to obtain a pilot for the intricate "lead," the passage to Bergen. He called at the islet of Utvaër, inhabited by fishermen who at first were shy; but, on finding that he was not English, invited him into one of their huts and regaled him with fresh milk, a wonderful treat for a youth two months at sea. Calbraith returned on board with two fishermen who piloted *President* into Bergen harbor, the famous Vaagen; she was the first American man-of-war to visit a Norwegian port. After exchanging 17-gun salutes with the castle, Rodgers welcomed the American consul and gave liberty to most of his officers, who were hospitably treated by the inhabitants. In return, the ladies and gentlemen of Bergen were twice entertained on board *President*, and flotillas of small craft containing the common people who were not invited rowed around the ship out of curiosity.

Departing Bergen 2 July 1813, Rodgers sailed "northabout" around Scotland, took a few prizes, missed an opportunity to engage a British frigate through faulty ship identification, then shaped a course for home. On 23 September 1813 near Nantucket Shoals, *President* had an amusing encounter with five-gun schooner *Highflyer*, Lieutenant George Hutchinson RN, which illustrates the use of deception in days of sail. Rodgers started the game by raising British colors. This misled Hutchinson into mistaking *President* for H. M. frigate *Sea Horse*, so he bore down and hove-to under her stern. Rodgers dressed one of his officers in a British uniform and sent him on board *Highflyer* to "pay his respects" and request Hutchinson to return the call and lend him a signal book. The lieutenant, delighted to be invited on board a fine frigate, handed over one of his signal books, came on board, and was conducted to the Commodore's cabin. There he placed in Rodgers's hands a bundle of dispatches for his superior, Admiral Sir John Borlase Warren, and informed his host that Sir John's main objective was to capture or destroy the *President!* The Commodore, dissembling a bit longer, inquired, "What kind of a man is Rodgers?" To which the lieutenant replied, "An odd fish, and hard to catch." "Sir," said Rodgers, "do you know what vessel you are on board of?" "Why yes, sir," he replied, "His Majesty's ship *Sea Horse!*" "Then, sir, you labor under a mistake," said Rodgers. "You are on board the United States frigate *President*, and I am Commodore Rodgers, at your service!" At that the band on the quarterdeck struck up "Yankee Doodle" and the American ensign was displayed. Poor Hutchinson was very down in the mouth at this revelation, especially over being in the power of Commodore Rodgers; for he had served under Admiral Cockburn when that notable marauder plundered and burned Havre de Grace a few months before, and had even carried away a sword from Rodgers's home Sion Hill as his share of the loot. Hutchinson had been warned to be especially careful "not to fall into the hands of old Rodgers, for if *he* comes across you, he will hoist you upon his jib-boom and carry you into Boston!" But the gallant Commodore treated the lieutenant with complete courtesy, and after reaching Boston set him free on parole.

Three days after this humorous encounter, on 26 September 1813, *President* entered Narragansett Bay and proceeded upriver to Providence. She had done well on this cruise, having captured 12 ships and made 271 prisoners. But she missed the glory of a good slam-bang fight with a British warship, such as most of the other frigates had enjoyed.

At Newport, Midshipman Matthew Calbraith Perry received the good news that on 24 July, upon recommendation of his commanding officer, he had been promoted acting lieutenant, a rank corresponding to our present lieutenant junior grade. There was a joyous family reunion, to which news came of big brother Oliver's glorious exploit in the Battle of Lake Erie, with little brother, twelve-year-old Midshipman James Alexander Perry, on board. Four Perrys in the navy at once — two on salt water and two on fresh!

Oliver H. Perry and the Battle of Lake Erie

Among the curious paradoxes of this War of 1812 — which lasted until 1815 — is the fact that the only decisive naval actions were fought on fresh water. These were Commodore Oliver H. Perry's victory on Lake Erie, 10 September 1813, and Commodore Thomas Macdonough's Plattsburg battle on Lake Champlain a year later. The one led to American recovery of the Northwest, and the other not only halted an invasion of the Hudson valley but persuaded the British government to conclude peace.

Oliver H. Perry's victory must be recounted here, both because Oliver was the pattern for his adoring younger brother Calbraith, and because the controversy over who won the battle bedeviled the entire Perry-Rodgers connection for at least thirty years.

Master Commandant O. H. Perry went to Presque Isle (now Erie, Pennsylvania) early in 1813 with orders to build and command a fleet strong enough to wrest control of Lake Erie from the British. This was no small task in that outpost of civilization. Noah Brown and his foreman Sidney Wright, New York shipbuilders sent there to do the construction, required ten days to reach Erie. With a maximum force of 200 men they managed in a few months to build "from the stump" two 20-gun, 110-foot, 500-ton man-o'-war brigs, *Lawrence* and *Niagara*, and four 60-ton armed schooners. Considering that they had to send men into the woods to cut the timber, and that all guns, munitions, oakum, iron, cordage, canvas and other necessary materials had to be hauled overland from Pittsburgh or sailed from Buffalo, this accomplishment thrusts into the shade some of the much vaunted feats of World War II shipbuilders. During all this time Oliver H. Perry, working by Brown's side, with about three-score sailors whom he had brought with him from Rhode Island, showed frantic energy. But, had it not been for Wright's invention of 90-foot "camels" (floats) to lift the larger vessels over the bar, Perry could not have got his flagship out of Erie harbor. Once outside the bar on 6 August 1813, Perry was joined by Commander Jesse D. Elliott, bringing two more schooners from Buffalo.

Elliott now became captain of *Niagara* and second in command to Perry, a position which evidently did not please him. Although junior in the navy list to Perry, he was thirty-one years old to Perry's twenty-eight, already had some minor successes to his credit on the Lakes, and thought he should have been named Commodore.

The nine American vessels were well armed, but short of men. They should have had a total complement of 740, but obtained only 490. Of these, fewer than two hundred were of the navy, and another one hundred were militia from Kentucky and Pennsylvania lent by General Harrison nine days before the battle. Perry made them marines overnight, and they paid their way as sharpshooters. He also had hastily recruited Indians, frontiersmen, and one Russian "who couldn't speak a word of English." "Full one-fourth" of the American crews, according to an eyewitness, were "blacks," whose pluck in battle was of the best. Thirty-two men in the flagship were down with cholera morbus and dysentery at the time of the battle, and Perry himself was recovering from a touch of "Lake fever" which left him very weak. But he showed no weakness during the fighting.

Perry now sailed his squadron to the western end of the lake, and after considerable maneuvering anchored at Put-in-Bay among the Bass Islands. His object was to challenge the British Lake Erie Squadron under Commander Robert H. Barclay RN to come out and fight. Barclay had built up this squadron under difficulties equal to Perry's. Headquarters were at Malden (Amherstburg), Ontario, where the Detroit River empties into Lake Erie. That place was chosen because a new sloop-of-war H.M.S. *Detroit*, of about the same tonnage and armament as Perry's two brigs, was there being rushed to completion. Barclay's logistic difficulties should have been less than Perry's, owing to his control of water transportation, but actually were greater. He too had only a minority of naval ratings, plus Indians who had no stomach for "walk-on-the-water" fighting, and Canadian militia who, he said, were not "worth their salt." Since no guns for *Detroit* arrived, he had to make do with ordnance dismounted from the fort at Malden. As the back-country thereabouts was largely wilderness, little or no food could be obtained, and the many thousand of Tecumseh's Indians encamped around his base consumed most of the rations. Barclay would fain have waited another month to receive reinforcements, but a serious shortage (only two days' supply of flour and one of rum) forced him out, fatally, on 9 September.

Upon receiving word of Barclay's resolution, Perry held a conference of his commanding officers on board *Lawrence*, drew up a line of battle,

Commodore Oliver Hazard Perry, by Gilbert Stuart

exhibited a flag he had made for her, displaying the alleged last words of Captain Lawrence of U.S.S. *Chesapeake:* DON'T GIVE UP THE SHIP, and ordered each member of his squadron to engage her opposite number of the British line. He clinched this order with a paraphrase of Lord Nelson's celebrated words: "If you lay your enemy alongside, you cannot be out of your place." Unfortunately, that is just what Elliott did not do.

The tenth dawned, a beautiful September day with not a cloud in the sky and a light southwest wind. At sunrise, when he sighted Barclay's squadron hull down, he weighed and steered directly for it. The wind at 10 A.M. shifted to southeast, which gave the Americans the weather gauge, a lucky break, and thwarted Barclay's plan to run down and board them. From this diagram of the two fleets as they approached — Barclay's hove-to waiting for Perry - – it will be seen that each commodore had placed his heavier ships in the van, separated by a small schooner-gunboat, with one or two ahead, and the rest tailing. Barclay's heavy ships were H.M.S. *Detroit* and *Queen Charlotte;* Perry's were *Lawrence* and *Niagara.* Although

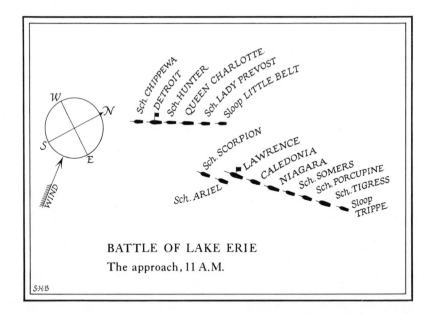

BATTLE OF LAKE ERIE
The approach, 11 A.M.

these two British were ship-rigged, giving them better maneuverability than the brig-rigged Americans, their armaments were almost identical in numbers, 20 to 22 guns, or 10 to a broadside. But there was one essential difference. All but two of Perry's guns in the brigs were carronades; all but two of Barclay's were long guns. The carronade was a short-barreled 32-pounder, invented during the War for American Independence.

It was known as a "smasher" since it was lethal at ranges from 250 yards down, but decreasingly efficient as the range opened. The long guns, however, were accurate up to a mile or more, if properly served.

Before the battle opened, Perry repeated by flag hoist and speaking trumpet his instructions of the night before that each of his ships should closely engage her opposite number in the British line. This meant for *Lawrence* to attack *Detroit*, and *Niagara* the *Queen Charlotte*. Perry formed his line at 11 A.M. and raised the DON'T GIVE UP THE SHIP flag. All hands cheered, and at the Commodore's orders spliced the main brace.

At 11:45 A.M. a bugle sounded on board H.M.S. *Detroit*, her band struck up "Rule, Britannia!" and her first gun spoke, shooting a 24-pound cannon ball that fell short. A second shot hit *Lawrence*, then a mile distant. Perry, knowing full well that trading shots at that range would be fatal to him, held his fire and calmly closed range on *Detroit*. By 12:15 P.M. he had arrived within musket shot and the battle began in earnest. Had Elliott in *Niagara* then followed orders and borne down to engage *Queen Charlotte*, the battle might have been won then and there; but Elliott kept out of the way, well to windward, and Captain Figgis of *Queen Charlotte*, unable to reach this "reluctant dragon" with carronades, of which he had 14, thrust ahead to support *Detroit*, which had only two "smashers." Thus the two biggest British ships were able to concentrate gunfire on the American flagship, with 18 carronades and two long guns; H.M.S. *Hunter*, a schooner armed with eight long guns and two carronades, also contributed to Perry's undoing.

Lawrence bravely held this station for the space of two hours and a quarter, inflicting almost as much damage on the two big British ships as she received. By 1:30 P.M. her sails, spars and rigging were so cut up that she lay dead in the water, a sitting duck for British guns. Yet for another hour Perry sustained this unequal contest, supported to some extent by schooner *Caledonia* (which was largely engaged with her opposite number *Hunter*), but not at all by *Niagara*, which continued to hug the wind at a safe distance. The American schooner-gunboats in the van engaged their opposite numbers in the British van, rather ineffectively, but the four American gunboats in the rear were such slow sailers compared with the square-riggers that they never got into the fight at this stage.

Finally, at 2:30 P.M., when *Lawrence* was so disabled that not a single gun could be worked, and her decks were covered with dead and wounded, the Commodore made his famous decision. Taking his little brother Midshipman James Alexander Perry (who had slept peacefully below all through the uproar), his blue pendant, and the "motto flag," he had himself rowed to *Niagara* in his only intact boat. *Niagara* (as Barclay later testified) was still "far to windward" of every other ship and "per-

fectly fresh," having received but one hit. By this time she had pulled up
abreast of *Lawrence*, distant about half a mile. The row took fifteen minutes with shots falling around the boat most of the way, Perry standing
erect so he could assess the situation.

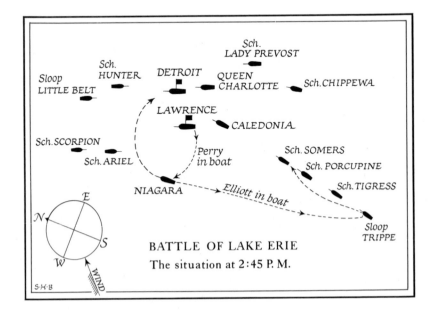

BATTLE OF LAKE ERIE

The situation at 2:45 P. M.

Elliott, meeting him at the gangway of *Niagara*, asked, "How goes the
day?" "Bad enough," answered Perry, "but why are the gunboats so far
astern?" "I'll bring them up," said Elliott, "Do so!" ordered Perry. Elliott
jumped into Perry's boat, went on board *Somers*, one of the several small
craft which were becalmed to leeward, ordered them to break out their
sweeps and pile in, which they did — but too late to affect the result.

In the meantime the officer in charge of *Lawrence*, himself wounded
and with only nine men and not one gun fit for duty, had struck his colors
to save further loss of life. Fortunately the British were too busy to lower
a boat and take possession; so before the end of the battle the Stars and
Stripes were again displayed in *Lawrence*.

Now came the crucial moment of the battle. The wind (which seemed
determined to help the Americans) freshened. Perry promptly set all *Niagara's* sails and covered the distance to the head of the British line —
about a mile — in a quarter of an hour. He thrust in between schooner
Hunter and the flagship, his double-shotted carronades engaging both simultaneously; and he also took on *Queen Charlotte* which had fouled *Detroit* and could not get clear. *Hunter* was completely clobbered, and the

two big British ships, already badly shot up by *Lawrence* in the earlier part of the action, had little fight left. At about 3 P.M., after receiving one or two broadsides, Barclay struck, surrendering his entire squadron.

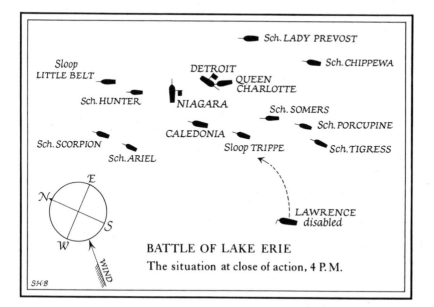

Sch. *LADY PREVOST*

Sch. *CHIPPEWA*

Sloop
LITTLE BELT

DETROIT

QUEEN
CHARLOTTE

Sch. *HUNTER*

NIAGARA

Sch. *SOMERS*

Sch. *PORCUPINE*

CALEDONIA

Sch. *SCORPION*

Sloop TRIPPE

Sch. *TIGRESS*

Sch. *ARIEL*

E

N

S

W

WIND

LAWRENCE
disabled

BATTLE OF LAKE ERIE

The situation at close of action, 4 P. M.

S·H·B

As soon as Perry satisfied himself that victory was secure, he wrote in pencil on the back of an old letter the dispatch to General Harrison that has helped to seal his fame: —

> We have met the enemy and they are ours:
> Two Ships, two Brigs, one schooner & one Sloop.
> Yours, with great respect and esteem
> O. H. PERRY

Perry returned to *Lawrence* (her deck still slippery with blood), and received on board four of Barclay's commanders or seconds in command. Captain Figgis of *Queen Charlotte* was dead, and other C.O.'s wounded. When the British officers presented their swords, Perry refused them, and inquired with real concern about the British commodore. Poor Barclay, who had lost an arm at Trafalgar, had the other arm disabled here and was wounded in four other places; but he survived, and Perry saw that he received the best medical attention that the Americans could provide. The ceremony of surrender completed, Perry sent his first battle report to the Secretary of the Navy, beginning, "Sir, — It has pleased the Almighty to give to the arms of the United States a signal victory over their enemies on this lake. The British squadron . . . have this moment surrendered to the force under my command after a sharp conflict."

A sharp conflict it was, uncommonly bloody for that era. *Lawrence's* casualties were 22 officers and men killed and 61 wounded out of 110 on board. Total for the squadron was 29 killed, 91 wounded. *Detroit* and *Queen Charlotte* lost 30 killed and 62 wounded. Total for the British squadron was 41 killed, 94 wounded. *Detroit* and the *Queen* were too much banged up to be of any use to their captors, but the schooners were soon put to work as United States transports.

This American victory was decisive not only tactically but in a strategic sense. It reversed the ill effects of General Hull's surrender of Detroit, and enabled General Harrison to win the Battle of the Thames, which recovered control of the Old Northwest. These results were final; the enemy made no comeback. As Washington Irving put it, "The last roar of cannon that died along the shores of Lake Erie was the expiring note of British domination."

Captain Mahan, who studied this battle in detail, with his wealth of background on the age of sail, concluded that it was Perry's victory, and his alone. "As Perry's action on first standing down insured decisive action, so by him was imparted to the *Niagara* the final direction which determined victory. The influence of the rear gunboats brought up by Elliott was contributive, but not decisive." Unfortunately, there were many at the time who felt otherwise and gave the palm to Elliott. Perry let himself in for that by praising his second in command in his official report of 13 September. Before he boarded *Niagara*, he said, "The wind springing up, Capt. Elliott was enabled to bring *Niagara* gallantly into close action," and throughout "he evinced his characteristic bravery and judgment, and since the close of the action, has given me the most able and essential assistance." Perry so reported, in my opinion, owing to an amiable trait he shared with his younger brother Calbraith: a desire to give everyone who served under him a pat on the back. But he deeply regretted that he had done so, and retracted later. Congress took what Perry wrote *au pied de la lettre* and voted gold medals both to the Commodore and to Elliott. Things might have remained in this pleasant state of covering up faults and mistakes had not junior officers tattled by word and pen.

Perry's friends pointed out there was no physical reason to prevent *Niagara* from fanning down to engage *Queen Charlotte* when Perry attacked *Detroit*. *Niagara* never got into close action until Perry took over her command while Elliott rowed off to rally the schooner gunboats. Of *Niagara's* relatively light casualties — 4 killed and 20 wounded — all but two occurred under Perry's, not Elliott's command. Elliott's friends, on the contrary, persuaded him that Perry was a poltroon to abandon his flagship, that *Niagara* was prevented from closing because schooner *Caledonia* got in her way, and that she had already begun to do so when Perry came on board.

Elliott was a very odd fish, even for a naval officer. His career is studded with quarrels, challenges, duels and courts-martial, and some of his letters and speeches suggest that he had a "screw loose." The facts of this battle, as we have related them, cannot be denied; but one may speculate endlessly as to what was in Elliott's mind. Did he, like Captain Landais in Paul Jones's battle off Flamborough Head, deliberately withhold support in the hope that his commodore would sink and he himself win the victory? Or was it mere funk? In favor of the latter explanation is an incident that took place on board gunboat *Somers* near the close of the battle. A gun captain, seeing Elliott duck when a cannon ball screeched over the quarterdeck, was so indiscreet as to burst into laughter; the Captain then beat the unfortunate man almost senseless with his speaking trumpet. And Elliott's alacrity in shoving off from *Niagara* as soon as Perry came on board, instead of sending a junior officer to rally the gunboats, suggests that close-in fighting was not his dish.

Henry Adams thus concluded his spirited account of the battle: — "No process of argument . . . could deprive Perry of the fame justly given him by the public, or detract from the splendor of his reputation as the hero of the war. More than any other battle of the time, the victory on Lake Erie was won by the courage and obstinacy of a single man." He had shown the shining mark of a really great military commander — the ability, in a fluid, uncertain tactical situation, to make a decision that snatched victory from defeat.

Nevertheless, attempts to deprive him of credit, in favor of Elliott, extended over the next thirty years and afforded Calbraith and all the Perrys infinite chagrin.

Calbraith Marries

Lieutenant Matthew Calbraith Perry was detached from *President* in the fall of 1813 and ordered to Commodore Decatur's flagship *United States*. His duty on board that frigate was frustrating. She, together with Decatur's prize *Macedonian*, and sloop *Wasp*, were bottled up in New London harbor by the British blockade. Perry had nothing to do but go through ship routine and make recruiting expeditions to various ports along the coast. Since there seemed little likelihood of *United States* being able to break out, the Navy Department in April 1814 transferred most of her officers, including Commodore Decatur and Lieutenant Perry, to *President*, then moored in New York harbor.

The following summer and winter were very anxious months for the navy and the country. England, having disposed of Napoleon permanently (as she thought), was free to concentrate on winning the war with America. More frigates were available for blockading the coast, more troops for expeditionary forces. One invasion, mounted in Montreal, was stopped by Commodore Macdonough's fresh-water navy on Lake Champlain in September 1814. Another ravaged the shores of the Chesapeake, marched on Washington, burned the Capitol and the White House, then retired and raided Baltimore. A third was being planned against New Orleans, and a fourth on Savannah. Nobody knew where the enemy would strike next. Commodore Decatur's squadron had the duty of protecting New York City in case that were the selected target.

Lieutenant Perry, in the meantime, became intimate with the Slidell family. John Slidell, a New York merchant married to one of the Scots Mackenzies, had a seventeen-year-old daughter named Jane. Her the twenty-year-old lieutenant courted; and on Christmas Eve 1814, the very day the peace treaty was signed at Ghent, he and Jane Slidell were married at Grace Church by the Reverend Nathaniel Bowen. Raymond, presumably, acted as Calbraith's best man, but it is not likely that any other Perrys were present. The parents could hardly have got there when the sea route from Newport was interdicted by the British blockade, and Oliver, as commander of the new U.S.S. *Java*, was bottled up in Baltimore.

With so many United States ships blockaded, junior officers were in long supply, and Lieutenant Perry had no trouble in obtaining a honeymoon furlough. That is why he had the good fortune not to be on board U.S.S. *President* when she sailed from New York on 13 January 1815. The very next day a situation arose, the reverse of the *Belvidera* affair. Commodore Decatur ran into the fatal embrace of a British blockading squadron. *President* was now the hare; H.M.S. *Endymion* and three other frigates, the hounds. As in the earlier action, only one ship caught up with the quarry in time to engage her before nightfall. *Endymion* and *President* banged away at each other during five glasses, at the end of which both were badly crippled, *Endymion* worse than *President*. The American clapped on all sail to escape, but she leaked so badly that H.M.S. *Pomone* and *Tenedos* closed during the night. After another exchange of gunfire in the early hours of 15 January, Decatur surrendered his flagship. A court of inquiry exonerated him, but the British gained a fine frigate. There is still a *President* in the Royal Navy, as for many years there was a U.S.S. *Guerrière, Macedonian, Java,* and *Cyane*.[1]

The War of 1812 was over, but its consequences were far-reaching.

---

[1] Until about 1840 the U. S. Navy followed the old British custom of naming new ships after old ones captured from the enemy; and the Royal Navy has continued so doing. The present H.M.S. *President* is a training ship moored to the Thames embankment in London.

CHAPTER VI

Family Affairs and First Mediterranean Cruise
1814–1819

L IEUTENANT Matthew Calbraith Perry's marriage to Jane Slidell proved
to be as important for his career as war service. It not only brought
him a devoted wife who bore him ten children, but allied him with a
wealthy and influential family of New York. A Freeman, a Barber, a Hazard, and a Raymond had already brought successive Perrys up in the
world; now Jane Slidell brought Calbraith up another notch, and their
children continued the same pattern.

John Slidell, son of a soap and tallow merchant, carried on his father's
business but branched out to become a shipowning merchant and banker.
The Slidells are not mentioned as dinner guests in the famous diary of
Philip Hone, but neither are the Astors nor the Vanderbilts; and Hone himself, before he became arbiter of fashion in New York and entertainer of
distinguished foreigners, had been an auctioneer and commission merchant.
Except for the old Knickerbocker families, who remained disdainfully
aloof, New York society from 1800 to 1840 consisted largely of merchants,
very few of whom had more than a common school education. John Slidell
owned a house at 50 Broadway when his daughter married Lieutenant
Perry, and an office and warehouse at 41 South Street. His choice as vestry-
man of Grace Church testifies to his respectability.

Officers of the United States Navy, even long subsequent to the Civil
War, enjoyed no great social status. The time would come (as Colonel
Calverly sang in *Patience*):

> When I first put this uniform on,
> I said, as I looked in the glass,
> "It's one in a million
> That any civilian
> My figure and form will surpass!"

Jane Slidell (Mrs. Matthew C.) Perry in
middle life

Lieutenant Matthew C. Perry, Jr., USN

Purser Nathaniel H. Perry USN

Mrs. Caroline Perry Belmont

But in the era that we are considering, gold lace distinctly had no "charm for the fair," and still less attraction for papa and mama. They, in accordance with American social usage, provided no dowry for their daughters but expected them to marry men who could properly support a family. Officers of the army and navy were not considered good catches.[1] They were no Beresfords, Joinvilles or Mountbattens, but simple fellows with no financial resources but their meager pay and a little prize money after a war. They generally married, for love, nice home-town girls. Nor did the navy guarantee a young officer a career; most of them were discharged at the end of hostilities and had to seek other employment. In the northern part of the United States, the blue-water merchant marine enjoyed great prestige; on Cape Cod it used to be said of a bright, pretty girl of good family, "She's good enough for an East India captain!" But no Cape Codder ever said that about a naval captain.

We may surmise that Lieutenant Matthew Calbraith Perry obtained the consent of the Slidell parents, partly because of the glory that his elder brother had won on Lake Erie, partly for his personal qualities. I suspect that Jane was a rather plain girl who did not attract the young bucks of New York, but whom Calbraith saw as a girl of character whom he devotedly loved, and who returned his love.

If the reader wishes to know more of her, he will not find it here. None of her correspondence exists; not one letter from her to him, hardly twenty from him to her. If any of those tender, intimate letters between man and wife, which tell so much, survive, this writer has been unable to find them. They disappeared in the holocaust of documents indulged in by Jane and her heirs. Jane's tread through the secret channels of Calbraith's life is so noiseless that, like the second Mrs. Ralph Waldo Emerson, only a rare footfall reaches the ears of the questing biographer. Let the reader study her face in the one known portrait of her in middle life, and draw his own conclusions.

This we do know, that the marriage was both happy and prolific, and that as Jane matured she became really beautiful, in a rather somber, dignified way. Calbraith, like his brother Oliver, was called a "family man" in the navy, sometimes in admiration, sometimes with a sneer. He consistently repelled the advances of sirens in foreign ports. And there was never a breath of scandal against Jane.

With Jane, Perry acquired three brothers-in-law. The eldest, John Slidell who had graduated from Columbia College when Calbraith was at sea in *Revenge*, became an idle "young man about town," got into trouble over a duel, and was shipped off by his father to New Orleans. There he

---

[1] The writer recalls his debutante friends bewailing the fact that Beatrice Ayer was "throwing herself away" on a young army lieutenant named George S. Patton, whom she married in 1910. But this attitude completely changed in World War I.

married a Creole belle, became a successful lawyer, and eventually United States senator. As a Democrat in a period when Democrats were generally in power, John Slidell was a valuable connection for a naval officer. Thomas Slidell, Jane's favorite brother, followed John to New Orleans and became chief justice of the state supreme court. The youngest, Alexander, entered the navy, became the biographer of Oliver H. Perry, and a valued brother officer to Calbraith.

Other Perrys of this generation made advantageous alliances. Commodore Oliver H. Perry married Elizabeth Champlin Mason of a prominent Rhode Island family. Raymond, the next elder brother, married in 1814 Mary Ann D'Wolf, daughter of James D'Wolf, the leading merchant-shipowner of Bristol, Rhode Island. The following year, Calbraith's eighteen-year-old sister Anna Maria married Lieutenant George W. Rodgers, a younger brother of the Commodore who had been an officer of U.S.S. *Wasp* in her fight with H.M.S. *Frolic*. This, and other marriages later, brought two important naval families into close alliance. Sister Jane married William Butler, a naval surgeon from South Carolina; one of their sons became a general in the Confederate Army. The youngest of Christopher R. Perry's children, Nathaniel Hazard Perry, married Lucretia M. Thatcher of a prominent New London family and made his naval career in a purser's rating. We shall encounter him briefly on board U.S.S. *North Carolina*.

Thus six children of Captain Christopher and Sarah Alexander Perry married into important families — Slidell, Mason, Rodgers, D'Wolf, Butler and Thatcher — three of whom had money as well as brains. Matthew Calbraith Perry throughout his life was intimate with all, and they were loyal to him.

As the War of 1812 drew to a close, a joyous family reunion took place in Rhode Island. The navy, frustrated by the extension and tightening of the British blockade, prepared two "flying squadrons" of brigs and schooners to harass the enemy, break up convoys, and raid his coasts, Oliver H. Perry, designated to command one of these squadrons, came home to build its flagship, named *Chippewa* after one of his prizes on Lake Erie. She was a 400-ton, 16-gun brig of war, and her construction at Warren, Rhode Island, became a Perry family enterprise. Oliver himself drew the plans and oversaw the building. Calbraith, as soon as his honeymoon furlough expired in January 1815, reported to his brother, who made him the recruiting officer for *Chippewa;* brothers Raymond and James Alexander acted as Oliver's aides.

Alexander Slidell,[1] Calbraith's eleven-year-old brother-in-law, Oliver appointed acting midshipman. He has left a charming picture of this fam-

---

[1] He added Mackenzie to his name, from that of a maternal uncle, around 1838, and was known as Alexander Slidell Mackenzie.

ily group. Captain Christopher R. Perry, whom he describes as "a man of elegant and commanding" personality, had taken a house at Bristol a few miles from the shipyard where *Chippewa* was building. There he played a patriarchal rôle, entertaining the homesick little Slidell from New York with anecdotes of his naval career, occasionally pointing a moral that might later be useful. His wife Sarah's "flow of interesting and agreeable conversation" was equally delightful. Sarah junior and the two teen-age Perry boys, James and Nathaniel, lived with them; and the three elder brothers — Oliver, Raymond and Calbraith — "occasionally joined the domestic circle, which was the perpetual scene of affectionate and cheerful intercourse." Calbraith and his bride, and Commodore and Mrs. Oliver H. Perry, lived in a nearby house and frequently visited their parents. Oliver used to entertain all hands by playing the violin and the flute, and to his music the younger brothers and sisters danced with their friends. Slidell never forgot the "freshness of feeling," the "warmth of affection" in that Perry household.

Constructing the *Chippewa* again illustrated Oliver Perry's skill in getting things done. In five months she was built, equipped, armed and ready for sea. But by that time the war was over.

After the war, the government appointed Captain Christopher Perry to a sinecure, collector of federal taxes for the Newport district. Having sold his old house at the Point, he bought a better one on Church Street, Newport, hard by Trinity Church, and there he died on 1 June 1818. Sarah, his widow, continued to live there for several years, but found it rather depressing. Newport never recovered her former importance as a seaport, nor did she revive as a summer resort until the 1830's when wealthy citizens of the eastern cities began erecting handsome Greek revival villas. So, after two of her sons had died in naval service and all but one of her daughters had married, Sarah moved to New London, possibly to be near her husband's Raymond relatives. The Marquis de Lafayette, visiting New London in 1824, paid his respects "to Madam Perry, mother of the late commodore." She died in 1830.

News of the treaty of peace, signed at Ghent on that same Christmas Eve when Calbraith and Jane were married, arrived at New York 10 February 1815. The treaty, a very advantageous one to America, was consented to by the Senate and ratified by President Monroe with almost indecent haste. But it took some time for the word to reach warships at sea, and some of the sharpest fights of the war took place after the peace treaty had been signed.

Shortly after the war was over, John Slidell offered his son-in-law Matthew Calbraith Perry command of a merchant vessel loading at New York for the Netherlands, provided he could obtain a furlough. He jumped at the chance. Guessing from what had happened in 1783 and 1801 that most of the navy would be sold or laid up in ordinary when no longer needed to fight, he preferred to enter the merchant service. That was far more profitable for a young officer than being a naval lieutenant waiting for slow peacetime promotion. He applied for a furlough. It was not granted, because another war was in the offing.

During the war with Great Britain the Dey of Algiers, one of the most powerful pirate princes of the Barbary Coast, had been capturing American merchant ships and enslaving their crews. Since he did not even trouble to reply to protests, Congress declared war on Algiers shortly after the war with England was over. In May 1815, Commodore Decatur with frigates *Guerrière, Constellation* and *Macedonian,* two sloops-of-war, three brigs and two schooners, was sent over to deal with the Dey. *Chippewa,* not completed in time to join them, formed part of a second squadron under Commodore Bainbridge, who wore his flag in U.S.S. *Independence,* our first ship-of-the-line. Lieutenant Matthew C. Perry, after a last leave, joined the squadron when it sailed from Boston 3 July 1815.

U.S.S. *Chippewa* was a smart little man-o'-war brig with a complement of ninety officers and men, commanded by Lieutenant George C. Read. Calbraith Perry was his second in command, the executive officer as we should call him today, or "First Luff," as the holder of that post was then called. Young Alexander Slidell shipped as a midshipman. Her cruise, uneventful as far as fighting was concerned, taught Perry a great deal about handling a small ship in a squadron. Before Bainbridge arrived in the Mediterranean, Decatur had done the required job very neatly. After capturing the Algerian flagship, he forced the Dey at gunpoint to release American captives and sign a peace treaty, and then made hostile demonstrations off Tunis and Tripoli, to enforce better behavior on the part of their rulers. These pirate princes would promise anything, tongue in cheek, when threatened by a strong naval force, knowing that no naval squadron could hang around the Barbary Coast indefinitely. Imagine their dismay when a second American squadron, that of Commodore Bainbridge, appeared! This had a very happy influence in checking the pride and rapacity of the Barbary chiefs. And it proved a precedent for what the younger Perry did at Naples in 1832, and in Japan in 1853-54.

Decatur's and Bainbridge's squadrons rendezvoused at Gibraltar in September. Thence they sailed home, leaving four warships to protect American commerce in the Mediterranean. Lieutenants Read and Perry had greatly enjoyed their cruise. *Chippewa* took them to exotic coasts and to Gibraltar, where the British naval officers were friendly and hospitable. Consistent with his passion for self-improvement, Calbraith managed to teach himself Spanish on this voyage. As proof of this achievement, he translated a Spanish book on Mediterranean hydrography, navigation and piloting into a blank book which is still preserved in the museum of the Naval Academy at Annapolis.

Chippewa made Newport on 15 November 1815, and once more the Perry family was united. Oliver's command, frigate *Java*, had been so badly built that work on her had to continue for a year after the war was over. On 7 January 1816, using a commodore's privilege, Oliver sailed her into Newport harbor for a last visit to his family and friends before proceeding to the Mediterranean. Three days later, on an intensely cold morning when the wind was blowing a gale from the southeast, Commodore Perry was eating breakfast in his home on Washington Square when word reached him of a shipwreck outside the harbor. Schooner *Eliza* of Newport had hit Seal Rock off Brenton's Neck, the surf was dashing over her, and the crew were in imminent danger of being swept off. Although this would ordinarily have been a job for a junior officer, Perry himself took charge, alerted his barge, and in her was rowed to the wreck with a crew of twenty stout fellows, one of whom had helped him in the ship-to-ship passage on Lake Erie. It was a tough pull of five or six miles to Seal Rock where the eleven sailors still alive were lashed to the quarterdeck, drenched with freezing spray. Perry directed the barge as it took everyone off, and rowed them back to Newport where they were revived. His readiness to risk life to save lives of seamen, a leading trait of Oliver H. Perry, was equally strong in his younger brother, as we shall see in due course.

Calbraith was not in Newport at the time of this notable rescue. *Chippewa* had been placed in ordinary, and all her officers and crew discharged or detached. He then applied for a furlough, seeing no further prospect of active duty. In December 1815 it was granted, and later twice extended, into 1819.

Little is known of his movements at this period. He commanded one or more of John Slidell's merchant ships on voyages to Europe. The only surviving scrap of evidence is a letter of October 1817 from Commodore O. H. Perry at Newport to his brother in New York. Oliver, it seems, had asked a friend in New York to procure for him a barrel of Virginia hams. The friend, finding Calbraith's ship in port with a cargo of Westphalia hams, bought them instead. That was all right with Oliver, and in the same letter he promises to pay off a debt to the younger brother because he is "going to housekeeping." This probably means that Jane, after living with her parents, had persuaded Calbraith to rent a house. His name does not appear in the New York City directory until the issue of 1822-1823, when he is listed as a "shipmaster," living at 33 Mercer Street; but by that time he was back on active duty in the navy. His first four children were born in New York between 1816 and 1821. And no record of his voyages survives, except for the Westphalia hams and a manuscript in Calbraith's handwriting entitled "Remarks on Harbors in the Gulf of Spezia, and on Genoa and Elba." This we may call the dark period of his life.

A darker one, in a different sense, was about to open. Before it does, we may mention some of the characteristics that young Calbraith had so far shown. Conscientious devotion to duty comes first; there are no over-stayed liberties, no escapades, no girls, no jolly brawls in young Perry's record, somewhat to the regret of his biographer. Ambition to improve himself as a naval officer and a citizen is a trait that marks him off from most of his brother officers. The evidence is a lively curiosity not only on professional matters but in a wide range of human knowledge — history and ethnology, horticulture and botany, conchology and science in general. Scattered about in libraries and documentary collections are manuscripts by Perry going back to his youth, not only on these subjects but on how to launch a ship, consumption of ammunition in battle, ordnance, lighthouses, and Africa. And all this in addition to making himself a master in his profession. Sainte-Beuve, in *Profils anglais*, remarked that Benjamin Franklin would have been an excellent sailor, owing to his qualities of courage balanced with prudence, and caution with observation. This balance is just what Perry had, and which, in addition to something indefinable, made him a great seaman.

Although Calbraith adored his elder brother Oliver, he was a very different person from the hero of Lake Erie. Oliver was dashing, ebullient, quick to anger and prompt in action, subject to sudden furies, unforgiving, relentless. Calbraith was calm, deliberate, slow to anger, considerate of others' feelings, forgiving. There was a certain glow about Oliver that Calbraith lacked. Oliver fascinated people when he talked; Calbraith could only convince them, and people were apt to find him stiff or even stuffy until they knew him well. Oliver had a high standard of duty, rectitude and intelligence that he applied ruthlessly to others; Calbraith had equally high standards for himself, but a tolerance for human differences and failings. This, in the end, made him a great fleet commander and an even greater diplomatist.

Both Perrys were practising as well as believing Christians. Calbraith always took a Bible to sea with him and read it through, or almost through, on every cruise. As a communicant of the Episcopal Church, he also loved the Book of Common Prayer, and read divine service in ships which had no chaplain. Although Calbraith's letters are not studded with the conventional pious expressions that were common in his era, there is no doubt that he was sincerely religious, and that he took no part in the breakdown of traditional faith that followed new scientific discoveries about the universe.

Before Oliver's brief and brilliant career ended, he had one more bout with Captain Elliott over the Battle of Lake Erie. Elliott started it by demanding a naval court of inquiry because a newspaper which reported Commodore Barclay's postwar court-martial in England stated that *Niagara* was "making away" from the battle when Perry boarded her. The court, after examining a few witnesses, rendered a verdict on that point only: — *Niagara* was not "making away," although she sailed well to windward, practically out of harm's way.

This was in 1815. The following year, Commodore O. H. Perry sailed to the Mediterranean as captain of U.S.S. *Java*. On that cruise, his hot temper got him into trouble with a captain of marines, whom he struck; a court-martial followed, and an odd sort of duel in which Perry refused to shoot and the marine missed. Elliott, taking advantage (as Perry thought) of the furor over this case, began feeding disparaging remarks about the Commodore to the newspapers and wrote to him a disagreeable, insulting letter, obviously intended to provoke a duel. Perry, in reply, told Elliott that his statements had lost him the character of a gentleman, which entitled him to challenge or be challenged.

The Commodore's next move was to demand a court-martial of the Captain, in the hope of clearing up the whole business. In 1818 he preferred very severe detailed charges against his antagonist. Charge one: — After the Battle of Lake Erie, Elliott was guilty of "pursuing a series of intrigues, designed to repair his own reputation at the expense and sacrifice of his said commanding officer." There were eleven specifications to this charge — reported oral statements by Elliott, some to the effect that when Perry boarded *Niagara* he was in despair and ready to surrender the squadron, but was dissuaded by Elliott; another, the most ridiculous and irritating, that Perry, abandoning his flagship, should properly have rowed to the *Detroit* and surrendered his fleet to Barclay! Charge two: "Conduct unbecoming an officer, and manifesting disregard of the honour of the American flag," with four specifications. Charge three: Elliott's "oppression towards certain officers and men under his command on Lake Erie," such as beating up the seaman who laughed when he ducked a shot. Charges four and five were Elliott's failure to obey his commodore's orders in the battle, especially by "keeping the wind instead of bearing down," and "through cowardice, negligence or disaffection," not doing his utmost to destroy *Queen Charlotte*, his opposite number in the British line.

This was strong language, even for those days. The charges, dated August 1818, were accompanied by eight officers' affidavits in support, and additional charges against Elliott when later commanding U.S.S. *Constitution* in the Mediterranean. President Monroe ordered the whole thing to be pigeonholed; this was the "Era of Good Feelings" and he did not wish to stir up a disagreeable subject.

Oliver Perry now intended to retire from the navy. With the prize money coming to him from the battle — $7140 to which Congress added $5000 — he built a cottage on the ancestral farm in the Narragansett country, where he raised horses, and bought a town house on Washington Square, Newport. But there was no rest for him. In response to a special appeal from the Secretary of the Navy, Oliver accepted a difficult mission to South America. He was to interview General Simón Bolívar and dissuade him from countenancing the pirates who, under cover of blank letters of marque issued by him, were plundering friend and foe alike. At the mouth of the Orinoco, Perry shifted his flag from sloop *John Adams* to the small armed schooner *Nonsuch*, in order to ascend the river to Angostura (now Ciudad Bolívar). She had to run three hundred miles against the current under sail alone, her crew tortured by heat and mosquitoes. Reaching Angostura on 26 July, Perry found General Bolívar to be absent, and had to deal with a procrastinating vice president. While waiting for him to make up his mind whether or not to call off the pirates, a large part of the crew came down with yellow fever; and by the time *Nonsuch* began her descent of the river the Commodore, too, was fever-stricken. It was impossible to do much for him, confined to a tiny cabin in debilitating heat. Off Port of Spain he was transferred to his flagship *John Adams;* but on 23 August 1819, three days after his thirty-fourth birthday, Oliver H. Perry died.

Sir Ralph Woodford, Governor of British Trinidad, saw to it that the Commodore received a funeral worthy of his rank and fame. The procession from the wharf to the cemetery at Port of Spain was preceded by the 3rd West India Regiment with arms reversed. The regimental band followed, playing the Dead March from *Saul*. Then came the commander of the garrison and staff, with white scarves and hatbands, the British Army's symbols of mourning. The funeral car was flanked by local officials on foot and officers on horseback. Behind it marched the officers of *John Adams* and *Nonsuch*, followed by "a great number of respectable inhabitants," and 120 American seamen. Sir Ralph himself on foot closed the procession. A minister of the Church of England read the funeral service, and British troops fired volleys over the grave.[1]

The country lost one of her greatest naval officers in the very flower of his life; and Calbraith lost a beloved brother.

---

[1] In 1826 his body was transferred to Newport on an American warship, and on 4 December was buried there in the Island Cemetery.

CHAPTER VII

Founding Liberia

1817–1823

Cruise in the Cyane

In the meantime, Matthew C. Perry became involved in a philanthropic enterprise which led to the Republic of Liberia. He may well have heard of this as a lad, since the project of repatriating American Negroes to Africa originated with the Reverend Samuel Hopkins of Newport in 1773. Funds were collected, and a group of prospective Negro leaders of the colony matriculated at Princeton to be properly educated in theology; then the War of Independence broke out and the business was shelved. English emancipators such as Wilberforce picked up the idea, and in 1787 began sending to Sierra Leone homeless Negroes from London, and emancipated slaves of American loyalists who had taken refuge in Nova Scotia and the Bahamas. After much suffering and despite (or possibly because of) the sending of fifty irreclaimable London prostitutes to the colony, it became a moderate success.

Early in 1817 a group of public-spirited Americans founded at Washington the American Colonization Society, dedicated to emancipating Negro slaves in the United States and colonizing them in Africa. The principal leaders were Henry Clay, the Reverend Robert Finley of Princeton, William Thornton the architect of the Capitol, Francis Scott Key of "Star-Spangled Banner" fame, and Charles Fenton Mercer, a Virginia congressman. The vision of these founders, and of the early officers of the A.C.S., which included Chief Justice Marshall, President Monroe, General John E. Howard and Justice Bushrod Washington, was noble indeed. They aimed to do for the American Negro what the Republic of Israel has done for the Jews — to give him back his homeland, or at least a part thereof.

The plan fitted in with the "universal benevolence" that was the subject of countless sermons, and assuaged a bad national conscience. Almost every white man of brains and family in the United States, for forty years after independence, was ashamed of slavery and wanted to get rid of it. Here was a chance! For the greatest obstacle to Negro emancipation was not greed, but the problem of what to do with the freedmen, in view of their difficulty in adapting themselves to American society, and the bitter antagonism of the meaner sort of white people. The founders of the American Colonization Society, assuming that the African Negro would never fit into a predominantly white society except on a basis of permanent inferiority, believed that he could only realize his potentialities through a government of his own in his ancestral continent.

Obviously the A.C.S. could not hope to repatriate all slaves in the United States, who numbered about a million and a half; nor even all the free Negroes, who numbered over 230,000. But many planters were eager to emancipate their slaves, provided they could be removed to Africa instead of becoming victims of their own improvidence and of persecution by neighboring "poor white trash." The A.C.S. encouraged this movement in every way. It hoped that respectable free Negroes in the United States would provide leaders for the emigration, and become missionaries to spread Christianity throughout the dark continent. Nobody was forced to leave; the colonists were all volunteers, although some were emancipated on condition that they would go to Africa.

This scheme was neither harebrained nor lightly entered upon. England's free Negro colony in Sierra Leone had taken care of two or three thousand former slaves, at least half of them from America. A prosperous Massachusetts free Negro named Paul Cuffee, who commanded his own trading schooner, brought to Sierra Leone at his own expense a trial shipload of thirty-eight American freedmen in 1815, but died before he could make a second voyage.

Perry, whose curiosity about Africa may have been stimulated by his voyage in *Chippewa*, must have heard about the formation of the Colonization Society, even before his long furlough ended in 1819. For a part of this period he was attached to the Brooklyn Navy Yard. Newspapers were full of the Colonization Society's plans, everyone discussed them, and abundant funds were raised by private subscription. Richard Rush, in whose home Perry's parents had been married, was a vice president of the A.C.S.; Judge William A. Duer, connected by marriage with the Slidells, was an officer of the New York branch. Thus, in marked contrast to later abolitionist societies, this scheme of emancipation was eminently respectable, even fashionable. It appealed to a man of Perry's background; he had heard from his brother and father that the Negro race could produce leaders such as Toussaint L'Ouverture. So Perry knew very well what he was about when, at his own request, on 3 August 1819, he was appointed First Lieutenant of U.S.S. *Cyane*. Her mission was to escort the first A.C.S. group of free Negroes to Africa.

Corvette *Cyane*, built in 1796 for the Royal Navy, had been captured by U.S.S. *Constitution* in her last battle of the war, and incorporated into the United States Navy. She carried a complement of 180 officers and men under thirty-five-year-old Captain Edward Trenchard. She mounted 32 carronades and a four 9-pounder "long toms." *Cyane* was a smart sailer. To be her First Luff was a distinct promotion for Perry, and as good a billet as a twenty-five-year-old lieutenant could expect in time of peace.

Congress in 1819 passed an act declaring the African slave trade, long declared illegal by most of the states, to be piracy. The navy now had the duty of capturing slave ships wherever found, and Congress appropriated $100,000 to enable slaves thus rescued to be returned to Africa. *Cyane*, consequently, had a fourfold mission: to escort the first colony of repatriated American Negroes to their destination, to cruise along the Guinea coast in search of slavers, to return to Africa any slaves she might recapture, and to nurse the new colony during infancy.

For transporting this first Afro-American colony overseas, the A.C.S. chartered a merchant brig named *Elizabeth*. Had she sailed promptly, the colonists would have enjoyed a fair summer passage, arrived on the West Coast in the dry season, and got off to a good start. Unfortunately this "Liberian *Mayflower*" suffered as many delays as had the Pilgrim Fathers' ship two centuries earlier. It took months to select and assemble the pioneer company, provision the ship, provide tools and building materials and emergency rations, and get ready for sea. Thirty families were recruited, comprising some eighty-eight free Negroes of both sexes and all ages. Mostly they were farmers, but a few tailors, carpenters and other artisans were included from New York and Philadelphia; not many came from Maryland and Virginia, and none from further South. After an emotional farewell service at the Colored Methodist Church in New York, the passengers boarded *Elizabeth* on 3 January 1820. Shepherding them were the Reverend Samuel Bacon and two other agents — one appointed by the Federal government to select a site for the colony, and one employed by the A.C.S.

While enduring this exasperating delay, Lieutenant Perry received the bad news of the death of brother Oliver in the Gulf of Paria. This is doubtless why his and Jane's third child, born at the end of October 1819, received the somewhat peculiar name for a girl of Jane Oliver Hazard Perry. Calbraith sent news of her birth to his older brother Raymond in a letter of 13 November, in which he also records that he had received a slight injury from jumping a fence in pursuit of a deserter from *Cyane*. Raymond was temporarily out of a command, and Calbraith advises him to obtain that of U.S. schooner *Spark* if he can manage it. "Service for old Lieutenants," he concludes, "is getting daily more difficult to be obtained."

Ill fortune hit the prospective African colony as soon as the people were on board ship. A spell of sub-zero weather set in, locking *Elizabeth* and *Cyane* in harbor ice. The brig finally managed to break away on 6 February, after the A.C.S. had paid for cutting a channel from her anchorage to open water. *Cyane* was frozen in for four more days. She then spent five days cruising off the entrance to New York Bay, searching in vain for *Elizabeth*, whose skipper had decided to profit by a westerly wind rather than await his escort. *Cyane's* passage to Africa was uneventful, except that on the last day of the month she spoke the French ship *Jerome*, whose "Captain politely furnished us with files of French papers from which we received the intelligence of the death of George III of England." To Lieutenant Perry, born when George III had already been on the throne for thirty-five years, this must have seemed the end of an era, as the death of Queen Victoria did to my generation.

On 13 March, after *Cyane* had passed the Cape Verde Islands but before raising the coast of Africa, there is a significant entry in Lieutenant Perry's Journal: —

The coast of Africa is generally considered an unhealthy station, and, as we are to remain there for a considerable length of time, it becomes necessary for us to adopt every precaution to guard against the diseases incident to that climate, exposure to the night air, the meridian Sun, intemperance, and fatigue are considered the principal causes of disease. The precautions observed by us as preventives, are to compel the men to wear flannel, never to allow them to sleep on deck, or to remain in wet cloathes for a moment if it can possibly be avoided, to pay the strictest attention to their cleanliness, and never to turn them out in the night unless absolutely necessary, to have fires burning upon the Birth deck a part of the day, for the purpose of dispersing the foul and introducing fresh air. To fumigate and, whitewash, the Birth deck every day, and to use every method of exhilarating the spirits of the crew; on our arriving more immediately upon our cruising ground, we shall put in practice such other means of preserving the health of the crew, as local causes (which we are yet unacquainted with) may recommend.

Since Perry later became noted in the navy for enforcing these regulations very strictly, it is evident that he "sold" them to Captain Trenchard. But where did Perry get these ideas? They are so similar to those of Sir Gilbert Blane, printed in an English medical journal in 1815, as to suggest that Perry's inquiring mind had obtained and studied a copy of it in preparation for this voyage. Sir Gilbert stressed the need for good ventilation below decks, for dryness produced by portable coal stoves, for cleanliness of the seamen, wool clothing, and fresh provisions. An earlier writer, Winterbottom, also included an absolute prohibition against sleeping ashore in a fever-stricken country or anchoring close to a swampy coast, and Perry observed these cautions too. Of course none of these sanitary precautions got at the real root of yellow fever — its transmission from an infected individual by mosquito bite. But they kept sailors out of mosquito-infested regions and made them more resistant, both to "African fever" and to other fevers and agues common on the coast. A prevalent theory that the fever was spread by "noxious exhalations" caused the ships to anchor far off shore outside the mosquitoes' flying range; and forbidding seamen to sleep on deck gave the pesky insects few targets if they did reach the ship. As for "exhilarating the spirits of the crew," Captain Trenchard had laid in a set of musical instruments, and Lieutenant Perry, who knew something of music from playing the flute, organized a shipboard band which performed for the sailors almost daily and rejoiced the natives who overheard the concerts.

Cyane reached the agreed rendezvous at Cape Mesurado on the Grain Coast on 27 March 1820. There she heard that brig *Elizabeth* had already called, but continued westward to Sierra Leone. So *Cyane* followed her thither. She received proper honors from the British authorities, but that did not help the colonists in *Elizabeth*, who had had a rough, miserable passage and moreover were completely unfitted to establish a colony. It never seems to have occurred to the kind people who organized the A.C.S. that the objects of their benevolence needed special training to cope with conditions in West Africa, or that native Africans would be hostile to the project. Actually, these regarded the Negro colonists much as American Indians regarded English colonists. The Governor of Sierra Leone refused *Elizabeth*'s passengers asylum on the mainland, forcing them to settle on swampy, malarial Sherbro Island. Captain Trenchard lent them a few of *Cyane*'s crew under Midshipman John S. Townsend, to build houses. But the rainy season had already set in, the colonists were appalled by unfamiliar conditions, and were terrified by native Negroes who swarmed about their settlement making threatening gestures and emitting blood-curdling whoops and yells.

Reverend Samuel Bacon now requested the officers of *Cyane* "to observe the different Head Lands as we passed to leeward and enquire whether the natives would be willing to dispose of a tract of land for the accommodation of the American settlers." En route, off the mouth of the River Gallinas on 10 April 1820,[1] *Cyane* chased and captured a fleet of seven brigs and schooners suspected of slavery: one owned in Baltimore; one from Charleston, which had changed both name and colors to Spanish at sea; a New Yorker which had done likewise; a Spanish brig, and three others. Having taken these without resistance, tireless Captain Trenchard

---

[1] Gallinas River (on modern maps called Sulima or Moa) is in eastern Sierra Leone near the Liberian border.

turned *Cyane* back to Gallinas roadstead and there picked up two more sail, one from New York and one from Baltimore, making a total bag of nine. Two were released, the slaves on board were sent to Sierra Leone, and the vessels destroyed. The Americans among their crews were sent to the United States in four of the prize schooners, each under command of one or two officers detached from *Cyane*.

Continuing her cruise to the eastward, *Cyane* raised Cape Mesurado on 13 April 1820. Perry in his ship's journal, described it as "the most elligable [sic] situation for a settlement I have yet seen. The Natives are pacific in their dispositions, engage but little in the Slave Trade, and . . . express a willingness to admit our Countrymen among them. The land is extremely rich and is capable of producing Rice, Coffee, Sugar Cane, Indigo, Cotton and the common fruits and vegetables of Tropical climates." There is "a fine bay, where vessels may anchor near the shore in 10 fathoms water." Healthy sites for a fort and town are present. "It is to be hoped that the advantages of this place will induce Mr. Bacon to remove his Colony hither."

To prepare the way, Perry exchanged letters next day with the one civilized resident of the Cape, "Mr. J. S. Mill, an intelligent Mulatto who had received his education at Liverpool." Perry told him about the colonization project and requested his good offices in purchasing a tract of land. Mill replied that he could promise nothing, but he sent runners into the interior "to convene the Kings and Chiefs of the Country . . . to consult on the nature of your propositions." The ship remained in Mesurado roadstead long enough to receive their favorable reply, then sailed back to Sherbro Island to inform Dr. Bacon. Thus, the eventual success of Liberia derives from Perry's choice of this healthy site.

Cyane now ranged the Guinea coast looking for more slavers. In the roadstead off Grand Bassa, on 15 April, she spoke H.M.S. *Snapper* and persuaded her captain to take charge of "those of our prisoners who called themselves Englishmen." She then left the coast for the Cape Verde Islands.

On her way thither, "Alexander Scott, a most excellent seaman," died of yellow fever, the second victim among *Cyane*'s complement of 180 officers and men. Both casualties were members of the first cutter's crew, which had been constantly employed in shore duty as well as speaking ships, affording them unusual exposure to the anopheles. The approximately fifty others who took the fever were cured by "an immediate application of purgation . . . before it got entire hold of the system." In the two fatal cases the men's condition was "exasperated by intemperance." (*Cyane* was a dry ship except for the grog ration, but the boats' crews always managed to get liquor from the ships or shore establishments that they visited.) Lieutenant Perry adds: —

In my opinion, we may conceive ourselves fortunate, in not losing more of our men. The sudden transition from a very cold, to an extremely hot climate, would naturally effect the health of any Crew. I do not therefore conceive the Coast of Africa (in the dry season) a peculiarly unhealthy station. The most strict attention to cleanliness ought however to be observed.

On 19 May *Cyane* put in at Porto Praia in the Cape Verdes, saluting the Portuguese governor with 17 guns. She only received 15 in return; but that, as the Governor explained, was because the fort ran out of ammunition. His Excellency hustled up enough powder in the town for two more bursts, and American honor was vindicated. *Cyane*'s band of music had created such a sensation on the coast that its reputation reached Porto Praia ahead of her. As soon as the matter of the salute had been adjusted, the Governor invited Captain Trenchard and his officers to take tea, and intimated that a band concert would be welcome, "as the evening will be rendered delightful and pleasant by a full moon." It was, and the invitation was repeated for the following Sunday.

Lieutenant Perry, ever watchful for useful information, inserted in his Journal a not very flattering description of Porto Praia. The two hundred soldiers who made up the garrison were paid only three dollars a month, from which they were obliged to find their own food and clothing. Consequently "it is not infrequent to find a Soldier on guard at the Governors house (or Palace as it is called, a common two-story frame house) without shirt, shoes or Coat." The island is capable of producing an abundance of corn, coffee, cotton, sugar and indigo, but the people are too indolent "to labour more than absolute necessity compels them." They produce enough surplus, however, to make this a favorite port of call for vessels bound to the Pacific or Brazil to obtain fresh provisions and water. Turkeys cost only a dollar apiece, fowls three dollars a dozen, pigs from one to three dollars each, and a 250-pound bullock, twenty dollars. As there was no good chart of the harbor, Perry made one, to be circulated in the navy. The harbor is safe, he says, but there is no wharf and the ocean swell sets in, making landing on the beach very difficult at times. He vividly describes the fix *Cyane* got into by anchoring too far up the bay. The anchor came home when getting under way, and she almost drifted onto Quail Island before a second anchor brought her up.

At Santa Cruz, Tenerife, *Cyane* had a cold reception. The Spanish governor refused to return her salute, on the ground that King Ferdinand VII had given him orders to take no notice of any republican flag. Nevertheless, Perry found much good to say of Santa Cruz; the town was the most beautiful Spanish one he had seen, "streets wide and perfectly clean, the houses airy and commodious, and the people kind and hospitable." *Cyane* broke two anchors in the harbor, but he did not blame it on the bottom;

the navy had recently been supplied with chain cables, which were too strong for old anchors.

U.S.S. *Adams* and *Hornet* joined *Cyane* in September, and, returning to the West Coast, captured four more slavers. Perry's journal indicates his enthusiasm for this duty, and his interest in the native Negroes. Kroomen, the expert surf boaters of this coast, were employed to take passengers and cargoes ashore in their dugout canoes, and also as sailors on coastwise vessels. When putting Kroomen on the payroll, *Cyane*'s yeomen, unable to translate their names into English, allotted fancy names such as "John T. Chew Tobacco," "Pot of Beer," "Sam Coffee," "Three Fathoms," and "Drawbucket." These were very pleasing to the savages, who not only adopted them as official cognomens but handed them down to their children. Occasionally a native crew brought out a chief to the ship. If he intended to trade, the potentate brought along his "scroff" or treasurer, who carefully counted and appraised the "cut-money," the coins. When cautioned to tell the truth or confirm a covenant, an oath was taken by dipping a finger in salt mixed with earth, raising it toward heaven, and then sucking off the salt, to them a sacred mineral. Scores of Kroomen were hired by Captain Trenchard at $1.25 a week, to relieve feverstricken sailors of their heavy labor. All this was strange and amusing to the American sailors, but the heavy rains and intense heat prostrated many members of the crew; and despite Perry's sanitary regulations, not only yellow fever but scurvy broke out.

Had Dr. Bacon promptly taken Perry's advice to remove to Cape Mesurado, many lives, including his own, would have been saved. When *Cyane* next called at Sherbro, she found the colonists reduced to the utmost misery. Every one of the eighty-eight Negroes had caught "African fever," and twenty-three had died. Dr. Bacon and every other white leader but one were dead. Midshipman Townsend of *Cyane*, "a very excellent young officer" according to Perry had perished, along with the entire crew who had been left at Sherbro to help the Negroes. The survivors were leaderless, listless, and too depressed even to grow their own food. We shall later hear better things of this colony, when transferred to Monrovia. Perry paid this just and generous tribute to the departed leader in his journal: —

Mr. Bacon died of actual exaustion. "Buoyed up as he was by the pleasing hopes of carrying into execution the philanthropic views of the Colonizing society: The small spark of life which previous sickness had left him, blazed forth in his generous zeal"; and he appeared, when I last saw him, in the full vigour of health. But on his return to Sherbro the evident ingratitude and bad conduct of many of the Colonists, the villiany of Kerell, on whom he placed the utmost confidence; the loss of all but one of his white companions, and the death of many of the Blacks, sunk his spirits from the pinnacle of hope into the deepest despondency. Yet were his exertions unabated, he assisted in the most toilsome labour, threw himself into the River and brought the luggage from the Schooner on his shoulders, attended the sick with the most affectionate care, deprived himself of rest, and the common comforts of life, until his weak and debilitated frame sunk under these accumulated hardships and miseries and sickness came upon him. By the advice of a trader from Sierra Leone he endeavoured to reach that place, that he might there obtain medical aid and the comforts he stood so much in need of, but Death overtook him on his way, and he breathed his last at the British Factory on Cape Shilling.

Captain Trenchard now decided that it was time to sail home, the navy department having authorized him to do so when he thought best. On 4 October *Cyane* departed Sierra Leone, and after a very foul-weather passage reached New York on Christmas day 1820. Captain Trenchard's health had been so undermined by the African cruise that he caught pneumonia and died when still in his thirties.

Lieutenant Perry, who fortunately had escaped contagion, passed the rest of the holiday season at home. And before the twelve days of Christmas were up, Jane was pregnant again. Long-desired Matthew C. Perry Jr. was born in New York on 6 October 1821 after his father had returned to sea.

Cruise in the Shark

Disagreeable as this first African cruise had been in many respects, Perry was eager to return. He believed in the objectives of the A.C.S., he liked the coast and the people, he was eager to put into effect on other ships the sanitary regulations that he had worked out to preserve sailors' health. While *Cyane* lay at the Brooklyn Navy Yard awaiting orders, he enjoyed extended leaves to spend with his little family. Then, at his own request, on 21 July 1821, he was ordered to Washington to take command of the United States armed schooner *Shark* on an African voyage.

This was his first independent command. He had been promoted lieutenant commandant, corresponding to our lieutenant commander. *Shark*, which had just been built at the Washington Navy Yard, was a fast 200-ton schooner of Baltimore-clipper type, 86 feet in length. She carried a complement of 70 officers and men, and mounted 12 guns. Perry was delighted with her. To his old commodore, John Rodgers, he wrote from New York on 24 July 1821, just before she sailed for Africa: —

From the period of our leaveing Washington, we have contended against bafling adverse winds, but during the whole time the Schooner has behaved in a manner highly satisfactory, not only as regards her sailing, but the ease with which she carries her guns, her stiffness and buoyancy, are equally the subject of admiration among the numerous Vessels fallen in with during our passage

. . . speak in admiring terms of her appearance, good accommodations, and excellent fitment, while the Pilot, and Mr. Floyd, think her precisely what a man of war Schooner ought to be. . . . I regret that I cannot give so favourable a representation of her spars, her lower masts complain at the slightest Puff, particularly the Foremast, which indicates serious weakness a little below the Hounds, her topmasts are by no means to be depended on, as a proof of which we sprung our Fore Top Mast in two or three places, when the Schooner was going but 4½ knots, wrap full, water smooth and the breeze very moderate, the manner of its breaking is also an indication of its weakness, as it broke without splintering in the least, like a dry stick.

Perry's orders were to convey Reverend Eli Ayers to Africa as United States commissioner for the Negro colony. We are fortunate to have two original accounts of this voyage, one by Midshipman William F. Lynch who describes Dr. Ayers as "an intelligent and prepossessing gentleman, with whom we were much pleased," and the other by the skipper himself. His journal reflects his pride and pleasure over having this command at the age of twenty-seven, as well as a charming naïveté. For instance, "I imagine myself on the Inner edge of the Gulph Stream, but unfortunately I have no certain means of ascertaining the fact, as I broke the only Thermometer in the Vessel, the day of our Sailing." He takes great pride in overhauling merchant vessels, although unable to carry full sail on the weak foremast. Another entry shows the curiosity over wonders of nature that Perry maintained his life long. The men fished out of the sea an object which they called a "Beach Beau." The sailors believed it to be a "marine production," but the skipper guessed that it was the fruit of some tree which had drifted so long on the Gulf Stream as to be "completely covered with barnacles." My oceanographic friend Dr. Henry B. Bigelow feels pretty sure that it was a piece of driftwood to which long goose barnacles had attached themselves.

Shark had a pleasant summer passage. Her first landfall (1 September 1821), Santa Maria in the Azores, caused the skipper some chagrin as it proved his reckoning to be fifty miles out. He was somewhat consoled by the fact that his officers figured out an even more inaccurate position. Had he known that Columbus and his pilots had made similar and even greater mistakes on their return from the New World in 1493, he might have felt better. Another week's sail brought the schooner to Funchal, Madeira. In order to make a good impression there, Perry "employed the crew in turning in the Fore Rigging a fresh, setting it up, Rattling it down, &c., Painting Boats, caulking the Spar Deck, &c. &c." Almost every day the "great guns" were exercised. One seaman was "punished at the Gangway (6 lashes) for insolence" — moderate punishment, according to the standards of that era. Passing ships gave Perry news of the death of Queen Caroline of England, and of Napoleon, and both were duly logged.

Next landfall was on Tenerife, on 12 September. "At 11 P.M. discovered the loom of the land ahead and at midnight, when the moon had disappeared, could distinctly discern the land." *Shark* hove-to off Port Oratava, picked up a pilot, and passed the Grand Canary. Perry then had the satisfaction of overhauling an English vessel bound from Guernsey to Rio de Janeiro and giving her skipper his true position: "If he had not fortunately fallen in with us, he probably would have shared the fate of many others by running upon Cape Blanco."

At Santa Cruz, Tenerife, Perry filled his water casks. Since he had called there in *Cyane* the year before, there had been a revolution in Spain which made Ferdinand VII a constitutional monarch, and the new governor of the island "cheerfully returned" *Shark's* 13-gun salute, gun for gun. Perry observed with pleasure that the Canary Islanders were now enjoying "many of the rights and priviliges of free men," although these would not bear "comparison with those of our happy Citizens." The principal victims of the new regime were the priests, thousands of whom had been unfrocked and their convents converted into barracks. The laity now go so far in "insulting and contemptuous conduct toward their priests, that even foreigners who before dispized them for their superstitious bigotry now equally dispize them for their wanton disrespect to men who, if they are not immaculate, are not as bad as is generally supposed by their religious opponents."

"Fine, pleasant Trade winds," Perry's journal records for 21 September 1821, after leaving the Canaries. He practises the crew firing at a target with small arms, "Musquett or Pistol," and finds them "rather awkward at first, but I am in hopes a few exercises will make them more expirt." Firing at targets was very unusual in that era; "exercising the great guns," which we find noted in ships' logs from the time of John Paul Jones, meant merely going through the motions of firing, or firing blank charges; cannon balls were too valuable to waste. Realizing that *Shark* is "now getting on to a Cruising ground where there is a great prospect of falling in with vessels contravening National Laws," Perry takes no chances and misses no opportunity. He chases one suspicious-looking sail for two hours, only to find her to be a whaler bound for the Pacific, but he has the satisfaction of pointing out to the Nantucket skipper that he is one hundred miles east of his reckoning. Two more sail are overhauled after a long chase; one proves to be English, bound for the South Shetlands; the other, a Portuguese brig from Boa Vista to Fayal with salt.

On 28 September *Shark* is off Porto Grande on the island of São Vicente. Perry wishes to enter this familiar harbor, best in the Cape Verdes; but, seeing a big armed vessel inside with no colors displayed, he cautiously sends his first lieutenant in a boat to check. The suspicious ship hoists "Buenos Ayrean Colours" — the blue and white flag of the new

Argentine Republic. Perry, reassured, sails into Porto Grande, anchors, and exchanges visits with Captain Mason of the Argentinian warship *Heroine*. Two New Bedford whalers, a Salem trading schooner and a Philadelphia brig are also in the harbor, and Perry visits them. One is impressed by the sociability of Atlantic trading routes in days of sail, as compared with nowadays when one can cross and recross the ocean without sighting anything but aircraft.

Perry now sails south through the Cape Verdes, chasing and overhauling three or four ships en route, and decides to take a look at English Road off the island of Maio. There, says the official *Africa Pilot*, "Landing is usually bad." It was very bad in 1821. Perry sent in the cutter under Lieutenant Montgomery to speak two brigs anchored in the roadstead, hoping that one might be bound for America and could carry dispatches to the Navy Department. Perry cautioned Montgomery not to land because a big surf was breaking on the beach; but the Portuguese fort fired on the boat so the Lieutenant decided he had better land and show his credentials. The Governor, who had mistaken *Shark* for a "patriot vessel" — a Portuguese revolutionary craft — "made some difficulty, but ultimately permitted the Boat to leave." Perry, observing the firing, stood in as close as he dared "to protect the Boat and if necessary to fire on the Town." Fortunately that was unnecessary. *Shark* recovered her cutter and sailed for Porto Praia, Santiago, in order to fill water casks. That harbor is but a few miles distant from Maio, but *Shark* ran into a flat calm and the passage took 36 hours. At 5 P.M. 10 October, "Having provided ourselves with fruit & vegetables, two Bullocks & four sheep for the men, I got under way and stood to sea."

Between Porto Praia and Sierra Leone, *Shark* chased and spoke several vessels. One, which Perry overtook in a dead calm by making his crew man the sweeps, turned out to be H.M.S. *Thistle* from Gambia, bound to Sierra Leone. Her skipper, Lieutenant Commander Hagan RN, had lost every one of his officers through yellow fever. Perry invited him on board for dinner and offered to lend him officers to help work *Thistle* into Sierra Leone. Hagan felt he could cover that small distance without American help, but was glad to have *Shark* sail in company.

Before the end of October Perry landed Eli Ayers at a bay near Freetown, where the survivors of the unhealthy Sherbro Island colony had been permitted by the governor to settle. Since Perry's last visit, another shipload of Negro colonists had been landed here from brig *Nautilus* under the guidance of two missionary couples, the J. B. Winns and the Ephraim Bacons, and the Reverend Mr. Andrews. He and both Winns were already dead, and many of the blacks too, although yellow fever generally did not affect them as seriously as it did the whites. During Perry's absence his suggestion of transferring the colony to Cape Mesurado had been acted upon by Ephraim Bacon. Ayers promptly sailed to the site in U.S. armed schooner *Alligator*, commanded by Lieutenant Robert F. Stockton, another young naval officer destined to be famous. They rounded up King Peter and other native chiefs who lived thereabouts, and bought the site of Monrovia for an assortment of axes, hatchets, cloth and other trading truck. Ayers then returned to Sierra Leone and chartered a British schooner, which brought the first of the Sherbro Island survivors to Cape Mesurado on 7 January 1822. In August of that year, after *Shark* had sailed for the West Indies, the Reverend Jehudi Ashmun, who is regarded as the Great White Father of Liberia, brought out 52 new colonists, some lately released from a captured slaver. All surviving American Negroes in Sierra Leone were then shifted to Cape Mesurado.

Unfortunately an attack by the natives was coming up. Despite their sale of land, the native Africans took a very dim view of this irruption of American "do-gooders" to evangelize them and suppress their only lucrative business, the slave trade. There might have been no trouble for some time, had not the American colonists violated another precious native prerogative — not confined to Africa — of plundering every trading schooner that ran aground. An English schooner having grounded near Cape Mesurado, the American Negroes protected her crew, helped them float her off, and were rewarded for their pains by the gift of a brass cannon complete with ammunition. This humane action being regarded by the natives as utterly abominable, they decided to wipe out the free Negro colony. In October 1822 a chief of the Dey tribe known as King George led a force of several hundred tribesmen against the American settlement, where only twenty-seven men were strong enough to bear arms. Under the inspiring leadership of Jehudi Ashmun, helped by skillful serving of the brass cannon, this forlorn remnant repulsed the attack.

Stout courage was rewarded, the colony made a fresh start. Officers of a British armed schooner negotiated peace between natives and colonists, who were also helped by the crew of a privateer under Colombian colors; and in the spring of 1823 the crew of U.S.S. *Cyane* built a Martello tower as key to the colony's defense. Over a hundred free Negroes came out from Virginia in 1824, the year that Ashmun named the colony Liberia, and the town Monrovia after President Monroe. A temporary constitution was adopted, and new settlements were deliberately scattered along the coast between Sierra Leone and Cape Palmas in order to suppress the slave trade.

After landing Eli Ayers, *Shark* patrolled the West Coast in search of slavers and made two captures, the first on 8 November being a French schooner named *Ys*, owned by the Governor of Guadeloupe. Her cargo, consisting of about a thousand gallons of rum, seven thousand pounds of tobacco and a trunkful of umbrellas (in great demand by the West Coast

Negroes), convinced Perry that she was "unquestionably waiting for a cargo of Slaves." But he could find no evidence permitting him to capture her, so she was allowed to proceed.

"Having examined that part of the Coast from the Bissago Islands to Cape Mount," continues Perry in his journal, "and executed the orders of the Department so far as it relates to my African Cruize, I shaped my course to the West intending to pass along the edge of Soundings, in the hopes of falling in with some more Slavers." On 10 November he discovered a strange sail and "called all hands to Chase Ship. Employed wetting Sails." That procedure was supposed to increase a ship's speed; probably it did, since the sailcloth of that era was rather loosely woven. At 4:30 P.M. "Out sweeps. At 6 the Chase made all sail endeavoring to Escape. I cleared for action, hoisted American Colours and fired the Larboard Bow Gun 8 times successively, the last 6 shotted. At 9 sent the Gig and Cutter ahead to tow. At 10:45 Fired a muskett, when the Chase hove too and showed French Colours. Hoisted Spanish Colours and sent 3 officers and a crew on board, and in return brought back the Capt. with his papers and 7 of his Crew. The Stranger proved to be the French schooner *Caroline*, Victor Ruinet Commander, 3 days from Cape Mount with a cargo of 133 Slaves." Here Midshipman Lynch takes up the story: —

> The slaver . . . was bound to the French West India islands. The overpowering smell and the sight presented by her slave-deck, can never be obliterated from the memory. In a space of about 15 by 40 feet, and four feet high, between-decks, 163 [*sic*] negroes, men, women, and children, were promiscuously confined. In sleeping they were made to dovetail, each one drawn up to the shortest span, and the children were obliged to lie upon the full grown. They were all naked, and to protect from vermin not a hair was permitted to grow upon their persons. Their bodies were so emaciated, and their black skins were so shrunk upon the facial bones, that in their torpor, they resembled so many Egyptian mummies half-awakened into life. A pint of water and half a pint of rice each, was their daily allowance, which is reduced if the passage be prolonged. The passage is performed in from fifty to seventy days.
>
> I never saw the sympathies of men more deeply moved than were those of our crew. Immediately after taking possession, while the papers were being examined, we hoisted up a cask of water, and some bread and beef, and gave each poor slave a long drink and a hearty meal.

After inspecting the schooner's papers, which were French and in good order, Perry decided that he had no authority to capture her, since France was not yet a party to the international treaty to suppress the slave trade. He "reluctantly permitted" her to proceed, after taking into custody an American member of the crew. *Shark*'s officers, indignant at letting the slaves go, offered jointly to reimburse their captain for any loss he might sustain for illegal capture. He declined, but before releasing the *Caroline* made her French captain sign a paper solemnly promising "never to be directly or indirectly hereafter, Engaged in transporting Slaves . . . from the Coast of Africa," that he "hereby abjures the Slave Trade forever," and further pledging himself "to treat with humanity and kindness the Slaves now on board during our passage to Martinique." This curious pledge, the fulfillment of which we have no means of checking, was signed under oath by "Le Capitaine V. Ruinet, in presence of M. C. Perry, Esq., Commander, T. B. Timberlake, Purser, J. S. Wiley, Act'g Surgeon." "With feelings that I cannot undertake to express," wrote Lynch, "we saw the schooner fill away and steer to the westward bearing into life-long captivity the unhappy wretches whom we had inspired with a hope of freedom."

U.S.S. *Shark*, we gather from Midshipman Lynch, was a taut but not too happy a ship, since "the 'Rodgers' system of discipline was strictly enforced; the ruling feature of which is, to render every one as uncom-fortable as possible." This "Rodgers system," of which we shall have more to say, Perry had imbibed as the Commodore's midshipman in U.S.S. *President*. Its object was not to make all hands uncomfortable but to keep them healthy, under good discipline, and get as much work as possible accomplished. The leading features were a minimum of shore liberty, keeping everyone occupied, and corporal punishment. Lynch does give Perry credit for keeping *Shark*'s crew healthy by his strict regulation of their diet and clothing. He missed no opportunity to procure fresh vege-tables, and required every sailor to turn in with flannel next his skin.

From Africa she sailed before the trades to the West Indies in late No-vember 1821, following the track of homeward-bound Guineamen. Perry hoped to encounter a few, but did not. Arriving at Cuba, he sent the ship's boats up rivers looking for pirates. Only one did he manage to overhaul, and she was at sea off Havana. "I found her full of Rogues," says his journal, "and as I could not obtain sufficient proof against her my Self, I determined on delivering them into the hands of the Governor General of Cuba for punishment." He sent by boat a letter to His Excellency in Ha-vana, who in returned thanked Commander Perry and "pledged himself to have them tried as Pirates."

At Kingston, Jamaica, Perry received orders to sail directly to New York. It was a tough passage. From Cape Hatteras *Shark* had to beat against a northeast snowstorm. No fires could be lighted, and "when we reached port," writes Midshipman Lynch, "our schooner, from the truck to the water's edge, was a pyramid of ice; and as fast as we were detached from her, each one, who possessed a home, made what haste he could to reach it." There were bad cases of frostbite; but it was Perry's proud boast that the schooner had lost not one of her complement after six months in fever-infested regions.

Perry was not through with *Shark;* a very interesting tour of duty lay ahead. But before that came about, his family sustained another loss. The youngest brother, Lieutenant James Alexander Perry, who as a tiny reefer had been with Oliver in the Battle of Lake Erie, was drowned in the harbor of Valparaiso while trying to rescue a shipmate who had fallen overboard. The widowed mother, Mrs. Christopher Raymond Perry, petitioned Congress for a pension on the ground of inadequate income, as she was now cut off from the financial help that this son had afforded. "Your petitioner," she wrote, "is destitute, and her support, small as it is, is thrown on hands but inadequately able to bear it" — meaning, no doubt, Calbraith with his three small children. "She knows not that she has any other claims on the liberality of her country, than to say that she has reared five sons for its service." The petition was not granted.

Perry did not pay for his interest in Liberia with his life, as had Captain Trenchard, Dr. Ashmun, and scores of others; but his selection of the site of Monrovia deserves to be held in grateful remembrance by the Republic. Twenty years later, when the A.C.S. and Liberia were being viciously attacked both by Garrison abolitionists and pro-slavery advocates, Perry remained loyal to the generous concept of his youth. In another chapter we shall describe his later services to the Negro republic.

Every captain of a naval or merchant vessel is "the Old Man" to the sailors, no matter what his age; and Perry as commanding officers of *Shark* had earned a nickname that stood by him through life — "Old Bruin." Other sobriquets also he had, such as "Old Matt" and "the Old Hoss"; but "Old Bruin" best fits his character, as well as the powerful voice with which he roared out orders to the men.

CHAPTER VIII

"Old Bruin" Hunts Pirates in the West Indies

1822–1823

C OMMODORE Oliver H. Perry's mission to Angostura, in the course of which he lost his life, we have already described. At that time the liberated South American nations' practice of issuing letters of marque in blank to armed vessels manned by desperadoes of all nations (including the United States) was causing havoc to peaceful American merchantmen. A letter signed by presidents of six Boston insurance companies to President Monroe, on 1 December 1819, listed 44 American vessels which had already been plundered or captured in the West Indies that year.

The Commodore's efforts bore fruit. Privateers acting under commissions from Mexico, Colombia and other Latin-American republics were now under fairly good control. But worse was to come, from pirates based on Cuba and Puerto Rico. The Spanish authorities of those islands, resenting the sympathy and help given by the United States to their revolted colonies, winked at far worse practices than the new republics had condoned. Pirate ships based on Cuban and Puerto Rican harbors, some flying the traditional Jolly Roger but mostly showing the fashionable pirate colors, a plain blood-red ensign, began capturing American trading vessels off shore. Armed barges jumped peaceful traders within sight of the Morros, made off with the plunder, and escaped to the bush after killing and even torturing their crews.

To deal with this menace, the Navy Department in 1822 set up a West Indies Squadron, to which Perry's schooner *Shark* was attached as soon as she returned from Africa. Captain James Biddle, the commodore, wore his flag in captured frigate *Macedonian*.

Shark sailed from New York 26 February 1822 and arrived at Key West next month. As the treaty with Spain ceding Florida to the United States had just been ratified, Skipper Perry had the honor of formally taking possession and raising the Stars and Stripes at Key West, then called Thompson's Island; Perry named the harbor Port Rodgers, but neither name stuck.

As José María de Heredia wrote, the Caribbean was *le pays du fable* for Europeans and North Americans. Sailors repeated to one another the quip that in the West Indies one saw "mountains of sugar, rivers of rum, and fish that fly in the air"; and the observation by a returned sailor's mother that she could take the first two, but flying fishes — "Don't tell me such lies!" Typical of Caribbean yarns was that of the Yankee skipper who sailed Ralph Waldo Emerson to Europe. In the 1820's he had been captured in the Caribbean by a pirate, who cut up his vessel's sails into pants for the pirate crew, and stripped her copper sheathing to make brass instruments for his band, which the skipper was required to conduct under pain of death, and to play masses for the pirate casualties!

Perry's first success in these waters took place off Tampico, Mexico, on 5 May 1822. *Shark* chased a suspicious-looking schooner ashore. "Old Bruin" sent Lieutenant Young, with gig and cutter, "to undeceive the crew, as I naturally inferred that they took us for an enemy." But the crew fled to the bush, and an examination of the schooner showed that she had been looted. Perry concluded that these men were pirates and so informed the Governor, Don Felipe la Gaiza. The schooner was too hard and fast aground to be floated off.

Later that year, *Shark* operated off the north coast of Cuba, accompanied by schooner *Grampus*, commanded by Lieutenant Francis H. Gregory. At Sagua la Grande, a notorious pirate rendezvous, they captured an outlaw schooner. As Midshipman Lynch describes the fight,

I was attached to one of the boats directed against the schooner, and as we neared her, the scene became more and more exciting. Besides the boom of the cannon fired from the schooner and the battery, the lake and the shore around rang with the incessant peal of musketry, and the hurling of the iron and lead around us was dreadful. But as oar would drop, and form after form sink from its place, the louder became the shout, the more vindictive the fury of our men. Ourselves upon the bow, the other boat farther astern, almost simultaneously, we laid the pirate aboard. To grapple the side, spring on the bulwark and leap upon the deck, amid muskets, pikes and brandished knives, was the work of an instant. With courage equal to our own, the pirates rushed forward to repel us, and a desperate hand-to-hand conflict ensued.

The musketry had now ceased, and a pistol shot was but occasionally heard, but the clash of steel was incessant, and the silent but deadly thrust became more frequent. The shout of an officer as he cut down the swarthy pirate with whom he was engaged, was responded to by a wild cry of exultation from the men, and animated as by one spirit, we bounded forward with a cheer. A better cause and far more numerous force, could not have withstood our charge. The pirates gave way, slowly at first, but when our leader called out "push home, men! and no quarter!" and the cry "no quarter! no quarter!" was fiercely re-

peated, they turned, and springing to the side, leaped overboard, and endeavored to escape by swimming. Many of our men plunged after them sword in
hand; others jumped to the boats, and pursuing, cut them down as they overtook them, while another portion, from the deck of the captured vessel, deliberately shot them as they struggled in the water.

On the part of those wretches, not a cry was raised — not a supplication uttered. When too hotly pursued, they turned to grapple where they could, and
in silence they received the death wound, and in silence they sunk, their throats
gurgling the water which was deeply crimsoned with their blood. . . .

When those in the battery saw their fellow-pirates leap overboard, they also
took to flight. They were relentlessly pursued, and the scene which had been
enacted upon the water was repeated on the land. But few escaped; and destroying what we could not preserve, we gathered their booty, and bore our prize
away in triumph.

Score two for "Old Bruin" and the *Shark*.

Three days later the two American vessels gave chase to a pirate
schooner which had the appropriate name *Bandera de Sangre* (Bloody
Banner). She was commanded, says Lynch, "by the most desperate and
remorseless of the ruffians." His men, less brave than himself, fled after a
few ineffectual shots, some in boats and others by swimming. The American bluejackets followed them ashore; but most of the pirates, well acquainted with the locality, escaped. Both captured schooners and three
prisoners were sent to the United States for adjudication.

Shark now swept the north coast of Cuba between Sagua la Grande and
Matanzas. She forced ashore one pirate schooner flying a red shirt in lieu
of ensign, and after the crew had escaped to the bush floated her for use as
a "lookout boat." Perry himself put off from *Shark* in one of her armed
boats, and for six days "scoured the coast of Cuba from Sugar Key to
Matanzas," as he reported to Commodore Biddle. "My several Expeditions
have become acquainted with a system of abominable fraud, rapine and
[*torn*] openly permitted by the Spanish Authorities and encouraged by
the most wealthy men in the Island. There is not a Fisherman who is not a
Pirate, nor a canoe that is not a Pirate Vessel in miniature. The plundered
goods are publickly sold at the large Commercial Towns, and the First
Merchants become the purchasers."

During this West Indian cruise, *Shark* encountered a waterspout and
squall, subject of the only known picture of the schooner, which we have
reproduced. Note the men on the bowsprit who have just taken in the flying jib, sailors on the yards trying to furl the flapping royals and topgallants, and the main sail "scandalized" — the old sea term for reducing its
pull by dropping the peak.

After this north coast operation there developed the consequences of
exposure to mosquitoes, and want of food and rest. Perry himself had a

U.S.S. *Shark*, artist unknown
Struck by tornado in the Caribbean; foresail has been brailed up, mainsail
let go, men are furling topgallant and royal and handing the jib

touch of the fever. "This climate makes sad inroads upon my naturally strong constitution," he wrote to his old commodore, "and I am now labouring under the effects of a severe indisposition, the Consequence of great exposure during our late Boat Expeditions." Men with serious illness were transferred to larger vessels, and *Shark* sailed for Key West.

Even Perry's precautions did not prevent yellow fever breaking out in *Shark* after she reached there, Key West being then as much infected by malignant mosquitoes as any place in the Caribbean. Writes Lynch: "Our hastily erected and scantily furnished hospitals were soon crowded with the sick, the dying and the newly dead. . . . He alone, who has laid on a rude pallet in the ward of a hospital, crowded with the victims of a malignant disease, can realize the horrors of such a state."

The West Indies Squadron operated with no great success in 1822. Pirates were too nimble, the Spanish authorities uncoöperative, and the ravages of yellow fever decimated the American crews. Flagship *Macedonian* was obliged to leave for Norfolk in July after losing forty-nine officers and men, with eighty-four more on the sick list. Eventually one hundred members of that crew died of the fever. Biddle, like Captain Christopher Perry in 1799, ascribed this outbreak to "impure and offensive air" issuing from the hold, and blamed it on officers of the Boston Navy Yard for sending her to sea without a thorough cleansing. A court of inquiry headed by Commodore John Rodgers cleared the Boston officers; this made Biddle furious, and in a private letter he accused Rodgers of fumbling the *Little Belt* affair, of running away from the enemy during the war, and of many other things. It is probable that a part of this enmity was transferred to Matthew C. Perry, whose bold and energetic actions are not mentioned in Biddle's reports; but later they became good friends.

A new chapter in this quasi-war opened in 1823 when David Porter relieved Biddle as Commodore of the West Indies Squadron. Congress having appropriated half a million dollars for pirate suppression, Porter purchased and armed eight small Chesapeake Bay schooners which he called the Mosquito Fleet, to operate in shoal water, and substituted sloop-of-war *Peacock* for the unlucky frigate as flagship. On 3 March he wrote to the Secretary of the Navy announcing his squadron's arrival at St. Thomas: "I have dispatched Lieutenant Commandant Perry with the *Shark* and three small schooners, to scour the south side of Porto Rico, and shall sail tomorrow with the rest of the squadron to St. John's, where I have been informed that several privateers have been fitted out which have done considerable injury to our commerce." A welcome addition to the squadron was "steam galliot" *Sea Gull*, second steamer in the U. S. Navy — *Fulton* having been the first. A converted Long Island Sound side-wheeler with light draft, burning wood and mounting three guns, she proved very useful in overtaking suspicious vessels in a calm, and penetrating shallow harbors and creeks. Commodore Porter, often as not, wore his broad pendant in *Sea Gull.*

Shark in the meantime had been operating in Mexican waters. She was sent to cruise between Veracruz and Tampico (according to a letter from Perry to a friend on 2 February 1823) "for the protection of our commerce and the Security of the friends of American citizens coming from Mexico. The Government is also desirous of inducing the Old Spaniards residing in Mexico, to send their Specie to the U. States in preference to the usual mode of transmitting it to England." That would have been fine for Perry, because commanding officers in those days were allowed a cut of one or two per cent of the value of specie carried in their ships. Unfortunately the "Old Spaniards" regarded *Shark* as no safe means of shipping their specie abroad, and she captured no pirates in the Gulf.

From *Sea Gull,* anchored at Key West, Commodore Porter wrote to the Secretary on 10 May 1823, "I shall despatch the *Peacock* today for La Vera Cruz to relieve the *Shark,* and shall now be left with only my small vessels." But nimble *Shark* was already elsewhere. On 26 April, Perry wrote to his commodore from Port Royal Bay, Jamaica, that on her passage thither from Cartagena, Colombia, "being under snug sail, the Top Gallant Masts and Fore Yard on deck," she sprung her foremast "two feet below the partners of the Spar Deck." As a mast sprung so low could not safely be fished, he bought a new spar from the British dockyard for $330, and his crew were engaged in fashioning it to a new foremast. Next day, he informed the Commodore that he had purchased "bread, spirits and a few other trifling articles of Stores," with bills drawn on the Secretary of the Navy, and that he would soon sail for home as ordered. *Shark* arrived New York 8 July 1823, with "officers and crew all well," and Perry had a couple of weeks with his family before proceeding to Norfolk. He wrote to Commodore Porter thence on 8 August, about setting ashore his brother Raymond, who was to have commanded U.S.S. *Decoy* but came down with fever. And before the end of that month Perry was relieved from the command of *Shark* by his brother's old friend Lieutenant Thomas Holdup Stevens.

U.S.S. *Shark,* after refitting and shipping a fresh crew, returned to the West Indies Squadron and operated with it through the year 1826 under two successive commanding officers. By that time the squadron had pretty well cleaned up the pirates, and the authorities of Cuba and Puerto Rico were coöperating by rounding them up ashore and hanging them. Lieutenant Gregory's *Grampus,* Perry's partner in 1822, captured the most notorious pirate, Cofrecina. Governor Miguel de Torres of Puerto Rico caused him, with twenty-eight others, to be executed, and their quartered remains were sent to the outports to be exhibited as a warning against piracy.

Perry was ordered in August 1823 to report to the receiving ship at Brooklyn for duty in the navy yard. For exactly what duty we do not know; but he had been at sea for over two years on very exacting and enervating tasks, his health had suffered, and the department probably wished to give him a year with his family to recuperate. Never one to be satisfied with routine or perfunctory performance, Calbraith doubtless found something significant to occupy him at the Brooklyn Navy Yard, which at that time was commanded by his brother-in-law George W. Rodgers.

The still young naval couple — Calbraith only reached his thirtieth birthday in 1824 and Jane was three years younger — lived at 33 Mercer Street in New York City. This was in a residential district, about a two-mile walk along Grand and Walnut Streets from the navy yard ferry. Already blessed with three children — five-year-old Sarah; Jane Oliver, aged four; and Matthew Calbraith Jr., aged three, "Old Bruin" lost no time in begetting another cub — Susan, born in May 1824, who died in infancy.

This year ashore with his family enabled Perry to participate in the relatively simple New York society of that era, when the city had fewer than 150,000 inhabitants. Members of the upper-middle class, to which the Slidells and Perrys belonged, had plenty of friends. They attended plays and concerts, owned horses, and rode or drove out into the open country where Central Park was later established, or even to Harlem. A relative who introduced the Perrys to such meager literary society as then existed in New York was William Alexander Duer, judge of the state supreme court, later president of Columbia College. The Duers were considered one of the first families of New York, since the Judge's mother was "Lady Kitty," daughter of General William Alexander, who claimed to be the sixth Earl of Stirling. Perry must also have known J. Fenimore Cooper, five years his senior and already famous for *The Spy*, since he was chosen by a group of naval officers who wished to give a dinner in Cooper's honor to write the invitation.

A gossipy letter from Perry to his old friend Thomas Breese, then purser in U.S.S. *Constitution*, indicates that he kept in touch with what was going on, nationally, as well as with former shipmates: —

New York, March 3d, 1824

My Dear Friend —

. . . As to the news in this quarter of the globe I have something very interesting to communicate. Congress is at present employed in legislating on the bill for the revision of our present tariff. The western members are in full force against the representatives from the Atlantic States, and I fear might succeed in their plans of destroying commerce and consequently the Navy. Their object is to impose so high a duty on imports, as will in fact amount to a prohibition of foreign manufactures. This will of course throw the whole Wealth of the country within the controul of the manufacturing and agricultural community, and have a direct tendency to dry up the source from whence we have heretofore drawn our revenue.

Much interest is felt in relation to the election of our next President, and the papers, you will have recd., contain all the information on the subject. It appears that the most imposing candidates at present on the carpet are Messrs. Adams, Crawford, and Genl. Jackson. Mr. Calhoun I understand has withdrawn in favor of Genl. Jackson. Each of these gentlemen have their party and much will depend on the run of the cards as to the ultimate success of either.

The Bill before the House of Representatives for the creation of Admirals, Commodore, &c, I fear will not pass, and I also fear that nothing will be done for the benefit of the service until the Presidential question is settled.

How are all your shipmates and our friend Turner? His family were all well at New Port when I last heard. Tell Parker that I passed his House today and saw his wife & two of his little ones playing at the window. They looked extremely well. Tell Booream that midshipman Booth dined with me yesterday and is but two or three days from Norwich where he has lately spent two months. Mrs. Booream and her pretty little child are remarkably well. I had the pleasure of seeing them myself in Sept. last in passing through Norwich. Inform Ellery that his family are all well and that his brother Charles started on Monday last in company with his bride for Newport.

Remember me in the most friendly manner to Aulick, Beckham and others of your messmates of my acquaintance.

Yours Most Truly,

M. C. PERRY

The tariff bill that he mentions did pass, but had no such tragic consequences as he predicted. The bill to create the ranks of rear admiral and commodore failed, as did, for almost forty years, every other attempt of the navy to obtain a rank higher than that of captain. On the presidency, Perry is rather cagey in this letter, as befitted a junior naval officer; only from other sources do we know that he followed his Slidell relatives in favoring Jackson. But when election day came, he was at sea.

That summer, the great event was Lafayette's visit in August. Jane and the children doubtless watched the parade from the windows of one of their friends' houses, but Perry missed it. For in July he received his sea orders, and a new phase of his naval career began, in the Mediterranean.

CHAPTER IX

First Lieutenant of *North Carolina*
1824–1828

"First Luff" and His Duties

ON 26 July 1824, one year less three days after his discharge from *Shark*, Lieutenant Commandant Perry was ordered to Norfolk to report on board U.S.S. *North Carolina*, of which he had been appointed First Lieutenant. He left his family in New York and moved into lodgings in Norfolk until his quarters were ready on board ship.

She was one of nine battleships authorized by Congress in 1816 and designed by William Doughty, a veteran naval constructor who had drafted the plans of frigate *President*. Congress doled out money for the navy so parsimoniously that the first two, *North Carolina* and *Delaware*, were not completed and ready for sea until 1825 and 1828, respectively. Ten more years elapsed before *Ohio* and *Pennsylvania* were ready to join the fleet, and the building of the other five dribbled along so that they became obsolete before completion. Two were still on the stocks when the Civil War broke. Nevertheless, this act of 1816 committed the country to building a balanced fleet in peacetime comparable to those of the leading European powers, and the vessels constructed under it were the capital ships of the United States Navy for a generation.

North Carolina was a noble ship, pride of the navy and the nation. Measuring 196 feet overall and 33-foot beam, she mounted 102 guns capable of throwing a greater weight of metal than any man-of-war afloat at that time. She carried a total complement of 832. The main yard was 124 feet long, and her main truck towered 225 feet above the waterline. Square-rigged, she carried on each of her three masts a lower course, topsail, topgallant and royal, in addition to a fore-and-aft spencer and spanker on main and mizzen, a dozen or more trysails, jibs and staysails, and a whole flock of studdingsails. Although not so beautifully proportioned as frigates of the *Constitution* class, and not so fast, *North Carolina* was "a sight for sore eyes" when under sail. She had been allotted to Commodore

John Rodgers as flagship for the Mediterranean Squadron, and he flew his broad pendant, thirteen white stars on a blue field, at her main truck.

Since the last war Commodore Rodgers had been one of three Navy Commissioners, corresponding to the present General Board. Now senior naval officer on active duty, he had a reputation for rigid discipline, which was the principal reason for his being given a sea command at the (then considered) advanced age of fifty-three. Junior officers on the Mediterranean station had lately disgraced the flag by dissipation, brawls with foreigners ashore, and lethal duels among themselves; and as bad manners aft communicate themselves forward, the morale of enlisted men suffered. It is probable that the United States Navy fell in with the Royal Navy system of allowing swarms of prostitutes to come on board in foreign ports, as an alternative to Jack's raising hell ashore.[1] However that may be, Navy Secretary Southard believed that the old Commodore's strong hand was required to enforce decency and restore discipline.

This great ship was not ready to move out into the stream until the New Year. In the meantime most of her crew lived on board the "guardo," as they called the receiving ship at the Norfolk Navy Yard. After the usual mess and clutter made by carpenters and riggers had been cleared away and all was "shipshape and Bristol fashion," *North Carolina* sailed in January 1825 for a shakedown cruise in Chesapeake Bay. Off Ragged Point, Maryland, Commodore Rodgers was escorted on board by an official party headed by President Monroe, so greatly was he esteemed in Washington. She then dropped down to Hampton Roads and sailed for Europe on 27 March.

Some ten years later, when one of Perry's favorite junior officers, Lieutenant William C. Nicholson, was appointed 1st Luff of *North Carolina*, he requested his former commander to write him a letter on duties appertaining to that billet. Perry replied that it "involves a great responsibility and demands a reflecting and circumspect course of conduct." The first lieutenant "is the second in command and in fact the business Officer of the Ship." In the captain's absence he has complete responsibility. Some commanding officers and commodores are "content with the name and privileges of the station" and leave practically everything to the first lieutenant; others constantly meddle with details, "either from ignorance or conceit." But the first lieutenant must always remember that his authority is not independent, but delegated by the captain. Consequently there

---

[1] Scott Claver *Under the Lash* (1954) reprints (pp. 187-95) an appalling official report of 1821 on "Certain Immoral Practices in His Majesty's Navy." Although I have seen no positive evidence that this was done in the U. S. Mediterranean Squadron, I heard from an old retired naval officer in the early 1920's that it was practised when American naval ships put in at West Indian ports before the Civil War.

should be "a free and harmonious interchange of thought and opinions" between them.

If the first lieutenant is vigilant, he will know everything of importance that happens on board, be it reported to him or not. Upon joining a ship he should "make himself acquainted with her stowage and trim," the weight of "ballast tanks, casks, water, provisions, armament, powder, shot and other munitions," and check both the quality of the stores and their stowage so they can be got at quickly when wanted. Particular attention should be devoted to the powder magazine, to prevent accident by explosion, to apportioning the proper charges of powder for each gun, to stowing of the gun-wads and shot, and to the furniture of the "great guns" themselves. A man-of-war "when she trips her anchor for a cruise should be in readiness for any service, whether for action, pursuit or flight." Lessons of the *Chesapeake* affair of 1807 had evidently been well learned.

The first lieutenant, "under the instruction of the Captain," must draw up station bills for officers and men under all conceivable circumstances (action, making sail, weighing anchor, wearing, reefing topsails, etc.) and superintend gun drill. "He is to berth and mess the midshipmen and see that they are properly equipped with Quadrant, Journal, and other necessary articles; to aid those of recent appointment with necessary advice, and extend to them reasonable indulgence."

Having rendered the "fighting department" of the ship as perfect as possible, captain and first lieutenant should direct their attention to improvement of her rigging and her sailing quality. In this department, observes Perry, "neatness, lightness and dandyism in rigging have become so fashionable of late that masts have been stripped of their proper support and are blown away by the first sharp squall." This is exactly what happened to American yachts a century later, and for the same reason, to avoid excessive windage.

Next come "police and discipline." At the beginning of a cruise, captain and 1st Luff must establish a code of regulations which the latter, "being the executive officer," has the duty to enforce. "Every individual, even to the smallest boy, should have some daily and hourly employment involving a responsibility, however trifling." Lieutenant Nicholson is familiar with the "additional bills" established by Perry in *North Carolina* and *Concord*, which, "if they have no other merit, they certainly secure to the . . . industrious man protection from the impositions of skulks who, whether of high or low degree, whenever they can do so, invariably palm their portion of duty on their Shipmates." But "it is not necessary that severe or frequent punishments should be resorted to." "Never inflict punishment in anger. It is better to confine a culprit at first, and arrayn him after time has given opportunity for reflection, and the man a chance for explanation." Perry concludes with a set of "cardinal qualifications necessary to the composition of a superior first lieutenant": —

A prompt, cheerful and unconditional obedience to all lawful orders.

An equal determination to enforce obedience from juniors.

A perfect command of temper and a kind and respectful deportment to all, whether senior or junior.

A parental interest and regard for the improvement and welfare of the Midshipmen; and an equal regard for the health comfort and cheerfulness of the Crew.

A patient and unevinced industry; and, last of all, a *disinclination to leave the Ship.*

"Marine Eden" or "Hell Afloat"?

It is evident that Perry advocated a "taut ship," but advised corporal punishment to be applied with discretion, never in anger. It is therefore disturbing to find that, according to one of *North Carolina's* seamen, he disobeyed his own precepts. This cruise in the Mediterranean, which a former biographer of Perry described as a "Marine Eden," was "Hell Afloat" from one maintopman's point of view, and the principal devil was our hero. The maintopman's name was James Garrison. A brother to William Lloyd Garrison, the famous abolitionist, James was the black sheep of the family, frequently getting into trouble over strong drink and being bailed out and set up again by his distinguished brother. He had already served in the Royal Navy and the American merchant marine when, a hopeless alcoholic at the age of twenty-three, he signed on as seaman in *North Carolina* and was assigned to duty as a maintopman.

Here are Garrison's damaging anecdotes about his 1st Luff. An elderly seaman washing his clothes in a bucket on deck — the only method sailors then had of keeping their clothes clean — was noticed by Perry. "Who are you?" said he. "I am a man," was the reply. Boatswain's mate was called, and "the poor old tar" given thirteen lashes of the cat-o'-nine-tails for insolence. At a general inspection, when the seamen stood by their hammock nettings facing inboard, a man stepped on Garrison's toes and he whispered, "Get off!" Perry observed this, called Garrison out of the ranks, and in the morning had him given a dozen for moving his lips, swearing at him into the bargain. At Poros in the Aegean, Garrison had charge of a boat sent to pick up the ships' armorers, who had been doing a bit of work ashore. He refused to accept them as the boat had just been cleaned and their gear was filthy. This was reported next day to Perry, who "use'd the most obscene and blasphemous language that I ever heard flow from mans mouth," had Garrison given thirteen lashes, stopped his grog and shore leave, and made him "ride the bow gun" — lashed astride a

cannon — every day for a week. At the same time two men were punished for urinating directly overboard instead of using the head. "Not
content with giving them 13 lashes [and] stoping their grog he [Perry]
order'd the master at arms to take them up to the head, and fill their face
and eyes with the excrescence of man and rub it well in."

Equally startling are Garrison's stories of collusion between Matthew C.
Perry and his twenty-three-year-old brother Nathaniel, purser of *North
Carolina*. Pursers in those days were paid only $480 a year, but were ex-
pected to make money by selling clothing and other items to the seamen,
at a substantial profit. While the ship was still lying in Hampton Roads,
the First Lieutenant, whenever he saw a seaman without a peajacket, ordered him to draw one from the purser's "slop-chest." One cold winter's
morning, when the topmen began climbing aloft wearing jackets, Perry
ordered them removed and left on deck. He then told "Jemmy Legs" (the
master at arms) to pack the jackets in bags, and bundled them ashore in
the pilot boat. "Thus was poor Jack robbed of his jacket which cost him 8
dollars from the Purser."

How much of this are we to believe? Not much. Fortunately we have
the official journal of *North Carolina*, and Commodore Rodgers's own
journal and two midshipmen's journals to check. From them it is clear that
Purser Nathaniel Perry did not join the ship until June 1826, when she
was in the Gulf of Smyrna, and that he was detached at Gibraltar before
she returned home. Thus, either the peajacket story is a fabrication or, if
true, another purser was responsible. Garrison's punishment of twelve
lashes is logged on 9 July 1826, but it was "for leaving the boat while at
Tenedos" (not Poros), not for refusing to let the armorers on board.
On the same day, Sunday, a marine for sleeping on post, and two sailors
for "riotous conduct," were given a dozen lashes each; and a third sailor
received two dozen "for striking a Boatswain's Mate and disobedience of
orders." The three contemporary shipboard authorities mention only
twelve other cases of corporal punishment in two years, mostly for
drunkenness and absence without leave in port. This seems not excessive
for a ship with over eight hundred men on board. Garrison's narrative was
not written until after he had brooded over his wrongs for fifteen years,
nor was it published for almost another century; thus Perry had no opportunity to answer his charges — as he did those preferred by John Randolph of Roanoke. Garrison's accusation that Perry used obscene and
blasphemous language is also unbelievable, since Perry throughout his
naval career was noted for moderation in speech and absence of profanity.
Either Garrison was working off an old grudge by telling lies, or he had
confused Perry with some other officer, as he did in the case of the purser.

A few commanding officers in the navy refused to use the cat-o'-nine-
tails or the less severe "colt" — a three-strand rope frayed out at the end.

This, used mostly on the boys, was applied over the culprit's shirt, not on his bare back as was the knotted "cat." As we observed from Midshipman Lynch's narrative of *Shark*, Perry was a practitioner of the "Rodgers system" of discipline, *North Carolina* was the Commodore's flagship, and Rodgers was becoming elderly and irascible. Stories of the Commodore's undignified rages were current even after his death. Chaplain Alden of U.S.S. *Delaware* heard that one day, when Rodgers was inspecting the forecastle, a halfwitted country bumpkin who had shipped as landsman, failed to rise but addressed him politely. Rodgers called him horrible names and felled him with his fist. And "in one of his maniacal acts of madness he struck a pilot over the head with a spy-glass, and he fell dead at his feet."

The log book of frigate *United States* in 1842-1844 records 163 floggings in a fourteen-month cruise, more than half of them for drunkenness or smuggling liquor. Chaplain Alden of *Delaware* in 1841, when David G. Farragut was acting Captain, has this to say about the first flogging he witnessed after leaving Rio de Janeiro: —

All hands were called to witness punishment. The brig was cleared — two rec'd 36 lashes each by sentence of court martial. Once more there are no prisoners on board, an accident which has not happened since we left Hampton Roads. Many in my position have complained of the frequency & the severity of the punishment inflicted. Such is not my opinion of that on board the *Delaware*, tho' from the great number of men, discipline is much more difficult to enforce & be kept up, than in a smaller ship. I cannot conceive that an executive officer on board of a line-of-battle ship could come so near, as Capt. Farragut to the injunction of the Church to her Bishops, "Be so merciful, that you be not too remiss: so minister discipline that you forget not Mercy."

Alden became so used to these scenes that in a spell of chilly weather he cynically remarked, "Jack must get a thrashing now and then to keep his back warm."

North Carolina was not the toughest ship in the Navy, from the forecastle point of view. Garrison admits that later he received worse usage in frigate *Constellation*. McNally states that in U.S.S. *Fairfield*, in which he served as a seaman from 1828 to 1831, not one day elapsed without a flogging; and he records "flogging through the fleet," a cruel old British practice which was forbidden by U.S. Navy Regulations but occasionally practised nevertheless.

These disciplinary methods, inherited from the Royal Navy of Great Britain, were common in all navies and merchant marines at least to the middle of the nineteenth century. Most naval officers considered corporal punishment necessary because of the drunkenness, depravity and general cussedness of many seamen. But independent young Americans seldom enlisted, owing to their natural distaste for such ignominy. It was very difficult to obtain good seamen for the navy by the existing practices of naval recruitment. These were no different from those in the War of Independence, except that no bounty was paid, and crimping was resorted to. A new crew was enlisted for every new vessel. The term of enlistment was two years for boys, three for men; but when a ship returned from an extended cruise, it was the custom to pay off every sailor who wished it, even though his term was not up, and recruit a fresh crew when the ship fitted out for her next cruise.

In many cases the recruiting service, to complete the crew of a vessel, had to resort to "crimping." The crimp, usually a waterfront boarding-house keeper, supplied a recruit with the prescribed outfit of clothing and mess kit, and delivered him (usually drunk) on board the receiving ship, where an officer examined the collection and paid the crimp $36 — three months' able seaman's pay — for articles not worth $10. Others, like Garrison, were persuaded to enlist by their relatives, to get rid of them, or in the hope that sea life and stiff discipline would effect a reform. After a few days or weeks at sea, poor Jack had run through the shoddy clothing, paper-soled shoes and flimsy straw hat, and had to draw another outfit from the purser, which set him back another two or three months' pay. The enlisted man of that era had to provide his mess kit, tobacco, clothing, and materials for mending and resewing the purser's issue, which came in only two sizes — "large" and "small." The only item with which the government provided a sailor besides pay and rations, was a bar of salt-water soap to keep himself and his clothing clean; no small matter, when all the hemp-rope standing rigging was tarred down, and he did all his washing, of himself and his clothes, in a bucket. His pay was docked 20 cents per month for hospital dues. Thus the American man-o'-warsman often had nothing to take home after a three-year term of service but a few dollars and a sore back. The grog ration — a gill of very poor whiskey diluted with water — gave him just enough thirst so that all spending money advanced for shore liberty, and much of his clothing too, went for drink; and once discharged, the cycle began all over again. No wonder, then, that a considerable proportion of the naval seamen at this epoch were floating foreigners or native derelicts.

Perry had ample opportunity to ponder the effects of this system while recruiting for *North Carolina;* as early as January 1824 he ventured to write to the Secretary of the Navy pointing out its defects, and recommending that an apprentice system be adopted in order to attract young Americans of good character into the navy. Sixteen years elapsed before this highly desirable reform was adopted, and then, as we shall see, it went by the board as a result of the *Somers* mutiny. In the meantime, Perry had to do his best to maintain discipline among riffraff recruited by the old methods.

Many good men managed to survive this system and attain the rating of able seaman or petty officer. These were the cream of the fleet — upstanding fellows who did more than their duty on board, and presented a handsome appearance in their white blouses with blue collars, blue bell-bottom trousers, and black tarpaulin hats of straw covered with oilcloth. A seasoned man-o'-warsman who had learned to handle his drink was as fine a specimen of mankind as one could see anywhere. Take, for example, "Jack Chase, our noble first captain of the top," immortalized by Melville in *White Jacket:* —

No man ever had a better heart or a bolder. He was loved by the seamen, and admired by the officers; and even when the captain spoke to him, it was with a slight air of respect. . . . No man told such stories, sang such songs, or with greater alacrity sprang to his duty. . . . He had a high conceit of his profession as a seaman, and being deeply versed in all things pertaining to a man-of-war, was universally regarded as an oracle. . . . Jack had read all the verses of Byron and all the romances of Scott.

Chase, incidentally, was English-born; Perry himself stated in 1824 that most of the boatswains, gunners' mates and other chief petty officers in the United States Navy at that time were foreigners. He had an excellent boatswain in *Shark*, who followed him into *North Carolina*.

Another good example is a nameless Jack Tar described in the log of the *Delaware*. That ship of the line was getting under way in a rough roadstead off Montevideo. A pampero was blowing and heavy seas made up. The cable was roused in and the anchor lifted to the surface, but it still had to be catted — i.e., a hook from a triple-purchase block attached to the ring so that it could be hauled inboard. Jack went out on the bowsprit nettings to do it. At every plunge of the bows he was ducked completely under water. The heavy cat-block flailed about within an inch of his head, and the anchor, weighing over a ton, slewed below his feet. Yet he managed to grasp the block and hook it to the ring. "Napoleon planted the French standard in the midst of the thickest fire of his enemy," observed Chaplain Alden, "but Napoleon never catted an anchor of a line-of-battle ship." No particular notice was taken of this exploit. Naval seamen in those days received no commendations, no medal-ribbons, no bonuses, no fringe benefits. The most they could look forward to was promotion to chief petty officer, and $20 per month. There was no possible way for such a man to become a commissioned officer.

The summer uniforms in the picture of the sailor and the lieutenant were those of the *North Carolina*. Note the black, stiff tarpaulin hat; how did the sailors ever keep them from blowing away? [1] Or their fluttering

---

[1] This tarpaulin hat was the ancestor of the boater with club hatband worn by men in summer for over half a century, and the sailor straw hat worn by ladies around 1905.

Lieutenant and Bluejacket, one of the Huddy and Duval prints of 1839-42

ribbons from catching in the rigging? What the contemporary writer called a frock, since it was formerly worn outside the trousers and came down to the knees, is now tucked into the trousers and would eventually be called a blouse.[1] The material at this era is linen, but owing to pressure by Southern senators, cotton duck was later substituted. Perry, writing from the Mediterranean, said he preferred linen as easier for the sailors to clean, but he would not object to cotton if the department would issue a stronger salt-water soap. Note that bell-bottom trousers, blue sailor collar with rows of white tape, and black neckerchief of World War II uniforms are already in use; only the stitched-on blue bib has disappeared. Observe also the dainty pumps or slippers of the wheelsman; he wore these ashore or at muster, but had stout leather shoes for going aloft. The days of barefooted sailors were over, at least in the navy.

In favor of the "Rodgers system" is the significant fact that the old Commodore was very popular. When Perry was recruiting a crew for *North Carolina* in New York, frigate *Constitution* was fitting out for a cruise under Captain Thomas Macdonough, hero of the Battle of Plattsburg. Perry was astonished to have seventy men already assigned to *Constitution* request transfer to *North Carolina*. "When we take into consideration the popularity of the *Constitution*, and the known lenity of Capt. McDonough, I was somewhat surprised that her men should wish to leave her," he wrote to Commodore Rodgers. He could have enlisted "two-thirds of the crew of that ship," had it been proper to do so. We have noted, in Perry's letter on the duties of a First Lieutenant, his detestation of "skulks," as he called shirkers; and for the same reason, the best seamen liked a taut ship in which the lazy and insubordinate were held to strict account. Captain Arthur H. Clark, who commanded a clipper ship before the Civil War, told me around 1920 that the abolition of flogging in the merchant marine was a mistake; it was the only way to prevent malingering, insolence and drunkenness by the lazy and disreputable portion of a crew, for whom detention in the brig was a pleasure. The good seamen who did their duty, he said, resented the abolition of flogging because it meant they had to do the work of the shirkers. Rodgers and Perry would have agreed. Nevertheless, the flogging of sailors, like slavery, was one of the things that outraged humane feelings in an age of "universal benevolence," and was too often abused by inconsiderate or sadistic officers.

The system certainly bred efficiency. In time of battle all grudges were forgotten and the crew, who had "exercised the guns" weekly, fought like demons. Charles Nordhoff, who from his experience in the old navy corroborated everything we have said about excessive punishment and pursers' graft, reports that his ship, in a sail exercise, took in and furled

---

[1] Origin of the sailor blouse with square collar, favored by small boys and young girls for almost a century, and still the uniform of schoolgirls in Japan.

every sail, even the studdingsails, in eight minutes. Chaplain Alden, in his journal of the *Delaware's* cruise in 1841-1842, describes the rescue of a man who fell over the side. From the first cry of "Man overboard!" through shooting the big ship into the wind, backing her yards, lowering a boat and picking up the man, only seven minutes elapsed. Even more remarkable is an incident told by a former seaman of sloop *St. Mary's.* During the Mexican War, when a norther made up in the Gulf, her commander had all three topgallant and royal masts sent down on deck, together with their yards; even the lower yards were lashed athwartship, bulwark to bulwark. After she had ridden out the gale safely, all hands were called to send up the top hamper. They secured the six upper masts with their standing rigging, crossed all twelve yards, and had the running rigging rove, in exactly seven minutes.

Mediterranean Cruise

U.S.S. *North Carolina* made Gibraltar 30 April 1825 after a rough passage of thirty-three days, overlong for that season of the year. During the last three days before the expected landfall, a great deal of extra work was done. "Baggy wrinkles," the unsightly bunches of chafing gear, were removed from the rigging, "holidays" (bare spots) on the standing rigging were touched up with tar, and woe betide a sailor who dropped tar on the decks, holystoned cream-white! The jeers were rigged, the special tackle for sending topgallant and royal masts on deck as soon as the ship anchored, in order to reduce her windage when moored. Brasswork was given an extra polish, dirty hammocks scrubbed clean, the boats' gripes loosened so that they could be lowered smartly. Officers were particularly eager to make a good impression in Gibraltar, where the Royal Navy was only too ready to pick flaws in a Yankee ship.

Awaiting the arrival of *North Carolina* at the Rock was Perry's twenty-two-year-old brother-in-law Lieutenant Alexander Slidell, who had taken advantage of a long furlough to make a tour of Spain. In his *A Year in Spain* he thus describes the arrival of the line-of-battle ship: —

After much weary expectation, the ship was at length signaled from the tower, and, climbing to the top of the Rock, I saw her coming down before a gentle levanter, with skysails and studdingsails — a perfect cloud of snow-white canvas. By and by the lighter sails were drawn in and disposed of. Europa was doubled and left behind, and the gallant ship stood boldly into the harbor, with yards a little braced, sails all filled . . . and hull just careening enough to improve the beauty of the broadside. . . . Nothing could exceed the beauty of the spectacle.

Slidell came on board just as the Commodore was going ashore to pay his visit of ceremony to the British admiral commanding Gibraltar. The sailors were drawn up before the mainmast, officers and marines on the quarterdeck ready to salute the departure of the commander. "A splendid band of music, dressed in Moorish garb" — this being one of Rodgers's eccentricities — was stationed at the stern. "At length the Herculean form and martial figure of the veteran commodore was added to the number." Everyone, officer or man, raised his hat, the marines presented arms as he stepped over the side, and the band played a martial melody. Slidell thought he "had never seen any array so soul-inspiring, so imposing."

While waiting for the rest of the Mediterranean Squadron, then at Messina, to join him, Commodore Rodgers took *North Carolina* to Malaga and Tangier. By mid-June the whole squadron had arrived — frigate *Constitution*, corvettes *Cyane* (Perry's old ship), *Erie* and *Ontario*. *Cyane* was sent to her old cruising ground off Liberia; the rest sailed on 9 July 1825. Their first port of call was Tunis, whence they sailed for the Aegean. Rodgers's orders were to protect American commerce during the war for Greek independence that was being waged. He also had a special mission, to sound out His Excellency, Capudan Pasha Khosew, Lord High Admiral of the Turkish Navy, about a treaty. President Monroe's emissary to the Sublime Porte had found it impossible to do business in Constantinople, since the ambassadors of European powers used their influence to prevent the Sultan from negotiating with the United States. He had been tipped off, however, that if the two sailors got together, things might be started favorably — as indeed they were.

The stately squadron now sailed through the Sicilian and Malta channels — scenes of great naval exploits in 1943 — across the Ionian Sea, rounded Cape Matapan and Cythera, and entered the Aegean. Here they first called at the island of Poros to replenish fresh water and give officers an opportunity of "examining the relicks of antiquity," according to Perry. It was here that the Commodore, according to Garrison, lost his temper with a shore party which preferred a fresh-water bath to "relicks." But another and chivalrous side of the old boy was revealed by a curious incident. Greek slave traders brought out to the flagship eight Turkish women — two white and six colored — whom they had captured at Corinth and enslaved, offering to provide the Commodore with a ready-made harem at $40 a head. After much dickering, bawling of threats and brandishing of weapons on both sides, Perry was sent in the gig to the Turkish boat, and bargained to such good purpose that the Commodore acquired the lot for $50. His only object was to set them free, no easy task. The captives, one a lady of quality, begged to be taken to America since all their Corinthian relations had been murdered and in Turkey they would be unable to follow any other profession than that of prostitute. The Commodore's gallantry, however, was unable to encompass shipboard hospitality to eight Moslem women for several months, so he landed them at Smyrna, next port of call, where they had to shift for themselves. They probably picked up enough English on board *North Carolina* to be useful to sailors on shore liberty.

During their stay at Smyrna, the crew of *North Carolina*, under Perry's leadership, turned out to extinguish a big fire on the waterfront. They returned on board drenched and exhausted, and Perry in consequence developed a rheumatism from which he never wholly recovered.

The squadron now crossed the Aegean to Nauplia in the Gulf of Argolis. There the Greek revolutionary government was holding out against the army of Ibrahim Pasha, which had overrun the Peloponnesus. The Greeks, naturally, were grateful for this visit and hoped it meant intervention by the United States in their favor; but there was no chance of that, now that isolationist John Quincy Adams had become President of the United States. Commodore Rodgers, unable to obtain word of the whereabouts of the Turkish admiral, left U.S.S. *Ontario* to protect American commerce in the Aegean and sailed the rest of his squadron west to Gibraltar. There it was joined by frigate *Brandywine*, which had brought Lafayette home from his last visit to America. On 25 October 1825, when Captain Patterson was detached to take command of the *Constitution*, Perry became Acting Commander of *North Carolina* and served as such for the next two years. He still had the Commodore on board "breathing down his neck," but Rodgers trusted him and interfered very little.

Before the end of November the squadron arrived at Port Mahon in the island of Minorca to spend the winter of 1825-1826. Minorca, the original home of the Decaturs and the Farraguts, had been a British possession for most of the eighteenth century, but Britain returned it to Spain in 1783 and kept Gibraltar — a poor exchange. Port Mahon is a magnificent deep-water harbor that runs up miles into the land, and is much more defensible than the Rock. By arrangement with the Spanish government, the United States Navy received every facility there and it became a favorite liberty port. The common people were miserably poor — children fought for scraps from the sailors' mess tables — but Jack's meager advances from the purser went a long way, and the girls were kind. For the officers there was a hospitable local aristocracy whose womenfolk, though well protected by duennas, were beautiful, amorous, and occasionally accessible through stratagem. Unfortunately for the common sailors, it was part of the "Rodgers system" to deal out liberty very, very sparingly, since no means had yet been found for preventing them from abusing it. Chaplain Alden of *Delaware*, for instance, wrote at Rio de Janeiro in 1842: "The conduct of some of our men on shore has been disgraceful in the extreme: . . . A sailor usually considers himself as out of the pale of respectable society, and he longs for an opportunity to become the only thing he thinks he can be — a brute!" At Port Mahon a shore party once managed to outwit the officers. The crew were becoming so restive at confinement on board that Perry allowed about a hundred men to go ashore for a "run" on the uninhabited side of the harbor opposite the town. No sooner were they ashore than a jocose bugler in the party sounded a well-known ditty, "Over the Hills and Far Away." Then, relates Garrison, there was "such scampering and scudding it was laughable; every man running for the head of the harbour to get into town." Perry, seeing what was happening, ordered the gun signal "Recall" to be fired, and sent boats away to enforce it. About thirty men obeyed, but the rest spent the night in Port Mahon. Next morning they came on board, to be served with a dozen lashes after breakfast; all except one who escaped punishment because he pleased the Commodore by telling the truth when asked where he got the money for drink: "I sold my jacket!"

There is no doubt that Port Mahon was a demoralizing place. Commodore David Conner, not a malicious gossip, recorded that Captain Daniel T. Patterson acquired a mistress there, and renewed relations with her when he returned as commodore of the Mediterranean Squadron in 1832, notwithstanding the fact that Mrs. Patterson and three grown daughters came out to join him. This enterprising Mahonese lady saw to it that the squadron procured supplies only from persons with whom she had a financial interest. She took a cut on all uniforms made ashore for the officers, and even put *la mordida* ("the bite") on the bumboat men who sold fruit, liquor and souvenirs to the sailors.

Teen-age Minorcan boys were very eager to join the United States Navy in order to avoid being drafted into the Spanish Army. Hundreds of them obtained billets as mess attendants or musicians and most of these stayed in the United States. One was Manuel Fenollosa, father of the poet Ernest Fenollosa, pioneer historian of Japanese art.

The winter of 1825-1826 passed quickly enough. On 10 April the squadron departed Port Mahon, each ship towed by her boats through the narrow neck of the harbor. The Commodore now decided to make another attempt to contact the Turkish admiral. His squadron called at Algiers, Tunis, Milos, Poros and Delos, and arrived at the roadstead of Vourla, twenty miles from Smyrna, on 19 June.

Lieutenant Commander Perry showed great interest in the ruins of Greek civilization, and saw to it that as many of the junior officers as possible visited the classic sites, not only in the Aegean but on the mainland near ancient Troy. But he was not above the average tourist's urge to record himself. Over a century later, one of his descendants visited Delos and found carved on the base of a statue of Apollo, "M. C. Perry, Captain U.S.N., 1826." It is amusing that he upped his own rank. He had, to be sure, the courtesy title of captain because he temporarily commanded

North Carolina; but he did not attain the rank of captain for another eleven years. At Smyrna, however, he learned that the previous March he had been promoted master commandant, corresponding to the modern commander.

North Carolina departed Smyrna 30 June in search of the Turkish admiral, and anchored off Tenedos three days later. The governor of the island was polite but evasive about meeting His Excellency, who answered the problem himself by sailing out of the Dardanelles at the head of an imposing fleet. One of the Turkish ships hit a rock between Tenedos and the mainland. Rodgers took advantage of this accident to send Master Commandant Perry, in command of schooner *Porpoise* and accompanied by an interpreter, to offer assistance to the grounded frigate. Perry found her to be commanded by a Capudan Bey, next in rank to the Capudan Pasha who, he said, was at the Hellespont and would gladly receive the American commodore.

That turned out to be unnecessary. The Lord High Admiral had himself rowed to Tenedos to inspect the damage to his grounded ship. There followed an interesting conference, which doubtless gave Perry a few hints about dealing with Orientals. The Capudan Pasha's flag lieutenant and dragoman, on being piped aboard *North Carolina,* intimated that the unfortunate Capudan Bey would be decapitated unless the American commodore interceded for him. So, on 6 July, Rodgers, somewhat agitated, paid a visit of ceremony to the Capudan Pasha, an imposing three-tailed Pasha of the highest rank, with a yard-long beard. After an exchange of compliments, the American interceded for the unfortunate officer. Capudan Pasha remarked, with humor reminiscent of Pooh-Bah in *The Mikado,* that he would spare his subordinate's life if Rodgers would have him flogged on board *North Carolina!* The Commodore naturally declined to enter into any such bargain; but apparently the Turkish captain got off free, since Perry observed the Capudan Pasha giving him oral orders, which the interpreter translated, "Go to hell or to Mytilene and await my arrival!"

As an additional courtesy, Rodgers sent Perry, in charge of schooner *Porpoise,* to convey the Capudan Pasha across the Strait of Tenedos, which so often had been traversed by the "black ships" of the Argive fleet in the famous siege of Troy. The Turkish admiral chose to make the crossing in the magnificent gilded rowing barge that had brought him from the Dardanelles, but he condescended to pass a towline to *Porpoise.* "Thus ended," wrote Rodgers to the Secretary of the Navy, "our first interview with the Captain Pacha, who in the course of crossing the Strait frequently expressed to Capt. Perry and Lieut. Commdt. Cooper the great delight his meeting us had afforded him." After towing the barge as near the Trojan shore as the depth of water would permit, *Porpoise* cast off the

Mediterranean Squadron sorties from Port Mahon; left to right: *North Carolina, Constitution, Brandywine, Erie, Ontario;* painting by A. Corlotta, 1825

Perry's Quarters, Charlestown Navy Yard

towline and gave the Capudan Pasha a salute of 21 guns, normally accorded only to heads of state.

These courtesies oiled the really important conference that followed at
Mytilene Roads in Lesbos (anciently the abode of Sappho), where
Rodgers's squadron next anchored. The Turkish fleet arrived on 14 July.
Rodgers, prior to the Turkish flagship's anchoring, dispatched Perry to
present his compliments and prepare the admiral to receive another 21-
gun salute. Next day the Capudan Pasha made his ceremonial visit to
North Carolina in a stately 20-oared barge. He was received with the
honors due to his rank as third personage in the Ottoman Empire. Upon
his departure the yards of every American ship were manned by seamen
in white uniform, and His Excellency received another 21-gun salute.
Rodgers returned the visit on the 16th, and was honored not only with 21
guns but by the imperial flag being displayed at the main, as if the Grand
Turk himself were on board. That had never before been done for an
officer of any Christian navy; the Capudan Pasha explained that he did it
"as a Signal Mark of Respect and Friendship of the Turkish Government
for the Flag and Government of the United States." Presents were exchanged, the American squadron got under way, and each ship upon coming abreast of the Turkish flagship clewed up her topsails, topgallants and
royals, manned her yards and gave the Capudan Pasha three cheers while
the band played "Hail, Columbia!" They then made sail in a matter of
minutes and departed in high feather. All this from the Commodore's report to the Secretary of the Navy.

It is obvious that when Rodgers wanted an officer to perform a ceremonial and semi-diplomatic mission he called on Captain Perry. It was a good
choice. Perry (wrote one of his midshipmen, John Jay Almy) was "a fine-
looking officer in uniform . . . generally stern in his manner." He had a
sense of protocol and native dignity, particularly useful when dealing
with Orientals. Over a quarter-century later, he had opportunity to put
this experience to good use.

Ceremonies completed, and negotiations begun which led to the first
treaty between Turkey and the United States, the fleet returned to
Vourla near Smyrna, then to Port Mahon. *North Carolina* now visited in
succession Toulon, Marseilles and Tunis, then sailed past Pantelleria and
Sicily to Sardinia, and returned to Port Mahon. On the last leg of this
voyage she encountered a violent norther — the mistral — with which she
wrestled most of the month of January 1827. As all sailors know, wind
and sea in the "Med" can be as nasty in winter as anywhere in the seven
seas. Owing to frequent drenching and unusual exertions, many officers
and seamen came down with pulmonary diseases, and the dreaded smallpox broke out. When more than 130 officers and men were on the sick list
and provisions were running low, Commodore Rodgers bore up for Malta

and on 20 January 1827 ran into Valetta Harbor where, by courtesy of the British vice admiral Sir Henry Neal, no fewer than 117 of the sick were transferred to the Royal Navy's hospital. The ship was quarantined and, under the expert direction of Perry, thoroughly fumigated, scrubbed, cleaned and painted. On 17 February she was able to leave Malta, and on 3 March, after arriving at Port Mahon, Commodore Rodgers reported that the smallpox patients had recovered and the health of his crew was never better.

Welcome news reached the ship at Port Mahon: orders to return home. The sailmakers made up a long homeward-bound pendant, and *North Carolina* sailed in mid-May, calling at Gibraltar, Cape Haitien, Port au Prince, Havana, and Key West. On 28 July 1827 she passed the Capes and next day anchored in Hampton Roads, after an absence of twenty-eight months. Among those who welcomed Commodore Rodgers home was his friend the author James K. Paulding, former secretary to the Navy Commissioners, who wrote, "You have by your firmness and steadiness restored the discipline of the squadron under your command to what it ought to be. For this you deserve the thanks of the whole country."

Captain of the Boston Navy Yard

If Perry received thanks for his important part in restoring strict discipline, it is nowhere recorded. In those days there were no navy crosses, bronze stars or letters of commendation for officers who did more than their duty.

Jane did her duty, too. On 20 May 1828, nine and one-half months after her husband was detached from *North Carolina*, she presented him with a seventh child, William Frederick Perry. This "blessed event" occurred at New London, where Jane was probably staying with her husband's mother, old Mrs. Christopher R. Perry.

In the meantime, on 17 August 1827, Calbraith had been assigned "to command the Naval Rendezvous at Boston." This post corresponded to the modern captaincy of a naval shipyard. He superintended the recruiting service in New England, but his duties included almost anything assigned by the commandant, who at that time was Commodore Charles Morris. Many new shore facilities were being constructed — timber sheds, a ship house, storehouse and quay walls; the great stone dry dock, still used for smaller naval vessels in the 1960's; and the magnificent ropewalk where expert ropemakers made the navy's big hawsers for over a century. Morris used his influence to give this new construction the "solidity as well as the simplicity" which, in his opinion, "national works should possess," and hoped that "the example once given would be followed in future constructions."

The Perrys moved into one of the new officers' quarters in the Charlestown Navy Yard. Their next child, Caroline Slidell Mackenzie Perry, the future Mrs. August Belmont, was born there on 23 August 1829. By that time there was quite a collection of little Perrys under one roof — eleven-year-old Sarah; ten-year-old Jane; Calbraith Jr., a stocky seven-year-old who had already decided on a naval career; Oliver, aged four; and one-year-old baby William, destined for the marine corps. Two had already died; two more were to come. And for a time they had the company of their first cousin Oliver Hazard Perry Jr., son of the late Commodore. There has survived a charming childish letter from Sarah Perry to "dear Oliver," telling how they miss him in Charlestown and hope he may soon return.

Although "Beantown" did not wean the Perrys from New York, they enjoyed the social life which Boston, more than any other American seaboard city, shared with naval officers. The Master Commandant made as full use as his time would permit of the city's literary and scientific facilities. His principal civilian friend was the talented Henry A. S. Dearborn, president of the Massachusetts Horticultural Society, who stimulated his interest in botany. Perry was elected a corresponding member of his society in 1829, the year it was founded, and from whatever foreign port he visited, he sent dried specimens of plants for its herbarium. Perry doubtless attended Harvard commencement, and saw graduate in 1829 young Oliver Wendell Holmes, who astonished the country next year with his poem "Old Ironsides." U.S.S. *Constitution* was then at the Charlestown Navy Yard awaiting the scrap heap. Holmes's

> *Aye, tear her tattered ensign down!*
> *Long has it waved on high!*

created such a wave of sentiment that the navy revoked the order for her demolition, and she was the first ship to be put into the new dry dock for complete rebuilding.

CHAPTER X

Commanding U.S.S. *Concord*

1830–1832

To Russia with Randolph

PRESIDENT John Quincy Adams persuaded Congress in 1825 to authorize the building of ten new sloops-of-war, a class much more useful to the United States Navy at that time than frigates or 74's, and far less expensive to build and operate. These sloops or corvettes were designed by Samuel Humphreys, son of old Joshua Humphreys of *Constitution* fame. They were 127 feet long overall, 33 feet 9 inches beam, mounted 18 to 24 guns, and carried a complement of 190 officers and men. Master Commandant Perry, on 22 April 1830, was ordered to command one, the *Concord*, which had just been completed at the navy yard in Porstmouth, New Hampshire. She was a much more formidable warship than schooner *Shark;* fast, able, and beautifully proportioned.

Perry loved being at home with his family, but like many other sailors he became fed up with shore duty — dealing with raw recruits, bossing navy yard workmen, arranging repairs and upkeep for vessels that came into port, and the endless teas, dinners and receptions in a "navy town" such as Boston. So he was delighted to command this fine new sloop-of-war. Had he known what lay ahead, he would rather have taken shore duty anywhere from chilly Portland to feverish Pensacola. For his first mission, after a shakedown cruise, was to embark at Norfolk and convey to his post the new Envoy Extraordinary and Minister Plenipotentiary of the United States to the court of Nicholas I, Emperor of All the Russias. Said E. E. and M. P. was John Randolph of Roanoke, one of the most cantankerous, eccentric, delightful and disagreeable statesmen in the early history of the Republic.

It had long been the custom, in England and the United States, to send diplomatic officials to their foreign posts in warships. This was supposed to save the government passage money in a packet, and to enhance the envoy's dignity. Naval officers hated this duty. Diplomats, unless they happened to be sea-minded like the Adamses, were prone to throw their weight around on shipboard, interfere with the captain's authority and demand that he take in sail to cater to their comfort, or alter his route to meet their whims.

All this and more did John Randolph, already a sick old man at fifty-seven. As congressman and senator, Randolph had been a gadfly to every administration since Washington's. Every President had felt the barb of his wit, the lash of his invective, and the sting of his sarcasm. Randolph hated Yankees, hated every state except his native Virginia (and hated most Virginians too). He hated democratic manners and customs, but nourished a deep affection for England, which he had visited twice before. He accepted this mission partly because he hoped to include a sightseeing tour of the Old Country, partly because the salary would help to retrieve his losses as a Virginia planter. Why President Jackson made so unsuitable an appointment — for Randolph knew nothing of Russia and cared less — is a matter of speculation. The ostensible reason was to send a "famous statesman" to negotiate a new commercial treaty. Randolph's earliest biographer thought it was to reward Randolph for his help in defeating John Quincy Adams. That was part of it; but I suspect that foxy Martin Van Buren, Jackson's Secretary of State, wanted Randolph out of the country before he could launch a bitter attack on this administration as he had on all its predecessors — and eventually did on Jackson's.

A few days before sailing, Randolph was tendered a banquet by the citizens of Norfolk, at which his self-esteem was further inflated by being called the greatest Virginian since George Washington. He sent on board in advance of sailing (according to the log of *Concord*) "the following for the Hon. J. Randolph, 1 coffee pot, 1 d° Mill, 4 Mattrasses, 4 Blankets, 4 pillows, 4 boxes, 1 Saddle and Bridle, 1 demijohn & 2 casks of Porter, 1 chest of Tea, 1 Bag of Coffee, 1 Bag of Sheets & Pillow cases, 1 Keg of meal, 4 bottles Brandy, 1 chicken coop & chickens, 1 Keg hams, 1 Keg rum, 1 box books, 3 boxes papers, 3 Sheep, & 1 Portmanteau."[1] Next day Randolph brought on board with him his kinsman John Randolph Clay as secretary of legation, three Negro body-servants named John, Juba and Eboe, mountains of baggage, boxes of books to be rebound in London, and a caged mockingbird to remind him of Virginia.

Randolph's latest adoring biographer, William Cabell Bruce, admits that he should not have been offered the Russian mission, and never should have accepted it; and, he might have added, should not have been sent to St. Petersburg (now Leningrad) in a man-of-war. For Randolph hated the

---

[1] *Concord* Log, 27 June 1830. This diplomatic baggage was moderate in comparison with Minister Caesar Augustus Rodney's, when Captain Biddle took him to Buenos Aires in *Congress* in 1823. Rodney insisted on loading 107 chairs, 11 bureaus, 86 boxes, 54 barrels, 26 trunks — and four goats!

navy, had never been on board a naval vessel, and knew nothing of the immemorial usages of the sea which perforce make the commanding officer an absolute monarch.

Nevertheless, this cruise began with the best of good feelings. Perry looked forward to having as passenger one of the great wits of the age; Randolph, after being tendered a salute of 13 guns, with yards manned, and being introduced to the junior officers, sent ashore on 28 June 1830, the day *Concord* sailed from Norfolk, a letter to President Jackson in which he said: —

> The *Concord* is a fine ship and I have but one fault to find with my situation — it is, that Capt. Perry's politeness has induced him to give up his own state Room and dressing Room to me, and I fear to straiten his own quarters. I have every accomodation that the most fastidious person could possibly desire. Nothing can surpass Captain Perry's polite and kind attentions to myself and Mr. Clay.

In addition to giving up two cabins for Randolph's personal use, Captain Perry had partitioned off a generous portion of the berth deck and fitted it up for Secretary Clay and the three slaves.

The first unpleasantness, so far as we know, occurred on the Grand Bank of Newfoundland. Having encountered a fleet of Banks fishermen, Captain Perry spoke one, backed *Concord*'s main topsail, lowered a boat and sent it on board, in charge of Midshipman Noland, to procure fresh fish. "At 10:40 the boat returned with fish for Ships Company," states the Journal. But that was not all. As the laden boat approached the *Concord*, Randolph, who had stationed himself on the quarterdeck alongside Perry, screamed out, "Mr. Noland, how much did those Yankees charge you for those fish?" "Not a cent, sir, not a cent!" replied the middie, who also came from Virginia. "As soon as the skipper learned that we were the *Concord*, and that *you* were on board, he insisted on presenting the fish to us, out of respect to you, sir." "Well, well, well! Who ever heard of such a thing!" shrilled Randolph. "This is the first time in my life that I ever heard of a Yankee giving something for nothing!"

That could pass for wit; but although the Captain informed him that presenting fish to passing vessels was an old custom of New England and all other fishermen, Randolph, when the codfish was served up, and for days after, elaborated in his falsetto voice on the exceptional circumstance of Yankees making a free gift. Since the Captain and at least four of his officers were Yankees, this became rather tiresome.[1]

The next subject that attracted Randolph's attention was naval training

---

[1] The writer heard this story in the early 1920's and has had it confirmed by Dr. Francis L. Berkeley Jr. of the University of Virginia, who got it from his great-great-uncle, Midshipman Noland, who "never got over his humiliation that his captain should have been so treated by a fellow Virginian."

and discipline. Coming from a region where the whipping of Negro slaves was a daily occurrence, Randolph was profoundly shocked at seeing members of the master race under the lash. Some fifteen months later he wrote to President Jackson: —

The scenes which I witnessed on board the *Concord* were so revolting, that I made up my mind never to take passage again on board of a vessel of War — at least with a newly shipped crew. The men were raw; some of them landsmen; most of them fishermen (not whalemen — *they* are the best of seamen) utterly ignorant of the rigging, or management of a square rigged vessel. The Midshipmen had to shew them the various ropes, etc.; the very names of which they were ignorant of, and knew not where to look for them — the lieutenants were worn down performing not their own proper duties only but those of the midshipmen also, who, in turn, were discharging the duties of able bodied seamen. Punishment by putting in irons, and by the *Colt* was continually going on. I do not know whether the *Cat* was used or not, as I always retreated to my stateroom to avoid the odious spectacle that surprised and shocked my negroe slaves. In seven years the same quantity of punishment would not be distributed among the same number of slaves as was inflicted in a voyage of three weeks from Hampton Roads to Portsmouth.

Respecting the untrained crew, Randolph correctly observed the effects of existing recruiting methods which Perry had long been trying to change. His account of flogging, however, was vastly exaggerated. After a speech of Randolph's, to the effect that *Concord* was a hell-ship, had been reported in the newspapers, Perry took pains to refute it in a letter to the Secretary of the Navy, producing a copy of the special log he kept of shipboard punishments. This proved that during the passage from Norfolk to Russia he had confined to the brig only nine men, "of which number, four of the most aggravated cases were punished by flogging, and the other five forgiven." These facts, he observed, "fully disprove the unfounded statements of Mr. Randolph." The junior officers of *Concord* corroborated Captain Perry's statement.[1] These letters, as well as Perry's, gave Randolph the lie, unequivocally; and Jackson evidently believed them rather than the former envoy, since Perry was never reprimanded.

The outward passage was short — twenty-two days from Norfolk to the Isle of Wight. Wind blew westerly most of the way, and the ship's journal records little except the frequent making and taking in of sail, daily to

---

[1] Perry to Levi Woodbury, Syracuse, 16 Feb. 1832, *Concord* Letter Book at Hist. Soc. Pa.; the original is in Master Commandants' Letters Jan.–June 1832 (National Archives). Enclosed is "Extract from the Register of Punishments kept on board U.S. Ship *Concord*" 29 June-10 Aug. 1830. One ordinary seaman got "12 lashes with Cat for theft," a marine "10 lashes with the Cat" for sleeping on post, a second O.S. "12 lashes with Cat for drunkenness," and a third O.S. "9 cuts with a Colt" for beating a boy. The offenses of those forgiven were drunkenness. All were confined on 4 July, date of punishment not noted, but must have been within a few days. Obviously the seamen had been celebrating the Glorious Fourth too vociferously.

thrice daily soundings in the chops of the Channel, and vessels sighted. On 10 July, "discovered an iceberg to leeward bearing NNW, at 11:30 made two other icebergs on the lee Bow . . . made a short leg on the Starboard Tack . . . to pass them further to windward. . . . Equally pleased with the gratification of our curiosity and the prospect of escaping from its dangerous and chilly neighborhood." Perry was evidently taking unusual pains to give his distinguished passenger a safe, pleasant and speedy passage. Studdingsails were set more than half the time, and when a squall threatened, *Concord* stripped to reefed topsails and the royal yards were sent down. A typical entry is the following: —

From 8 to Meridian fresh breezes and pleasant weather, 8:15 set both main topmast steering sails, hauled up the spencer & spanker, hauled down the fore topmast steering sails,[1] at 9 set the fore royal & both main royal steering sails, at 9:30 set the Larboard lower & fore topmast steering sail, at 9:45 set the Larboard fore Topgallant steering sails, at 11:15 set the Larboard fore royal steering sail, mizzen topgallant sails and royal.

In such wise, spreading every sail, with foam at her bows and in her wake, *Concord* approached the coast of Old England. She picked up an English Channel pilot in the small hours of 19 July and in a strong west wind with five studdingsails set, roared past Eddystone, the Start, Berry Head and Portland Bill. At 8:30 A.M. July 20 she was off the Needles, at the entrance to the Solent, between the Isle of Wight and Hampshire. She stood in for the Mother Bank and at 10 A.M. "anchored in 7 fathoms water off Ryde. . . . The quarantine officer came on board, furled sails and sent down Topgallant and royal yards."

Now a fresh subject of altercation arose between Captain and Envoy, over anchorages. Perry had been instructed by the Secretary, "Should Mr. Randolph desire to touch at any of the English or other ports on the way, you will accede to his wishes," and he constantly endeavored to please. The object of anchoring in the Solent was to enable the Envoy to land at Portsmouth and proceed to London. Spithead would have been nearer Portsmouth, but Perry selected the Mother Bank after consultation with Randolph, because the British admiral at Spithead insisted on being saluted, but refused to return gun for gun; and the United States Navy could accept no less.

Shortly after *Concord* anchored, the American consul came out to the ship from Ryde, and Randolph elected to go ashore in his small boat rather than wait for the *Concord* to be granted pratique, when he could have been taken properly in the Captain's gig. It was a long, rough boat trip, and the Envoy got wet. When Perry landed later the same day, he

---

[1] A common spelling at that time for "studdingsails," pronounced "stuns'ls."

was astonished to receive an angry letter from Randolph complaining
both of him and the pilot. To this missive Perry made the following calm
reply: —

U.S.S. *Concord*
Tuesday July 20th 1830

Sir,

In reply to your letter received this morning from the hands of Mr. Clay I
have to express my extreme regret that any misconception of mine of your
wishes in regard to the place of anchorage of the Ship *Concord* or any mis-
conduct of the Pilot should have put you to the least delay or inconvenience:
it has been my sincere wish to contribute all in my power to your comfort expedition and convenience and as you have determined to embark at Cowes, I
shall depart immediately on my return to the Ship, in order to have her in
readiness, at that anchorage for your reception when you return.

If I had known previously to my leaving the Ship that her anchorage was not
satisfactory to your wishes — I could have removed her without the least delay
or inconvenience.

After hearing from Randolph that he was proceeding to London and
proposed to rejoin the ship at Dover, Perry, after making a brief trip to
London himself, engaged a North Sea pilot, "received on board 2 sheep
for the Hon. John Randolph," and made sail 24 July. On the evening of
the 25th, *Concord* anchored a mile off Walmer Castle in the Downs, the
classic roadstead between Goodwin Sands and the Kentish shore. Since
time immemorial big ships outward bound from London had called there
to take on mail; and those inward bound, to drop impatient passengers for
London. Dover then had no harbor capable of receiving a ship of *Concord*'s 17-foot draught. Deal, where there were many expert boatmen, was
the usual place for ships in the Downs to communicate with the shore. So
Perry sent Lieutenant Nicholson ashore with orders to proceed to Dover
and learn the Envoy's pleasure as to time and place to embark. Perry respectfully suggested that he embark at Deal, where a ship's boat would
await him between 4 and 8 P.M.

But Randolph was not ready. He wished to visit Ramsgate, and sent his
secretary on board with a "memorandum" demanding that he be picked
up there. To this Perry replied on the 26th, after consulting with the
pilot, that *Concord* could anchor between four and six miles off Ramsgate,
requiring a long, rough boat trip compared with that from Deal; he suggested Margate as an alternative, and said he was sending Lieutenant Marshall to Ramsgate in the cutter, either to bring the distinguished passenger
on board, or to convey His Excellency's wishes for a different port.

His Excellency, making himself as disagreeable as possible, sent back
word by Lieutenant Marshall that he wished to consult the pilot person-

ally: — "Mr. Randolph again requests of Capt. Perry, another interview with the Pilot, to ascertain whether Mr. R. rightly understood that officer, in the first conversation had with him, by Capt. Perry's permission, first sought and obtained by Mr. Randolph."

Perry replied the same day: —

In answer to Mr. Randolph's note this moment received, Capt. Perry respectfully states that he has directed the Pilot to wait on Mr. Randolph.

Capt. Perry takes this occasion to observe that he considers himself bound by his instructions to take the Ship to any port Mr. Randolph may designate and into which the Ship may safely enter, and that he shall use every possible exertion to hasten the Ship on her passage to whatever destination Mr. Randolph may point out.

After talking with the pilot, Randolph decided he had better embark from Ramsgate, and did so on the 27th at 8 P.M. But he had already taken a fancy to visit Yarmouth on the East Coast, and ordered Perry to sail him thither. The prospect of landing at that fishing port, with its narrow and difficult approach, alarmed both Perry and the pilot. And as Captain and Envoy were no longer on speaking terms, Perry had to convey this news by letter, as follows —

> U.S.S. *Concord*
> At Sea, Off Yarmouth
> July 28th 1830

Sir

Mr. Bates the North Sea Pilot informs me that the Ship in standing off and on cannot approach nearer to Yarmouth than 8 miles owing to the sands; if therefore you would prefer the Ship's going into the Harbour, I will take a Harbour Pilot and run in, otherwise I will approach as near to the town as the sands will allow and hire a pilot boat to tow one of our Boats in and out — which latter arrangement will save the risk and delay of taking the Ship in and be more expeditious.

To this Randolph returned an equally formal reply: —

> Half past 8, July 28 *Concord*
> off Yarmouth Roads

Lieut. Inman has just delivered to me a verbal communication which, after what has passed, I feel myself most reluctantly compelled to decline receiving. Yet in self-protection I take this method of stating that it is no wish of mine that the *Concord* should enter Yarmouth Roads.

You will therefore govern yourself by my written requisition of yesterday formally exacted by you yesterday.

If however it will be productive of no additional delay, nor of any the least risk whatsoever, I have no objection to shewing the third Sea-Port of England on the German Ocean & the great county of Norfolk perhaps the first ship of her Class in equipment as well as naval architecture in the world.

I have the honour to be respectfully
Sir, your obedient Servant

J.R. OF ROANOKE

The Captain still remained amiable. *Concord's* log reads: "10 P.M. Standing to Yarmouth Rhodes [*sic*], hove to . . . called all hands to bring ship to an anchor, Yarmouth pilot came on board, at 11:30 came too off Yarmouth with the Larboard anchor, in 7 fathoms." And, for the 29th, "At 2 John Randolph Esqr. left the ship . . . at 6:30 Mr. Randolph came on board. At 7 mustered the crew at quarters, hoisted up the boats and got under weigh."

While the Envoy was seeing Yarmouth, Captain Perry wrote the following letter to his old Commodore, John Rodgers: —

U.S. Ship *Concord*
Yarmouth Roads, England
July 28th 1830

PRIVATE.

Sir:

I have but a moment to inform you that we touched at this Port this morning at the request of Mr. Randolph, being the third British Port I have entered upon his Requisition. Mr. R. notwithstanding his well known character for strangeness and eccentricity, has actually out done himself since he came on bd this ship. His conduct & deportment has been that of a man out of his wits and he has shown a degree of malevolence against me & others truly astounding. I have borne with him with great patience & intend to continue to do so, but it appears that he gets in a rage because he cannot make me commit myself. His conduct has been so strange that all the Ward Room Officers have of their own accord & unsolicited by me, addressed me letters, in which there will be found evidence enough to prove Mr. R. almost any thing. To day he is in one of his rational fits, and he has sent his Secty. to inform me, that whilst at London he wrote to the President complaining of me and that he now repents it. He has gone onshore with a determination to write again to the Prest. & Sect. of the Navy, to do away any unfavourable impression his other letters might have made.

Perhaps to night he will refuse to speak to me. This very morning I sent a Lieut. to him with a message relative to our coming with this Port, and he refused to receive a verbal message but requ[este]d a written Communication.

I am almost worn out with his vagaries. I hope my dear Sir if he writes to the Secy. Mr. Branch that you will request that gentleman not to form any opinion to my prejudice without giving me an opportunity of explaining. I can do so to his entire satisfaction, and shall not fear the fullest scrutiny of my Conduct but would rather court an investigation.

From Elsinour, I will send you all the particulars. In the mean time I beg you not to permit the Prest. or Mr. Branch to suppose that I have in any way committed myself with Mr. R. tho' I have been surrounded with snares & vexations. Will you be good enough to consider this as confidential.

You will laugh when I enform you that we have come to this Port to take onbd. a few Reams or quires of paper which Mr. R ordered from London to be sent to Yarmouth. I remonstrated but he insisted, referring me to the Secretary's order to me to go to whatever Port he wished. I know not what Port he will next require the Ship to touch at.

With the assurance of my unfeigned Esteem & regard I subscribe myself

Very Respectfully & Truly
Your friend & obt. Servt.

M. C. Perry

P.S. You may rest assured that I can prove myself perfectly free from all blame in my intercourse with Mr. R. He cannot say as much.

Between Yarmouth and Elsinor, where Perry delivered dispatches for the American minister to Denmark, Randolph kept to his cabin with an "indisposition." He was sufficiently ill-disposed to write acidulous letters to Martin Van Buren and President Jackson complaining of Perry's conduct: —

J.R. of R. to M.V.B.   *Concord* off Copenhagen
    private   Augt. 2, 1830 9 A.M.

Dear Sir:

*   *   *

I refer you to an extract of a private letter to Mr. Branch for a refutation of idle reports. The truth is that I bore my faintness so weakly about me that our worthy Capt. began to doubt whether I might not be induced to give up the control which the Govt. had given me over the ship. He behaved not with courtesy but lack of it after I joined the *Concord* at Ramsgate, but as I thought it due to the credit of the service that nothing of this sort should appear before the publick, I took effectual steps to that effect by keeping copies of all that passed between us. This self protection required me to do. They shall never be produced except in the last resort & in self defence. . . . I have no fear that Capt. P. will make this affair an object of publick discussion — but who can answer for the discretion of young midshipmen etc. writing to their friends.

Note especially the phrase, "the control which the Govt. had given me over the ship." Randolph evidently considered the *Concord* his private yacht and Captain Perry the owner's sailing master who must go where he wished, regardless of wind, tide, or the ship's safety. Randolph insolently sent copies of these letters to Perry, who was therefore able to get off a letter to the Secretary defending his conduct.

The Envoy was not through with sightseeing. Since Copenhagen lay on the direct route from Elsinore to the Baltic, there was no objection on Perry's part to calling there. Nevertheless, Randolph ordered him to do so in the following coldly offensive note: —

> *Concord* — Cattegat
> Off Anholt Light
> Augt. 1, 1830. Half past Six A.M.

Sir

In conformity with the authority vested in me by the President of the United States I require that this ship do touch at Copenhagen in her passage to Cronstadt.

> I have the honour to be, Sir
> Your obedt. Servant
>
> J. RANDOLPH OF ROANOKE

The ship stopped at the Danish captial for a few hours on 4 August, long enough for Randolph to gratify his curiosity and to decide (as he wrote to Martin Van Buren, in the same letter) that "The History of Denmark is already written. It is finished. Her career is ended."

On the evening of 9 August, after exchanging 13-gun salutes with a passing Russian ship of the line, *Concord* dropped anchor off Kronstadt. She saluted the fort with 13 guns, the fort replied, and at 10:30 A.M. August 10 the governor of the fortress and a Russian admiral came on board, giving occasion for exploding more gunpowder. Randolph, describing this visit in a letter to his friend Nathan Loughborough, remarked, "Our Captain's wine being none of the best, I pressed upon them some fine old Cercial and some brown stout that had crossed the Atlantic twice. . . . They declared by more than words . . . that they had never tasted such beer and wine." It is not surprising that Perry, whose salary as Master Commandant was $1,174 per annum with no allowance for entertainment, owned wine inferior to the Sercial Madeira of Randolph, who received $6000 for his "outfit" in addition to a $10,000 salary.

At Kronstadt, after receiving a 13-gun salute with yards manned, the Envoy, suite, baggage, and mockingbird in cage, boarded a steamboat for St. Petersburg at 2:15 P.M. August 11. The diplomatic baggage by this time had been augmented (according to *Concord*'s log) by "6 Boxes, 3 barrels and 2 bags of bread, 2 sugar loaves, 3 Packages papers, . . . 2 cases, 2 casks and 3 demijohns of wine, . . . one of ship's whiskey, furnished at the request of Mr. Randolph." Once ashore at the Russian capital, Randolph put up at a hotel, hired a coach and four, made the proper diplomatic calls, presented his credentials to the minister of foreign affairs, and in court dress was received by the Emperor.

Captain Perry and some of his officers went ashore within a day or two, to pay their respects to the Emperor. Perry, before sailing from the United States, had been so foreseeing as to obtain the services as captain's clerk of Joseph William Jenckes, a good linguist. Jenckes doubled as assistant schoolmaster to the midshipmen on the outward passage, and Perry brought him to the Winter Palace as interpreter of the imperial French to himself, and of his English to Nicholas I. Despite Jenckes's "sweetening the conversation greatly," it was a very formal, stand-up interview in the great hall of the palace. The Emperor was stiff so Perry was stiff; but, according to the interpreter, Nicholas asked many questions about the United States Navy and then offered to make Perry a flag officer if he would join the Russian Navy. This Perry politely but firmly declined. Possibly he recalled John Paul Jones's unfortunate experiences as a Russian rear admiral.

Perry had been ordered to sail for the Mediterranean immediately after landing Randolph. Unfortunately for him, a sprung foremast required a week's detention at Kronstadt; and before that time had expired, Randolph requested *Concord* to wait a few days in order to carry his first dispatches from Russia to England, for transmission to Washington. "Altho' my instructions do not direct me to wait for the dispatches of Mr. Randolph," wrote Perry to the Secretary, "I have thought it most advise-able to delay the ship a reasonable length of time for the purpose of facili-tating the transmission of these documents." Perry sent Lieutenant Williamson to St. Petersburg in the hope of expediting matters, but Randolph put him off from day to day, and on 17 August wrote the following

> Demouths' Hotel
> Tuesday 2 P.M. Augt. 5th 1830 — 17th — new Style

Mr. Randolph has the Honour to apprize Capt. Perry, through Lieutenant Williamson, that in consequence of his own extreme ill health & that of Mr. Clay (much worse) he cannot by possibility get his despatches prepared before tomorrow Evening (at the earliest) in time for the afternoon Steamboat say 5 o'Clock, very probably Mr. R. shall not be able to finish before the next morning's boat.

Perry wrote daily to Williamson or to Randolph, begging him please to make haste with his dispatches. The crew of *Concord* became sickly from drinking River Neva water, one died, and the ship was required to shift her anchorage to the uncomfortable outer roadstead. Randolph, consulting his own convenience, kept Perry waiting day after day; then, to the consternation of officers and crew, decided to come on board himself! For, after spending some ten days in St. Petersburg, he felt that the heat, dust and insect life of the Russian capital were too much for him, and that to restore his poor health he must hasten to London and spend the winter there, of all places.

The unwelcome passenger and most of his baggage (the food apparently left ashore for Clay to consume) returned on board *Concord* in Kronstadt Roads on Sunday, 22 August. She sailed early next morning and reached Copenhagen September 6. No incidents are recorded of this passage, except that the weather was boisterous and the winds unfavorable. Undoubtedly Captain and Envoy did not speak. There is a light touch in Perry's Journal for 31 August: — "In breaking out the Spirit Room this afternoon the Master's Mate discovered a quarter cask supposed to contain wine, marked imperfectly J. Randolph." Let us hope that this was some of the famous Sercial, and that it was allowed to replace the ship's whiskey which Randolph had taken ashore with him at St. Petersburg.

Concord called at Margate Roads on the 16th. Since Randolph did not choose to go ashore, she proceeded to Cowes where, to the delight of all hands, Randolph, the three slaves and baggage left the ship for the last time. He remained in London during the following winter, occasionally urging the Russian ambassador at the Court of St. James's to discuss a treaty (which His Excellency refused to do) and enjoying his stay in the only country that he considered civilized. President Jackson finally sent James Buchanan to St. Petersburg as envoy extraordinary, and he negotiated a treaty in December 1832.

Irony is added to this episode by the fact that both John Randolph and President Jackson were professed enemies to corruption, jobbery and waste in government. Randolph's junket cost the taxpayers over $20,000 in addition to the payroll of U.S.S. *Concord;* and he accomplished absolutely nothing. But Perry learned from his disagreeable passenger how to exercise self-restraint in the face of boorish megalomania.

Abolition of Flogging

To do Randolph justice, it must be admitted that he was humane and compassionate. As early as 1812 he introduced a bill in Congress to abolish flogging in the army, and his complaints of conditions on board *Concord,* exaggerated as they were, seem to have borne fruit. Secretary Woodbury, in a circular issued 24 September 1831, ordered that no man in the navy be flogged "but by order and in the presence of the Commanding Officer." This had long been Perry's practice. And in his annual report of 1832 Woodbury recommended that corporal punishment be abolished. Nothing was done for twelve years, when Senator John P. Hale of New Hampshire, a noted antislavery man, took up the matter seriously.

So we may now conclude that unpleasant subject. Congress on 3 August 1848 directed the Secretary of the Navy to make a complete report of all naval floggings in 1846-1847, and he complied. The details are fascinating.

For example, brig *Somers* in the first six months of 1846 had 45 cases of flogging, mostly for "fighting and insolence," one for "taking meat from harness cask" (where salt beef and pork were kept), others for drunkenness and "tapping liquor in spirit room." All punishments in the fleet were from 5 to 12 lashes with the cat or, in the case of boys, the colt. There were a few exceptions, such as a court-martial sentence of three seamen in *Saratoga* to 50 to 100 lashes for desertion and mutinous conduct. But Commodore Perry reduced this by half. A man in U.S.S. *Columbus*, court-martialed for "drunkenness and striking an officer," got "50 lashes with cats." That ship had 176 corporal punishments between 23 February and 22 August 1846. Toughest of all was frigate *United States*, which between 18 August 1846 and 18 May 1848, inflicted corporal punishment 466 times, an average of over five floggings per week.

Some of the offenses logged are "seditious conduct in cursing the ship when ordered to go in a boat," 12 lashes; "dropping slush bucket from aloft," 6 lashes with colt; "entering cabin and stealing champagne therefrom," 12 lashes. Perry's flagship at that time, U.S. Steamer *Mississippi*, had very few punishments. For the quarter ending 31 December 1846, "by order of Commodore M. C. Perry," there are only 15 cases, mostly for drunkenness, insolence and gambling.

The Secretary also asked for the opinions of senior naval officers, not only on abolishing flogging but on omitting the grog ration. Perry replied in a long report dated 1 March 1850. He was unqualifiedly in favor of abolishing grog, but recommended the substitution of a wine ration. (When he had tried this in the Mediterranean, the sailors despised it!) As for abolishing flogging, Perry said he feared the effect on discipline. He consulted nine of the oldest seamen on board *North Carolina* at Brooklyn, men who had served from nine to twenty-six years in the navy, and found that every one was opposed to abolition, pointing out that the threat of flogging was the only way to control the shirks and the insubordinate.

Congress responded to the Secretary's report by adding a rider to its annual naval appropriation act of 2 September 1850, declaring "that flogging in the navy and on board vessels of commerce . . . is hereby abolished." The final fillip which led to this almost casual liberation of American seamen from corporal punishment is said to have been the publication of Herman Melville's *White Jacket* the previous April. That gifted author painted a true picture of the sadism he had witnessed on board frigate *United States* a few years earlier.

Perry did not welcome this decision. To William Sinclair, his confidential friend in the Navy Department, he wrote in May 1851, "I would not care to go to sea under the present state of discipline of the Navy." And when he did go to sea, in obedience to orders to open Japan, he wrote from the Indian Ocean (10 March 1853), "I can see a wide difference in the discipline and efficiency of the crew since I left the Gulf, the want of legal means of punishing men for the thousand faults they are daily committing, has weakened the authority of the officers, and Congress may be assured that unless some remedy is applied, the Navy as an institution will go to the devil."

After Perry had gone to sea minus the cat, and in consequence of petition to the Senate by some diehards to have flogging restored, the subject came up for debate. Commodore Stockton, now Senator from New Jersey, argued against flogging, but Senator Mallory of Florida, the future secretary of the Southern Confederacy's navy, begged that it be restored, with arguments such as: "Is this the time to discontinue a usage consistent with so much naval glory when we had gallant men in the service, when now we have worse *material?*" But flogging was not restored. And the United States Navy disproved Perry's gloomy predictions by proceeding to greater glories without benefit of cat or colt.

Mediterranean Cruise

Now well rid of Randolph, Perry was free to enjoy his ship as she made her southing from Ushant to Gibraltar. *Concord* is "an admirable vessel in every particular," he wrote to Commodore Charles Morris after a week in the Mediterranean. She "sails well under any sail, but her best is on a wind in smooth water, under single or double-reefed topsails." She "steers well under all circumstances" never misses stays, lays-to comfortably under balanced-reefed spanker and fore spencer, rides easily at anchor with no strain on her cable, and can beat any other ship of the squadron except frigate *Brandywine* under press of canvas in a heavy head sea. He reported her only fault to be a waist so deep that in heavy weather green water came over the hammock rails, and hatches had to be battened down. "Harmony and order" prevailed on board; not one officer drank spirits, but all chipped in to buy light sherry from "the house of Gorden at Xeres." The crew, recalcitrant members having been "licked into shape," gave no more trouble. Midshipmen were kept hard at work, Perry having decided to emulate his elder brother and make *Concord* an informal school ship for young officers. "My midshipmen are kept constantly at their studies," he wrote to Morris from Gibraltar on 28 November 1830. "I have two excellent Instructors, one a noted schoolmaster who conducts the English and Mathematics Class, and the other the Clerk who is perfectly competent as teacher of the French, Spanish and Italian languages. My forward Cabin is appropriated as a school room and we have regulations which require a most rigid attendance at school between the hours of 9 and ½ past 11 A.M. when the midshipmen are called up to take the sun — and between the hours of 3 and 4 in the afternoon, which is exclu-

sively devoted to their French and Spanish studies." Perry brought with
him a selected library of ancient classics in translation, and books on the
history and antiquity of Mediterranean lands. The "young gentlemen"
were invited to browse in them, and at every port of call where there
were interesting ruins or monuments, "Old Bruin" organized a sightseeing
tour.

Brandywine joined *Concord* at Gibraltar, whence they sailed in company, arriving Port Mahon 2 December 1830. There *Concord* spent the
usual winter season very pleasantly.

About the first of April 1831, James Biddle, now commodore of the
Mediterranean Squadron, sent *Concord* on a cruise, during which she
called at Cartagena, Málaga, Marseilles, Genoa, Leghorn and Naples. After
another sojourn at Port Mahon, she kept Christmas 1831 at Syracuse and
there remained until March 1832, when she proceeded via Malta to Alexandria.

Perry gave his officers opportunity to visit Rosetta, Cairo and the Pyramids, and *Concord* received a state visit from the Khedive of Egypt, Mo-
hammed Ali, generally known at that time as Mehemet Ali Pasha. For him
the yards were manned and the battery fired a full 21-gun salute. Mehemet's chief interpreter wrote to the United States consul at Cairo that His
Highness had experienced "peculiar satisfaction" over this visit, and that
"the attentions there received from the Hon. Commander Capt. Perry,
from the officers and from the whole ship's company, have been deeply
felt by His Highness." There is a cryptic entry in *Concord's* letter book:
— "Sent the bears as a present to the Pacha." Did Randolph bring two
bear cubs on board with him at Kronstadt, and had they grown too big
for shipboard pets? Perry and his officers were sumptuously entertained at
the khedival palace, where Mehemet Ali presented the Captain and First
Lieutenant Kennedy with costly shawls for their wives, and enlarged the
ship's stand of small arms by thirteen handsome Mameluke swords.

Perry cultivated his lifelong interest in botany by collecting Sicilian
plants, grapevine cuttings, and roots of the black currant from Zante, for
the Massachusetts Horticultural Society. To his friend Henry A. S. Dearborn, president of the society, he wrote suggesting the name of an Italian
botanist as corresponding member. Dearborn answered that not only
would the society be glad to elect anyone nominated by Perry, but that
"the deep interest you have evinced for the advancement of horticulture,"
and "the repeated favours we have received from you, excites our most
lively gratitude." He wished that more naval officers would take a similar
interest and improve their many opportunities for collecting exotic plants.

From Alexandria to Nauplia *Concord* had as passenger the wife of Sir
John Franklin, then assisting the Greeks in their War of Independence.
Lady Franklin and Perry became good friends, although she rather bored

U.S.S. *Concord* and *Brandywine* off Malta, 1831, artist unknown

him and the wardroom by talking endlessly about her husband's exploits. After landing her ladyship at Nauplia with "five trunks, saddles, numerous carpet-bags and umbrellas," Perry received the compliment of a state visit from Admiral Kanaris of the Greek Navy, one of the heroes of the War of Independence. His two fireships had attacked a Turkish fleet at Tenedos in 1822, and virtually destroyed it.

Concord now stretched across the Aegean to Smyrna, and by 1 May was at Vourla where a seaman was given a "dozen for disobedience to orders and neglect of duty." This is the only flogging logged for a cruise of over a year.

Boston at that time enjoyed a valuable trade with Smyrna. Small brigs and barques carried lumber, West India goods and "Yankee notions" to that emporium of ancient Lydia, and brought back opium, Turkey carpets, oranges and dried figs, which Boston distributed throughout the United States. Captain Perry conceived it his duty to protect this trade from the inhabitants of the Cyclades who were profiting from the war by exercising their traditional piracy. As *Concord* was escorting across the Aegean brig *Smyrna* of Boston, with $180,000 in specie on board, she spoke brig *Bruce* of Boston, which had been robbed by a gang of over fifty pirates who boarded her from a big armed barge. The skipper and his small crew saved their lives by escaping in the brig's boat, but upon their return found *Bruce* stripped of everything, including the compass. Using Caribbean tactics, Perry manned his ship's boats with seventy-five seamen and marines, and sent them to scour the shores of Poros, Sipheros, Seriphos and Mikonos. This turned out to be a wild-goose chase, as the islanders gave his men false information and the pirates were always one jump ahead of them. "Although we have not caught any of the Scoundrels," wrote Perry to the American consul at Smyrna, "I am convinced that our close pursuit of them will have the effect of intimidating them, or at all events to make them wary in venturing out into the open passages. . . . But I am perfectly convinced that they have their friends and agents in all the Islands." The Commodore had ordered *Concord* to return to Port Mahon in early June, but Perry, looking for duty as usual instead of taking the easy way, postponed his departure from Smyrna until he could collect a convoy of merchant shipping to escort around the Peloponnesus. He also gave an American missionary free passage to Athens.

Entering Port Mahon 25 June 1832, Perry reported that he had "shown the flag" in ten ports, although 64 days out of 80 had been spent at sea. The health of the men was excellent, and the officers had improved their education by visiting scenes of ancient civilizations. *Concord* remained at Minorca, partly under quarantine imposed by the local authorities, until 26 August. She was then chosen by Commodore Biddle, who had just been relieved, to sail himself together with forty-two cases of luggage and five casks of wine, to Marseilles. It may be assumed that they did not discuss politics during the crossing; for the Commodore, brother to Nicholas Biddle of the Second Bank of the United States, was a violent anti-Jackson man. But they became warm friends. Biddle presented Perry with a pair of silver goblets as souvenir of a pleasant passage.

Nobody can accuse President Jackson of pursuing a weak foreign policy. After he had settled by negotiation most of the outstanding controversies with Great Britain, he proceeded to enforce the payment of claims against other powers for spoliations on American commerce during the Napoleonic Wars. France agreed by treaty in 1831 to pay $5 million. Collection of a smaller bill due from the Kingdom of the Two Sicilies dragged along. John Nelson, American chargé des affaires at Naples, wrote on 12 July 1832 to the Secretary of State, Edward Livingston, that the foreign office had repeatedly put him off, that only coercive measures could get results, but he made the quaint suggestion that payment might be made in works of art, in which Naples was rich, instead of money. The prospect of a museum of Neapolitan art in Washington did not appeal to the Jackson administration — one can well imagine a furor over "statues of naked women!" — but that of coercion did, and collection of this bill was entrusted to the guns of the Mediterranean Squadron. Jackson placed implicit confidence in Commodore Biddle's relief, Commodore Daniel T. Patterson, and Patterson had equal confidence in Perry, who had been his 1st Luff in *North Carolina* in 1825. Hence, when Patterson, on the excuse of illness — but probably from reluctance to abandon his double life in Port Mahon — decided not to visit Naples, he entrusted this none-too-delicate mission to Master Commandant Perry, as acting commodore and C.O. of his flagship U.S.S. *Brandywine;* a proud command indeed, since she was the newest, crack frigate of the United States Navy. And he also had frigate *Constellation* and sloops *John Adams* and *Boston.*

Either Patterson or Perry worked out a smart operation plan which Perry executed — one which probably suggested his strategy in the Japan mission. It consisted in making a cumulative impression by sending the squadron to the Bay of Naples in echelons. First to arrive, on 23 July 1832, were *Brandywine* and *Constellation.* The King of Naples at that time was Ferdinand II, later lampooned as "King Bomba," because in fighting Garibaldi he bombarded his principal cities. On this occasion, however, Ferdinand was on the receiving end of an incipient bombardment. His palace overlooked the inner harbor of Naples — passenger liners moor under its windows today — and within easy range of anchored warships. Ferdinand happened to be away when the two frigates arrived, but was immediately sent for. "Great uneasiness was felt upon the occasion," wrote Minister Nelson, "and vigorous preparations were made for the defense of the

City, which its Inhabitants had the weakness to suppose, was about to be attacked."

Brandywine and *Constellation* sailed back to Port Mahon in August, and Naples drew a long breath. But Perry, after delivering Commodore Biddle to Marseilles in *Concord*, sailed directly to Naples, arriving 17 September. *John Adams*, already there, had not created much alarm, but the arrival of *Concord* did the trick. Prince Cassaro, minister of foreign affairs, now condescended to negotiate with Nelson, and Perry assisted the negotiation by entertaining members of the Neapolitan aristocracy on board.

Those shipboard balls in the Mediterranean, in days of sail, were something to remember; Herman Melville reminisced about one on board U.S.S. *Ohio* at Naples in his long poem *Bridegroom Dick* —

> Lo, Genteel Jack in hurricane weather,
> Shagged like a bear, like a red lion roaring;
> But O, so fine in his chapeau and feather,
> In port to the ladies never once *jawing;*
> All bland *politesse,* how urbane was he —
> *"Oui, mademoiselle — Ma chère amie!"*

> 'Twas Jack got up the ball at Naples,
> Gay in the old *Ohio* glorious;
> His hair was curled by the berth-deck barber,
> Never you'd deemed him a cub of rude Boreas;
> In tight little pumps, with the grand dames in rout,
> A-flinging his shapely foot all about;
> His watch-chain with love's jewelled tokens abounding,
> Curls ambrosial shaking out odours,
> Waltzing along the batteries, astounding
> The gunner glum and the grim-visaged loaders.

On 14 October 1832 Cassaro signed for the King a treaty promising to pay the United States 2,100,000 ducats within nine years. It was now Perry's duty to carry the American negotiator home with the treaty. After his experience with John Randolph, the prospect must have made him shudder. Nelson turned out to be an agreeable gentleman, but in a dreadful hurry, eager to reach Washington in time for President Jackson to mention the treaty in his annual message to Congress. *Concord,* accordingly, got under way the very day after the treaty was signed, cut a scheduled call at Lisbon, and for twenty consecutive days battled gale-force headwinds in hope of meeting the presidential timetable. When Cape Cod was finally sighted on 4 December it was too late. Nelson consented to be landed at the nearest port to leeward, which happened to be Portsmouth, New Hampshire, *Concord*'s birthplace. There she was laid up in ordinary, the crew discharged, and Captain Perry, after conscientiously overseeing this operation, which detained him another fortnight, returned to his home and family at 95 Spring Street, New York City. He had been absent over two years.

If President Jackson had been shaken in his opinion of Perry by the diatribes of John Randolph — and there is no evidence that he was — confidence was restored by his performance at Naples. But that performance entailed a good deal of money from the Commander's pocket. Perry and five other master commandants, including Sloat, Gregory, and Stringham, printed a leaflet appealing for support of a bill "for the more equitable compensation of the Officers of the Navy." They pointed out that officers of their rank received the "degradingly low" compensation of $1174 per annum, less than that of majors of the army and the marine corps or clerks in the Navy Department, and no entertainment allowance. Yet, as commanding officers of American warships, they were obliged to entertain ladies and gentlemen in foreign ports, and "invarably return from sea deeply in debt." Perry personally received in 1835 a special grant of $1500 from Congress "for extra services and expenses incurred by him while commanding U. S. Sloop of War *Concord*, in obedience to orders, and more particularly in the reception on board his ship of Mehemit Ali, the Pacha of Egypt, and numerous suite."

This cruise in *Concord* concluded Perry's service in the Mediterranean. As with all his other naval duties, he reflected on his experience and suggested improvements. In "Thoughts on the Navy," which he and his brother-in-law Alexander Slidell wrote four years later, the Mediterranean was "an admirable school" for naval officers. Not only did it afford them an opportunity to learn foreign languages, but to acquire culture "by visiting a thousand sites crowned by the pure monuments of a classic age and consecrated by undying associations." But it was a mistake to allow warships to "remain there like so many fixtures during three entire years"; there should be more interchange. And, owing to the stormy nature of the Mediterranean winter, "which is always passed there in idleness, and sometimes in dissipation and discord in some snug port," the squadron, all but one vessel, should then be transferred to "the temperate regions of the coast of Africa," Brazil or the West Indies. He discreetly failed to mention the Circean attractions of Port Mahon for an American Ulysses.

Nothing was done about these suggestions. Service in the Mediterranean continued to be enjoyed, and service in Africa and the West Indies abhorred, by officers and seamen alike.

CHAPTER XI

Navy Reformer
1833–1842

The Brooklyn Navy Yard

PERRY applied for and obtained command of the recruiting station in New York on 7 January 1833. As earlier in Boston, he was now Commander of the Naval Rendezvous, or, in modern terms, Captain of the Yard. His primary duty was to direct the recruiting service in New York, but he also assisted in divers ways the successive commandants.

The decade of shore duty which thus began turned out to be one of the most productive and enjoyable periods of Perry's life. Jane's father John Slidell had lately died. He had lost a large part of his fortune, but left enough to Jane for the Perry family to live like other gentlemen's families in that era. They bought a house at 95 Spring Street in lower New York west of the Bowery and somewhat nearer to the Brooklyn Navy Yard ferry than their former residence. There their ninth child, Isabella, was born in 1834. Jane enjoyed a rest from childbearing for over three years, but celebrated her husband's promotion to Captain USN, which took place on 19 February 1837, by producing Anna Rodgers, her tenth and last child. This little girl, who lived less than a year, was buried in the Slidell family vault at St. Mark's "in the Bowerie," where, twenty years later, the Commodore was destined to join her.

Captain Matthew Calbraith Perry succeeded Captain Renshaw as Commandant of the New York Navy Yard in 1841. Perry thus acquired the courtesy title of commodore, since he now had the command over all United States naval vessels in New York harbor. He flew the broad blue pendant, designating flag rank, in his old ship *North Carolina*, now receiving ship for that naval district, but lived in the official headquarters in the yard. That small, handsome mansion with oval dining room and extensive grounds had been designed by a pupil of Bulfinch and built in 1810; it has survived the abandonment of the Brooklyn Navy Yard in 1966, serving as quarters for Commander Eastern Sea Frontier. Matthew C. Perry Jr.,

COMMANDANT'S QUARTERS, BROOKLYN NAVY YARD

Photograph of the 1860's

The drawing room in 1965

already a midshipman, was now at sea, and the older Perry daughters followed the family pattern by making good matches. Jane married John
Hone, great-nephew of the famous diarist, in October 1841. Three
months later, Sarah married Robert S. Rodgers, son of the old Commodore. Both weddings took place in the drawing room of the Commandant's headquarters. Sarah's marriage was a delight to both parents; and
young Rodgers, a lawyer, looked to Captain Perry for guidance, since his
father the Commodore had died. Jane's wedding to young John Hone
was equally happy, besides being another upward step in the social world
of New York. The Hones were now at the top of the heap, John's
mother being a De Peyster, and he a successful lawyer and trustee. His
great-uncle attended "the nuptials" at the navy yard and noted in his
diary: — "The wedding was handsomely conducted, everything genteel
and in good taste and the company most respectable. The clergyman who
made my young friend a happy husband was the Rev. Dr. Eastburn of the
Church of the Ascension."

The Perrys not only participated in the social life of Brooklyn and New
York; as Commandant and lady they did a great deal of official entertaining. Since New York City then had few attractions for visitors — no art
museum, no tall buildings, not even a zoo or an aquarium — the usual
entertainment for visiting foreigners was to inspect the navy yard and
lunch or dine with the Commandant. During his predecessor's frequent
absences; this duty devolved on Captain Perry, who tried in vain to obtain
an entertainment allowance from the government; and these expenditures
became even heavier after Perry himself became Commandant. To Captain David Conner he wrote, "This is a confounded expensive station I
have, which with Princes, Lords, Governors, &c, I have my hands
full, with *empty* pockets." He hoped that the Navy Commissioners would
provide official quarters with a cook and steward, but they never did, and
Jane had to squeeze the enhanced wage and grocery bills out of her house
money. Even as a Captain USN, Perry's salary was only $3500. He partici-
pated in most of the city's official functions; for instance, he was a guest at
the dinner given to Lord Ashburton at the old Astor House in City Hall
Park, on 2 September 1842.

During these ten years at New York, Matthew C. Perry accomplished
things for the navy and the country along four general lines: steam navigation, ordnance, improved lighthouse service, and the education of naval
officers and enlisted men. He promoted and helped to organize the navy's
Pacific Ocean exploring expedition, and he was offered the command but
declined, feeling that someone particularly skilled in hydrography and
chart-making should head the expedition. Such a man was his friend Lieutenant Commander Charles Wilkes, an excellent choice. "I rejoice with
you," Perry wrote to a friend in September 1838, "that the Expedition is

at last fairly afloat. May it have good success say I with all my heart."

Perry's promotion to Commandant in 1841 came as a surprise because the Whigs were in power, and he and his Slidell connections were Jackson Democrats. The Brooklyn Navy Yard having fallen victim to Jackson's spoils system, with consequent loss of efficiency, Secretary Badger instructed the new commandant to disregard political considerations when choosing workmen, and to forbid electioneering in the yard. Perry obeyed these instructions so faithfully as to displease the local Whig leaders, with the result that before the end of this command he found himself in the Tyler administration's doghouse. But that did not prevent him from tightening up discipline in the yard and seeing that the government's money was properly spent.

Beginnings of a Steam Navy

In a leading article of the *Naval Magazine* for January 1837 entitled "Thoughts on the Navy," Perry gave free expression to his ideas on naval improvement. He deplored the "languid and ineffectual support" that the navy was receiving "from the representatives of the people." It had fallen to eighth place in the navies of the world, after England, France, Russia, Turkey, Holland, Sweden and Egypt. Its weakness with respect to the first two powers, the only ones likely to challenge us to a war, was striking:

WARSHIPS IN COMMISSION, 1836

	Royal Navy	French Navy	U. S. Navy
Ships-of-the-line	23	15	2
Frigates	15	13	7
Sloops and corvettes	51		14
Brigs and schooners	25	} 65 {	7
Steamships	21	23	0

In addition to this relative decline in numbers, "Our naval architecture has rather retrograded than advanced of late years, during which we have launched some ships that would be a disgrace to the Chinese Navy." None built since the War of 1812 were equal to the old *United States;* a school of naval architecture was badly wanted. Gunnery practice had been neglected, and in naval ordnance the French had run away with the efficient shell-throwing gun which the Stevenses of Hoboken invented in 1814. Now, under the name of Paixhans, a French artillery officer who picked up the idea and developed it, these shell guns had been installed in all capital ships of the French Navy.

Perry came to be known in American naval circles as "the father of the steam navy." As a young lieutenant in New York, in the fall of 1814, he had witnessed the launching of U.S.S. *Demologos*, renamed *Fulton* after her designer's untimely death. He had observed the steam galliot *Sea Gull* pursuing pirates up Caribbean estuaries. Congress in 1816 authorized the President to acquire engines and other materials for constructing three steam-propelled "floating batteries," the idea being that these floating fortresses could proceed by their own power to any seaport threatened in time of war. Perry had no use for this purely defensive concept, which suited the popular taste. What he wanted was a seagoing steam warship. And he got an experimental prototype when Secretary Mahlon Dickerson, a friend of his, used the 1815 authorization to build another U.S.S. *Fulton*.

Perry watched over the three-year construction of this second *Fulton* at the Brooklyn Navy Yard like a hen hatching her first clutch of eggs. She was a 700-ton sidewheeler, 180 feet long, armed with four 32-pounders, powered by two locally built engines totalling 625 horsepower. With four tall stacks, big paddlewheel boxes, and three masts rigged for sail, she was a weird sight. Launched in May and commissioned in December 1837, her initial commanding officer, most appropriately, was Perry himself, who carried this responsibility in addition to his shore duties.

This imposed on Perry a new task of organization. The department had given him no authority to obtain engineers or firemen. He worked out details on wages, qualifications, duties, and status of engineers in the navy, and his long letter to the Navy Commissioners, dated 11 September 1837, is regarded as the foundation of the engineer corps. He already had a competent chief engineer, Charles H. Haswell, who had designed the engines; but in order to operate them he needed four assistant engineers at $500 to $800 per annum, six firemen at $25 to $30 a month, and four coal heavers at $15 per month. These were lower than the wages paid by Long Island Sound steamers, and he "respectfully invited the attention of the Commissioners" to their tenure.

The Commissioners stalled at making a decision until the end of October 1837, when Perry reported the *Fulton* ready to get up steam. They then authorized him to procure the necessary complement at the suggested rates of pay; and, such was the novelty of this experiment, he got them. On her trial trip in New York harbor she raised steam in half an hour and traveled at the marvelous speed of 10 knots! Despite this preliminary success, Perry encountered deep prejudice against steam power on the part of many senior officers and especially of James K. Paulding, the elderly literary gentleman whom President Van Buren unaccountably appointed Secretary of the Navy. Paulding is reported to have declared "he never would consent to see our grand old ships supplanted by these new and ugly sea-monsters." This situation made Perry the more zealous to make *Fulton* a success and to give engineer officers a status equal to that of line officers in the navy. He selected lively young men for line officers of

Fulton and ordered them to receive the engineer officers as equals. In a report to the Navy Department he wrote: —

The officers of a steamer should be those of established discretion, not only that great vigilance will be required of them, but because much tact and forbearance must necessarily be exercised in their intercourse with the engineers and firemen who, coming from a class of respectable mechanics and unused to the restraints and discipline of a vessel of war, may be made discontented and unhappy by injudicious treatment. . . .

I am solicitous of establishing the [steam] service on a footing so popular and respectable, as to be desired by those of the navy who may be emulous of acquiring information in a new and interesting field of professional employment.

Perry designed the engineer officers' uniforms to be identical with those of line officers, adding an olive-branch and paddlewheel device on the collar. He promoted a training school for naval engineers and firemen apprentices. These suggestions were approved by the Secretary in 1838, and Commodore Ridgely was directed to appoint five apprentice engineers to *Fulton*. This was, in effect, the nucleus of the engineering course at the future Naval Academy.

Fulton's first venture outside New York harbor was not brilliant. Her condensing apparatus which produced fresh water for the boilers failed to function properly and the four tall stacks woefully reduced her speed. Perry reported: "The *Fulton* will never answer as a sea-vessel, but the facility of moving from port to port, places at the service of the Department, a force particularly available for the immediate action at any point." The new year 1838 was not two weeks old when Captain Perry received orders to take her on a coastwise cruise. In Long Island Sound she did well, making 28 miles in a little less than two hours. Everyone assumed she could break up a blockade, such as the port of New York had suffered during the last war. Perry even made the pregnant proposal that *Fulton*'s engines be protected by inclined ironclad bulwarks, "so as to cause all shot striking them from any direction to ricochet" — exactly what happened when C.S.S. *Virginia* (ex-U.S.S. *Merrimack*) sortied in 1861.

Although Perry realized that *Fulton* could never be really seaworthy, she was at least a beginning and as early as 17 February 1838 he reported to the department "that seagoing war steamers of 1400 or 1500 tons could be built to cruise at sea even for twenty days, and yet be efficient and as safe from disaster as the finest frigates afloat, while the expense would be considerably less." In May 1838 he managed to sail *Fulton* to Washington, D.C., where she was inspected by President Van Buren and other important people in the government. This was a wonderful stroke politically; it convinced many senators and congressmen that a steam navy was practical, and well disposed them toward Perry's far-reaching proposal.

As a result, the Naval Appropriation Act of March 1839 provided for three steam warships "on such models as shall be most approved." These three emerged as U.S.S. *Mississippi, Missouri* and *Union*, the first of which Perry was destined to command in the Mexican War, and on the Japan Expedition.

In 1839, after his return from the lighthouse mission which we shall describe shortly, Perry used *Fulton* for gun practice, and established proving grounds at Sandy Hook for testing guns, shells and shot. He had Paixhans and ordinary cannon sited ashore, set up a variety of targets at 800 to 1200 yards' range, and anchored *Fulton* off the beach to fire from her guns. All were practised with different kinds of explosive shells and fuzes, solid shot, grape and canister. The results were a demonstrated superiority of the Paixhans-type 64-pound shell gun, the need for a new type of gun carriage (unchanged since the Revolution), and the surprising inaccuracy of solid shot. This, said Perry, was owing to the method of stowing it in damp places on board ship, making every cannonball more or less rusty. To cure this, he suggested dipping each ball, as it came from the foundry, into some rust-resistant substance. He concluded, "This may appear to many a refinement of precaution altogether unnecessary, but when it is remembered that without guns and shot a ship of war is a useless machine and . . . that the vessel and her crew are intended only to accommodate and to manage the guns, it would seem that the first care should be given to that which is of the first importance." These practical tests were very important. Paixhans guns were installed in sloops *Portsmouth* and *Plymouth*, completed in 1844, and in almost every large naval vessel before the Mexican War broke. Although far more destructive than round shot, the shell guns had not the range of the old-fashioned long cannon which threw solid shot, and so did not altogether replace them for many years.

Fulton's coal bunkers had so little capacity that she spent most of her short life moored in New York harbor, occasionally getting up steam to go in aid of vessels in distress. But one more naval innovation came out of her before 1842, when she was laid up in ordinary. Upon returning to New York after a brief sortie, she refused to answer her helm and rammed a merchant brig with devastating effect. Profiting by the accident, Perry proposed that the ancient practice of ramming an enemy be revived as appropriate for heavy steam vessels. The idea took, and ramming became recognized naval tactics in the Civil War, in European naval wars, and throughout the century. Even at the time of the Spanish American War the U. S. Navy had a specially constructed ram named *Katahdin*. By that time the improvement in naval ordnance made it virtually impossible for a ram, or warship equipped with ramming beak, to approach a surfaced enemy near enough to do its stuff. But there were many instances of destroyers, not so equipped, ramming surfacing submarines in World War II.

Perry corresponded with Thomas Aspinwall, the American consul at London, asking him to obtain data of cost per horsepower of the engines and boilers used by Cunard's West India steam packets, and to find out how long it took to complete them. His keen interest in steam power was recognized by the Navy Commissioners in Washington appointing him president of a Board for Steam Models and Machinery, and it was this board which approved the model of U.S.S. *Mississippi*. The Commodore also became general consultant on proposed new naval gadgets such as "Gilbert's Balance Floating Dock," which he advised the navy not to buy; and he himself invented a collapsible smokestack for U.S.S. *Missouri*, which was adopted after approval by William C. Redfield.

That gentleman, who started life as a saddle-maker in Conecticut, became the leading American meteorologist of his age, and an expert in other scientific branches as well. Perry wrote to him from London in September 1838, "The warfare that is now raging in the U. States in reference to the Navy, and the relative qualities of steamers &c, will result in . . . improvements in a branch of the Service (*a steamer force*) which has hitherto been neglected by our Government. . . . Every intelligent man that I have conversed with seems to be fully impressed with the opinion that the destinies of the great maritime nations of the world are henceforward to be in a measure controlled by a power for which steam will be the great governing element." Although steam propulsion and the shell gun were fast making sailing navies obsolete, only a few officers in the United States Navy, a devoted band led by Perry, Stockton and Franklin Buchanan, could see it. The Tyler administration undertook a big building program, but spent nine-tenths of the money on sailing warships. American mechanics seemed unable to construct dependable marine engines, and naval constructors hated to spoil the sleek lines of a hull with clumsy paddlewheel boxes.

Perry also advocated an equally significant innovation, the iron ship, especially for river gunboats, owing to "their superior speed, buoyancy, cleanliness and safety." Their planned prototype was the steam frigate *Princeton*, an iron warship with engines and propeller designed by John Ericsson, built at Philadelphia under the superintendence of Commodore Stockton. Her two 12-inch Paixhans-type guns were tested at Perry's Staten Island proving grounds and found satisfactory; but the American-built gun, inappropriately named "Peace Maker," burst on board *Princeton* in February 1844 when she was carrying President Tyler and an official party down the Potomac, killing six people, including two cabinet ministers. Whilst this disaster did not cause the navy to lose confidence in shell guns, it eliminated Ericsson from government employment until the Civil War, and gave Congress an excuse to hold up construction of more steam or iron warships.

Naval Education

Thoroughly dissatisfied with the haphazard method still in vogue of appointing midshipmen, Perry tried to do something about it. Congress had discovered in middies' warrants a new and juicy form of patronage. Prominent politicians, of whom President Tyler's Secretary of War is an outstanding example, used the navy to get rid of young troublemakers. So well was this understood that one politician, asking Perry to endorse his request for a warrant for his son, wrote, "*I am not one to dump my black sheep on the Navy!*"

Even more dissatisfied was Perry with the "learn by doing" system through which the navy attempted to educate warrant midshipmen to qualify as passed midshipmen. (He did not live long enough to find this to be a favorite principle of "progressive education.") Apart from acquiring practical seamanship, for which a cruise in a sailing ship could not be bettered — even today — the middies were supposed to learn mathematics, navigation and French from the chaplain. According to Navy Regulations of 1802, the chaplain "should perform the duty of a schoolmaster, and to that end he shall instruct . . . in writing, arithmetic, and navigation, and in whatsoever may contribute to render them proficient." But, says J. Russell Soley, historian of the Naval Academy, "It was only in cases of fortunate accident that they knew anything about a subject before they were called to teach it." *North Carolina* and her sister ships of the line rated each a special "schoolmaster" (salary $300 per annum); but, in the frigates and smaller men-of-war, the chaplain still had to double as instructor of the young.

Like many other self-educated Americans and Englishmen, Perry was eager to promote the acquisition of knowledge by those who did not share his drive and persistence. As we have seen,[1] he personally promoted this process in *Concord* in 1830–1832 by acquiring a well-educated chaplain, a schoolmaster, and a library of books. But Commander A. S. Mackenzie, writing in 1840, declares that in all his naval service, which began in 1814, he had known no naval officer except the Perry brothers to take seriously the shipboard education of junior officers.

During the War of Independence, John Paul Jones urged the establishment of a naval academy for the training of young gentlemen as officers, such as England had had since 1733. Both Presidents Adams recommended

---

[1] Above, Chapter XI.

it, but democratic jealousy of the navy outlasted even the War of 1812. In the J. Q. Adams administration, Representative Lemuel Sawyer of North Carolina predicted that the glamour of a naval education would "produce degeneracy and corruption of the public morality and change our simple Republican habits." Senator William Smith of South Carolina, after pointing out that neither Julius Caesar nor Lord Nelson attended a naval academy, predicted that American bluejackets "would look with contempt upon trifling or effeminate leaders," such as a naval school might produce. Around 1830 a poor substitute was adopted — naval schools held at the navy yards of Boston, New York and Norfolk to instruct midshipmen "not otherwise employed." The "reefer" had to pass an examination at one of these schools to earn the rank of passed midshipman and his first stripe; yet the total number of pupils in 1833 was only 52, and they were taught by four civilians, each of whom was paid $981.75 per annum. At the same time the seagoing teacher-chaplain's pay was upped to $100 a month. This enhanced the faults of the old system by loading chaplains with work foreign to their profession.

In the meantime, many naval officers had been pressing for a naval academy. Perry, in his "Thoughts on the Navy," pointed out that a naval academy would be an "easy check" on political appointments; incompetents would be "bilged" before graduation. Secretary Paulding urgently requested this of Congress in 1838, but another poor compromise was adopted. At Philadelphia the navy maintained a snug harbor for aged and indigent seamen, known as the Naval Asylum. Two civilian professors and two naval lieutenants were now attached to this institution as teachers, and midshipmen were encouraged to enroll in order to be coached for their promotion examinations. There was little or no discipline; middies came and went as they pleased, and the presence of the ancient and decrepit mariners, whose asylum it was, did not encourage the young.

An important contribution by Commodore Perry to the education of adult officers was the establishment of the United States Naval Lyceum. The lyceum system, then being extended across the northern part of the United States, was the first comprehensive American scheme of adult education, catering to an insatiable popular appetite for self-improvement and scientific knowledge. A group of citizens in a town, or even village, would form a lyceum, raise money by subscription, attract lecturers such as Emerson and Horace Mann on all manner of literary and cultural subjects, and scientists such as Silliman and Henry to lecture on their specialties. The men of science brought specimens and apparatus and performed experiments before admiring audiences. Often, as an offshoot, a public library was organized or a botanical and mineralogical collection started, and scholarship funds were collected to send bright local boys to college.

Feeling that naval officers needed culture as much as any class of the

American people, Perry in 1833 set about founding the United States Naval Lyceum. This institution provided for officers stationed at the Brooklyn Navy Yard, or on board ships under repair, a higher form of recreation than the dubious establishments that lined Sand Street. The constitution of the Naval Lyceum declared that it was formed "in order to promote the diffusion of useful knowledge, to foster a spirit of harmony and a community of interest in the service, and to cement the links which unite us as professional brethren." It had its own insignia with the motto *Tam Minerva quam Marte*. Perry persuaded the Navy Department to add an extra story to the office building then being put up in the yard, and there the Lyceum had its lecture hall, cabinet, library and reading room, open daily from 9 A.M. to sunset, where the leading periodicals of the Western world were taken in. Every Tuesday at 8 P.M. a meeting was held for papers and discussion. Admission fee was five dollars; army officers and midshipmen could use the library without charge. The cabinet contained paintings of naval scenes, busts of George Washington and William IV the "sailor king," "a large and beautiful collection of Sicilian Lava"; and, after Perry had made a start with his conchological collection, Commodore Patterson contributed three barrels of Mediterranean shells. The Lyceum recorded weather data at Brooklyn, persuaded other lyceums around the country to do the same, and reviewed the first book by Midshipman Matthew Fontaine Maury.

The *Naval Magazine*, modeled on the Royal Navy's *Nautical Magazine*, was launched in 1836. Perry and his brother-in-law Alexander Slidell were on the editorial board, contributing articles such as "A Pilot's Story of a Shipwreck," "Steamers of War," and "Thoughts on the Navy," from which we have quoted. Unfortunately this excellent quarterly did not obtain sufficient support to continue after its second year. But the Lyceum continued for another half-century. A progress report of 1839 indicates a flourishing institution. In four years the library had increased by five hundred volumes, many of them valuable and expensive works such as Dumont D'Urville *Voyage de la Corvette l'Astrolabe* (29 volumes), presented by the French Minister of Marine; and fifty-six Admiralty charts "presented through Capt. M. C. Perry, U.S.N., by Capt. F. Beaufort, R.N." The manuscript "Book of Donations" lists Perry's initial gift of shells, coins, mosaics, specimens of lava and of Parian marble, and engravings of Decatur and brother Oliver. Apparently the Naval Lyceum did not engage lecturers from the outside, possibly for lack of funds, but more probably because the members found plenty of topics to discuss at their weekly meetings.

After the Civil War the Naval Lyceum declined. No more meetings were held, and in 1892 the entire collection was shipped to the Naval Academy Museum in Annapolis, which still has the inventory. There were paintings and engravings of naval ships and battles, and ship models, many of which are on display at Annapolis. The library comprised some three thousand volumes of voyages and travels, naval and general history, classic and modern literature, government documents, navigation and international law. To Annapolis went Perry's collection of shells, and case after case labeled "curiosities"; just such things as mid-century museums featured — stuffed birds, minerals, ancient pottery, Indian relics, specimens of exotic fish in alcohol, a Turkish tombstone and brass cannon, chips off the Pyramids, a stuffed leopard and an Egyptian mummy of a sacred cat, and a Russian work on conchology, Perry's favorite scientific subject. Dr. Usher Parsons, Oliver H. Perry's fleet surgeon in the Battle of Lake Erie who had since become professor of anatomy and surgery at Brown University and president of the Rhode Island Society of Natural History, contributed two boxes of shells, together with a catalogue of the collection owned by Dr. John C. Jay, who later wrote the report on Japanese shells for the official Narrative of the Japan Expedition.

In Perry's view, the status of naval officers was important as education. At present, he wrote in "Thoughts on the Navy," the highest rank in the United States Navy was that of captain, corresponding to a colonel of the Army or Marine Corps. Why, he wondered, did Congress consistently refuse to create the rank of rear admiral, which (with vice admiral and admiral) every other respectable navy then had? The want of higher ranks to look forward to had created "a system of death-like stagnation among the officers of our Navy suited to smother hope, ambition and every generous sentiment." Young, ambitious officers "are doomed to pass . . . their best years in subordinate drudgery, reserving the era of command for that declining age, when the broken voice, the failing vision, . . . counsel retirement."

Nothing was done about this for another quarter-century. Democratic resentment of the rank of admiral, inexplicable in view of the avidity of every tin-pot politician to be called "General," prevented the Navy from having even a rear admiral until 1862. And the "death-like stagnation" that Perry described has been characteristic of several between-wars periods of our history. It is true now as always, that wartime operations are the final test of a naval officer's character and capacity. Only through war with its trials and casualties, or a period of vigilance, patrol and testing new weapons such as the "cold war," can human deadwood be eliminated and the eager, competent officers receive commands commensurate with their ability.

Lighthouses and Irish Politics

Among other things placed under the responsibility of the Commander of the Naval Rendezvous at Brooklyn were the local coast guard and lighthouses; and the latter soon became objects of Perry's reforming zeal. Tremendous improvements had been made in European lighthouses since 1820, especially in France, where Frédéric Fresnel had invented a lenticular lens that magnified whale-oil lamplight and projected it miles further than before. But the coastal lights of the United States, still using simple basin-shaped reflectors instead of lenses, were among the world's dimmest. This is not surprising, since lighthouse keepers were still regarded by the average American as pawns in political patronage. A candidate for high office in Lowell's *Biglow Papers* remarks: —

> Ef you git *me* inside the White House,
> Your head with ile I'll kin' o' 'nint
> By gittin' *you* inside the Light-house
> Down to the eend of Jaalam Pint.

"In this country," wrote Perry, in contrast to England and France where any absent lighthouse keeper would be fired, "it is notorious that some of our principal light-houses are left for days in charge of incompetent and irresponsible persons," while the keeper was drunk or giving himself a vacation. "It is a peculiarity of the people of this country," he concluded with his usual philosophy, "that a proper regard to the preservation of human life enters too little into the concerns of the every-day transactions of the community." Thus, "lights which are established to guide the anxious seaman along the dangerous coast or into the distant port" are neglected. And there were very few of them — not even one hundred in the entire United States.

Captain Perry wrote two reports on the subject which were printed as government documents. The first was the result of an examination in 1837 by himself and two other naval captains of lights and other aids to navigation in New York Bay and adjacent waters. They queried pilots, masters of vessels and officers of marine insurance companies and cruised through the waters in a revenue cutter. They recommended a $300 "beacon light" at South Amboy, buoys and beacons in the Kill Van Kull, an improved light at Prince's Bay, Staten Island, and that Sandy Hook be more efficiently lighted. An average of 2500 vessels bound foreign, or coming from foreign ports, and at least 10,000 coasters, passed Sandy Hook annually, and the number of people and amount of property involved warranted a greater expenditure for aids to navigation.

The report did not envisage any change from reflectors to lenses. But

Perry himself, having long suffered from the paucity and inefficiency of American aids to navigation, and being cognizant of European developments, managed by personal persuasion to stir up Senator Davis of Massachusetts and the Navy Department to do something. "Honest John" Davis, as the Senator was called, obtained a congressional appropriation to purchase two sets of French lenticular lenses, and the department sent Perry to Europe to study lighthouses in 1838, and to obtain the new lenses, or improved reflectors, or both.

This being a subject of interest to every maritime power, Perry had no difficulty obtaining coöperation. In France he made friends with Fresnel's younger brother, who undertook to superintend the manufacture of two sets of lenticular lenses on the inventor's model; and with other important people too. He was even invited to a family dinner at the Tuileries with King Louis Philippe. These were very jolly affairs, with the attractive royal princes and their wives present, Queen Marie-Adelaide at one end of the table and the host at the other. Whatever the menu, Louis Philippe always had a large cold ham set before him, and carved it himself in wafer-thin slices; an art which, he genially observed, he had learned when an almost penniless exile in England.

Perry examined some of the greater lighthouses in northern France, and in his report presented a description of the lighthouse at Barfleur, "which is of the first class and will answer in application to all others in the country." And he made a special study of the illuminating oil used in French lighthouses. Finding that it came from the colza plant, he visited the region where it was cultivated, procured ten pounds of the seed, and promoted its cultivation in America as a means of rendering the lighthouse service less dependent on whale oil. (But the whaling interests prevented anything being done about that.) He then proceeded to England, enlisted the aid of Andrew Stevenson the American minister, and of Trinity House, which controlled all British aids to navigation. He consulted with members of the several lighthouse boards, who were most helpful in providing him "with a great variety of books, drawings, estimates, charts, manuscripts, &c," containing "the best possible information on the subject." "With a view to brevity," he writes, he reports on only one lighthouse in each district of the United Kingdom — South Stack on Holyhead, Inskerth in Scotland, and Poolbeg near Dublin. The British lighthouses, although in process of adopting Fresnel lenses, were using parabolic reflectors so "infinitely superior" to those used in America that Perry ordered fifteen of them, complete with lamps. Boston Light got all but one — for the only way to enhance the candlepower of a lighthouse in those days was to provide a battery of oil lamps.

Before leaving London, Perry became involved in a ridiculous though embarrassing controversy. The Irish leader Daniel O'Connell, at an abolitionist meeting in Birmingham on 1 August 1838, not only slandered the character of George Washington but accused Minister Stevenson, who came from Virginia, of being "a slave-breeder, one of those beings who rear up slaves for the purpose of traffic." Stevenson, upon reading the newspaper report of this speech, consulted both Captain Perry and his old Newport schoolmate General James Hamilton of South Carolina, who happened to be in London. Both advised the minister to go slow, and before challenging the Irishman to a duel, to inquire whether the press report was correct. O'Connell replied that, in substance, it was; but he meant it "in a Pickwickian sense" as it were — nothing personal! Stevenson then let the matter drop. Hamilton unfortunately published in an American newspaper his version of the affair, bringing in Perry's name as a possible second to the duel that never took place. John Quincy Adams, now a representative in Congress, tried to make political hay out of the incident by calling for an investigation of Stevenson, Hamilton and Perry; but all he got out of that attempt was a letter from a gentleman of Alabama threatening to shoot him on sight. Perry commented in a letter to Stevenson: —

Mr. Adams, as you will have noticed, has been playing some of his mad pranks in reference to the O'Connel business. He owes both you and General Hamilton a grudge and I am brought in for the sake of Consistency.

Although much has been written, and said, on the subject, I am still satisfied that of the two dilemmas in which the villainy of O'Connel placed you by his speech at Birmingham you chose that which was the most judicious, and if it has produced no other good effect, it has opened the eyes of the Irish beggar's friends and this Country to his unparalleled mendacity.

Many Americans of proper feeling must assent to your course in this unpleasant affair, the most honourable solution. I am sure that all your Southern friends do. . . . I send you Mr. Clay's speech in which he alludes to you and O'Connel.

Perry was particularly irritated with Adams's reaction to this incident because he and his elder brother had consistently tried to stop dueling in the navy. Oliver, it is true, was forced to a duel with the marine officer he had struck in a fit of passion, but he refused to fire his pistol, and Calbraith not only found an honorable way out from a duel with which he was threatened, but successfully prevented dueling among his junior officers.

Back in New York in mid-January 1839, Perry, after a few days with his family, proceeded to Washington full of ideas, plans and suggestions, and his final report on the lighthouse mission was submitted in 1840. As usual with his recommendations, they were carried out years later. What was done with the two French lenses he obtained, we do not know; but reflectors were still required by law until 1852, when the United States was maintaining 325 lighthouses and light-ships on Atlantic, Gulf, Lake and Pacific coasts. In that year the Treasury Department (responsible for aids to navigation), after trying a French lens at the Highlands of Navesink and ascertaining that "the lenticular apparatus could be managed by the average light-keeper after instruction," began substituting Fresnel lenses for reflectors. At the same time President Fillmore implemented another Perry recommendation, appointing an independent Lighthouse Board, to replace haphazard control by the Treasury Department. The first Board had a very distinguished membership: Commodore W. S. Shubrick chairman, General Totten, chief engineer of the army, Professor Bache, superintendent of the Coast Survey, Joseph Henry of the Smithsonian, and Commander S. F. DuPont USN. They drew up regulations for installing and operating Fresnel lenses, and pushed their replacement of reflectors in all important lighthouses.

The Apprentice System

"Next to the formation of an efficient corps of officers," states the Perry-Slidell article, "is the creation . . . of a class of seamen, peculiarly its own." In 1836 the haphazard and wasteful system of recruiting, which we have described in Chapter IX, was still in force. A naval vessel "wasted the months that should be passed in cruising," in sailing from one naval rendezvous to another "in vain efforts to fill up the complement of her crew; draining the country of its able-bodied seamen," and obtaining a disproportionate number of drunks, misfits and foreigners. The navy should be authorized to enlist 3000 apprentices, fourteen years of age and upward, to serve until their majority, and undertake to feed, clothe and educate them.

Those who are unacquainted with the Navy cannot understand the transition that takes place in a poor half-fed and half-clad boy, when taken from the streets and wharfs of our great cities and entered on board a man-of-war. The cleanliness, which is particularly enforced among the younger portion of the crew, by the daily muster, under the vigilant eye of the master-at-arms at seven bells, the comfortable clothing, and the sufficient food, all make an instantaneous change for the better in his physical condition. He starts up to grow and spread in a manner almost magical. His character too developes itself rapidly, as he begins to learn, and make himself useful in the duty of the ship. There is, perhaps, no pleasure which the benevolent officer experiences in a man-of-war greater than that which he feels in watching the growth and daily improvement, in appearance, character and usefulness of an active lad, aspiring to the dignity of an able seaman, with an ambition unsurpassed by any thing that we see in the loftier walks of life.

Every ship of the line should take at least 300 apprentices to sea; every frigate, 150. "In this way our Navy would soon be manned entirely by Americans, among whom it is not now popular, owing to the existence of a harsh system which has grown out of the unlimited introduction of foreigners." Nine-tenths of the merchant seamen employed in vessels operating from New York were foreigners. The writer urged the immediate "establishment of a school-ship" to berth the first hundred apprentices, and begin their naval education. He had asked for this before, expecting that "business men flushed with such signal prosperity" would support it, but they were blind to their own interest in turning into a patriotic profession the youngsters then hanging about our streets and wharves.

On no other subject was Perry so eloquent and persistent as on this apprentice system. He had been at it since 1824. Congress authorized the navy in 1837 to recruit an indefinite number of apprentices between the ages of thirteen and eighteen, to serve until their majority, and to be paid at the rate of $7.00 a month. Navy Secretary Upshur, in his annual report of 4 December 1841, declared that the experiment was already a success and that a thousand boys had been enlisted. "An extension of the system is contemplated, so as to give to boys in the interior of the country an opportunity to join the service, without subjecting them to the expense of a journey to the rendezvous on the seaboard."

The smart new brig *Somers* was assigned as the first schoolship, with Perry's brother-in-law and collaborator Alexander Slidell Mackenzie as commander. This promising experiment, as it worked out, ended in tragedy and became the greatest disappointment in Perry's life.

So, this reform went down the drain, and, though crimping was abandoned, the receiving ship system of training recruits continued for more than a century because nobody had the imagination to think up anything better. As late as the beginning of World War II, so Rear Admiral Francis C. Denebrink informed me, the "debilitating influence of receiving ships" continued. Recruits "were just vegetating" in them. Finally, in 1943, "boot camps," training ships and stations and specialist schools were set up under a new Operational Training Command.

The Battle of Lake Erie Controversy

While Perry was stationed at Brooklyn, the Elliott-Perry controversy over the Battle of Lake Erie again raised its ugly head. It had never completely disappeared. Copies of the charges against Elliott which Oliver H. Perry preferred before sailing on his last cruise, and which President Monroe quashed, had been left with Captain Stephen Decatur. That gallant officer was killed in a duel by Captain James Barron in 1820, Elliott being Barron's second. Someone then leaked the documents to the press without Matthew C. Perry's knowledge. Since the documents were somewhat garbled in printing, the devoted younger brother, self-appointed guardian of Oliver's reputation, decided to publish them with additions in a pamphlet. *Documents in Relation to the Differences . . . between O. H. Perry and J. D. Elliott*, was printed at Washington in 1821 and at Boston in 1834. Next, appeared anonymously a substantial volume of 480 pages, *A Biographical Notice of Com. Jesse D. Elliott*, in which the battle was fought again. It included a number of affidavits by members of *Niagara*'s crew, some to the effect that Perry never came on board until the battle was almost over and Elliott had the British licked. This book received little attention, and the Perrys took no notice of it; but two almost simultaneous publications in 1839 stirred things up violently. One was a booklet by Tristram Burges, formerly chief justice of Rhode Island and a member of Congress, giving a fresh account of the battle, with Perry's charges of 1818 in an appendix. The other was J. Fenimore Cooper's *History of the Navy of the United States*. This work, by a leading American author of undisputed competence to write naval history, had been eagerly awaited by the public. Since Cooper had joined the Naval Lyceum at Brooklyn when organized, and contributed to the *Naval Magazine*, and Perry headed a group of officers who, expressing their "fraternal regard" for the author of *The Pilot*, proposed to give him a banquet; and since Perry at a later date, at Cooper's request, invited him to dine to meet Senator Hayne of South Carolina, Perry regarded the novelist as a friend. Accordingly, when he heard that the *History* was being written, he wrote to its author the following letter: —

New York, March 13, 1839

My dear Sir

My friend Captain Stephens[1] has informed me some time since, that you had approached in the progress of the work on which you are now engaged, that part of the Naval History of the U.S. that will embrace an account of the Battle of Lake Erie, that you were desirous of obtaining every information in reference to that memorable event; and suggested the propriety of my writing to you, and of transmitting such papers as I possess, in illustration of the circumstances of that battle.

Captain S. was more anxious for this as he was impressed with a belief that you had received false information on the subject, and might possibly be influenced by such representation.

In the latter respect I think differently from my friend: believing as I do that his warm and kind hearted zeal for the memory of my brother had led him to suppose that the machinations and falsehoods of others had diverted your mind from the true merits of the battle.

It appears to me, that I know you well enough to satisfy myself that you never could be influenced by such reports, that you are too intimately acquainted with naval matters to be deceived as to the evolutions of vessels, their

---

[1] Captain Thomas Holdup Stevens of South Carolina, C.O. of *Trippe* in the battle. He was one of Perry's strong supporters in this controversy.

means of getting into action, or of keeping clear of the shot of an enemy; and can judge as well as others, of the influence of the same wind upon all alike, and can estimate the preponderating evidence undeniably standing against the *Niagara* until Commodore Perry assumed command of her, and to this fact all, excepting those belonging to that vessel, bear ample testimony; and that their opinions are corroborated by the British officers, who could have been influenced by no personal views. . . .

> I am, Dear Sir,
> Very Respectfully
> and Truly Yours,
>
> M. C. PERRY

According to Elliott, Perry later called on Cooper in Philadelphia, gave him a package of documents on the Battle of Lake Erie, and some time after was told by Cooper that those documents were "controverted"; that he sought the "truth" and would mention the name of Elliott with respect. This is probably a garbled version of the fact that Perry on 18 May 1839 sent Cooper a number of copies made from Commodore Rodgers's letter book of the War of 1812 for use with his History, but did not allude to the war on the Lakes. In any case, he was too late, as the work was already in the press. To seek the truth, of course, was wholly proper (and somewhat unusual) for a novelist turned historian. Cooper, in the first edition of his *History of the Navy of the United States*, which appeared in May, wrote on the whole a stirring and accurate account of the battle. But Cooper loved controversy, the more venomous the better; and in the *History* he threw a few barbs into the Perry clan. He not only omitted essential facts, such as Oliver Perry's repeated orders to his captains to engage their opposite numbers in the British line, but indulged in snide remarks about the Commodore, such as, "An officer seldom went into action worse, or got out of it better." And in a long, provocative footnote he compared Perry's boat trip at the height of the battle unfavorably with Elliott's from *Niagara* to the gunboats, because Elliott's was over twice as long; omitting to mention that Perry's journey was accomplished under heavy gunfire whilst Elliott's, out of the enemy's range, was not so annoyed.

William A. Duer, President of Columbia and uncle to Alexander Mackenzie, reviewed Cooper very severely in three successive numbers of the New York *Commercial Advertiser*. Mackenzie himself, already engaged in writing a biography of Oliver H. Perry, called Cooper to task in a long review-essay in the *North American Review*. He praised the greater part of Cooper's history, but took pains in some detail, although with good taste, to point out the author's *suppressio veri* and *suggestio falsi* in his account of the controversial battle.

The fat was now in the fire, and for years the stink rose. Cooper sued the owner of the *Commercial Advertiser* for libel; the case, subsequently referred to arbitrators, earned him $250 damages. He also recovered damages from another journal, but did not sue Mackenzie, obviously because there was nothing actionable in that review.

Cooper was the sort of historian who never retracts; for him, anything he had published was the truth, not subject to revision. And the next move in this unseemly controversy was a small volume by him entitled *The Battle of Lake Erie; or, Answers to Messrs. Burges, Duer and Mackenzie.* It was printed by a job printer in Cooperstown early in 1843, probably because no publisher would take it, the public being thoroughly sick of the dispute. This work added heat to the controversy, but no light. Cooper asserted that everyone who supported Perry was either a member of the Perry-Rodgers-Slidell "family clique" or "a parcel of western militia" or a native of Rhode Island. Once more he sneered at Perry's boat trip, but the invective is directed more against Mackenzie than Perry. Dark hints are dropped of suppressed evidence, and there is a deal of nonsense about Elliott's duty to "hold the line," as though the obsolete British fighting instructions of the eighteenth century were still doctrine in the United States Navy. The booklet concludes with typically Cooperian cracks at all three of his critics: — Burges regards the battle as "part of the maritime affairs of Rhode Island," Dr. Duer "fancies a little schoolboy Latin will wrap fallacies, misquotations and professional ignorance from the vulgar ken," and Mackenzie foolishly hopes that "all mankind are to view his hero, and his acts, with the same subservient senses and judgment as he submits to himself."

Although Cooper fancied that he had "finished" Mackenzie, he joyfully seized another opportunity to attack him, and incidentally to annihilate the entire Perry clan. On 14 December 1842, before the *Battle of Lake Erie* booklet was finished, U.S.S. *Somers* arrived in New York harbor with the startling news that Captain Mackenzie had hanged at the yardarm three men for attempted mutiny. And one of the victims was Midshipman Philip Spencer, son of the Secretary of War.

CHAPTER XII

The *Somers* Mutiny

1842–1843

The Fatal Cruise

DURING the summer of 1842 Commodore Perry concerned himself with finishing, equipping and manning a smart new man-o'-war brig, U.S.S. *Somers*. Designed by Samuel Humphreys and built under his and the Commodore's supervision at the Brooklyn Navy Yard, she was an exquisite example of marine architecture. One hundred and three feet long on deck and 25-foot beam, she was no bigger than many sailing yachts of today or fishing schooners of yesterday; but she carried a press of square sail. Four yards crossed each of her two tall, raking masts. In addition to her square sails, three or four jibs could be set on her monstrous long bowsprit; spencer and spanker were bent on foremast and mainmast, and there were ample light sails. She carried a complement of 120 officers and men, and ten guns peered out of square ports on her spar deck. Together with her sister ship *Bainbridge* and the three slightly larger brigs *Truxtun*, *Lawrence* and *Perry*, built almost simultaneously, she was designed along Baltimore clipper lines — wineglass-shaped cross-section and sharp ends — primarily for speed. These were the fastest ships in the United States or perhaps in any navy, but badly over-rigged; two of the four capsized in squalls, with heavy loss of life. With the sloops-of-war built about the same time, they were the last of our war vessels designed with no other view than wind power, and the brigs were the first to be named after naval heroes.

Commodore Perry had *Somers* assigned for an experimental schoolship cruise by naval apprentices. He took particular pains in selecting the officers. To command her, he chose his brother-in-law Master Commandant Alexander Slidell Mackenzie, whom we have frequently encountered since the building of U.S.S. *Chippewa*. At the age of thirty-nine Mackenzie, already an old hand in the navy, had managed to educate himself and establish a literary reputation. When pursuing pirates in the West Indies

Squadron, he suffered two attacks of yellow fever, obtained a furlough to recover his health, traveled in Europe, and wrote *A Year in Spain.* This book earned him the friendship of Longfellow and Washington Irving, for whose *Life of Columbus* he plotted the discoverer's courses. In 1830–1832 he was attached to *Brandywine,* Commander Biddle's flagship in the Mediterranean. After that he took a two-year furlough, traveled in Europe, published three more books, and in 1835 married Catherine Robinson. Returning to active duty in 1837, he visited Russia and Brazil as First Lieutenant of U.S.S. *Independence,* and in Brazil was made commanding officer of the new man-o'-war brig *Dolphin.* After a year or two in her, chasing slavers along "the Brazils," he took another long furlough to repair his health, bought an estate at Tarrytown, wrote a biography of John Paul Jones, and the *Life of Oliver Hazard Perry* that stirred up J. Fenimore Cooper. Returning again to active duty in 1841, he was assigned to the new war steamer *Missouri* and from her transferred to the command of brig *Somers.* As Commodore Perry's shipmate since 1816, close collaborator at the Brooklyn Navy Yard, and sharer in his ideas for naval improvement, he was the natural choice.

Despite the navy's congenital suspicion of officers who write books, Mackenzie had won golden opinions from the captains and commodores under whom he served, and his attractive personality made friends for him elsewhere. "Mackenzie is one of the . . . kindest, plainest men I know," wrote Francis Lieber, the publicist; "very quiet, yet so kind and mild, so true and unaffected, that one cannot help liking, nay, cherishing him." Professor Felton, a Greek scholar who later became president of Harvard College, remarked on Mackenzie's "calmness, gentleness and refinement." Such was the man whose resolute action to preserve the lives of his men and the honor of his flag has been presented by the malignant and the sentimental as that of a savage martinet, a sadist, or a coward who preferred hanging innocent men to taking risks.

Four other members of the Perry-Rodgers clan were on board *Somers.* Lieutenant Matthew C. Perry Jr., twenty-one years old but already eight years in the navy, served as Acting Master, officer next junior to First Lieutenant. Calbraith, as the family called him, was a rather stolid young man, brave and loyal like all the Perrys, but relatively undistinguished during a long naval career. Oliver H. Perry II, the Commodore's seventeen-year-old son, was on the roll as captain's clerk. His father had failed to get him a midshipman's billet, since the navy then had a superfluity of reefers, but once the cruise started, Mackenzie created him acting midshipman. Young Oliver, too, showed that he had the guts to help quell a mutiny, but the experience left him somewhat shaken. Henry Rodgers, younger son of the old Commodore, was another *Somers* midshipman, and Adrien Deslonde of Louisiana, a brother of Mrs. John Slidell, who had

Commander Mackenzie at the Inquiry

U.S.S. *Somers*

lived in the Perry household as a young lad and been recommended for a midshipman's warrant by his uncle Calbraith, was also on board. All four proved towers of strength to Mackenzie in time of trouble, as did the First Lieutenant, Guert Gansevoort. That member of an old Knickerbocker family, thirty years old, had already served nineteen years in the navy.

Perry and Mackenzie hoped that the prospect of a foreign cruise in a smart new brig would persuade respectable parents in country towns to send their best; but the reputation of naval ratings was such that the commander could not procure many boys of that class. Even so, he selected 74 out of the 166 apprentices on the receiving ship and got rid of some of the worst after the shakedown cruise. Whether the Navy Department or Mackenzie selected the able seamen and petty officers to season *Somers's* crew and teach raw boys the ropes, is uncertain; but someone made two very bad choices. Samuel Cromwell, a great brute of a man about thirty-five years old, bearded and whiskered, became boatswain's mate and senior petty officer; Elisha Small, of about thirty, a shifty little fellow but an excellent sailor, was captain of the main top. Both had served in slavers before entering the navy; and Cromwell, if not at one time a pirate, had acquired an intimate knowledge of piratical procedure. But the worst assignment, the fatal one, came from the Navy Department and Commodore Matthew C. Perry. That was the appointment of Midshipman Philip Spencer, aged nineteen.

This youth belonged to one of the first families of New York. His grandfather Ambrose Spencer had been chief justice of the State Supreme court. His father John Canfield Spencer, one of the ablest lawyers of the Albany bar, was Secretary of War in President Tyler's cabinet. Philip was young in years but old in vice. At Hobart College, whence he had been dropped or expelled, he was chiefly remembered for his favorite reading, *The Pirate's Own Book*, and for having boasted that he would become a pirate. He spent a few months at Union College and dropped out there. Now obtaining an acting midshipman's warrant through his father's influence, he was first assigned to U.S.S. *North Carolina*, receiving ship for the Brooklyn Navy Yard. Passed Midshipman William Craney, to whose cabin and care he was assigned, could do nothing with Spencer and was twice struck by him — a serious offense which, when reported to the Navy Department and Commodore Perry, was ignored. The Commodore then assigned Spencer to U.S.S. *John Adams*, bound for Brazil. At Rio where she spent a month, Spencer (as one of his shipmates recalled) passed most of his shore liberty in "the reeky bagnios" of the Rua Sabôa, and on one occasion became so obstreperously drunk as to be reported to Commodore Charles Morris of the Brazil Squadron. That Commodore, like Perry, evidently fearing that proper punishment of the lad would get him in wrong with the administration, had Spencer transferred to frigate

Potomac for return to the United States, "there to receive the decision of
the Secretary of the Navy." On board both her and *John Adams* (so he
later confessed to Lieutenant Gansevoort) he had plotted mutiny. Secretary Upshur, after perusing "with pain" the correspondence transmitted
by Commodore Morris, and too easily believing in Spencer's penitence,
ordered him in August 1842 to report to Commodore Perry for duty in
U.S.S. *Somers*, then fitting out at Brooklyn.

Commander Mackenzie, who knew Spencer's record, refused to accept
him but offered to transfer him to another ship. Spencer then went over
Mackenzie's head to Commodore Perry, who made the fatal mistake of
having him reinstated as a midshipman in *Somers* — his second intervention in the young rascal's favor. One can only guess at the Commodore's
reasons. Among other arguments for the apprentice system, he claimed
that it would cure juvenile delinquency; here was a chance to prove it.
And, one may surmise, Perry wished to please the Tyler administration,
since he and his kin had been conspicuous in the Jackson camp. However
you look at Spencer, he was a prototype of what nowadays is called a
"young punk," and Commodore Perry's giving him another chance was a
singular instance of very bad judgment.

One striking thing about this cruise of the *Somers* was the youthfulness
of her crew — 70 per cent of them under the age of nineteen. Commander
Mackenzie at thirty-nine was the oldest man on board, and only three
others — Quartermaster Charles Rogers, boatswain's mate Cromwell and
carpenter's mate Thomas Dickerson — were over thirty. She had five senior officers, including the commander, the purser and the surgeon, and
seven midshipmen. Three of the middies were twenty years old and up,
the other four between sixteen and nineteen years of age. She had eight
petty officers, nineteen enlisted seamen (only five of whom were aged
twenty or up), and eight cooks and stewards, mostly American Negroes.
All 74 apprentice boys were minors, 22 of them under sixteen years of
age. Most of them had never been to sea before. With a total of 121 on
board, *Somers* was badly overcrowded; her sister ship *Bainbridge* carried
only 100 officers and men including 16 marines; and when sunk in the
Mexican War, *Somers* had a total complement of 76.

In June-July 1842, prior to Spencer's assignment, *Somers* made a shakedown cruise under Commander Mackenzie to Puerto Rico and back, in
which everything went well. She now made a gala departure from New
York on 13 September 1842, officers' and apprentices' relatives flocking to
see her off as if she had been a flash packet ship on a pleasure cruise. In
order to give her a mission, she carried dispatches for U.S.S. *Vandalia*,
then cruising on the West African coast looking for slavers. Prosperous
winds attended *Somers* on the outward passage. As far as Madeira, where
she arrived 5 October, she was a happy ship. Since naval mutinies fresh in

the public mind, such as the one on H.M.S. *Bounty* and those at the Nore and Spithead, had been caused by "cruel hard treatment of every degree" as the old chanty puts it, there was an effort at the subsequent inquiry and court-martial to prove that Commander Mackenzie had been another Captain Bligh. Every one of the enlisted men and boys interrogated testified that they had enjoyed good usage; that Mackenzie showed unusual interest in their welfare, sending delicacies to seasick boys from his own table, buying fresh fruit and vegetables for them in the islands, giving plenty of liberty, and never losing his temper. Only a few of the boys had to be punished, and they with the comparatively mild colt rather than the cat. Boatswain's Mate Cromwell, however, cuffed the boys so frequently that Mackenzie had to reprove him more than once and even threaten that if he continued he would lose his rating, to which Cromwell made an insolent reply. The only odd feature of the outward passage was the conduct of Midshipman Spencer, who neglected his duties, shunned his messmates, but chatted endlessly with the boys and enlisted men on deck, gave them cigars and tobacco, and even put up a steward to filch brandy from the wardroom to distribute among his cronies. There was no grog ration in the *Somers*, and the boys were not supposed to use tobacco; but Spencer got around that with his gifts.

After calling at Tenerife (8 October) and Porto Praia (21 October), she sailed to Monrovia in search of *Vandalia*, arriving 10 November. The frigate having already sailed for home, Mackenzie decided, as his orders allowed, to follow. He departed next day, shaping a course for St. Thomas, where he hoped to encounter *Vandalia*, intending to reach New York before Christmas.

On this return passage, and especially after departing from Africa, the atmosphere of the ship changed. Orders were obeyed grumblingly, or after repetition, rather than cheerfully and with alacrity. "The elder portion of the crew," testified Matthew C. Perry Jr., "were surly and morose in their manner." And this manner "daily grew worse until the execution." Spencer was observed holding extended conversations with Cromwell and redoubling his efforts to curry favor with the crew; whilst the big boatswain's mate laid off cuffing the apprentices, became playful and palsy with the older boys, and threw coins on the deck to be scrambled for by the young ones. There was nothing you could put a finger on, as Mackenzie later admitted, hardly anything you could express in words; but the sum total of attitudes told any man who knew sailors that something sinister was cooking.

On 25 November things began to happen. Spencer took James W. Wales, the purser's steward, to the booms. That was the place amidships where the brig's boats were lashed down and the spare yards and studdingsail booms were stored. Here, partly in the presence of Small, the renegade midshipman unfolded a plan startling for ingenuity as well as its utter criminality. He would kill the officers, capture the *Somers*, and turn her into a pirate ship. The key members of this conspiracy were Spencer himself, Cromwell, Small, and Wales if willing. Spencer had a list of the "certain," and "doubtful," and those "to be kept *nolens volens*," concealed in his neckerchief. The rest, unwilling sailors and useless boys, the majority of the crew, were to be "disposed of." The mutiny would be sparked off before reaching St. Thomas, during the mid-watch when the captain was below, Spencer on duty, Midshipman Rodgers officer of the deck, McKinley (one of the "certain" conspirators) at the arms chest, and McKee (one of the "doubtful") at the wheel. Cromwell and Small would start a mock fight with some of their pals on the forecastle head. Rodgers, on Spencer's appeal, would come forward to stop the fight and, when he reached the gangway, be overpowered and pitched overboard. McKinley would distribute firearms (Spencer having given him the key to the chest), Spencer would dive into Mackenzie's cabin and murder the sleeping captain "with the least noise possible," and then, with Cromwell and Small assisting, penetrate wardroom and steerage and cut the throats of Lieutenant Gansevoort, Master Perry, Purser Heiskell, and a few midshipmen for good measure. Spencer would then call all hands on deck, select "such as would suit his purposes," and cause the rest to be tossed overboard. The brig, now in possession of mutineers, would proceed to Cape St. Antonio or the Isle of Pines off Cuba, where Cromwell had friends among the pirate fraternity. With professional cutthroats added to her complement, she would scour the North Atlantic trade routes as a pirate ship, plundering and sinking defenseless merchantmen and murdering all hands, except that any "females" on board would be taken to the brig "for the use of the officers and men, using them as long as they saw fit; after that, to make way with them." The pirates, after gorging themselves with lust and plunder, would put in at a Cuban port, sell the brig, and live in luxury.

Fantastic as this scheme may now appear, it was practicable. *Somers* could outsail anything afloat except her sister ships, overhaul any merchantman, and overpower any vessel smaller than a frigate. And she would have been far more difficult to catch than C.S.S. *Alabama* in the Civil War or the German raiders of the two world wars.

Spencer picked on Wales to join the gang because he had had an altercation with Commander Mackenzie on the shakedown cruise and, Spencer assumed, cherished resentment. Wales, however, was a loyal man and decided at first opportunity to get word of the plot to his captain. That was easier said than done.

At this point we must glance at the deck and cabin arrangements of *Somers*, to appreciate what Mackenzie was up against. A flush-decker, her

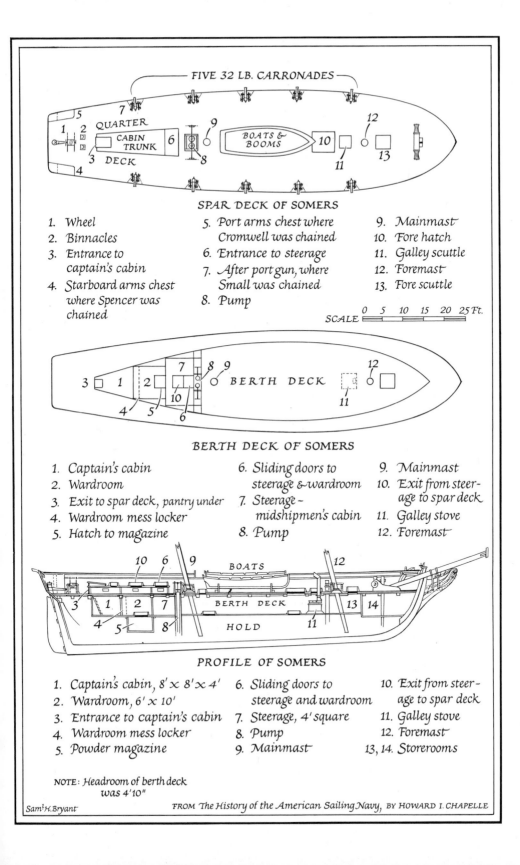

FIVE 32 LB. CARRONADES

SPAR DECK OF SOMERS

1. Wheel
2. Binnacles
3. Entrance to captain's cabin
4. Starboard arms chest where Spencer was chained
5. Port arms chest where Cromwell was chained
6. Entrance to steerage
7. After port gun, where Small was chained
8. Pump
9. Mainmast
10. Fore hatch
11. Galley scuttle
12. Foremast
13. Fore scuttle

SCALE 0 5 10 15 20 25 Ft.

BERTH DECK OF SOMERS

1. Captain's cabin
2. Wardroom
3. Exit to spar deck, pantry under
4. Wardroom mess locker
5. Hatch to magazine
6. Sliding doors to steerage & wardroom
7. Steerage – midshipmen's cabin
8. Pump
9. Mainmast
10. Exit from steerage to spar deck
11. Galley stove
12. Foremast

PROFILE OF SOMERS

1. Captain's cabin, 8' x 8' x 4'
2. Wardroom, 6' x 10'
3. Entrance to captain's cabin
4. Wardroom mess locker
5. Powder magazine
6. Sliding doors to steerage and wardroom
7. Steerage, 4' square
8. Pump
9. Mainmast
10. Exit from steerage to spar deck
11. Galley stove
12. Foremast
13, 14. Storerooms

NOTE: Headroom of berth deck was 4'10"

Sam¹ H. Bryant

FROM The History of the American Sailing Navy, BY HOWARD I. CHAPELLE

quarterdeck was merely that part of the gun or spar deck abaft the main-mast, not raised above it as on sloops, frigates and 74's, so not easily defensible against mutineers. Along the midships fore-and-aft section of the quarterdeck rose a rectangular house, like the cabin trunk of a modern yacht, affording light and air to the captain's cabin, the wardroom, and the steerage. At the after end of the cabin trunk, and only two feet four inches forward of the binnacles, a booby hatch led down to the captain's cabin; and at the forward end of the trunk a companionway and ladder led to the steerage where the midshipmen slung their hammocks and ate their meals. Sole access to the tiny wardroom (eight by ten feet) where four officers slept, ate, and worked out their navigational problems, was by a door from the steerage, a compartment only eight feet long and four-teen wide. Forward of the steerage, separated from it by a flimsy bulkhead and sliding door, lay the berth deck where the seamen, petty officers and apprentices lived. Its headroom measured only four feet ten inches. Normal access to berth deck from spar deck was through a hatch just abaft the galley, which snuggled close to the foremast. The brig could not have been better planned for a surprise attack. Even if the afterguard managed to rally, they would find it almost impossible to defend quarter-deck and three cabins from determined mutineers.

It took some time for Wales to get his startling news into the right ears, for in a crowded vessel like the *Somers* privacy was a rare commodity. Not until next day, Saturday 26 November, was he able to confide the portentous secret to Purser Heiskell, who carried it to Lieutenant Ganse-voort, who told the Captain. Mackenzie at first refused to believe the story; he did not want to believe it. But Lieutenant Gansevoort did, and made it his business to find evidence. He was told about Spencer's lengthy conferences with Cromwell and Small, and that he had been seen examin-ing a chart of the Isle of Pines. At evening quarters, acting on Gansevoort's advice, Commander Mackenzie summoned Spencer to the quarterdeck, ordered Master Perry to take the wheel, and confronted the midshipman with Wales's story. Spencer admitted that the steward had reported him correctly, but insisted it was all a joke. "This, sir, is joking on a forbidden subject," said Mackenzie. "This joke may cost you your life. . . . You must have been aware that you could only have compassed your design by passing over my dead body, and, after that, the bodies of all the officers; it will be necessary for me to confine you, sir."

At the Captain's command, Gansevoort arrested Spencer, took away his sword, seated him on the starboard arms chest close to the wheel, chained him to the bulwarks and handcuffed him as an additional precaution. Each successive officer of the deck was ordered to put Spencer to death imme-diately if he tried to communicate with the crew, but in the meantime to see that he was properly fed and that his other necessities were taken care of. Gansevoort covered him with his own cloak during rainsqualls.

Shortly after this arrest Midshipman Rodgers, searching Spencer's sea chest in the steerage, found in his razor case the paper of which he had spoken to Wales, listing five "certain," ten "doubtful" and eighteen "to be kept *nolens volens*," and assigning posts at wheel, arms chest, cabin, wardroom and steerage during the mutiny. Spencer, thinking to conceal his sinister design, had used the transparent schoolboy device of writing names and directions in Greek letters. The forms of many letters were wrong, but it was not difficult for Rodgers, who knew some Greek, to translate them. He brought the result to the Captain. There were only thirty-three names on the list, leaving more than eighty to be murdered or thrown to the sharks. Spencer did not even contemplate the humanity of the *Bounty* mutineers, who allowed officers and loyal men to depart in a well-provisioned boat.

Armed with this evidence of who was or might be in the plot, and pondering his next move, Mackenzie decided, largely on the basis of an incident that happened next afternoon (Sunday the 27th), to arrest Cromwell and Small. The tradewind had moderated, *Somers* was making only 7.5 knots (she was capable of 12). The Captain, eager to make best speed, ordered main skysail and royal studdingsails to be set, and sent a boy to the main royal yard to help. Cromwell, Wilson, and others high on Spencer's Greek list went to the main top, which was not their proper station but, owing to the rake of the mainmast, lay directly over the quarterdeck. Midshipman Hays, officer of the deck, ordered the weather royal yard brace to be let go. Small, who was at that station, instead of obeying the order, hauled in the brace "very violently" with the aid of a boy, and belayed it "very hard." [1] Consequently the topgallant mast and royal yard with the sails bent onto them came tumbling down on deck, and the boy on the yard narrowly escaped going overboard by grabbing the lee royal shrouds. It looked as if this was a plan by Cromwell and his cronies to rescue Spencer by taking advantage of the confusion, especially if a boat had to be lowered to pick up the boy. Fortunately Lieutenant Gansevoort rushed on deck and efficiently took charge of clearing up the mess of spars, sails and lines. After dark the same day, when the topgallant mast was about to be swayed up into place, and Rodgers ordered four or five men to help on the quarterdeck, some twenty men and boys rushed aft, stamp-

---

[1] Much of the discussion turns on whether this was accidental or not. Every yachtsman knows that if you tauten a vang and let out the mainsheet you risk breaking the gaff, and that shrouds too taut may break a wooden mast. It is inconceivable that an old seaman like Small could have hauled in and belayed the weather brace accidentally, especially when ordered to do the contrary, and when the ship was rolling to leeward.

ing their feet in a way unusual and unallowable on a man-of-war. Gansevoort jumped onto the cabin trunk and, pointing his pistol at the tallest man, threatened to shoot anyone who put his foot on the quarterdeck. This, again, looked very much like a rescue attempt.

Mackenzie now decided to arrest Cromwell and Small. The boatswain's mate was seated on the port arms chest of the quarterdeck, facing Spencer and ironed to the rail; Small forward of him next the after gun.

Somers was rolling along, sailing large with the tradewind on her starboard quarter; but the wind appeared to be diminishing, an additional anxiety to Mackenzie. Unless he encountered *Vandalia* at St. Thomas and turned the prisoners over to her, he would have to go on to New York and have them tried there. But could he safely make even St. Thomas, at least a week's sail distant? Discipline was disintegrating. *Somers* had no brig where prisoners could be confined, and no marines to guard them. After the event, shore-side critics of Mackenzie asked why he could not have confined them to the hold or chained them to pad-eyes in his own cabin — a trapezoidal-shaped cubbyhole eight feet long, eight feet broad forward and two feet broad aft. And the bulkheads between captain's cabin and wardroom, as between wardroom and steerage, were so flimsy that a strong push could have breached them. The hold was full of ballast, water casks and stores to within a few inches of the berth deck; anyone confined there would have suffocated. What was Mackenzie to do, with this sinister plot simmering, and no possible help from anyone outside the ship? What might not happen in a sudden squall at night? Mackenzie knew perfectly well a stern fact which Admiral Nimitz recalled to the Pacific Fleet a century later: — "The time for taking all measures for a ship's safety is while still able to do so. Nothing is more dangerous than for a seaman to be grudging in taking precautions lest they turn out to have been unnecessary. Safety at sea for a thousand years has depended on exactly the opposite philosophy."

Let us pause a moment to consider the dramatic contrast between the brightly illuminated setting, with the dark designs of the plotters and dismal apprehensions of the intended victims. Sailing west to "the Indies" in the winter northeast trades is perhaps the most beautiful sailing in any ocean; and *Somers*, rolling and dipping in the long swells, had the wind just where she wanted it, on the quarter, to make best time over a sapphire ocean flecked with whitecaps. Flying fish flashed silver past the foam at her bow. Puffy tradewind clouds raced her overhead, and occasionally one lashed her with rain. No throb of engines assaulted the ear; there were no sounds but the striking of the ship's bell, the creaking of spars and timbers, lines slatting against the sails, and the rush and gurgle of great waters. Every few hours the square sails changed color: golden gossamer when the last-quarter moon rose, polished silver just before dawn, ruddy at sunrise, and cream-white at high noon. But the fatigued, harassed and anxious officers, and the conspirators guessing whether or not they were found out, had neither taste nor time for aesthetic appreciation. Sailors collected in knots to exchange gossip. Officers, divided "watch and watch" (eight hours on and eight off), armed themselves with two pistols and a cutlass each, and even in their watch below kept continually moving about the vessel, to break up any attempt at rescue. Thus Monday passed, and Tuesday, with increasing tension and fatigue on the part of the loyal officers and increasing insubordination on the part of the crew. Orders were obeyed sullenly after repetition; the men "would go growling along as though they did not care," said Wales. Knives and other lethal weapons were discovered in handy spots. Four suspects failed to appear at muster, and it was always they who brought food to the prisoners, hoping perhaps to communicate with them. On the night of the 29th there was another ominous rush aft when the spanker boom preventer tackle carried away, and young Calbraith Perry had some difficulty chasing unwanted hands off the quarterdeck.

On Wednesday morning, 30 November, Mackenzie arrested four suspects whose names were high on Spencer's Greek list: sailmaker's mate Wilson, landsman Daniel McKinley, and apprentices McKee and Green. Seven prisoners were now chained to the bulwarks of the quarterdeck, their presence interfering with the proper handling of the ship.

The Commander's next action was to order the four wardroom officers (Lieutenant Gansevoort, Purser Heiskell, Surgeon Leacock and Master Perry) and the three senior midshipmen (Rodgers, Thompson and Hays) to deliberate, take evidence, and give him their collective advice. They met in the little wardroom the rest of that day and most of the night, thirteen to fourteen hours in all, discussing the affair and questioning several older members of the crew. All oral evidence strengthened the case against Spencer, Cromwell and Small. The witnesses agreed that Cromwell was the most dangerous man on board, the brains of the conspiracy. Spencer's piratical ambitions might have remained the mere fantasies of a depraved youngster's mind, had not Cromwell showed him how to make the dream come true. But Cromwell, who was very "cagey" — using an alias on Spencer's Greek list — would hardly have conspired without Spencer, the son of a cabinet member whose influence could be counted on to get them off if anything slipped.

At nine in the morning of Thursday, 1 December, five days since Wales had communicated the mutiny plot to Mackenzie, the seven officers reported in writing that they had "come to a cool, decided, and unanimous opinion" that Spencer, Cromwell and Small were "guilty of a full and determined intention to commit a mutiny," and that the uncertainty as to who was in their gang, and "the impossibility of guarding against the contingencies which 'a day or an hour may bring forth,' " had convinced them "that it would be impossible to carry them to the United States; and that the safety of the public property, the lives of ourselves and of those committed to our charge, require that . . . they should be put to death, in a manner best calculated . . . to make a beneficial impression upon the disaffected."

Mackenzie had already reached the same conclusion — that the three ringleaders be put to death. His authority he found in an Act of Congress passed in 1800: "If any person in the navy shall make or attempt to make any mutinous assembly, he shall on conviction thereof by a Court Martial, suffer death." The council of officers was not a court-martial, and Mackenzie had no authority to call one; but it was the best substitute at hand. He felt that since Spencer, Cromwell and Small were the only three men, other than the loyal officers, capable of navigating a ship, their removal would discourage any attempt to carry out Spencer's diabolical plan. But could not Mackenzie have waited until his ship reached Danish St. Thomas, which she did on 5 December, or squared away for a nearer island? There the prisoners could have been incarcerated ashore, to await safe transportation to New York for trial. Mackenzie, however, considered "that a naval commander can never be justified in invoking foreign aid in reducing an insubordinate crew to obedience." He had hoped to encounter U.S.S. *Vandalia* in St. Thomas and turn over the prisoners to her; but, owing to "the daily and hourly increasing insubordination of the crew," he dared no longer delay the execution of the ringleaders.

Once the decision was made, Mackenzie proceeded to the execution. All three men were informed that they were about to die, and had better make their peace with God. Spencer, who hitherto had been sneeringly confident, counting no doubt on a big public trial in New York and his father engaging the best legal talent to get him off, now fell on his knees, blubbering, and confessed his guilt. But he exonerated Cromwell. The boatswain's mate also knelt and begged for mercy, but protested his innocence. Small kept a stiff upper lip but freely confessed his guilt.

Three whips, as the tackles used for hoisting in stores were called, were now rigged to the main yardarm, two on the starboard arm for Cromwell and Small, one on the port arm for Spencer. The condemned men were given time to read the Bible and pray. Spencer said, "There are few crimes that I have not committed; I feel sincerely penitent." All three asked the loyal officers and men to forgive them; Cromwell begging Lieutenant Gansevoort to forgive him was the nearest he came to confession, and he tried to shake off his guard and jump overboard. Little Elisha Small died a manly death. He admitted that the Captain was doing his duty, told him, "I honor you for it; God bless that flag!" He made a dying speech to the ship's company, warning them against mutinous intendments and against slaving. " 'Twas going in a Guineaman that brought me to this." He concluded, "Now, fellow topmen, give me a quick death." The nooses were put in place, one around Spencer's neck as he stood on the quarter-deck under the port yardarm, one around each of the others as they stood on the bulwarks under the starboard yardarm. Spencer's face was covered with a black handkerchief, those of Cromwell and Small by sailors' blouses. Two men were detailed to haul on each whip, and officers were stationed beside them, with cutlasses drawn and orders to cut down any-one who faltered. Spencer was offered the privilege of giving the word for the execution signal gun to be fired, but his nerve failed him and he asked the Captain to do so. Mackenzie called, "Stand by, Fire!" A boy applied a live coal from the galley to a touch-hole, the cannon roared, the men at the whips hauled away, and within a minute three dead men were dangling from the main yard.

Mackenzie now called the crew aft and delivered a sermon on truth, honor and fidelity. He concluded by calling for three cheers for the flag. "They gave three hearty ones," and this seemed to relieve the minds of all from the prevailing gloom. The crew were now piped to dinner. Macken-zie was shocked that some of the boys, as they went below, pointed at the dead bodies and laughed. But was that not natural? They were now safe from mutineers who had planned to throw them to the sharks.

Dinner is eaten. The bodies are lowered and prepared for proper burial at sea. Mackenzie, a stickler for doing everything properly, orders Spen-cer, as an officer, to be buried in uniform in a coffin, and "Chips" claps together two sea chests to make one, weighted and bored with holes for a quick sinking. The enlisted men are sewed up by messmates in their own hammocks, the last stitch being taken, according to ancient sea custom, through the nose, and a cannonball placed at each man's head and feet for quick sinking. During these preparations a black squall passes over *Somers*, as if a last salute by the powers of darkness. There is a delay while the three bodies, laid out in order of rank, are decently covered with tarpau-lins.

By the time the squall is over, the short tropical twilight has faded, the new moon has set, and battle lanterns are broken out to light a solemn scene on the spar deck. Prayer books are handed around. While *Somers* sails slowly through the velvety tropical night under the star-studded fir-mament of heaven, with no other music than the swish of parting waters, Captain Mackenzie reads from the Book of Common Prayer the office for burial of the dead at sea. Bearded men and smooth-faced boys, gathering on the booms and in the gangways, speak the responses reverently, and the four men in irons whisper what they can remember of the service.

We therefore commit their bodies to the deep, to be turned into cor-ruption, looking for the resurrection of the body (when the Sea shall give up her dead), and the life of the world to come, through our Lord Jesus Christ.

There are three loud splashes as the corpses drop into a three-thousand-fathom deep. Ensign and pendant, half-masted for the burial, are now two-blocked and *Somers* continues on her course — west and by north — from which she had never deviated during these five days of fear and tension.

There was no further trouble about discipline on board. The arrested men were kept below deck most of the passage to New York, and took their meals with the others. The crew obeyed orders cheerfully, apparently greatly relieved, although the presence of four enlisted men in irons reminded them that justice was not yet satisfied. After calling a few hours at St. Thomas on 5 December, the brig proceeded to New York. She had a quick passage, nine days later anchoring off Brooklyn Navy Yard. No visitors were allowed on board, and nobody was granted leave or liberty. Mackenzie dispatched Acting Midshipman O. H. Perry II to Washington with his report, then took his entire crew ashore and marched them to the nearest church to give thanks for the preservation of ship and company from capture and murder. The officers were so fagged out with their extra duties and lack of sleep that, when they crossed the lawn to the Commandant's quarters, they reeled and staggered like drunken men.

The Inquiry and Trial

For Commodore Perry, father of two officers in *Somers*, uncle by marriage to a third, and brother-in-law of the commander, this affair provided the most severe trial of his life. Rightly anticipating that Secretary Spencer would clamp down on Mackenzie, he wrote to his congressman in Washington, General Aaron Ward, trusting he would stand up for *Somers's* commander. Ward answered not too hopefully that Secretary Spencer was trying to get Mackenzie tried for murder by a civilian jury, and that he had won over Secretary Upshur to that view. Perry then sent Ward this stout letter: —

Navy Yard

Confidential   Brooklyn Dec. 27 1842
My Dear Genl.

I write a line to ask you in the name of our friend McKenzie who you know is like myself a constituent of yours that you will watch after his interest at Washington.

I fear that there is some influence at work which may do him harm unless it is checked. You know the character of McKenzie well & you know that he would not hurt the hair of a man's head unless from stern necessity.

His conduct is born out by every one in this quarter. The Clergy, Judges,

Lawyers, Women & Children all praise him & his officers for having crushed in the bud a most diabolical scheme of rapine and murder.

He asks nothing but fair and open justice and he conceives that there should be no influence exerted by persons in power to prejudice the case. He has done what he would do again under like circumstances and what every honorable officer placed under the same responsibility ought to do but there are few who would have sufficient firmness to meet the contingency.

So far as my two sons have been concerned in this melancholy affair they have my unmeasured approbation and they would have been spurned by me if they had acted otherwise. *No man is fit for the Navy if he is not ready at all times to interpose his life in the preservation of the integrity of the American Flag and the Safety of the vessel entrusted to his and their Charge.* . . .

> With great Regard
> I am, D. Genl., Truly Yours
>
> M. C. Perry

First procedure after the arrival of *Somers* in New York waters, a naval court of inquiry, convened on 28 December 1842 aboard Perry's old ship *North Carolina*, moored off Brooklyn Navy Yard. The court consisted of three commodores on active duty, veterans of the War of 1812, with Charles Stewart as president. Ogden Hoffman Esq., federal attorney general for New York, also a naval veteran of the last war, served as judge advocate. Commodore Perry's son-in-law John Hone acted as Mackenzie's secretary, and there was a heavy attendance by officers of the army, navy and marine corps. Every officer of *Somers*, 22 enlisted men (including six Negro cooks and stewards), and 68 of the 74 apprentices were questioned. The court sat until 19 January 1843, and next day Commodore Stewart announced its findings: "The immediate execution of the prisoners was demanded by duty and justified by necessity." The conduct of Mackenzie and his officers "was prudent, calm and firm, and he and they honestly performed their duty to the service of their country."

That did not end the matter. Even before the court of inquiry adjourned, Secretary Upshur at Commander Mackenzie's earnest request took the unusual step of ordering him to be tried by court-martial. Mackenzie felt that only thus could he properly be cleared, and that otherwise he might have been indicted for murder in a civil court, for which Secretary Spencer and Cromwell's widow were working. Tried he was, on five counts — murder, oppression, illegal punishment, conduct unbecoming an officer, and cruelty.

The court-martial, consisting of eleven naval captains and two commanders, with Captain John Downes as president, met on board *North Carolina* 2 February and shortly after adjourned to the chapel in the navy yard. The judge advocate, William H. Norris Esq., was a relative of Spencer's. Principal counsel for the defendant was his friend Theodore Sedg-

wick Esq., third of that name, a famous lawyer and publicist. Sessions
were public, and freely commented on by the press. Most of the evidence
merely repeated what had come out in the inquiry, but cross-examination
brought out some new facts in Mackenzie's favor, which was not what the
judge advocate wanted. Cromwell had threatened, in the presence of several members of the crew, to pitch Mackenzie overboard when he was
sitting on the taffrail. Two apprentice boys had overheard Spencer and
Cromwell discussing a piratical cruise. Two others had heard Spencer ask
Cromwell if he could disguise the brig and Cromwell replied that he could
easily do so. Cromwell acted "beside himself" when Spencer was arrested.
Seaman Neville had seen Spencer and Cromwell discussing a paper "not
English writing," and Spencer invited him to sail on "his" ship. Cromwell
and Small had been overheard exchanging data on the notorious pirate
rendezvous the Isle of Pines, where, Cromwell said, soon they would be.

Lieutenant Gansevoort, stalwart witness for the defense, stood up under
vigorous cross-examination, reiterating his belief that the brig could never
have been brought into port but for the executions, and that "Spencer or
Small had made his plot known to at least twenty of the crew." Asked a
member of the court, "Did you see in Commander Mackenzie any traces
of unmanly fear, of a despotic temper, or any conduct unbecoming an
American officer?" "I did not," replied the First Lieutenant. "His course
was that of a brave man and good officer — such as to inspire us with high
respect for him as an officer and warm friendship for him as a man."

On 1 April 1843 the verdict was issued. The last two charges were
dropped. On every other charge the verdict was "not proved." On the
most important one, of murder, it was said in the newspapers that three of
the twelve members then sitting dissented. But the entire court voted, *nem.
con.*, to "acquit Commander Alexander Slidell Mackenzie of the charges
and specifications preferred by the secretary of the navy against him."
Secretary Upshur confirmed the verdict.

During the nearly four months of inquiry and trial, the *Somers* affair
was discussed all over the country. No case of the century, prior to the
assassination of President Lincoln, aroused as much interest and passion.
Naval opinion was not unanimous; Captain Robert F. Stockton even refused to serve on the court, alleging that he had already made up his mind,
and would have voted to hang Mackenzie. Several hundred merchants of
New York and Boston signed memorials to Mackenzie, praising his conduct; they knew very well what damage the *Somers* might have done
under the black flag. Charles Sumner, the rising young Boston lawyer,
published an account of the case in the *North American Review*, highly
praising Mackenzie: "We thank him, and the country thanks him, that he
did not hesitate." And Sumner made an excellent legal case for the Commander by pointing out that the planned mutiny placed *Somers* "for the

time being, in a state of war." Strong support for the Commander also came from a series of letters to the press by Richard Henry Dana, author of *Two Years Before the Mast*, who knew life at sea from the common sailor's point of view. Dana was answered by Captain William Sturgis of Boston, an old China hand. He argued that as shipmaster in the China trade, he had kept discipline among characters more desperate than those on board *Somers* without hanging any, and he believed that Cromwell was innocent. Mackenzie was both vigorously defended and viciously attacked in the press; some even attempted to make political capital out of the affair. It was probably fortunate that the brig reached port after the November elections.

A strong anonymous attack on Mackenzie, probably by a Whig journalist, was a 102-page pamphlet *Cruise of the Somers: Illustration of the Despotism of the Quarter Deck and of the Unmanly Conduct of Commander Mackenzie* (New York: 1844). Far more powerful, from the pen of the leading naval historian, was that of J. Fenimore Cooper, still nursing his wounds from the Battle of Lake Erie controversy. Cooper, like "the last of the Mohicans," never forgave an injury. Here was a perfect opportunity for revenge, and he made the most of it. In his 81-page *Review of the Proceedings of the Naval Court Martial* (New York: 1844), he used every argument good or bad to prove Mackenzie to be a jittery, incompetent martinet. He sneered that *Somers* was more of a "family yacht" than a man-of-war, and boasted how he himself could have handled the situation better. Cooper flattered himself that his tract would "finish" Mackenzie as a naval officer, which it certainly did not. It should have finished Cooper as a competent authority on naval affairs.

Every few years there appears an article or book on the *Somers* case exonerating Spencer and his accomplices. Arguments and innuendoes of the sort which have become familiar in discussions of Pearl Harbor and the assassination of President Kennedy, are freely used: — Why was not so-and-so examined? Everyone available testified, except some of the younger boys. Why was Wales's story of the plot accepted by Mackenzie without corroboration? There was plenty of corroboration, especially from Sergeant Garty, whom Spencer tried to suborn, boatswain's mate Browning, carpenter's mate Dickerson, and others. Why were the four men whom Mackenzie brought to New York in irons as accessories, not proceeded against? Because the judge advocate found insufficient evidence against them, and Mackenzie felt that there had been enough punishment. And, did not the skipper provoke a mutiny by cruel treatment? There is abundant evidence that Mackenzie had been a mild and indulgent commander, slow to take offense.

Although Commodore Perry was pleased that his brother-in-law, in whom he never lost faith, had been exonerated, he was deeply grieved by the effect of the *Somers* affair on the apprentice system. All boys who had served in the brig were discharged, and no more wanted to sign on. The plan was quietly dropped, and not revived until 1864 when a freshly re-cruited group made a successful start. Yet some good came out of the attempted mutiny. The principal culprit offered a perfect illustration of the effect of appointing midshipmen haphazardly, and by favor. Navy and public were now convinced that a school must be established for the edu-cation of naval officers. The final fillip which brought it about was Presi-dent Polk's appointment of historian George Bancroft as Secretary of the Navy in 1845. Commodore Perry was a member of the board of examiners of midshipmen who met that year at the Philadelphia Naval Asylum and were asked by the Secretary to prepare a plan for "a more efficient system of instruction for the young naval officers." They complied promptly, drafted a table of organization and plan of studies, and Secretary Bancroft cannily got a bill for it through Congress by persuading the army to give up obsolete Fort Severn, Annapolis, thus avoiding the expense of a new building. On 10 October 1845, the Academy opened with Perry's close friend Commander Franklin Buchanan as superintendent.

On 1 December, three years from the day that Philip Spencer's body swung from the *Somers's* yardarm, Secretary Bancroft made a notable pre-diction in his annual report. The Naval Academy, by affording midship-men preliminary instruction before their first cruise, by extending "an affectionate but firm supervision" over them and providing "suitable cul-ture" thereafter, and "by rejecting from the service all who fail in capac-ity or in good disposition to use their time well," would "renovate and improve" the navy.

No prophecy about the navy has been more amply fulfilled. The Naval Academy's course has kept pace with changing conditions of naval war-fare, and its discipline is such that nobody even remotely resembling Philip Spencer has since obtained a naval commission.

So much for the *Somers* mutiny. There will always remain the teasing thought that Mackenzie might have risked a rescue attempt for four more days, when he could have had his prisoners confined at St. Thomas and later tried in New York. Opposed to that concept is the hard fact that every man on board with maritime experience and proved loyalty be-lieved that execution was necessary. They felt that matters had reached a boiling point on 1 December 1842, and that Mackenzie was justified mor-ally, if not legally, in putting Spencer, Cromwell and Small to death.

On that conclusion, the present writer rests.

CHAPTER XIII

Commodore of the Africa Squadron
1843–1845

Back to the West Coast

A MONG the few family letters of this period which have survived is one of 23 April 1843 from the Commodore's eighteen-year-old son Oliver H. Perry II, veteran of the *Somers*, to Mrs. Robert S. Rodgers at Havre de Grace. "Dear Sister," he begins, "Father has left for Washington, having received orders to command the African Squadron a week ago; mother is wearily preparing for another move." He expects, he continued, Cousin William P. Rodgers to go with father as captain's clerk; and William did. Cousin Christopher Raymond Perry Rodgers, about to marry Julia Slidell (younger sister of Jane Perry) is also going as a midshipman in father's flagship U.S.S. *Saratoga*. Oliver himself feels that he has had enough of naval life and is planning to enter Uncle Tom Slidell's office at New Orleans and read law. But, as it turned out, he liked that even less.

The move that Jane contemplated — her ninth or tenth in twenty-eight years of married life — was to the country. The Perrys, when living in New York City, used to spend part of the summer in hired cottages at Sing Sing or Tarrytown, near Mackenzie's farm. They loved that part of the Hudson Valley, with broad reaches like the Tappan Zee bordered by hills. In 1839 the Commodore, after returning from his lighthouse tour to Europe, purchased a farm in the northern part of Tarrytown, bordering on the Hudson. There he built a stone house, which he appropriately named The Moorings, planted a garden, and employed the few leisure hours he could snatch from his duties, gardening and setting out trees. This somewhat ambitious purchase for a naval captain was financed partly from Jane's inheritance, partly from several thousand dollars lent by Perry's affluent friends and relatives. Washington Irving of Sunnyside, and Colonel James Watson Webb, editor of the New York *Courier and Enquirer*, were neighbors. Until the Hudson River Railroad penetrated these

rural solitudes of Westchester County in 1848, the usual means of transport from New York was a packet sloop owned and skippered by a genial
Tarrytowner. Perry and Irving were often fellow passengers on this trip,
which took from two to ten hours, depending on wind and tide. They
became warm friends and corresponded when Irving was United States
minister to Spain.

Before sailing on his next mission, Calbraith saw Jane settled at The
Moorings as a year-round residence. Daughters Caroline and Isabella, son
William until he joined the marine corps, and Anna (Perry) Rodgers, the
widow of George Washington Rodgers, lived under the same roof. Francis Lieber, who visited Tarrytown in 1843, described Jane as "an exceedingly goodlooking grandmother, I believe of not more than 40." Jane
would have been flattered — she was then 46.

Command of the U. S. Naval Forces, West Coast of Africa, commonly
known as the Africa Squadron, was far from being a blue-ribbon assignment. Opportunities for amusement, common to every other station, were
almost wholly wanting. Hard work, yellow fever, frustration and adverse
criticism were the usual rewards for African service. Commander Joel
Abbot wrote to a friend from U.S.S. *Decatur* in 1843, "There is no fun, I
can assure you, in being upon this African Station. Scorching sun &
drenching rains with numerous privations & disagreeable circumstances is
one's common lot, to say nothing of a good chance of dying." One suspects that the African mission was given to Perry because Whigs were in
the saddle at Washington, and the Perry-Slidell-Rodgers clan — Democrats all — were in the doghouse owing to the *Somers* affair. The Commodore wrote to John Slidell from on board U.S.S. *Macedonian* at sea, 23
March 1844, "I am no favorite with the present administration for reasons
with which you and many others are acquainted."

However that may be, Perry was glad to have an opportunity again to
visit Liberia, in whose founding he had been concerned, and to help suppress the slave trade, which he regarded as wholly abominable. If "Old
Bruin" found the Guinea coast somewhat less miasmic than the atmosphere of New York engendered by the *Somers* case, he needed all his bear-
like qualities, together with diplomatic finesse, to cope with West African
conditions and personalities.

As flagship Perry was given sloop-of-war *Saratoga*, recently built at the
Portsmouth, New Hampshire, Navy Yard. She was 150 feet long,
mounted 22 guns, and measured 882 tons. The other vessels of the squadron were *Decatur*, a smaller sloop of 16 guns; *Macedonian*, the prize
ship of 1812 which had been razeed to a 36-gun sloop; and brig *Porpoise*,
the same handy little vessel that had towed the Capudan Pasha's barge
from Tenedos to Troas. These three were to rendezvous with Perry at the
Cape Verde Islands. He went on board *Saratoga* at her anchorage inside

Sandy Hook on 5 June 1843, broke his commodore's broad pendant, and received an 11-gun salute.

With a prosperous wind behind her, *Saratoga* rolled along the Gulf Stream, logging more than five hundred miles in two days. The gale finally blew itself out, and Purser Bridge gives us a good description of fun during the dog watch in summer seas: —

All day, the wind has been ahead, and very light. This evening, a dead calm is upon the sea; but the sky is cloudless, and the air pure and soft. All the well are enjoying the fine weather. The commodore and captain walk the poop-deck; the other officers, except the lieutenant and young gentlemen of the watch, are smoking on the forecastle, or promenading the quarter-deck. A dozen steady old salts are rolling along the gangways; and the men are clustered in knots between the guns, talking, laughing, or listening to the yarns of their comrades — an amusement to which sailors are as much addicted as the Sultan in the Arabian Nights. But music is the order of the evening. Although a band is not allowed to a ship of our class, there are always good musicians to be found among the reckless and jolly fellows composing a man-of-war's crew. A big landsman from Utica, and a dare-devil topman from Cape Cod, are the leading vocalists; Symmes, the ship's cook, plays an excellent violin; and the commodore's steward is not to be surpassed upon the tambourine. A little black fellow, whose sobriquet is Othello, manages the castanets, and there is a tolerable flute played by one of the afterguard. The concerts usually commence with sentimental songs, such as "Home, Sweet Home," and the Canadian Boat Song; but the comic always carries off the palm; "Jim along Josey," "Lucy Long," "Old Dan Tucker," and a hundred others of the same character, are listened to delightedly by the crowd of men and boys collected round the forehatch, and always ready to join in the choruses. Thus a sound of mirth floats far and wide over the twilight sea, and would seem to indicate that all goes well among us.

Twenty days out, *Saratoga* raised the Peak of Tenerife, a hundred miles distant. Next day she anchored in the harbor of Santa Cruz, where an eight-day quarantine was imposed by the Spanish authorities. Perry protested without success, but the delay afforded him opportunity to give the ship a thorough cleansing. By 4 July, fortunately, pratique was granted and the entire crew were given shore leave in relays, which, wrote Perry, "will contribute much to their health and spirits." He wrote to Washington Irving at Madrid, asking him to protest against the quarantine, and to report the local authorities' want of courtesy in not returning his official visit. Irving replied eight months later that he had not been able to do anything about either. *Cosas de España.*

From Tenerife, *Saratoga* sailed to the Cape Verde Islands. After calling at Porto Grande on São Vicente to fill water casks, she proceeded to Porto Praia on Santiago, his old port of call in *Cyane* and *Shark*. There Perry received a letter from the commander of the British Africa Squadron, proposing to coöperate and exchange signals. The United States Africa Squadron later received unjust criticism for spending time in the Cape Verdes. Actually it was ordered to do so, and could hardly have done otherwise. The coast of Liberia afforded no safe anchorage; even at the best off Monrovia, officers' staterooms might be inundated by an unusually heavy swell rolling a vessel scuppers-under, and the breakers on the bar rose so high that communication with the shore became impossible. Furthermore, as Perry wrote to the Secretary on 17 May 1844, the entire West African coast from Gambia River to the equator was so unhealthy that any attempt to establish there a "Naval Depot or General Rendezvous for refreshment and refitment would result in the most serious consequences . . . to human life," and, without benefiting Liberia, would raise such a resentment in America that the colonization cause would suffer.

To feed and clothe a thousand sailors for eight weeks required an enormous amount of stores, even with the simple wants of those days — ship biscuit, flour, salt beef and pork, beans and coffee. At Monrovia, provisions were always in short supply; and although Liberian coastal waters teemed with edible fish, the native Negroes refused to sell any to ships, believing that their offal thrown overboard would frighten away the living fish. Santiago lay some nine hundred miles northwest of Monrovia, but a ship could count on fair winds both going and coming. Porto Praia, the rendezvous of vessels in the Brazil trade and of Yankee whalers, afforded fresh provisions and fruit grown on the island. Owing to the impossibility of obtaining fresh provisions in Liberia, Edmund L. DuBarry, the fleet surgeon, begged his Commodore to obtain "Lemon syrups, tamarinds, and such acid and refreshing drinks and diet, . . . at any cost," which he did. Perry repeatedly, but in vain, begged the Navy Department to send to this island a storeship which could double as hospital; and he arranged with the Portuguese government to establish a depot there for ships' stores sent out from the United States. The harbor, although open to the southeast and unsafe in the rainy season (July to November) was far better than the open roadsteads off the Liberian coast; and the smaller but more protected Porto Grande on the island of São Vicente, about 120 miles to the northwest of Santiago, afforded good shelter from southerlies. The British Africa Squadron, similarly, used the lee side of Ascension Island as their base, since their own colony of Sierra Leone had proved fatal to unacclimated white men.

On 24 July, two days after *Saratoga* departed Porto Praia, the rainy season struck in, and the Commodore put into effect sanitary regulations that he had worked out in the *Cyane* years before.[1] They caused "considerable mirth and some growling," recorded Purser Bridge. One rule was

---

[1] See above, Chapter VII.

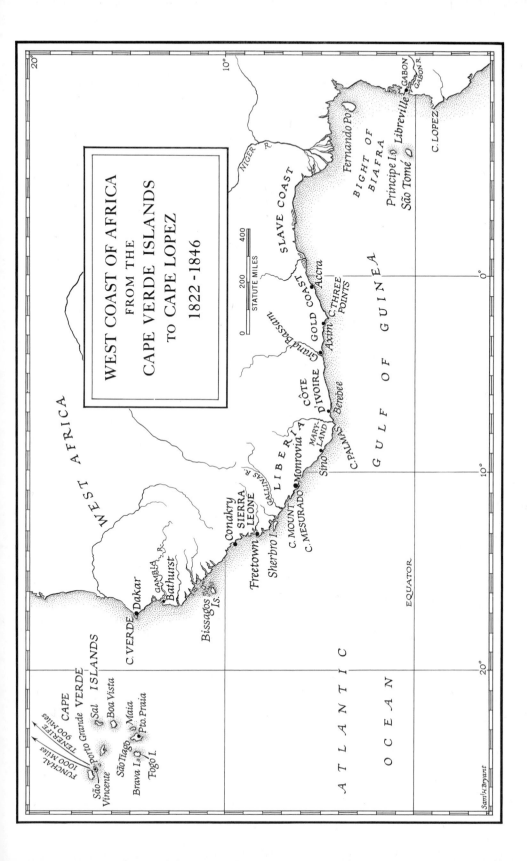

WEST COAST OF AFRICA
FROM THE
CAPE VERDE ISLANDS
TO CAPE LOPEZ
1822-1846

STATUTE MILES
0   200   400

WEST AFRICA

CAPE VERDE ISLANDS

São Vincente
Porto Grande VERDE
Sal
Boa Vista
São Tiago
Maia
Brava I.
Pto. Praia
Fogo I.

CAPE

FUNCHAL 1000 MILES
TENERIFE 900 MILES

C. VERDE
Dakar
GAMBIA R.
Bathurst
Bissagos Is.

Conakry
SIERRA LEONE
Freetown
Sherbro I.
GALLINAS R.
C. MOUNT
C. MESURADO
Monrovia
LIBERIA
Sino
MARY-LAND
C. PALMAS
Berebee
CÔTE D'IVOIRE
Grand Bassam
GOLD COAST
Axim
C. THREE POINTS
Accra
SLAVE COAST

NIGER R.

Fernando Po I.
BIGHT OF BIAFRA
GABON
Libreville
GABON R.
Principe I.
São Tomé
C. LOPEZ

GULF OF GUINEA

EQUATOR

ATLANTIC OCEAN

20°
10°
0°
10°
20°

Sam'l.H.Bryant

that every man wear a flannel undershirt night and day, and turn into his hammock wearing a cloth jacket and pants; another, that every sailor scrub himself clean once a week. Fresh air, supplied through the hatches from canvas windsails, and encouraged to circulate by a system of fans and bellows, was dried by portable anthracite stoves between-decks. Ill-smelling smudges were lighted to discourage vermin. Irksome and resented as these orders were, they probably saved the lives of hundreds who otherwise would have succumbed to malaria and yellow fever. Nobody then knew that both diseases are communicated by a mosquito; but Perry, by requiring everyone to terminate shore liberty by 8 P.M. and come on board for the night, unwittingly baffled the insects. On one occasion, two officers and six men, capsized when making for their ship at Cape Mount, Liberia, spent the night on shore; everyone caught the fever, and one died. Even with these precautions, a number of sailors stricken with the fever on the West Coast died after their ship reached the Cape Verdes; and there, as Protestants, they were not allowed Christian burial. Perry bought land and established at Porto Grande a seamen's cemetery, which was also used by the Royal Navy.

Brawls and Diplomacy in Liberia

Saratoga on 1 August anchored off Monrovia, where brig *Porpoise* was already riding. Perry's principal business then began. The Africa Squadron had been set up by virtue of the Webster-Ashburton treaty of 1842 which (it was hoped) had solved the touchy matter of visit and search. Each contracting party, the United States and Great Britain, agreed to maintain a squadron of at least 80-gun strength on the West Coast to search its own nationals. Statements by the late William E. Burghardt Du Bois and other historians of the slave trade to the effect that both the administration and Perry were halfhearted or insincere in their efforts to suppress this abominable traffic, are completely contrary to fact. Perry's orders from Secretary Upshur, dated 30 March 1843, are so detailed and explicit as to leave no doubt on the subject:

"You are charged with the protection of American Commerce in that quarter, and with the suppression of the Slave Trade, so far as the same may be carried on by American Citizens or under the American Flag. . . . The United States are sincerely desirous wholly to suppress this iniquitous traffic and with that view have declared it to be piracy. They have recently, by their treaty with England, come under specific stipulations upon the subject, to which your particular attention is called." Perry is not to allow the American flag to be used for evasive or criminal purposes. He is warned in detail about the tricks of the slave traders. He shall cruise from Madeira and the Canaries to the Bight of Biafra, and from the

African coast to long. 30° W. He is to establish a depot for stores and provisions at Porto Praia, and every two months to send each vessel thither, or to some other insular port, for rest and replenishment. Nothing was said in these instructions about helping the American colonists in Liberia to protect themselves against hostile natives, but the Commodore took that upon himself in addition to his other duties.

The American Colonization Society, by purchasing tracts of land along the Grain Coast between Sierra Leone and Cape Palmas, and planting new colonies of American Negroes, had effectively suppressed the slave trade on Liberian shores and rivers. But there was plenty more work to be done. Perry was pleased to find that Monrovia, whose site had been selected by him, had become a neat colonial capital where stone houses were being built, and American cultural and political standards were maintained. The Governor, appointed by the American Colonization Society, was Joseph J. Roberts, a remarkable man of color. The son of free Negroes in Virginia, Roberts was a great man by any standards; he did more to keep the colony going than anyone since Jehudi Ashmun. The Commodore gave the Governor an 11-gun salute and invited him and his colored cabinet to dine in his cabin, entertaining them with a performance by the ship's band. Roberts and Perry there worked out an operation plan for chastising the tribes which had been plundering American vessels. But the Governor warned the Commodore against lingering on the coast at that season, when strong south winds raised such heavy seas that even Kroomen could not cross the bars.

The squadron now paid a brief visit to Porto Grande where, on 9 September, it rendezvoused with *Decatur*, Commander Joel Abbot, and *Macedonian*, Captain Isaac Mayo. To the latter frigate (now razeed to a sloop) Perry shifted his broad pendant. That was his characteristic method of solving an insufferable situation with his flag captain in *Saratoga*, Josiah Tattnall. Joel Abbot's journal for 30 November 1843 states, "Called on bd. *Saratoga* to see Capt. Tattnall. Found Capt. Mayo there. We had some animated conversation on matters touching the feelings of Capt. T. in regard to matters between him and Comr. P. Capt. M. and myself tried to calm the feelings of Comdr. T. & to act a friendly part to all concerned." What that gallant officer's grievance may have been against Perry does not appear. It may have arisen in 1840 when Tattnall, a year junior to Perry, served under him in ordnance experiments, but it may have developed on this cruise. I strongly suspect that the trouble arose over the Commodore's sanitary and health regulations, that Tattnall found them too strict and was lax in enforcing them. For we find that shortly after the Commodore left *Saratoga* she became infested with yellow fever and other sickness, whilst *Macedonian* had not a single case on board at the end of November 1843.

Joseph J. Roberts, President
of the Republic

John B. Russwurm, Governor of
Maryland in Africa

It is true that not every officer in the navy liked Perry,[1] but his bad relations with Tattnall were exceptional. On this African cruise he became close friends with the other ships' commanders, especially Mayo and Abbot. These two, together with Commanders Franklin Buchanan and Raphael Semmes, who were elsewhere at that time, became as intimate as Lord Nelson's "band of brothers," and were proud to be under Perry's command anywhere. Abbot, when he became Perry's flag captain, played backgammon or chess with him almost every evening. Tempers became very taut on the Africa station, and the Commodore had to compose a number of serious quarrels and prevent duels being fought. But, despite his strict discipline, "Old Bruin" always remained a favorite with the enlisted men. No one, enlisted or commissioned, ever questioned his courage or ability.

The Africa Squadron, now complete, sailed to Cape Palmas, arriving 19 October. Here the Maryland branch of the A.C.S. had established a colony called Maryland in Africa, with villages named Harper and Tubman after the benefactors of the Society. There were both Catholic and Episcopalian missions, and an able colored governor named John Brown Russwurm whom Purser Bridge recognized as a former fellow student at Bowdoin College. Russwurm was the illegitimate son of a Jamaican slave and a white American, whose wife adopted him and saw to his education. Disheartened by his status as editor of a Negro newspaper in New York, Russwurm emigrated to Africa and became governor of the African Maryland in 1836. His community now comprised about 650 colonists; and the natives, with whom its relations were somewhat touchily friendly, had villages of conical huts nearby.

On 23 November 1843 the squadron with Governor Roberts and other Liberian notables on board left Monrovia for Sinu, arriving on the 27th. Here on a sandy-shored bay, one of the most pleasant and fertile places on the coast, the Mississippi branch of the A.C.S. had settled over a hundred freedmen from that state, and more were shortly expected; they named their village Greenville. The chief difficulty was an intrusion by the Fishmen, formerly middlemen between Bushmen who caught the slaves, and the traders who brought goods to exchange for "black ivory." Fishmen resented the American Liberians for having broken up this trade; they in turn were resented by tribes already on the coast who were friendly to the Americans. Against these, as well as against the colonists, the Fishmen were "acting ugly," pilfering and threatening, and recently they had mur-

---

[1] Shortly before this African cruise, Secretary Paulding had to compose a quarrel between Perry and Captain Francis H. Gregory, who felt that the Commodore had done him out of a command of one of the new steam frigates. Captain Thomas Ap Catesby Jones used such bad language about Perry at the Navy Department that the Secretary apologized for him. Later, as we shall see, the Commodore had a run-in with Farragut, and Joel Abbot turned against him in Japan.

dered two sailors of the American schooner *Edward Burley*. Commodore
Perry, determined to see that justice was done, held a palaver with the
chief men of the natives. Here is Purser Bridge's description of the palaver
at Sinu: —

At 9 A.M., thirteen boats left the different ships, armed, and having about
seventy-five marines on board, besides the sailors. Entering the river, with
flags flying and muskets glittering, the boats lay on their oars until all were in
a line, and then pulled at once for the beach, as if about to charge a hostile
battery. The manoeuvre was handsomely executed, and seemed to give great
satisfaction to some thirty colonists and fifty naked natives, who were assembled
on the beach. The officers and marines were landed, and formed in line, under
the direction of Lieutenant Rich. The music then struck up, while the Commodore and Governor Roberts stept ashore, and the whole detachment marched
to the palaver-house, which, on this occasion, was the Methodist Church.

The Commodore seated himself behind a small table, which was covered
with a napkin. The officers, with Governor Roberts and Doctor Day occupied
seats on his right, and the native chiefs, as they dropped in, found places on
the left. If the latter fell short of us in outward pomp and martial array, they
had certainly the advantage of rank, there being about twenty kings and headmen of the tribes among them. Governor Roberts opened the palaver in the
Commodore's name, informing the assembled chiefs, that he had come to talk
to them about the slaughter of the mate and cook, belonging to Captain
Burke's vessel.

The facts brought out in the palaver were that Captain Burke of the
Edward Burley, in retaliation for an African doing him out of $4, seized
two native canoes and detained their crews prisoner. He then sent his
mate and cook in the schooner's boat, armed, in pursuit of a third canoe.
These two were overwhelmed by the natives and killed. Commodore
Perry and Captains Mayo, Tattnall and Abbot, as well as Governor Roberts, concluded that although the murders were unjustified, Burke had
been the aggressor. Observe that Tattnall and Mayo, from slave states, did
not subscribe to the principle "the white man is always right." One of the
murderers was apprehended, but the affair did not end there. The colonists,
in coöperation with members of the friendly tribes who resented the
Fishmen's intrusion, helped to destroy their village and chase the erring
tribesman back to the bush.

Governor Roberts thus describes the Commodore's palaver with the
friendly Africans: —

He assured them that it was the wish of his government to cultivate a
friendly feeling with all the native tribes, and would pledge himself that so
long as the natives behaved themselves, and treated with proper respect and
kindness American and other traders, his Government would look upon them
as friends and treat them as such. He told them he had not been sent to Africa

to oppress or ill-treat the natives, but to protect the American Flag from insult, and the persons and property of American citizens from imposition and outrage, such as has been practiced by certain tribes along the coast. This duty he should do to the utmost of his ability. He however assured them that notwithstanding he should punish to the fullest extent such as deserved it, he should also respect the rights of the natives and as far as possible prevent any abuse from American traders. And told them should any American visiting their coast ill-use them, or any of their people, to make a proper representation to him or to the commander of any American vessel of war and their grievances should be looked into and if possible their wrongs redressed. The kings were very much delighted with the commodore's expression of good feeling, thanked him, and promised that nothing should be wanting on their part to maintain the good understanding already existing between them; and assured him that their future conduct should be such as to merit a continuation of the good opinion of the American people. An interchange of presents now took place. The kings presenting a couple of bullocks, and the commodore a few pieces of cloth, some tobacco, &c., &c. The next morning Commodore Perry and myself received a formal invitation from the king and headmen, requesting us to make a visit of ceremony to their town. This of course was accepted, and we parted good friends.

Naval versatility is illustrated by the Commodore's next exploit — saving the life of a native accused of witchcraft. Upon landing at Cape Palmas and observing a muster of black men, Perry learned that they had come to witness the death agonies of a wretched man forced to undergo the sassywood ordeal, drinking a concoction of that poisonous bark. The Commodore and most of his officers ran to the spot, persuaded the crowd to give him up, and handed him over to the fleet surgeon to administer an emetic, which saved his life. But the real business which brought the squadron back to Maryland in Africa, was the approach of a hostile tribe which threatened to wipe out the colony. The naval officers were about to sit down to dinner at Governor Russwurm's when an alarm gun was heard from the colonists' fort on Mount Tubman, and a breathless messenger announced that the Barroky tribe was attacking. Commodore and Governor, mounted on the only two horses in the official stable, Purser Bridge on a tiny donkey, and about thirty marines on foot, proceeded on the double to the scene of conflict, only to find that the garrison had already repelled the assault. Apparently the report of a saluting cannon that morning had suggested to the Barroky that war was on between Maryland and her neighbor King Freeman, so they decided to move in and share the spoil. Since Freeman and his Grebo tribe had been acting suspiciously of late, the Commodore and his captains held a palaver with him and his fellow chiefs, he dressed in a robe of crimson damask trimmed with gold lace. And there was no more trouble of that kind at Maryland in Africa.

The next important palaver concluded with an undignified scuffle which adds a touch of humor to these rather tedious proceedings. It took place east of Cape Palmas, on the Ivory Coast, which later became the French colony of Côte d'Ivoire and is now an independent republic. This had been the scene, two years earlier, of the capture of an American trading schooner, *Mary Carver* of Salem, and the murder of her entire crew. With a cargo valued at $12,000, she had anchored off a Fishmen village called Little Berebee to trade with the natives. Captain Farwell imprudently went ashore unattended and was assaulted, tortured, and killed by the Fishmen, who then took the schooner apart and murdered her crew. There was no pretense of Farwell's having abused the natives; it was just a "catch," as they called the piracy of a vessel. A conference of naval officers with the two governors on board *Macedonian* decided that reparation must be demanded and the surviving criminals be tried by their fellow tribesmen. Perry, of course, had to enforce it; and there ensued a brawl which seems comic in retrospect, although anything but funny while it lasted.

On 13 December 1843 all boats of the squadron rendezvoused alongside *Macedonian* off Little Berebee, embarked some two hundred marines and bluejackets, and pulled for the shore, line abreast. To preclude the danger of entering a village of hostile natives, Perry caused a tent to be pitched on the beach as a palaver house, and summoned King Ben Krako and five or six of his men to attend. Krako was a prodigious black of formidable strength. In the palaver, conducted through a native interpreter who had been one of the murderers, Krako's defense was so fantastic that Perry told him he would have no more of that nonsense, and ordered the marine guard to approach. On signal from a shot in the nearby village, the interpreter started "running like a deer," but before he had gone far was felled by a rifle shot fired by Commander Tattnall. Krako, too, tried to bolt. Perry seized him by his long calico robe which carried away, then grabbed the royal loincloth and, holding on for dear life, was dragged through the sand for fifteen or twenty yards. At that point a sailor conked Krako with the butt end of his musket and others jabbed him with bayonets. He pretended to be dead; but, seeing a musket on the ground, leaped to get it. Captain Mayo of *Macedonian* lunged at the same time, but Krako got the musket and grappled with Mayo. That resourceful captain gave the Negro a mortal stab with his pistol bayonet. Firing, in the meantime, had become general. The landing party drove the Fishmen out of their village and burned it, while the guns of the Squadron lent fire support. All Americans were re-embarked with no loss. The dying Krako was taken on board the flagship, but did not live long. That evening, says Captain Abbot, there was "some unpleasant conversation" between Captains Tattnall and Mayo and the Commodore, which "happily terminated amiably. I did all I could to sooth the parties. I retire much fatigued."

Next day the Commodore proceeded to Grand Berebee, located on a 120-foot cliff, and there held a palaver with sundry kings who not only disclaimed any part in the capture of *Mary Carver* but approved the killing of "that very bad man" Krako. They cheerfully signed an agreement to refrain from plundering trading ships or molesting missionaries. This Treaty of Grand Berebee was immediately followed by the return of prisoners captured several months earlier by U.S. brig *Porpoise*. Each received a sailor suit and other gifts, and Prince Jumbo, the king's son, was honored with an officer's frock coat. His reunion with his father, who had given him up for dead, made a tremendous impression all along the West Coast. And that treaty was never violated.

Late in December 1843, when the squadron's provisions were running out, it departed for the Cape Verdes, calling at Cape Palmas and Monrovia to land passengers. Governor Russwurm and the two missionaries at Maryland in Africa wrote letters of thanks to the Commodore, Russwurm saying, "Our hearts now swell with gratitude to you for the deep interest expressed in our future well-being." Governor Roberts, in his annual report to the American Colonization Society, paid a notable tribute to the Commodore and his officers: —

Commodore Perry, as you will at once see, is entitled to much credit for the able manner in which he has conducted the whole of these palavers. No one could have managed them better.

In every instance he has been most successful in obtaining satisfaction for outrages committed on American citizens, and of impressing the natives with a proper respect for the American flag. Though firm and decided in all his intercourse with them, he used no unnecessary threats or menaces, but invariably treated them kindly, — heard what they had to say — admonished them as to their future conduct, — and warned them of the punishment that would certainly follow any outrage committed upon Americans or insult offered to the American flag.

By this course he has gained the confidence and esteem of the natives along the whole coast. So averse was he to taking life, that even at Berebee when the natives commenced the attack, he would not allow them to be pursued or fired at more than was absolutely necessary for the preservation of his own men.

Commodore Perry was well sustained by his officers in all his operations along the coast. They seem to know, and do their duty; and a more gentlemanly set, I think I have never seen. I am personally indebted to every one for the kind attention shown me, and the great interest they manifest for the prosperity of Liberia.

And Perry's then flag captain, Joel Abbot, wrote to a friend in December 1843: —

Our noble Commodore has so far done what I consider just and right, and I have no doubt he will continue such a course to the utmost of his power and ability. The natives on the African Sea Coast are not, as you may suppose, like the ignorant African Negro Slave of Our Country. Their every feature is stamped with Sagacity and intelligence. I can assure from what I have witnessed at the several palavers I have attended, that they have their Daniel Websters & Henry Clays, and their native Eloquence, graceful posture, and dignified bearing would command respect and would not be disparaging to them, their advantages considered, alongside those two mighty champions. . . .

I think the admirable manner in which Comre. Perry has punished crime and aggression on this coast, and caused a settlement of difficulties between the colonists and natives in a way calculated to extend and protect our trade & at the same time foster a friendly feeling on the part of the natives to our country, is worthy of all praise. I hope all his measures and exertions in detail may be published, & I have no doubt they will be. I have only given an imperfect scanty sketch or reference to them.

It must be remembered that Perry had received no orders to do anything for the American colonists, and his dispatch from Monrovia the previous 3 August to the Secretary, asking for instructions on that subject, was never answered. He took it on himself to protect them, and even on one occasion extended assistance to an English colonial settlement. Hearing that natives were threatening to wipe out Bathurst on the Gambia River, he sent U.S.S. *Preble* to the rescue. She frightened away the aggressors, but in that narrow, mosquito-infested river, Perry's sanitary precautions proved inadequate. The men were allowed to sleep on deck and go on "sporting expeditions," and mosquitoes had most of the sport. There were 90 cases of fever and 19 deaths in a crew of 144.

Lieutenant Thomas W. Freelon, C.O. of *Preble*, wrote to the Commodore on 13 January 1845 from Porto Grande, expressing gratitude for his "deep interest" in that vessel since her visitation of African fever: "Your personal sympathy with the afflicted Officers and men, your anxiety to see them comfortably lodged on shore, the efforts you have made to supply the ship with water, provisions and medicines, in some cases absolutely depriving your own ship of necessary articles in order that the sick might not suffer," and his exertions to provide a suitable cemetery there for the dead, "entitles you to the warmest thanks, not only of myself but of every individual in the ship."

Fleet Surgeon Edmund DuBarry reported to the Commodore on 21 December 1843 that the health in the fleet was still fairly good, and that the chief trouble was a "general debility" from living so long in tropical heat and dampness. But the brawl at Berebee had had a bracing effect.

A storeship, which the Navy Department had dispatched to Porto Praia with supplies, managed to get herself wrecked en route, leaving "the squadron very much straitened" for provisions, and Perry wrote rather sharply to the Secretary of the "absolute and positive necessity" of "a more regular supply of provisions for this Squadron." So, partly in search of food, partly for recreation, he sailed his squadron to Funchal, Madeira, where officers and men enjoyed the festive season and the horse races. The Commodore engaged a group of native musicians as flagship band; unfortunately, they could play no American tune but "Hail, Columbia!" and so bored the officers with its repetition that one made the indiscreet remark that if they could not play something else at sea, they would be flogged. That suggestion so alarmed the musicians that they jumped ship.

At Madeira the Commodore took on board a consignment of the famous wine produced in that island for his New York friend and connection Frederick De Peyster. It was a genial custom in days of sail for commanders to purchase and bring home Madeira for their friends; a tropical voyage in a man-of-war's hold was supposed to be good for the wine, and each consignment was always referred to by the name of the ship that brought it over. We still have the invoice of De Peyster's "Macedonian Madeira" — a quarter-cask of "Fine Old London Particular, Vintage 1835," at $55.00, two half quarter-casks of the same, vintage 1836, at $27.50, and one half quarter-cask of "Choicest Old Sercial Madeira Wine" for the same "very advantageous price," as Perry described it in a letter.

The squadron next called at Monrovia. There the Commodore and his officers enjoyed the hospitality of the principal merchant, Colonel Hicks, a former New Orleans slave who dressed for dinner, where his colored wife presided "with genuine elegance and taste." And at Cape Palmas began a cruise to the eastward along the coasts of the present-day African republics of Côte d'Ivoire, Ghana, Togo, Dahomey, Nigeria, Cameroon and Gabon. Perry had been instructed to patrol this coast down into the Bight of Biafra, in hope of intercepting American slavers. None of those gentry were encountered, but interesting visits were paid to the British, Dutch and Danish forts at Axim and Accra, and to Gabon. There, at the site of Libreville, the French government was about to found the colony that later became French Equatorial Africa. Purser Bridge observed that all American vessels trading along the Guinea Coast were from Salem, and that both Protestant missionaries at Gabon, Benjamin Griswold and John Leighton Wilson, were Yankees. Mrs. Wilson, however, was a Southern lady who had emancipated her slaves, devoted her fortune to missions, and had been at this post for six years. Her husband had learned the native language well enough to preach in it. Dr. Albert Schweitzer's famous hospital at Lambaréné, was established in 1924 on the site of an offshoot of that earlier American mission.

After a call at the Portuguese island of São Tomé, which they found altogether charming, the squadron, with larboard tacks aboard, sailed to Porto Praia. It made another visit to Monrovia in September, and that was the last time that Perry saw Africa. At Porto Praia, on 20 February 1845, he was relieved in command of the Africa Squadron by Commodore Charles W. Skinner.

In late March 1845 he sailed on a perfect day, with a northwest wind blowing off the land, roadstead crowded with shipping, and everyone's eye on *Macedonian* to see how smartly she got under way. Topsails are set and braced so that she lies still in the water, like a great bird waiting to take off. Anchor detail at the capstan bars sing a chanty as they walk around, heaving. "Anchor's apeak, sir!" cries the petty officer in charge. "Well, break it out!" says the 1st Luff. "And stand by jib halyards, stand by fore braces!" Another heave on the capstan, and "Anchor's aweigh, sir!" "Well, hoist jib and flying jib, haul weather sheets!" and, to the man at the wheel, "Helm hard up!" Gracefully she turns to leeward, as anchor detail cats and fishes the big hook. A three-gun salute to the Portuguese governor ashore roars out, and is returned by the fort. Topgallant sails are hoisted and sheeted home. Merrily she heels to the breeze and bowls down the familiar roadstead, easily clearing Quail Island and Punta Temerosa. The long, whiplike homeward-bound pendant is broken out, and the men sing the old chanty "Goodbye, farewell, we're homeward bound!"

Macedonian arrived New York 28 April 1845 just as war clouds with Mexico were gathering. Although absent from home almost two years, Perry could proudly report that there was not one case of illness in his flagship.

As usual, Perry brought back curiosities and specimens which he presented to academies and scientific societies. The National Institute for the Promotion of Science received a breadfruit and "a curious fish" from the Cape Verdes, a "native iron" from East Africa, a "Cartridge Box of a Celebrated War Chief of West Africa" — probably Krako — and "a mask worn by the Grand Devil, whose haunt was on the Cavillo River near Cape Palmas." Perry explained that every tribe had such an unholy man who lived in the bush where he was consulted by the tribal chiefs and delivered delphic responses to queries. These were favorable or otherwise according to the value of the consultant's offering. Perry must have placated the oracle, for from now on there were no more mutinies, no embarrassing passengers, no contretemps with the Navy Department. A glorious career in the Mexican War and a productive four years' shore duty lay ahead, and they were followed by his greatest achievement, the Japan Expedition.

CHAPTER XIV

Mexican War Opens
1845–1846

PERRY had now reached a turning point in his career. At the age of fifty-two he received an important command, of the Gulf Squadron, in the one major war of his mature life, the war with Mexico. Had he failed to measure up to this opportunity, he would have been largely forgotten like the officer he relieved off Veracruz, and the one whom he relieved as commodore of the East India Squadron. Both responsibilities he fulfilled so well that in due course his name became one of the most famous in American naval history.

Although war between the United States and Mexico did not formally begin until May 1846, it had long been anticipated. Unpaid claims, the annexation of Texas, President Polk's ambition to acquire California, and the disinclination of the Mexican government to negotiate — all contributed to the outbreak of a war that could easily have been avoided by less aggressiveness on one side and more realism on the other. Yet neither country had prepared for war. The United States Navy, with several fine new frigates, sloops and brigs built to fight a blue-water war with a European power, lacked both light-draft steamers and sailing vessels which could operate profitably along the Gulf Coast and up the rivers of Mexico. Even so, it was overwhelmingly superior to the Mexican Navy. A small squadron of enemy warships could have steamed right up to New York and shelled it, so feeble were the city's defenses. But Mexico had no ships capable of steaming that far. Her only war vessels with respectable fire power were taken over by their English builders for want of payment before seeing action; and two war steamers being built in New York for Mexico were commandeered by the United States and named *Vixen* and *Spitfire*. American bluejackets, from their supposedly vast knowledge of women, referred to these vessels as "the two Pollies." They proved to be a godsend to the Gulf Squadron, and Perry so persistently asked for others like them, or smaller, to be sent out that he got the backs up of the older officers about the Navy Department, and received a reprimand from the Secretary.

The Mexican War was not generally popular in the United States, except in the West and lower South. It was a party and sectional war. Sentiment on the Eastern seaboard in general was against it. All Whig statesmen such as Clay and Webster, and also John C. Calhoun, were opposed. The United States Navy, however, was eager for the fray. Perry probably reflected the general feeling when he wrote of the Mexicans, "They are all villains," and proposed keeping more of the conquered territory than President Polk thought wise. Almost the entire Perry-Rodgers-Slidell clan got into the war, in navy, army, or diplomatic corps.

Notwithstanding his detestation of Mexicans in general, Perry like many other officers of the United States Army and Navy approached their country with keen interest and anticipation. William H. Prescott's *Conquest of Mexico*, which appeared in 1843, became an immediate success; sailors of U.S.S. *Delaware* petitioned the Secretary of the Navy to give them a set for their ship's library, and Secretary Mason liked the book so well that he ordered one for every vessel in the United States Navy. Equally popular was a book that Prescott introduced the same year, *Life in Mexico* by Madame Calderón de la Barca, as told in a series of her letters; these gave a lively picture of Mexican society and personalities. Perry must have read Calderón and Prescott, since everyone who read anything did; and it is also likely that he read the Lockhart translation of Bernal Díaz del Castillo's *Historia Verdadera* of the conquest by Cortés, which appeared in 1844. At any rate, he knew that Cortés began his conquest in Tabasco, and it is probably more than a coincidence that in his second Tabasco expedition Perry modeled his strategy on that of the great conquistador. Also widely read before the war began were John L. Stephens's *Incidents of Travel in Central America* (1841) and *Incidents of Travel in Yucatán* (1843). These first told the English-speaking world about Maya monuments such as Chichén Itzá and Uxmal. Perry would dearly have loved to have visited Uxmal, but Yucatán was in such a turmoil that he could not risk the mule-back journey. He did, as we shall see, make a great effort to visit the ruins of Palenque in Chiapas, described both by Stephens and in Lord Kingsborough's *Mexican Antiquity*.

The Home Squadron of the United States Navy, which Commodore David Conner commanded, assembled in the Gulf of Mexico on 2 April 1845, when Texas was about to be received into the Union. Thenceforth it was generally (though never officially) known as the Gulf Squadron. Conner at that time wore his flag in frigate *Potomac*. Under him were the new war steamers *Mississippi* and *Princeton*, sloops-of-war *Saratoga, Falmouth, John Adams* and *St. Mary's*, and brigs *Somers, Lawrence* and *Por-*

poise. Conner anchored behind Sacrificios Island, so called because the Spanish explorers there found remains of the Aztecs' human sacrifices. But this anchorage was too close to Veracruz to be comfortable if war should break out, so the Commodore began to make use of the Antón Lizardo roadstead, some eleven miles farther south.

Early in 1846 the smart new frigate *Cumberland* was dispatched to Veracruz to strengthen the squadron. We are fortunate to have a description of her approach to the Mexican coast from her chaplain, F. W. Taylor. On a clear winter morning the gleaming white conical summit of Orizaba, "Mountain of the Star," 18,851 feet above sea level, is sighted a hundred miles away. The wind being fair, Captain Breese claps on sail in order to reach his anchorage before dark. By midafternoon the sierra has become a backdrop, Punta Morra at the north and Punta Antón Lizardo at the south appear to be embracing the frigate from afar, and a white line of breakers marks the reefs and low islets that protect Veracruz harbor. The church towers and domes of Veracruz can now be made out through a glass and the squadron masts appear over Sacrificios. All hands are aloft or on deck awaiting orders, and some of the old salts are growling, "What's the old man think he's doing? We'll be aground in no time!" The officer of the deck, Lieutenant Hazard, judging the opportune moment, calls through his speaking trumpet, "Stand by to take in the studdingsails — man the clewlines, sheets and downhauls — stand by to furl royals — man the royal clewlines!" The men quickly take their stations. Then comes the order, "In studdingsails and royals!" In a moment the little "kites," fluttering like big handkerchiefs, are pulled into the tops or down on deck, and the royals are clewed up and furled. With topsails and topgallants set, the frigate weathers Anegada de Adentro, the outermost reef, then Isla Verde, and stands in toward Pajaros reef. Between them the city of Veracruz is plainly visible, and the cone of Orizaba looms over it like a white cloud. "Man the lee braces — haul taut!" cries the lieutenant. The men brace every yard up sharp to weather the last obstacle. She rounds the southeast tangent of Sacrificios Island in seven or eight fathom of water, the yards are squared again, and *Cumberland* fairly roars down toward the crowded anchorage.

Foretopsail and foretopgallant are thrown aback to check her headway, lower courses are clewed up, and the jack is raised on the mizzen truck to signal for a pilot. A boat brings the pilot on board, she fills away again and bears down in gallant style on the anchored ships where hundreds of critical eyes are watching, ready to remark on the slightest mistake. The guns are already charged for saluting, and 1st Luff, after being assured by chief gunner's mate that all rigging is clear, gives the order "Starboard, fire!" then, "Larboard, fire!" And so on, until the full 13-gun salute to Commodore Conner is rendered. Flagship *Potomac* replies in kind. *Cumberland*

now makes for the berth indicated by the pilot, directly astern of a
French corvette, and as her way is checked she makes a running moor,
drops her starboard bower anchor and pays out chain while the well-
braced yards and close-hauled spanker help her to round into the wind.
All sails are furled, all lines neatly coiled, and the frigate lies snug to two
anchors as the sea breeze dies away and the moon rises from the Gulf.

Raphael Semmes, Commodore Conner's flag lieutenant, waxed lyrical
over the scenery. "Nothing can exceed the beauty of that portion of the
Mexican coast in the vicinity of Veracruz," he wrote. The sea-breeze
gradually dies away as the sun declines and the lofty mountain range
stands up boldly to view, with its giant peaks Orizaba and the Cofote, rosy
at dawn and red at sunset. Nor is this the only spectacular scenery on the
Gulf Coast. Some fifty miles east of the Antón Lizardo roadstead, where
the squadron usually anchored, one sights the Sierra de San Martín, which
rises straight from the sea and cradles the Laguna Catemaco, a beautiful
mountain lake. There are three volcanoes in this sierra, the highest being
the San Martín Tuxtla. "When in an active state, says the *Central America and Mexico Pilot*, "the flames by night and the column of smoke by
day afford an excellent landmark." Bible students like Perry must have felt
that they were indeed favored! He had to pass the Sierra de San Martín at
least twenty times during his service in the Gulf Squadron.

In mid-September 1845 President Polk sent to Mexico City John Slidell,
Perry's brother-in-law, with a reasonable offer to settle all controversies
between the two nations, and about the same time he ordered Perry to
come to Washington and offered him the Gulf Squadron command. Commander Franklin Buchanan, after the war was over, wrote to Perry describing the circumstances. In September 1845, he said:

I was with Mr. Bancroft in his private library at his residence in Washington
on business connected with the Naval School. After that business was arranged
we conversed freely on Naval matters. During our conversation he handed me
a Navy Register and remarked "Name the Commodore of the Home Squadron." I at once named yourself and after a short conversation he said, "I will
offer Commo. Perry the home squadron." Shortly after this conversation his
front door bell rang. Mr. Bancroft looked at his watch and remarked "It is
Commo. Perry he has come to dine with me, and you must remain also." I
did. As I left him to join you in the parlour, I asked him if he had any objection, to my mentioning to you his intentions, respecting the Command of the
Squadron. This reply [was] "No certainly not" or words of that import. I did
mention the circumstance and you justly appreciated the Compliment or
rather honor for it certainly was a great one. The same day at dinner he
tendered you the command of the Squadron, which you promptly accepted,
remarking at the same time, that it was unexpected and unsought by you, but
it was a command too important to decline. Your conversation then continued

Vice Commodore Matthew C. Perry, portrait by J. Beaufort Irving

Commodore David Conner, engraving by Samuel Sartain

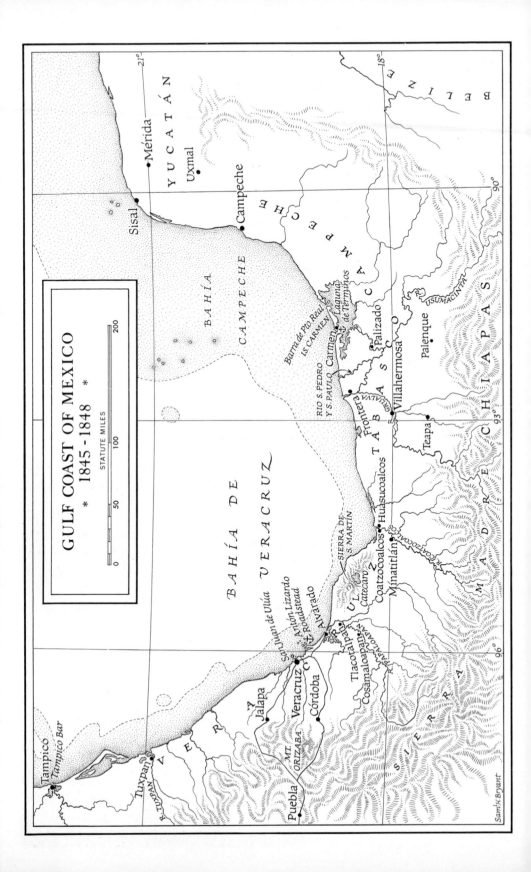

GULF COAST OF MEXICO
* 1845 - 1848 *

STATUTE MILES

0   50   100   200

Tampico
Tampico Bar

Tuxpan
R. TUXPAN

VERA

MT. ORIZABA
Puebla
Córdoba
Veracruz
Jalapa
Anton Lizardo
Roadstead
San Juan de Ulúa
Alvarado
CRUZ

Tlacotalpa
Cosamaloapan
R. PAPALOAPAN

SIERRA DE S. MARTÍN

U.L. 265
catecaro

Minatitlán
Coatzcoalcos Huasucoalcos
R. COATZACOALCOS

BAHÍA DE VERACRUZ

BAHÍA CAMPECHE

RIO S. PEDRO
Y S. PAULO
Barra de Pto. Real
IS. CARMEN
Carmen
Laguna de Términos

Frontera
TABASCO
Palizado
Villahermosa
VATVIA
Teapa

USUMACINTA
Palenque

SIERRA MADRE CHIAPAS

BELIZE

Sisal

Mérida
Uxmal
YUCATÁN

Campeche
CAMPECHE

21°
18°

90°

93°

96°

Sam.H.Bryant

when it was understood that you were to relieve Commo. Conner at his convenience or when he returned to the North. Mr. Bancroft said, "Commo. Conner's health was very bad" and "he would return." During the conversation you said you would write to Commo. Conner that you were old friends and you would regret doing any thing that did not meet his wishes. Mr. Bancroft said he would also write to him and mention the circumstance.

Perry, accordingly, wrote to Conner, stating Bancroft "offered to me unsolicited" the command. But, as he had only returned from African duty in April, Perry hoped to have "as long a time at home as possible" before proceeding to Mexico. On 16 October he wrote again, inquiring when Conner wished to be relieved. There was no answer. On 10 December 1845 Bancroft wrote to Conner, "It is my wish that you should retain the command as long as it is agreeable to you. I think it would be well for your reputation that you should retain it till our affairs in Mexico are fully adjusted. . . . It is not my purpose to relieve you before the expiration of a three years' command unless you yourself desire it." Two days before Christmas Conner replied from Pensacola that he wished to retain the command "until our affairs with Mexico are in such a train, as will have no doubt of their amicable adjustment." Neither Bancroft, nor Conner, nor anyone in a responsible position, then expected Mexico to fight.

Here was the germ of one of those command controversies which from time to time have bedeviled the United States Navy. Commodore David Conner, two years older than Perry, had the reputation of a highly capable officer. After a brilliant record in the War of 1812 as a lieutenant of U.S.S. *Peacock*, for which he had been voted two silver medals by Congress, he had rounded Cape Horn in command of the twelve-gun schooner *Dolphin*, and served on the Board of Naval Commissioners and in the bureau of construction, equipment and repair. But he enjoyed very poor health, being subject to a recurring *tic douloureux*, a painful tri-facial neuralgia, and Secretary Bancroft feared that he might break down. On 7 May 1846 the Secretary wrote to Conner, hinting (as delicately as he could) that his resignation would be acceptable, having heard with a regret that the Commodore's health had suffered from the Mexican climate. But "the Department is prepared to relieve you as soon as you desire. Justice to you demands that the opportunity of relief should be placed before you for your own free election." Conner had no intention of asking to be relieved, since, assuming that Mexico would not fight, he wished to serve out his term as commodore.

Nevertheless, war was imminent. After the Mexican government refused to receive Slidell, President Polk ordered General Zachary Taylor's army to advance to the Rio Grande. Mexican cavalry engaged in a skirmish with it there on 25 April 1946, and on 12 May Congress declared war on Mexico. Perry made no immediate move to leave the United States; he was busy superintending the outfitting of *Vixen* and *Spitfire* at New York. On 8 May he wrote to "My dear Conner," introducing the Blunts, authors of the then standard *Coast Pilot*, who were joining the squadron to make a much needed hydrographic survey of Mexico's Gulf Coast, and saying nothing about relieving the Commodore. He was behaving with his usual courtesy and circumspection in a ticklish situation.

President Polk ordered a blockade of both Mexican coasts on 13 May 1846. The Gulf Coast stretches roughly a thousand miles from the mouth of the Rio Grande to Campeche, bordering a coastal plain through which several navigable rivers flow into the Gulf. A few miles up each river are small trading towns, the most important being Tampico, Tuxpan, Alvarado, Coatzacoalcos, and Frontera. Only Veracruz could be approached without crossing a shallow bar, and for this reason had become Mexico's principal port of entry; but all had to be watched lest Mexican privateers get out, or blockade runners slip in. Since Mexico had become enemy territory, logistic supply for the blockaders, even fresh water, had to come from New Orleans, Pensacola or Norfolk. The lean and efficient George Bancroft was succeeded as Secretary of the Navy in September 1846 by fat, easy-going John Y. Mason, and the department's bureau of construction, equipment and repair (nicknamed "bureau of destruction and despair") had no conception of how to keep ships on foreign service properly supplied with provisions and ammunition. Commodore Dudley W. Knox, who seldom criticized the navy, has this to say about the situation in his *History:* —

The Navy Department was also very remiss in not meeting the commodore's frequent requests for a proper means of supply. The only base was at Pensacola, nearly nine hundred miles from Vera Cruz, and it was very poorly equipped with facilities and supplies. For example, thirty days were required to bake enough bread there to last the flagship three months, and even fresh water was difficult to obtain in sufficient quantities. There was no coal, and more than two months elapsed after the first three small steamers arrived, nearly three months after war began, before a cargo of coal reached Pensacola. Obviously the Department was poorly organized for conducting a war which it had fully expected for nearly two years, and great credit is due the naval personnel at the front for carrying on so well under these severe handicaps.

It has well been said that Mexico's Gulf Coast is guarded in winter by storms and in summer by pestilence. From April into September or October, when the rainy season prevails, fever-bearing mosquitoes swarm over any ship anchored near shore, transmitting malaria and the *vómito negro*, or yellow fever. From September or October into April is the so-called dry season. At any moment a sudden, fierce *norte* may spring up, unheralded by weather forecasters and playing havoc with shipping. This norther is a whole gale accompanied by heavy rain. Nowadays its approach can be signaled from the coast of Texas where it makes up; but in the 1840's sailors had to depend on their own knowledge of the local signs. These are very variable; not necessarily a falling barometer, but such things as "a glittery appearance of the sea" and "birds flying southward." The modern *Central America and Mexico Pilot* cautions vessels always to be prepared for northers, which "often come without any warning whatever. The best way to moor is with the two bowers ahead with a good scope of chain, the sheet anchor under foot, and the stream anchor astern." And for ships at sea, the sudden burst of a *norte* meant heaving-to in a hurry, sending down topmasts when the vessel was rolling and pitching, decks swept by heavy seas, boats carried away, men swept overboard. Madame Calderón de la Barca's description of going through *nortes* both approaching and leaving Mexico is enough to discourage anyone from crossing the Gulf of Mexico in the winter season.

Perry enjoyed almost a year's shore duty after being told he would eventually relieve Conner. Upon the declaration of war he became eager for active service, and Bancroft wanted a commander with his aggressive qualities in Mexican waters. The Secretary wrote to him at Tarrytown on 12 August 1846: "Commodore, you have expressed a strong desire for active service, in the Gulf of Mexico. I am about to detach Capt. Fitzhugh from the Command of the Steamer *Mississippi*. If acceptable to you, the Department will give you the Command of that Ship, to be held until such time as you may succeed to the Command of the Home Squadron. An early answer is requested."

The answer was favorable, Bancroft promptly sent Perry south in U.S. steamship *Vixen*, and she arrived Antón Lizardo on 23 September. Perry's orders from the department were to take command of U.S.S. *Mississippi*, fly a vice commodore's red pendant if he thought "proper," and relieve Conner as commodore of the Gulf Squadron when Conner was ready. (He was also reminded, thriftily, that being appointed vice commodore would not increase his pay.)

After lying at Antón Lizardo for two weeks, Perry wrote to his son-in-law John Hone, "Commo. Conner, who holds on to his command with a pertinacity very extraordinary, shows no disposition to vacate, and as I have made up my mind not to remain as second in command, for which I have many reasons, the most prominent are: that I do not choose to share the odium of a mismanagement which every one talks about even in the squadron, when I have not the power to prevent or avert it."

The Commodore did, on 6 October, order Perry "agreeable to your instructions from the Department," to relieve the captain of *Mississippi*, but chose to ignore the order that he was to be second in command. So Perry asserted it. On 8 October he sent formal notice to Conner, "By virtue of authority vested in me by the Honorable Secretary of the Navy, and in accordance with a verbal communication made to you this morning, a red broad pendant has been hoisted on board this vessel." The red pendant — a red burgee with 28 white stars — was the flag of a vice commodore.

Conner had no intention of relinquishing his command in the near future; but most of his officers were delighted at the prospect of a new and vigorous commodore. For instance, Lieutenant Charles Kennedy of sloop *St. Mary's* wrote to Perry that the "near prospect of commanding the Squadron" caused his arrival to be hailed with joy. Perry, however, thought better of not remaining "second in command," since he soon discovered that there was plenty of work in those waters for a vice commodore. Before mid-October he was ordered to command an offensive.

So far, Gulf Squadron operations had been such as to justify Perry's remarks about "mismanagement." Conner's first aggressive move, an effort to capture Alvarado near the mouth of the Papaloapan River and a few miles south of Antón Lizardo, was a failure. Protected by a bar at the river mouth, Alvarado could never be very useful as a fleet anchorage, but a secondary road led thence to Mexico City, and several small craft of the Mexican Navy were upstream. On 7 August steamship *Mississippi* (not yet under Perry's command) and *Princeton* were to tow two frigates across the bar. Bombardment of one of the forts protecting Alvarado opened late that afternoon, but a strong current prevented the steamers from closing the range sufficiently to do any damage, and when darkness fell Conner ordered Cease Firing. He planned a boat expedition upriver for the following day, but indications of an unseasonable norther caused him to call it off. The attack force returned ignominiously to the squadron anchorage, and the predicted norther never blew up. Conner decided to postpone his attack until the flooded river subsided, the weather became settled, and more light-draft gunboats had been attached to his squadron.

Midshipmen and junior officers who had been "sharpening their swords, loading their pistols, eating hard tack and salt junk, and boasting of what they intended to do," were disgusted with Conner's hesitation. "Nothing was easier than a capture of the whole place," wrote Lieutenant John A. Winslow three days later. "We were foolishly frightened away. All the officers and men in the other ships are indignant." There were about two hundred Mexican troops on the beach to dispute the landing, but the Commodore's imagination blew them up to a thousand. Midshipman Parker of *Potomac* declared in his *Recollections* that Conner was "an educated man and a brave officer; but during the war he always seemed to be too much afraid of risking his men; he lacked moral courage, would not take the responsibility his position imposed upon him."

It has been conjectured that an element in Conner's indecision was his expectation that Mexico would soon quit the war, so why risk his sailors' lives unnecessarily? He had good reason so to believe. President Polk recalled to active duty Commander Alexander Slidell Mackenzie, formerly commander of *Somers*, in order to sound out at Havana the exiled Mexican General Santa Anna. If the General gave assurance of readiness to make peace with territorial cessions, Mackenzie had authority to pass him through the blockade. Santa Anna managed to deceive almost everyone with whom he came in contact, even President Polk and Madame Calderón de la Barca, so it is not surprising that he pulled Mackenzie's leg too. He obtained the *laissez-passer* and Conner allowed him to enter Veracruz on 16 August. But at Mexico City Santa Anna made himself dictator, and, instead of negotiating peace, prosecuted the war more vigorously.

That was the situation when Perry arrived in Mexican waters and raised his red pendant in *Mississippi*. Perry's principal duty was to help enforce the blockade, and blockading is probably the most difficult and boring duty that sailing navies were called upon to perform, exceeded only by escort-of-convoy in World War II. Raphael Semmes pointed out the particular irksomeness of this blockade. Until Veracruz was taken, and except when an upriver raid was on, all hands were confined to their ships. And those sailing vessels, crowded and devoid of ventilation below decks, became almost insupportable in the summer months or the winter gales. Officers frequently had to live on the men's salt meat and hardtack rations, and wash in salt water. When not cruising off the coast looking for blockade runners, the ships anchored in Antón Lizardo roadstead. There they had the protection of a chain of islets, reefs, shoals and sandbanks which break the seas and make it "as secure as many harbors," according to the *Central America and Mexico Pilot*. But the holding ground is bad to indifferent, and there was trouble over dragging anchors in every big blow. Commodore Conner established on Salmedina Island, one of those that protected the roadstead, a boat depot, repair shop, and tent hospital which was crowded with fever victims throughout the war. From the logistic point of view Antón Lizardo was no improvement over Sacrificios, as neither water nor provisions were obtainable, and an evening walk on the deserted beach constituted the only recreation.

Commodore Conner put into effect the sanitary regulations that Perry had worked out in Africa: — 'tween decks ventilated and kept dry with stoves, men required at sunset quarters to exchange their cotton duck frocks and trousers for woolens. In spite of all precautions, the health of his squadron disintegrated during the summer and fall of 1846, and morale declined accordingly. Rations, when actually supplied, were more varied and abundant than in the days when Perry was First Lieutenant of

North Carolina;[1] but for four months that winter the crew of at least one ship had no fresh provisions. Scurvy broke out, and the captain only managed to check it by raiding the coast under British colors and buying cattle and poultry which the natives sold in the belief that the landing party were friendly Englishmen. Dysentery and yellow fever also appeared; there were 29 cases of the *vómito* in one frigate alone. *St. Mary's,* a crack ship reputed to be the most efficient blockader in the squadron, suffered a near mutiny. Seaman Samuel Jackson, a handsome fellow like Billy Budd, reputedly an Irish nobleman's son who had enlisted under a false name, exploded with rage when the officer of the deck, finding his shoes under a gun after inspection, kicked them overboard. Jackson knocked the officer down twice and told him what he thought of him. He was tried by court-martial for striking an officer and for "mutinous and seditious words," and sentenced to death. Commodore Conner confirmed the sentence and the wretched man was hanged from the yardarm on 17 September at Antón Lizardo in view of the entire squadron. Unlike the hanging of three mutineers in *Somers,* this passed off without much notice being taken by the public.

The only way to make the blockaders' duties less arduous was to capture one or more bases on the enemy coast. But, with the exception of heavily fortified Veracruz, every one of Mexico's Gulf ports lay several miles up a river, and all these rivers had bars at their mouths, too shoal for frigates and sloops-of-war to cross.

By mid-October 1846 when he had several more light-draft vessels under his command, including two revenue cutters, Commodore Conner decided to take another crack at Alvarado. Since the August threat, the Mexicans had installed a couple of new breastworks on the high bluffs bordering the river between Alvarado and the river bar, and strengthened the garrison. This was supposed to be a desperate venture, and Flag Chaplain Taylor received a pack of "last letters home" from the sailors who were to take part. Perry longed for the command, but the Commodore took it himself, on 16 October. The Vice Commodore's job, in *Mississippi,* was to engage the attention of the outer fort while the other ships crossed the bar. But long-legged *Mississippi* could not close near enough to do the fort any significant damage, and heavy surf on the bar so frightened the pilots that they refused to take the ships across. It was not so heavy, however, as to prevent Perry from sending Midshipman Henry Rodgers in a boat to sound the bar, and Rodgers reported a least depth of twelve feet

---

[1] Bruell in his *Sea Memories* pp. 13-17 says that weekly rations were 3 pounds pork, 2 pounds beef, 1 pound flour, ½ pound rice, ¼ pound dried fruit, 6 dozen sea biscuits, 14 ounces sugar, 1¾ ounces tea, 4 ounces butter, 1½ pints beans, ½ pint molasses and ½ pint vinegar. Coffee was still an officers' drink; tea the standard beverage for enlisted men. Bruell tells how each mess brewed its own in a big pot and let it "cook" for half an hour before serving!

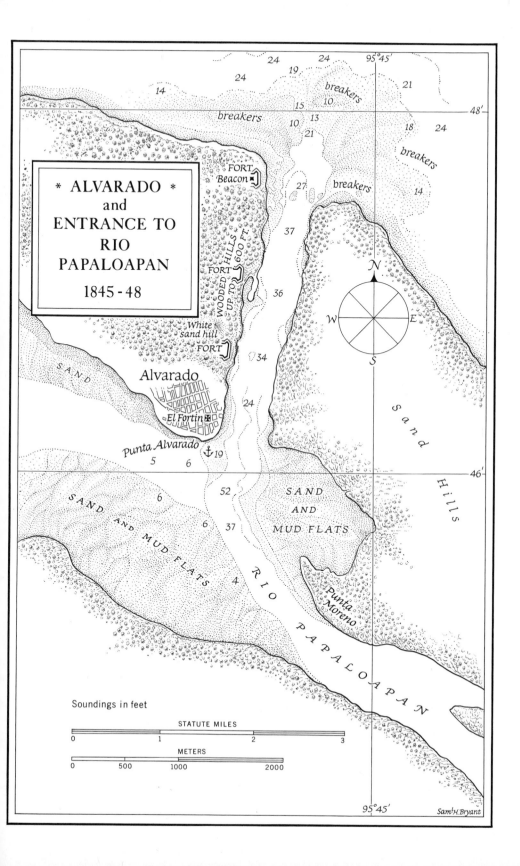

* ALVARADO *
and
ENTRANCE TO
RIO
PAPALOAPAN
1845-48

24
24
24
19
21
14
breakers
10
15
18
24
breakers
10
13
10
breakers
21
FORT
Beacon
27
breakers
14
37
N
36
W   E
White
sand hill
S
FORT
34
Alvarado
Sand
Hills
24
El Fortín
Punta Alvarado
19
5   6
46'
6
52
SAND
AND
MUD FLATS
SAND AND MUD FLATS
6
37
4
RIO
Punta
Moreno
RIO PAPALOAPAN

FORT
WOODED HILLS UP TO 600 FT.

S A N D

95°45'
48'
95°45'

Soundings in feet

STATUTE MILES
0   1   2   3

METERS
0   500   1000   2000

Sam'.H.Bryant

— good enough. And as the waves subsided, Commodore Conner at noon, after conferring with his captains, ordered the bar to be crossed in two columns, one led by himself in *Vixen* towing two schooner-gunboats; the second led by revenue cutter *McLane* towing three gunboats. *Mississippi* again rendered gunfire support. At about 1:30 P.M., as the two parallel columns approached the bar, the vessels yawed badly and could make little headway against the current. The flag column crossed safely, but *McLane* grounded and her towed gunboats fouled one another. Upon seeing their distress, the Commodore turned to his flag captain and said, "Well, Sands, what's to be done now?" To which Commander Sands replied, "Go ahead and fight like hell!" But Conner had no stomach for such heroics. He ordered his column to reverse course and retire, which it did after exchanging shots with the nearest fort. Both sides evidently were very bad marksmen since nobody was killed, and only a few men wounded. *McLane* floated off, but Conner ordered the whole expedition back to Antón Lizardo.

Mexico was greatly elated by the repulse of this expedition, and its government became foolishly confident of beating off any attack by the United States Navy.

CHAPTER XV

Vice Commodore Perry[1]
1846–1847

First Tabasco Expedition

"OLD BRUIN" was delighted with his ship — "The *Mississippi* is a paragon," he wrote to Conner. Influential in designing her hull and engines, he had frequently journeyed to Philadelphia to watch her construction, and helped the department to select competent officers, especially engineer officers. Two hundred and twenty-nine feet long, drawing 19 feet, measuring 1692 tons, she carried two 10-inch and eight 8-inch shell guns of the Paixhans type. She was barque-rigged, spread 19,000 square feet of canvas, and sailed well. Her coal-burning power plant consisted of two side-lever engines which operated two paddlewheels, each 28 feet in diameter. Both wheels and their boxes were so strongly constructed that even a heavy sea could not wrench them off. In twenty years' service in two wars, interspersed by two voyages around the world, *Mississippi* never got into serious trouble until she ran aground off Port Hudson, blew up and sank, in 1863. In the new steam navy her prestige corresponded to that of frigate *Constitution* in the old sailing navy.

The Vice Commodore chafed under Conner's command but tried not to show it; and his disgust over the Alvarado fiasco did not last long. For the Commodore, appreciating Perry's energy and intrepidity, immediately sent him on an independent mission to the State of Tabasco to retrieve the Navy's reputation and capture a substitute for Alvarado.

Tabasco is the Mexican state between the Isthmus of Tehuantepec and the Yucatán peninsula, and north of the State of Chiapas. Almost its entire surface is a fertile coastal plain, one of the richest in Mexico. The Grijalva River, rising in the Sierra Madre near the Pacific Coast, becomes navigable

---

[1] Perry was never independent of Conner as long as Conner was Commodore; the oft-repeated statement that Conner had charge of the sail, and Perry of the steam vessels, is incorrect. Like any task force commander, Perry was virtually independent as soon as his force was under way and beyond signaling distance; but he was always subject to Conner's orders.

at Teapa, meanders northward across the state and empties into the Gulf six miles below a town called Frontera. About halfway between Teapa and Frontera is the provincial capital, La Villahermosa de San Juan Bautista, which we shall refer to for short as Villahermosa.[1] In 1845 it was a pretty town with a few thousand inhabitants garrisoned by two to three hundred troops. But it had a very important trade. In 1845 no fewer than 70 vessels of twelve different nations entered and cleared from Villahermosa, and some 178,000 pesos in customs duties were collected.

Certain Tabasqueños, disgusted with the central Mexican government, had been working for secession, like Yucatán; and Conner hoped to find coöperation from them. But in the meantime the provincial governor and captain general, Don Juan Bautista Traconis, an energetic and flamboyant character, rallied the state to Santa Anna and prepared to defend it against *los barbaros norteamericanos*, as he called the American invaders.

Conner and Perry, in consultation on board *Cumberland* the afternoon of the Alvarado fiasco, decided on this raid. Before sunset 16 October, the Commodore set up a Tabasco task force and issued an operation order. Vice Commodore Perry, wearing his red pendant in *Mississippi*, commanded steamer *Vixen*, revenue cutter *McLane* and schooner-gunboats *Reefer, Boneta, Forward* and *Nonata*. The last-named was a smart Mexican schooner which brig *Porpoise* had captured and the United States Navy taken over. Embarked was a landing party of some 253 sailors and marines commanded by Captain French Forrest of frigate *Cumberland*. Perry's orders were to examine the coast from the Isthmus of Tehuantepec to Carmen, then enter "the river of Tabasco," secure Frontera or any other river town he could reach, destroy enemy military stores and equipment, and capture any Mexican vessels encountered. Nowadays an expedition of this nature would be called a reconnaissance in force. Perry was not expected to capture and hold the provincial capital, unless he found friendly local authorities.

Nobody dragged his feet in this operation. The Tabasco expedition sailed from Antón Lizardo at 9 P.M. 16 October. Next morning it came upon an American merchantman in treasonable communication with the enemy, and made prize of her as well as of the Mexican schooner *Telegraph*. During the next five days, mostly stormy, the task force sailed east and examined the mouth of the SS. Pedro y Paulo River, where the bar breaks all across. But at the Grijalva Perry had the good luck to find a fair depth on the river bar. Even so, the bar was too shoal for *Mississippi*, so at noon 23 October Perry shifted his flag to *Vixen*, to lead the procession. She was a stout little schooner-rigged sidewheeler, 118 feet long, carrying three guns, commanded by Joshua R. Sands, a small, slight officer but a

---

[1] In 1846–48 Americans generally called both river and town Tabasco. The constituent hot pepper of the famous tabasco sauce, *Myrtus tabasco*, is a native of the state.

terrific scrapper. *Vixen,* towing one-gun schooners *Forward* and *Boneta,* crossed the bar safely; but the inept skipper of *McLane,* which led the second column, again managed to find a shoal spot and grounded. *Nonata,* which she was towing, gallantly sailed upstream without benefit of power, and the boats which *McLane* had been towing were rowed against a 4-knot current the six miles to Frontera. There the river widens to over half a mile, making a natural harbor where the Spaniards and Mexicans had established a brisk little town.

At 3 P.M. the lookouts in *Vixen* made out two steamers at the Frontera quays firing up to depart. Perry promptly cast off his tow, poured on coal, and made best speed to the town. Impressed by this show of force, the *alcalde,* the masters of the steamers and of all other Mexican vessels present, surrendered without a shot. This was a valuable bag, especially river steamer *Petrita,* which had been built in New York for the Richmond-Norfolk run. She and *Tabasqueña* were promptly converted to United States gunboats. Two more schooners were taken at the same time, and a third (*Amado*), which tried to flee, was captured by *Boneta.*

Perry wasted no time gloating over this easy conquest, which gave the Gulf Squadron a base at least equal to what Alvarado might have been. Leaving a small garrison of marines to hold Frontera, he embarked most of Captain Forrest's landing force in captured *Petrita* and, at 9:30 A.M. 24 October, shoved off for Villahermosa, whch lay some seventy miles upstream. *Vixen* towed *Forward* and *Nonata; Petrita* used her own power. All that day and all night they proceeded cautiously. The banks of the Grijalva, now occupied by cattle ranches and cornfields, were then covered by a heavy hardwood jungle which harbored thousands of howling monkeys and birds which screamed at the invaders.

The expedition safely rounded an S-turn in the river which the Mexicans called El Torno del Diablo — The Devil's Bend — because it was the site of collisions whenever the wind dropped and the current — or the devil — took control. Shortly after eight bells ushered in the morning watch on 25 October, *Vixen* sighted an enemy breastwork at a place the Americans called Acachapan,[1] commanding part of this S-turn. *Petrita* landed a body of marines who found the breastwork deserted and spiked the guns.

During the forenoon watch nothing was heard but the chunking of the squadron's paddlewheels. Shortly after noon, Villahermosa came in sight, and at 1:40 P.M. Perry anchored his ships off the town in line of battle. Captain Forrest, Captain Sands, and Calbraith Perry Jr. went ashore with a flag of truce to demand immediate surrender of the town. Don Juan

---

[1] Acachapan is not a place but the name of a district which extends from the Devil's Bend almost to Villahermosa. See chart in Chapter XVII below, for this section of the Grijalva.

Bautista refused; dared the squadron to open fire. Perry took up the challenge, and *Vixen's* third shot brought down the red, white and green tricolor that flew over the Esquipulas barracks. It was soon displayed again, over another building. Perry now landed marines under Captain Alvin Edson, and bluejackets under Lieutenant John A. Winslow. They fought their way into the Plaza Mayor, at no great distance from the river, and occupied that part of the town; but when night fell the Commodore, "apprehending from the proverbial heedlessness of sailors" that they might be ambushed in the narrow streets, ordered them back on board ship. In the meantime, the squadron had scooped up every Mexican vessel anchored off Villahermosa — two brigs, two schooners and two sloops; Winslow was complimented for his courage and given the command of a prize.

During the night Perry got word that the merchants and principal inhabitants wished to surrender but were overruled by Traconis, who proposed to fight it out street by street. Perry doubtless wished to capture Villahermosa as a matter of prestige, but he had no authority to do so unless the local authorities coöperated, which Traconis's attitude prevented. So, as he had insufficient force to hold an inland town which could easily be reinforced by the enemy, Perry determined "from motives of humanity, not to fire again, but to pass down to Frontera" with his prizes. Traconis, however, feeling that Mexican honor required a bloodletting, opened fire at daylight 26 October on the American ships. They replied with cannon shots at the customs house and other public buildings. At 7 A.M. a white flag appeared ashore, Perry ceased firing and sent Captain Forrest to investigate. He returned bearing a letter from foreign consuls and merchants requesting him to desist in order to spare their property and the lives of noncombatants. Perry agreed, and at 9:20 raised a white flag in *Vixen*. At the same time he ordered the masters of his prizes to raise white flags and drop downriver. One of them, sloop *Desada*, grounded in front of the town. This was too much for the Mexicans. Thinking her helpless, they opened a brisk fire under cover of waterfront houses, and extended it to other ships as well. The Commodore, seeing *Desada* hard pressed, sent Lieutenant Charles W. Morris in an armed boat to render assistance. She ran a gauntlet of hot musketry, which killed one seaman and mortally wounded Morris.

Perry, incensed at what he considered treachery during a truce, resumed cannon fire on the public buildings of Villahermosa. According to the Mexicans, the fleet fired 170 shots in half an hour. One fell on a house occupied by a mother and three sons, killing all four. This indeed was unfortunate; but Mexican accounts of the cannonade admit that this family comprised all the civilian casualties, that consulates and private houses were spared, and that the American guns concentrated on public buildings, which they battered very effectively. *Desada* floated without further loss, and at 11 A.M. *Vixen* weighed anchor and dropped downriver with the rest of the squadron, firing as they passed the town. Perry, sending the news to Conner, praised the "enterprise and spirit" and "zeal and energy" of all ship commanders except the skipper of *McLane*, who had bungled at the bar.

Such is the laconic account by Perry of his first raid into Tabasco. That of Don Juan Bautista Traconis reads very differently. According to a proclamation that he issued at noon 26 October, he considered that all American ships displaying a flag of truce should have withdrawn beyond cannon shot of the town; since they were anchored near enough to threaten it, he was within his rights to resume fire. This obviously was a mere excuse — his troops had little or no fire discipline, and the apparent helplessness of *Desada* was too tempting. The American ships, said Traconis, "waging a savage war of vandals," fired indiscriminately on the town, "sparing not even the consulates where numerous women and children had taken asylum." But he neglected to say that nobody in the consulates was even wounded. His valiant troops forced *los barbaros norteamericanos* to retreat, empty-handed, in "shameful flight." Anglo-American pride had been lowered, Mexico avenged. A service of thanksgiving was held that evening, and the four victims of the alleged North American barbarity were given a state funeral.

It was certainly not much of a fight. Total Mexican losses were five soldiers and four civilians, and damage to the post office, the customs house and other public buildings. The Americans lost two men killed and two drowned. Perry's "shameful retreat" had been decided upon the night before fighting was renewed, and his failure to press the attack on Villahermosa was due to his desire to spare human life. Moreover, he did not retire empty-handed, as Traconis asserted. For principal booty, in addition to steamers *Petrita* and *Tabasqueña*, taken at Frontera, he carried away Mexican schooner *Laura Virginia*, which he renamed U.S.S. *Morris* in honor of the Lieutenant, brig *Yunauta*, three schooners, a sloop and a brig. The other prizes, being of no value, were destroyed, except that Perry returned *Desada* to her skipper in recognition of "his excellent conduct when his vessel was attacked." Nine vessels in all he presented to Commodore Conner at Antón Lizardo, where he arrived 1 November, and all would have been converted by the U. S. Navy, had three not foundered at Antón Lizardo in a November norther.

Perry, as usual, gave high praise to his officers and men, especially to Captain Forrest for pulling *McLane* off a shoal, and Commander Sands of *Vixen*, his flag captain. Perry's relationship with Sands, a man of his own age but junior in the service, became very intimate; and in his old age retired Rear Admiral Sands paid this tribute to his former commodore: "His many excellent qualities of heart and head were encased in a rough exterior. . . . He was a man of great personal bravery, as were all the Perrys, of undoubted courage and gallantry, bluff in his manners, but most hearty and warm in feelings, and with that genuine kindness which impresses at the moment and leaves its mark on the memory. . . . As a friend he was most true and constant, and his friendship was always to be relied on. . . . The impression he made on my mind and affections was such as to make me desirous of following him to the cannon's mouth, or wherever the fortunes of peace or war should appoint our steps."

"The objects of the expedition were fully accomplished," reported Secretary Mason, "and, by the capture or destruction of every vessel and steamer of the enemy, . . . a check has been given to a commerce by which . . . munitions of war were introduced into Mexico from Yucatán. Much praise is due to Commodore Perry and to the officers and men under his command, for the skill, judgment, and courage manifested throughout the expedition." It also afforded the Gulf Squadron a welcome break in the monotony of blockade, a much needed lift in morale, and secured a convenient port for anchoring small craft and obtaining cattle. As a watering place, however, Frontera was a disappointment; vessels had to push up the Grijalva for thirty miles to find pure drinking water. Don Juan Bautista Traconis, despite his heroic proclamations and paeans of victory, was toppled by a local revolution at Villahermosa the following month.

Tampico Captured

Next on Commodore Conner's program was the capture of Tampico, a port of entry for the State of Tamaulipas which bore slight resemblance to the bustling oil-export city of that name today. Once over the bar, the lower fifteen miles of the Pánuco river made a good harbor. This the Washington administration coveted, under the erroneous impression that a road led thence to San Luis Potosí on the main route from Monterrey to Mexico City. Unfortunately the road turned out to be a mere mountain trail, useless for military purposes. This the navy ascertained before the expedition started, but went ahead with it as a diversion, hoping to deceive Mexico into transferring troops from the main theater of war. But Santa Anna did the unexpected, ordering his garrison to evacuate Tampico and transfer the coast-defense guns upriver to Pánuco.

Commodore Conner, not knowing that Tampico was undefended, set up a formidable task force to capture it: two big steamers, two frigates, a sloop, the "two Pollies" and four schooners. Orders were issued on 11 November 1846 to rendezvous off the bar.

Midshipman Parker of *Mississippi* tells an amusing story of the passage from Antón Lizardo to Tampico. During the night, when a norther blew up, the officer of the deck cast off schooner *Boneta* which *Mississippi* had in tow, without informing Perry. Early next morning the Vice Commodore came on deck and asked, "Where's the *Boneta?*" The officer of the deck told him she had been cast off. Perry, "not noted," says Parker, "for his *suaviter-in-modo*, though strong on *fortiter in re*," said, "Send the master to me!" Upon his appearance "Old Bruin" roared, "Where's that schooner?" Master Brown, never at a loss for an answer, said, "She is south-southeast, sir, fifteen miles distant." "Very well, alter the ship's course to south-southeast." In about an hour's time the lookouts made out the masts of a schooner — but she turned out to be a mere merchant vessel. Perry, furious, sent for Brown and said, "Did you not say that schooner *Boneta* bore fifteen miles south-southeast?" "No, sir," said the Master. "You asked about a schooner but did not say *what* schooner!" Perry was silenced for once, and *Boneta* eventually reached Tampico under her own sail power.

Sloop *St. Mary's* and brig *Porpoise*, which had sounded Tampico bar, were already in the roadstead when Conner's task force arrived on the morning of 14 November. The attack was a pushover. Conner in *Spitfire* led the first division, towing two schooners and several ships' boats full of men; Perry in *Vixen* led the second division, similarly made up. There were no casualties on the bar, a white flag appeared as the vessels approached Tampico, and the city fathers after considerable bargaining surrendered the city.

In the meantime the invaders captured three more Mexican gunboats and a schooner, which were added to the United States Navy under the names *Union*, *Tampico*, *Mahonese* and *Falcon*. The first-named, placed under the command of Lieutenant Winslow, shortly after hit a reef and became a total loss. Another casualty of Mexican winter weather was our old acquaintance U.S.S. *Somers*, now under Lieutenant Commander Raphael Semmes. She capsized 8 December 1846 in a sudden squall off Veracruz when chasing a blockade runner and sank in ten minutes, taking down 32 officers and men of her crew of 76. Owing to the brave efforts of sailors belonging to Spanish, French and British warships anchored nearby, the swimming survivors were rescued; and these included Semmes. In view of the famous battle in 1864 between Captain Semmes of C.S.S. *Alabama* and Captain Winslow of U.S.S. *Kearsarge*, it is amusing to find that as lieutenants who had lost their ships, the future adversaries shared a cabin in frigate *Raritan* while awaiting reassignment.

Perry personally thanked the commanding officers of the foreign warships, and Congress voted medals to them and to their crews who effected the rescue. Tampico became a useful staging point in the next operation against Veracruz. It had no road to San Luis Potosí, but it did have one to Monterrey. This enabled two divisions of General Taylor's army to march down and embark in transports for Veracruz.

Conner remained at Tampico until 13 December, to organize a provisional government. Since his landing force was not strong enough to garrison the town, he dispatched Perry north in *Mississippi* to Brazos Santiago roadstead near the mouth of the Rio Grande, to obtain troops from the American army stationed nearby, and with orders to continue to New Orleans on a similar quest. Calling at the Brazos 16 November, Perry sent a message to the army commander at Matamoros, who promptly embarked part of a regiment in a steamer and sent her to Tampico. Perry continued to New Orleans, arriving 20 November. His Slidell connections doubtless helped him to obtain quick action from the Governor of Louisiana. With a few score infantrymen and a field artillery battery embarked, *Mississippi* departed New Orleans the very next day, arrived at Tampico on the 29th after a boisterous voyage, and landed passengers and supplies on the last day of November. This was a record turnaround for that era.

That Perry was becoming increasingly irked over Conner's delay in relinquishing the blue pendant, is evident from the first paragraph of a long letter which he wrote to Secretary Mason, immediately after departing Brazos Santiago: —

U.S. Steamer *Mississippi*
At Sea, Nov. 16th 1846

Sir — Being at present only Second in command of the Gulf Squadron it is not in my province to communicate directly with the Government on matters connected with the command, but at this conjuncture, and when there was no time for Commo. Conner to write in detail, it seems to be my duty to put the Department in possession of such information as may be useful, and I am less scrupulous in thus departing from the usual course from the presumption that in accordance with repeated assurances I shall soon be placed in chief command, and that the remarks now made may be considered rather an exposition of the plan of operations I should suggest when placed in that position.

After reinforcing Conner's pleas for giving Tampico an army garrison, he continues with his views on how to win the war: —

The Department has I presume been already made acquainted with the attack by a detachment of small vessels & barges under my Command upon the Town of Frontera & City of Tabasco. The sweeping of the River along its entire navigable extent a distance of 80 miles, of every vessel and craft, the utter annihilation of its present commerce & the locking up of its mouth by the placing of small vessels within the Bar.

There are many rivers emptying into the Gulf, the entrances to which are obstructed by dangerous bars, upon these Rivers are situated numerous flourishing Towns, some of them enjoying Considerable trade.

It is by taking possession of these Rivers by vessels of light draft, and by cutting off the entire trade from the Rio del Norte, to Cape Cartouch, that the people occupying the Eastern Coast of Mexico & the adjacent province of Yucatán can be brought to listen to the repeated proffers of peace made by the U. States. They are far from being well affected to us, and can only be brought to terms by the infliction of severe chastisement.

Previous to the capture of Tabasco an undisturbed trade had been carried on to that and the neighboring Ports and the whole Country was supplied with every necessary article of provision & Military Munitions not only indirectly by the way of Yucatán, but directly from Europe & the United States, many cargoes of Cotton from New Orleans had been landed to supply the Mexican Manufactories, and even now considerable Illicit trade is doubtless carried on with the United States, all this can & should effectually be put a stop to. . . .

In landing detachments from the ships we have found the want of Artillery — to remedy this I would suggest that each Frigate & large Steamer be supplied with Two light Field Six pounders, with all the appurtenances Munitions &c. complete and each Sloop of War with one. I believe it is now the practice in the English & French Navies to provide their large vessels with field Artillery, a most excellent and necessary arrangement with all cruising ships, and particularly with regard to vessels upon this station, where they have difficulty from the shallowness of the water in approaching within gunshot of the Forts.

All vessels on this station are short of officers & men, an extra number of which are necessary to supply vacancies constantly occurring. The greater number of officers that can be furnished to landing parties, the better as their presence tends to preserve order & efficiency.

In conclusion I may repeat the remark, that from my observations the Mexicans are extremely prejudiced against the Americans. So far from appreciating the benevolent policy of our Government in its desire of conducting the war upon principles of humanity they seem to ascribe the motive to a spirit of indecision and a desire to temporise and build thereupon hopes of ultimate success in the war.

The Mexicans are not deficient in personal courage, nothing is wanting to make them good soldiers, than military discipline & a national ardour which cannot be expected of men impressed as they are into service, in the most cruel & ruthless manner.

With Great Respect,
I am, Sir,
Your Obt. Ser.,
M. C. PERRY

Perry's surprise at the Mexicans' lack of appreciation for the "benevolent policy" of the American invasion is certainly naïve; but his comments on the several armistices consented to by Taylor and Scott were justified. These seemed evidence of indecision to the Mexicans, took the pressure off them, and gained nothing for the United States.

Yucatán Visited

Having returned to Tampico, Perry was ordered by the Commodore on 1 December to tow *Vixen, Boneta* and *Petrel* to Antón Lizardo. That duty performed, he received orders on the 16th to perform a far more interesting mission, to Yucatán.

Yucatán, which then comprised the present state of that name together with Campeche and Quintana Roo, was a special case, as Perry indicated in the letter we have just quoted. Yucatán had been in and out of the Mexican Republic since the revolution from Spain. At one time La República Chica (the Tiny Republic as it was nicknamed) became very friendly with the Republic of Texas, and even borrowed a squadron of the Lone Star Navy for protection against Mexico. She again became a state of the Mexican Republic, but on 1 January 1846, shortly before war began with the United States, seceded for the second or third time. John L. Stephens, author of *Incidents of Travel in Yucatán*, who happened to be in Washington in the spring of 1846, believed that the state could be kept neutral during the war if tactfully handled, and convinced Secretary Bancroft that something should be done to promote it. The Secretary, accordingly, ordered Commodore Conner to send a warship to Yucatán to coöperate with the state authorities, and Conner complied in June by sending brig *Somers* to Campeche, with instructions to assure "the young republic" of his friendly disposition, and to salute her flag (if she had one) with 21 guns. Her C.O., Commander D. N. Ingraham, after consulting the American consul, became satisfied that the secession of Yucatán was genuine, and released a couple of prizes which belonged to her citizens. But this situation did not last long. The union party, inspired by Santa Anna, gained ascendancy and proclaimed Yucatán's reincorporation with Mexico on 2 November. And, a month later, the secession party issued a *pronunciamento* repudiating this! In any case it soon became obvious (as Perry reported in his long letter of 16 November which we have quoted) that the Mexican dictator was getting plenty of supplies from La República Chica. Consequently the Commodore decided to send a detachment of the Gulf Squadron to blockade Yucatán; and as base, occupy the town of Carmen, or Laguna as it was then generally called.

The twenty-mile-long island of Carmen, a barrier to the great salt Laguna de Terminos, covered the main route of supplies from Yucatán to Mexico City, and still did in 1965. The main federal highway from Campeche to Mexico D.F. runs along Carmen Island, with which it is connected by ferries, and proceeds thence to Villahermosa. Mexico imported war supplies from Cuba, Europe, and even the United States, which were transshipped at Campeche into small cargo vessels. These slipped into the lagoon at its eastern entrance, the Barra de Puerto Real, out again into the Gulf at the Barra Principal next the town of Carmen, entered the Grijalva River at Frontera, sailed or steamed up to Villahermosa and even to the head of navigation a hundred miles from the sea, whence the munitions were sent by road to the capital. Many a cargo of arms and munitions was concealed under a topping of coconuts and sweet potatoes, and Tabascan products returned by the same route to Yucatán. This was the situation which caused Commodore Conner to send Perry to occupy Carmen — the bottleneck of this contraband traffic. His orders, dated 16 December 1846, were to take possession of the town, destroy cannon and other public property, leave two vessels in the harbor to stop the contraband traffic, order neutral vessels to depart within fifteen days, buy provisions for *McLane,* which at that time was blockading the Grijalva River mouth, and return to Veracruz, en route scouring the coast for blockade runners.

Perry, besides his "paragon" of a flagship, was given *Vixen, Boneta* and *Petrel.* Transferring his red pendant to *Vixen* (since *Mississippi* drew too much water), Perry towed the two schooners and four barges across the Barra Principal and anchored off the waterfront of Ciudad de Carmen after nightfall, 20 December 1846. Next morning he sent two officers ashore to demand the unconditional surrender of the town, "which demand, after some little demur, was submitted to." He then took possession of the two forts, spiked their guns, and raised American colors.

Carmen was a valuable acquisition, furnishing the Gulf Squadron with much-needed fresh fruit, vegetables and beef. The Vice Commodore might reasonably have indulged in a few days' leisure at this pleasant place, but being Perry he had to keep on the move. Leaving his flag captain, Joshua R. Sands of *Vixen,* as military governor of Carmen with *Petrel* to help maintain the blockade, he departed on 22 December. He ordered Commander Sands to cultivate the friendship of the Yucatecos "by acts of judicious forbearance and kindness," to respect their lives, property and religion, but keep their coast under strict blockade and take no stock in their professions of neutrality. But Commodore Conner, as soon as he heard of Yucatán's 8 December declaration of neutrality, ordered the blockade lifted. So Campeche merrily resumed its export of logwood to Havana, America and Europe.

Mississippi towed *Boneta* to Frontera, where she joined *McLane* in blockading the Grijalva River, and at Frontera Perry spent most of Christmas Day. But there were no "twelve days of Christmas" for the Vice Commodore. "On the evening of the 25th," he reported, "I shaped my course to the westward, and traced the coast along, sufficiently near to discover the smallest boat, looking into the mouths of the principal rivers." Off Alvarado he captured two more blockade runners, and anchored in Antón Lizardo roadstead on the 27th.

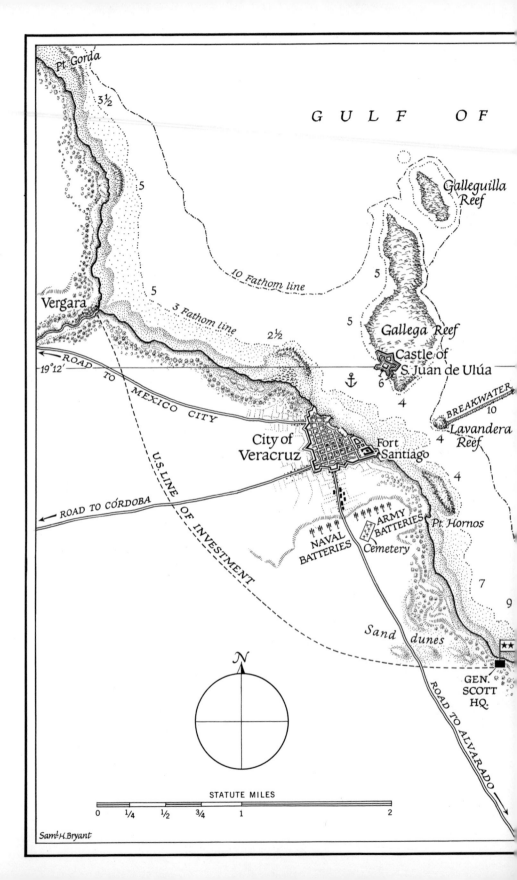

GULF OF

Pt. Gorda

3½

5

Galleguilla
Reef

10 Fathom line

5

5

Vergara

5

3 Fathom line

2½

5

Gallega Reef

ROAD

19°12'

TO

MEXICO CITY

Castle of
S. Juan de Ulúa

⚓

6

4

BREAKWATER

10

City of
Veracruz

Fort
Santiago

4

Lavandera
Reef

U.S. LINE

ROAD TO CÓRDOBA

OF

4

INVESTMENT

NAVAL
BATTERIES

ARMY
BATTERIES

Cemetery

Pt. Hornos

4

7

9

Sand   dunes

★★

GEN.
SCOTT
HQ.

N

ROAD TO ALVARADO

STATUTE MILES

0   ¼   ½   ¾   1   2

Saml H. Bryant

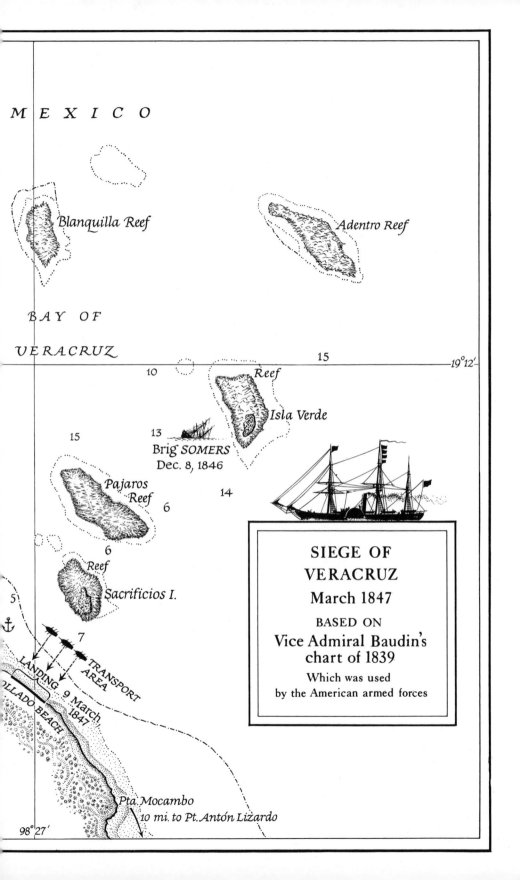

M E X I C O

Blanquilla Reef

Adentro Reef

BAY OF

VERACRUZ

15   19°12′

10

Reef

Isla Verde

15

13

Brig *SOMERS*
Dec. 8, 1846

Pajaros
Reef   14

6

6

Reef

Sacrificios I.

5

7

TRANSPORT
AREA

LANDING 9 March, 1847

OLLADO BEACH

Pta. Mocambo
10 mi. to Pt. Antón Lizardo

98°27′

SIEGE OF
VERACRUZ
March 1847

BASED ON

Vice Admiral Baudin's
chart of 1839

Which was used
by the American armed forces

Logistic problems were a cross to Commodores Conner and Perry that winter. The Navy Department had no conception of what it took to supply a fleet in regions which yielded neither coal, fresh provisions, nor fresh water in sufficient quantities. Pensacola was little more than a supply dump, and the nearest dry dock was at Norfolk. Terms of enlistment of sailors in the frigates were expiring, and the vessels themselves, some of which had been on the Gulf station for almost two years, were in need of upkeep. Among these was *Mississippi*. Her bottom was foul, and all three boilers needed attention. Having no condensers, she used salt water for her boilers which were supposed to be good for only eight months without a thorough cleansing; but *Mississippi* had been at sea sixteen months, and used steam one-quarter of the time. The pipes, leaky from the strain of tossing in the heavy seas, were spitting steam through bleeding joints, and the crew had to pump for seven hours out of every twenty-four to get rid of the resulting water. On 11 November 1846, Perry informed Conner that the boilers could hold out for two months at best. One month later, writing, "Ignorant as I am of the plan of operations," he could not decide whether or not to advise risking his flagship remaining longer on station. Conner now ordered *Mississippi* to Norfolk for repairs. She sailed shortly after returning to Antón Lizardo from the Carmen expedition, and arrived at Norfolk 13 January 1847.

Thus Perry was absent during a crucial part of the Veracruz operation — the landings.

The Veracruz Landings

President Polk, doubting General Taylor's ability to advance much further south by land, determined on 17 November 1846 to send General Winfield Scott along the classic route of Cortés to Mexico City, with a fresh army to be landed at Veracruz. Commodore Conner, as soon as he heard of the administration's plan, became desperately eager to accomplish it early in the new year. For Veracruz lay in a bad yellow fever belt, and any army that did not reach the highlands before late April would certainly be decimated by the dreaded *vómito negro*.

This landing at Veracruz was the biggest amphibious operation in which the United States Navy participated prior to the invasion of North Africa in 1942, and probably was not exceeded by that of any other power prior to the attempt of the Western Allies to capture Gallipoli in 1915.[1]

Veracruz, although captured several times, had acquired a reputation as the most strongly fortified place in the Americas. About half a mile off

[1] In the Union attack on Fort Fisher in January 1865, biggest amphibious operation of the Civil War, there were only 44 ships and 2000 men.

the heavily walled and fortified city, on the Gallegos Reef which protects the harbor, lies the formidable castle of San Juan de Ulúa, commanding the harbor, the town, and all seaward approaches. Dating from the sixteenth century, it had been built up, extended and strengthened to such good purpose as to hold out for almost three years after Mexico had become independent. But a squadron of French frigates under Admiral Baudin in 1838 forced the castle to surrender by sea power alone. That exploit caused a sensation; the Duke of Wellington is said to have remarked that it was the only example known to him of a strong fort being reduced by naval force alone. The instrument of this unusual feat was the Paixhans shell gun whose projectiles penetrated the soft coral stone walls, exploding inside and showering the garrison with rubble. Commander David G. Farragut, who observed this action from U.S.S. *Erie*, reported on it to the Navy Department, as Commodore Conner probably knew; and since the Gulf Squadron mounted plenty of shell guns, he proposed that naval action alone could force both Veracruz and the castle to capitulate. But General Scott vetoed this suggestion, largely because faulty intelligence had greatly exaggerated the strength of San Juan de Ulúa.

Assuming that the castle could not be carried by naval bombardment and escalade without unacceptable loss of life, Scott insisted that his army be landed on the coast beyond the range of the castle's guns, take the city from the rear, and then deal with San Juan. That was the classic method of capturing a strong coastal position. He asked for fifty transports to lift 14,000 men and a large siege train, and 140 surfboats. These were the first landing craft specially constructed for an American amphibious operation. Designed by a naval officer, costing about $800 each, they were flat-bottomed, double-ended wooden rowboats built in three sizes from 35¾ feet up to 40 feet long so as to nest in the transports' holds. Each had a capacity of 35 to 45 troops. Only 64 surfboats arrived in time to be used in the landings, but they proved to be sufficient.

The Veracruz expedition was partly staged through Brazos Santiago, where transports picked up General Worth's division and other units of General Taylor's army, and partly through Tampico, whither two divisions marched overland from Monterrey. Other units came directly from New Orleans or Mobile in transports, and all rendezvoused at the Lobos Island roadstead. The transports began arriving at Antón Lizardo roadstead on 4 March 1847 — it was a noble spectacle to see them sail in until almost one hundred ships were present. General Scott, who arrived next day in army transport *Massachusetts*, joined Conner and other officers in personally inspecting possible landing beaches from steamer *Petrita*. During this reconnaissance she was bracketed by shots from San Juan de Ulúa. Her passenger list suggests that if the Mexican gunners had found the right deflection, the American Civil War might have had a very different history; on board were Captains Robert E. Lee and Joseph E. Johnston, and Lieutenants G. T. Beauregard and George C. Meade.

Scott and Conner agreed to land on Collado Beach, facing Sacrificios Island and some two and a half miles south of Veracruz, but beyond the range of the castle's guns. It was an excellent choice. The beach gradient was right for prompt retraction of surfboats, the land behind was clear of trees or other cover, and although a range of sand dunes commanded the beach, the Mexicans had not fortified them.[1] There being an average range of only nineteen inches between high and low water at Veracruz, tide did not have to be considered. The trouble with Collado Beach was a limited anchorage. The three-fathom line lies about 400 yards from shore, leaving about 900 yards' deeper water between it and Sacrificios Island — not space enough to accommodate even half the transports. This difficulty was surmounted by Scott's adopting Conner's suggestion to concentrate the landing force on a few vessels which could anchor in the roadstead. The operation opened on 7 March at Antón Lizardo, where the 64 available surfboats were launched and organized in divisions of ten. Each boat was manned by a coxswain and six seamen, with a midshipman or petty officer in command. Each was provided with a kedge to keep the boat head-on to the beach and prevent broaching.

In contrast to the high-powered, elaborately organized amphibious operations of World War II, the Veracruz landings were simple and hand-powered, but adequate. Conner and Scott worked the plan out together, and although Scott never relinquished overall command, he gave Conner full responsibility to organize both the approach and the ship-to-shore movement. The "two Pollies" and four light-draft gunboats steamed ahead of the attack force, anchoring about 90 yards from the beach to render close fire support to the landing craft. Frigates and sloops were expected to contribute gunfire from a greater distance. The surfboats were to rendezvous at what we would now call a line of departure, and land in three waves. The navy already had letter-code flag signals, but General Scott's staff made up a fresh set with four special flags — red, yellow, red-and-white vertically, red-and-white diagonally. Lieutenant Parker, usually a harsh critic of Commodore Conner, admitted that his landing arrangements were "simply perfect."

After one postponement, owing to an expected norther, the operation came off on 9 March 1847. It was a perfect day with bright sunlight, a

---

[1] Collado Beach was the same in 1965 as in 1847, except that the beach proper is somewhat narrower and a wooden sea wall has been built over part of it, to stop further encroachment by the sea. The city of Veracruz has expanded beyond Point Hornos, and the sites of the American siege batteries are now covered with streets and houses.

Collado Beach, Site of the 1847 Landing in 1965
Above: Most of the landings took place here
Below: West end of beach; General Scott's headquarters were near the
white building on right

The U. S. Navy Battery Bombarding Veracruz 24-25 March 1847, from a
contemporary painting by Lieutenant Henry Walke USN

gentle southerly breeze, and smooth sea. At first light the surfboats at Antón Lizardo began ferrying troops from non-participating transports to those designated to carry them to the anchorage area. These were frigates *Raritan* and *Potomac*, sloops *Albany* and *St. Mary's*, brig *Porpoise*, steamers *Princeton* and *Petrita*, and five army transports including General Scott's command ship. This movement was completed at 10 A.M. The four fire-support gunboats were already approaching their stations at 11:30 when the entire force got under way for the eleven-mile run to the anchorage off Collado Beach. Commodore Conner, leading in frigate *Raritan*, and General Scott standing in full-dress uniform on the quarterdeck of *Massachusetts*, acknowledged cheers from all hands as they passed through the fleet. It was a brave sight, as an eyewitness described it: the tall ships of war sailing leisurely along under topsails, their decks thronged with masses of troops, brass and bayonets glittering in the sun, bands playing popular and patriotic airs, schooners under all plain sail with crowded decks, steamers chuffing along with strings of surfboats in tow; and the snowy cone of Orizaba hovering over the land.

Between 1 and 3 P.M. the ships reached their assigned anchorages, surfboats cast off towlines, and each rowed to the vessel designated to fill her with troops. During these preparations, Mexican cavalry appeared on the sand dunes behind Collado Beach, and everyone afloat expected a fight to get ashore; but the enemy commander, impressed by this force of overwhelming strength, prudently decided to fall back on the town. (Similarly in 1944, when American amphibious technique became irresistible, the Japanese refused to contest it at the water's edge but fell back into prepared positions.) At 3:30 General Scott caused a red, a yellow and a red-and-white flag to be hoisted at the mainmast of *Massachusetts*, which meant: Prepare to Land. Soldiers of the first wave had been swarming over the bulwarks into their surfboats; and these, when filled, attempted to form a line parallel to and 40 yards off the beach. Here occurred the only confusion in the entire operation. Strong currents swirling through the roadstead made it impossible for oarsmen to hold loaded boats at the line of departure. This was straightened out by *Princeton's* ordering them to make fast to her in two long lines. At 5:30 the General added the fourth flag to his signal hoist, meaning: Land! All hands sent up a cheer, the close-fire-support ships began shooting, and in swept the boats toward the beach, to land on a 400-yard front. A few minutes later Worth's division of regulars, constituting the first wave, touched down and the General leaped out of the first boat. His troops splashed ashore, rushed up the sand dunes and planted a flag, upon seeing which the bands on a dozen ships struck up "The Star-Spangled Banner." Every surfboat retracted to load and land Patterson's division of volunteers; then a second time to bring ashore Twiggs's regulars. There was little confusion and no opposi-

tion. By the time eight bells marked the beginning of 10 March, between
8600 and 10,000 men of Scott's army were ashore, without expending a life
or a boat. When we think of the foul-ups of even unopposed amphibious
operations in World War II, this at Collado Beach near Veracruz stands
out as a really brilliant achievement of General Scott and Commodore
Conner.

The General now set up headquarters ashore, more troops and supplies
landed, and the army began making dispositions to encircle Veracruz.
Trenches were dug in preparation for a siege, although siege guns were in
short supply. The ship-to-shore movement continued around the clock.
General Scott wrote home on 17 March, "Everything of course must be
landed in surf-boats, and from an average distance of more than a mile, on
the open beach of the sea. Commodore Conner's squadron is indefatigable
in assisting us." As soon as one ship was emptied of men and supplies, she
returned to Antón Lizardo where another stood by to take her place in
the narrow anchorage. Requirements of troops in those days were simple
— rations, ammunition, tents and sutlers' supplies. Hence there was not
much to get lost or mislaid, and there were no such humorous incidents as
occurred in World War II — ping-pong tables and plastic toilet seats coming ashore before the ammunition! From all accounts, no man ashore went
hungry or thirsty within reach of the fleet, although he sometimes had to
breakfast on cold salt pork and hardtack. Collado Beach began to look like
a small town. Boat crews managed to pick up meals at the army camp, and
some even picked up mounts. One sailor passed army headquarters riding
on the rear end of a donkey. "Hey, Jack, move up amidships!" shouted
one of the officers outside the tent. "Gentlemen," said the sailor, drawing
rein, "this is the first craft I ever commanded, and I shall take charge of
the quarterdeck as long as there is a timber head left!"

Change of Command

Dispositions were already made for a joint army-navy bombardment of
the city when the axe fell for Commodore Conner. On the afternoon of 20
March U.S.S. *Mississippi* arrived off Sacrificios, bearing Vice Commodore
Perry with orders to take over command of the Gulf Squadron immediately.

What had happened to deprive Conner of the fruits of victory?

Mississippi, sent home to have her boilers overhauled, arrived Norfolk
in mid-January 1847. The navy yard reported that it would take six weeks
to make the necessary repairs. That did not suit Perry. He hastened to
Washington, found Engineer-in-Chief Charles H. Haswell who had been
his chief engineer for the old *Fulton*, and persuaded him to come to Norfolk and make a fresh survey. Haswell promised, by working the yard

crew day and night, to finish necessary repairs in two weeks; but the navy yard took six weeks just the same. Perry was not idle during this period. The Secretary ordered him to supervise fitting out several small vessels designated to reinforce the Gulf Squadron — steamers *Scourge* and *Scorpion*, brig *Decatur*, storeship *Electra*, and four bomb brigs named after volcanoes: *Vesuvius, Hecla, Etna* and *Stromboli*. These were converted 80-foot coastal schooners, each armed with a single pivoted 10-inch shell gun between the masts. None reached Mexico in time to fire on Veracruz, but all proved useful later, especially *Vesuvius*, because her executive officer was Lieutenant Henry Walke the artist.

Perry's duty gave him an opportunity to visit his family in Tarrytown, but not for long. He returned to Washington at Secretary Mason's orders to report to him orally. What transpired we shall probably never know, since neither man talked about it; but certain officers who knew nothing about it asserted that Perry "intrigued" to wrest the command from Conner. Perry, as we have seen, had been offered the command, unsolicited, as early as September 1845 and ordered to relieve Conner when the Commodore was ready; but Conner never had been ready. The Vice Commodore would have been less than honest had he not reported to the Secretary several instances of Conner's indecision and the opinion of many senior officers in the Gulf Squadron that his health might break down at any moment. But he also reported that Conner's complaints on the quality and quantity of the squadron's logistic support were justified. Perry must have had some frank talks on that subject with the Secretary and with his old friend Commodore Morris, chief of the bureau of construction. For there was an immediate improvement in logistic support, the department even anticipating some of Perry's requests instead of mulling them over for weeks before doing anything. A few months later, the Commodore returned a loaded collier from Veracruz to Pensacola, having more coal on hand than his steamers could burn.

One thing Perry did not sell to Secretary Mason was a plan to win the war. He proposed to let the navy do it by occupying every Mexican seaport, maintaining a tight blockade, and collecting duties; American troops would be withdrawn from the rest of the country, excepting Upper California. He predicted that blockade alone would force Mexico to make peace. This made little sense; Mexico could have lived off her own fat for years. Naval blockades are important strategical weapons, but they must be followed up by military strikes at the enemy's heart, to be really effective. It is, however, a common delusion of naval strategists that blockades alone can win wars.

Perry had two interviews with President Polk on 26 March before leaving Washington, one alone and the other with Secretary Mason present. What would we not give to know what was said! But closemouthed Polk and closemouthed Perry let nothing out. The President, as we know from his diary, was anxious because the two commanding generals, Taylor and Scott, both Whigs, were making unmistakable noises of becoming presidential candidates. Moreover, Commodore Robert F. Stockton of the Pacific Ocean Squadron, who had campaigned for Harrison and Tyler, was winning fresh laurels in California with exploits calculated to make him a popular hero. Polk felt more easy to have a hard-hitting Jackson Democrat with no political ambitions in command of the Gulf Squadron.

Whatever may have been thought or said, both President and Secretary had decided before interviewing Perry[1] that it was high time for Conner to go. The public demanded action from the navy and was not likely to get it from him. The only thing he had accomplished, so far as they then knew, was the unopposed capture of Tampico. Conner himself, having overstayed the three-year limit for wearing the blue pendant, knew that his health could not hold out much longer; on 2 March, the day before orders for his relief were issued in Washington, he wrote to his wife, "As I told you in my last letter . . . it was my intention to apply at once to be relieved. . . . I have just got over the longest and most severe fit of the *tic* that I have ever had . . . the anxiety and vexation that I suffer here is intolerable." But the Secretary's orders of 3 March 1847, which Perry brought south to Conner, were rather brutally worded: "The uncertain duration of the war with Mexico, has induced the President to direct me no longer to suspend the rule which limits the terms of command in our squadrons, in its application to your command of the Home Squadron." Upon Perry's reporting, "You will transfer to him the command of the Naval forces of the United States in the Gulf of Mexico, composing the Home Squadron, transfer your pendant to the Steamer *Princeton*, and proceed in her to the port of Philadelphia."

Whilst this change of command was generally welcomed in the squadron, it was bitterly resented by some of Conner's particular friends, coming as it did on the eve of victory at Veracruz. But the charge of Perry's "intriguing" to obtain the blue pendant is ridiculous in view of the fact that it had been promised to him by Secretary Bancroft in September 1845, that he had been in Mexican waters, under orders to relieve Conner whenever the Commodore was ready, since September 1846, and that Conner's three-year term expired in November. During that long interval Perry's attitude toward Conner had been loyal and correct.

On 6 March, the day before sailing from Norfolk, Perry addressed the following tender little epistle to his eleven-year-old daughter Isabella, who

---

[1] Perry states in a letter of 25 February 1847 to John Hone that he had already been told to relieve Conner upon arrival at Veracruz; and the President, recording his interviews on the 26th, described Perry as one "who has been ordered to relieve Commodore Conner."

was staying with her Aunt Kate (Mrs. Alexander Slidell Mackenzie) at
Rockwood in Tarrytown.

> U.S.S. *Mississippi* Norfolk
> March 6th, 1847

My Dear child

I was very much pleased by the receipt of your letter with the guard chain
which I shall wear in all my expeditions in the Gulf, not that I shall require it
to remind [me] of my darling who is always in my thoughts, but it will be preserved as a precious gift from one for whom I cherish the most abiding love.
and I hope my child that whenever you look at the ring I sent you by your
uncle you will offer up your silent prayers for the preservation of your devoted
& affectionate

> FATHER

If Bella was moved to tears by this sentiment, she probably felt differently when she turned the page and read the P.S.: —

I hope, my dear child, you will apply yourself industriously to your studies.
I am sure, you duly appreciate and are deeply grateful for the kind attention
of your Aunt Kate to your improvement, in a little time you will be grown,
when you will experience the want of a proper education.

After assuming command of the Gulf Squadron, Perry used the same
title that Conner did: Commander-in-Chief of United States Naval Forces
in the Gulf of Mexico.

CHAPTER XVI

Commodore Perry of the Gulf Squadron
1847–1848

Capture of Veracruz

T HE twenty-first day of March was busy and eventful for Perry and his
flagship. At 8. A.M. Commodore Conner, who had been informed of
his relief the previous afternoon, made this signal to the fleet:

COMMODORE PERRY COMMANDS THE SQUADRON.

A heavy norther was making up. No sooner had Perry taken command
than word reached him that S.S. *Hunter*, together with a French blockade
runner that she had captured, and a pilot schooner, had gone ashore on Isla
Verde (Green Island) a few miles offshore from Sacrificios. The shipwrecked vessels had some sixty people on board, including a mother and
child. Perry got up steam, slipped his cables and bore out in the teeth of
the norther to assist these vessels in distress. Captain Isaac Mayo, four
officers and a number of seamen volunteered to man *Mississippi's* barge to
effect the rescue, and by making several trips through rough water they
managed to bring all sixty people safely on board the flagship. This is the
spirited scene depicted by the artist officer, Lieutenant Walke.

Having steamed back to the Sacrificios anchorage, Perry and Commodore Conner conferred with General Scott about army-navy coöperation.
Perry succeeded in selling to the General a project already promoted unsuccessfully by Conner — to land navy guns to strengthen the army's
siege train. He insisted that these pieces be served by sailors, not soldiers.
This was not interservice rivalry but common sense; Perry had experimented with the new Paixhans type of naval ordnance at Staten Island,
and had officers and men who knew how to handle it without being more
of a menace to themselves than to the enemy. The same, to a less degree,
was true of the old-fashioned naval guns that threw cannonballs. General
Scott saw the point, and gave his consent.

Having settled this important question, the new Commodore, when
wind and sea abated toward evening, staged a scene typical of his sense of

theater. Manning *Mississippi's* barge with her smartest sailors, and wearing the blue pendant on a jackstaff, Perry in full-dress uniform (blue frock coat, sword, yards of gold lace, two heavy gilt epaulettes and fore-'n'-aft hat) took his stand in the stern sheets and had himself rowed under the stern of every ship in the roadstead, announcing through a speaking trumpet that he had taken over and that the Squadron was to land guns and crews promptly to help the army invest Veracruz. John H. Upshur, a junior officer, later recalled: —

> Cheer after cheer was sent up in evidence of the enthusiasm this promise of a release from a life of inaction we had been leading under Perry's predecessor inspired in every breast. In a moment everything was stir and bustle, and in an incredibly short space of time, each vessel had landed her big gun, with double crews of officers and men. . . . Perry announced that those who did not behave themselves should not be allowed another chance to fight the enemy which proved a guarantee of good conduct in all. . . . Under the energetic chief who succeeded to the command of a squadron dying of supineness, until his magic word revived it, the navy of the United States sustained its old prestige.

A similar feeling, this writer remembers, animated the South Pacific Force in 1942 when Admiral Halsey took over that command. Conner belonged to the age of sail that was passing; Perry was the embodiment of the new age of steam power and shell guns, which forced the navy to wrap itself in iron and steel to survive. He, like Halsey, showed firm decision and vigorous action.

Landing and siting naval ordnance occupied the new commodore for several days. Each gun had to be lowered very gingerly into a ship's launch, laid athwart-ship, manhandled ashore and slung under the axle of a two-wheel truck brought in by the army. Every piece then had to be dragged by as many as two hundred soldiers and sailors to the chosen emplacement for bombarding Veracruz, through loose sand and a shallow lagoon. But there were plenty of volunteers for this onerous duty. Sailors of the fleet, bored with the blockade, fell over themselves to serve ashore, and Perry gave as many as possible a chance by assigning to the guns double crews, which relieved each other every 24 hours.

The siege of Veracruz began in earnest on 22 March when the American batteries opened fire. It was only a question of time how long the city could hold out. Santa Anna, instead of concentrating his forces there to contain the American invasion until the rainy and sickly season set in, ordered troops away to the north; and when General Don Juan Morales, the local captain general, sent a messenger to Mexico City to request help, he was told "not a man or a peso" would he get. General Scott, before opening the bombardment, offered to postpone it until Morales could

U.S.S. *Mississippi* Rescuing Crews of French Barque and American Pilot
Boat off Veracruz 21 March 1847, by Lieutenant Walke

Attack of U. S. Gunboats on Veracruz and San Juan d'Ulúa, 22-25 March
1847, by J. M. Ladd, USN; left to right: *Falcon, Reefer, Vixen, Petrel,
Boneta, Spitfire, Tampico*

evacuate civilians, but the Mexican proudly refused.[1] And he so neglected to provision the city for a siege that after two days of bombardment the flour, bread and meat were exhausted. Nevertheless, he commanded a formidable garrison of 1,030 officers and men in the castle and 3,360 in the city, on whose walls numerous pieces of artillery were mounted. And the castle had some new Paixhans guns.

Perry ordered the "two Pollies" and five schooner-gunboats to open the assault by bombarding Veracruz. Although Captain Josiah Tattnall disliked Perry and did not mind showing it, the Commodore gave him this chance for distinction, which he gladly embraced. Tattnall asked for specific directions as to what point he should attack, to which Perry replied, "Where you can do the most execution, sir!" Tattnall, who asked for nothing better, anchored his "mosquito division" off Point Hornos about a mile from the city walls at 5:45 P.M. March 22 and began shooting at the plaza and the market gate. San Juan de Ulúa answered after a fashion for an hour and a half, but made not a single hit; and the cannonballs hurled by Tattnall's small ordnance were hardly more effective. This operation was repeated early next day, the 23rd. The Mexican gunners now got the range, and their near-misses beat up so many splashes around the little ships that Commodore Perry, anxious for their safety, signaled them to retire. Tattnall, with a Nelson touch, failed to see the signal and banged away for another hour, still invulnerable. Perry finally sent Captain Mayo in a boat to give a positive order to retire, and Tattnall's division returned to the anchorage without losing a man wounded or killed. It was greeted with cheers by troops ashore and from the French, Spanish and British warships who were watching with keen interest. The Mexican gunners excused themselves for bad marksmanship on the ground that the Yankees thrust in so close that cannon could not be sufficiently depressed to hit them! Perry, though provoked by Tattnall's insubordination and by the need to send Mayo's boat crew through enemy gunfire to reach him, generously "directed the commanders of all vessels engaged to express to the crews his sense of their gallantry," as Tattnall himself acknowledged. "All expected to see us sunk, and that we escaped without a loss is a miracle. . . . All four generals complimented me."

By this time Scott had some 13,000 men ashore, enough to invest the city completely on the land side and cut off sources of supply. Another norther on the 23rd prevented further landing of ammunition; but on the 24th the naval battery of three 68-pound 8-inch shell guns and three long 32-pounders went into action for the first time. This changed the bom-

---

[1] Later, when things got hot and civilians were being killed, Morales asked for an armistice to remove civilians; this Scott properly refused, pointing out that if Morales wished to spare lives he should surrender the city.

bardment from a somewhat ineffective throwing of solid cannonballs into smashing shellfire which opened breaches in the walls of Veracruz.

The Mexicans promptly opened fire from one of the forts in Veracruz, and the naval battery replied. Lieutenant Walke's painting which we reproduce well depicts the scene. Some well-known names are in the caption. Commander Mackenzie of *Somers* fame, now ordnance officer of frigate *Potomac*, served that ship's 32-pounders, with Lieutenant James S. Biddle second in command. Lieutenant Charles Kennedy commanded *St. Mary's* 68-pounder, a Paixhans. Lieutenant Oliver Hazard Perry Jr., son of the hero of Lake Erie, commanded a similar gun from sloop *Albany*, and Lieutenant Sidney Smith Lee, elder brother of Robert E. Lee, operated another shell gun from *Mississippi*. Lieutenant Raphael Semmes, having lost the *Somers*, played second to Lieutenant Harry Ingersoll with a 32-pounder from frigate *Raritan*. The smaller cannon, firing solid shot at a range of 700 yards, knocked breaches in the city walls, and the shells exploded on barracks and casemates. Mexican counter-battery fire and "bombs bursting in air" killed four sailors and wounded six, including the young gentleman whose horse is seen rearing in the foreground of the painting. The naval battery ceased fire at 2:30 P.M. when its ammunition was expended, but the army artillery continued to pour out shot during the night of 24-25 March.

Next morning at 8, says our anonymous eyewitness, "the gallant Perry and his brave associates, having finished the mounting of their guns, . . . opened with a tremendous roar the Naval Battery upon the west side of the city, and were immediately answered from four distinct batteries of the enemy." Mexican counter-battery fire this day became more effective. At 2:30 P.M. when the Mexican guns fell silent, Captain Mayo ordered his men to stand on the parapet and give three cheers. The Captain then mounted a horse and galloped off to report to Commodore Perry, who had established a temporary command post on the beach. En route he encountered General Scott at army headquarters, predicted that the enemy would never fire another shot, and was so warmly embraced by the General as to keep his seat with difficulty. Scott thanked him in the name of the army for the day's work and gave him a spot promotion to the rank of Commodore, which the navy unkindly did not confirm. Mayo galloped on to report to Perry, whose report of the bombardment, as usual, gave high praise to all participants.

On 25 March Scott decided that if no white flag were displayed at Veracruz he would storm the city next day. He and Perry agreed that one of the three assault columns directed against the sea wall of the city be composed of sailors and marines. Scaling ladders were fashioned from the studdingsail booms of *Mississippi;* and Perry, spoiling for a real fight, proposed to lead this assault in person. But the Mexicans thwarted him. A flag of truce came forward at 5 P.M. and General Scott sent officers back with it to the city to negotiate surrender. Although provisions were exhausted and the city council begged for a capitulation to save civilian lives, General Morales lacked the moral courage to decide. He allowed his second in command, General Don José Juan Landero, to take the responsibility. Generals Worth and Pillow and Captain Aulick negotiated for the United States, three colonels for Mexico, and Commander Mackenzie, fluent in Spanish, acted as interpreter.

The armistice initiated by these surrender negotiations proved to be timely. That very night there blew up a norther, the worst in Perry's experience, raising the devil in the anchorage. *Mississippi* parted one of her cables, and more than twenty of the schooners, storeships and small craft dragged ashore and became a total loss. General Scott ordered a cease fire at 8 A.M. 26 March as the norther was almost burying his shore batteries in sand. During two days the naval battery had fired a thousand shells and eight hundred round shot, almost half of the total from all North American cannon. On the afternoon of 27 March, from "Head Qrs. of the Army, Camp Washington, before Vera Cruz," General Scott wrote a four-page letter to Commodore Perry in his own hand, saying that consuls and neutrals could, if they wished, take refuge on board their ships of war as the consuls had begged to do; but the plan made no sense as Veracruz "will have surrendered before ten o'clock tonight." He apologized for not including Perry among the negotiators, on the ground that the Mexican proposal to treat reached him when the norther made it impossible to send word. The articles of capitulation were signed at Point Hornos on 27 March. Greatly to the surprise of the Americans, General Landero surrendered not only the city but San Juan de Ulúa, which had been expected to hold out for weeks or months. The terms agreed upon appealed to Mexican sense of honor: officers allowed to keep their side-arms, horses and all personal property; garrison to march out with colors flying and after stacking arms to be released on parole.

On 29 March occurred the ceremony of surrender. First the castle and then the city fired a salute of 21 guns and struck their Mexican flags; the Stars and Stripes were hoisted over both strongholds and duly saluted, the Mexican garrison marched out and Americans marched in. "With infinite satisfaction," wrote Perry to Secretary Mason that morning, "I announce to you that the city of Vera Cruz and the Castle of San Juan de Ulloa were this day occupied by garrisons of the United States troops." And at 1 P.M. the same day: "I write this from within the castle. The batteries in the city are now saluting the American flags already hoisted on the forts of the city." The Commodore issued a general order to all his ships, declaring, "Never at any period of our naval history has the true spirit of professional gallantry been more strongly exhibited than at the present time."

Perry was right. The alleged Gibraltar of America had been captured at the cost of only 14 officers and men killed and 59 wounded. Mexican casualties were reported by the senior British naval commander present to have been 80 soldiers killed and wounded, and one hundred noncombatants killed. The city itself was a mess; streets filled with rubble and corpses lying about, but the army soon cleaned it up, fed the populace, and restored normal traffic with the interior.

General Scott promptly recognized the naval contribution to this astounding result. In his general order of 30 March he thanked "the entire Home Squadron, under the successive orders of Commodores Conner and Perry, for prompt, cheerful and able assistance from the arrival of the army off this coast."

Immediately after the fall of Veracruz, General Scott began his brilliant march on Mexico City with many fewer troops than he had asked for, too many political appointees among the officers, and so long a supply line that he was often forced to live off the country and fight with captured ammunition. After winning the Battle of Cerro Gordo, he advanced to Pueblo and there remained for three months to receive replacements. Resuming his march, Scott reached the continental divide on 10 August. He then consented to an armistice while peace commissioner Nicholas Trist negotiated with Santa Anna without success. In September Scott again took the offensive and, after some tough fighting, entered Mexico City in triumph on the 17th. Santa Anna abdicated and months elapsed before Trist and Scott could find any Mexican government willing to negotiate, but the peace treaty was finally signed on 2 February 1848.

Greatly to Perry's grief, all marines in the Gulf Squadron, now numbering around two hundred effectives, were ordered by Secretary Mason to join Scott's army, which already had assigned to it a fresh marine battalion from New York. Perry protested, arguing that he could not garrison captured seaports without marines, since bluejackets were notoriously unfit for such duty. General Scott referred him to General Franklin Pierce, to whose brigade the squadron marines were to be attached. The future President of the United States saw the point, and accepted from the Commodore a token force of one officer and 28 men from the squadron. On 16 July, the newly arrived marine battalion began to march inland to be incorporated with General John A. Quitman's 4th Division. The leathernecks' fighting qualities offset the ill-trained and undisciplined volunteers, and well they earned the opportunity to put "The Halls of Montezuma" into their famous hymn.

"Old Bruin," who now anchored his flagship in the harbor of Veracruz when not scouring the coast, remained on excellent terms with army commanders throughout this war. When Alexander Perry Rodgers, son of his sister Anna, was killed in the campaign against Mexico City, General Worth wrote to the Commodore on Christmas Eve 1847, "Your nephew had given appearance of future distinction and fell in a manner worthy of his blood." Perry, controlling sea communications at Veracruz, took pride in sending war news to Washington, and some of his reports of Scott's victories, the first to reach the United States, were printed by Congress. There was a slight unpleasantness when a drunken sailor was picked up by military police and punished by a military commission; but on receiving Perry's protest, General Twiggs, army commander at Veracruz, agreed that in future any misbehaving sailors would be sent on board a United States ship to be dealt with there.

Veracruz was by far the most important Gulf Coast conquest in which the navy took part. It was the second city in Mexico for wealth and numbers, and here began the lifeline to General Scott on his march to the capital. Unfortunately it was very unhealthy and a summer epidemic of *vómito negro* and malaria was taken for granted.

Alvarado and Tuxpan

Since Perry knew even before the fall of Veracruz that his squadron would get no more marines and might even lose those already on board, he began in March 1847 to organize the first infantry brigade in the history of our navy. This provided a landing force for future upriver expeditions. Sailors were glad to become "doughboys" — the nickname for infantry that originated in this war — so long as they were drilled by their own officers and usually slept and ate on board ship. So many volunteers came forth that at one time the Commodore had over two thousand men and ten brass cannon organized and drilling daily on ships' decks or on the beach. In the Tuxpan operation they received their baptism of fire.

After the fall of Veracruz Perry commanded, in Secretary Mason's words, "the largest squadron ever assembled under the American flag." It comprised ship-of-the-line *Ohio*, frigates *Raritan* and *Potomac*, sloops *John Adams*, *Albany*, *Germantown* and *Saratoga*, three brigs, steam frigate *Mississippi*, five small steamers, seven gunboat-schooners — most of them Perry's converted prizes — and the four volcanic bomb brigs. His first duty was to continue and tighten the blockade. But he also attempted an odd naval mission — to round up horses for the army, which was very short of mounts. General Scott ordered General Quitman to march south on the hitherto invincible Alvarado, principal market town for horse kind and beef cattle south of Veracruz, and expected Perry to help.

Naval coöperation in this enterprise, for reasons beyond the Commodore's control, was frustrated by the excessive zeal of Lieutenant Charles

G. Hunter. He commanded U.S.S. *Scourge*, a converted iron screw steamer formerly on the Boston-Bangor run, which the navy had purchased and armed with a single gun. Perry sent her ahead to blockade Alvarado until his own task force and the army column arrived. Lieutenant Hunter, instead of obeying orders, crossed the bar, and after firing a few shots at one of the forts which were not returned, received the surrender of Alvarado. He then steamed up the Papaloapan River and obtained the surrender of Tlacotalpan. A glorious day for Hunter, this last of March; but the next proved to be April Fool's day for the Commodore. After *Mississippi* and twelve other ships had crossed the bar, Perry heard that the town had already surrendered to Hunter and was garrisoned by a midshipman and two men! This could have been laughed off; and, to do him justice, General Quitman did laugh heartily when the midshipman gravely presented him with the town of Alvarado. But Hunter's jumping the gun frustrated the main object of the expedition. He warned the Mexicans in time for them to drive away their herds of horses, and also to burn several small craft of the Mexican Navy lying in the river. When *Scourge* reappeared from Tlacotalpan and Hunter arrogantly took his time reporting to the Commodore, "Old Bruin" emitted one of his loudest roars, and for disobedience and contempt of a superior officer had Hunter arrested and court-martialed. The Lieutenant's defense was that, having crossed the bar merely to take a crack at the fort, a boat bearing a white flag came out and offered to surrender the town. What else should he have done but accept? That, however, did not excuse his steaming upstream, firing on everything that moved and stampeding the cattle. The court found him guilty and sentenced him to be relieved of his command, dismissed from the Gulf Squadron and sent home.

Most officers in the Squadron thought that "Old Bruin" had been rather stuffy and the court too severe, but Perry wrote home that Hunter's conduct had been "perfectly ridiculous and vainglorious," involving no risk whatever to him and his ship. In any case, the Gulf Squadron was well rid of Hunter. In New York his cause was taken up by opposition journals. In their view, Alvarado became a "second Gibraltar" taken by a hero in an old Boston-Bangor steamboat. The Lieutenant was tendered banquets, presented with swords of honor, escorted to his home in Trenton, New Jersey, by a regiment of militia. Nicknamed Alvarado Hunter, the young officer had a beautiful time being wined and dined as a martyred hero. The poor fellow became utterly spoiled. President Polk, to Perry's indignation, quashed the court-martial sentence and gave Hunter another command, during which he got into financial difficulties. From these he was rescued by admirers; but on his third and last command, of U.S.S. *Bainbridge*, he disobeyed his commodore's orders because he did not approve them, sailed directly home, and issued an address to the public justifying his action. That was too much. President Pierce dismissed him from the navy.

One thing never explained is why Alvarado, which had twice driven off Commodore Conner, fell such easy prey to Lieutenant Hunter and his tiny boat. Probably Santa Anna had withdrawn to his own army most of the garrison which had defied the Americans, and had left the town dispirited. But some Mexican soldiers must have been there, since Perry reported that "the enemy, before evacuating the place," burned all public vessels and spiked or concealed most of the guns; his men found no fewer than 60 pieces on several forts which looked formidable.

Leaving Captain Mayo to garrison Alvarado and round up for the army any horses which had not been removed, Perry led his task force back to the Antón Lizardo roadstead. Secretary Mason now gave him a new duty, to collect customs duties in the seized ports, "in relief of our own treasury." Perry himself had suggested this during his visit to Washington. This feature of the blockade gave it a different character from the Union blockade of our Civil War, or the Allied blockades of the twentieth century, which endeavored to strangle the enemy's economy. The American blockade of Mexico not only permitted normal fishing and coastal traffic under the Mexican flag, but a great deal of neutral traffic as well. About half a million dollars in duties was collected by the United States at Mexican ports on both coasts during the war. This was not much in comparison with the cost of the conflict (variously estimated at $100 million to $186 million); but it is evident from advertisements in the Veracruz newspaper under American occupation that the inhabitants were procuring provisions and consumer goods from abroad and exporting their own products freely.

By 10 April 1847 every important Mexican town on or near the Gulf was under American control except Tuxpan, halfway between Tampico and Veracruz. Thither Perry now directed his attention. He considered this expedition "a point of honor," since the Mexicans had fortified Tuxpan with guns from U.S.S. *Truxtun*. That man-o'-war brig was lost because her commanding officer naïvely employed the master of a Mexican schooner which he had captured, to pilot him along the coast. The Mexican managed to run her on a shoal near the mouth of the Tuxpan river, and her crew had to surrender. The gallant enemy gave the captured officers a ball, but salvaged the guns.

Tuxpan looked to be a tough place to capture. The town lies eight miles up the likenamed river, whose average width was about 300 yards, and was protected not only by the usual bar but by prepared defenses within two miles of the town. There the river narrows to 150 yards, a 40-foot cliffy promontory juts out into the stream, commanding the approach with a formidable-looking battery called La Peña. Further upstream there was battery La Palmasola on the edge of the right bank, and another on the left bank under Hospital Hill, as this hill is still called. General Don Martín Perfecto de Cos, a brother-in-law of Santa Anna, commanded an ample garrison.

Perry decided that the defenses of Tuxpan required a joint attack by land and water. For the former he had 1489 officers and men, and four guns of his naval landing force from nine different ships of the Squadron; and for naval support, steamers *Spitfire*, *Vixen* and *Scourge*, three schooner-gunboats, and three bomb brigs. The expedition rendezvoused at Lobos Island roadstead and arrived off Tuxpan river on 17 April 1847. As there were only eight feet of water on the bar, and that only in one spot, a channel had to be buoyed, and Perry ordered the two bigger steamers to remove their masts to lessen their draft. That operation took their crews all night, but they worked with a will, supported by an extra ration of grog and the prospect of a good fight next day. Early in the morning of 18 April, the landing party, commanded by Captain Samuel L. Breese, boarded vessels designated for the dash upriver, filling some thirty barges to be towed. Perry anchored *Mississippi* off the bar in five fathom, transferred himself and a fieldpiece to *Spitfire* (Captain Tattnall), and led *Vixen*, *Scourge*, three schooners, and the laden barges across the bar and upstream.[1]

At 2:30 P.M. the flotilla came under fire by the battery on top of La Peña. Perry now ordered the steamers to cast off their tows, and the boats and sailing vessels to continue under sweep and sail. *Spitfire* pushed gallantly ahead under a dangerous head of steam, followed by the whole flotilla. "The enemy beginning now to use grape and canister," recalled Raphael Semmes, "the affair began to be a little serious." The surface of the river was whipped up by a shower of all kinds of missiles, but the boats only rowed the faster, as if in a regatta. Commander Franklin Buchanan with the landing detachment from *Germantown* won the race to the foot of La Peña; Commodore Perry ordered him through his speaking trumpet to "land and storm." Buchanan leaped ashore first and at the head of his foot sailors rushed the hill. "The Mexicans, dropping rammers and sponges, fled in every direction, and in a moment more a loud cheer, re-echoed by the rest of the fleet, . . . greeted the Stars and Stripes as they were planted on the crest of the Peña."

It was now 3 P.M. *Spitfire* received a volley of musketry from Mexican

---

[1] In 1847 the banks were low and marshy for the first five or six miles, but levees have been built and the land is now well cultivated. By building jetties at the mouth of the Rio Tuxpan the least depth over the bar has been increased to 17 feet. Tuxpan is now an export center for oranges, fish and oil, and a center for sport fishing.

Attack on Tuxpan, 19 April 1847, lithograph by Lieutenant Walke

La Peña, 1965

soldiers concealed in bushes on the water's edge, severely wounding Tatt-nall [1] and three other officers. The painting by Lieutenant Walke here reproduced depicts this scene. As usual he exaggerated heights, and for effect telescoped places some distance apart into one scene. La Peña and the green slope beyond (now site of a yacht club) are shown accurately enough, but Hospital Hill, a mile and a half upstream, invisible from La Peña since it is around a bend, is shown close and blown up to at least thrice its height. The town of Tuxpan is correctly placed, but the Puy-de-Dôme-like mountain behind does not exist. Buchanan's men have already raised the flag on La Peña. *Spitfire*, minus her masts but wearing the Com-modore's blue pendant on her port paddlewheel box, is in the lead and returning Mexican fire from the right-bank shore battery. *Vixen*, also un-masted, is standing by under La Peña; steamer *Scourge*, her sails brailed up, is in the right foreground and the three schooner-gunboats are under sail. Several barges are about to land men on the left bank to take a battery under Hospital Hill; the Commodore's son, 2nd Lieutenant William F. Perry usmc, was the first to leap ashore there. By 4 p.m. the Americans had secured all the outer defenses and were about to occupy the town, with a loss of only two killed and twelve wounded. The night passed qui-etly except for a mild uproar when the sailors discovered a stock of cham-pagne, sherry, Madeira wine and cigars which General de Cos had laid out at his quarters to celebrate an expected victory over *los gringos*.

"If the dispositions for defense were judicious," reported Perry, "the defense itself was feeble; though, had it been more obstinate, the results would have been the same, for I cannot exaggerate the intrepidity of our officers and men, or say too much of the spirit that animated them." He proceeded to render Tuxpan useless to the enemy by destroying the forts and carrying off the guns which had belonged to wrecked U.S.S. *Trux-tun*. After an occupation of only four days Perry evacuated on 22 April 1847, leaving Captain Breese with *Albany* and *Reefer* to watch the river mouth, and ordering Commander Buchanan to conduct a boat expedition upstream. Semmes, who accompanied Buchanan, wrote an idyllic descrip-tion of the lush foliage and superb scenery in this part of Veracruz prov-ince.

"Manifest Destiny"

Perry's second raid into Tabasco, in June 1847, is considered his finest exploit in the Mexican War. The two months which separated it from the Tuxpan expedition were, on the whole, frustrating. His small steamers were breaking down and badly in need of overhaul. On 12 May he took

---

[1] Perry sent Tattnall home a few days later, and in a letter to the Secretary of 1 May 1847 praised his "great energy, gallantry and skill."

possession of Coatzacoalcos because it was rumored that Santa Anna was about to embark thence for Cuba. The Mexican general had no such intention, but the unopposed occupation of that little port with the long name gave Perry an opportunity to promote what he regarded as America's destiny. On the 13th he sent a surveying party in *Scorpion* and *Vixen,* including Commander Mackenzie, to sound the Coatzacoalcos River. For the Isthmus of Tehuantepec, which this river almost bisects, had long been talked about as the site of an interocean ship canal; and Perry had become, emotionally, one of the Manifest Destiny group which wished to annex the isthmus, if not all Mexico and Central America. A second surveying group pushed twenty-four miles upstream to Minatitlán and returned with what Perry felt to be "valuable information." Most valuable of all was a map which Mackenzie obtained from a surveyor employed by a British company which was looking into this canal route. Perry forwarded it to Washington with the following letter to Secretary Mason, on 24 May: —

The persons engaged in surveying the route to the Pacific are employed by an English Company, but it has occurred to me that if a Canal is ever to be opened across the Continent of North America, it should be executed by the Government or people of the United States. Destiny has doubtless decided that the vast Continent of North America from Davis' Straits to the Isthmus of Darien shall in the course of time fall under the influence of the Laws and institutions of the United States, hence the impolicy of permitting any European Power or interest to obtain a footing within the prescribed Latitudes. With such a consideration in view I deemed it politic to take formal possession of the Coatzacoalcos as far up as I ascended, and to invite the submission of the populous Towns, mostly inhabited by Indians, which are situated near its headwaters. In a treaty of Peace with Mexico I presume the exclusive right of way across the Continent could be secured by stipulation, but whether my views may or may [not] be considered visionary and chimerical, the explorations which I propose to make as soon as other occupations shall permit, cannot but contribute to some useful end.

That was as far as Perry's grand design went. Lieutenant Matthew Fontaine Maury of the navy's bureau of charts and instruments reported on it discouragingly and Perry had to admit that his reconnaissance, showing a river depth of 12½ feet, was not very promising for a ship canal. He returned to the subject in October, urging the government to authorize a joint army-navy expedition to cross the Isthmus to the Pacific and set up a cordon of forts which would cut off Tabasco and Chiapas from Mexico. Secretary Mason thought well enough of this to send it to President Polk to read, but nothing came of it.

During the peace negotiations Commissioner Trist was unable to persuade the Mexican government to disavow the English concession and

President Polk set his face firmly against demanding annexation of territory in that quarter. He was more than willing to pluck the Mexican
eagle's tail feathers, but not his breast. After the conclusion of peace the
Mexican government granted the United States a right of transit over the
Isthmus of Tehuantepec, but the difficulties of building a canal there have
been insurmountable to this day. Coatzacoalcos remained a sleepy little
river port for another half century, then leaped into sudden prosperity
when an English company made it the Gulf terminus of a trans-isthmian
railway. The name of the town was then changed to the ambitious Puerto
México. But the railway company went bankrupt, owing to Panama Canal
competition, and Puerto México became Coatzacoalcos once more. In the
twentieth century, the discovery of extensive sulphur deposits on the
Isthmus has set the town booming again. It even has a Hotel Ritz — which
we do not recommend!

While Mackenzie and his colleagues were hopefully expecting to gaze
on the Pacific Ocean via the Coatzacoalcos river, Perry, around 20 May
1847, paid a quick visit to the Laguna de Terminos in *Mississippi* with three
other ships. Commodore Conner had been so favorably impressed by the
Yucatán ordinance of secession on 8 December 1846 that he ordered the
American garrison to withdraw from Carmen, but to maintain the blockade of the Laguna. Perry, very skeptical of Yucatán's neutrality, reoccupied Ciudad de Carmen and stiffened the blockade, much to the indignation of the Yucatecos; but he allowed them to export logwood.

CHAPTER XVII

Second Tabasco, Yellow Fever, and Guerrillas
1847–1848

Second Tabasco Expedition

Perry wrote to Secretary Mason on 24 May that he could see no good
reason for a second attack on Villahermosa, "as we have quiet possession of the mouth of the River, which, with the occupation of Laguna,
completely shuts the Tabascans from the sea." But within a fortnight he
decided otherwise. Supplies and reinforcements were reaching the main
Mexican armies through Villahermosa. *Raritan* and *Albany* were about to
go home for upkeep, weakening the blockade. And the Commodore admitted that he was "also influenced by a desire to give the officers and men
of these two Ships another opportunity of displaying their gallantry and
zeal." So he decided to take the risk of thrusting up the Grijalva immediately, at the height of the rainy and sickly season.

The Grijalva River and Villahermosa, on paper at least, were much better defended than at the time of the first attack in October 1846. Just
above Devil's Bend there was a new breastwork extending from the river's
edge to impenetrable chaparral and commanding a flock of underwater
obstructions calculated to hold up waterborne invaders. Although these
obstructions were simple pilings, they may be considered ancestors of the
"horned scullys" and other sinister gadgets that wrought such havoc
among landing forces in World War II. One mile further upstream was a
new Acachapan breastwork; a mile and a half further, another breastwork, La Independencia. One mile below Villahermosa several large-
caliber cannon pointed downriver from the parapet of new Fort Itúrbide,
and others of smaller caliber commanded the road from Acachapan. In
these defenses and the town itself were some 900 troops under the new
governor and captain general, Don Domingo Echagaray.

His bombastic predecessor Traconis was at least a brave and honest
man; but Don Domingo was both inept and corrupt. "Dominated by an
insatiable thirst for gold," writes Ghigliazza the historian of Tabasco,

"and set on accumulating it by the most reprobate means," he pocketed customs duties, the garrison's pay, local taxes, and even the funds of a military hospital. "Sad indeed was the situation of the soldier in Tabasco. Without clothes or shoes, almost naked, deprived of his pay, in a deadly climate and subject to the despotism and impudence of a *jefe* deprived of all virtue, he had no other hope but to beat the Americans again, and to support with honor the noble duties that his country imposed on him in this afflicting crisis."

Perry, well apprised of the new construction, planned this operation meticulously, using his entire naval brigade and all the ships he could spare from blockade duty. *Spitfire* even carried two new gadgets for amphibious warfare, electrically activated charges to blow the obstacles; and if that did not work, Captain G. W. Taylor's "patent India rubber camels" — inflatable rubber floats for lifting ships. *Mississippi* and the sailing frigates anchored outside the bar of the Grijalva, across which the attack force was towed in two divisions. First, in the early morning of 14 June 1847, steamers *Scourge*, *Scorpion*, *Spitfire* and *Vixen* towed two bomb brigs and two schooners up to Frontera, then returned to pick up the ships' boats and surfboats, crammed with men, and towed them across the bar. This is the subject of the spirited scene by Lieutenant Walke. Executive officer of bomb brig *Vesuvius* of the task force, Walke used an artist's license in depicting the scenes of this second Tabasco expedition, but his conception of the waves at the bar is not exaggerated. They became such a menace to ships entering this vital river artery that the Mexican government later dug a canal from bay to river, about three miles south of the bar. Some vessels still prefer crossing the bar to paying canal tolls, and a small freighter was waiting for a pilot there, off the lighthouse, when we visited the spot in 1965.

Returning to Walke's painting, *Scorpion* (Commander Tattnall), flying the blue pendant of Commodore Perry, who may be seen conning his temporary flagship from atop the port paddlewheel box, is followed by three steamers, each towing a string of boats whose passengers are obviously in for a lively tossing. The bar was passed without incident; nobody capsized or touched bottom. Perry filled his steamers' bunkers from the coal pocket at Frontera, took river pilots on board, and at 3:25 P.M. signaled the force to get under way. *Scorpion* passed hawsers to *Vesuvius* and schooner *Washington*; *Spitfire* towed *Stromboli* and *Boneta*; *Scourge* towed a schooner, and *Etna* trailed *Vixen*. Each had a string of boats. Every deck was thick with sailors; the 40 pulling boats carried 1050 men, and seven surfboats lifted each a brass field gun as well as Captain Taylor's "sub-marine apparatus" and "patent camels."

All night 14-15 June the squadron worked its way cautiously upstream, the decks occasionally swept by overhanging branches which knocked

Scorpion Leads Gulf Squadron across Grijalva Bar, 14 June 1847, by Walke; *Spitfire, Vixen* and *Scourge* follow, with 40 loaded barges in tow

The Devil's Bend in 1965, photograph by S. E. Morison

men overboard. At 3 A. M. June 15, two Indians encountered in a dugout canoe warned that Mexicans were posted on the banks to ambush the invaders. Sharpshooters were then stationed on the vessels' tops. The morning passed without an attack, but at 4:15 P.M. when the task force came abreast of a hamlet called Santa Teresa (since disappeared from the map), a heavy volley of musketry opened from the left bank. The Mexicans overshot and did little damage. Perry, feeling that he could ignore such inept marksmen, continued without taking the trouble to land a force to silence them. At a point just before entering Devil's Bend, *Scorpion* was met by a fusillade of musketry out of the chaparral, directed by Colonel Miguel Bruno, a famous fighter. Her upper works, including the awning from under which Perry directed operations, were riddled with bullets. She and *Washington* retaliated and soon silenced the Mexican infantry. During this exchange of fire the masthead lookout in *Vesuvius* sighted a cavalry troop about a hundred strong. The bomb brig then earned her keep by dropping a 10-inch shell which stampeded the horses. A lone Mexican avenged this insult by picking off one of the brig's sailors with a rifle shot.

By this time darkness was falling over the beautiful river and its lush banks. Perry decided to anchor for the night and deal with the underwater obstructions next day. The men slept on their arms behind hammock and nettings. They were not molested by the enemy during the night — but very much molested by mosquitoes.

At first light 16 June, a fair day with a light breeze, Perry moved up his ships to cover a landing and sent a boat to examine the underwater obstacles. Mexicans behind the breastwork called La Colmena, now impossible to locate, fired on the boat, severely wounding the lieutenant in charge and driving the boat away. Perry, doubting whether the obstacles could be removed in time for the ships to proceed upstream, decided to land his landing force and advance on Villahermosa by road. Commander Franklin Buchanan selected a bluff on the left bank of the river as a good place to go ashore dryshod. This bluff, adjoining a spot called by the Americans Seven Palms, by a curious coincidence seems to be identical with the Punta de Palmares where Cortés on 13 March 1519 landed Alonzo de Ávila with one hundred men to march on the town by land, while he and the boats proceeded by water. The very tactics that Perry followed![1]

While *Spitfire*, *Scourge* and *Boneta* swept the objective with grape, musketry and shellfire, a landing party of 89 officers and 1015 men, from eleven different ships, formed up. Commodore Perry, with Captain Mayo

---

[1] To Spaniards and Mexicans *palmares* meant royal palms; coconut trees were not called palms, so we have conjecturally chosen the place shown in our photograph, although the bluff is a mere bank not more than 8 feet high. No 20-foot bluff can now be found on the river.

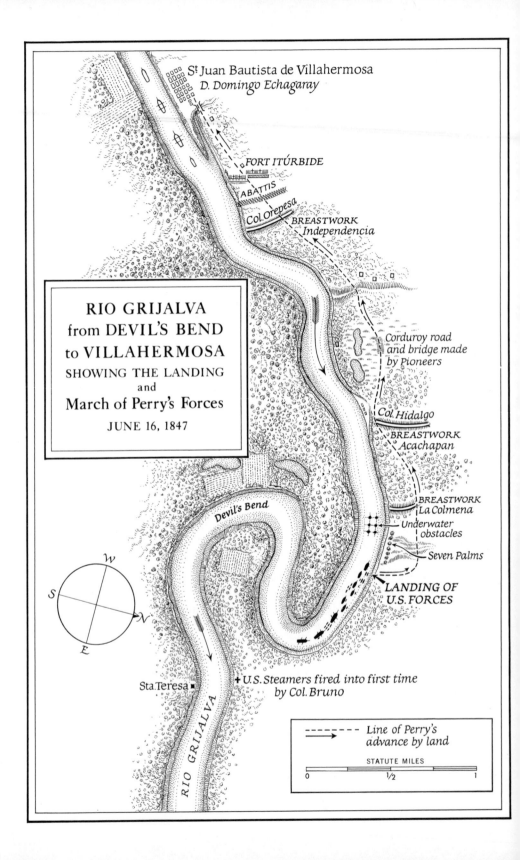

St Juan Bautista de Villahermosa
D. Domingo Echagaray

FORT ITÚRBIDE

ABATTIS

Col.Orepesa

BREASTWORK
Independencia

RIO GRIJALVA
from DEVIL'S BEND
to VILLAHERMOSA
SHOWING THE LANDING
and
March of Perry's Forces
JUNE 16, 1847

Corduroy road
and bridge made
by Pioneers

Col. Hidalgo

BREASTWORK
Acachapan

BREASTWORK
La Colmena

Underwater
obstacles

Seven Palms

Devil's Bend

LANDING OF
U.S. FORCES

W

S

N

E

Sta.Teresa

+U.S. Steamers fired into first time
by Col. Bruno

RIO GRIJALVA

- - - - - - - Line of Perry's
advance by land

STATUTE MILES

0   ½   1

as adjutant, boarded his barge, had himself rowed to the head of the line, and then gave the classic order for executing an amphibious operation: — "Land the Landing Force!" Perry leaped ashore first and ran up the slope at the head of his men, followed by an orderly carrying his command flag. When the squadron saw the blue pendant planted on top of the bluff and "Old Bruin" with drawn sword leading, sailors in the boats and on the vessels gave three loud cheers. Walke recorded this scene with substantial accuracy.

By 8 A.M. the whole naval brigade was ashore with seven fieldpieces, and before half an hour had elapsed the force of over 1100 men began marching along a rough road toward Villahermosa. Lieutenant Maynard's pioneer and scouting party, leading the column, had to fell trees to corduroy the road so that the wheeled pieces could pass. Next came the few marines whom the department had allowed Perry to keep, led by Captain Alvin Edson USMC. Behind them marched "Old Bruin" and staff; next came artillery under the ubiquitous Commander Mackenzie. The landing force's main body under Captains Breese and Forrest followed, and a field ambulance closed the rear. Perry, in his report, referred to the "universal enthusiasm" of his men afloat and ashore.

Since the landing party's route bypassed La Colmena, their first obstacle was Acachapan breastwork where Colonel Hidalgo commanded 300 infantry, about the same number of cavalry, and two guns. Mackenzie sited his artillery for preparatory fires, Mayo deployed the infantry, and Perry, with a sailor following him displaying the blue pendant, took his stand in advance of the troops, fully exposed to the enemy. A few rounds of grape caused the defenders of Acachapan to waver; Perry then ordered "Charge!" and as the Mexican soldiers beheld this muster of sailors rushing on them pell-mell, they forgot their "noble duties," abandoned the breastwork and fell back on Villahermosa.

It was now between 9:30 and 10 A.M. In the meantime, the ships anchored below the landing place had been very busy. Captain Taylor found it unnecessary to inflate his rubber camels. Anticipating the frogmen and demolition teams of World War II, he caused swimmers to place charges of dynamite at the bases of the wooden piles, connected them with electric batteries in the boats, and blew a channel. Lieutenant David D. Porter, future admiral of the Union river fleet, directed the bending of hawsers to the loosened logs and towed them clear. At 10 A.M. *Scorpion, Spitfire* and *Boneta* resumed their passage against the current, passing Acachapan after the landing party had taken it. The camels were used later to lift *Etna* and *Scourge* over a shoal spot on the river and to raise ships' bows or sterns far enough to effect underwater repairs without docking or careening.

Perry reformed the landing force under the shade of enormous ceiba trees, and resumed his advance. It went slowly, as the pioneers had to

Perry's Landing at Seven Palms on Grijalva River, 16 June 1847, by
Lieutenant Walke
"The Landing was effected in 5 minutes after the Commo. gave the order
(in the face of the enemy entrenched) by about 1000 American Seamen
and Marines, armed with muskets and 10 brass fieldpieces."

Seven Palms in 1965, photograph by S. E. Morison

build a corduroy bridge to cross a swamp; the guns, thoughtlessly landed without their limbers, had to be hauled by hand, and the gunners carried their own ammunition. The heat was excessive. "It was heartbreaking and backbreaking work, and many men succumbed," wrote Lieutenant Porter. In the meantime, the warships were fast thrusting ahead. At 10:32 they came under innocuous fire from battery La Independencia, then rounded a point into Fort Itúrbide's field of fire, suffering several hits and one man wounded. This fort has disappeared not only from the terrain but from the knowledge of today's Tabasqueños. Commander Abraham Bigelow, in temporary command of the flotilla, pressed on, passed the fort, and poured a deadly fire into it from the rear. Lieutenant Porter of *Spitfire* then landed at the head of 68 men, who had no trouble driving the enemy out of Fort Itúrbide. When the ships arrived abreast of the town, no Mexican flag was flying, Don Domingo having "abandoned the capital out of prudence," as he announced, and fallen back on the upriver village of Tamulté. There he pompously reviewed his ragged and hungry troops and promised to lead them back shortly and send the Americans reeling downstream. Villahermosa was surrendered by its prefect, the Stars and Stripes were raised on the roof of Don Domingo's official residence, and when Perry at the head of his landing force entered the town at 3:30 P.M. there was nothing to do but park artillery in the plaza and seek food and shelter. The ships provided the food, and shelter was offered by the public buildings just in time to escape a torrential rain. As the town fathers had decamped, along with most of the civilians, Perry appointed Commander Gershom J. Van Brunt temporary *alcalde.* Quietly passed the night of 16-17 June.

Perry had taken the last important Gulf port in Mexican hands, at the cost of only five men wounded. This well-organized and gallant exploit greatly enhanced his reputation, even though the resistance was miserably weak and ineffective. That is no reflection on the Mexicans; when an amphibious force is overwhelmingly superior to the defenders, the best thing they can do is to retire.

Franklin Buchanan, in a letter written 22 July 1847, said that Perry was perfectly fresh after his walk from the landing place. "He is at present certainly the man for the navy; in many respects he is an astonishing man, the most industrious, hard working, energetic, zealous, persevering, enterprising officer of his rank in our navy. He does not spare himself, or *any one* under him. This *I like;* his great powers of endurance astonish every one; all know he is by no means a brilliant man but his good common sense and judgment, his sociable manner to his officers, no *humbuggery or mystery,* make him respected and esteemed." David D. Porter, who as first lieutenant of *Vixen* commanded a detachment of the landing party at Tabasco, confirmed this verdict on Perry many years later: — "He had a

solid matter-of-fact way of doing things which pleased me mightily. . . .
Commodore Matthew C. Perry was one of the finest officers we ever had
in our navy — far superior to his brother Oliver."

The Commodore remained five days at Villahermosa, superintending
the salvage or destruction of munitions, and demolishing the fortifications.
Leaving a company of marines to garrison the town, and three small vessels to support them if necessary, he returned to flagship *Mississippi* off
the bar. Doubtful whether to hold Villahermosa or abandon it, as in the
previous raid, Perry asked the Navy Department for instructions. In the
meantime Mexican troops infiltrated the town every few nights to pick
off Americans; this was the kind of fighting they liked, and they were
good at it. Commander Bigelow of *Scorpion* decided to clean up on Echagaray's army at Tamulté, and dispersed it; but dispersing Mexicans was no
more effective than chasing hungry deer out of a vegetable garden. They
always drifted back, to take pot shots at the "gringos."

As late as 5 July Perry wrote to General Franklin Pierce, in command
at Veracruz, that he had determined to hold Villahermosa; that "it would
be madness . . . to evacuate the place at this moment, especially as Commander Bigelow has all the means to hold it and to drive the Enemy
back." But Bigelow had to attack Tamulté again on 16 July, and by that
time one-third of his garrison had contracted yellow fever. So, after visiting Frontera and consulting with Bigelow, Perry decided to evacuate
without waiting for instructions from home. On the 22nd the ships embarked the garrison and dropped down to Frontera, unopposed. And that
was the end of the Second Tabasco Expedition.

From on board *Mississippi* off Frontera, Perry issued a general order on
25 July thanking officers, seamen and marines of the attack force "for
their zeal and courage." They were disappointed, he wrote, that the Mexican troops, despite their "extensive and judicious arrangements" for defense, "did not stand more firmly to their arms." Perry was particularly
chagrined at having no opportunity to lead a real hand-to-hand fight as his
elder brother had done, and as every naval officer worth his salt hoped
some time to do. Generously, as usual, he named in his official report almost every officer who took part in Second Tabasco.

Various Contretemps

Perry now began sending some of his larger ships home and receiving
replacements. He was becoming dissatisfied with "paragon" *Mississippi* as
a flagship, because she had no commodore's cabin, only a small semi-ellip-
tical captain's cabin at the extreme stern. That was well enough for sleeping, but there was no place except the wardroom to conduct the paper
work incumbent on a squadron commander. And that paper work was

very extensive, for an officer with only one clerk, and all in longhand. Perry not only had to write to the Secretary every time an officer died — and that was every few days in the summer — but deal with logistics and all sorts of petty matters. For instance, the "aged mother" of one of his bandsmen, through her congressman's importunity, persuaded Secretary Mason to request he be sent home as "necessary for her support." Perry replied somewhat testily that he was "the only flute player in the band and his services cannot be dispensed with." The indispensable flautist, he continued, had $110 to his credit in the flag purser's books, which he could send home instead of squandering it on his next shore liberty; and he could make an allotment of pay to support his aged mother throughout the war.

Perry wrote that he had put up with the discomfort of *Mississippi* because of her speed and handiness, but he "earnestly requested" a frigate like *Cumberland*, with a poop cabin which would give him "the retirement and privacy of a separate apartment, as well as to keep myself aloof from the usual bustle of a large mess."

A fire broke out in *Mississippi's* coal bunkers early in July 1847. It was quenched "by good order and discipline," wrote Perry; but for fear it might flare up again, some 500 tons of coal were jettisoned. Shortly after this accident, fevers, both yellow and malaria, broke out in the flagship. "We have had much sickness in the Squadron," wrote Perry to his neighbor James Watson Webb on 16 August. This he believed to be "the consequence of great fatigue & exposure. Myself and youngest son have had the yellow fever, and the elder son the Intermittant, all of us are much prostrated, so much so in my case that I may be obliged to abandon my command. But I shall hold on somewhat longer, or as long as I can in the hope of Peace though at present I see very little prospect of it."

Perry thought the fevers were caused by rotten coal in the filthy bilges, which had not been cleaned in six years. An intense "putrescence" arose from the mixture of coal, cinders and salt water, and bad smells were still supposed to cause fever. The actual cause must have been the breeding of fever-carrying mosquitoes in the wet hold. And the flagship was not the only victim. Yellow fever spread throughout the squadron to such an extent as to cripple its operations; frigate *Potomac* alone had 150 to 200 cases. The surgeon of *Vixen* deserves good marks for closing all hatches and ports and filling her hold with live steam from the boilers, which ended the epidemic on that vessel. He thought that this had been effected by killing the rats and cockroaches, but of course it killed the mosquitoes too.

Altogether, this summer of 1847 proved to be a misery for the squadron. Engines of the small steamers broke down, the schooners and brigs had to slip into port in every blow, all were plagued by fever. After transferring some of the sickest men to the Salmedina Island hospital — 202 patients were there on 4 August — Perry shifted his blue pendant to frigate *Germantown* and sent *Mississippi* and *Decatur*, the two ships worst hit by the fevers, to Pensacola, to give their crews a fair chance of recovery. Together they had 170 cases, of which seven proved fatal.

By the end of September the fever began to abate.

Another nuisance broke out that summer — guerrilla attacks on the captured ports. In response to a cry for help from Alvarado, Perry sent the "two Pollies," sister *Scorpion*, and a bomb brig to steam up and down the Tlacotalpan River. That scared the "bandits" away — temporarily.

In the spring of 1847 sloop *Saratoga*, commanded by Captain David Glasgow Farragut, had relieved *Decatur* off Tuxpan, and soon had more fever cases on board than any. Farragut, a great sailor and the naval hero of the Civil War, had an irascible side. He had never served under Perry, disliked being subordinate to anybody, and now accused the Commodore of partiality in assigning him boring blockade duty from April to July, instead of including his ship in the Tabasco task force. Before the end of the summer he had an unfortunate run-in with Perry on another matter.

Royal Mail Steam Packet *Teviot* arrived Veracruz 12 August with mail and passengers, including General Paredes, an ex-president of Mexico who was planning a comeback. His inclusion in the passenger list was a violation of neutrality. *Saratoga* happened to be the biggest American ship then in harbor, but Captain Farragut neglected to search the steamer and for that oversight received a roar from "Old Bruin" when he learned that Paredes had got clean away. Farragut defended his inaction, first, on the ground that if anybody searched the ship it should have been the army, which ran the port of Veracruz; and that, anyway, his officers could never have identified Paredes, who was traveling under a false name and disguised by a beard. General Paredes accomplished nothing in Mexico, so his escape had no military consequences, but the Polk administration made an issue of *Teviot's* unneutral act, complained to the British government. Lord Palmerston the foreign minister actually apologized — which he seldom did to anyone — and ordered the steam packet's company to suspend its erring master from command. Perry now issued strict orders that every neutral or merchant ship entering a Mexican port must be visited and searched by a naval vessel. And no more suspicious characters got through the blockade.

Unfortunately this incident inspired a very unfair attack by Farragut on Perry. After an article had appeared in the New Orleans *Times* blaming Farragut, the peppery captain, scenting Slidell influence, blew up. To William Loyall (his father-in-law) in Norfolk he wrote on 16 December 1847: —

I know not what will be our next move, & as I have applied to be either ordered home in the ship or relieved, I do not care much how we are imployed during the next 3 months. I will do my duty to the best of my abilities & Perry may do his worst. Still I do not wish to be court martialed nor will I patiently submit to his injustice without complaining to the proper authority, as I am clearly of opinion that the more a man submits the more he will be oppressed. . . . Only to think of all the sacrifices & exertions I made, to get out here, to lead such a life as I have. But I hope all will yet come right.

While writing this letter, he continues: —

The Com° came past in a steamer, & ordered me on board, & after some minutes conversation he struck the wrong key, & I went off, & told him my mind honestly. He ordered me to silence: that I should not talk so to him & that if I had any complaints to make to do it in writing. Whereupon I left him & returned on board & sent him a letter to forward to the Honl. Sec'ty of the Navy, in which I speak the honest truth & ask to be relieved from Perry's command either by sending the ship home or relieving me from him. . . .

[Same letter] Dec. 15th. I have seen two or three persons who say the Comre. told them "he never had such a setting down" as I gave him, but declared "that he never had the intention to do me injustice." At least I have brought him to his senses. He has not answered my communications but before I sail I will ask him if he has forwarded my letter to the Honl. Secty. of the Navy.

Perry behaved with his customary dignity and forbearance. He made no official complaint of Farragut, overlooked his outrageous language to a superior officer, and forwarded his letter of complaint to the Secretary. In a covering letter Perry, after disclaiming prejudice against Farragut, whom he did not know and had hardly seen, pointed out that as commodore he was the sole authority over his squadron's distribution; that in his judgment the exigencies of blockade required newly arrived *Saratoga* to cover Tuxpan, thus releasing ships for Tabasco which had long been blockading. He added that off Tuxpan *Saratoga* was less exposed to yellow fever "than any vessel of the squadron," but tactfully refrained from mentioning that she acquired more cases than any.

Flagship *Germantown* now anchored under the castle of San Juan de Ulúa, but the Commodore, for the first and only time during the war, established temporary headquarters ashore, in a house belonging to the Veracruz Navy Yard. That gave him more quiet than living on board a ship, with its noise and bustle night and day, exchanging gun salutes with every armed vessel that entered or departed. For a few weeks Perry enjoyed the acme of an old-time sailor's happiness — "in all night and beans for breakfast!"

Despite these alarums and excursions, the events of 1847 reflected glory on the United States Navy. Secretary Mason, who had been almost apologetic for the Gulf Squadron's performance the previous year, proudly reported in December: —

Alvarado, Tuspan, Laguna, Fronteira, the mouth of the Goatzacoalcos, and the city of Tobasco, eighty miles in the interior, the capital of one of the richest and most fertile of the Mexican states, were successively captured and occupied by our naval forces. In many of the operations which led to these results, the service was arduous, the exposure to unhealthy influences, great, and the localities gave to the enemy decided advantages of successful resistance; yet, with an indomitable courage and fortitude, the officers and men met and overcame all difficulties, and still hold these important points except the city of Tabasco, which was voluntarily evacuated, because of its extreme insalubrity. Blessed with vigorous health and a robust constitution, the Commodore, has, in person, encountered the hardships and exposure to which those under his command have been subjected.

Whilst Perry appreciated the compliment, he must have spread a wry smile over the reference to his "vigorous health." The attack of fever that summer left him very weak, and before mid-1848 he had to request relief.

But the Gulf Squadron had plenty of work still to do.

CHAPTER XVIII

Yucatán Complexities
1847–1848

Cosas de Yucatán

IN mid-May 1847, when Perry visited Carmen, he sent sloop *Albany* (Commander Samuel L. Breese) to Campeche with Commander Mackenzie as interpreter, to investigate the political situation. The two commanders exchanged lengthy notes with Don Joaquín Garcia Rejón, the local secretary of state, who endeavored to persuade them that Yucatán was completely independent of Mexico. Consequently the occupation of Carmen was an insult to her dignity and honor. Logical indeed; but Perry, faced with a condition not a theory, pointed out that as the Yucatecos were incapable of suppressing contraband traffic themselves, he must reoccupy Carmen. Bomb brigs *Etna* and *Vesuvius* sustained that occupation, and the inhabitants of Carmen, having their commerce restored and escaping both Mexican and state taxes, became increasingly happy. They even stopped the salaries to teachers, priests and curates — but Protestant Perry made the municipality pay up!

Next, Perry sent sloop *John Adams*, Commander H. A. Adams, to Campeche. On 17 September 1847 he reported that he had talked with Governor Mendez and other important people in Yucatán, and that an Indian uprising was threatened, but they thought they could handle it. Adams added that the "lukewarmness" of the United States toward La República Chica, and the American occupation of Carmen, were "sources of mortification and discontent to the party now in power."

Yucatán politics continued to puzzle the Commodore as long as the war lasted. The secession party, fearing lest the Peninsula be "thrown to the wolves" at the conclusion of peace, sent to Washington Don Justo Sierra O'Reilly to demand recognition as an independent state, and the end of the occupation of Carmen. At Veracruz he was piped on board flagship *Germantown*, cordially received by the Commodore in his *esplendido gabinete de receptiones*, and a day or two later tendered *un esplendido banquete*. Perry toasted the prosperity and grandeur of Yucatán and the success of O'Reilly's mission. The envoy left by steamer for Washington on 27 September 1847, armed with a letter of introduction from the Commodore to Secretary of State James Buchanan. At the same time Perry wrote to Secretary Mason, insisting that the occupation of Carmen must continue, no matter what O'Reilly might say, although he would not oppose handing over the customs duties collected there to the Yucatán authorities. All Yucatán flag vessels, said the Commodore, now enjoy the same privileges as those of the United States in trading with Carmen and other occupied Gulf Coast ports; the real reason for the Yucatecos' protest about the occupation is that they wish to resume contraband trade with Mexico. Letters from the commander of bomb brig *Vesuvius*, stationed off Campeche, indicate that the Yucatecos are "at sixes and sevens"; the pro-Mexico party has revolted at Mérida and destroyed the unity of the Mendez government, whose pledges cannot be relied on. The navy cannot do much to influence them until *Mississippi* returns from Pensacola.

Return she did on 22 October 1847, and next month Perry, again raising his blue pendant on her mainmast, made another visit to Yucatán, hoping to talk with Mendez; but the Governor was absent. The Indians' revolt was rising, but Perry thought the white Yucatecos could take care of it — and how wrong he was! *Mississippi* was still a fever ship despite her trip north. "It is the opinion of many," wrote Perry, "that the hold of the vessel is still infected" — after all, it had not been thoroughly cleansed for years. He was back at Veracruz by mid-December. In early January of 1848 after the flagship had lost two assistant engineer officers, he asked the department to let him send her and the two faithful "Pollies" home, and give him a few small steamers as substitutes.

Perry himself was soon on the sick list. On 10 January 1848 he wrote to Secretary Mason requesting relief by 1 April owing to protracted convalescence from his summer's attack of the fever, "incessant toil" and long absence from home. The Secretary refused, on the ground that the Squadron could not afford a change of command, and pointing out that Perry had not yet served his full term. This was very disappointing. And what made it worse was an implied reproof from the department in a recent letter from the Secretary: — "I am aware of the harassing and engrossing cares which constantly absorb you, in your important duties, and am not therefore disposed to remark on the tone in which on more than one occasion, you have commented on the orders of the Department. I have no reason to believe that they are intended to be disrespectful and have not regarded them in that light."

In reply Perry wrote that he was "pained" over the Secretary's taking exception to the "tone" of his letters.

I had supposed that my communications had been couched in the most respectful and decorous language. . . . I have always thought it to be of the highest importance . . . that the communications of a Commanding Officer abroad to the functionary, at the head of his particular department at home, should be constant, free, and undisguised. . . . In this view of my duty, I have, it would appear, (though unconsciously to myself) in the earnestness of my disposition, and in the hurry of other engrossing occupations, been less careful than I should have been, in the arrangement of my remarks. But, be it as it may, I trust the Department will acquit me of an indecorum of which I believe myself incapable, and that is, of bearing myself in any other manner than with the greatest respect, towards all the high functionaries of the Government, and Especially towards yourself, from whom I have received much personal kindness.

In general, officers and men of the blockading squadron experienced a less unhappy winter in 1847-1848 than that of the year before. Tampico, Veracruz, Alvarado, Coatzacoalcos, Carmen and Campeche being in American or friendly hands, there was more shore liberty for the seamen, with opportunities to indulge their taste for wine and women; in Yucatán the local gentry entertained American officers. Commodore Perry, always on the move, inspected these captured ports during the winter. He even sent a landing force far up the Papaloapan River to occupy a place called Cosamaloapan, on a rumor that the Mexican governor of Orizaba was there, plotting mischief. But the governor anticipated his coming and fled in time. Throughout this constant activity the Commodore, owing to continual poor health, was unhappy. On 15 February he wrote to his wife from frigate *Cumberland*, off Veracruz, that he hoped his health would improve after another trip to Yucatán, and that he suffered from lack of exercise, "though I ride every afternoon a short distance on a Mexican Poney which I captured at Tabasco." This steed he described as "a very pretty animal, though somewhat spirited," brown with black points; he gave him to his son William the marine officer, but hoped to ship him home. And the very day after, Perry wrote to Jane, "The war seems to be at an end — every thing is very dull out here and the weather is already become warm. . . . Alexander and William are well and so I believe are Calbraith and George Rodgers. Love to Caroline, Ann, Julia & Raymond." [1]

On the same day "Old Bruin" wrote to Secretary Mason that despite increasing debility, he was about to return to Yucatán where the situation had become very serious. The Maya Indians, who still comprised a great majority of the inhabitants, were now really on the warpath under the lead of a chief known as Jacinto Pat, and driving all before them. The

---

[1] Alexander means Mackenzie; and William, Perry's son then serving on the staff of Gen. Robert Patterson. After receiving permission from the Navy Dept., Perry shipped two ponies home on storeship *Fredonia*.

white Yucatecos, instead of making strong efforts for their defense, were yelling for help from anyone and everyone — except (for the time being) Mexico. On 16 May there had been a demonstration at Campeche by the national guard in favor of annexation to Spain; soldiers ran about the streets waving Spanish flags and shouting, *¡Viva la Reina Ysabel y la España!* Perry, writing from Veracruz, thought that this had been cooked up at Havana "to suit some commercial speculations." He was not aware that a Spanish warship had already arrived at Sisal with munitions and other help for the white Yucatecos, or that in March the government of La República Chica offered simultaneously to cede its "dominion and sovereignty" to the United States, Great Britain and Spain, in return for help against the Maya.

Perry returned to Yucatán on 13 March 1848 in *Mississippi*, with *Scorpion*, *Iris*, *Water Witch* and *Vesuvius*, hoping by an impressive demonstration of naval force to give the Indian rebels a scare; but as they were all back in the bush they did not even know of his presence. And the shore at Campeche was so shelving that vessels drawing more than nine foot could not approach within cannon range of the town. Perry was disgusted with the white people of Campeche. They "have become panic stricken and seem to have lost all courage." Their soldiers behaved disgracefully. He proposed to give them some Mexican arms captured at Veracruz, but could do nothing in the way of a landing force without instructions.

President Polk who (wrote Secretary Mason to Perry) "heard with regret of the ferocious and murderous conflict now raging," approved of Perry's sending arms to the whites. At the instance of Don Justo O'Reilly, Polk had already dispatched a cargo of cannon powder to Sisal in the vessel *Mary Ann*, and gave Perry discretionary power to distribute it. The President became agitated by the suggestion that European powers were "intriguing" to take over New World territory. Polk never advocated outright annexation of the Peninsula, but on 29 April 1848 he sent a message to Congress warning it of foreign intervention and requesting authority to intervene for "humanitarian" reasons. This touched off an angry debate in the Senate. Hannegan of Indiana asserted that he had "authentic information" of perfidious Albion "at this very hour taking steps to acquire Yucatán." Senator Houston described the gentle and vegetarian Maya Indians, whose average stature was around five feet, as giants, "ferocious in their dispositions, loathsome in their habits, who rioted on human flesh." But by this time the war with Mexico was over, the Manifest Destiny senators were outvoted, and in early June a bill authorizing the President to occupy Yucatán failed to pass.

Nevertheless the situation, especially in the Campeche section, remained serious. Perry was informed, and believed the information to be correct, that prior to 1 March some 30,000 armed Indians had occupied or destroyed 100 towns or villages, 38 haciendas and 852 ranches, displacing more than 162,000 white people. Governor Mendez informed the Commodore that the whites could not hold out much longer without American or other foreign aid, both troops and munitions. A Baltimore paper reported, correctly, that Perry now believed this to be necessary. A somewhat amusing byproduct of this deplorable situation was a complete change of attitude by the Yucatán authorities about the American occupation of Carmen. It was no longer an "affront" to the "dignity and honor" of La República Chica; she wanted more of it, especially at Campeche, Sisal, anywhere the Americans would send a landing force. The only concession that Perry consented to, was to secure Palizada, a little town on the river of that name, about forty miles above the Laguna de Terminos. General Miguel Bruno, a former defender of Villahermosa, had occupied Palizada, and was threatening to descend the river and sack Carmen. So Perry sent a small armed sloop upriver under Commander Bigelow, and Bruno promptly retreated.

This happened in early April 1848. In the meantime Perry had been shuttling back and forth between Veracruz, Carmen and Campeche. He attempted to cure the sickness on board *Mississippi* with certain "disinfecting agents" (apparently nitrate and muriatic acid acting on zinc) applied in person by their inventor, "Professor" Robert Grant, not otherwise known to fame. The mosquitoes breeding in the bilges certainly did not like the Professor's medicine and the *vómito* ceased, although "intermittent fever" (malaria) continued for some time. Perry even found time in March to make an interesting six-day river trip in the *Scourge*. She steamed up the Usumacinta River, which joins the Grijalva not far from Frontera, to Tenoisique, 224 miles upstream. He had been told that this place lay an easy distance from the famous ruins of Palenque. Learning upon arrival there that it would be a long, difficult trip through the jungle, he regretfully gave up his visit to Palenque, descended the Usumacinta to where it forks, and took the right fork, the Palizada River, to the Laguna de las Cruces which empties into the Laguna de Terminos.

Perry's personal exertions did a good deal for the beleaguered whites of Yucatán, although he despised them for their "extraordinary example of disgraceful cowardice" and would fain have left them to their fate, but for their women and children. He not only brought about one thousand stand of captured Mexican muskets to Campeche, but from Veracruz he dispatched war steamer *Iris* (Lieutenant Commander William L. Herndon) thither with food for the refugees, reported to be starving on the beach, and *Falcon*, with muskets, flour and gunpowder. From the leading inhabitants of Carmen Island, which the rebel Indians had not reached, he received a petition asking that the United States annex them outright. If that were impossible, they begged America not to abandon them when

making peace with Mexico. "The undersigned," they concluded, "suppli-
cate you most earnestly, that you will continue in the military occupation
of this island, until Mexico shall send sufficient forces to occupy and defend it."

The American public had become so much interested in the Yucatán
situation that Secretary Mason gave to the press Perry's letter from Veracruz of 15 April 1848 — discreetly omitting the paragraph about the
white Yucatecos' "disgraceful cowardice" that we have already quoted,
and some routine matters: —

> Flag Ship *Cumberland*
> Vera Cruz, April 15, 1848

> The *Iris* has this moment arrived from Campeche, bringing letters from
> Commander Bigelow, as late as the 12th Inst., and from Commander Engle at
> Frontera, up to the 10th.
> In Yucatan, the Indians were still gaining ground, and the whites without
> attempting the least defence, continued to fly towards the coast. The U.S.
> Schooner *Falcon* had taken to Campeche more than an hundred of the poorer
> classes who were found on the Coast in a destitute condition.
> Governor Mendez has resigned in favor of his political rival, Señor Barbe-
> chano, which measure has, it seems, produced increased dissensions among the
> troops.
> Lieutenant Commandant Herndon, of the *Iris*, informs me that the inhabi-
> tants of Campeche are preparing to abandon that stronghold to the Indians.
> The Department is, I presume, aware that Campeche is a strongly fortified
> place, being entirely surrounded by thick and high walls, rendering it defen-
> sible against a very large force, especially of half-armed Indians, unprovided
> with a battering train.

Campeche did not fall, but the War of the Castes, as this racial war has
been named, dragged on. In a letter of 12 May, Secretary Mason authorized Perry to use his landing force to protect Carmen if threatened by the
Indians, but he must not invade the interior of Yucatán. This letter was
crossed by a proposal of Perry's to garrison Campeche with bluejackets.
But the end of the war with Mexico being in sight, President Polk felt
that without congressional authorization he had no right to order American armed forces to participate in a civil war.

Although two thousand armed Indians were reported to be within
thirty miles of Campeche on 10 May, and no preparations to meet them,
they never reached the coast, owing to dissensions among their leaders.
And as soon as the peace treaty was concluded (news of its ratification by
the Mexican government reached Veracruz 23 May) President Herrera, at
the request of the Union party in Yucatán (now back in power), intervened. He sent an army to Yucatán which defeated the Indian rebels and
restored white rule. La Republica Chica now returned to the arms of

Madre México; but thousands of the Maya taken prisoner were sold as slaves in Cuba.

This was not the last blow-up of the Maya. The War of the Castes broke out intermittently as late as the 1920's.

End of the War

"I am becoming quite feeble," Perry wrote to John Hone from frigate *Cumberland* at Veracruz on 28 March, "and have no appetite, though my boils are in no way lessened." Nevertheless, he resumed riding one of the liberated "poneys" and even did some shopping for the family — a set of Mexican chairs for the dining room at The Moorings. He also found time to indulge his curiosity in natural history. William C. Redfield, the Yankee saddler turned scientist and collector, whom Perry had known well in New York, wrote to him asking for specimens of Mexican fishes; the Commodore obliged by encouraging his men to fish in the harbors and rivers of Mexico, bottling the catch in alcohol, and bringing them to Redfield in New York; he was disappointed, however, in being unable to obtain a specimen of manatee or sea-cow, which used to be exhibited in American country fairs as a "genuine mermaid."

For another friend who had a taste for exotic birds he acquired an aviary — whistling ducks, royal Mexican pheasants and chachalaca[1] — and brought them home alive in his flagship. To Redfield he brought a specimen of a bird with a yellow tuft, "the celebrated hanging bird of Mexico. Very curious in its habits." This, evidently, was *oro pendula*, the yellow-tailed blackbird which builds a long, hanging nest like an oriole's.

The Commodore even dabbled in Mexican archaeology, although gravely disappointed at being unable to visit Palenque. Some of his junior officers, guided by a Mexican, unearthed near Tlacotalpan what they called an "Aztec idol" and wished to take it home; but the Commodore, suspecting that the object meant something to the Mexicans, forbade it. This may well have been one of the remarkable pre-Columbian statues that now adorn the Museo de Antropologia of Mexico City. In any case "Old Bruin" deserves a word of thanks for his refusal to countenance the universal practice of sailors filching "souvenirs" from an enemy country. The ponies and everything else that he took home were paid for. "In letters written to his biographer by fellow officers," says Griffis, "are many instances of 'Old Matt's' shrewdness in preventing and severity in punishing wanton pillage."

On 28 May 1848 the Commodore received official word from Washington that the Treaty of Guadalupe Hidalgo, already ratified by President

---

[1] The chachalaca is a sort of quail which cries constantly in flight; its name has become a synonym for "chatterbox" in Mexico.

Polk, had been ratified by Mexico. He began immediately to return all customs houses and occupied ports to the Mexican authorities, and presided over the embarkation of 18,000 American troops at Veracruz. All vessels still remaining in the Gulf Squadron were routed to home ports. From Veracruz he wrote to Major General Robert Patterson on 10 June that he was hastening this process because of a veritable epidemic on board his flagship. All four lieutenants, most of the officers and one hundred of the crew were down with fever, mostly malaria. The fleet surgeon wrote urgent letters to Secretary Mason on 6 and 7 June, the first recommending *Cumberland*'s immediate dispatch home since the fever was increasing daily (14 cases yesterday, 15 today); and the second declaring the Commodore's health to be "such as to render his immediate return to a northern climate a matter of absolute necessity." "As early as November last," he added, "it was the opinion of Fleet Surgeon Jackson & myself, that the Commodore's health required his departure from the station before the approach of the sickly season. Since that time the vigour of his constitution has been so exhausted by the combined influence of the climate and an energetic application to the laborious duties of his command, that a few weeks more within this tropical climate, under the epidemical state of the atmosphere now prevailing, will in my opinion deprive the Government entirely of his services."

Authorization from Washington must have crossed these letters, for on 15 June 1848, wearing his blue pendant in frigate *Cumberland*, the Commodore said farewell to Veracruz, Orizaba and Mexico. She arrived New York 23 June. Out of consideration for the inhabitants of Carmen, Perry before his departure beefed up the garrison there to 250 marines and four pieces of artillery and, for another six weeks, kept Commander Bigelow on station as senior naval officer with four or five armed schooners, Carmen was finally evacuated on 30 July.

The war was really over.

Perry's career in the Mexican War was notable for energy and intelligence. His flagship, whether under the red or the blue pendant, was constantly on the move. The quick turnaround at New Orleans, where his Slidell relatives would gladly have entertained him for a week or more, is a case in point; and in early 1847, when waiting for *Mississippi* to be repaired at Norfolk, he kept busy superintending the completion of new warships instead of taking home leave. In Mexico, when not engaged in some upriver expedition, he sailed to Yucatán to get in touch with the situation, or to captured ports to see how the garrisons were doing and that customs levies were being properly collected. Tarrying in Veracruz harbor was not his idea of doing his duty, and as soon as he could get on top of his paper work, he would be off again. This strategy of movement was primarily dictated by Perry's preferences, and his desire to employ the squadron to best advantage; but it also had the effect of keeping the crews in better health. There is nothing that destroys the morale of a sailor more quickly than "swinging around the hook" in a harbor where no liberty can be allowed; or that keeps him happier than constant movement and frequent action. Thus, gruff "Old Bruin" emerged from this war as a very popular naval officer with the enlisted men.

Henry Coppée, later a noted writer and president of Lehigh University, encountered Perry when, a second lieutenant of artillery, he carried messages for General Scott to the Commodore. Asked for his impressions of Perry some thirty-five years later, Coppée reported that he was "blunt, yet dignified, . . . heavy and not graceful, . . . held somewhat in awe by the junior officers and having little to do with them, seriously courteous to others" — among others being this twenty-five-year-old lieutenant. *"The ship seemed to have a sense of importance because he was on board."* That sentence is very significant. Perry carried an aura of dignity, distinction and authority wherever he went, or whatever he did.

CHAPTER XIX

Four Years' Shore Duty
1848–1852

Family and Home Affairs

Now, for the first time in his life, Perry received public recognition. Shortly after his arrival in New York in July 1848, the mayor and corporation tendered him a civic reception, conferred on him "the freedom of the city" with a big gilt key, and an engrossed parchment thanking the officers and crew of *Cumberland* for their "gallantry and good conduct in the late war with Mexico." Some years later, commenting on American lack of recognition of military exploits, Perry remarked, "It is true that a public dinner is sometimes offered to officers of the Army or Navy, which in consideration of many of the persons to whom such compliment is paid amounts to no compliment at all, apart from the painful obligation imposed on the guest of making a bad and sometimes unintelligible speech."

The Commodore, now fifty-four years old, cared little for public applause, although he may have reflected wryly that Alvarado Hunter received more praise for disobeying orders than he got for doing his duty and commanding the Gulf Squadron. But he did very much care to see that officers who served well under him were recognized. Every report to the department included the names of those he thought especially meritorious, and whenever one was detached from his command, he was followed by a letter setting forth his good qualities. When the Maryland Legislature after the war proposed a vote of thanks to her two native sons, Commander Franklin Buchanan and Surgeon Ninian Pinkney, Perry's letters warmly commending them were printed in a leaflet. On the other hand, Perry never made the mistake that his brother had done in the Elliott case, of commending an officer who did not deserve it.

As commodore of the Home Squadron, flying his blue pendant from frigate *Cumberland* anchored off the Brooklyn Navy Yard, Perry still had plenty of work to do, what with laying up ships in ordinary and repairing others so that they would be fit for instant service. He was relieved from that command on 20 November 1848, and on the same date given a new appointment, just created: General Superintendent of Mail Steamers. This responsibility, from which he was not relieved until March 1852, gave Perry a long stretch of shore duty. During most of it he was living in Tarrytown.

Family affairs and The Moorings had been much on Perry's mind throughout the war. City-bred Jane did not enjoy winters in the country without her husband, although she had his sister Anna, widow of George W. Rodgers, as a permanent guest, and Kate Mackenzie for neighbor. Perry's letters from Mexico to John Hone were filled with exact directions about spring planting, cutting timber, and the like, and his missives to Jane generally concluded with instructions for their gardener, known as Jaypee; but Jane took little interest in grounds or garden. The Commodore had financed building the house through borrowing on mortgage from Anna and Julia Rodgers, James Watson Webb his Tarrytown neighbor, and his Madeira-drinking friend Frederick De Peyster. Although these loans amounted only to $7300, the expense of interest and upkeep was too great for an officer on captain's pay, and Perry had such a horror of indebtedness that in 1847 he seriously contemplated selling the place. A couple of windfalls enabled him to pay off these debts: at least $880 in prize money,[1] and $7000 cash which John Hone managed to extract from the Hudson River Railroad for a right of way along the river front.

Perry suffered a severe loss in 1848 when his brother-in-law, shipmate and neighbor Alexander Slidell Mackenzie, having returned from Mexican War service broken in health, died of a heart attack while riding horseback. Alvarado Hunter now renewed his diatribes against both Perry and Mackenzie, whom he regarded as the villain of the wartime court-martial. Hunter published two open letters to Perry, in which he alluded to him and Mackenzie in a highly offensive manner. Perry requested a formal inquiry of Hunter to put an end to the Alvarado business, and he got it; but the results were very unsatisfactory, exonerating Perry and mildly rebuking Hunter. The young officer, instead of being reprimanded for printing disparaging remarks about his superior officers, received a new command before the end of 1850. "That infernal blackguard Hunter," as Senator Slidell called him, had been made such a pet of by the Whigs that the Taylor-Fillmore administration could not bear to dismiss him. But, as commander of U.S.S. *Bainbridge*, Hunter's conduct was so flagrantly insubordinate that he had to be dismissed.

Fortunately there were several events to delight the Perry-Rodgers-Slidell clan. Most important was the marriage of Caroline, the Perrys'

---

[1] This was up to July 1847. He must have received more after the end of the war, but I have been unable to find the total in the archives.

twenty-year-old daughter, to August Belmont. How Tiny, as the family called her, met that wealthy German-born financier we do not know; probably her elder sister Mrs. Hone introduced her into New York society, and Belmont wooed her in the Hone drawing room. At the age of thirty-three he had become one of the richest men in New York, the biggest catch from the point of view of the mamas, and the most romantic from that of the young ladies. For, having resented a slur on a lady's reputation, uttered by some young man about town, August challenged him to a duel and received a bullet in the leg.

The New York *Herald*, first American newspaper to print social gossip, had this to say about the wedding: —

It was whispered, confidentially, a short time since, that Auguste Belmont, the agent of the celebrated banking house of Rothschilds, had popped the question and solicited the hand of the beautiful daughter of a well-known and gallant naval officer, whose career had reflected honor on his country. Soon the rumor spread, and created a buz in parlors and drawing rooms up town. It was hardly credited by the wealthy dames with marriageable daughters, when they first heard it, but soon all doubts were removed by the announcement that Mr. Belmont was positively engaged to the charming Miss Caroline Slidell, daughter of Commodore M. C. Perry, and that the wedding day was fixed. But the friends of both parties were doomed to encounter a little touch of disappointment before they should have the pleasure of witnessing the tying of the nuptial knot; for a day or two previous to the time appointed for the interesting ceremony to take place, the bride became indisposed, and a delay of a short time was deemed advisable. New cards were issued as soon as she was convalescent, and another day, the 7th inst., appointed for consummating the engagement. On that day the sun shone most brilliantly, the atmosphere was as balmy as the bride was beautiful; not a cloud could be observed in the heavens; and before twilight set in, "the twain were one flesh," the marriage ceremony having been performed by the Rev. Francis Vinton, D.D., in the Church of the Ascension in this city.[1]

This marriage, a very happy one, provided the bride's father with another anchor in the Democratic party. August Belmont, unlike most New York financiers, was an ardent and generous supporter of Lewis Cass, James Buchanan and Tammany Hall. According to Mrs. Van Rensselaer, historian of New York's "four hundred," he "gained entrance to New York Society through the social position of his wife, coupled with his own participation in national affairs." He settled on his wife a valuable tract of real estate, the entire square between Fifth and Sixth Avenues and 19th and 20th Streets, and built for her a house on the corner of Fifth Avenue and 19th Street. Mrs. Belmont, who "had magnificent gowns and the ability to wear them magnificently," within a few years became the

---

[1] Reverend Francis Vinton, who married Elizabeth Mason Perry, daughter of Commodore Oliver H. Perry, at this time was rector of Grace Church, Brooklyn.

acknowledged leader of New York society and a founder of the new summer colony in Newport.

Immediately after the Perry-Belmont wedding came a jolly Christmastide reunion at The Moorings. A letter from the Commodore tells how Jane accommodated everybody in that not very large house. "August and Tiny," the newlyweds, occupy the lower bedroom; the Hones have "Anna's room," as Anna will keep Christmas with the Rodgerses at Sion Hill; "Raymond and Julia" (Commander and Mrs. C. R. P. Rodgers) share "Billy's room," since Lieutenant William Frederick Perry USMC cannot come home for Christmas. Small children will be "colonized in the parlor" with their nurses. Also present were fifteen-year-old Isabella, the Perrys' one unmarried daughter, and Oliver H. Perry II. That young hopeful had already returned from his "forty-niner" trip to California, much to the "chagrin" of his father, who in a letter to Calbraith Jr. hopes he "may now buckle himself to his work, and commence helping himself in earnest." William Frederick, the lieutenant of marines, unfortunately had acquired a weakness for alcohol. Before the end of the Mexican War the Commodore proposed to send him home, writing that he needed a guardian, and hoping that Jane and John Hone would keep him "strait." Bill nevertheless managed to survive all but two of his nine brothers and sisters, without accomplishing anything noteworthy. Calbraith (M. C. Perry Jr.), the eldest son, could not get home for Christmas as his ship was abroad. He had a creditable naval career, receiving his fourth stripe in the Civil War.

Doubtless to Jane's delight, Perry sold his country estate shortly before sailing for Japan, and bought or built a house "away up town" in New York City — 38 West 32nd Street — where he and Jane and daughter Isabella lived from 1855 to his death, and his widow lived until 1870. To finance that deal he received a loan of $20,000 from August Belmont. It became one of the self-assumed duties of that gentleman, one which his likenamed son inherited, to assist indigent or financially embarrassed members of the Perry clan. This has been done cheerfully and unostentatiously for more than a century.

Steam Triumphs and Tragedies

These four years of Perry's next-to-last shore duty were a period of national euphoria. A tough little war had been brilliantly won, Texas secured, California and New Mexico annexed, and a lion's share of the Oregon country wrested from Great Britain. The gold rush to California and an economic upsurge followed. Territorial acquisitions aroused bitter antagonism between pro- and anti-slavery forces; but the Compromise of 1850 appeared to have settled all that. Dreams of Pacific empire now unfolded. Islands of that ocean, perhaps all Far Eastern countries, were ripe to be brought under the aegis of Western civilization through the energy of the Yankee race and the piety of Protestant missionaries. The European revolutions of 1848 paid tribute to the principles of 1776; all the world seemed to be going republican and democratic. These were the years of some of the greatest American books (Hawthorne's *The Scarlet Letter*, Whitman's *Leaves of Grass*, Melville's *Moby Dick*, Longfellow's *Golden Legend*, Emerson's *Representative Men*), which were read wherever English was read. In fine arts, the Hudson River school of painting reached its apogee and Andrew Jackson Downing dictated the designs of gentlemen's country estates along the Hudson; but Perry could not afford to employ him. Thomas Crawford and the Greenough brothers were producing notable works of sculpture in Rome and Florence. New colleges and universities were being founded, and free public education pushed west with the frontier. In the great international exposition at London's Crystal Palace in 1851, American inventions, gadgets and machinery won the reluctant admiration of Europe. And, the same year, the schooner yacht *America* won her famous race around the Isle of Wight against almost the entire English yachting fleet. The star of Young America was in the ascendant.

This too was the clipper ship era. American designers and builders of those glorious full-rigged sailing ships hung up records that have never been broken; Donald McKay's *Flying Cloud*, for instance, sailed around Cape Horn from New York to San Francisco in 89 days in 1851, a speed never surpassed and only twice equaled, once by herself. It was the heyday of New England whaling, and of the schooners, brigs and barques running along the East Coast or down to the West Indies and South America, and over to the Mediterranean and Africa. But there was one great and growing branch of navigation in which America lagged behind England and France — steam navigation. American patriots were mortified because the Cunard Line, starting in 1840, had taken the cream of transatlantic freight and passenger traffic away from crack New York sailing packets. Similarly the Royal Steam Packet Company's smart steamers (*Teviot* which occasioned the Perry-Farragut dispute was one) had captured the passenger and fast freight service to the West Indies and Mexico. Both lines managed to do this only by dint of generous subsidies from the British government in the form of mail contracts. During the enthusiasm of the Mexican War, Congress authorized the postmaster general to make an important contract with Edward K. Collins and associates. They were to build five ocean steamships of two thousand or more tons each, to make twenty round voyages annually between New York and Liverpool, and to receive $385,000 a year for carrying the mails. In the enabling act it was provided that these steamships be built "under the inspection of a naval constructor in the employ of the Navy Department . . . and so constructed as to render them convertible at the least possible cost, into war steamers of the first class."

In addition, there were two other subsidized lines of American steamships, whose construction came under Perry's superintendency. These were the Law Line from New Orleans to Havana and Chagres (Caribbean terminus of the road across the Isthmus of Panama), and the Aspinwall Line from Panama City to San Francisco and Astoria. Each of the three companies, down to 1 February 1852, received a little short of a million dollars in mail subsidies. All their ships, including the five Collins liners, were built in New York, and each had a special "superintendent in charge" appointed by the navy. Perry, appointed General Superintending Agent of Mail Steamers 20 November 1848, had the duty "to exercise over them a parental official influence." He must "watch the progress of construction of those not yet completed or commenced, in view of suggesting such timely arrangements as will render them more readily available for vessels of war." He will inspect each vessel upon her completion and report to the Secretary of the Navy whether or not the contract has been complied with, especially whether the ship could be converted to a warship. He is assured that "the Department will readily adopt any suggestions which will add to your efficiency or guard against any collision with the private interests of the contractors."

As an enthusiastic advocate of steam navigation, Perry took this duty very seriously, and spent almost every weekday watching the construction of one ship or another; the new Hudson River Railroad enabled him to live at The Moorings and commute to New York City. But he labored under several handicaps: the vagueness of his orders; the department's refusal, after several requests, to clarify them; and the Secretary's failure to answer letters. Was he supposed merely to report observed defects, or had he authority to order them remedied? He does not wish to be a "Meddlesome Matty," but in June 1849 he ventures to urge that, since the first Collins liners are almost complete, he "be made acquainted with the present views of the Department" with regard to his "precise duties." He was hampered by having taken no part in making the contracts, and the hulls of Collins's first two steamers were already completed when he became General Superintendent. In his reports to the Secretary, he intimated that had he been consulted on the contracts, or had been able to oversee building from the keel up, the Collins liners would have been less "extravagantly showy" and more practical. "If these vessels," he reported, "had been originally constructed conformably to the *spirit* (though it was not called for by the letter) of the contracts, as they should have been — and all English mail steamers now are — *in anticipation of their possible conversion into war vessels*, the cost of converting them would be much less. . . . Most of them were completed before I was ordered to their supervision." Perry's old friend Charles H. Haswell, chief engineer of the navy, and the naval constructors assigned to each vessel, were even more critical of the new steamers.

Nevertheless, the Commodore acquired such a reputation as an expert that Baron von Roenne, minister to Washington from the short-lived Germanic Confederation, sounded him on the possibility of coming to Germany to be the government's adviser on building a new navy. Perry replied that he could not accept as a civilian; only if so ordered by the Navy Department. No such orders were issued. He was too valuable at home to be spared.

For about a month in the spring of 1849, Perry served on a court-martial at Newport News, where he suffered from a painful return of the rheumatism to which he had been subject since his first Mediterranean cruise. "This is the first time, within my recollection," he wrote to Secretary Preston, "that I have asked to be excused from any duty assigned to me, and I feel mortified that circumstances altogether beyond my control should have rendered it necessary now."

The Collins liners became the nation's pride and the favorites of transatlantic travelers. George Steers, architect of yacht *America*, designed and leading New York shipbuilders built them; and the first four — *Atlantic, Pacific, Arctic* and *Baltic* — were ready to sail in 1850. Constructed with white oak frames strengthened by iron rods, and planked with 5- to 7-inch yellow pine, they were (on an average) 280 feet long, measuring 2700 tons, were powered by side-lever steam engines operating two 35-foot paddlewheels, and cost the unprecedented sum of $675,000 each. These and the Law liners *Illinois* and *Ohio* were then the biggest and fastest steamships in the world. *Pacific* in April 1851 made the first Liverpool–New York passage in less than ten days: 9 days 20 hours 15 minutes. *Arctic* clipped off three hours next year, and *Baltic's* record of 9 days and 13 hours westbound in August 1852 stood for twelve years. That was the last time that an American ship won this "blue riband of the Atlantic" until *United States* recovered it exactly a century later. And the Collins liners, provided with auxiliary sail, could make 9 knots under canvas alone.

Perry warned the department that "under no circumstances . . . can a steam vessel, built expressly for the transportation of freight or passengers, be made, in any manner, equal in convenience and efficiency to a vessel originally intended for war purposes." No Collins liner could possibly be transformed into another *Princeton* or *Mississippi*. Yet that was exactly what the enabling act of Congress required — that they be convertible "into war steamers of the first class." Perry also reported that the builders had spent too much money on elegant and luxurious appointments which would have to be ripped out upon conversion.

These interior fittings, as much as the speed, attracted the traveling public to the Collins Line. This was the first ocean steamship company to endeavor to persuade passengers that they were living in a luxury hotel, not on board a seagoing ship — a trend which has continued to dizzy heights in the present century. Collins Line first-class cabins were steam-heated, lighted by the latest type of French oil lamp, provided with beds instead of bunks, "rich curtains" and bell pulls. The dining saloon, in which five meals a day were served, was separate from the cabins, with ports looking outboard "as pleasantly as those of any parlor" instead of (as in early Cunarders) exchanging smells and sounds with the private cabins. The grand saloon, wainscoted with "rare and costly woods, luxurious sofas and arm chairs, and a profusion of rich gilding," had marble-topped tables, stained-glass windows, and "handsome spittoons" disguised as flower vases. An "air of elegant comfort" prevailed, combined with "Oriental magnificence." But precautions for safety at sea were grossly inadequate.

Perry said nothing about that side of naval construction in his reports to the Secretary. In the first place, it was none of his business; the department was not interested in safety, only in convertibility, and seeing that the building specifications were followed. Second, as a naval officer, he was not particularly concerned with safety at sea. As today, when sailors live on top of a cargo of high explosives, they are not much bothered by the prospect of drowning. The navy did not even provide lifejackets in 1850, and the warships' boats were not designed for lifesaving, although each had its own crew well trained in rescue work, as we observed when *Mississippi*'s barge took sixty people off three grounded ships in March 1847. The Collins liners did provide lifejackets for all hands, but when the test came most of them leaked and proved useless. They had lifeboats, some of the latest metal type, for perhaps one-fifth of the passengers; but no crews trained to handle them. Nobody seems to have suggested transverse bulkheads to confine a leak to one part of the ship, although European builders were already installing them. Most extraordinary, to our way of thinking, was Collins's failure to provide his ships with steam whistles. When fog rolled in, a deckhand was stationed forward to blow a fisherman's tin foghorn.

For almost four years the Collins Line prospered. It carried more first-class passengers, at $125 a head, than the Cunard Line obtained for the same or less. Fortnightly sailings were maintained except in the dead of winter. Congress, delighted with this symbol of American supremacy in steam as well as sail, increased the subsidy in 1852. Two years later, when Perry was no longer Superintendent, disaster struck.

Arctic, westbound on 27 September 1854 with a full complement of passengers and crew, collided at 13 knots with the French iron steamer *Vesta*, making 10 knots, in a heavy fog off Cape Race. *Vesta* lost her bow, but, since her builders had provided watertight bulkheads, she made St. John's in safety. She might also have taken on board *Arctic*'s passengers and crew; but the American master, with singularly bad judgment, elected to make a run for the coast. Seawater pouring through two great breaches quenched her fires and she began to founder. A disgraceful *sauve qui peut* followed, firemen and coal heavers thrusting aside women and children in a panic-stricken rush for the few lifeboats. Only 23 out of 282 passengers and 65 out of 175 officers and crew were saved, and the survivors included not one woman or child. And, as if this were not enough to humble American boosters and boasters, Collins liner *Pacific* sailed from Liverpool in January 1856 and was never heard from again. Transatlantic passengers now shunned the Collins Line, Congress reduced its subsidy, and the panic of 1857 finished it. Three surviving steamships were auctioned off at $50,-000 for the lot.

Although it does not appear that Perry was in any manner blamed for the *Arctic* tragedy, he like any other seafaring American felt deeply humiliated. In 1855, when he was returning to the United States in her sister ship *Baltic*, he wrote a letter to Thomas B. Curtis of Boston who had printed a pamphlet on safety at sea. Perry made several good suggestions, some of which have subsequently been adopted. He approved Matthew Fontaine Maury's plan for designated eastbound and westbound steamer lanes. He wanted a safe maximum steam pressure required by law, to keep down excessive speed; a hopeless proposal when every line was trying to win speed records. He wanted all lifeboats to be the metal type invented by Joseph Francis, each to be stocked with emergency rations and gear, and enough provided to float most of the ships' complement. At the beginning of each passage, he said, a "collision bill" and a "fire bill" should be drawn up and posted, assigning specific duties and stations to each passenger and crew member in an emergency. Since he considered it impossible to have enough lifeboats on deck for an entire ship's complement, he endorsed a scheme of Henry Evans of New Bedford, to have parts of the promenade or saloon decks so constructed that they would automatically float off as rafts if the ship sank. This proposal was revived after the *Titanic* disaster of 1912, but shipbuilders rejected it as impractical.

A curious fatalism on the part of sailors, and niggardliness on the part of shipowners, has prevented for more than a century the full adoption of Perry's suggestions. Lifeboats are more numerous in modern transatlantic steamers, but never enough; lifeboat drills are often regarded as a joke; fire and collision bills for all hands are used only in the navy. Thus, owing to human frailty, greed and ignorance, we continue to suffer from marine disasters.

CHAPTER XX

Isolated Japan
1600–1851

In my former commands upon the coast of Africa and in the Gulf of Mexico, . . . I found no difficulty in conciliating the good will and confidence of the conquered people, by administering the unrestricted power I held rather to their comfort and protection than to their annoyance. So I believe that the people of [Japan], if treated with strict justice and gentle kindness, will render confidence for confidence, and . . . the Japanese will learn to consider us their friends.

— PERRY TO SECRETARY KENNEDY, *14 December 1852*

DURING the last week of January 1852 Perry received this telegram from Navy Secretary Graham: BE READY TO COMMAND THE EAST INDIA SQUADRON. As we shall see, he had just protested against this assignment, but, as a good naval officer, he obeyed. Thus began his greatest achievement: persuading a great empire, sealed for over two centuries from external contacts, to make a limited opening to the world, without the application of force or the loss of a single life. "Old Bruin" managed this delicate and unprecedented mission, as he proposed in his letter quoted above, in such manner as to earn the respect and gratitude of the Japanese people. It was a triumph which may well be compared with that of General Douglas MacArthur after World War II. Yet, paradoxically, Perry did not want it, tried to get out of it, and only through a series of accidents had it thrust upon him.

Until 1853 Perry never once gazed on the Pacific. His overseas experience had been in the Caribbean, on the West Coast of Africa, and in European waters. Now, at the age of fifty-seven, his highest ambition was to command the Mediterranean Squadron. But, like other farsighted Americans, he had become deeply interested in the Pacific. For the Mexican War and the Oregon settlement had given the United States four major ports — Seattle, Portland, San Francisco and San Diego — looking out over that vast ocean which Magellan had been the first to cross. And in the winter of 1850-1851 Perry wrote to President Fillmore's Navy Secretary a memorandum — now lost — on the wisdom and timeliness of sending a naval expedition to obtain a treaty with Japan.

Hitherto, and from that day in 1784 when the ship *Empress of China* of New York showed the Stars and Stripes near Canton, American policy toward the Far East had been a trading one. Salem, Boston, New York and Philadelphia built up a thriving commerce with the Orient, and the navy protected it. An American Pacific Squadron had been set up in 1822, and renamed the East India Squadron in 1835. About that time the whaling industry of New England began to find the North Pacific a profitable cruising ground. The navy attempted without much success to police rowdy whalemen ashore in the Pacific islands, but it had considerable success in what used to be called "gunboat diplomacy," protecting peaceful traders from murderous onslaughts by natives. In 1830, for instance, frigate *Potomac* punished Quallah Battoo in Sumatra for having massacred the crew of a Salem merchantman. And, as the result of long efforts by John Quincy Adams, first American statesman to regard the Pacific as our sea of destiny, the navy in 1838 sent forth the Wilkes Expedition to explore and chart that ocean. But there was no attempt to rival England and France by annexing islands.

A new turn in American Far Eastern relations came in 1844. England, as fruit of victory in her Opium War with China, forced the Emperor to cede Hong Kong and to open five treaty ports to British commerce. President Tyler sent Caleb Cushing to procure a similar treaty for the United States, and Cushing succeeded. The Treaty of Wanghia, which he signed on 3 July 1844, opened five ports to American trade, granted most-favored-nation treatment and extra-territorial rights for American citizens resident in China, and prescribed the customs duties that China could levy on imports from the United States.

The next obvious move was to obtain a treaty with Japan. But that country was far more difficult to deal with than China, as at least four European nations had learned. Japan had been effectively sealed against foreign contacts for more than two centuries. Around the year 1600 the Japanese government, hitherto favorable to Christian missionaries and traders, began to eliminate or expel all foreigners and to suppress native Christianity. It began because the Shogun Ieyasu, who had successfully established the supremacy of his House of Tokugawa over Japan, feared lest native Christians set up a fifth column for Spanish or Portuguese invaders. This movement culminated in 1638 with an absolute prohibition of intercourse with the outside world. Nowhere else in modern times has there been such drastic national seclusion. No foreigner could enter the country, no foreign vessel could call at a Japanese port or land people on her coast. Japanese subjects were forbidden to leave home or to build seagoing ships; their fishermen and coastal craft were forbidden to communicate with foreign vessels. If a Japanese junk crashed on a foreign shore, the survivors were not allowed to return lest they bring "forbidden thoughts" with them. Consequently the industrial revolution of the nineteenth century had never reached Japan. The country which within a century would build the biggest warships and tankers in the world, in 1850 had no steam engine, locomotive or stationary, no forge capable of casting a cannon, no factory in the modern sense, no telegraph, no ships bigger than 50-foot junks, no modern firearms or fortifications other than earthworks armed with ancient cannon. And, amazing to relate, the ladies and gentlemen of Japan adopted no new fashions in wearing apparel!

But, before dismissing the Shogunate as hopeless old fogies, we should remember that in their two and a half centuries of seclusion they created things of priceless value to any nation: — peace, a feeling of unity, and devotion to a symbol. That is what China conspicuously lacked until the communists took over and imposed an alien ideology on a people who had no common purpose.

The only crack in this rigid isolationist shell was a strictly regulated Dutch trade at Deshima, a small island off Nagasaki. There the Netherlands government maintained a permanent factory (agency) and thither sent annually one or two Dutch vessels bringing materials that Japan lacked and taking away Japanese products that Europe wanted. This trifling concession, Japan's only legal link with the Western world until 1854, was maintained by the Dutch for profit, despite insulting regulations. Every so often the factory had to send a delegation to Edo, the future Tokyo. They were required to approach the Shogun across the audience Hall of a Hundred Mats crawling on their bellies — no small feat for a Dutch merchant — and then put on a song-and-dance act and play drunk, to amuse His Highness. No religious services were allowed at Deshima, no Bibles or other European books could be taken ashore. Once or twice annually all Japanese employees of the Dutch were required to prove their hostility to Christianity by trampling on a cross. All books on board the foreign ships were supposed to be collected and sealed up in a cask at Nagasaki, but many leaked into Japan nevertheless.

Through this peephole a few Americans obtained a peek at Japan. During the Napoleonic wars, when the Dutch East India Company was unable to send vessels to the Indian Ocean, it chartered annually an American ship for the Japan trade. *Eliza* of New York in 1797, and six or seven others, visited Nagasaki wearing the Netherlands colors and were accepted as such. The captains, as their "privilege," brought home Japanese bronzes, lacquered boxes and furniture that the Nagasaki artisans made for the Dutch trade. But these visits led to nothing, and from around 1807 until Perry's arrival not one American ship managed to traffic with Japan.

Many attempts were made by European nations to break down this system. Russia, advancing eastward into the Pacific, was the most persistent. From 1804 on, several rather rough attempts were made by Russian naval vessels to force a trade, and in 1852 Emperor Nicholas I organized a Japan Expedition like Perry's which arrived shortly after his. Lieutenant Fleetwood Pellew RN of H.M.S. *Phaeton* entered Nagasaki harbor in 1808 and obtained food and water on threat of sinking all Japanese ships in the harbor, as Perry found to be angrily remembered in 1854. At about the same date a Russian ship landed men on Hokkaido and so terrorized the inhabitants that when Perry's "black ships" appeared off Hakodate in 1854 townspeople fled to the hills. British ships at various times sent parties ashore to get wood, water and provisions, and when these were refused, plundered them. These and other illegal descents on the coast of Japan had the cumulative effect of showing up weakness in the Shogun's government; but almost nothing was done to strengthen coastal defenses, owing to the ease with which American ships were driven off in 1837 and 1846. It is characteristic of the Japanese to adopt a polity that can be changed only by violence or by outside influence — they might be called a reactor people who need a fuze to set them off. The Kodo-Ha movement did it from within in 1931-1940, the atomic bomb did it from without in 1945, and Perry's Expedition in 1853-1854 began a movement that ended in the reopening of Japan to foreign trade and intercourse.

Incidentally, Perry knew about many, though not all, of these incidents of "barbarian violence" against Japan, and determined that only under deep provocation would his squadron ever resort to rough stuff. He wished his visit to leave a pleasant impression; and it did, surviving even a decade of violence in Nippon-American relations. Today, Perry and MacArthur are the two most respected foreigners in Japanese history.

The United States was not far behind other Western powers in trying to crack the Japanese shell. In 1832 President Jackson sent Edmund Roberts to the Far East in U.S.S. *Peacock* to conclude treaties with Oriental powers. He succeeded in so doing with the King of Siam and the Sultan of Muscat, but died at Macao before embarking for Japan. In 1837 an Anglo-American firm of China traders at Canton sent ship *Morrison* to Japan, ostensibly to repatriate seven Japanese sailors who had been cast away at the mouth of the Columbia River, but really in the hope of opening trading relations and introducing Christian missionaries. *Morrison* was fired upon by Japanese forts at Uraga and Kagoshima and retired without even landing the castaways. Her supercargo, Charles W. King, wrote a book about this voyage, in which he urged the American government to consider this incident an insult and to demand a treaty to prevent its recurrence. From that time on, the opening of Japan seldom dropped out of sight in Washington. And the American Protestant missionary societies, having already enjoyed considerable success in Africa, India, China and Polynesia, were eager to open a new field for conversion.

Two different matters combined to make the subject urgent in 1850. The first was the New England whaling industry, then reaching its zenith. Until the Civil War, American home lighting and the lubrication of machinery depended on oil brought in by whaling vessels. Perry in 1852 ascertained that some $15 million was embarked on this business in the North Pacific alone. With scores of ships annually pursuing their big game in the Sea of Okhotsk and Japanese coastal waters, there were bound to be shipwrecks, and any sailors who managed to get ashore were thrown into jail and eventually reached home, if at all, through good offices of the Dutch at Nagasaki. Repatriating Japanese castaways, too, was illegal under Japanese law; but whaleship *Manhattan* of Sag Harbor, having rescued 22 Japanese sailors from a shipwrecked junk, was allowed to land them at Uraga in 1845 and obtain provisions. As this seemed a good augury, President Polk instructed Commodore James Biddle, who had been sent to China in U.S.S. *Columbus* to exchange the ratifications of Cushing's treaty, to have a try at Japan.

Commodore Biddle, Perry's old friend of U.S.S. *Concord* days, was no diplomat. He had messed up negotiations with Turkey after Perry's good opening with the Capudan Pasha. On 20 July 1846 the Commodore in ship-of-the-line *Columbus*, with sloop-of-war *Vincennes*, anchored off Uraga at the entrance to Edo Bay, where they were immediately surrounded by hundreds of armed guard boats. Biddle, surprisingly for a Philadelphia patrician, tried a "folksy" approach to the Japanese. He showed himself freely, let sightseers swarm over the ships, accepted gifts, and entrusted the President's letter to the hands of a minor official at Uraga who forwarded it to the government at Edo. Abe Masahiro), the Shogun's senior councilor, refused to accept the letter and instructed the governor of Uraga to order the ships away. This the official did in a curt note, adding that they must never return. The officer in charge of the Japanese guard boat which brought out this reply ordered the Commodore to come aboard and get it. Biddle at first refused, then made the mistake of complying. In full uniform he was about to step on board the vessel when a rude Japanese soldier (in Biddle's words), "gave me a blow or push which threw me back into the boat." The Japanese authorities expressed their regret; but since Biddle had orders "not to do anything to excite a hostile feeling or distrust of the United States," he simply departed in peace, an action interpreted by the Japanese as weakness. Commodore Perry took note of Biddle's lack of dignity and resolved never to place himself in a position where a Japanese could insult him. And he insisted on bringing steam warships to Japan. For, as a crowning indignity, Commodore Biddle's two windjammers, becalmed, had to be towed out to sea by Japanese guard boats.

Shortly after the Mexican War ended, word reached the East India Squadron that fifteen shipwrecked American seamen were awaiting repatriation at Nagasaki. These men, from whaleships *Lagoda* and *Lawrence*, had been cruelly treated and their lives spared only through the pleas of the Dutch at Deshima. U.S.S. *Preble*, Commander James Glynn, was sent from Canton to pick them up. Learning at Okinawa, where he called first, that the story of Biddle's visit had reached the Ryukyus as a "Japanese victory over the American big ships," Glynn stood for no nonsense at Nagasaki. He sailed *Preble* through the cordon of boats, anchored within easy gunshot of the city, and, after two days' discussion, promised to open gunfire if the seamen were not forthcoming. Delivered they were, and in very poor condition too. During the palaver Glynn learned that Japanese officials had followed events of the Mexican War with keen interest and were highly impressed by our capture of Veracruz. He reported to Washington that conditions were favorable for another attempt to open Japan, but that a strong naval force should be sent to do it.

Glynn was right. The time was ripe for making an impression on the Japanese government, and pressure on the American government to do it increased after the war. Not only the protection of castaways but the need for coaling stations brought matters to a head. Without means to coal en route, transpacific steam navigation would be impossible. England was already linked to the Chinese treaty ports by steamer — the Peninsular & Oriental began monthly service from Calcutta to Hong Kong in 1845, and shortly after set up an Egypt-India line. But no California-China service was possible, owing to the distance. The marine engines of that era burned so much coal that a steamship could carry enough for crossing the Pacific only at the expense of leaving little space for cargo. In 1867, after the Japanese had established a coaling station at Yokohama, the big paddlewheel steamships of the Pacific Mail Line began nonstop runs from San Francisco to Yokohama, where they coaled before proceeding to Hong Kong, but even they had room for only 2000 to 2800 tons of cargo.

The trading motive for breaking down Japanese isolation appealed to certain American manufacturers whose one-man Washington lobby, Aaron Haight Palmer, bombarded President and Congress with pamphlets setting forth glittering prospects of trade with the Orient. He demanded a special mission to make treaties not only with Japan but Abyssinia, Persia, Burma, Cochin China, the Moro Islands, and the Indian Archipelago! Palmer also got up petitions to Congress by China traders and others. His efforts could not have been very effective, since Perry was disappointed at the lack of interest in his Expedition shown by the businessmen of New York.

Conditions in Japan, too, were relatively favorable for an opening. Isolation was still theoretically firm, complete and immutable, but cracks and fissures were beginning to appear in the monolithic structure of the Tokugawa Shogunate. Scattered throughout Japan, a number of so-called "Dutch scholars" were reading European books smuggled in through Deshima. They realized that Japan must voluntarily open to some extent or risk being forced open in a humiliating manner, as China had been by the Opium War. Takashima, a Japanese of high standing, devoted his energies and private fortune to improving Japan's means of defense, purchasing muskets and cannon in Holland, and translating European military works into Japanese. It was probably lucky for Perry that Takashima's ideas had not got very far by 1853, and that earthen forts equipped with small smooth-bores were all that Edo Bay had for defense. Through the Dutch, European medicine reached Japan, and physicians were the only "Dutch scholars" tolerated by the authorities. Still others, such as Sakuma and Yoshida, whom we shall encounter later, hoped to make the government more receptive to European ideas, and to overhaul a system which not only excluded bright young men from official posts but kept the bulk of the people ignorant and illiterate. But vested interests against change were so strong that these bewildered and unorganized young liberals could never have broken the ironclad system or brought about the end of the Shogunate in 1868, but for the entering wedge inserted by Perry.

Much was known about the United States in 1853 by top-echelon Japanese. At least two books of description and history had appeared in Japan before Perry's arrival. Important information also reached Japan from Manjiro, a Japanese castaway. Shipwrecked on a small Pacific island and rescued by whaleship *John Howland,* he was carried home by her master, Captain William H. Whitfield, and in 1843 sent to school at the age of sixteen in Fairhaven, the next town to New Bedford. Manjiro joined the '49 gold rush to California, made his way to Honolulu, and there met two other castaways with whom he planned a return to their fatherland. Knowing that this was forbidden under pain of death, they tried to enter via the Ryukyus, but were arrested and sent to Kagoshima for interrogation by the Daimyo of Satsuma. That potentate, having the sense to see that decapitating the castaways would cut off an important source of information, sent them to Nagasaki, where officials pumped Manjiro dry of everything he knew about the United States. His account of the Mexican War made a deep impression, and his insistence that America entertained no "imperialist" ambitions in the Orient was reassuring, if not convincing. Manjiro also gave his questioners an interesting account of American manners and customs, even mentioning the thrifty New England custom of catching up on one's reading while sitting on the john! These lengthy interrogations, along with the books Manjiro had smuggled in, were sent to the Bakufu, the central government at Edo. There Manjiro was given samurai rank, a new name (Iwakara), and appointed official translator of English documents. Later, on a foreign mission, he revisited his old friends in Fairhaven.

Thus, the upper ranks of Japanese society probably knew as much about America in 1853 as literate Americans knew about Japan. But it is easy to exaggerate the extent of pre-Perry foreign influence in Japan. The vast majority of the samurai and all farmers, fishermen, handicraftsmen and other simple people remained completely ignorant of everything beyond their own shores; for them the "outer barbarians" were hairy-faced pirates who plundered and kidnapped. Almost everything in government and society remained exactly as it had been when Shogun Ieyasu adopted his seclusion policy. The people still wore their traditional dress, home-made and handwoven, and were confined within rigid class lines. The 260 daimyo, the great feudal lords, did pretty much as they liked in their own domains, and traveled in lacquered sedan chairs carried by retainers accompanied by a guard of two-sworded samurai who cut down or killed any common people who got in their way or who failed to do proper obeisance. These samurai, a hereditary class of warriors, were the original "gentlemen of Japan." Although for the most part poor, living on whatever their master chose to give them, and uneducated in everything except sword-play, they were completely loyal to the rulers, the customs and traditions of old Japan. Thus to say that Japan was ripe for an opening in 1853 and that Perry was simply the agent of an inevitable event, is about as sensible as to say that America was ripe for discovery in 1492 and Columbus nothing more than a symbol.

On the American side, the project of a naval expedition to open Japan came to a head in 1851. On 10 June Captain J. A. Aulick USN, about to depart in U.S.S. *Susquehanna* to take command of the East India Squadron, received instructions from Daniel Webster, President Fillmore's Secretary of State. He should enter Edo Bay and demand a treaty providing for repatriation of shipwrecked mariners and granting the American merchant marine permission to buy Japanese coal. The "godlike Daniel," in one of his flights of rhetoric, described coal as "a gift of Providence deposited by the Creator of all things in the depths of the Japanese islands for the benefit of the human family." What the Shogun would have made of this amazing statement we shall never know, because the Aulick expedition never came off. The Commodore lost his command, partly because of a breakdown in health at Canton, partly owing to malicious gossip; it was alleged, untruthfully, that he had given his son a free ride to the Far East and had tried to shake down a Brazilian diplomat who left the ship at Rio. What Aulick, a run-of-the-mine naval officer, would have done with a Japan expedition had his health improved is a matter of conjecture. His appointment had been made hastily, and probably both Navy and State Departments were glad for an excuse to clear the decks for Perry.

Which was the last thing that "Old Bruin" wanted!

CHAPTER XXI

Organizing the Japan Expedition
1851–1852

> The delays and difficulties which have beset me in the
> equipment of the vessels, designated to form the Force to be
> placed under my Command . . . have been notorious. . . .
> They were not calculated to advance the reputation for Sci-
> ence, Skill or energy of those who had the direction at the
> time.
>
> — PERRY, *manuscript Journal of the Japan Expedition.*

Perry to Command East India Squadron

IF a computer system had been invented by 1851, and officers' records
kept on I.B.M. cards, a query as to what naval officer was best qualified
to negotiate with Japan, would have elicited a punched pattern spelling
out "Matthew Calbraith Perry." Nobody in the navy even approached his
record for diplomacy. He had negotiated with the Capudan Pasha, the
Kingdom of Naples, the President of Liberia, sundry African chiefs, and
with Yucateco leaders during the Mexican War. He had kept his temper
during the trying voyage with John Randolph of Roanoke and had patiently dealt with irascible naval officers such as Farragut and Tattnall.
Even Perry's physical appearance qualified him as an Oriental negotiator:
he was dignified, impressive, and had become somewhat portly. The regulation naval frock coat accented his "corporation," as a Chinese mandarin's gown would have done; this served him well because Orientals regard a full belly as an emblem of affluence and honor. Whilst the
daguerreotype of him in profile (now owned by the Naval Academy
Museum) shows his features to have been strong and serene, the full-faced
photograph showing the corners of his mouth turned down, gives him a
stern appearance. This *hsiung* expression (as the Chinese call it) conformed to the conventional Japanese manner of depicting a warrior: he
should look fierce, intense, determined. The Commodore's hair, so luxuriant for a man of his age that Nathaniel Hawthorne mistook it for a wig,

Commodore Perry in 1852

still held its dark brown color. All in all, Perry had a very distinguished presence, enhanced, in the opinion of contemporaries, by a deliberate manner of speaking which nowadays might seem pompous.

Far from intriguing to relieve Aulick, as certain people charged, Perry had done his best to obtain a different assignment, as his letters to William Sinclair and to Secretary Graham prove. Sinclair, a friend of the Perrys since 1811 when he and Oliver commanded gunboats in the same squadron, had risen to headship of the bureau of provisions and clothing. Commodore Perry hated self-promotion, loathed personal lobbying, and avoided Washington whenever possible, but he needed an intimate friend in the department to keep him in touch with service politics and wrote confidential letters to Sinclair which reveal his intimate thoughts.

In May 1851, three weeks after Aulick's appointment to the East India Squadron, Perry wrote to Sinclair declaring his eagerness to command the Mediterranean Squadron. The August Belmonts were planning to spend the following winter in Europe, taking with them the entire Perry family not otherwise occupied — Jane, her youngest daughter Isabella "to complete her education," the John Hones, and possibly a few Slidells and Rodgerses. "No one disapproves more than I do the residence of females of high or low degree on board ship," wrote Perry, but in view of the fact that most of his family would be in southern Europe, "It would be particularly desirable that I should be on that station . . . that I might, as convenient, communicate with them." He adds that but for this projected European trip he would not care to go to sea again "under the present state of discipline of the Navy" — an allusion to the abolition of flogging.

The summer passed without any decision being made about Perry. He wrote to Sinclair, 21 October 1851, begging him to smoke out the department's intentions "with regard to the Mediterranean Command." Sinclair replied that intentions were negative. On 18 November 1851 Secretary Graham recalled Commodore Aulick from the East India command, and on the same day ordered Perry to "proceed to Washington immediately." Perry complied, but found the Secretary too busy to do more than broach the subject of his relieving Aulick, hear his objections, and hastily promise to send him to the Mediterranean.

Somewhat offended by this brush-off, Perry wrote a long letter to Graham on 2 December, expressing his views firmly and frankly. It would be "a serious disappointment and cause of personal inconvenience not to go to the Mediterranean, as I was led to believe that it had been the intention of the Department." He feels "a strong disinclination" to go to the Far East, "as the mere relief or successor to Commodore Aulick," an officer who had served under him in the Mexican War. But if — a very big if — "the sphere of action of the East India Squadron and its force should be so much enlarged as to hold out a well-grounded hope of its conferring distinction to its Commander," he will not object. Supposing, however, that "it is not intended to augment" the East India Squadron "in view of carrying out the important object with respect to Japan," he will respectfully but firmly hold the Secretary to his "kind promise" to give him the Mediterranean command. Perry then described the proper composition, objectives and methods of a Japan expedition, all remarkably close to what was done, and concluded by referring the Secretary to a paper he had written on the subject "last winter and marked Private." Thus, although Perry did not want the command, he had given the subject careful thought. And this is confirmed by a letter that he wrote on 18 December 1851 to Captain Joseph C. Delano of New Bedford, a leading whaleship owner who was eager for action with respect to Japan:

I am prepared and shall cheerfully undertake the service to which you refer and with respect to which we have already had some correspondence, *provided* I am entrusted with the authority, and the means of securing a *reasonable* chance of success, but without these powers, and the necessary force, I shall not willingly embark on an enterprise, which if unsuccessful, saying nothing of my own mortification, would fatally retard the ultimate accomplishment of the desired end: — the opening of a friendly intercourse with Japan and the adjacent Islands and the emancipation of the unfortunates of which you speak, now suffering in cruel & hopeless captivity.

Perry adds a jocose paragraph, indicating that he had no sympathy with the popular hero Kossuth, or with "Young America's" aspirations to "liberate" the Old World and set up republics:

The present time would be propitious for the undertaking now that the Jenny Lind fever has subsided, were it not that all the sympathies of our excitable foreigners were embarked in the cause of Hungarian liberty (alias socialism & Red republicanism) poor Jack must wait, as he has been wont to do, for a more fitting time, or in other words until we learn to let our neighbours affairs alone, and look out for our own. Fortunately the President and Cabinet have so far escaped the epidemic.

What, then, happened to bring Perry into the picture? Obviously the reading of his "paper marked Private" referred to above, coupled with an appreciation of his diplomatic experience. Possibly a push from President Fillmore, whom Perry accompanied on a junket in May 1851 to Dunkirk, New York, to celebrate the opening of an important new stretch of the Hudson & Lake Erie Railroad. The President made a favorable impression on the Commodore, and it may be assumed that the feeling was mutual. Both were eager to enlarge the commerce and advance the prestige of the United States, and Fillmore was anxious to get the long-planned Japan expedition off the ground. So was Secretary Graham, a good judge of men, a former state governor and senator, and one of the best navy secretaries of that century.

At any rate, Perry's last plea for the Mediterranean command failed.[1] On 14 January 1852 Secretary Graham wrote, "Commodore Perry will proceed to Washington and report to the Secretary of the Navy without delay. Report in person at the Department." Report he did, to be told that although he must go to Japan, he could have any available ships to augment the East India Squadron, appoint his own officers, and spend any reasonable amount of money on equipment and presents; in other words, "write his own ticket." His oral orders to command the expedition were dated 22 January. On 3 March he was relieved of the superintendency of mail steamers, and on the 24th he received written orders for Japan.

Perry quickly became reconciled. On 8 April 1852 he wrote to Captain Delano, "For myself I would much rather be engaged in duties which involve trial and responsibility, than in those which tend to ease & comfort." There's the real "Old Bruin"! Secretary Graham promised to beef up the East India Squadron to twelve men-of-war, and actually furnished ten, including three storeships.

The Commodore rebuilt the squadron around his old flagship, to which he returned as commanding officer on 13 May. "The *Mississippi* has always been a favorite with me," he noted at the opening of his journal. "As the Flag Ship of a former Squadron under my command she has rendered good Service, and with God's Providence, I may still hope with her and other vessels of my Squadron to accomplish something that may redound to the honor and credit of the Country." In preparation for this extended cruise, her coal bunkers were enlarged from 450 to 600 tons' capacity. She had no flag quarters, but Perry intended to shift his pendant to the more commodious *Susquehanna*, a barque-rigged sidewheeler, best of several steam warships which the navy had built since the Mexican War. Perry also had her sister ship *Powhatan*, whose engineer officer reported that her engines ran as if "set in music"; they lasted until she was broken up in 1887. Steamers *Alleghany* and *Princeton* were also assigned to him, but their engines broke down and they had to drop out; this was probably fortunate because the logistics problem was exceedingly difficult. Perry had to arrange for fuel supply by echelons of chartered colliers in addition to the three storeships. The rest of the squadron consisted of four sloops-of-war of the sailing navy: *Saratoga*, Perry's flagship en route to Africa in 1842; *Macedonian*, in which he had returned from Africa;

---

[1] In the Dartmouth College Library is a "Private" letter of Secretary Webster to Samuel Jaudon of Philadelphia, dated 25 January 1852. He says that if "the Commodore had made known his wishes while here, they could have been readily accomplished." He supposed Perry "to be quite desirous" of the East India command. So, Perry may have missed getting the Mediterranean command at the last minute because of failure to call on Daniel Webster!

Plymouth, built in 1843; and *Vandalia,* a real old-timer partly rebuilt in 1848.[1] Graham promised him ship-of-the-line *Vermont* but Perry never got her for the curious if conclusive reason that the department had no funds to pay the big crew required by a ship of that size.

Perry chose his officers well. "The selection," he wrote to Joel Abbot, "was made from those who served with me in the Mexican War." Three close friends, Commanders Franklin Buchanan, Sidney S. Lee, and Abbot himself, were appointed commanding officers respectively of *Susquehanna,* *Mississippi* and *Macedonian.* Commander Henry A. Adams, who had shown great discretion in Yucatán, became the Commodore's chief of staff with the title Captain of the Fleet. Lieutenant Silas Bent, another stalwart of the Gulf Squadron, became his flag lieutenant. As secretary, Perry appointed his chronically unemployed son Oliver and, to avoid the unfriendly gossip that had been Aulick's undoing, paid his fare to Canton by merchant ship. Except for this son, and Lieutenant John Duer, there were none of the Perry-Rodgers-Slidell clan among the 190 to 200 officers of the squadron — J. Fenimore Cooper's taunts of nepotism evidently had rankled, and Perry did not wish to have them revived. Two of the Commodore's most successful selections were a seagoing Frenchman as *chef de cuisine,* and an Italian bandmaster to train and conduct his flag musicians. Perry, no gourmet himself, had observed that naval enlisted cooks were incapable of tickling foreign palates; he knew that good eating and drinking was the oil of diplomacy. And he valued music not only to entertain the natives, but to maintain shipboard morale.

For his ships' crews and replacements for vessels already in Far Eastern waters, Perry advised his captains to recruit mostly landsmen and boys who would "in a very short time become more effective men in a steamer than middle-aged men of questionable constitution." He feared lest "old salts" prove difficult to handle without the threat of flogging. "We shall now learn how the philanthropic principle of moral suasion answers," he wrote to Commander Buchanan.

The gathering of accurate information about Japan engaged Perry's earnest attention. Flag lieutenant Silas Bent had been to Nagasaki with Glynn in *Preble.* Perry entered into an extensive correspondence with Captain Joseph C. Delano, asking innumerable questions and adding jocosely, "Applying the adage that 'the old coach horse loves the crack of the whip,' perhaps you may find relaxation from the monotony of a shore life in traversing in imagination the remote seas and Countries to which I have invited your attention, at all events I may hope so." He visited Delano at New Bedford in April 1852 and queried many whaling captains who had sailed in the Japan seas, notably Mercator Cooper who had been

---

[1] See list of the squadron with dimensions, etc., at end of Chapter XXV, p. 356.

a castaway. He requested the American minister to the Netherlands to find out what he could there. The Dutch were very helpful, furnished some important charts of Japan, and forwarded to the Japanese government Secretary Webster's official announcement that an American naval squadron would visit their country in 1853.

Perry obtained copies of all important European books about Japan. The most authoritative was *Nippon, Archiv zur Beschreibung von Japan* (Vol. I, Leyden: 1832) by Philipp Franz von Siebold, a German physician and naturalist attached to the Dutch factory at Deshima in the 1820's. Von Siebold accompanied the head of the factory on an embassy to the Shogun's court at Edo and there obtained permission to instruct Japanese physicians in western medicine. Owing to his arrogance and indiscretions, Von Siebold was eventually expelled from Japan, but not before he had learned more about her than had any European since 1600. A popular work based largely on his *Nippon*, called *Manners and Customs of the Japanese*, appeared in London and New York in 1852. As soon as this learned German got wind of the American Expedition he begged to be enrolled as guide, interpreter and adviser; but Perry sized him up as *persona non grata* in Japan who would make trouble, and, also suspecting that he was in Russian pay, turned him down. Von Siebold then attached himself to the Russian Japan Expedition under Admiral Putiatin which reached Nagasaki several weeks after Perry's first visit, and after returning to Europe published a pamphlet which aroused the Commodore's violent indignation. He claimed that he and Russia, not Perry and America, had opened Japan!

A surprising number of books on Japan were available. Second only to Von Siebold for accurate information is the English translation of a Dutch work by Engelbert Kaempfer, *The History of Japan*. A popular abridgment entitled *An Account of Japan* came out in 1853, reaching Perry in time for his second visit.[1] Captain Golownin of the Russian Navy, held prisoner in Japan for years after being shipwrecked, wrote a book of fascinating *Recollections* (3 volumes, 1824); and Père Charlevoix S.J., of Canadian fame, also wrote a history of Japan. Recent works were *Japan and the Japanese* (1852) by Talbot Watts "late of the Hon. the B.E.I. Company's Service"; Charles MacFarlane's *Japan, an Account Geographical and Historical* (1852); and a volume by Dubois de Jancigny in Didot's great series *L'Univers* (1850). Perry took with him the potted Von Siebold and Kaempfer, Charlevoix, Golownin, MacFarlane, and Thunberg (to be mentioned shortly); and before leaving Hong Kong he asked interpreter Williams to lend him other books on Japan from his own library.

Most of these works were well illustrated and presented a fairly accu-

---

[1] The Harvard copy is inscribed, "Geo. Henry Preble, U.S.N. On board U.S. Ship *Macedonian*."

rate and comprehensive picture of the history, society, manners and customs, religion and commerce, currency, weights and measures, of Japan. Even the tea ceremony, the geisha, and the dwarf trees were described. The fanciful Professor C. P. Thunberg, of the University of Upsala, presented Japan to his readers in his *Travels* of 1795 as a veritable Utopia, and gave a completely erroneous description of the government, where "are to be found neither Throne, Sceptre, Crown, nor any other species of Royal Foppery, . . . no Lords in waiting, nor Maids of Honor," etc. No European or American managed to understand the Japanese government. Westerners with a knowledge of the two consuls of Rome assumed that Japan had two emperors: one whom they called the Mikado or Daïri, supposedly a sort of high priest who lived in seclusion at Kyoto; the other, the secular emperor whom they called the Tycoon, living at Edo. Actually there was only one emperor, in whose name the hereditary Tycoon or Shogun of the house of Tokugawa had governed since 1600. Neither Perry nor his predecessors comprehended this peculiar Japanese dualism, but the double-emperor hypothesis turned out to be a useful error. Perry was satisfied with having the President's letter to the Emperor delivered to the Shogun at Edo; never, short of invading the country, could he have reached Emperor Konei at Kyoto.

The Bakufu (literally, "government behind a curtain"), as the Shogunate was called, had interesting methods of keeping Japan under strict control. Each daimyo or feudal lord had to spend part of every year in Edo (the future Tokyo) and leave his family there as hostages for good behavior when he returned home. Any member of the Shogun's appointed *rujo* (council of elders) could propose an amendment to the laws, but if it was not adopted, the proposer had to commit harikari. In 1853 Abe (Masahiro) Ise no kami, the senior councillor and a fairly intelligent man, was running the Bakufu because the Shogun was ill and had no mind of his own. A wonderful system indeed for maintaining stability and security, which Japan badly needed after centuries of foreign war and civil turmoil. And there was nothing "primitive" about it; at Edo where each important daimyo maintained a palatial town house with a beautiful and extensive garden, the arts flourished, and the sophisticated, aristocratic society which we read about in *The Tale of Genji* continued as in the Middle Ages. Perry, through his reading, knew that he had to deal with a highly civilized, proud and essentially powerful nation whose system of government had become incapable of coping with the machine age or the realities of nineteenth-century international intercourse.

Perry had a broader conception of the Japan Expedition than originally did the administration, but President Fillmore and the cabinet came to share his views. In the realm of high strategy he conceived of it as the opening move of an eventual struggle between the United States and

Great Britain for control of the Pacific. A bad prophecy, to be sure; Perry would have been surprised and grieved to learn that the nation he helped to bring out into the bright light of the nineteenth century would force an all-out war on the United States before another century elapsed.

In the realms of geography, natural history, and sociology, Perry considered the Expedition an opportunity to make a comprehensive report on Japan. He wished to correct false statements by earlier writers and to bring out the true nature of Japanese society, commerce, fisheries, and agriculture. To that end he, or the department, sought an appropriation from Congress for a scientific corps to accompany the Expedition, analagous to Napoleon's in Egypt,[1] but Congress refused. He also had the precedent of the Pacific Exploring Expedition of 1838-43, for which Commander Wilkes was allowed to recruit civilian artists and scientists at salaries up to $2500 a year. Wilkes enlisted several specialists, but the experiment was not altogether successful; naval officers and men of science did not get along well, and Congress was very slow to publish their scientific reports — the last did not appear until 1871. Since the Navy Department regarded the Japan Expedition as primarily and essentially diplomatic, it refused to make any special provision for civilian scientists. Hence the only way Perry could obtain experts was to persuade them to accept a naval rating of acting master's mate and pay of $25 per month. As he explained to Captain Abbot, they were so rated "by special authority of the Department to give to certain scientific persons some definite position, and to make them amenable to Naval Law." An example of the simple way in which Perry accomplished this may be seen in a note from him to one of his captains on behalf of John P. Williams of Utica, a telegrapher. If the Captain finds Williams to be "a robust healthy young man," enlist him as a master's mate for the East India Squadron. He did, and Williams set up the first telegraph line in Japan; but though pronounced both robust and healthy, the young man died at Hong Kong and is buried at Macao.

Two artists, William Heine and Eliphalet Brown Jr., were selected from several score who applied; their paintings and sketches make a valuable pictorial record of the Expedition. Brown, a pioneer photographer who gave up a valuable business in New York to join, brought along a daguerreotype camera and a large supply of plates, with which he took four or five hundred "stills" of scenery, and of Japanese officials sitting very stiffly with retainers behind them. Perry presented most of these to their subjects; and of the balance, twenty or more were engraved for the official Narrative. Peter Bernard Wilhelm Heine, to use his full name, was

---

[1] Perry probably had seen a set of the magnificent *Déscription de l'Egypte* at the home of William H. Eliot, one of his former hosts in Boston, or at the Harvard College Library to which Eliot presented it around 1829.

only twenty-five years old and had been in the United States but three years. He painted the illustrations of Oriental scenery and Japanese ceremonies, which were lithographed for the official Narrative, and made some excellent paintings of fruit and flowers for Perry's manuscript Journal.

The only civilian who made trouble for the Commodore was Dr. James Morrow, a thirty-three-year-old physician who had experimented with tropical plants on his father's Carolina plantation, and whom the Secretary of State appointed "agriculturist" of the Expedition without consulting Perry, and sent out to join him in Hong Kong. Morrow proved to be a good collector; but his egotism, as we shall see, thwarted the Commodore's plan to have an entire volume of the official Narrative devoted to botany. A biographer who has tried to rescue Morrow from oblivion has stated that Perry "inflexibly opposed the appointment of any civilians to the expedition." That is false. He badly wanted civilian artists and scientists, but few were young and adventurous enough to accept naval pay and rating. And, by exception, three interpreters and Bayard Taylor were signed on in China without these conditions.

Perry combed the navy for officers who might enhance the Expedition's intellectual capability. The most useful person in this category was flag chaplain Reverend George Jones, whom he had known in the Mediterranean Squadron. A graduate of Yale, rector of Christ Church, Middletown, seagoing navy chaplain for twelve years and to the Naval Academy for two years, Jones had managed to acquire a considerable knowledge of geology and astronomy, and at the age of fifty-three was bursting with energy. Several other officers, most of them surgeons, wrote reports on botany and geology; and at least a score of the juniors made useful reports on hydrography.

"It is my duty," wrote Perry in his Journal, "and it certainly is a pleasure to say, that the President and every member of his Cabinet evinced the liveliest interest in the Expedition, and extended towards me the utmost kindness and consideration, authorized the most liberal equipment of the vessels, invested me with extraordinary powers, diplomatic as well as Naval."

The government gave Perry *carte blanche* to purchase presents for the Emperor and lesser officials, and these he assembled with great care. To prove that Americans were no uncultured barbarians, he bought copies of Audubon's two magnificent elephant folios, *Birds of America* and *Quadrupeds of America*, published at $1000 each. The Shogun, who received them, probably better enjoyed the baskets of champagne, barrel of whiskey, cask of Madeira and case of arms donated by Mr. Colt of Hartford. Nor were the royal ladies forgotten; Jane saw to it that the flagship laid in a supply of mirrors and French perfumes for the Queen Mother of "Loo

Choo" and the Empress of Japan. Assuming that the Japanese would be mainly interested in machinery and gadgets, Perry loaded an assortment of farming implements, clocks, stoves, a daguerreotype camera, a telegraph instrument, and a quarter-size steam locomotive with tender, coach and track which he had specially built in Philadelphia.

Samuel F. B. Morse, inventor of the electric telegraph, instructed one of Perry's lieutenants at Poughkeepsie in the Morse code and how to set up and exhibit the instruments. Perry, when studying lighthouses in Paris in 1838, had met Morse, then trying to interest l'Académie des Sciences in his invention, and now wrote to him: "I hope you will pardon this intrusion upon your time. I feel almost assured, however that you will take a lively interest in having your wonderful invention exhibited to a people so little known to the world." Perry spent the first half of 1852 traveling between Boston, Albany, New York, New Bedford, Philadelphia and Washington, gathering information and accumulating equipment. At the end of June he wrote to William Sinclair that after completing the transfer of his Tarrytown estate to its new owner, he would hasten to Philadelphia and Washington to cope with a new situation.

Down-East Interlude

Midsummer of 1852 brought Perry a political check which postponed the start of his Expedition for months. The Whig national nominating convention put up General Winfield Scott for president and Secretary Graham for vice president. Graham thenceforth took slight interest in Perry or Japan, and resigned from the cabinet to devote himself to politics. His replacement as Navy Secretary was the novelist John P. Kennedy, who had an immediate problem to deal with — the long-standing fisheries dispute with Canada; and Perry became involved.

This particular row concerned Yankee fishermen encroaching on the territorial waters of the Maritime Provinces. The Anglo-American Convention of 1818 forbade United States fishing craft to operate inside a line three miles off the coasts of New Brunswick, Nova Scotia and Prince Edward Island. As the number of New England fishing vessels increased, their crews became more bold and aggressive. Canadian fishing interests petitioned the British government to do something to restrain them, and in 1841 the British Admiralty imposed a serious restriction. The permitted line would no longer follow the beach, but be drawn from headland to headland across every bay. Thus, the Gut of Canso, Northumberland Straits and the entire Baie de Chaleur, as well as a number of other bays in deeply indented Nova Scotia, became forbidden waters to Yankees. Many refused to respect this order, defiantly pushed their operations even within the three-mile limit, and landed to buy bait and firewood. Britain then sent out a formidable naval squadron under Vice Admiral Sir George Seymour RN, which proceeded to police the Yankee fishing fleet. His alleged highhandedness created indignation in the United States. There arose a rumble of anti-British oratory in Congress, especially on the part of the Democrats who, in view of the forthcoming election, hoped to pin something on the Whigs. So, it had to be Perry to the rescue — a quick transition from Far East to Down East!

In *Mississippi* Perry sailed from New York on the last day of July 1852, with instructions to pour oil on these troubled waters. After communicating with a fleet of eighty mackerel fishermen in the Gulf of Maine, he raised the Machias Seal Islands, passed through Grand Manan Channel, and threaded Quoddy Roads to Eastport, a ticklish bit of navigation even at high water. There, Perry gathered information from officials and shipowners, visited Campobello where a British warship gave him a 13-gun salute, and proceeded to St. John, New Brunswick, where he spent a week listening to provincial complaints of Yankee fishermen. *Mississippi* now crossed the Bay of Fundy and rounded Cape Sable to Halifax where Admiral Seymour's flagship *Cumberland* lay at anchor. After plenty of gunpowder had been expended in salutes by both navies and the harbor forts, Perry and Seymour conferred. As two old sailors they understood each other. Seymour promised to restrain his over-eager lieutenants from exercising the disputed right of visit and search, and Perry promised to warn Yankee fishermen against being too rambunctious. Before leaving Halifax the Commodore wrote to Jane, "I think I shall get through this delicate duty much to my & to all satisfaction if the government will not interfere." He did, and the government gratefully accepted it.

At Halifax, Perry entertained on board the Most Reverend Dr. Walsh, Archbishop of Halifax, Archbishop John Hughes of New York, and "a Suite of Bishops, also by the Commander of the Forces at Halifax." Refreshments were served and more gunpowder burned. A forthcoming consecration explains this episcopal muster and a sumptuous banquet at the Bishop's Palace which Perry and forty others attended.

Perry also did a little business for the Japan Expedition. Sir George, with whom he dined on board his flagship, promised to procure for him copies of the most recent charts and sailing directions of the eastern seas. And a box from the Admiralty containing four books and eighty charts arrived at Norfolk just in time for Perry to take to Japan.

Mississippi now steamed along the outer coast of Nova Scotia and through the Gut of Canso into the Gulf of St. Lawrence, frequently stopping American fishing vessels to question the skippers and caution them against landing or otherwise exceeding their rights. The ship's surgeon boarded schooner *Ocean Star* of Camden, Maine, "to give Medical attention to one of her sick." A fleet of 54 mackerel schooners was encountered off Prince Edward Island, and every one boarded and questioned. "These vessels," Perry reported, "generally had a copy of the Treaty on board. They complained, however, of a want of precision in it in reference to the Bays, Inlets, and Indentations of the Land. . . . All seemed anxious to get permission to fish inside the Bay of Chaleur. It may be remarked that they all seemed aware of the necessity of compliance with the Treaty with Great Britain, and that if they were caught fishing inside the limits it was at their own responsibility. The crews of these Vessels appeared stout, healthy and American."

Returning to New York on 1 September, Perry after sifting all complaints reported to the Secretary of the Navy that the "British outrages" amounted to exactly four American vessels seized in the years 1848-1851 and later released; and that the "Yankee aggressions" consisted of a few fishermen resisting arrest by arms, and brawling ashore with Nova Scotia "Bluenoses." Some 2500 American vessels and 27,500 men were engaged in fishing, and although both fishermen and Royal Navy had occasionally been over-aggressive, clashes were few, and the British authorities were inclined to be reasonable. The net effect of Perry's report was to allay excitement in the United States, a happy and necessary prelude to concluding a reciprocity treaty with Canada in 1854.

Thus Perry had one more diplomatic mission to his credit.

Instructions and Final Preparations

During Perry's absence, little had been done to forward the Japan Expedition. The Commodore accordingly sought and obtained permission from Secretary Kennedy to depart in his flagship with *Princeton* only, trusting that the other ships not already in Chinese waters would be dispatched as soon as possible. Then there was the matter of his instructions which, in view of Perry's diplomatic status, President Fillmore decided should be issued by the State Department. Perry called on Secretary Webster in Washington to obtain them. He found the New England colossus a mere shadow of his former self, suffering from cirrhosis of the liver, almost incapable of doing business. James Watson Webb, a friend to both, after discussions with Perry, had had several interviews with Webster, "who not only entered into the question with great zeal, but took an enlarged view of the manner in which the expedition should be got up — its imposing character, etc., and he authorised me to say to you that you should not only have all the strength you desired, but that you should be clothed with full and discretionary powers." Webb accompanied the Commodore in his interview with the Secretary of State, who confirmed the promise that Perry could "write his own ticket."

Shortly after this interview Webster retired to his home in Marshfield, and died there on 24 October 1852. The last but not least achievement of this great man is that amid his suffering he grasped the full importance of the Japan Expedition. Few people did outside the government. Most of the press ignored or sneered at it. Perry himself was distressed by the indifference of the business community and urged his friend Delano to stir up the merchants' associations to write letters and pass resolutions. The Japanese historian Nitobe, searching the American periodical press of 1852, was astonished at the absence of public support of the enterprise. The Philadelphia *Public Ledger* regarded it as "romantic"; the Baltimore *Sun* called it "humbug" and "a matter of ridicule."

Although no documentary proof can be found of Perry having written his own orders, the Instructions he received, dated 5 November 1852, in the form of a letter from State to Navy, certainly expressed his ideas. After a brief review of the abortive efforts by Western nations to deal with Japan, and Japan's ill treatment of castaways, the Instructions state: —

The objects sought by this Government are: —

1. To effect some permanent arrangement for the protection of American seamen and property wrecked on these Islands, or driven into their ports by stress of weather.

2. Permission to American vessels to enter one or more of their ports in order to obtain supplies of provisions, water, fuel, &c, or, in case of disasters, to refit so as to enable them to prosecute their voyage.

It is very desirable to have permission to establish a depôt for coal, if not on one of the principal Islands, at least on some small uninhabited one of which, it is said, there are several in their vicinity.

3. Permission to our vessels to enter one or more of their ports for the purpose of disposing of their cargoes by sale or barter.

The next clause, which Webb definitely attributed to Perry, is highly important, as proof that the United States was not asking for exclusive privileges: —

This government, however, does not seek by this expedition to obtain any exclusive commercial advantage for itself, but on the contrary desires and expects that whatever benefits may result from it will ultimately be shared by the civilized world.

It is manifest from past experience, that arguments or persuasion addressed to this people, unless they be seconded by some imposing manifestation of power, will be utterly unavailing.

The Secretary of the Navy will, therefore, be pleased to direct the Commander of the Squadron to proceed, with his whole force, to such point on the coast of Japan as he may deem most advisable, and there endeavor to open a communication with the government, and, if possible, to see the Emperor in person, and deliver to him the letter of introduction from the President with which he is charged.

He will express the President's friendly feelings toward Japan, his grief over her treatment of shipwrecked mariners, and his fervent hope that a reciprocal arrangement may be made for the return of the castaways. A further object of the Expedition will be to establish commercial intercourse, "a difficult, but perhaps not an impossible task." Since "the deep-seated aversion of these people to hold intercourse with Christian nations" originated from "the indiscreet zeal" of Portuguese and other Christian missionaries, Perry will point out that the United States tolerates all religions and does not attempt to proselyte for any. Since our language is English, and the fears of the Japanese are excited against the British owing to their recent annexation of Hong Kong, the Commodore must make it very clear that the United States is no part of, not even an ally, of the British Empire, or any other European country. He shall point out that our wealth and population are rapidly increasing, that California lies only twenty days' steaming from Japan, that the Pacific "will soon be covered with our vessels," and that even a limited Japanese-American trade would be mutually profitable.

Any concessions on these points "should be reduced into the form of a treaty for negotiating which he [Perry] will be furnished with the requisite powers." But "if, after having exhausted every argument and every means of persuasion," the Commodore is unable to extract any concession from the Japanese, "he will then change his tone and inform them . . . that if any acts of cruelty should hereafter be practised upon citizens of this country, whether by the government or by the inhabitants of Japan, they will be severely chastised."

He will bear in mind that as the President has no power to declare war his mission is necessarily of a pacific character, and will not resort to force unless in self-defence in the protection of the vessels and crews under his command, or to resist an act of personal violence offered to himself or to one of his officers.

What we may call the key paragraph of the Instructions follows: —

In his intercourse with this people, who are said to be proud and vindictive in their character, he should be courteous and conciliatory but at the same time, firm and decided. He will therefore submit with patience and forbearance to acts of discourtesy to which he may be subjected by a people whose usages it will not do to test by our standard of propriety, but, at the same time, will be careful to do nothing that may compromit, in their eyes, his own dignity or that of the country. He will, on the contrary, do every thing to impress them with a just sense of the power and greatness of this country, and to satisfy them that its past forbearance has been the result, not of timidity, but of a desire to be on friendly terms with them.

This paragraph was certainly drafted by Perry. His belief in dignity, firmness and forbearance is manifest from his early career. His close conformity to those principles, and patience with the irritating evasions and procrastination of the Japanese, will be manifest from events to come.

As the State Department cannot in these Instructions provide for every contingency, "It is proper that the Commodore should be invested with large discretionary powers and should feel assured that any departure from usage or any error of judgment he may commit will be viewed with indulgence." Perry will call at Hong Kong and Macao to support certain claims by the United States on China; he will, if he has time, explore the coasts of Japan and conclude treaties with any independent sovereignties he may encounter — meaning presumably the Ryukyus. And he may draw on Baring Brothers of London, the department's English bankers, for extra expenses in the Orient, and for the purchase of presents.

Strangely enough, nothing is said in the Instructions about Perry asking for Japanese consent to designate certain harbors as ports of refuge. The Commodore, rereading the document on the first leg of his outward passage, noted that omission, pointed it out to the Secretary of State in a letter from Funchal, and proposed that if Japan proved recalcitrant he might obtain permission from the government of "Loo-Choo," the Ryukyus. In reply, Secretary Everett on 15 February 1853 wrote that President Fillmore fully concurred, and believed that his best chance would be at Okinawa — a good guess. Perry must visit the Ryukyus, and "forbid and at all hazards prevent plunder and acts of violence on the part of your men toward these simple and unwarlike people; — for such they are described to be. Let them from the first see that your coming among them is a benefit and not an evil to them. Make no use of force, except in the last resort for defence if attacked, and self-preservation." And pay for all supplies that the Okinawans furnish.

Everett concludes: —

The President is gratified to perceive that you are impressed with the importance of the enterprize confided to your direction, the success of which will mainly depend upon your Prudence and address. It will attract a large share of the attention of the civilized world; and the President feels great confidence that the measures adopted by you will reflect credit on your own Wisdom and discretion and do honor to your country.

Other documents were necessary, especially a presidential letter to the "Emperor" at Edo. Edward Everett drafted President Fillmore's letter of 13 November 1852 to his "Great and Good Friend" the Shogun. Even the most distinguished Americans in those days knew nothing about proper forms of address to Oriental potentates, and so resorted to a sort of diplomatic pidgin as though the addressee were a child. Everett's letter was somewhat less supernatural than Webster's undelivered one of the previous year, but it had high points: "Commodore Matthew C. Perry, an Officer of the Highest Rank," is about to visit Your Imperial Majesty's dominions. He been directed to assure Your Imperial Majesty that the President entertains "the kindest feelings" toward his person and government, and that the one purpose of this mission is to propose "that the United States and Japan should live in friendship and have commercial intercourse with each other." The United States of America "reaches from ocean to ocean," and Japan is only 18 days' steaming from California, where gold, silver, "and many other valuable articles" are produced. "Japan is also a rich and fertile country, and produces many very valuable articles," as well as people "skilled in many of the arts," the Emperor is informed. The President is aware "that the ancient laws of Your Imperial Majesty's Government do not allow of foreign trade . . . but as the state of the world changes . . . it seems to be wise, from time to time, to make new laws." At the period "when the ancient laws of Your Imperial Majesty's Government were first made," America was being discovered and settled by Europeans. "For a long time there were but a few people, and they were poor. They have now become quite numerous" and (it is hinted) very rich. If Your Imperial Majesty does not deem it wise to repeal his ancient laws of exclusion, he might consider suspending them "for five or ten years so as to try the experiment." If this does not work, he can restore them.

Next, the poor whalers are mentioned. "It sometimes happens, in stormy weather, that one of our ships is wrecked on Your Imperial Majesty's shores. In all such cases we ask, and expect, that our unfortunate people should be treated with kindness. . . . We are very much in earnest in this." And there is the touchy subject of coal. "Our steamships, in crossing the great Ocean, burn a great deal of coal, and it is not convenient to bring it all the way from America." The request is made that "Your Imperial Majesty appoint a convenient port, in the southern part of the Empire, where our vessels may stop," to purchase coal, water and provisions. "We are very desirous of this," too. Thus, friendship, commerce, coal and kindness to castaways are the only objects of this expedition. "May the Almighty have Your Imperial Majesty in His Great and Holy Keeping! Your good friend, Millard Fillmore."

Such was our State Department's contribution toward unscrewing the inscrutable empire of Japan. Could we but know what the Shogun's court made of it! The letter was properly engrossed on parchment and sealed with the Great Seal of the United States enclosed in a gold case and attached to the document by silk cords. With Perry's letter of credence similarly engrossed and sealed, it was placed in a rosewood casket with inlay, hinges and clasps of gold. Unfortunately these samples of American calligraphy and jewelry were destroyed by a fire at Edo in the last century.

Perry's letter of credence gives him full powers "to negotiate, conclude and sign a convention or treaty . . . concerning the friendship, commerce, and navigation of the two countries." This created him envoy extraordinary and minister plenipotentiary, as well as a naval commander, and raised the Japan Expedition from what might have been a mere demonstration of naval power to the status of a diplomatic mission. President Fillmore on 11 November ordered the Great Seal of the United States to be affixed not only to the above-mentioned documents, but to five copies of the Letter of Credence "in blank," names of addressees left out in case Perry should find it convenient to visit other Oriental countries. Exactly what Ferdinand and Isabella did for Columbus in 1492!

A very significant thing about these documents is their failure to demand reparation for past injuries. Every European power in its relations with Oriental countries (and the United States, too, in relations with China and Central America) initiated negotiations by demands for redress of outrages, real or imaginary, payment of financial claims, and the like. The United States might have done this with respect to the maltreated whalemen, the firing on *Morrison*, and the indignity to Commodore Biddle, but forebore. Japanese-American relations started on a clean slate.

With the Commodore at the helm, things began to move. "Is Secretary Kennedy coming to New York in *Powhatan?*" he writes to Sinclair on 2 September. If so, he will await him there. The time had come for farewells to family and friends. Among them was his nephew Christopher Grant Perry, a son of Oliver. The Commodore patted the head of Christopher's seven-year-old boy Tom and said pleasantly, "How'd you like to go to Japan as Uncle Calbraith's cabin boy?" Tommy allowed he would, rushed upstairs, packed a carpetbag, and reported for duty! Thomas Sergeant Perry afterward regarded as the greatest disappointment of his life the revelation that Uncle Calbraith was only joking. Forty-five years later he was compensated by becoming professor of English at one of the new universities of Japan.

In *Mississippi*, towing *Princeton*, Perry departed New York in early September 1852 for Baltimore, where new engines were being constructed for that unlucky screw steamer. In a letter to Sinclair the Commodore explodes over the contractor's delay in finishing these engines, promised nine months earlier, and rightly predicts that "when these contracts are completed there are three chances to one that the work will prove defective." So it turned out. "That unfortunate ship the *Princeton* is fast on the mud at Baltimore," wrote Perry from Annapolis on 16 November.

While waiting for her to float, the Commodore writes from Washington on 31 October to Jane, then staying with the Rodgerses at Havre de Grace, that he has had a long interview with the Navy Secretary, who suggests that he had better stay in Washington until *Princeton* is ready. Rapid progress is being made in fitting out *Vermont, Macedonian, Vandalia* and *Allegheny*,[1] and they will follow him to China. Jane, Sarah, Bill and Calbraith are to join him at Willard's Hotel and see husband and father off.

Still waiting, Perry at Annapolis entertained on board *Mississippi* President Fillmore, Secretary Kennedy, and the rest of the now "lame duck" administration. For the Whig ticket had been decisively defeated at the polls by the Democrats. Fortunately for the Japan Expedition, Perry had always been a Democrat, and his friendship with President-elect Franklin Pierce began during the Mexican War. So the new administration's support of the Expedition was assured, despite the Whigs having the credit for getting it under way.

But not yet. When steaming down Chesapeake Bay, *Princeton's* new engines stalled, and a hurried examination by the fleet engineer officer revealed that they were defective beyond repair. Perry, probably glad to be rid of this hoodoo ship, towed her back to Baltimore and then proceeded to Norfolk, where *Powhatan* awaited him. On a last visit to Washington he received his final letter of instructions from Secretary Kennedy, together with an order to "consider as your guide" the long letter of 5 November from State to Navy. "In prosecuting the objects of your mission to Japan you are invested with large discretionary powers, and you are authorized to employ dispatch vessels, interpreters, Kroomen, or natives, and all other means which you may deem necessary to enable you to bring about the desired results." He will explore the coasts of Japan and of the adjacent islands, and collect the necessary data for charting them. He is to gather all manner of information about countries and places to be visited, and "to these ends you will call into activity the various talents and acquisitions of the officers under your command." A very important paragraph follows, in the execution of which Perry incurred criticism from shipmates who had an itch for publication, since they fancied it was due to his personal selfishness: —

A subject of great importance to the success of the expedition will present itself to your mind, in relation to communications to the prints and newspapers, touching the movements of your squadron, as well as in relation to all matters connected with the discipline and internal regulations of the vessels composing it. You will, therefore, enjoin upon all under your command *to abstain from writing to friends or others upon those subjects.* The journals and private notes

---

[1] *Allegheny*, an iron-hulled steam sloop, broke down and, like *Princeton*, never made it.

of the officers and other persons in the expedition *must be considered as belonging to the government*, until permission shall be received from the Navy Department to publish them. . . .

Tendering you my best wishes for a successful cruise, and a safe return to your country and friends for yourself, officers and companies of your ships,

I am, very respectfully, your obedient servant,

JOHN P. KENNEDY

At Washington a gentlemen's club gave Perry a dinner. Among those present were Secretaries Kennedy and Everett, Senators John J. Crittenden and Jefferson Davis, and some fifteen other notables. An agricultural expert named Horace Capron, one of the last survivors of this company, and himself in later years a benefactor of Japan, recalled Perry's clear and well-defined answers to questions, and the highly favorable impression that he made on all present. Capron even added that "the Almighty Disposer of all things" must have guided the administration in selecting Perry. However that may be, Fillmore certainly appreciated Perry. Announcing the Expedition in his annual message of 6 December 1852, the President described the Commodore as "a discreet and intelligent officer of the highest rank known to our service," gave a brief resumé of his Instructions, thanked the King of the Netherlands for good offices in announcing the coming Expedition to the Japanese, and promised that any privileges obtained for the United States "will be equally enjoyed by all the other maritime powers." Perry had the gratification of reading this in the Hong Kong newspaper of 13 April 1853, *Mississippi* having sailed from Norfolk on 24 November 1852. For, as he wrote in his Journal, "Finding that unless I sailed alone, and trusted to the chances of being joined at uncertain periods by the vessels assigned to my command and under equipment, I might be detained several months longer, I determined with the consent of the Department to proceed with this Ship without further delay." Even *Powhatan* did not accompany her, as she had to await the receipt of a ratified treaty with the Sultan of Borneo which the State Department wished Captain McCluney to exchange at Brunei.

Thus Perry departed unescorted. With his blue pendant flying, *Mississippi* became the nucleus of the East India Squadron and the Japan Expedition; it mattered not if she had no company this side of China, because, as Henry Coppée said after the Mexican War, every naval vessel acquired "a sense of importance" once Perry was on board.

CHAPTER XXII

Bound Away
November 1852 – May 1853

He will bear in mind that as the President has no power
to declare war his mission is necessarily of a pacific character, and will not resort to force unless in self-defence in the
protection of the vessels and crews under his command, or
to resist an act of personal violence offered to himself or to
one of his officers.

— *Perry's Instructions*

THE outward passage to China afforded the officers of *Mississippi* plenty
of sightseeing, thanks to her need for coal. First she called at Funchal,
where all hands enjoyed galloping about on ponies or taking ox-drawn
sledge rides on the lava pavements. Madeira wine cost only a dollar a bottle, and that was a 150 per cent markup for the Americans' benefit. Perry
laid in, at $55 each, fifteen quarter-casks of what the shipper described as
"the most perfect wine that can be exported" for his New York friends,
and another lot, presumably less perfect, for the wardroom and entertainment. The flag band of twenty-three instruments, with its talented bandmaster, amused the ship's company and entertained the populace wherever
they called.

Assuming the dignified title "Commander in Chief United States Naval
Forces Stationed in the East India, China and Japan Seas," Perry now
issued General Orders Nos. 1 and 2, and later extended them to his entire
command. Order No. 1 was an absolute prohibition to officers and men to
send home journals, notes, drawings, curiosities or specimens without his
permission, or to allow their letters to be given to the newspapers. This
order, which would have seemed perfectly reasonable in World War II,
aroused considerable resentment in 1853. Officers and men did not understand why, in time of peace, they should not collect souvenirs or have
their letters printed in hometown newspapers. The order, conforming to
Perry's official Instructions, probably had been conceived by him, since

the printing of gossipy or malicious letters in the American press had annoyed him in Africa and Mexico. Now embarked on a voyage essentially diplomatic and exceedingly delicate, he did not care to risk compromising future relations with Japan by indiscreet and untimely revelations.

General Order No. 2, again following official Instructions, "requested and directed" that every officer under his command "employ such portions of his time as may be spared from his regular duties and proper hours of relaxation" to collect information on a variety of subjects. Perry anticipated our modern questionnaire by providing a printed check-list mentioning twenty-one different subjects, such as hydrography and ichthyology, against which every officer was requested to check his special interest. Despite Perry's assurance that they would receive credit for whatever they did, few officers, and those mostly of the medical corps, availed themselves of this opportunity for fame. One noted exception was the flag chaplain, Reverend George Jones, "a man of great energy of character," according to a shipmate, with a flair for scientific discovery. On the Funchal-St. Helena leg of this outward passage, Jones carefully observed the zodiacal lights, which "were very brilliant, and so remarkable that they proved an object of great interest to all on board." Zodiacal lights are defined by Bowditch as "a faint glow . . . along the ecliptic before sunrise and after sunset, attributed to the reflection of sunlight from quantities of meteorological material." It is a beautiful phenomenon, as you sail in the southern trades; a soft light in the east telling you that another day is about to break.

After passing the Canaries, Captain Lee caused the buckets to be removed from *Mississippi's* paddlewheels and her stack laid flat, and proceeded under sail alone. But the anticipated northeast tradewinds faded after a few days, fires had to be relit, the stack hoisted into place, and buckets replaced. Christmas was kept at sea, and the equator crossed with due ceremony on 3 January 1853. From St. Helena, where the ship spent a few days, *Mississippi* proceeded under sail to Capetown, where officers and most of the men went sightseeing. The Commodore, "having provided himself with a barouche drawn by four beautiful stallions," visited the celebrated vineyards of Constantia. On the way back he called on a Kaffir chief named Seyolo who had been taken prisoner by the British in their war with the natives, together with five of his wives. Seyolo was so pleased with the Commodore's attention that he invited him to take his pick of the wives. This became a subject of merriment in the Perry family, children asking the Commodore, "Why didn't you accept?" and to Jane, "What would you have done if Papa had brought one home?"

At Capetown, *Mississippi* took on board a dozen oxen, fourscore sheep, and a quantity of fresh vegetables to augment the official rations of "salt horse," hardtack, and beans. As an additional antiscorbutic, the Commodore caused the daily grog to be laced with lime juice. As usual, and ever since his African cruises, Perry's efforts on behalf of shipboard health were not appreciated; the shellbacks grumbled over tending cattle and having "limey-juice" in their grog, like the Royal Navy.

The flagship made a record run of fifteen days from Capetown to Port Louis, Mauritius, beating the Peninsular & Oriental steamers and H.M.S. *Sphynx.* At Mauritius, where they spent the last ten days of February, Perry and his officers were entertained both by the British authorities and the French merchants. Everyone of any education in western Europe and the United States had read, and most readers had wept over, Bernardin de St. Pierre's *Paul et Virginie,* the scene of which was laid in this island. To attract tourists, an enterprising inhabitant had erected a "tomb" of Paul and Virginia (admission one shilling). Perry snorted over this and wrote to Jane that it passed his understanding how there could be a tomb of fictional characters; the two lovers never existed! But he ascertained that this "beautiful though fabulous story," as he called it, was founded on an actual shipwreck in which a young French lady was drowned because modesty forbade her to undress before attempting to swim ashore in her lover's arms.

One is impressed by the excellent logistics of the Japan Expedition, especially the timing of sailing colliers. Perry evidently had worked out a schedule with his friend Sinclair in the Navy Department. *Mississippi* coaled at Port Louis from a vessel dispatched for that special purpose by Howard & Aspinwall of New York, and then proceeded to Point de Galle, Ceylon, where another collier awaited her. En route, Perry wrote to Sinclair that he needed more midshipmen — he had only six on board, and with nearly four hundred middies on the navy list it was a "crying shame" that "a full complement cannot be found for any one ship. . . . They prefer any but the legitimate employment for which they entered the Navy." But no more came. He complained, too, of the effect on discipline of abolishing flogging. "The want of legal means for punishing men for the thousand faults they are daily committing, has weakened the authority of the officers, and Congress may be assured that unless some remedy is applied the Navy as an institution will go to the devil."

A poor prophecy indeed, but the Commodore was not the only officer to regret the abolition of flogging. Surgeon Wheelwright of *Powhatan* wrote home from Mauritius, "Everything now is so different from what it was even a few years ago in the Navy. There is no order or system. Officers are dissatisfied and crews disorderly." Bayard Taylor, a civilian, agreed.

Point de Galle, port of call for the P. & O. and other steamship lines, has a neat little harbor and town surrounded by a wall built by the Portuguese and the Dutch before England took over Ceylon. Here the Americans had

their first sight of typical far eastern scenery — backdrop of high mountains, green-clad foothhills, heavy surf all along the outer shore, coconut
palms nodding on the beach. Perry noted in his journal that the "spicy
breezes" which (according to Bishop Heber) "blew soft o'er Ceylon's
isle" were greatly exaggerated; give him a Southern magnolia in full bloom
or a newly mowed field of clover on the Hudson! *Mississippi* spent five
days at Point de Galle. A warship displaying the white elephant ensign,
indicating that she belonged to a King of Siam, lay in the harbor. Perry,
desirous of improving the good relations established by Roberts with
Thailand, entertained the commanding officer on board and gave him a
sword and a Bowditch, together with a Colt pistol for his monarch. The
King, greatly pleased by these attentions, invited the Commodore to pay
him a state visit before returning home.

Departing Point de Galle 15 March 1853, *Mississippi* passed Dondra
Head, southernmost point of Ceylon, crossed the Bay of Bengal, entered
the Straits of Malacca between Great Nicobar Island and Achin Head, Sumatra, enjoyed a fair wind through the Straits, and reached Singapore on
the 25th. Although founded only thirty-four years earlier by Sir Stamford
Raffles, Singapore had become a booming free port with godowns,
wharves and shops, visited by hundreds of ships of all nations. Perry tarried only long enough to add to his collection of shells, visit a Chinese
temple, pick up descriptions of exotic plants and fishes, and load 230 tons
of coal borrowed from the P. & O. depot, to be repaid at Hong Kong.

The next leg of the voyage, the passage of the South China Sea, worried
Perry because he could not make sense of its tides and currents. "But as I
am a new-comer in this part of the World," he noted in his Journal, "I
shall not venture . . . to explain what I do not comprehend myself." His
luck held, and *Mississippi's* steam power enabled her to make the 1500-
mile passage in a little more than a week. She reached Macao roads on 6
April, and the same day crossed the Pearl River estuary to Hong Kong.
There she anchored amid a flurry of salutes from other ships present of
the East India Squadron: *Plymouth*, *Saratoga* and storeship *Supply*. Next
day, more gunpowder was expended exchanging salutes with the British
forts and with French frigate *Capricieuse*. But, to Perry's chagrin, he
found no *Susquehanna*, to which he intended immediately to transfer his
blue pendant. Humphrey Marshall, the new United States minister to
China, had arrived a fortnight earlier with a numerous suite, eager to proceed to Peking; and Commander John Kelly of *Plymouth*, senior officer
of the Squadron pending Perry's arrival, assigned *Susquehanna* to give the
Marshall party a lift to Shanghai. "This extraordinary and injudicious exercise of a doubtful authority has greatly embarrassed me," wrote Perry.
They should have waited for him, since he was anxious to consult the
minister, and to make haste to Japan. He promptly dispatched *Plymouth*

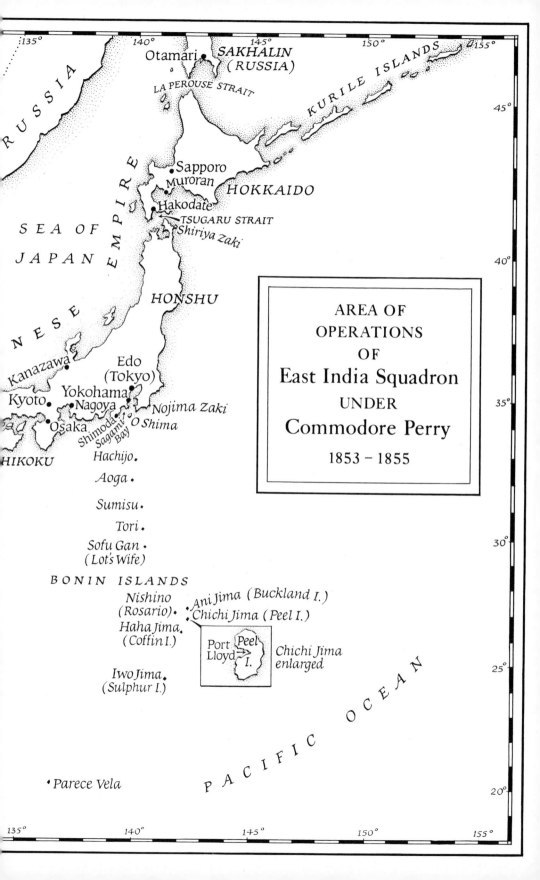

to Shanghai with orders to Commander Buchanan of *Susquehanna* to await his arrival, and hastened to complete coaling and other necessary business at Hong Kong. With Chinese methods of doing business, that took three weeks.

All hands had a chance to admire the scenery of Hong Kong, mountains rising incredibly high from the sea, pretty coves and a waterfall on the south side, and the city of Victoria, with stone buildings, godowns, schools, churches, banks and clubs that the British had built during the twelve years of their possession. Officers exchanged visits as well as salutes with the British authorities, and the men had a chance to shop in "Chinatown" or across the harbor in Kowloon, not yet annexed to the crown colony. Perry enjoyed the foreign society of the treaty ports, although somewhat shocked by their ostentatious luxury. At Hong Kong he met conchologists with whom he compared and exchanged shells. Wherever they went, American naval officers were expected to pick up shells to improve the Commodore's cabinet and that of the Naval Lyceum in Brooklyn.

"In no instance, during a long service in foreign countries," wrote Perry, "have I experienced any want of hospitable attention," especially from the British; adding that he wished Congress would give naval officers on foreign stations an adequate entertainment allowance. (After the lapse of over a century, United States naval officers are still wishing.)

The Commodore could never long stay still. *Mississippi* presently stood up Pearl River to the old Pagoda anchorage in Whampoa Reach, a terminus for China traders when only Canton was open. Canton seemed very dirty and run-down in comparison with Hong Kong, but Perry bought a dress for daughter Isabella, and ordered a set of dining room furniture for the new house on West 32nd Street, and a chest of tea for every member of his family — two for Jane. Here the Commodore made contact with the old Boston firm of China traders, Russell & Company, through the then head of the house, Paul S. Forbes. The firm offered — and the Commodore accepted — the hospitality of their guest house at Macao, the tiny Portuguese colony at the mouth of the Pearl River estuary. Perry and a number of his officers were entertained there, and it proved a welcome retreat from shipboard and city bustle. Similar hospitality was accorded at Shanghai, where Russell & Company had another splendid establishment, staffed with Chinese, the most efficient house servants in the world.

At Canton the Commodore acquired a valuable addition to his staff in the person of Samuel Wells Williams. As a young man he had come to China as printer for the American Board of Commissioners for Foreign Missions, the principal Protestant body then operating in China. He learned mandarin Chinese and on the ill-fated *Morrison* expedition picked up Japanese from the castaways. His book *The Middle Kingdom* and other works on Chinese history, description and linguistics, gave him a well-deserved reputation as the leading American sinologist. Williams felt complimented by Perry's invitation to be flag interpreter, but somewhat embarrassed since his knowledge of Japanese was very slim. But he consented to serve, with the stipulation that he remain a civilian, would be given "comfortable accommodations," and that the old naval slogan, "No sabbaths off soundings," would not apply to him. Perry accepted, and left *Saratoga* at Macao to bring the interpreter to Okinawa, where he joined the Squadron. As an amateur botanist, deeply interested in Oriental flora, Williams was of even greater assistance to Perry as a scientist than as an interpreter; communication with the Japanese would have been difficult, except for the efforts of a Dutch-Japanese interpreter named Antón Portman whom Perry engaged at Shanghai. Williams brought with him a Chinese assistant, a confirmed opium eater who shipped in the hope that a sea voyage would break the habit. So it did, radically. Deprived of the drug, the poor fellow's stomach refused all food, he became a living skeleton, expired in convulsions, and was buried at sea.

On 28 April 1853 *Mississippi* stood out of Lymoon Passage for Shanghai, in company with *Plymouth* and *Supply*. A difficult run this proved to be, with fog, irregular tides, and a winding, unmarked channel to negotiate at the mouth of the Yangtze. All three vessels touched bottom but got off without damage and anchored off the Bund.

Shanghai, one of the new treaty ports, was becoming an international city, with English mercantile houses and clubs, a racecourse, and all the apparatus of European life. Perry and twenty officers were ceremonially carried in sedan chairs to the palace of the Chinese provincial governor, and regaled with tea, champagne and cake. Now the Commodore ran into political complications, which may have reminded him of Yucatán in 1847–1848. The Taiping Rebellion, led by a remarkable character named Hung Hsin-Ch'uan against the Manchu Emperor, was going full blast. Hung had already captured Nanking and the mercantile community at Shanghai was apprehensive lest its turn come next. Perry, sizing up the situation, wrote home in May 1853: —

The whole empire seems to be in a state of agitation arguing some mighty revolution. . . . At the head of the rebel force is a very sagacious man, who . . . at first had only a few followers, but in the course of time multitudes flocked to his standard. . . . This man professes a faith somewhat similar to that of the Mormons in America, and gives forth that he has constant communion with God, and has been acknowledged as his Son. His ignorant and lawless followers profess to believe in his pretended revelations, and with them he has acquired great power by his religious devices. He . . . argues that all

Christian nations . . . should aid him in driving out . . . the present usurping family, and putting on the celestial throne a true son of heaven, a believer of the decalogue, and a scion of the old Chinese monarchs.

This was a shrewd estimate; the rebel troops seldom molested foreigners. But the panic fears of these foreigners proved a constant embarrassment to Perry as long as he was in the Orient; they were always bawling for a warship to protect them in one port or another. Russell & Company, and other leading American and British trading houses in Shanghai, petitioned Minister Marshall to order Perry's squadron to stay there to protect them, and even proposed that the Commodore organize a landing force to defend the city. Perry naturally refused to intervene in a Chinese civil war without positive instructions from home. Marshall urged him to consider whether the emergency in China was not more important than the mission to Japan, and wanted the squadron to convey himself and staff to the mouth of the Peiho River, whence they might communicate with the imperial government. Perry, eager to get on with his primary mission, declined, but consented to leave U.S.S. *Plymouth* at Shanghai to placate the Americans and Europeans. During his stay of ten days in Shanghai he transferred flag and belongings to *Susquehanna*, inferior to *Mississippi* as a war steamer but provided with relatively commodious flag quarters. He also visited the private botanic garden of an Englishman named Beale, where Heine painted some of the exotic flowers; one of the azaleas Beale named *Perryana* after the Commodore.

At Shanghai Perry recruited another important civilian: Bayard Taylor, a twenty-eight-year-old American man of letters already famous for his poems and essays. Young ladies swooned over his "Bedouin Song": —

> From the Desert I come to thee
> On a stallion shod with fire,
> And the winds are left behind
> In the speed of my desire. . . .

Taylor very much wanted to visit Japan, as he was doing a travel book on the Orient; and the Commodore, favorably impressed by the young man, not only invited him on board but gave him permission to send letters to the New York *Tribune* for immediate publication. In return, Taylor consented to have his notes and journals of the Expedition impounded like those of the other civilians, and the official Narrative made very good use of them.

On 15 May 1853, Perry wrote to his wife: —

My dear Jane

As we sail tomorrow for Loo Choo preparatory to our visit to Japan I write a few lines to say that we are all well. Oliver is on board and has commenced on his duties. . . .

The Governor has sent me as a present a piece of straw coloured silk, which I shall send home by the first vessel of the squadron returning to the U.S. I shall also send some tea and a few trifling articles for the children. Every thing is high here but there is great temptation to purchase, but not having the means I shall be careful.

The Customs of China as practised by Europeans and Americans tend to great luxury. I am now staying & have been since my arrival at the house of Mr. Forbes, brother of Miss Forbes, who is very wealthy. Some ten other guests are also here, and every one is made at home. The society of the place is very good — dinner parties, balls &c are of constant occurrence, and the Americans seem to be prosperous.

As an example of Russell & Company hospitality, Perry once remarked at their table that the only mineral water which agreed with him came from the Congress spring at Saratoga. Next morning, No. 1 Boy unostentatiously placed a bottle of Congress Water on the Commodore's bedside table. He had undoubtedly scoured the entire foreign community until he found it. Perry concluded:

I must expect to meet many cares and responsibilities, and must be prepared to bear them the best way I can. . . .
God bless you all. With my love to all.

Ever your affect. husband

C

The squadron coaled, provisioned, and loaded five tons of Chinese cash. These copper coins, worth about one twelfth of a cent, were reported to be the only medium of exchange in Japan. On 17 May 1853 the first echelon set forth from Shanghai: flagship *Susquehanna* (Commander Franklin Buchanan); *Mississippi* (Commander Sidney S. Lee); storeship *Supply*, and a chartered collier, the American barque *Caprice*. "The day of departure," says the official Narrative, "was unusually clear, and the cultivated banks of the river, with their orchards and fields of grain, never appeared more beautifully green. With . . . the inspiriting music of the band, which struck up a succession of lively airs, the crowds of spectators on the shore, and the natural enthusiasm of all, . . . the departure from Shanghai was in a high degree animating." *Mississippi*, using both sail and steam, towed *Supply*. After being delayed three days by foul weather they enjoyed fair winds on their southeasterly passage across the East China Sea, and on the morning of 26 May raised the island of Okinawa.

CHAPTER XXIII

Loo Choo and Bonins
May – July 1853

First Visit to Okinawa

THE island group which Perry called Loo Choo or Lew Chew, and which the Chinese then pronounced Liu Kiu, is identical with what we call the Ryukyus. That name is the Japanese pronunciation of a Chinese original which means "The Floating Horned Dragon," suggested by the appearance of the group as you approach by sea. Okinawa, the biggest island, foreigners then called The Great Loo Choo. Almost a century later the United States conquered Okinawa, last stage on the long road from Pearl Harbor to Tokyo, at the cost of some 12,500 men killed on our side, and even more on the enemy's, together with the loss of 32 United States naval vessels and 763 naval aircraft; and it has since become an imposing American military base, by agreement with the Japanese government.

The Ryukyus are inhabited by a race apart, a mixture of Chinese, Malayan, and Ainu. From early times there were kings of the Ryukyus, and a single dynasty ruled from 1187 to 1879, when the islands were formally annexed to Japan. During the Middle Ages the king paid tribute to China, principal source of such culture as his people acquired; but as a result of an invasion around 1600 by the Daimyo of Satsuma, in southern Japan, the king acknowledged his sovereignty, paid him also tribute, adopted the Japanese polity of seclusion, and (at the daimyo's command) a very un-Japanese pacifism. Okinawa produced superior lacquer, pottery and a peculiar type of cotton cloth, but the Americans were never allowed to see, much less purchase, any of these.

European visitors found the Okinawans polite but suspicious and evasive, anxious to protect themselves from prying foreigners, and with no armed forces whatsoever. Captain Basil Hall, on his way home in 1816 after a visit to Okinawa, talked with Napoleon at St. Helena. When he described the Okinawans to the Emperor:

Nothing struck him so much as their having no arms. "*Point d'armes!*" he exclaimed, "*c'est à dire point de canons — ils on des fusils?*" "Not even muskets," I replied. "*Eh bien donc — des lances, ou, au moins, des arcs et des flèches?*" I told him they had neither one nor the other. "*Ni poignards?*" cried he, with increasing vehemence. No, none. "*Mais!*" said Buonaparte, clenching his fist and raising his voice to a loud pitch, "*Mais! sans armes, comment se bat-on?*" I could only reply that as far as we had been able to discover, they had never had any wars, but remained in a state of internal and external peace. "No wars!" cried he, with a scornful and incredulous expression, as if the existence of any people under the sun without wars was a monstrous anomaly.

Complete disarmament continued until after Perry's visit. During the several months that the Americans were in Okinawa they never saw a gun, a cannon, a sword, a spear, or a poignard. They did not know that when deprived of weapons the Okinawans invented *kurata*, the method of bare-hand defense that is now taught to many of the world's armies.

Perry proposed to visit these islands before Japan. Having read of the Okinawans' inveterate pacifism, he rightly guessed that they would be more easy to deal with than the martial Japanese, and that a call there could be a sort of dress rehearsal for his main mission, as well as a means of securing a coaling station if Japan refused to grant one. The Commodore also had a shrewd appreciation of the strategic value of Okinawa, which has now made it an important military outpost of the free world — the keystone of the Pacific. In a letter home he observed that Britain, by establishing bases at Singapore, North Borneo and Hong Kong, already had the power to control every entrance to the China Seas from the westward. An American base at Okinawa would enable the United States Navy to control access to these same waters from across the Pacific, and balance British power in the Far East.

The Okinawan government had developed evasion and procrastination to a high degree in order to discourage visitors. If a foreign ship entered harbor, usually in search of water and fresh provisions, she would be furnished with them gratis, but politely urged to sail away and never return. Nobody was supposed to go ashore, and any sailors who did manage to land were followed, surrounded, and isolated by a swarm of police, while the populace retired behind closed doors and shops refused to sell. So, as there was little to buy anyway, the discouraged "barbarians" departed. Perry was prepared for this treatment, but determined to surpass the natives both in patience and obstinacy.

En route, the Commodore issued a general order informing members of the squadron that the countries they were about to visit were "inhabited by a singular people" who had been sealed off from the world for centuries, that his orders called for an attempt "to overcome these prejudices by

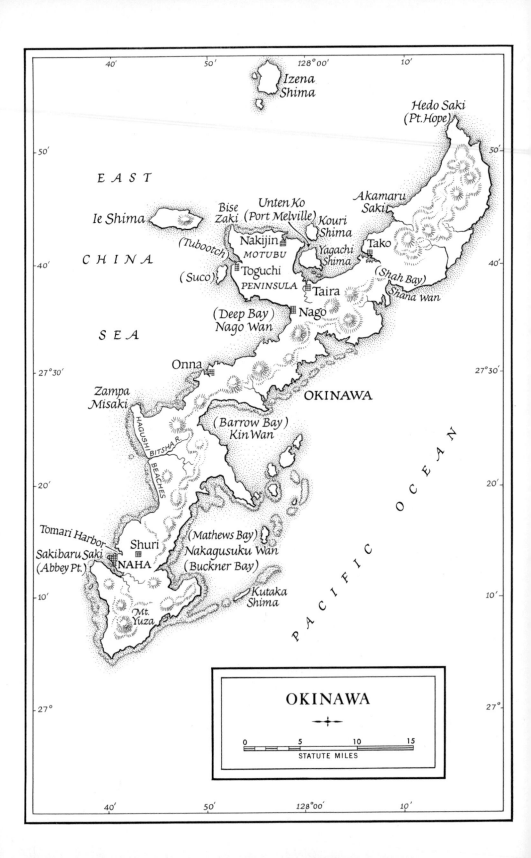

40' 50' 128°00' 10'

*Izena
Shima*

*Hedo Saki
(Pt. Hope)*

50' 50'

E A S T

*Akamaru
Saki*

Ie Shima

C H I N A

*Bise
Zaki*

*Unten Ko
(Port Melville)*

*Kouri
Shima*

Tako

(Tubootch)

Nakijin
MOTUBU

*Yagachi
Shima*

(Shah Bay)

40' 40'

(Suco)

Toguchi
PENINSULA

Taira

Shana Wan

*(Deep Bay)
Nago Wan*

Nago

S E A

Onna

27°30' 27°30'

*Zampa
Misaki*

OKINAWA

*(Barrow Bay)
Kin Wan*

HAGUSHI

BITSHAR

BEACHES

20' 20'

P A C I F I C   O C E A N

Tomari Harbor

*Sakibaru Saki
(Abbey Pt.)*

Shuri

NAHA

*(Mathews Bay)
Nakagusuku Wan
(Buckner Bay)*

10' 10'

*Kutaka
Shima*

*Mt.
Yuza*

27° 27°

OKINAWA

0   5   10   15

STATUTE MILES

40' 50' 128°00' 10'

a course of friendly and conciliatory measures" which would convince them that we were their friends, while refusing "to submit to insult or wrong" or to renounce the rights of hospitality due by the law of nations. Every man under his command must "exercise the greatest prudence, forbearance and discretion" in personal intercourse with the natives, extend "every kindness and protection," and not "molest, injure or maltreat them in any manner."

In other words, Perry had learned, before even going to Japan, that "rough stuff" such as the Russians and British had used would get nowhere with the Japanese any more than the "soft stuff" that Biddle handed out.

On 26 May the squadron raised the "Great Loo Choo." Fortunately Silas Bent, who doubled as flag lieutenant and chief hydrographer, had made notes on the narrow channel into Naha harbor when he entered in U.S.S. *Preble* years before. Okinawa impressed everyone as an uncommonly beautiful spot. Perry himself raved (as far as he ever raved) about it in a letter to William Sinclair: "It would be difficult for you to imagine the beauties of this island, with respect to the charming scenery and its marvelous perfection of cultivation." Bayard Taylor threw all his stock of adjectives into a description which is incorporated in the official Narrative. The island has an uneven surface and is intensively cultivated, with groves of umbrella pines and a small forest on the crest of the hills, resembling Italian landscapes in the background of Sienese paintings; but, instead of churches, the most prominent man-made features are enormous horseshoe-shaped structures, neatly whitewashed. Perry and his men thought they were a sort of temple, and a number of commanding officers in the Fifth Fleet in 1945 took them to be Japanese gun emplacements — as some of them then were. Actually they are a style of family tomb that the early Okinawans brought from South China. Gladioli and white madonna lilies grow wild in the fields in spring, and autumn brings out the white plumes of the suzaki grass.

On the starboard hand as the squadron approached Naha was a high promontory which sailors called Abbey Head (now Sakibaru Saki). The rocks have recently been razed and the site leveled to become part of Naha airport. On the port hand, as they proceeded toward the harbor entrance, they were astonished to see the Union Jack flying from a staff erected on a curious overhanging rock.[1] It marked the residence of the one person in Okinawa who was glad to see them — the Reverend Bernard Bettelheim M.D., a Hungarian-born and medically trained Jew, a naturalized British subject, Anglican convert and missionary. He had been

---

[1] Called the False Capstan by sailors. The site is now marked by the Naminoue shrine. In Perry's day it marked the eastern entrance to Naha harbor, which has been greatly reduced in area by filled-in land.

there with his family for seven years without making a single convert, except one whom the populace stoned to death. The government, unable to get rid of Bettelheim, allotted him an abandoned temple for residence and used his medical knowledge to good advantage, but forbade him to proselyte, and posted sentries to prevent his receiving unauthorized visitors. Not having seen another European or American for over a year, Dr. Bettelheim greeted the squadron with enthusiasm and made himself useful as interpreter of the Okinawan language or dialect. In his initial visit to the Commodore on board *Susquehanna*, Bettelheim was favorably impressed by Perry's *savoir faire* and the intelligent questions that he asked. During this colloquy the sailors plied the visitor's native boatmen with grog, which so confused them that they landed the Reverend three miles up the coast from his residence.

Prior to the missionary's call, the Commodore received an official visit from the island. A boat came out and the principal personage, clad in a salmon-colored robe and wearing a long beard, presented what appeared to be a yard-long visiting card inscribed with Chinese characters. These, said one of the Chinese servants whom Perry had enlisted at Shanghai, were "a *chin-chin*, or complimentary salutation." Since these people were obviously of inferior rank the Commodore refused to receive them. One recalls Lloyd George's remark at the 1919 Peace Conference when a mission consisting of persons of no consequence claimed to represent a small country: he declared he would not deal with "bottle-washers." That was exactly Perry's principle. Both Okinawa and Japan tried "bottle-washers" on him, but had to send men of rank before the Commodore would condescend even to show himself. At Okinawa, in the meantime, he did nothing, since he guessed that curiosity would eventually bring the high authorities on board.

So it happened. The Regent for the reigning monarch (a young boy) visited *Susquehanna* on 31 May. An elderly gentleman of innate dignity, he was received on board with the customary ruffles and flourishes, and a salute of three guns which so frightened some of his suite that they fell on their knees. Otherwise, "they were careful to preserve the most dignified demeanor," wrote Bayard Taylor, observing everything with interest, and the engine with considerable alarm. Through interpreters the Commodore and the Regent exchanged views for an hour and a half, and the ruler was piped over the side with full honors — excepting the salute.

Williams the interpreter, who had arrived in *Saratoga* and attended this conference, remarked that the Okinawa delegation showed "a melancholy set of faces, fixed, grave and sad, as if going to execution." They were probably apprehensive that the Daimyo of Satsuma would punish them for admitting these "outer barbarians," by loss of their profitable autonomy. The ruling class owned all the land and took four-fifths of its prod-

米利幹使節
ヘルリ肖像

副使
アーダムス肖像

暑通倭語
ウリヤ〻ス肖像

Williams, Commander Adams, and the Commodore
A popular Japanese portrait scroll of 1854

The Regent of the Ryukyu Kingdom

uce in rent and taxes; never had a people so ground down and exploited as those of Okinawa been seen by the Americans. But they could not help but be favorably impressed by the cleanliness and neat appearance of the ruling class. Their outer garments were similar in cut to the Japanese kimonos but made of locally woven *basah*, the fiber of banana-tree leaves, dyed in bright colors and stenciled with simple designs. All Okinawans dressed their hair in a closely tied topknot, pierced by two long hairpins whose heads of gold, silver or base metal indicated the wearer's rank.

During this interview the Commodore's announcement that he would return the visit at the royal palace in a few days produced horrified protests from the Regent and his councillors. Why should so eminent a person wish to enter their little castle? In comparison with the splendors of Canton and the luxuries of Shanghai there was nothing to see in their poor capital. Perry replied that he positively intended to visit the Regent in the palace at Shuri on 6 June and would "expect such a reception as became his rank and position as Commander of the Squadron and diplomatic representative of the United States."

An amusing byproduct of this conference was the rivalry between interpreters Williams and Bettelheim. The American noted in his journal that Bettelheim made grimaces, threw his arms about, interrupted, and messed things up generally; the missionary observed that the only Chinese known to Williams was the Cantonese dialect, and that he looked like a corpse. Williams's pale face and long nose are well depicted by contemporary Japanese artists; but he was a competent scholar in mandarin Chinese. Midshipman Sproston of *Susquehanna*, where Williams had his quarters, described him as a "remarkably disagreeable person," and Williams's own journal shows that he disapproved almost everyone from the Commodore down, and disagreed with Perry's policy. "The disregard of the Sabbath usual in this fleet" pained him. He thought that divine service should have been held daily instead of weekly and sneered at the Commodore's "tenderness for the crew that he would not keep them on deck in the cold long enough to hear a sermon" when it came on to rain. Bettleheim, on the contrary, was impressed by Perry's commanding personality, by his "paternal feeling toward his men," and by his gracious call at the mission. "He kissed my two girls, telling my boy that he kissed none but girls, then cast a penetrating eye into my poor study and promised me a pair of windows and some shoes." And he also had one of his sailors paint the dark woodwork of the study white.

Hitherto, Perry had tactfully restrained officers and men from going ashore; they merely rowed about Naha harbor, picking up shells and specimens of coral. At the interview, however, the Regent gave reluctant permission to the Americans to land, and land they did; but owing to the

Okinawan system of surrounding them with police and forcing the natives to hide, they got little satisfaction out of their liberty.

Perry employed several days prior to the state visit to organize an expedition to explore the interior. Chaplain Jones acted as leader, and several junior officers, Artist Heine, Surgeon Arthur Lynah, and Bayard Taylor, went along; also a squad of bluejackets, several Chinese coolies from Shanghai, and a number of Okinawan bearers. An amiable and portly "old fellow" named Pe-Ching acted as guide; the Americans brought their own food and tents. First they marched toward Shuri, where they were received in a "neat and elegant" official guest house and served tea by "a gentleman in a gray robe." Proceeding toward the citadel through "parklike scenery with strong contrasts of light and shadow," they selected a beautiful pine-shaded spot whence they sighted Nakagusuku Bay on the eastern side of Okinawa, pitched their tents and spent the night. Next day they left Camp Perry, as they named this place, and crossed the central ridge of the island "feathered with beautiful groves of Lew Chew pine, intermingled with terraced fields of grain and vegetables, while the plain below . . . was brown with its harvest of rice." On a rocky pinnacle which they named Banner Rock, they unfurled an American flag. They examined a typical Okinawa tomb and the ruined Nakagusuku Castle which dates from 1440. By quick marching they tried to outstrip their native guides but these always managed to run ahead and order the inhabitants not to talk, or even appear. An interesting discovery was made of three stone monuments which were obviously phallic. Unfortunately the artists did not sketch these records of the early Okinawans' fertility; or, if they did, dared not reproduce them.

On the following night the party camped in a village guest house, where Pe-Ching produced tea, eggs and fowl. Around a campfire they were watched from a respectful distance by two or three hundred natives. During the next four days they explored the interior, reached the west coast again, passed through the future site of Yontan Airfield hard by the Hagushi beaches where the Americans landed on Easter Sunday 1945, and camped at "one of the loveliest spots on the island," a village perched on a bold promontory named Ena — now Onna. It was "large, thriving, and as neatly laid out and hedged in as an English garden. The scrupulous neatness and regularity of the Lew Chew villages was doubly refreshing to one familiar with the squalor and filth of China." Here, at the *kung-kwa* or guest house, a pretty tile-roofed building, the explorers were given fresh fish, pumpkin and cucumber, well appreciated since their own provisions were reduced to hardtack.

At the end of the sixth day the exploring party returned to Naha without mishap. Everyone enjoyed the trip and several profited by it. Heine made sketches, Bayard Taylor took notes, Chaplain Jones reported on the geology, and Surgeon Lynah on the flora. They had passed through several climatic zones as distinct as Germany from the Mediterranean, and by their own calculation, walked over one hundred miles.

The formal call on the Regent at Shuri took place on 6 June after His Highness had exhausted every excuse to postpone or prevent it. He told the sad story of how a British naval officer, Captain Shadwell of H.M.S. *Sphynx*, had forced his way into the palace to present a letter from Lord Palmerston to the monarch, an intrusion which so frightened the Queen Mother that she had a nervous breakdown; the appearance of another barbarian in naval uniform might cause her death. This yarn made Perry the more determined to get in; if the Royal Navy got there, he must. He took care to do it in style, but refused to start before 10 A.M., in order to have plenty of time for landing and forming-up after the seamen's usual hour of breakfast.

His own means of conveyance uphill to Shuri posed a problem. No wheeled vehicle existed on the island, the only horse-kind were half-broken ponies, and it would compromise the Commodore's dignity to walk. So, having observed that the Regent arrived at the harbor in a sedan chair, the Commodore had one built for himself. *Susquehanna's* "Chips" and his assistants clapped together a convincing copy of an Oriental palanquin, brave with bright new paint, and in it Perry was borne to Shuri and back by eight coolies. This of course created a good deal of merriment among junior officers — "Does 'Old Bruin' think he's the Emperor of China, or what?"

More than two hundred bluejackets and marines, with two fieldpieces and *Mississippi's* band, landed at Tomari, a suburb of Naha which has its own little harbor. After being reviewed by the Commodore they formed marching order and started on the long uphill road to Shuri. Other officers watched the procession from a knoll with a pretty Japanese-style garden, where Brown may be seen sitting on a wall and making his sketch; Shuri is on the hill in the background. They marched along the main highway, "almost equal to the macadamized roads of England," between walls of unmortared coral rock. The highway, now called Katayoshi Dorii, is still there, but the arcadian beauty and simplicity depicted by Perry's artists is all gone, and one rolls up to Shuri nowadays between shabby car-repair shops, "beauty parlors" and junk heaps.

As a final dodge to avoid intrusion on the royal family, the Regent tried to steer the procession into his own house with the bait of refreshments; but Perry insisted on passing through the "Gate of Courtesy" [1] and enter-

---

[1] This was restored in 1958; the castle, which the Japanese used as a command post and artillery site, was completely demolished by American bombs and shells in 1945. The present Shuri High School is on the site of the Regent's house.

ing the castle in style — ensigns dipping and marines presenting arms as he passed, while the band played "Hail, Columbia!" After a very chilly and formal conference in the palace's main hall, known as "The High Enclosure for Fragrant Festivities," the Commodore consented to adjourn to the Regent's residence where "a most bountiful collation" was served. It consisted mostly of dishes the composition of which could only be guessed. For the first course there were twelve different kinds of soup. Pork, fish, cucumber, *daikon* (the big Japanese white radish) and many unidentifiable dishes followed, accompanied on both sides by both tea and *sake* "which had the taste of French liqueur." This was the Americans' introduction to *sake*, which their successors in Japan have taken to with enthusiasm. Perry proposed a toast to the Queen Mother and her son (neither of whom appeared), and "Prosperity to the Lew Chewans, and may they and the Americans always be friends." The Regent replied with a toast to the Commodore and his officers. A court interpreter, who had studied in Peking and could speak a little English, pleasantly surprised the American officers by praising George Washington as a "man whose peerless purity is the proud heritage of a common humanity the world over."

After presenting some rather trifling gifts, including "a handsome mirror and a quantity of French perfumery" for the allegedly prostrate Queen Mother, Perry ordered the procession reformed to start downhill. It was not quite so dignified a parade as the uphill one, since a few of the junior officers who had indulged too freely in *sake*, mounted ponies offered by their hosts and were run away with or kicked off, greatly to the joy of the bluejackets.

Apparently the subject of a treaty with Loo Choo was not broached during this first call; Perry decided to leave that for another visit. But he did receive a vague assurance that American vessels in distress would be welcomed, not molested, in Okinawan ports, and he wrote proudly to his wife: —

I have made greater advances than any of the foreign officers either English or French who have previously visited the Island. But I expect to have much more trouble in effecting any sort of intercourse with the Japanese. They are more powerful and have the means of resistance; and hence the uncertainty of any success with them but I shall have attained one of my objects in securing a foothold on this beautiful Island, and establishing here a Port of refuge for vessels of all nations, which have hitherto been excluded from all Ports in this neighbourhood.

Perry had indeed made a good beginning. Interpreter Williams thought that Perry was too rough on the Okinawans, and recent left-wing American writers have charged him with arrogance, conceit, and what-not in

The American Procession Returning from Shuri, 6 June 1853, by Heine and Brown; Shuri Castle is on top of the hill; the Commodore's sedan chair is in the center of the line of march

dealing with them, as well as entertaining "imperialist" designs.[1] Perry was imperious, but not imperialistic; firm, not arrogant; dignified, not conceited. His recognition of the dignity of his unwilling hosts, and his successful efforts not to harm the people physically or spiritually, are the outstanding features of his visits to Okinawa.

The Commodore, as we have seen by his actions in the Mexican War, was not one to let a ship swing idly around the hook. So, without awaiting the arrival of a collier from Shanghai, he sailed from Naha on 9 June in *Susquehanna*, with *Saratoga* in tow, for the Bonin Islands. This method of a steamer towing a sailing ship, both at the same time using sail, had the advantage of keeping together two vessels of very different speed potential. *Mississippi* and *Supply* remained at Naha under Commander Lee, with instructions to cultivate friendly relations, choose liberty parties with care, and survey the principal harbors.

The Bonin Islands

The Bonin Islands, which lie somewhat less than eight hundred miles east by north from Okinawa, constitute the principal group of the Nampo Shoto, the archipelago that trails south from Sagami Bay in Japan. They have a strange history. Discovered by the Spanish explorer Villalobos in 1543, rediscovered by a Japanese sailor around 1600, they remained uninhabited until British and American whaleships began frequenting that part of the Pacific in the nineteenth century. Captain Coffin of Nantucket whaler *Transit* landed in 1823 on the southernmost island of the group, which now bears the Japanese name Haha Jima. Perry felt that this gave the United States a good title to the entire group, and named this island after the Nantucket skipper. Four years after Coffin's visit the main island, now Chichi Jima, was visited by H.M.S. *Blossom*, Captain Beechey. He named it Peel Island after Sir Robert, and its excellent harbor Port Lloyd after the Bishop of Oxford. Beechey's voyage gave the British a claim to the Bonins.

The first settlers were a motley group consisting of Genoese, Hawaiians, a Dane, an Englishman and two Americans. One of these, Nathaniel Savory of Massachusetts, organized the party, obtained a schooner at Honolulu and in 1830 brought them to Port Lloyd. There they made an easy living with plenty of turtle, swine, corn and other vegetables and

---

[1] The "imperialism" charge is largely based on Perry's letter of 25 Jan. 1854 to Secretary Dobbin from Naha. He says that if Japan refuses to negotiate or to grant access to seaports, "It is my intention to take under the *surveillance* of the American flag, on the *ground of reclamation for insults and injuries committed upon American citizens*, this island of Great Lew-Chew. . . ." To this Secretary Dobbin replied, 30 May 1854, that he must not think of doing such a thing; and since by that time Japan had made a treaty, Perry never gave the subject another thought.

fruits which they sold to passing whalers. There were many of these — three called during the four days that U.S.S. *Susquehanna* lay at Port Lloyd. Other settlers arrived from time to time, but in 1853, when Savory was the sole survivor of the original group, the total had not reached forty.

Commodore Perry, who had heard about the Bonins from his New Bedford friends, became interested in Port Lloyd as a possible coaling station. Since no nation had ever exerted authority over the Bonins, he did not see why the United States, if it made an effective occupation, should not claim them by virtue of Captain Coffin's discovery. He arrived at Port Lloyd in *Susquehanna* with *Saratoga* on 14 June. Next day Peel Island, biggest of the group although but six miles long and two to three wide, was explored by two parties under Bayard Taylor and Surgeon Fahr. The Commodore sent a third party to reconnoiter the coasts of the two northern islands, Buckland (now Ani Jima) and Stapleton (now Ototo Jima).

Peel is a singularly beautiful island, resembling one of the Lesser Antilles like Montserrat, or the southern part of New Caledonia, rather than Okinawa. Mountains rising directly from the sea to over a thousand feet altitude meet in knife-edged crests; only on Port Lloyd, a submerged volcano crater, was there a small fringe of arable soil. Waterfalls tumble down the valleys directly into the sea. The Americans found a tropical jungle with dew dripping from the thick foliage and encountered wild boar, one of which they shot. And, although Japanese colonists later brought the steep slopes under cultivation and even planted cane fields in some of the mountain valleys, the island has largely reverted to jungle since the inhabitants were evacuated during World War II.

While the explorers were busy with wild nature, Perry went to work on the inhabitants, who were in a condition resembling Jean Jacques Rousseau's state of nature — no laws, no government; therefore no crime! Nathaniel Savory, born the same year as Perry, was a well-educated man who kept up with his New England relatives by the uncertain medium of the whaleships' mail. Asserting the authority due to his age and character, he had saved up money from trading with the whalers, but the settlement had been plundered by pirates a few years earlier, and both Savory's savings and wife were stolen. Hence he was delighted to have Perry appoint him an official agent of the United States Navy and to have a government of chief magistrate and council set up, with himself as chief. The Commodore still further pleased Savory by buying from him a fifty-acre tract of land on the ten-fathom hole at the head of Port Lloyd, turning over four neat cattle, five Shanghai sheep and six goats, and leaving a trusted seaman named John Smith to be his assistant. So, when Savory's new wife, a pretty Chamorro from Guam, bore him a son, he was named Horace Perry, honoring both the author of the *Eclogues,* and the Commodore.

CHICHI JIMA (PEEL ISLAND) IN 1966

Air view of Port Lloyd, Bonin Islands; ten-fathom hole in foreground

"Uncle Charlie" Washington and Nathaniel Savory at boundary of land
which Perry bought from Savory's great-grandfather for a coaling station

The fifty-acre grant, its boundaries defined for this writer in 1966 by a great-grandson of Nathaniel Savory, is now the site of the native village which the Japanese called "Yankee Town," and where the Savory clan maintained their English language and American loyalty through sixty years of Japanese occupation. Perry never intended this land grant for his own use, but for the United States if he could persuade his country to establish there a coal depot. Ever meticulous in matters of navigation, the Commodore enjoyed correcting Captain Beechey's coördinates of Port Lloyd — or so he thought. According to the impeccable Bowditch, both were half a mile out in latitude, and Perry was four miles out in longitude.

Perry now wrote a long letter to the Secretary of the Navy, describing his four-day visit to the Bonins and pointing out the convenience of Port Lloyd as a coaling station for transpacific mail steamers. He estimated the distance from San Francisco to Honolulu (where also they could coal) as 2093 nautical miles, Honolulu to Port Lloyd 3300 miles, and Port Lloyd to Shanghai 1080 miles. Thus mail steamers could reach China in 30 days from California, as compared with the 52 days required to transport the royal mail from England to Shanghai. "Apart from the advantages, and, I may add, the glory of perfecting a scheme so magnificent," states Perry, a transpacific line "would contribute largely to the benefit of commerce. Already many thousands of Chinamen are annually embarking for California, each paying $50 for his passage. These provident people are the most patient and enduring laborers, and must, by their orderly habits, add greatly to the agricultural interests of California." But there is one obstacle — the question of sovereignty. The American government should initiate negotiations with the British with a view to Queen Victoria relinquishing her claim to the Bonins, or sharing it with the United States as a condominium. "Should the Department, however, deem it desirable for me to take possession of the islands in the name of the United States, I will do so," and adopt the best means of holding them.

After his return to New York Perry pointed out that Port Lloyd was far handier than Naha for a coaling station and whaling rendezvous; and, despite his treaty with Okinawa, there were certain to be difficulties between its inhabitants and American whalers whose crews "are not remarkable for their orderly behavior or conciliatory deportment." A notable understatement! It would take very little time and money to establish "the nucleus of a religious and happy community" at Port Lloyd. Which is exactly what the Japanese did many years later.

On his return passage to Okinawa Perry could not resist the opportunity to do a little business for future navigators. He ascertained nearly correctly the position of a low islet west of Port Lloyd, then known as Disappointment or Rosario Island (now Nishino Shima). And he also checked the position of the uninhabited Borodino Islands (now Kita-daito Jima), 195 miles east of Okinawa.

Back to Naha and On to Japan

Susquehanna and *Saratoga* anchored in Naha harbor on 23 June, and found sloop-of-war *Plymouth* and storeship *Supply* already there. Perry was surprised to hear that the Regent who had entertained him had been deposed, and a younger man elevated to the sublime position; he never found out why. Probably the delicate Queen Mother punished the former Regent for allowing the Americans to penetrate her High Enclosure for Fragrant Festivities. The Commodore decided to invite the new Regent to a feast on board the flagship, and his invitation was accepted. On 27 June Regent Shang, the mayor of Naha, and about sixteen *ti-fu* (subordinates) were given a banquet in the flag cabin. Shang remained grave and taciturn, probably wondering whether Her Majesty would not throw him out too, but the others made merry. That is not surprising, as they were served French and German wines, Scotch and American whiskey, gin, Madeira and sherry and, with dessert, "a strong, smooth maraschino." At each sip of this liqueur the *ti-fu* rolled their eyes and smacked their lips with gusto. The dessert consisted of Bonin Island melons and bananas, fruits unknown in Okinawa, and so pleasing to the guests that they asked permission to take some home, and departed with their capacious sleeves and pockets bulging with the exotic fruit. In the meantime *Susquehanna's* band played on deck, and at dessert the Commodore caused its more expert members to enter the festive cabin and play solos on the flageolet, oboe, clarinet and cornet-à-piston. Their efforts did not make a hit; the native ears were not attuned to Western music,[1] and anyway they were much too busy eating and drinking to listen.

As everything now seemed to be going well between Americans and Okinawans, Perry decided to let the feeling ripen until his people were regarded as friends, before pressing for a treaty or a coaling depot. He had brought around the Regency to letting him pay for supplies, a great concession on their part, since the combination of free provisions and "get the hell out" was their long-tried method of disposing of unwanted visitors. The mayor of Naha, under protest it is true, had lent them a house where sick sailors could be cared for and shore parties might rest. The only unsatisfactory thing was the boycott of liberty parties. Before landing and

---

[1] A story about the flagship's band in Japanese waters, told by Sewall, is that the Japanese guests on board asked for an encore of the first number. This was done, but the interpreter explained that by first number they meant the tuning-up, which sounded more like their own music!

after returning to the boats, sailors could see Okinawan heads with the characteristic two hairpins stuck through a topknot, at every window and over every wall. As soon as they landed, policemen fastened themselves to the party and shooed every living person indoors or into the fields; market women even deserted their wares and fled. This system seemed odd even to Williams who had lived twenty years in China, but the Expedition was to experience more of the same in Japan. Probably it had been imposed by the Satsuma conqueror of the Ryukyus in the seventeenth century. The object in both places, like that of the harsh treatment of castaways, was thought control. The ruling class feared lest their subjects' contact with foreigners prove an entry for newfangled notions and dangerous thoughts. In Okinawa the people were friendly enough when caught off guard or without police about, as Silas Bent found when he sounded remote harbors in northern Okinawa.

Lieutenants Bent and Maury and other junior officers expert in hydrography, spent their spare time both on this visit and the two later ones in ships' boats, sounding, charting and compiling sailing directions for the several harbors of Okinawa. On the west coast they charted Deep Bay (now Nago Wan), and the entire shore thence around Bise Zaki into Port Melville (now Unten Ko), and Shah Bay (now Shana Wan). On the east coast they charted Barrow Bay (now Kummu or Kin Wan) and Mathews (now Buckner) Bay. In 1854, when U.S.S. *Lexington* brought out the promised printing press, the Commodore had sailing directions for several Okinawan harbors printed on board ship.

The last day of June was employed at Naha in coaling the two steamships from chartered vessels *Brenda* and *Caprice*, to insure their having enough fuel for a protracted stay in Japan. The colliers then sailed empty to Shanghai with orders to load another black cargo against the squadron's next visit. Leaving *Supply* to "hold down" Loo Choo as it were, the Commodore departed for Japan on 2 July 1853. *Susquehanna* towed *Saratoga*, and *Mississippi* towed *Plymouth*. "All seemed very satisfied to get away from Lew Chew," records the historian of the Expedition. "The picturesque interests of the island were . . . thoroughly exhausted, and the dull realities of life began to weigh rather heavily on the visitors." Enlisted men, in particular, were eager to get going. They had been unable to buy a drink or a souvenir; and the women, at least those of whom they obtained furtive glimpses, seemed "harridans beyond comparison." One can well imagine their relief at leaving this inhospitable island, and the boasts of what fun they would have with "them gay-shur gals" in Japan. But they were to have precious little of that.

Leaving to starboard Ie Shima where Ernie Pyle was killed in 1945, Perry passed up the chain of the Ryukyus, noting especially the second biggest island Amami-O-Shima (then called Oho Shima), which he hoped some day to explore. His ships celebrated the Glorious Fourth with a double ration of grog for all hands, but rough weather forced postponement of planned amateur theatricals. On the evening of the 7th, when the Squadron lay some 40 miles off the Izu Peninsula in central Japan, it stood off and on during the night. Next day broke fair and the bold Izu promontory could be seen rising out of the sea. While thousands of Japanese watched in amazement from the shore, the four ships, forming a single column, steamed at eight knots between the Peninsula and the volcanic island of O Shima, and entered Sagami Bay. On signal from *Susquehanna*, decks were cleared for action, cannon loaded, small arms made ready, and the men took battle stations. Soon the magnificent cone of Mount Fuji rose over the land through the mist, surpassing even Perry's memory of Orizaba. As the squadron approached the next peninsula, numerous junks and small craft were encountered, and their crews showed every sign of agitation. Passing through the six-mile-wide Uraga Suido, leadsmen at the chains crying the marks and deeps, the squadron at 5 P.M. July 8 came to anchor in twenty fathom off the harbor of Uraga, between one and two miles southerly from the lofty headland (Kannon Saki) marking the entrance to Edo Bay, now Tokyo Wan.

Nobody in the squadron ever forgot that first day in Japanese waters — the beautiful scenery, the flotilla of strange craft, the tense alertness and feeling that anything might happen. And the Japanese ashore were nervous and upset over the strange sight of smoke-belching ships moving against the wind. As anchor chains rattled out of hawsepipes, a fort ashore discharged two guns, leaving a ball of smoke in the air. That was a signal to the Bakufu, the government at Edo. It triggered a general alarm and mobilization of defense forces numbering over 20,000 men.

CHAPTER XXIV

First Visit to Japan
8–17 July 1853

> We pray God that our present attempt to bring a singular
> and isolated people into the family of civilized nations may
> succeed without resort to bloodshed.
> — PERRY, *Journal for 9 July 1853*

GOVERNMENT and people of Japan seemed to sense that this third day of the sixth month, sixth year of Kaei (8 July 1853) would be a milestone in their country's history. The sight of the two steam men-of-war — first steamships ever seen in Japan — each towing a sailing vessel, dashing along in a calm at nine knots, struck the natives with astonishment. On the fiftieth anniversary of this event an old man of Shimoda on the Izu Peninsula described how it felt: —

People in the town made such a fuss that I asked what was up and was told that off shore there were burning ships. With two or three men I climbed a hill. There we saw a big crowd of people jabbering about the ships. As they drew gradually closer to shore it became clear that they were not Japanese but foreign. What we had mistaken for a fire was smoke belching forth from these warships and they caused a great commotion. . . . When we came down the hill the whole town was astir. Some men rushed to Edo. . . . Today it may seem a laughing matter but I later learned that not only in Shimoda but also in Edo it was a matter of great concern. A popular doggerel of the time tells about the reaction in Edo when the ships first approached: —

> O what America has done with *jokissen!*
> It took only four to keep the Bakufu awake.[1]

All Edo was appalled. Perry's visit should have been no surprise; in 1852 the Dutch at Nagasaki sent them an official warning that the Americans were coming to Uraga to present a letter from their President to the Em-

---

[1] *Jokissen* is a pun; it can mean either a kind of tea drunk by Buddhist priests to keep themselves awake, or steamships.

peror and word had arrived from Okinawa that Perry was on his way. But, owing to the Bakufu policy of secrecy and procrastination, the recipients discounted the warning as a Dutch ruse to get more business for themselves and did nothing about it. Hence, when the American Squadron arrived, nobody knew how to receive it. Abe Ise no kami, Daimyo of Fukuyama, senior member of the *roju* (the Shogun's Council), had dealt with Biddle successfully; Edo Bay was supposedly so well fortified that no other stranger would dare enter, and so no preparations were made to deal with Perry. Abe was practically running the government, owing to the Shogun's feeble character and ill health. Nobody dared tell His Highness about Perry's arrival — he only heard of it by accident three days later while attending a *noh* play at Edo Castle, and the news threw him into such a tizzy that he went to bed, and stayed there.

A parallel situation would be an announcement by astronauts that weird-looking aircraft from outer space were on their way to earth; nobody would know how to receive them. Baba (Bun'ei), a Japanese historian at the turn of the century, describes the consternation at Edo Castle, seat of the Shogun. — "Fresh messages arrived one after the other," and when the *roju* met, the members were "too alarmed to open their mouths," but finally issued orders to the daimyo responsible for defense to mobilize at once to defend Japan from invasion. Dr. Ito, the gossipy court physician, noted that provisions became scarce, that plain suits of armor quadrupled in price, and the tailors were working around the clock to manufacture *jinbaori*, the cloaks worn over armor.

But Perry had not come to invade Japan. "I have come here as a peace-maker," he said in one of his interviews with Japanese officials — words selected by General Douglas MacArthur to be inscribed on the Opening-of-Japan monument at Shimoda. This first visit, as the Commodore wrote to his wife, was "a preliminary demonstration," with no immediate object except to deliver the Letter. With only four warships available out of the twelve promised before he left home, Perry expected the Bakufu to procrastinate about a treaty. Best therefore to try the old one-two tactics that he had employed in Naples: state his country's demands, sail away to give the government time to reflect, and return with a more imposing force.

The *kurofune* (black ships) as the Japanese called all foreign vessels, anchored off Uraga in line-of-battle. They were promptly approached and almost surrounded by Japanese guard boats. Each of these craft was rowed by six to eight stalwart oarsmen standing and facing forward. Each displayed a flag bearing the Tokugawa trefoil, together with sundry pendants and streamers, and carried a score of soldiers commanded by two officers. Fastening their painters to the ships, the guard-boat people tried to climb on board over the chains or the bobstay. Commodore Biddle had allowed that, to his subsequent undoing, and Commodore Perry was de-

U.S.S. *Susquehanna* off Uraga, 1853

This painting, by an unknown Japanese artist, is probably the only original of a Perry ship at the time of his first visit. It was widely and inaccurately copied in black-and-white woodblocks and news sheets, to satisfy Japanese curiosity about the "black ships." The inscription states it was purchased at a shop by Tokugawa (Nariaki), Daimyo of Mitro, when he took his son Yoshinobu (a future Shogun) to the seashore in 1854 to view Perry's squadron.

The tent-like deck coverings represent the canvas windsails which Perry had made to carry fresh air below decks, and awnings spread on the spar deck.

termined to prevent it. By his orders, the sailors cast overboard or cut the guard boats' painters, and repelled would-be boarders with pikes and cutlasses. No foreign ship had ever dared do that. The boats' officers roared angrily, and their crews kept up "an awful pow-wow and noise," hoping no doubt to intimidate the barbarians. What appeared to be the senior guard boat then approached *Susquehanna* near enough to hold up a scroll inscribed in large letters in French (supplied by the Dutch): "Depart immediately and dare not anchor!" A Dutch interpreter in the boat explained through Perry's interpreter that a high personage was on board and wished to be received. He was told that the commander of the American Squadron represented the President personally, and would see nobody under the rank of cabinet minister; but the high personage might board if he wished.

John Contee, Perry's flag lieutenant, interviewed the alleged dignitary, Nakajima (Saburosuke) by name. He, it turned out, was merely a *yoriki*, aide to a vice governor. Contee informed him that Perry's intentions were friendly; that his one object, which had been communicated to the Bakufu in 1852 through the Dutch, was to present the President's letter to the Emperor. Nakajima said that he knew nothing about the Dutch communication, but that in any case, if Perry wished to send a letter to the Emperor, his squadron must proceed to Nagasaki. That, Perry was determined never to do; it would not only involve him with the Dutch factory at Deshima and the degrading restrictions to which the Netherlanders had submitted, but (as the Russians discovered to their cost) would require three months to receive an answer from Edo. Through Contee he informed the Japanese official that the squadron had come to Uraga because it was near Edo where (he supposed) the Emperor resided; he refused absolutely to go to Nagasaki, and if the guard boats surrounding his ships did not immediately retire, they would be dispersed by force. Nakajima promptly went to the gangway and shouted an order which sent all but a few boats back to shore, and those few were chased away by an armed barge from *Susquehanna*.

Thus three important positions were gained initially: Perry would not talk with "bottle-washers," would not allow sightseers on board, and would not suffer his ships to be surrounded by a cordon of boats. A fourth position, already taken at Okinawa, he again maintained when a messenger from shore offered to supply food, water, and fuel. The Bakufu always gave supplies gratis to intrusive foreign ships, in order to afford them no excuse to tarry for want of necessities; and for that reason Perry gave strict orders to accept nothing except for money or some other *quid pro quo*. In this instance, a ship's officer told the messenger that the Commodore thanked him, but had plenty of provisions on board; however, as the American presence had apparently interrupted Uraga's usual supply of junk-borne food, "We shall be pleased to let you share our stock of provisions." This unheard-of reply left the Japanese speechless.

In the meantime, to take no chances, Perry kept his ships in top condition of readiness, maintaining every precaution against surprise attack. Himself he kept invisible to the Japanese. Not that he was confined to his cabin; *Susquehanna* had six-foot bulwarks, so the Commodore could walk on deck without any outsider catching sight of his stalwart figure. Perry's unapproachableness was regarded in some quarters as unduly formal, even stuffy. A former biographer accuses him of "playing Mikado," making himself "His High Mighty Mysteriousness, Lord of the Forbidden Interior," etc. Amusing, but beside the point. Perry, far better than most Americans of the twentieth century, knew the value of "face" when dealing with Orientals. He had observed the ill effects of Biddle's palsy-walsy approach. In the official Narrative he thus answered complaints of "un-Americanism": —

KEY TO NAMES ON COMMODORE PERRY'S CHART OF THE BAY OF EDO 1853–1854

Perry's Name	*Location, or Modern Japanese Name*
American Anchorage	Off Yokosuka Ko
Dobbin Point	Southern entrance to Kanazawa Wan
Fillmore Point	Koshiba Zaki
Goldsborough Inlet	Kanazawa Wan
Gorihama	Kurihama
Graham Bluff	Konosu Bana
Haneda	Haneda or Tokyo International Airport
Kamisaki, Cape	Kannon Zaki
Kennedy Point	Nojimaura
Macedonian Reef	Moroiso Ko
Marcy Point	Northern part of Yokosuka
Mississippi Bay	Negishi Wan
Morrison Bluff	Senda Zaki
Perry Island	Saru Shima
Pierce Point	Southern entrance to Nagaura Ko
Plymouth Rock	Ashika Jima
Powhatan Bay	Nagaura Ko
Rubicon, Point	Hatayama Zaki
Sagami, Cape	Tsurugi Zaki
Saratoga Spit	Futtsu Saki
Susaki, Cape	Suno Saki
Susquehanna Bay	Otsu Wan
Treaty Point	Honmoku Hanna
Webster Island	Natsu Shima
Woodawara Bay	Odawa, or Sagami Wan
Yedo, Bay of	Tokyo Wan

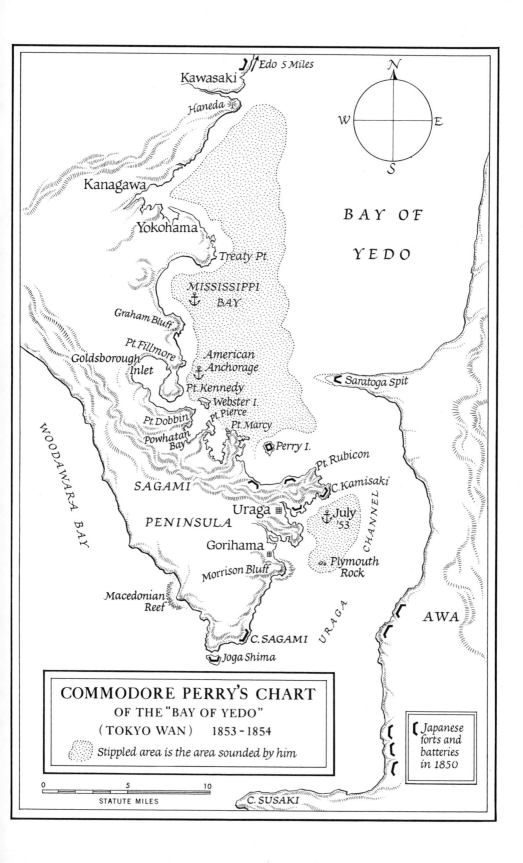

N
W — E
S

Edo 5 Miles

Kawasaki

Haneda

Kanagawa

BAY OF
YEDO

Yokohama

Treaty Pt.

MISSISSIPPI
BAY

Graham Bluff

Saratoga Spit

Pt. Fillmore

American
Anchorage

Goldsborough
Inlet

Pt. Kennedy

Webster I.
Pt. Dobbin
Pt. Pierce

Powhatan
Bay

Pt. Marcy

Perry I.

WOODAWARA BAY

Pt. Rubicon

SAGAMI

C. Kamisaki

Uraga

July
'53

PENINSULA

Gorihama

Plymouth
Rock

Morrison Bluff

URAGA CHANNEL

Macedonian
Reef

AWA

C. SAGAMI

Joga Shima

COMMODORE PERRY'S CHART
OF THE "BAY OF YEDO"
(TOKYO WAN)   1853 - 1854

Stippled area is the area sounded by him

⟨ Japanese
forts and
batteries
in 1850

0   5   10

STATUTE MILES

C. SUSAKI

The Commodore, also, was well aware that the more exclusive he should make himself, and the more unyielding he might be in adhering to his declared intentions, the more respect these people of forms and ceremonies would be disposed to award him; therefore it was that he deliberately resolved to confer personally with no one but a functionary of the highest rank in the empire. . . . He felt that it was well to teach the Japanese, in the mode most intelligible to them, *by stately and dignified reserve, joined to perfect equity in all he asked or did,* to respect the country from which he came, and to suspend for a time their accustomed arrogance and incivility toward strangers. The Japanese so well understood him that they learned the lesson at once. It was this feeling, and this only, which prompted him to refuse to see the Vice-Governor of Uraga, and to refer him to his aide for conference. He saw him enough afterward, when matters had been arranged between the governments, on terms of friendship and equality.[1]

"Stately and dignified reserve" is right. Perry acted imperiously, which the Japanese understood; never arrogantly, which would have offended them.

That night, beacon fires were lighted on the hilltops and along the shore of Edo Bay, placid as a lake. Silence was broken only by the tolling of a great bronze gong ashore, by ships' bells striking the half-hours, and by a lights-out gun from the flagship. Along the Bay, shrines and temples were thronged with worshippers supplicating their gods to raise another *kamikaze* (heavenly wind) like the providential typhoon which defeated a Mongol invasion fleet in 1570.[2] Shortly after eight bells ushered in the ninth day of July, a remarkable meteor appeared to the southward and crossed the sky, giving off sparks like a rocket, illuminating the roadstead during the midwatch, and reflecting a bright blue light on the hulls and spars of the American ships. To the Japanese, this seemed a portent, whether for good or ill they knew not; Commodore Perry noted in his journal that, like the ancients, we should regard it as a favorable omen, "as we pray God that our present attempt to bring a singular and isolated people into the family of civilized nations may succeed without bloodshed."

A bright morning sun dispersed the night mists and revealed a superb panorama of pine-tufted hills, cultivated fields and villages embowered in

---

[1] Dulles in *Yankees and Samurai* states, "Perry insisted throughout the negotiations on being called 'Admiral.'" This is not correct. The Japanese had never heard of a commodore but had heard of an admiral; so the Dutch interpreter referred to Perry as "the Admiral." He never assumed the rank himself. Similarly, "The Governor and his interpreter were requested to use the same designation in speaking of the President as by that which distinguished the Emperor," — Daïri. Such details were very important when dealing with a ceremonious nation like Japan.

[2] It was this same event of 1570 which gave its name to the famous Japanese *kamikaze* corps of crash-suicide aviators in 1944-45.

groves of trees, with Fuji towering over all. The same scene delights a sea or air traveler of today as he enters Tokyo Wan, although the coast from Kannon Zaki northward has become almost one continuous city. The shore was a scene of bustling activity, as mobilization decreed by the Bakufu began. Every daimyo responsible for the defense of Edo Bay sent a contingent, displaying banners emblazoned with their lord's arms, and great gilt tassels as emblems of his authority; for the Japanese were as keen on heraldry as medieval Europeans. There were caracoling cavalry, long-swordsmen, archers with eightfoot bows, musketeers carrying ancient smooth-bores, spearmen with ten-foot pikes; altogether a brave and beautiful spectacle, wholly new to Americans. There were already some twenty forts on the shores of Edo bay, mostly concentrated on the Uraga narrows, but now additional earthworks were thrown up, partly concealed by canvas screens; ancient smooth-bores were sited, and every other preparation that the Japanese then knew was made for defense, in case these "outer barbarians" were bent on conquest. Commodore Perry and his officers gazed unafraid upon this scene. The screened earthworks, which they called "dungaree forts," were not impressive, and through telescopes and binoculars they ascertained that the Japanese had no weapons which they need fear.

This mobilization, which included 17,000 soldiers exclusive of those at Kurihama, and all able-bodied males to act as labor troops, was the first reaction of the Shogun's government to the black ships. The Bakufu was really on a spot. If it did not get rid of these intruders as it had all earlier ones, it would lose face with the Japanese people; there might even be a revolution to depose the house of Tokugawa. An order was issued that people must not discuss the arrival of the black ships, but it could not be enforced. Perry evidently meant business, and the Bakufu had no means of defense against his weapons if he chose to land and march on Edo, or if he elected to blockade the heavily populated capital, all of whose provisions came by sea. Further, the high councillors of the Bakufu assumed that, if given an excuse, Perry would occupy territory as the British had done in China and set up an American Hong Kong; a useful misconception since it caused strict orders to be issued to withhold gunfire, no matter how insolent the barbarians might be, to avoid an "incident." So the Bakufu decided to accept the President's letter, but in reply to evade and procrastinate, hoping that another *kamikaze* would blow up; and if that did not happen, make as few concessions as possible to get rid of Perry. As a contemporary Japanese historian records:

The city of Edo and the surrounding villages were in great tumult; in anticipation of the war which seemed imminent, the people carried their valuables and furniture in all directions to conceal them in a house of some friend living farther off. . . . So at last they decided that it would be best to arrange the affair quietly, to give the foreigners the articles they wanted, and to put off sending an answer to the Letter; to tell the envoy . . . that he had better go away, and that in a short time he should get a definite answer.

The first important event of Saturday 9 July was a call from Kayama (Eizaemon) accompanied by a suite and two interpreters. The interpreters, possibly misunderstood, introduced him as the Governor of Uraga. Actually, Kayama was merely a *yoriki* or aide to the governor, doubling as chief of police, in which capacity he had dealt with Biddle and other unwanted visitors. He was obviously a shade higher than Nakajima in rank; but Perry, rightly guessing that he was not high enough, turned him over to Commanders Buchanan and Adams, keeping himself in the flag cabin and using son Oliver as go-between. Kayama again pressed the squadron to sail to Nagasaki. Perry again refused. If President Fillmore's letter were not properly received somewhere in Edo Bay, his only alternative would be to land with an armed force and deliver the letter in person at Edo Castle. Kayama, horrified at the impious suggestion, said he would send to Edo for further instructions but it would take eight days to receive an answer. Perry sent word that he would wait but three or four days before putting his dread alternative into effect. Kayama inquired, with a trace of malice, why four warships were required to deliver a letter to the Emperor? "Out of respect for him!" answered Perry, with his customary aplomb. Kayama hastened to the capital the same day and reported to Ido Iwami no kami, the new co-governor of Uraga, who admitted that he had received word from the Dutch of the Americans' coming but had not bothered to tell the other governor of Uraga, who would have to deal with the barbarians! Kayama advised him to receive the President's letter as soon as possible, and where Perry wanted; "so unmistakably did the countenances of not only the Commander but also of all the officers in the wardroom show their resolve to fight."

During this conference a boat from each American ship, with a white flag at the bow, began to sound and survey Edo Bay. Kayama, observing them, declared that they were breaking Japanese law, to which Commander Buchanan replied that the United States Navy operated under American law wherever it went. An international lawyer would be somewhat put to it to defend that proposition, but the big guns of the squadron, covering the boats, made it valid on this occasion.

On the following day, Sunday, 10 July, no visitors were allowed on board; the Commodore insisted on proper keeping of this, their first sabbath in Japan. The big capstan on *Susquehanna* was covered with a flag, on which the ship's Bible rested. Chaplain Jones read the office of morning prayer with the lesson for the day and preached one of his less lengthy sermons. To the accompaniment of the full band and the familiar tune

Sounding Edo Bay, off Village of Otsu
Watercolor by William Heine, 1853

"Passing the Rubicon"
Lieutenant Silas Bent in *Mississippi*'s first cutter confronts Japanese guard
boats, 11 July 1853; at left, a Japanese coastal junk

"Old Hundred," some three hundred lusty voices sang Isaac Watts's prophetic hymn: —

> Before Jehovah's awful throne
>   Ye nations, bow with sacred joy;
> Know that the Lord is God alone —
>   He can create and He destroy.

When the sounding parties resumed work on Monday morning the
11th, there occurred an incident painted by Heine and entitled "Passing
the Rubicon." A flotilla of thirty to forty guard boats filled with soldiers,
who "presented quite a bristling front with their spears and matchlocks,
while their lacquered caps and shields flashed brightly in the sun," confronted the flag launch under charge of Lieutenant Silas Bent, and the
senior Japanese officer made minatory gestures with his iron fan and
yelled orders which nobody in the American launch understood. The
Lieutenant, anxious to avoid a rupture, altered his collision course but
dispatched another boat to *Mississippi* to ask Captain Lee to move closer.
On the steamer's approach the guard boats retired. And Perry well named
the nearest point of land Point Rubicon, because no foreign ship had
passed it for three centuries.

Ignoring the Japanese batteries along shore whose guns were trained on
them, Silas Bent and his men sounded up to a point off the present Tokyo
International Airport, and *Mississippi* towed the boats back to their ships.
Perry's purpose was to locate the channel to Edo so that, in case no proper
person were sent to receive the President's letter, he could land a delegation near the Shogun's capital under the cover of his guns and deliver it
himself. Kayama, sent on board *Mississippi* to protest and inquire the reason for this intrusion, was told by Adams that they were charting the bay
in order to fight their way into Edo in case the Bakufu procrastinated too
long, or refused to receive the letter. This candor amazed the Japanese.
Any Oriental would have given ten different reasons, none of them
correct.

Incidentally the Americans indulged in the old discoverers' privilege of
naming places — not because Perry claimed them by right of discovery
but because he did not know the Japanese names. Thus Otsu Wan became, on Perry's chart, Susquehanna Bay, and Negishi Wan, Mississippi
Bay; Saru Shima, a pretty, well-wooded islet crowned by a three-gun battery, was named after Perry himself, and Natsu Shima called Webster Island to commemorate the late senator's interest in the Expedition. Other
points and headlands acquired temporarily the exotic names of American
presidents and navy secretaries. One of the surveying parties rowed up
Kanazawa Wan, an inlet bordered by villages and gardens, and named it
Goldsborough after the superintendent of the Naval Academy. Many in-

habitants rallied around and offered the men pots of sweet water and ripe peaches; officers of a guard boat invited the foreigners on board and enjoyed a social smoke with them, and the Americans amused their hosts by firing Colt revolvers. During this friendly gathering, "in which the Japanese seemed remarkably genial in manner and expansive in hospitality," a glowering official turned up and shooed off his countrymen like naughty children. All hands were "in raptures" over "the kindly disposition of the Japanese and the beauty of their country." Strange indeed was the contrast between simple popular friendliness and official alarm, confusion and standoffishness.

Boats rowing and flagship steaming up the bay caused even greater consternation in Edo than their initial appearance, because (according to Dr. Ito), "Since the age of our ancestral gods, it has been firmly believed that the hidden bank of Futtsu would prevent any foreign vessel from entering Edo Bay." [1] This advance touched off no hostile act, but from Japanese sources we learn that clashes were narrowly avoided. Retainers of two bellicose daimyo, of Aizu and Kumamoto, sent messages to their lords asking permission to open fire on the American boats, but were denied. One boat, unidentified, landed in front of a six-gun battery at Hatayama and, according to our Japanese source, "pointed drawn swords at our battery, jeered at us and were very overbearing." When the Japanese commander in a rage dashed forward with a spear pointed at the sailors, they retreated to their boat, laughed and clapped their hands. "There have been reported instances without number of insolence like this one."

On Tuesday morning 12 July a decorated barge brought Kayama, suite and interpreters to *Susquehanna*. Perry sent Commanders Buchanan and Adams to receive them. Kayama promised to have the letter received on shore at Kurihama by high officials in a specially erected building, but said that no answer could be delivered save at Nagasaki, through Dutch or Chinese intermediaries. To this Perry replied, "The Commander-in-Chief will not go to Nagasaki." Neither will he receive communications through foreigners. "He has a letter from the President of the United States to deliver to the Emperor of Japan, or to his secretary of foreign affairs, and he will deliver the original to none other." If it "is not received and duly replied to, he will consider his country insulted, and will not hold himself accountable for the consequences. He expects a reply of some sort in a few days, and he will receive such reply nowhere but in this neighborhood."

This exchange of views, which in Europe would have barely consumed

---

[1] Futtsu Saki sticks far out from the eastern shore, but even in 1853 there was a deep channel between it and the western shore. The ancestral gods were possibly appeased by *Saratoga*'s hitting the submerged part of the Futtsu shoal, but she got off with little damage, and Perry named it Saratoga Spit after her.

fifteen minutes, according to Japanese custom lasted three hours; and there was a second of similar length in the afternoon to discuss where the letter would be delivered and whether the high official would be authorized by the Emperor to receive it. Kayama assured Perry that he would, and the Commodore admitted that he expected no immediate reply but would return in a few months to receive it and enter into negotiations. Both parties agreed that there should be no discussion at the presentation, only an exchange of compliments, and the Japanese delegation was piped over the side after partaking freely of liquid refreshments. "During the whole of this interview the bearing of the Japanese was dignified and self-possessed," recorded Dr. Williams, to which the official Narrative adds that they "were disposed to be quite social, and shared freely and gaily in conversation." Perry commented on their "elegance of manners," "amiability of disposition," proficiency in Dutch and Chinese languages, and noted that they were "not unacquainted" with world geography. They knew something of the material progress of the United States, "asking, as they examined the ship's engine, whether it was not a similar machine, although smaller, which was used for travelling on the American roads." One of them recognized, and named, a Paixhans gun. Perry held nothing back from the Japanese; the working of guns, engines, and anything that attracted their interest, he had carefully explained to them.

Japanese mobilization to meet the "invader" was now almost complete. Dr. Ito observed that the entire western shore of Edo Bay was crowded with troops, every town and village had a garrison, and the roads were congested with gun carriages, carts hauling arms and provisions, laden pack horses and porters carrying heavy burdens slung on poles. The "state of consternation" among Bakufu officials was "beyond description," according to the Doctor; but those who dealt with the Americans put on a good show of imperturbability.

On the following afternoon Kayama returned on board, exhibiting a letter bearing the imperial seal to "His Highness Toda, Prince of Izu, first counsellor of the Empire," and "Prince Ido of Iwami" (as the names and titles were translated), authorizing them to receive the President's letter. A prefabricated wooden building had been erected especially for the presentation in Kurihama, a little village on a beach between the two headlands, about a mile and a half south of Uraga. This quiet spot had been selected because each headland to the harbor was fortified and the area behind the beach (now a baseball field) was level and broad enough to deploy thousands of troops. Further, to hold the ceremony there preserved the fiction that Uraga was the *ne plus ultra* for foreigners. Kayama, before going ashore, had a good look at the President's letter in its casket; and as he left the quarterdeck for his barge, he received a three-gun salute under the impression that he was Governor of Uraga and not merely chief of police. The intended compliment was lost on Kayama; he thought the Americans were saluting the letter, not him!

At this point one must consider a silly story to the effect that the Shogun dressed up a couple of servants or soldiers in princely garb and palmed them off on Perry as noblemen. Actually Toda and Ido were men of high birth, the former being Izu no kami and the latter Iwami no kami;[1] and each was *bugyo* or Governor of Uraga, a place so important for coastal traffic that two governors were required, one to reside there and the other in Edo. Toda had been resident governor for several years; and Ido, appointed co-governor several months before Perry's arrival, had previously been the Shogun's official in charge of maritime defense, thus enjoying a rank commensurate with an American secretary of the navy or a British first lord of the admiralty. His appointment to the Uraga post was a promotion carrying with it the honorable title of *kami*, which perhaps started the story of his being an *ad hoc* nobleman. Both men were eminently proper officials to receive a presidential missive to the Emperor. Toda set up a camp with three hundred retainers near Kurihama beach, and Ido had a hundred armed men in his headquarters.

Perry summoned his commanding officers to a conference, told them to allot so many bluejackets and so many marines from each ship, and all the officers who could be spared. At break of day Thursday, July 14, the two American steamers weighed, proceeded the short distance to Kurihama Wan, and anchored off the beach with springs on their cables so as to bring a full broadside to bear in case of a surprise attack. Kayama and Nakajima, dressed in bright-colored silk brocade turned up with yellow velvet and embroidered with gold lace, came out in official barges and were piped on board the flagship. Everyone on board could see that thousands of Japanese troops surrounded the village, so Perry sent his men ashore heavily armed. They numbered about 250 but were outnumbered by the Japanese at least twenty to one.

Fifteen launches and cutters under Commander Buchanan, filled with sailors and marines, now approached the beach in single line, flanked by the Japanese aides' barges as guides. The rest of the ships' boats followed, containing more sailors and bands from the two steamers. The Commo-

---

[1] The Japanese title *no kami*, (literally "of lord"), which Perry's interpreters translated "prince" and later writers, "lord" of, has no precise English equivalent. Suffixed to a place name, it meant that the man belonged to the feudal clan of that place; he might be only a remote cousin to the daimyo. The same word, added to a high position, meant something like our "honorable." Thus Toda Izu no kami means that his family name was Toda, and that he belonged to the same clan as the Daimyo of Izu; Hayashi Daigaku no kami (see Chapter XXVI below) means that Hayashi was head of the Daigaku, or university at Tokyo. Similarly the English speak of a "Lord Bishop" or "Lord of the Admiralty," although neither bishop nor admiralty official belongs to the nobility. The title of *kami*, however, could not be assumed by a cousin who had insufficient status; and to use it one had to have the Shogun's permission.

dore, saluted with 13 guns by *Susquehanna*, stepped into his barge just as Commander Buchanan, first American to set foot on Japanese soil, jumped ashore; and when the Commodore stepped ashore, the marines presented arms, sailors in the boats tossed oars, and the bands struck up "Hail! Columbia!" Major Zeilin's marines, heading the American procession, were followed by a band and a contingent of sailors. Two little ship's boys bearing the President's letter and the Commodore's letter of credence, came next. They were followed by two seamen of "stalwart proportions" bearing the American ensign and the blue pendant.[1] After them came the Commodore, marching between two orderlies, both tall and stalwart Negroes, since he wished citizens of color to take part. More bluejackets and the second band fell in behind them. The sailors were dressed in white frocks or blouses, with blue collar and black neckerchief, blue bell-bottom trousers, and the newly issued blue cloth cap, to which Perry caused to be added a hatband of red, white and blue horizontal stripes with thirteen blue stars on the white stripe. Marines wore blue jackets crossed by white bandoliers, white trousers and plumed shakos. The American formation and discipline impressed the Japanese. Kayama recorded, "The adroit maneuvers of the guards in the van as well as the rear, conducted just as if they had been marching into enemy territory, truly left us in amazement."

Drawn up to meet them behind the long *baku*, the canvas screens which were standard equipment for concealing troop movements, were some five thousand Japanese soldiers organized in brigades, each of which comprised a section of infantry armed with ancient muskets, one of pikemen, one of archers, and one of cavalry. The gaily colored banners that they displayed bore the arms of the four daimyo represented at Kurihama. The tall thin banners in our Japanese painting are the scarlet insignia of Ii Kamon no kami, Daimyo of Hikone, destined to become the *Tairo*, the Shogunate's first prime minister. Boats belonging to Matsudaira Higo no kami, who was responsible for maritime defense, flew blue banners with a character representing his ancestral castle of Aizu. Seven hundred men from Edo wore the livery of Matsudaira Tosa no kami, who, as a member of the Shogunate family, was privileged to display the Tokugawa arms. At extreme left can be seen the "nine star" arms (one big one in center and eight circling it) of Hosokawa Etchu no kami. The officers, each a two-sworded samurai, wore the traditional lacquered bamboo or leather-braided corselet, but most had discarded the branching steel helmet which made them look like human crustaceans. A very beautiful and impressive

---

[1] Perry brought the ensign home, and it is now in the Naval Academy Museum at Annapolis. Following a happy suggestion of General MacArthur's, it was displayed on the quarterdeck of U.S.S. *Missouri* during the surrender ceremony on 2 September 1945.

spectacle — "even the ranks of Tuscany could scarce forbear to cheer."

It was a tense moment when the Americans began landing; but not a man of the Japanese host raised hand or weapon to oppose them. Apparently ugly scowls on the faces of Japanese officers were merely the conventional ferocious expressions of the samurai. Excellent discipline on each side prevented an explosion which might have touched off a war instead of a treaty. The Americans never realized what a near thing it was. Many years later, Kashiwagi (Shigefusa), a samurai, recorded that he and about nine other two-sworded gentry were concealed under the floor of the reception hall with orders from Toda that if the visitors attempted any violence, they were to rush out and slay the Commodore and his staff.

Intensely dramatic was this confrontation of the Americans with a muster representing the gallantry and chivalry of medieval Japan. There had been nothing like it since Columbus met the caciques of Jamaica; never again could it happen, anywhere. To realize the deep significance of this meeting, imagine an England sealed up by Henry VII and his successors for three centuries, confronting a Napoleonic landing force with armored knights, archers and footsoldiers bearing the costumes and weapons of Bosworth Field and flaunting banners emblazoned with the arms of Richmond, Stanley, Norfolk and Northumberland.

The Japanese, too, grasped the meaning of this event, as is proved by their many extant paintings of the landing at Kurihama.

At the end of the short march from the beach the Commodore and about twenty-five selected officers entered a canvas pavilion which served as vestibule. The main building, hastily constructed of pine, was carpeted and hung with violet-colored silk on which were stamped the Tokugawa arms. Toda Izu no kami and Ido Iwami no kami, seated on camp stools, rose and bowed as the Commodore entered. They preserved an air of statuesque formality during the proceedings, speaking never a word and rising again only when the Commodore left. Had there been any doubt of their rank, it would have been dissolved by the deep prostrations before them of the two aides and all other Japanese present. Opposite them Perry and suite were seated on priests' thrones borrowed from Buddhist temples. An awkward silence was broken by the Japanese interpreter's declaring that their highnesses were ready to receive the documents, which should be placed in a scarlet dispatch case on a table in the center. Perry beckoned to the letter bearers and his Negro bodyguards, who marched up to the dais. The Negroes took the boxes from the boys, opened them, displayed the documents with their seals, and placed them, with the rosewood casket, on the lid of the imperial dispatch case. This flaunting of the documents had no visible effect on the Japanese; actually they were more interested in the Negroes, first they had ever seen. The two aides prostrated

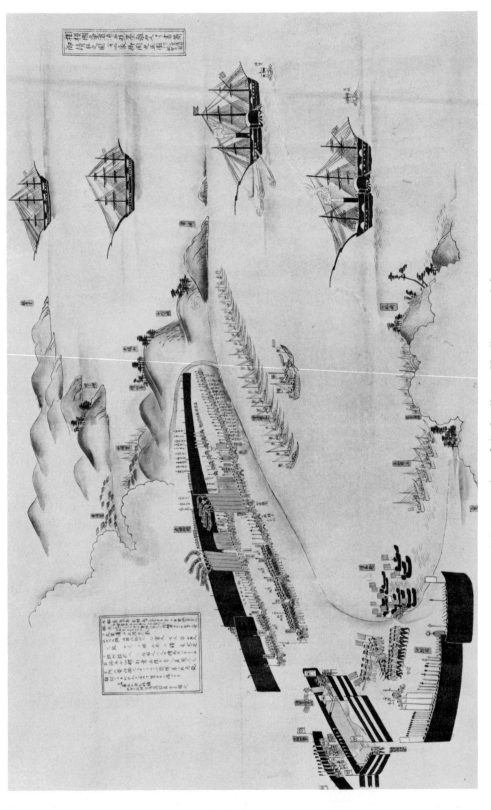

A Japanese view of the landing at Kurihama, 14 July 1853

themselves before Ido and received from his hand a scroll. It turned out to be a grudging receipt of the documents, which the Narrative translates as follows: —

The letter of the President of the United States of North America, and copy, are hereby received, and will be delivered to the Emperor. It has been many times intimated that business relating to foreign countries cannot be transacted here in Uraga, but at Nagasaki; nevertheless, as it has been observed that the Admiral, in his quality of ambassador of the President, would feel himself insulted by a refusal to receive the letter at this place, the justice of which has been acknowledged, the above mentioned letter is hereby received, in opposition to Japanese law. As this is not a place wherein to negotiate with foreigners, so neither can conferences nor entertainment be held. Therefore, as the letter has been received you can depart.

Delivery of this missive to the Commodore was followed by another long silence. Perry broke it by informing the Japanese through the interpreter that he expected to leave for Okinawa and Canton within two or three days, and would be pleased to convey any dispatches or messages from the imperial government. No reply. He remarked that he would return in the spring. "With all four vessels?" asked the interpreter. "Probably more," said the Commodore. The interpreter inquired the cause of the Tai-ping rebellion in China. Perry crisply replied, "Discontent of the people with the government." This so smacked of *lèse-majesté* that the interpreter dared not translate it. In Japan, people were not supposed to be discontented with their government.

Kayama and Nakajima fastened the dispatch case, informed Perry that the conference was over, and led the way out of the building. The procession formed in reverse order, and all hands returned to their ships, well satisfied with the day's proceedings which, as Perry recorded, were conducted in perfect courtesy and decorum, despite the abrupt order to depart and the coldly correct attitude of Ido and Toda.

With justifiable pride, Perry wrote to his wife after returning to Macao, "This achievement of mine I consider an important event in my life. The Pageant was magnificent and I am the only Christian that has ever before landed peacefully on this part of Japan or in any part without submitting to the most humiliating degradation." It was unprecedented, unpredictable, and, in view of the consequences, one of the most important events of modern history. "My next visit may prove still more eventful," continued Perry. It did indeed; but this first one, on 14 July 1853, set a pattern for the next.

Immediately after the ceremony Perry moved all four ships up Edo Bay in line abreast, running lines of soundings across the bay, and anchoring out of sight of Uraga in a roadstead that the Commodore named American

Anchorage, between Webster Island (Natsu Shima) and Point Fillmore (Koshiba Zaki). The two aides with suite bustled on board to inquire why the squadron anchored there? Because it was safer than the Uraga roadstead, said Perry. They forbade him to proceed further up the bay. Perry ignored the order but entertained the Japanese in the wardroom. "Quite a convivial scene ensued," says the official Narrative, "in the course of which abundant supplies of ham, ship's biscuit, and other stores, washed down by plentiful draughts of whiskey, quickly disappeared. The cheer seemed to be much relished." In accordance with Japanese custom, "substantial mementos of the pleasant feast" were "carried off in their capacious sleeves."

Although Perry decided to make his initial visit to Japan short, he felt obliged to explain his reasons to the Secretary of the Navy, in order to forestall criticism. Nothing was to be gained, and much lost, by hanging around Edo Bay for a month, the extreme limit of his food supply. The Shogun would certainly take longer than that to make up his mind, important presents for the Emperor such as the train of cars and the telegraph had not arrived, sailors' morale would suffer if given no shore liberty, and "incidents" might occur if they were turned loose. But he wished to show the Japanese that he could not be ordered out, and also to find out whether there was enough water for big ships further up the bay. So, transferring his pendant to *Mississippi* on 15 July, he steamed ten miles past American Anchorage to a point off Kawasaki, the southern suburb of Edo; then, at Kayama's earnest plea, turned back. "I might have gone still higher," wrote Perry, "but was apprehensive of causing too much alarm, and thus throwing some obstacle in the way." On Saturday the 16th he moved the squadron to a landlocked anchorage in Susquehanna Bay (Otsu Wan). Kayama came on board for a final call, bearing as presents, besides eggs and poultry, forty fans, five pipes and fifty lacquered soup bowls. Perry, observing that they were all cheap stuff, forwarded them from Hong Kong to President Pierce, trusting that he would receive better presents next year when he had better things to give. In return, the Commodore contributed rolls of calico, a bag of sugar and a case of wine described by the Japanese as *sanhauen* (champagne). He asked his officers to contribute any odd items that they could spare — such as a picture of a steamboat, an almanac from China, and a three-volume *History of the United States*, probably Richard Hildreth's. Kayama declared he was forbidden to accept anything, but finally consented, concealing books, bolts and bottles in his sleeves. After a final libation on board, Kayama shook hands all around and departed with tears in his eyes. He was last observed in his barge, knocking off the neck of a champagne bottle and imbibing its contents.

Kayama showed good judgment in consuming the wine quickly because

Abe (Masahiro) Ise no kami

Hayashi (Akira) Daigaku no kami

Toda Izu no kami

Ii (Neasuke) Kamon no kami

his boss Ido made a bonfire of the American presents and demoted him as punishment for being too friendly with the Americans. That was after Perry had left, and everyone from the Bakufu down had breathed a sigh of relief.

Dr. Ito the court physician noted in his diary that Perry's visit was "good medicine for the entire Japanese nation. The Bakufu for the first time realized how formidable a foreign nation might be." A junior councilor remarked to the Doctor, "These Americans are certainly different from the British and others. They seem to be sincere and honest. I hear that their military order is strict and they know the rules of politeness. From now on the Japanese had better stand on friendly relations with them." Ito marveled that any councilor could say as much; he regarded this as a revolution in thought.

Plymouth and *Saratoga* having joined *Mississippi* and *Susquehanna*, the Squadron weighed and sortied from Edo Bay on Sunday morning 17 July, steamers towing sailing vessels. Kannon Saki headland, the shores around Uraga, and hundreds of boats were thronged with sightseers to watch the Americans leave. Outside the bay *Plymouth* and *Saratoga* were cast off and made sail, with orders for Okinawa and Shanghai respectively. The two steamers made for Naha.

Upon returning to China, Perry wrote to his friend James Watson Webb, editor of the New York *Courier*, "It is up hill work to manage these very intractable people, and I have found it necessary to practice a very novel system of diplomacy with them, which I find works very well so far. I have been tolerably successful and hope to do something more when I again call upon His Imperial Majesty."

It would be difficult to criticize the Commodore's conduct during the eight days of this, his first visit to Japan. One false step, and there would have been no treaty, no opening, but a big fight in which the Americans, despite their superior fire power, might have been overwhelmed by sheer numbers. He had maintained the dignity of his government by insisting on a proper reception of an official document. He had surveyed Edo Bay sufficiently for any future contingency. He had been uniformly friendly and conciliatory, and called forth similar sentiments on the part of his hosts. Through careful organization and strict discipline no untoward incident had occurred. And not a gun had been fired, except for salutes and morning and evening colors.

CHAPTER XXV

China Interlude
July 1853–February 1854

Back to Naha and the Bonins

AFTER passing through a heavy gale without damage, *Susquehanna* and *Mississippi* made Naha at noon 25 July. They found storeship *Supply* rolling in the swell of the bay like a great log, but *Plymouth* riding nicely. Her skipper had no untoward incident to report since the Commodore's departure, but his shore parties were still bothered by swarms of police and spies and were unable to procure enough fresh provisions for the ships. Later, the Americans found out the reason for this petty harassment and refusal to sell. The government spies, if they saw any native selling for cash or barter, took the money or goods away from him. Similarly, the government requisitioned provisions from the farmers, and the squadron paid cash for them through Dr. Bettelheim, but the officials kept the money; so every farmer claimed his family would starve if he parted with any produce.

Perry let the Regent know, through the medium of a friendly mayor of Naha, that he was highly displeased with this conduct. "We must have a free trade in the market, and the right to purchase articles for the ships." He also wished, before sailing for China, to be guaranteed continued use of the rest-house, and permission to erect a shed for coal storage. An interview with the Regent was arranged for 28 July, in the *kung-kwa* or official guest house of Naha. Refreshments had been prepared, but the Commodore curtly refused to eat until after transacting business. A protracted dinner followed, during which Williams related, in Chinese, the high points of their friendly reception in Japan. After the *convives* had worked through ten or twelve courses the Regent delivered his reply, which Williams translated and read. It was humble and respectful, but evasive; the rest-house was really a temple, and wanted for worship; to build a coal shed would be embarrassing; the people who followed shore parties were not spies but guides; shopkeepers had nothing important to

sell anyway. Perry handed the paper back to the Regent, declaring that if
he did not receive a satisfactory answer within 24 hours, he would march
on Shuri, take the palace, and treat from there. Adams and Buchanan now
made a fresh approach to the Regent, who conceded everything. A coal
shed would be built and rented at ten dollars a month. The rest-house
would be maintained. "Guides," as he called the spies, would be fewer and
less officious. And a special fair would be held in the guest house early
Monday morning, 1 August, the day the Commodore had set for his departure. These concessions appear to have been expedited by the Regent's
hearing that *Susquehanna*'s "Chips" was tinkering with the famous sedan
chair in preparation for another ride to Shuri. The coal shed went up with
almost miraculous celerity.

On Saturday night the "dramatic corps" of *Mississippi* gave a theatrical
performance on board, attended by all the Bettelheims but avoided by
Williams. The Anglican recorded in his diary that the local "nobility" was
present in force and that "officers, boatswains, sailors and Negroes performed in a most remarkable way. The dancing and singing of the Negroes pleased my children exceedingly." Williams, jealous of Bettelheim,
accused him of winning everyone's dislike; but he was evidently appreciated in the squadron since he was repeatedly invited to preach on board
ship, and was presented with a silver loving cup for his services. His popularity may have been partly based on his following the famous Yale College Chapel principle, "No souls are saved after the first twenty minutes";
whilst Chaplain Jones preached what even Williams called "astronomical"
sermons. The Commodore, when he felt that a chaplain had talked long
enough, used to clear his throat loudly as a signal to pipe down; but apparently this had no effect on Jones.

At the fair, banana-fiber cloth, hairpins, lacquered boxes and various
cheap knickknacks were laid out, and the court interpreter served as
broker. Amusingly enough, the official Narrative uses the brisk trade
which followed as proof that Adam Smith was right: "As the demand
increased it was found, in accordance with the usual law of trade, that the
supply augmented; and the Lew Chew merchants were not backward in
illustrating this principle of political economy." Prices did not start high,
but the natives soon began to jack them up, and late comers to the bazaar
had to pay at least double the sum paid by early arrivals for a similar
article. Sales were for hard money; the Okinawans seemed to know the
value of silver dollars, and the Americans succeeded in spending over a
hundred of them.

On 1 August Perry departed Naha for Hong Kong with the two steamers. *Plymouth* he left behind with instructions to Commander Kelly to
cultivate the friendship of the natives and secure their confidence, to continue surveying Okinawan harbors, and to visit the Bonins. She spent most

of October there. On Peel Island (Chichi Jima), Nathaniel Savory and Seaman Smith were getting along well. The "constitution" had been promulgated, and flocks and herds were increasing. Unfortunately, a surveying party in the sailing cutter capsized in a sudden typhoon, Lieutenant John Matthews and all thirteen sailors were drowned, and even *Plymouth*, with topmasts and yards housed, dragged four anchors right across Port Lloyd and was saved from going ashore only by a shift in the wind. Commander Kelly also surveyed Haha Jima, southernmost island of the group, named Coffin by Perry after its Nantucket discoverer. Following Sir Francis Drake's precedent in California, Kelly nailed to a tree a copper plate claiming this island for the United States, and asserted the privilege of naming nearby islets Perry, Plymouth and Kelly. The Bonins were very popular with seamen of the squadron because their waters teemed with edible fish, and in Port Lloyd almost any day one could capture big green turtles whose flesh made a pleasant change from the navy's "salt horse." Also, the Hawaiian and other girls in Savory's colony were both pretty and kind.

En route to Hong Kong on 2 August, Perry met sloop *Vandalia*, Captain John Pope, which had sailed from Philadelphia 5 March. The encounter created great excitement; all three vessels hove to and Pope went on board *Mississippi* with letters and dispatches from home. They made Hong Kong together on the 7th, and shortly after, the Commodore made an official inspection of *Vandalia*. Yards were manned in his honor, then the men were piped down from aloft to quarters, where they were looked over and addressed by Perry, who pronounced "the ship the cleanest, and the men the finest looking set of men in the Squadron. As he left the ship the yards were manned and a salute of thirteen guns fired." It was his policy always to praise a taut ship and compliment the officers and men.

At Hong Kong the squadron was further augmented. Sloop *Macedonian*, Captain Joel Abbot, which had sailed from the United States 13 April, arrived at Cum Sing Moon anchorage on 26 August.[1] "You will be pleased to learn," Abbot reported to the Commodore, "that the *Macedonian* now sails remarkably well, and is one of the most formidable and powerful Ships in the Navy, when efficiently officered and manned." He claimed she had logged up to 14 knots, and to his wife he wrote that she "attracts great attention. . . . The Commodore seems to be very proud of her. He says she is the most splendid ship he ever saw. . . . The English Admiral . . . on his Arrival at Canton a few days since, remarked to numbers there that the *Macedonian* was the Most Magnificent Ship that had

---

[1] Cum Sing Moon (now Chin-hsing Men) is a harbor with 5-fathom depth and good holding ground about fifteen miles north of Macao, which then lacked a proper harbor. It was not a popular anchorage for the men, as the only amusement was to watch the movements of opium smugglers.

U.S.S. *Macedonian* homeward bound from Hong Kong, 2 February 1856

Photograph of Hong Kong waterfront, 1854; P. & O. steamer loading at right

ever been in these seas." Perry once said that "when he wanted anything done and well done in the shortest possible time under difficult and trying circumstances, he always sent Abbot." He was the Commodore's favorite captain, the only one in the Squadron whom he addressed by his last name, prefixed by "My dear." And he designated him vice commodore, so that he could fly a red pendant in *Macedonian.*

In September, storeship *Southampton* arrived from Norfolk. Her passage had been eventful. Off Formosa she reported a new volcano just risen from the sea, and off Cape Engaño, Luzon, she picked up some interesting castaways — six men and boys in a twelve-foot boat. Blown out to sea by a typhoon fifteen days earlier, they had drifted the entire length of the Philippine Archipelago, and were in bad shape. They puzzled every linguist and ethnologist of Hong Kong, since they resembled no race ever seen there, spoke no known language, and to every inquiry replied, "Salibaboo!" Perry, by poring over charts, ascertained that an island of that name existed in the Talaud group between Mindanao and Morotai. He transferred the Salibaboo boys to *Macedonian,* which next year carried them to Manila for repatriation.

Chinese Puzzles and Pleasures

With the arrival of *Powhatan* at Hong Kong from Okinawa on 25 August 1853, and of *Macedonian* from the United States next day, Perry's squadron was virtually complete. He was disappointed, however, to receive word from the navy department that he would not have the big three-decker *Vermont,* "as she cannot be manned without exceeding the seamen, &c, allowed by law." The train of cars, printing press, telegraph outfit and other heavy gifts for the Emperor had been off-loaded into the old and notoriously slow corvette *Lexington,* now converted to a storeship, and nobody could predict when, if ever, she would reach Hong Kong. But the letter concluded with a reassuring statement from James C. Dobbin, President Franklin Pierce's Navy Secretary, to the effect that the new administration would afford Perry "all proper aid," and had full confidence in his "ability, prudence and sagacity to bring about the desired results." Never was confidence better placed.

In a letter of 1 September from Perry to his friend Sinclair in the Navy Department, he gives an intimate picture of the state of his squadron: —

Mississippi is as near [the] city [of Canton] as she can reach, *Susquehanna* is preparing to take her place. *Powhatan* requires 60 days for repairs. She is as bad as the *Susquehanna* and that is saying enough to damn her as a war steamer. . . . Our *Mississippi* seems to be as staunch & fit for service as when she was in the Gulf, beating the *Susquehanna,* making better weather and consuming one-third less coal. But I shall nurse the two lame ducks, until I can finish my Japan business.

For God's sake do not talk about the return of the store ships until after my spring visit to Japan. I shall want them all, as well to make a show and thus to work upon the fears of the Japanese as to carry up coal and provisions to Yedo, for I cannot tell how long I shall be detained by those people.

In an official report written next day to the Secretary, Perry added that *Saratoga* was at Shanghai "protecting American interests," *Vandalia* at Cum Sing Moon anchorage, and *Plymouth* at Okinawa. Storeship *Supply*, "being the only vessel of the squadron of sufficiently light draft to ascend the river as far as Canton, has been ordered to take her station opposite the city for the protection of the merchants, in case of an outbreak, hourly expected; she will have a guard of marines temporarily attached to her." Anticipating that efforts would be made to compel him to concentrate on China guard duty at the expense of the Japan Expedition, Perry pled: —

I trust that there will be no change in my instructions that will divert me from this great object of my life. I had the assurance of the former administration, especially of Mr. Webster, that I should act alone in this responsible duty, and such was the understanding when I assumed command. As the service is one strictly naval, and must be managed by naval means, the free and uncontrolled command of my whole force is absolutely necessary to secure anything like success; a pursuance of the rules of ordinary diplomacy cannot have the least effect upon these sagacious and deceitful people.

This reference to "free and uncontrolled command" is significant. The Honorable Humphrey Marshall, high commissioner and minister to the court of Peking, proposed to employ Perry's ships exclusively in protecting American property from the Taiping rebels. Lord Lyons, British minister to Washington at the outbreak of our Civil War, wrote to the Foreign Office that every British consul in a Southern port demanded a warship; although (said Lyons) he didn't know what the warship could accomplish except to fire a salute to the consul! So it was in China in 1853-1854. Perry ordered storeship *Supply* on her way to Hong Kong from Okinawa to call at Amoy, which the rebels had taken. Her captain reported that the Taiping forces had "scrupulously respected" foreign persons and property, that there was no American trade with Amoy, and only three Americans in the city — two missionaries and the consul, whom he duly saluted. Nevertheless, Marshall wanted Perry to station a ship there, and one steamer each at Ningpo and Foochow. *Mississippi*, as we have seen, was already at Whampoa to protect the chief danger point, and *Supply* went right up to Canton. Before Perry left for Japan he chartered a shoal-draft British steamer named *Queen*, armed and manned her from the squadron with bluejackets and marines, and left her to defend Canton if need be; and he sent *Plymouth* to Shanghai instead of joining the squadron in Japan.

Thus it can hardly be asserted that the Commodore was indifferent to American persons and property. But he declined to be drawn into the rôle of No. 1 China policeman, or to be deflected from his main mission by dispersing his squadron all along the coast. He gave Marshall transportation in one of his warships from Shanghai to Canton, but when this restless diplomat asked for return passage Perry refused; he had to leave for Japan. To Secretary Dobbin, Perry vehemently protested against being subjected to Marshall's orders: "If the ships are placed at the disposal of diplomatic functionaries, the Commanding Officer can have little control over them." He was delighted over the prospect of having no "American merchants or diplomatic agents" in Japan.

In October Marshall was relieved as minister to China by Robert M. McLane, and "on the very day and precise hour" in January 1854 that Perry weighed anchor for Japan, he received a letter from Dobbin ordering him to meet McLane at Macao with a steamer to "be subject to his control until other orders reach you." With memories of John Randolph, the prospect of placing one of his best ships under a diplomat's control made Perry shudder, and he risked rousing the wrath of the government by procrastinating — a not exclusively Japanese method. He could not possibly detach one of his three steamers at that time; but as soon as his Japan mission was accomplished he would send *Susquehanna* to Macao for the minister to ride around in. The Commodore was particularly outraged at the prospect of being subjected to the orders of a young politician on the make such as McLane, who knew nothing of the Orient. He felt that even if their relations were placed on a civilian plane, his commission as envoy extraordinary to the Emperor of Japan would have precedence over McLane's later one. Had he seen McLane's commission accrediting him not only to China but to Japan, Siam, Korea and Cochin-China, his sense of outrage would have been even greater. But he did keep his promise to send *Susquehanna* to Hong Kong as soon as she could be spared from Japan, and she arrived before the minister did.

Diplomats and dysentery were Perry's greatest burdens in China. He never caught the tropical disease himself, but it made severe inroads on the health of the ships' crews and resulted in a dozen or more deaths. He established a temporary naval hospital at Macao, and the beds were kept full. A good deal of malaria, too, was contracted owing to commanding officers allowing their men to sleep topside in hot weather when anchored near shore. Nobody then understood that dysentery was caused by eating raw vegetables and fruit grown on land manured by night soil; it was attributed to the sailors getting drunk ashore. Actually their indulgence in alcohol must have prevented many cases of dysentery. Perry begged the

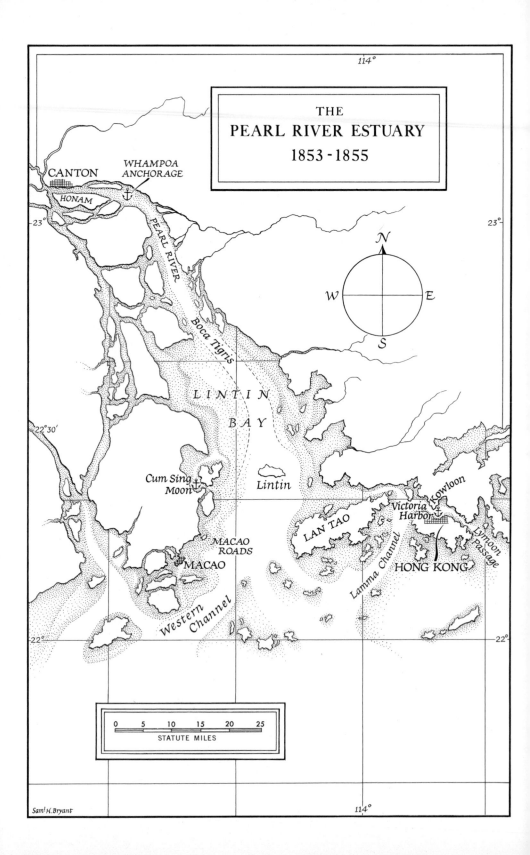

THE
PEARL RIVER ESTUARY
1853 - 1855

114°

CANTON

WHAMPOA
ANCHORAGE

HONAM

23°

23°

PEARL RIVER

Boca Tigris

N

W   E

S

22°30'

L I N T I N

B A Y

Cum Sing
Moon

Lintin

Kowloon

Victoria
Harbor

LAN TAO

HONG KONG

Lymoon
Passage

MACAO
ROADS

MACAO

Lamma Channel

22°

22°

Western
Channel

0   5   10   15   20   25
STATUTE MILES

Sam¹ H. Bryant

114°

Navy Department to send him replacements for the sick and the dead, but Secretary Dobbin replied that none were available; and to his plea for another ship to replace *Vermont* the Secretary replied, "The President is of the opinion" that the squadron is already strong enough. Perry must have exploded over "Frank Pierce" thinking he knew what it took to impress an Emperor! It turned out, however, that the President was right. The Commodore had enough gunpower to dictate a treaty; but if he had had to fight, it would have been another matter.

As usual, Perry's chief preventive medicine for naval distempers was to keep ships moving and the men busy. Units of his squadron shuttled between Hong Kong where there was plenty of fun for the sailors, Macao which was a sink of iniquity, and Cum Sing Moon where there was nothing but a dirty little village and a level space where the Commodore held a formal drill and review of 700 sailors and marines in mid-September. Next day, *Susquehanna*'s band, of which Perry was very proud, gave a Grand Concert in the Philharmonic Hall of Macao. Guests came even from Hong Kong by steamer. This concert was reviewed somewhat disparagingly by the *China Mail* of Hong Kong. Although the assemblage of beauty and fashion was well worth the trip, the critic found the program too ambitious and classical; a "stronger infusion of popular airs or better known music" would have elicited "enthusiasm instead of well-bred applause."

Perry's hired house at Macao had plenty of room for the flag office, and for the artists who were busy working up their sketches of Okinawa and Japan. He wrote to Jane: —

My health is so-so. My office labours are enormous, and I have little time for exercise. I am very comfortable, and the American and English families residing on Macao are very attentive to me but I have a charm for the ladies. I have my band on shore and they play two or three times a week. They have wonderfully improved and have become the best band in the Navy. There are two other bands in the Squadron but not to be compared with mine.

My expenses are larger from the fact that I have to entertain a great deal. I have already exchanged dinners with the Governor, French Minister[1] and the principal Merchants, and have entertained the Regent of Lew Chew. These are rather costly affairs, and work away a good many dollars, so that I have nothing to spare for purchases.

In contrast to Okinawa where there was nothing to buy, and to Japan where trade was forbidden, Hong Kong was, as it still is, a wonderful

---

[1] Sir George Bonham, Governor of Hong Kong, and M. de Bourboulon, Napoleon III's envoy. He was also friendly with the Governor of Macao, a Portuguese naval officer whom he had met in Africa, and at Hong Kong was entertained by the leading merchants. "The Commodore is highly applauded here by both English and Americans for the course he has taken," wrote Robert S. Maclay from Hong Kong 23 August 1853.

place for shopping. No sooner did a warship anchor than she was surrounded by sampans and presently her spar deck would be transformed into a bazaar, the bumboat merchants offering everything Jack wanted, and much more that he didn't want but was wheedled into buying. The "old China hands" belonging to *Susquehanna*, the knowing ones who had been out there for years, had found a much better way. You entered a shop, picked out at your leisure everything you wanted, placed the articles in a heap on the floor and started bargaining for the lot. That took some time, but the expert buyer usually ended by paying about one-third the original asking price.

Each paymaster of the squadron, warned doubtless by Perry's predecessors, brought out sacks full of Mexican or Spanish silver dollars, the principal medium of exchange in China. These cost the government less than $1.04 each at home, and the navy made its personnel a present of the four cents. China merchants were then so hungry for Mexican or Spanish dollars (since the Indian opium exporters would take nothing else except silver ingots which were in short supply), that in Hong Kong and Shanghai they were worth $1.50 to $1.60 United States each, and a Mexican dollar, usually 4s 2d in sterling, cost the British 5s 8d to 7s 8d. Thus, officers and men paid in "Mex" at Hong Kong could buy for $100 a Baring Brothers' draft on New York for $150. Perry prudently took advantage of this to invest a good part of his pay ($4000 per annum) in dollar drafts which he sent to Jane; but he had enough left to buy presents for all the family and a set of porcelain for their new home on West 32nd Street, New York.

All in all, China ports were a man-o'-warsman's paradise in the last century. There was much to do and see ashore, liquor and women were plentiful and cheap, and by the time a sailor had reached China he had worked off his "dead horse" — the two or three months' pay advanced before sailing — and had a pocketful of Mexican dollars coming to him. Commanding officers hired coolies at a few cents a day to relieve Jack of his heavier and more monotonous work, and the native life in sampans, on board which whole families lived, was fascinating to watch. Sampan dwellers did the sailors' washing for a trifle, consumed the ship's garbage, and if there was chicken for dinner John Chinaman was glad to pluck and draw the fowls free, if he could keep the entrails to feed his family.

On board ship, too, there was plenty of fun; amateur theatricals always followed Perry's blue pendant. Young Bill Allen, cabin boy of *Vandalia*, thus describes an evening's entertainment on board *Susquehanna*, to which other ships' crews were invited. The deck forward of the wheelhouse was the stage, with "well painted sceanes and stage properties." Female characters were represented by ships' boys "appropriately wigged and dressed." The entertainment commenced "with a very pritty tablieu formed of flags and arms draping a monument upon which were inscribed the names of some of the most renouned American naval heroes, while one of the men in Man O War uniform sang a patriotic song which was highly applauded and encored." There followed two one-act plays, *Bombastes Furioso* and *Family Jars*, interspersed with songs, all rewarded with rounds of applause "from the officers and crews of the various ships present besides whom there were several merchant captains attended by lady visitors." Commodore Perry has been accused of having no sense of humor, but he always attended these performances, laughed at the jokes and led the applause.

The Commodore could not, however, attend the "brilliant entertainment" of music or partake of the "magnificent supper" on board *Susquehanna* in Victoria Harbor, Hong Kong, around 1 December, since a renewed attack of arthritis kept him in his cabin. The *China Mail*'s Hong Kong rival, the *Friend of China* reported this entertainment in detail, enthusiastically: —

The *Troupe of Funny fellows*, as the Americans on board the U.S.S. *Susquehanna* denominate themselves, gave their promised Entertainment on the night of Monday last, and a very excellent entertainment it proved to be. A pleasant easterly breeze, and a smooth sea rendered the passage from the shore to the Vessel an agreeable trip, and the comfortable seats on the wheel bridge, forming the boxes of the Theatre, together with the polite attentions of the officers to the many visitors, including a good sprinkling of officers of H.M.'s 59th Regiment and of the several Men of War in port, were in excellent keeping with the endeavors of the crew, of whose means the theatricals were provided.

The pieces selected were the celebrated Drama of ROB ROY and the very laughable farce of "The Old Gentleman" with a miscellaneous interlude of Songs and a recitation. . . . We had not expected to hear such "gude braid scotch" from an American representative of Bailie Nicol Jarvie. . . . The parts of Helen McGregor, Rob Roy, the Osbaldistons and Dougal, were also excellently filled; — the Tartan dresses being apparently as well made by Chinese as if manufactured by Highlanders about the Clachan of Aberfoil.

But what may be said of the Comic singing? — simply that it was superlatively good. — Mr. Coursey's *encored* song of "I've been to California" being followed by Mr. Buck's recitation (in Nigger character) and "Walk your chalks Ginger blue" in first rate style. So enraptured indeed were the audience with Mr. Buck's dancing, that with a repetition of it the performance should have concluded. . . .

The great width of the *Susquehanna's* deck enabled the Amateurs to fit up a Theatre on the starboard side of the foremast as large, positively, as some of the minor places of performance in England; and the scenery and decorations were admirable. Personally we take this opportunity to return our sincere thanks to the *Susquehanna's* "troupe of funny fellows" for the pleasure their performance yielded, and trust that before their vessel leaves the harbour we shall again be enabled to report on their kind endeavours to amuse the public.

Nor did the *China Mail* deny praise to an entertainment on board *Powhatan* at Christmastide: —

One of the most pleasing performances witnessed in Hongkong, either ashore or afloat, was given on board the U.S. Steamer *Powhatan* last evening. The invitations were very general, from their Excellencies the Governor and Admiral downwards, and the welcome accorded to every visitor was of the most cordial description. The "Ethiopian Minstrels" performed their parts to perfection, amid roars of laughter. The theatre, on the ample deck, was most tastefully formed of the flags of all nations; and below, the tables groaned with good things for the refreshment, after the performances were over, of as many of the guests as could be accommodated.

So successful in fact were *Powhatan's* "Ethiopians" that the performance was repeated on or shortly after New Year's Day 1854. The Negro-dialect parody on Bulwer Lytton's romantic play *The Lady of Lyons; or, Love and Pride*, transferring the scene from the banks of the Loire to those of the Mississippi, was thought so funny that the *Friend of China* printed it in full, and the "Ethiopians" repeated it at every subsequent performance.[1] *Mississippi*, too, gave a concert before sailing for Japan.

Besides keeping his squadron up to top naval standards, Perry conducted quasi-diplomatic business which the United States ministers in China were unable or unwilling to handle. Governor Sir George Bonham of Hong Kong, instructed by his government to smoke out American designs on the Bonins, called on the Commodore to inform him that Queen Victoria claimed these islands by virtue of Captain Beechey's discovery. Perry countered with the earlier discovery by Captain Coffin, but assured Sir George that he did not presume to annex the group; his one interest was to make Port Lloyd a coaling station for transpacific steamers, and the land purchase from Savory was intended only to secure the most eligible site for a coal depot ahead of possible speculators. Sir George was mollified.

Through the Dutch Governor of Batavia, Perry received word from Japan that the reigning Shogun at the time of his July visit had died shortly after his departure, and the new Shogun would not be ready to deal with him in the spring. And a Russian ship which arrived at Shanghai 29 November reported that the Bakufu would not receive any foreign envoy for three years! Perry paid no attention to this discouraging hint, but he had to do something about a suggestion from an admiral of the Imperial Russian Navy that he and Perry combine forces on their next visit to Japan. Vice Admiral Putiatin, in command of a small squadron

---

[1] The humor of this parody has paled with lapse of time. It is a dialogue between Polly Ann, Ginger and Sam, such as "Polly Ann! — yer orter hab but werry few peccumdilloes ob yourn own to answer for — bekase you'm been de 'casion of such a book of follies in dis here 'sconsolate black Man."

ETHIOPIAN CONCERT,

UNITED STATES STEAM FRIGATE POWHATAN,

Hakodadi, island of Yesso, Empire of Japan. May 29th.

An Ethiopian entertainment will be given by the

JAPANESE OLIO MINSTRELS,

on board this ship, this evening, weather favorable, to which the OFFICERS invite your attendance.

PROGRAMME.

PART FIRST.

As "Colored 'Gemmen' of the North."

GRAND OVERTURE.

1. VIRGINIA ROSE BUD   .   .   *Mr. Dabney.*
2. DARKIES SERENADE,   .   .   "   *DeCosta.*
3. LADIES WON'T YOU MARRY?   .   "   *Tripp.*
4. SALLY WEAVER,   .   .   .   "   *Dabney.*
5. OH! MR. COON,   Duett,   *Messrs. Dabney & Reeves.*
6. OLD GREY GOOSE,   .   .   .   *Mr. Tripp.*

PART SECOND.

"As Plantation 'Niggas' of the South."

1. LIFE BY DE GALLEY FIRE,   ·   *Mr. DeCosta.*
2. GET UP IN DE MORNING,   .   "   *Reeves.*
3. MASSA'S IN DE COLD! COLD GROUND,   "   *Pablo.*
4. OLD AUNT SALLY,   .   "   *Dabney.*
5. SUSEY BROWN,   *Full Band.*

SOLO ON VIOLIN, by C. McLewee.

The whole to conclude with a *burlesque* on Bulwer's celebrated play,

THE LADY OF LYONS,

introducing a new and much admired *pas de deux*, with the following cast of characters:—

CLAUDE MELLNOTTE, *alias* SAM JOHNSING, *Mr. Dabney.*
PAULINE, *alias* POLLY ANN,   .   .   *Miss Tripp.*
GINGER, ...   *Mr. McLewee.*
MINSTRELS, &c.,   .   .   .   *By the whole band.*

Manager, Mr. W. J. Dabney.
Musical Director, Mr. C. McLewee.
Performance to commence at 7 o'clock, precisely.

Japan Expedition Press.

which, like Perry's, had been sent to obtain a treaty, stayed three months at Nagasaki and got precisely nowhere. It occurred to him that if he could tag along with Perry he might accomplish something. Perry politely but firmly declined, but the Russian's request altered his plans. Instead of waiting for spring and fair weather, he decided to depart immediately and brave winter gales rather than allow the Russians to get ahead of him.

On Christmas Eve Perry took time from his duties to write a long letter to Jane: —

U.S.S. Frigate *Susquehannah*
Hong Kong, Dec. 24, 1853

My dear Wife

I write to you at this particular season to convey to you the assurances of my undiminished affection and to wish you and all the members of my family and my friends about you, many happy returns of the year. . . .

This cruise will use me pretty well up, for my duties are very trying to my health. The operations of my Squadron have brought upon [us] the notice and inquiries of the English, French and Russian governments, and I have in consequence been drawn into Correspondence with the authorities of those nations. All this day and a part of the last night I have been engaged in replying to a Communication of the British Plenipotentiary in China, and without vanity I think I have been able to maintain my Position with all these people. . . .

My relations with the American Merchants of China are also very satisfactory, and they have treated me with unbounded kindness. So if I can only keep my health, I shall be delightfully situated, though the immense labour of the Command of so large a force and the official Correspondence which is imposed upon me keeps me constantly confined; which is favourable in one respect, as it gives me an excuse for declining the daily dinner to which I am invited; but tomorrow being Christmas I dine with the [British] Admiral and on New Years Evening one calls on me, on which Occasion I give a collation.

On Wednesday evening last, Capt. McCluney and the officers of the *Powhatan* gave a very handsome entertainment, having an exhibition gotten up by the sailors in imitation of Christie's Minstrels. The Governor, Admiral and many others of the élite were present and the affair went off splendidly. On Wednesday evening next the same party are to visit this ship on which occasion it will fall to my lot to give the entertainment.[1] All the high authorities will be present, and these parties are given in return for the many Civilities shown to us. A few days after I hope to sail for Japan, being in fact only detained awaiting the arrival of the *Lexington* nearly 200 days from New York. . . .

I shall bring you a great many things home. Let me know whether I had

---

[1] This party too was noted by a local reporter, who said that the theatricals were followed by supper and a ball, and none of the guests "seemed in a hurry to depart."

better bring some Canton Crape shawls. They are here from 8 to 50 dollars each. . . .

Ever your affectionate Husband

C.

Slow-coach *Lexington,* bringing the printing press and important presents for the Emperor, finally arrived at Hong Kong. Perry made very sagacious use of the little shipboard press, and the quality of its production was praised in the local newspapers. He employed it not only to disseminate Sailing Directions for this or that harbor, resulting from his many boat surveys, but to tell his officers and men what went on. By printing the President's letter to the Emperor, the Shogun's answer, and the texts of treaties and supplementary agreements, he kept everyone in the squadron informed, and so contributed to general morale. Unfortunately the government sent no paper with the press, and a hurried search of the Canton market before sailing produced only mulberry-leaf paper, the thinnest sort of gossamer. Stronger paper was procured on the next visit to Hong Kong, and the imprints on mulberry-leaf paper have become exceedingly scarce.

Nor did Perry neglect his responsibilities to science. To Secretary Dobbin he wrote from Hong Kong 9 January 1854 that with the assistance of Dr. Morrow and Purser Harris of *Susquehanna* he had been collecting seeds, and had shipped them home by merchant vessels. He had also "engaged some two hundred specimens of such Chinese plants of fruit or ornamental kinds which it would be desirable to introduce into the United States." The squadron was cheered by an editorial in *The Friend of China:* "If Commodore Perry came to Hong Kong with a design on the hearts and kindly feelings of a not over sociable community, we can but tell them . . . that they have most effectively succeeded; and their success in this respect augurs well for the result of an expedition which has for its chief aim the inducing an *un*-civilized set of *un*-sociables to take a position in the world's fraternity."

Okinawa Again

To avoid fresh complications with Humphrey Marshall, as well as to keep a jump ahead of the Russians, Perry made haste to depart on 14 January 1854. After saluting the flagship of Admiral Sir Fleetwood Pellew RN, Perry in *Susquehanna* led the column to sea by Lymoon Passage. *Powhatan* took one storeship in tow, *Mississippi* towed the other. *Macedonian, Vandalia* and *Supply* had already been dispatched; *Plymouth* and *Saratoga* were ordered from Shanghai to report at Okinawa.

From on board *Susquehanna* at Naha 3 February 1854, Perry wrote a long letter to William Sinclair, chief of the bureau of provisions and supplies. In view of Perry's prohibition of his officers and men to send letters to the newspapers, it is amusing that Sinclair promptly gave this letter to a Washington journal as that of "an officer on board Com. Perry's flag-ship to his friend in Washington," substituting "The Commodore" for Perry's "I."

With the people of this island we are getting along swimmingly; every day brings about some new concession from them which six months ago would not have been thought of.

To-day we visited the Regent at the Royal Palace in the city of Shui, about three miles from Naha accompanied by an escort of two companies of marines, three bands, and about forty officers, as by this sort of show the people of these countries are more readily influenced. We first visited the Regent at the Palace, and from thence went to the City Hall, where a grand entertainment was served to the whole party. On leaving, the Commodore invited the Regent and authorities to an entertainment on board the flag-ship, to come off on our return from Japan. They have already dined with him, but we intend on returning to give them a sort of dramatic show to be gotten up by the crew. . . .

We have explored the whole interior of the island and surveyed the entire coast. The people wherever our parties go attend upon them and supply them with lodgings and provisions. . . .

Hitherto our whaling ships have never dared to enter the ports of this Island; now they can do so with perfect safety, and be furnished with supplies at fair prices. . . .

We could not have managed at all without the assistance of the storeships; not a vessel could be chartered in China for transporting coal, and our whole cruise this Spring would have been defeated had it not been for their service.

The Commodore and the Okinawa government were not getting along quite so "swimmingly" as there stated. Perry felt obliged to send the Regent a protest against the continued harassment of his shore parties, and the difficulty of obtaining provisions. To this the Regent made an almost pathetically humble though evasive reply on 2 February 1854, of which the following is part of the official translation by Williams: —

Shang Hiung-hiun, Superintendent of Affairs in the Middle-Hill prefecture in the kingdom of Lewchew, high minister, & Má Liang-tsai, Treasurer, &c.,

Hereby petition in reply. . . .

This country is a little out of the way island in a corner of the sea, poor and unfruitful, producing nothing of consequence; and since the arrival of your ships in May last year, . . . the things required by them have been very numerous indeed. At present, the policemen and petty officers send persons all over the country to seek for things wanted in the orders, and though they may be very difficult to execute, there is no help for it. . . .

[You say that] "you do not, in what you agree to and promise, regard the truth or heed your words, but practice much falsehood, which shows your impertinence and disrespect." When we had the consultation the other day which your Excellency directed to be held, we had every desire to be "tremblingly obedient"; but the matter in hand was a difficult one to agree to, yet we trust that you will not in this impute disrespect to us, for how can we cherish any impertinence or disrespect? We humbly think upon your Excellency's vast kindness and commiseration for the poor, and consideration for those who have erred, always exhibiting humanity and kindness, to which goodness we look up.

As your Excellency has now stated these several particulars in your communication, we have respectfully replied to them in order, begging that kindness may be manifested towards this little country, and that you will condescend to regard it with compassion, and we shall be deeply moved at such incomparable goodness and regard.

One cannot help feeling sorry for the Okinawans. Here, "in a corner of the sea," they had lived peaceably for centuries offending nobody, asking for nothing, hoping to be let alone. Now, owing to incomprehensible forces, they were to be drawn into the web of international rivalries, and, ninety years after Perry's last visit, to become principal victims of a long and bloody campaign.

Perry did not take seriously the excuse of poverty and lack of products, as he had frequently seen junks leaving Naha loaded with rice, sweet potatoes and other products for Japan. But he had no further trouble on this score. And an unsigned letter of an American officer dated 6 February, which found its way into the New Bedford *Whalemen's Shipping List* of 23 May, states that relations with the Okinawans were on the mend. "The familiarity of the children in the streets is one of the most apparent signs of progress, for while they ran away from us before in every direction, they now come about us and seem under no restraint." A good sign indeed.

Perry had *Susquehanna*'s deck cabin taken apart at Naha and rebuilt on board *Powhatan*, since he planned to shift his flag to her in Japan and send *Susquehanna* back to China to be Minister McLane's yacht. The squadron departed Naha in echelons the first week of February, joining at sea. They passed along the chain of the northern Ryukyus, then bore away for Sagami bay, Honshu. On the 12th they sighted Mount Fuji, "completely clothed in its winter garb of snow." The uplands "were bare and desolate, while the distant mountains stood chill in their snowy drapery." *Macedonian* was found to be aground, as Captain Abbot had mistaken a cove on the Sagami Peninsula for the entrance to Edo Bay. She kedged off after extensive jettisoning of coal and other weighty objects (which the honest Japanese retrieved and returned), and *Mississippi* towed her clear, undamaged. The squadron then proceeded in single line, and at 3 P.M. February

13, 1854, reached American Anchorage off Yokosuka, twenty miles from Edo.

Now that the most crucial phase of Perry's mission begins, we may well take a glance at figures of the formidable squadron which he now had at his disposal.[1] The first three vessels were steamers; the others, three-masted, square-rigged ships.

Ship	Class	Built (Rebuilt)	Length	Tons	Offi-cers and Men	Guns		Commander
						Shell	Other	
SUSQUEHANNA	frigate	1850	257	2450	300	6	3	Comdr. F. Buchanan
POWHATAN	frigate	1852	253	2415	300	6	3	Capt. W. J. McCluney
MISSISSIPPI	frigate	1839	225	1692	268	12	0	Comdr. S. S. Lee
MACEDONIAN	sloop	1832 (1853)	164	1726	380	6	16	Capt. Joel Abbot
PLYMOUTH	sloop	1843	147	989	210	4	18	Comdr. John Kelly
SARATOGA	sloop	1842	150	882	210	4	18	Comdr. W. S. Walker
VANDALIA	sloop	1828 (1848)	127	700	190	8	16	Comdr. John Pope
SOUTHAMPTON	storeship	1842	156	567	45	0	2	Lieut. J. J. Boyle
LEXINGTON	storeship	1826 (1843)	127	691	45	0	2	Lieut. J. J. Glasson
SUPPLY	storeship	1846	141	547	37	0	4	Lieut. A. Sinclair

Perry shifted his broad pendant from *Susquehanna* to *Powhatan* on 18 February 1854.

[1] The number of officers and men on each ship is full complement; the actual number in Far Eastern waters must have been less. Not all these ships were present at any one time. *Saratoga* arrived Edo Bay 4 March, and *Supply* on the 15th. *Susquehanna* sailed for China on the 24th. *Plymouth* did not come to Japan on the 1854 visit; she was sent to take care of Shanghai. Not included are British S.S. *Queen* which Perry chartered, armed and manned from his squadron to defend Americans in Canton, and barque *Caprice*, chartered as collier.

CHAPTER XXVI

Negotiating the Treaty
February—March 1854

Perry was exceedingly anxious not to resort to strong measures if he could attain his object in other ways, and great praise is due to him for the combination of dignity, firmness and skill which he displayed in his dealings with a very difficult people, masters of evasion and procrastination.
— SIR GEORGE B. SANSOM, *The Western World and Japan*

Japan Is Willing; Perry Concedes

IT will be recalled that Perry, after promising the Japanese to return in the spring of 1854, upped the date to January. This is explained in an amusing letter of the previous December from Assistant Engineer Officer William A. Rutherford to his American sweetheart: "Commodore Perry has given an Order to every Captain in Squadron to have there Storm Sails bent by a certain date, . . . it looks like moveing. We have heard that the Russian Squadron has gone up to Japan and that there object is to open trade with them, &c. . . . The Admirals of the French and English Squadrons on this Station has informed *old Perry* that they intend to accompany him up to Japan *next spring* they had better keep there top eye open; for old *Sly Boots*, that is Perry, will certainly give them the Slip."

Which is just what he did, and none too soon. The Bakufu was ready to negotiate in February 1854, and the new Shogun Iesada had already appointed a diplomatic commission. Immediately after his accession senior councillor Abe (Masahiro), still the most powerful man in the government, took the unprecedented step of consulting the Emperor and more than a hundred daimyo, as to what should be done about the President's letter. The imperial circle at Kyoto and almost all the backwoods daimyo, assuming that the real American objective was conquest, that opening foreign trade would ruin the Japanese economy, and that the Tokugawa polity of seclusion must be maintained, advised that the American proposals be rejected, but negotiations prolonged to give time for defense. The Daimyo of Mito, an extreme isolationist, even suggested that to be consistent the Dutch be thrown out of Nagasaki — although only from the Dutch could Japan obtain modern guns! But the more sophisticated gentry, who knew something of the contemporary world, advised granting Perry's demands as a temporary measure while building up defense with a Western-style military organization and steam warships. Toda Izu no kami, co-recipient of the President's letter at Kurihama, went so far as to advocate opening trade with the United States, and Ii Kamon no kami added that Japanese trade overseas would bring good fruits in the future. As a first step, before Perry's return, the Council repealed the law against building large ships and applied to the Dutch to purchase a couple of warships.

Abe, in view of the imperial court's reluctance to treat, and the backwoods daimyo urging the Bakufu to "get tough," decided on a middle course: to promise kind treatment of castaways, and open Shimoda for coal and limited supplies if the Americans would have none of Nagasaki, but not for at least three years — preferably five. He also issued a warning that, in order to avoid incidents such as those which led to the Opium War in China, American visitors must be treated politely, furnished with necessities at low prices, and protected from "bad Japanese people." [1] And a conciliatory reply to the President's letter was drafted. Having already made the policy decision, the Bakufu was not embarrassed by Perry's early return, and ordered no special defense measures when his full squadron appeared off Uraga on 13 February 1854.

On that very day a local official named Kurokawa (Kahei) boarded the flagship at American Anchorage, accompanied by interpreters and sundry hangers-on. There then began a long and tiresome discussion about the place of negotiation. Perry's heart was set on the Shogun's capital, but the Japanese said emphatically, "You cannot be received at Edo." They proposed Uraga where they were already putting up a "treaty hall." Perry declined on the ground of insecurity of the anchorage off Uraga in winter; it was indeed exposed to the sea wind and swept by strong tidal currents. The Japanese then proposed Kamakura where the Sagami Peninsula thrusts out from the mainland. Since that place lay on an open roadstead with no shelter, Perry laughed it off. Day after day these parleys continued in perfect courtesy, with a frequent exchange of presents,[2] and

---

[1] Abe, humorously, also consulted the owner of the principal bordello in Edo, and her answer is still preserved in the archives: Send soldiers to the black ships, disguised as bumboat merchants, establish friendly relations with the crews, have drinking parties with them on board, start quarrels, and in the confusion blow up their powder magazines and kill the sailors one by one with small knives!

[2] Preble states, "Among the presents received by Com. Perry, was a box of obscene paintings of naked men and women, another proof of the lewdness of this exclusive people." But Manjiro reported the women of Fairhaven, Massachusetts, to be "lewd" because they kissed in public!

much consumption of Perry's store of liquid refreshments. As the Prince de Ligne said of the Congress of Vienna, "*Le congrès danse mais ne marche pas,*" one might say of these shipboard negotiations in Edo Bay, "Compliments were exchanged and alcohol consumed, but nobody got anywhere." The Japanese insisted on Uraga; the Commodore on Edo. Anyone who has tried to find an address in a remote part of Tokyo will appreciate how much patience one needs to deal successfully with Japanese; how long the explanations and excuses take with a people who use a hundred words in a polite circumlocution where a Westerner would use two words abruptly. Perry had that patience, up to a point; but once, according to the Japanese interpreter, he lost his temper and said "if his proposals were rejected, he was prepared to make war at once; that in the event of war he would have fifty ships in nearby waters and fifty more in California, and that if he sent word he could summon a command of one hundred warships within twenty days."

Commander Adams tried to break the ice by suggesting that the Japanese bring their wives on board for a dance; a proposal received with embarrassed giggles — nobody in Japan had ever heard of such a thing! This amiable effort having failed, Perry allowed his chief of staff and a few other officers to land at Uraga and parley with the Japanese Commissioners. That conference had to be postponed from 21 to 22 February because a violent southerly gale made up, forcing *Vandalia*, bearing the American delegation, to retire to a sheltered anchorage elsewhere. Every vessel in the squadron celebrated Washington's Birthday by dressing ship with flags and pendants, giving a band concert, and firing 21-gun salutes. These last created "tumultuous roars which frightened our people," says a Japanese chronicler; but they were satisfied with the explanation that it was the birthday of the "King of America."

The Uraga conference opened somewhat inauspiciously. Immediately after visiting cards had been exchanged, Izawa Mimasaka no kami closed his iron fan with a sharp crack which sounded like a pistol shot. The Americans, alarmed, grasped their sidearms "and assumed a resolute attitude," but the sight of the Japanese calmly putting on spectacles relieved them of anxiety. Everything was conducted amiably, but no decision was reached at this conference.

Before Commander Adams rejoined the squadron, Commodore Perry, hoping to expedite matters, moved his ships, preceded by surveying boats, up the Bay to a point whence the Shogun's capital city could be seen from the masthead; one could even hear the tolling of temple bells. He meant this as a hint to the Japanese that he could go to Edo if he would. Rutherford, in the leading survey boat, reported what a thrill it was to see Edo even from afar, not only because it was reputed to be the world's largest city but because no foreigner, save an occasional Dutchman, had been there for more than two centuries. "Mr. Maury having charge of the party ordered them to give *three cheers* in Honor of being the first Americans that ever saw the City of Yeddo." And friendly fishermen gave them some of their catch.

Surveying and sounding went on every day the weather was not too blustery; and, as the finished work indicates, Perry managed to compile an excellent chart of the western part of Tokyo Wan. Surveying had the additional advantage of keeping the sailors occupied and amused — eight boats or more were out daily, and the crews alternated. Guard boats no longer bothered the surveyors, and the people brought out bouquets of *Camellia japonica*, great swaths of whose white blossoms were now seen among the pines. One boat's crew under Lieutenant Preble had an interesting experience. As they approached the shore near Yokohama, where a number of Japanese had congregated, the native men intimated by unmistakable gestures that their women were easy; and the girls accented the invitation by opening wide their kimonos. Preble, disgusted at this "exhibition of lewdness," ordered his men to pull away, doubtless to their disappointment.

The Commodore allowed no shore liberty until a treaty was signed, but the men remained fairly cheerful. "Sailors are dancing on the forecastle" of *Macedonian*, wrote Lieutenant Preble to his wife; "I wish you could see them." Rival amateur actors on the different ships put on shows to while away the tedium. Naval rations, however, became very monotonous. *Powhatan*'s log for 19 February mentions "a quantity of vegetables, fruits and Fowls from the Japanese authorities" received on board and distributed through the fleet, but not many fresh vegetables were available so early in the year. Wild ducks were plentiful, but the Commodore forbade shooting them as he did not wish to break the local game laws. Since the Japanese at that time did not raise poultry for eating, only for egg-laying and as pets, the fowl obtained ashore for wardroom tables were exceedingly tough; Preble's messmates amused themselves by conjecturing whether one rooster served up for dinner could have crowed over the Portuguese evacuation two centuries earlier — or even have been the one that mocked St. Peter! On the other hand, there was an abundance of fresh sea food. Perry encouraged the sailors to fish, in the hope of discovering new species, and as soon as a desirable fish was painted and skinned it went to the galley.

During the three weeks that the squadron lay at anchor off Kanagawa, it "presented a very imposing aspect," recorded Lieutenant Sproston. *Southampton, Saratoga, Mississippi, Macedonian, Powhatan, Susquehanna, Lexington* and *Vandalia*, in that order north to south, were moored in a crescent, concave side facing the shore, where massive concrete breakwaters now enclose Yokohama harbor. When calm weather succeeded the winter gales, it was a pleasure to be on night watch. A waxing moon illuminated the shore, the ships, and even far-off Fuji. The band concert at evening colors, the striking of ships' bells and the calls of sentries and lookouts through the night made music agreeable to a sailor's ear.

In the meantime the Japanese Commissioners, whom Perry had not yet met, twice returned to Edo to confer with high officials of the Shogun's council, who ordered them at all hazards to resist Perry's demand to negotiate at Edo. If that were accepted, the Bakufu would be deemed incapable of defending its capital and probably be overthrown. But the delegation might compromise on some nearer place than Uraga.

That was done. Perry realized that to insist on Edo would threaten the regime, which he had no desire to overthrow; he was willing to settle for any convenient place on the shore of the bay with safe anchorage and a level spot where he could set up the train of cars and display his other presents. As a compromise the Japanese offered Yokohama, Perry accepted, and they began at once to put up a reception hall on shore. This treaty house, as the Americans called it, faced the southeastern bight of the harbor.

In "Notes of Transactions" that he appended to a dispatch of 20 March to the Navy Department, Perry thus defended his stubbornness about the site: —

In conducting all my business with these very sagacious and deceitful people, I have found it profitable to bring to my aid the experience gained in former and by no means limited intercourse with the inhabitants of strange lands, civilized and barbarian; and this experience has admonished me that, with people of forms, it is necessary either to set all ceremony aside, or to out-Herod Herod in assumed personal consequence and ostentation.

I have adopted the two extremes — by an exhibition of great pomp, when it could properly be displayed, and by avoiding it, when such pomp would be inconsistent with the spirit of our institutions; and never to recognise, on any occasion, the slightest personal superiority, always meeting the Japanese officials, however exalted their rank, with perfect equality whilst . . . making it known that I would communicate with none but the princes of the Empire. Up to this time, I have succeeded far beyond my expectations in maintaining this extreme point of diplomacy, and, as I believe, to very great advantage.

It is probable that arrogance may be charged against me for persisting as I did, and against the judgment of all about me, in changing the place of conference, and thus compelling four princes of the Empire to follow the Squadron, and subjecting the government to the trouble and expense of erecting another building; but I was simply adhering to a course of policy determined on after mature reflection, and which had hitherto worked so well.

Again, Perry acted rightly; he was imperious but not arrogant. And note that he acted "against the judgment of all" about him — meaning

Williams and the captains of his ships. We shall hear more of this later; suffice it here to point out that the Commodore was a "summit" in himself; a lonely figure in his own squadron, and his physical condition was far from perfect. "The Commodore is in bed with what *he* calls rheumatism," sneered one of the squadron's diarists. Rheumatism, as they called arthritis in that era, it was; Perry suffered from it for over thirty years.

At home Perry received adverse criticism for calling the Japanese "deceitful" in his published dispatches. But the Japanese were deceitful, and accounted it a virtue. This usually happens in a police or absolutist state where spies are everywhere and the only way a person can get on is by trickery and prevarication. As an example, when Commodore Perry caught Einosuke in a lie, and charged him with it, the interpreter took it as a compliment, duplicity being "one of the most cherished accomplishments of a Japanese official." Japan's reputation for treachery, for sudden, fierce attacks on an unsuspecting enemy in time of peace, explains why Perry sent his men ashore armed to the teeth and under cover of the squadron's guns. He did not care to risk their being the victims of a premature Pearl Harbor.[1] After the first two sessions at Yokohama, however, he went ashore with no armed guard; and the Bakufu showed equal confidence in American friendship by ordering no mobilization as it had at Perry's first appearance. The Daimyo of Kokura, responsible for the defense of Yokohama, had a moderate turnout displaying his arms of three superimposed red triangles on a white field, and he removed the canvas screens at Perry's request.

While the treaty hall was being put up, several parties for Japanese officials were given on board *Powhatan*. At one, a Japanese castaway from California who had enlisted in the squadron under the name Sam Patch, was confronted with Kayama. Poor Sam, thinking he was about to be delivered up and beheaded, grew green in the face, fell on his knees, trembled in every limb, and rose only when reassured by Commander Adams that he had nothing to fear. Later, Sam visited his family ashore and was urged to stay, guaranteed immunity from the usual castaway's punishment; but he preferred to continue as an American man-o'-warsman. He returned to the United States in *Mississippi*, and after being paid off lived in New York with a shipmate named Goble who became a Baptist missionary. The Reverend Jonathan Goble returned to Japan in 1860 with Sam as cook; and both died there.

---

[1] Naturally, qualities deemed virtuous for centuries did not simply disappear when Japan became a constitutional monarchy. In discussing the Pearl Harbor attack with Japanese friends after World War II, I found that the charge of treachery was not resented, but that they were gravely offended by my calling the Pearl Harbor strategy "idiotic."

The Negotiations Begin

After Commander Adams had inspected the new treaty house and found the grounds suitable for the display of official gifts, Perry made a ceremonious landing on Wednesday, 8 March 1854. With his usual care, the Commodore caused a detailed processional bill to be drawn up. Three ships' bands and five hundred officers, seamen and marines were to go ashore in 27 boats. The enlisted men were to wear white frocks, blue bell-bottomed trousers and blue jackets, and the blue cap which had recently been issued to replace the old tarpaulin,[1] officers the "undress" blue uniform with blue cap, frock coat, epaulets and sidearms; the Commodore alone in full-dress blue tailed coat, gold-striped trousers and *chapeau bras.* At 11:30, under Franklin Buchanan's command, all boats pulled for the shore line abreast. The men disembarked and formed two lines, making an aisle for the Commodore and his suite from wharf to treaty house, about five hundred yards distant. As eight bells struck, the Commodore stepped from *Powhatan* into his white-painted barge, and 17 guns roared a salute from *Macedonian* — the prescribed number for an envoy extraordinary and minister plenipotentiary, in which capacity the Commodore now acted. Upon his landing, drums rolled, marines presented arms, bands struck up "The Star-Spangled Banner," and oarsmen stood up and doffed caps. The Commodore, preceded by two colossal Negroes bearing the ensign and the blue pendant, was followed by officers in column of two, marching between lines of sailors and marines presenting arms. On each side of the entrance to the treaty house stood richly costumed samurai and their men, bearing banners, flags and streamers. As Perry reached this group, Japanese officials came out of the house uncovered (Commodore and suite promptly removing their hats) and with deep reverences conducted the Americans into the interior. As soon as they were within, and Perry had explained through his interpreter what to expect, howitzers mounted on the larger ship's boats floating near the shore, commenced firing a 21-gun salute in honor of the Emperor; and the Tokugawa trefoil, which the Americans supposed to be the Japanese imperial ensign, appeared on the main topgallant masthead of *Powhatan*.[2] Then the Japanese Commissioners received a 17-gun salute.

The treaty house had been erected on a farm near the then tiny village of Yokohama, facing the harbor and near what is now the official landing for ships' passengers. Ten years later, when Yokohama became the desig-

---

[1] On ordinary occasions and in summer, as Heine's pictures prove, the enlisted men wore broadbrimmed, low-crowned straw hats, with fluttering ribbons aft.

[2] The Rising Sun flag, which had been often used by Japanese junks for centuries, became the official ensign on 11 July 1854.

JAPANESE SCROLL OF THE LANDING AT YOKOHAMA, MARCH 1854

Left to right: *Mississippi; Macedonian* saluting *Powhatan; Susquehanna; Lexington*

Boat howitzers firing salute to the Emperor

Perry marching to treaty house between ranks of sailors and marines

nated residence for foreign consuls and merchants, this site was selected
for the British consulate, but a camphor tree which grew close to the house
was preserved as the one "under which Perry signed Japan's first foreign
treaty." In the great earthquake of 1923 which completely leveled Yokohama, the consulate burned down and the tree with it. But its roots survived, and in 1931 were transplanted in the courtyard of the new British
consulate. There the "treaty tree" has taken on new life, and in 1966 was
more than fifty feet high, last relic of the rural setting of this 1854
negotiation.

Perry, Adams and interpreter were given seats on the left of the dais,
the Japanese place of honor. The Commissioners, seated on the right, rose
and bowed as they entered. Chief Commissioner was fifty-five-year-old
Hayashi (Noboru) Daigaku no kami; i.e., Lord Rector of the University
at Edo, a position hereditary in his family for two centuries. His duties
included giving monthly lectures to the Shogun and a general oversight of
education and culture. An eminent Confucian scholar and a dignitary of
fine presence, benevolent expression and courtly manners, Hayashi had
often been consulted by the Bakufu on matters concerning foreigners.
Joined with him Ido (Satohiro) Tsushima no kami, the chief administra-
tor of Edo, Izawa (Mayayoshi) Mimasaka no kami, responsible to the
Bakufu for the administration of Uraga, and Udono (Choei) a *metsake* or
censor of the Bakufu, whose job it was to watch the others. Ido, about
fifty years of age, seemed elderly and somnolent; but Izawa, only forty,
appeared to be a young man "full of fun and frolic," keeping time to the
American band music with hands and feet. Their costume consisted of a
doublet, a pair of very wide, short trousers of figured silk, and white socks
laced to some distance above the ankles; over doublet and trousers a loose
gown of embroidered silk was secured to the waist by a sash, in which
were thrust the two swords which marked them as samurai. The three
kami also sported a white shirt exposed at the breast as a mark of their
rank.

At some distance from the Commissioners sat the official scribe, an un-
pleasant-looking character named Matsuzaki (Michitaro), who acted as
Hayashi's secretary and whom the Americans suspected of being an official spy. Einosuke the Japanese interpreter (who knelt throughout the
conferences) translated from Japanese into Dutch and vice versa, while
Portman translated from Dutch to English, and the reverse. The services
of Williams were not needed, but he contributed to good will by signing
fans. Every Japanese gentleman carried a fan, on which he liked to collect
signatures as Americans sign menu cards; and since Williams wrote good
Chinese characters his signature was greatly in demand. He claimed to
have signed a thousand fans in Japan. As his assistant, Williams had an
educated Chinese who passed the time exchanging fan signatures and orig-

CONTEMPORARY JAPANESE SKETCHES AT YOKOHAMA, MARCH 1854

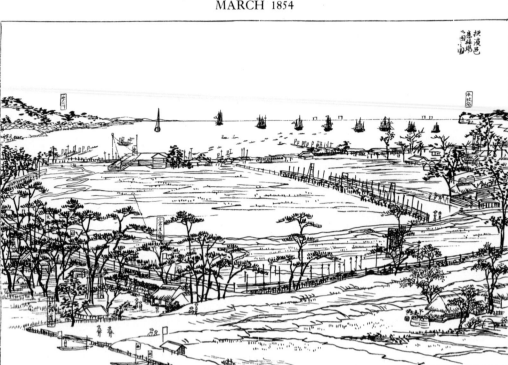

The treaty house area; note telegraph wire

The funeral of Private Williams, U. S. Marine Corps

Perry and his Negro color-bearer

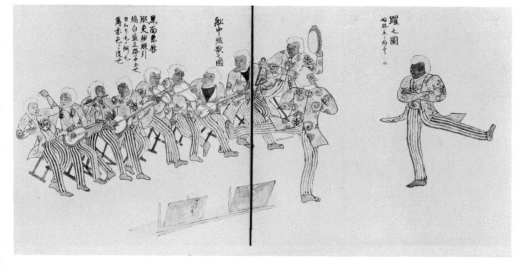

The "Ethiopian Minstrels" of *Powhatan*

TWO POPULAR JAPANESE SKETCHES OF THE AMERICANS

Japanese caricature of American guests at the official banquet

Marines testing the flesh of Sumo wrestling champion

inal poems with attachés of the Japanese delegation, while the real business went on indoors.

After an exchange of formal compliments, Perry and his immediate suite were ushered to an inner chamber, while those left out of this exclusive conference were consoled by a feast of fish, boiled seaweed, walnuts, shredded carrot, oysters, *sake* and tea.

Hayashi Daigaku no kami, at the opening session of the conference on 8 March, presented an official reply to the President's letter. Although authenticated by the Shogun's official seal, it was signed only by interpreter Einosuke. Perry, assured that this was the proper Japanese procedure for important state papers, offered no objection, especially since the reply was addressed to him as "ambassador" of "His Majesty" the President.

The reply opened with typical Bakufu double-talk: the Emperor (i.e., the Shogun who always acted in the Emperor's name) considered the American proposals to be "positively forbidden by the laws of our Imperial Ancestors"; nevertheless, to insist upon unalterable attachment to said "ancient laws" would be to "misunderstand the spirit of the age"; imperative necessity must govern. "We admit the urgency, and shall entirely comply with the proposals of your government concerning coal, wood, water, provisions, and the saving of ships and their crews in distress. After being informed which harbor Your Excellency selects, that harbor shall be prepared."

Pending the translation of this document, Hayashi opened proceedings by stating that the Emperor was ready to supply American ships with fuel, water, provisions and coal; and to treat shipwrecked sailors kindly; but that he could consider no proposal to open foreign trade. Absolutely none!

Perry, without replying to the Rector's emphatic negative, introduced an immediate problem. A private of marines named Robert Williams had just died on board *Mississippi;* could he be buried on Natsu Shima (Webster Island)? Hayashi offered condolences on the death of "one coming so far" from home, but insisted that burials were forbidden on that island, and proposed that the marine be temporarily interred at Uraga and later translated to the Dutch cemetery at Nagasaki. Perry, to whom the very name Nagasaki was anathema, said that would never do. The Commissioners then conceded that the marine could be buried in Yokohama. "Perry appeared to be extraordinarily grateful," recorded the Japanese scribe, "to the extent even of shedding tears." For "Old Bruin" had a heart, and every sailor and marine on board his ship he regarded as a member of the family.

Seldom has a dead marine been the subject of high diplomacy or accorded a burial service in two religions. All ships' ensigns were halfmasted next day, and at least a thousand Japanese watched the funeral procession respectfully. There was a guard of marines with reversed arms, a fifer and muffled drum which played the Dead March from *Saul*. The Japanese had been indoctrinated with such horror of Christianity (an official who picked up a prayer book on board the flagship dropped it like a hot coal when he saw the cross), that Chaplain Jones anticipated trouble and asked the Commodore for instructions. "Do exactly as you always do at home; no more, no less," said he. "But suppose I am interrupted?" "Go right on with your usual service," said "Old Bruin." No interruption occurred; Jones in his preacher's gown received every mark of respect from the Japanese spectators, and after he had concluded the burial service according to the Book of Common Prayer and the marine guard had fired three volleys over the grave, a Buddhist Bonze took over with gong, incense and prayers, concluding by throwing into the grave a *viaticum* consisting of rice, candles, a bag of money and a pass to get through the heavenly gates. These gracious gestures of the Japanese went further toward creating good will on the part of the American enlisted men than any other episode of this crucial visit to Japan. As cabin boy Allen of *Vandalia* recorded, they considered it "a most striking and convincing proof" of Japanese friendliness.

Williams's body was later translated to Shimoda and buried beside that of a sailor killed by a fall from a mast. The gravestones are still there beside the Gyokusenji temple.

Returning to the treaty conference of 8 March, Perry made a plea for kindness to shipwrecked sailors. He charged Japan with inhumanity and hinted that if she did not mend her ways she might expect a war, such as the one we had just waged against Mexico. Hayashi countered that Japan would fight if necessary, but that Perry's information about her treatment of castaways was false; all had been treated well except the crew of one American whaler who were bad actors.[1] He resented the charge of inhumanity, and scored a neat point by reminding Perry that Japan had enjoyed peace for three centuries, during which the Western countries had been almost constantly at war. Perry thanked him for consenting to the two points of castaways and ships' supplies, but went on to say, what about trade? "If you open your country to commerce it will bring to you great profit." The Lord Rector replied that whatever foreign commerce might mean to other countries, Japan wanted none of it; she produced everything she wanted, and had no wish to sell anything abroad. And he scored another point on Perry by reminding him that his principal objects, according to his own words, were "to have greater value placed on human life, and to have help given to ships. . . . Commerce has to do with profits, but has it anything to do with human life?"

---

[1] They had been treated the same as Japanese criminals, which is what Hayashi considered "well"; and the bad actors were deserters, not shipwrecked men.

Perry had to do a double-take on that. He "cogitated for some time, and then said, 'You are right. . . . Commerce brings profit to a country, but it does not concern human life. I shall not insist upon it.' " Nevertheless, he pulled out of his pocket and presented a little book containing the Chinese text of her recent treaty with the United States. He repeated that he would not insist, but hoped that the Commissioners would peruse this treaty "for information only." Hayashi graciously accepted it. He then "withdrew to the retiring room in order to indicate that his rank is higher than that of Perry," says the scribe, while the Commodore joined the inferior Commissioners at dinner. If Perry sensed the implied slight of Hayashi's dining alone, he chose to ignore it, and when interpreter Eino-suke boarded *Powhatan* next day, the Commodore expressed his appreciation of "the good will which inspires" the Lord Rector and his colleagues.

Interludes and Artists

The period when official notes were being translated and studied by both sides seemed a proper occasion to present gifts. Commander Adams went ashore on 12 March to set up the miniature railway with the help of engineer officers, to run a telegraph wire from Yokohama to Kanagawa, and tune the instruments at each end. He also brought ashore a patent metal lifeboat, the Audubon elephant folios, a telescope, sundry agricultural implements, a case of books, several cases of firearms, a barrel of whiskey, several baskets of champagne, all for the Emperor. In addition there were about three dozen Yankee clocks, seeds of American plants, and a quantity of wines and liquors for the Commissioners' consumption.[1] Captain Joel Abbot made a formal presentation next day. The miniature railway in particular was a *succès fou*. It consisted of a locomotive, tender, and passenger car, with a circular track of 18-inch gauge, 350 feet in diameter. Although the entire train was so tiny that the engineer had to

---

[1] Detailed lists are in *Narrative* I 356-57, Spalding pp. 242-43, *Powhatan's* log for 13-18 March, and Williams *Journal* pp. 131-35. The case of books comprised George Bancroft's *History of the United States*, 4 volumes of *Annals of Congress*, 16 volumes of *Natural History of the State of New York*, New York Laws, Documents, and Assembly Journals; Reports of the U. S. Lighthouse Board, "Farmers' Guide 2 vols.," and a work on Engineering by one Morris. Abe Ise no kami received two popular works on the Mexican War. For the Empress there were a "flowered silk embroidered dress," "toilet dressing box gilded," 6 dozen bottles of perfume, a lorgnette in case, a box of fancy soap, a clock — and a parlor stove! Other books, distributed among the Commissioners, interpreters, etc., were Lossing's *Field Book of the Revolution*, Owen's *Architecture*, the Brodhead *Documentary History of New York*, A. J. Downing's work on *Country Houses*, Owen's *Geology of Minnesota*, a dictionary, and a "list of U. S. post offices." Lithographs of American cities and steamships were also distributed, but not one volume of poetry or *belles lettres*. Griffis in 1871 saw the Audubons and some of the other books in storage at the house of the deposed Shogun.

sit in the tender to drive the locomotive, and the coach would hardly hold a six-year-old boy, many Japanese insisted on having a ride; and it was quite a sight to see a samurai on the roof of the car, robes flapping in the wind, while the train huffed, puffed and whistled around the track at 20 m.p.h. The Japanese easily learned how to run the train, but were baffled by the telegraph, probably because they knew absolutely nothing of electricity. American sailors mingled with Japanese soldiers and civilians, who showed intense curiosity about every item of American apparel and were only too ready to swap souvenirs and collect signatures on their fans. Among the dignitaries who came to view the presents was Ii Kamon no kami, Daimyo of Hikone.

A few days later conferences were resumed, and this time the Lord Rector and his colleagues traveled from Edo to Yokohama in *Tenchi Maru*, a magnificent two-decked barge, all gold and crimson, topsides emblazoned with princely arms, flying brightly colored silk banners and gigantic cylinders of golden silk indicating that she belonged to the Shogun. And, most significant, an unmistakable though inaccurate Stars and Stripes as courtesy flag; a compliment that Japan had never before paid to any nation.

Discussion now began as to which Japanese ports should be designated for American ships to procure water, coal and provisions. Perry proposed Yokohama and "five or six other ports"; Hayashi proposed Nagasaki; Perry would have none of that. Hayashi said that Perry should have mentioned what ports he wanted in 1853; the question must now be carefully studied at Edo. While the Shogun's advisers tried to figure out which ports could be conceded with least loss to national seclusion, there occurred a tremendous flap over the indiscreet caper of an American chaplain.

The Japanese had already allowed American sailors to land at Yokohama and stroll about the town, but forbade them to penetrate the interior. Chaplain Bittinger of *Susquehanna*, however, decided he must see Edo, and started to walk there alone. Japanese officials tried to stop him but he waved them off with his sword. They sent word to the Commodore, "who became very angry and ordered the officer to be recalled at once." Four cannon shots, the signal for recall, were fired, and Commander Adams sent a note to Bitty, as the men called him, with positive orders. The messenger caught up with him at the Rokugo River beyond Kawasaki, where the ferrymen refused to set him across; and return he did, in fear and trembling. Bitty had compounded his indiscretion by invading a Japanese shop, picking out of the till a handful of Japanese gold and silver coins against the owner's protest, and as payment throwing down $3.50 in American silver, a fraction of their value. "Old Bruin" would have liked to put Bittinger into the brig on bread and water, but as he could not do that to a chaplain, he had to be content with roaring at the footloose parson and requiring him to return the Japanese coins. He sent word to the Commissioners that no such incident would recur, nor did it. The Japanese returned the chaplain's $3.50, and so this affair terminated.

On 17 March the Commodore, with staff but no military guard, met the Commissioners at the Yokohama treaty house, mainly to discuss the question of ports. The Japanese, as usual, proposed Nagasaki which (Perry repeated) was inadmissible; he did not wish to hear it mentioned again. After a good deal of discussion, they offered the use of Hakodate on Tsugaru Strait, and Shimoda on the Izu Peninsula. Perry accepted the northern harbor, which he believed would prove handy for whaling ships, but preferred to take a look at the southern one before accepting. *Vandalia* and *Southampton*, sent to examine Shimoda, reported favorably and Perry consented.

While awaiting their report, Perry accepted a Japanese entertainment ashore, at which return presents were displayed. Those from the Shogun to President Pierce, naturally, were the best: a lacquered box and writing case, a bronze censer, and about thirty pieces of pongee and crêpe silk. Each Commissioner presented personal gifts to Perry, Adams, the interpreters, and the engineers who set up the railway; and the Shogun sent the squadron two hundred bags of rice and three hundred chickens. Perry's interest in conchology was catered to with over one hundred assorted shells. Most acceptable of the imperial gifts to President and Commodore were three spaniels, of a breed restricted to the use of the Emperor and Shogun, never seen outside palace grounds. They were so similar to King Charles spaniels that Perry inferred the English breed must be descended from a pair sent by an Emperor of Japan to Charles I in 1612. One dog he left with the Belmont family in The Hague, the other two were sent to the White House.

Following the presentation of gifts, some thirty *sumo* wrestlers were ushered in, and each of the monstrous fellows proved his prowess by carrying two 100- to 150- pound bags of rice from the treaty house to the boats. Koyanagi, champion of Japan, presented himself to the Commodore for examination, and a marine, at Perry's orders, ascertained that the huge body was muscle, not just fat. The *sumo* team then put on a series of wrestling bouts which, although bloodless and silent except for the wrestlers' yell of *yassa, yassa*, seemed brutal to Americans who were used to bareknuckled boxing matches of a hundred or more rounds. At the conclusion of the wrestling, Major Zeilin held an exhibition drill of marines. This greatly impressed the Japanese who, in that era, did not stress precision in military tactics.

Japanese illustrations of these scenes deserve a book in themselves. The imperial court at Kyoto, the Shogun's court at Edo, and many daimyo, intensely curious to learn about the American barbarians, their ships, arms and accoutrements, sent artists to Yokohama (and later to Shimoda) to describe and depict them on parchment scrolls and wood-blocks. Many individuals did likewise, and popular news sheets called *ka-waraban*, which were hawked through the cities and towns as ballad sheets used to be in London, carried the pictures to the remotest parts of Japan. If anyone still doubts the impact of the Expedition on Japan, he should consult these imprints in the many public and private collections.

There were two main ideas behind these graphic records: simple curi-osity, and ridicule of the "hairy barbarians," with assurance that they need not be feared. The demand was so heavy that certain artists made line sketches with india ink and sold copies to others who colored them for sale, with some rather odd results — Perry in a *happi* coat, naval officers in yellow jackets, marines in scarlet, and Old Glory with red, black and orange stripes.

The most popular subjects both for scrolls and wood blocks were the ships. They are usually drawn fairly accurately, but there are some spoofing caricatures of them as high-pooped junks with *sake* bottles for guns, a big umbrella for paddlewheel box, and a bespectacled American as figurehead. Second most popular subject was "Beriri" (Perry) himself. The writer has seen some fifty different Perry portraits in Japan. Most of them are honest attempts to depict the Commodore in different poses. There is a serene Perry, a prayerful Perry, a full-length Perry in uniform brandishing a sword, a smiling Perry, and a bookish Perry seated; but there is also a scowling, redbearded Perry, a long-nosed, baldheaded Perry, a piratical Perry with hair dressed in a topknot and skewered by an Okinawan hairpin, a Chinese war-lord Perry, and a ferocious Perry cap-tioned: "He wears woolen clothes and on his shoulder there are trimmings looking like chrysanthemum crest. His hair and beard are said to be friz-zled by the heated iron." A more complimentary caption is "Beruri, one of the three greatest foreigners"; the other two being Napoleon and a Turkish Sultan. Most of the caricatures depict Perry as a redbearded, slant-eyed monster snarling like a *shishi* lion, since that is what the public who bought the pictures expected a foreigner to look like. A scroll of the Commodore and his principal officers and interpreters was very popular; everyone has a long nose like General de Gaulle's, as that was the Ameri-can feature which most struck the Japanese. Spalding observed that the portrait artists drew a big nose first, and sketched the rest of the features around it.

One of the news sheets presents what the Bakufu wished people to be-lieve about the way it handled the Americans. Perry and his captains are prostrate before a scowling *Hangan* (the Japanese Uncle Sam) who has just given them a trifling present; they are weeping with joy and saying,

北亞墨利加人物　ペルリ像

"Portrait of Peruri, a North American"

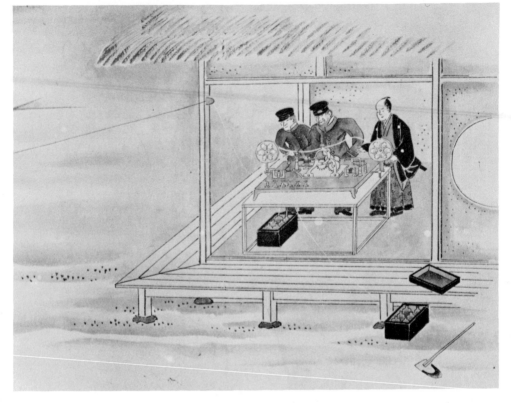

The telegraph instrument at Kanagawa

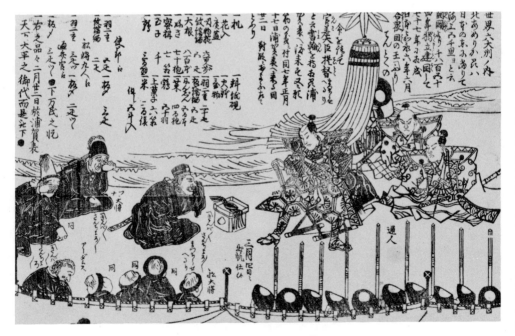

Kawaraban of a prostrate Perry

"Sank you, sank you!" Most of the *kawaraban* news sheets, however, are factual. All kinds of swords, cutlasses, and firearms, especially the Colt revolvers, are drawn and described, as are items of ship chandlery, from buckets to anchors, and the brass band instruments. Crude world maps are presented, to show where America lies. The train of cars is a favorite subject, and some pictures of the locomotive — obviously drawn by artists who never saw it — are nightmarish engines spouting fire and smoke. Every detail of officers' and enlisted men's clothing is depicted, and their possessions too: cigars, pipes, cigarettes, penholders, steel pens, wax wafers; cigar-box picture of a naked woman, and other items picked up in officers' cabins — even labels from their shoes and hats; bits of sugar-candy, and a tin can of French cauliflower. Seaman "Edward Yoring" contributed the tattoo of a girl embracing the Stars and Stripes on his arm. There are scenes on deck and below; sailors warming their hands at the galley fire, marines shooting craps, galley detail peeling potatoes. If any-one wishes to describe life in the United States Navy in 1854, he cannot do better than to study these Japanese scrolls and news sheets.

All the American gifts (including a cockatoo in a cage and a Chinese dog, not mentioned in the American records) are drawn, and there is a list of them in a printed pamphlet called *Amerika Zoto Ume no Ki* issued by the Bakufu in 1854. This little book observes that prices have risen unnec-essarily since the Americans arrived, that citizens should not be agitated, and that if there is any reason for alarm the fire brigades will pass the word by clappers, not shots. A dignified printed proclamation to the same effect was posted all along Edo Bay. It gives a brief resumé of the treaty, forbids citizens to engage in acts which might provoke hostilities, since Japan is not yet prepared to fight a naval force; exhorts all good Japanese to lead the simple life and make greater efforts for national defense. Some of the news sheets contain satirical ballads about the barbarians, with "cheeks hid in shaggy beards" under an "owlish-grave" Commodore, and hinting that if they return they may be received with bullets, not beans. But in general the theme of these *kawaraban* is simple curiosity, such as we might exhibit today upon the appearance of delegates from another planet.

Monday 27 March was gala. The Japanese Commissioners, attended by a numerous suite, were shown all over *Macedonian*, given two 17-gun salutes, and a banquet on board *Powhatan*. The Shogun's trefoil flew from the foremast, Hayashi's personal blazon adorned the mizzen, and the Com-modore's broad pendant showed at the main truck. The three ranking Commissioners had the privilege of dining with Perry in the flag cabin just forward of the wheelhouse; the remainder of the quarterdeck was cur-tained off with sails and flags, and two long tables set up. For the feast the Commodore had reserved live bullocks, sheep, game, poultry, as well as ordinary cabin stores of preserved meat, fish, vegetables, fruits, and a variety of wines. The cunning hands of the flag *chef de cuisine* made every dish attractive to the eye and appetizing to the taste.

Lieutenant Preble, who played host on the quarterdeck, gives a lively description of the main banquet, in which he had been instructed to make the guests eat and drink as much as possible. After they had worked through champagne, Madeira, cherry cordial, punch and whiskey, Preble mixed up tomato ketchup and vinegar

. . . which they seemed to relish with equal gusto. Following the custom of the country I encouraged them to pocket the remnants of the feast. I saw one fellow walk off with a whole chicken. . . . Altogether it was an amusing and animated scene. I have not enjoyed such a hearty laugh since we left the U.S. The Commodore . . . said the success of his treaty depended upon the success of the entertainment, so we did our best and I am sure it could not have gone off more to his or their satisfaction. They were highly amused when we toasted The Emperor of Japan, The President of the United States, The Commodore, The High Commissioners, and The Japanese Ladies. When the band commenced playing, several commenced shuffling and dancing — and to encourage them some of our greyest and gravest officers danced with them. A funny sight to behold — these baldpated bundles of clothes — and Doctors, Pursers, Lieutenants and Captains all jumping up and down to the music.

The Japanese, says the official Narrative, "kept shouting at the top of their voices, and were heard far above the music of the bands. . . . The rapid disappearance of the large quantity and variety of the viands profusely heaped upon the table was quite a marvel, even to the heartiest feeders among the Americans. In the eagerness of the Japanese appetite, . . . the most startling heterodoxy was exhibited in the commingling of fish, flesh, and fowl, soups and syrups, fruits and fricassees, roast and boiled, pickles and preserves. . . .

"When the Commissioners had been sufficiently mellowed in the cabin," said the Lieutenant, they "were brought on deck to witness a performance by the Ethiopian Band of the *Powhatan*, who style themselves 'Japanese Minstrels.' They enjoyed the imitations of the negro, and laughed very heartily." In his delight Matsuzaki, secretary to Hayashi, flung his arms around the Commodore's neck and remarked (as translated), "Nippon and America, all the same heart!" A senior officer asked the Commodore how he could stand that. " 'Oh,' said old Perry — 'if they will only sign the Treaty he may kiss me!' "

Thus, conviviality contributed to Japanese-American amity. One wonders whether the present bone-dry navy could have done as well.

Treaty Concluded

On the following day, negotiations were resumed at the treaty house; and as evidence of mutual trust Perry and his escort came ashore unarmed. The Lord Rector thanked the Commodore for his hospitality; Perry apologized at length (as Japanese etiquette required) for his "miserable, inadequate" entertainment, and announced that Shimoda would be acceptable as the second port open for ships' supplies. There followed a discussion as to whether American sailors would be allowed liberty in Shimoda, instead of being cooped on board as the Dutch were at Nagasaki. Perry proposed that they be allowed to walk ashore within a radius of ten *ri* from the town. Hayashi said that was too far. They finally settled on a radius of seven *ri* (about 17 miles) from Inubashiri Shima, the islet in mid-harbor. The Japanese did not wish to allow Shimoda or Hakodate to be opened for a year and a half. This looked like procrastination to the Americans, but there was a reason for it; in order to make these ports available for foreign shipping they had to be detached from their daimyo's fiefs and created imperial cities under the Shogun's immediate jurisdiction. It was finally agreed that merchant ships could enter three months after signature of the treaty, but that Perry could visit each port immediately.

A final controversy arose over the appointment of an American consul. The Japanese objected that this meant trade, a subject ruled out. Perry argued that we must have a consul in at least one port, to settle disputes that were certain to arise between sailors and natives. Hayashi saw the point and conceded it. And this proved to be a foot-in-the-door for commerce.

The Feast of Dolls, a traditional festival in which little girls dress up their dolls and visit one another, at that era fell on 31 March, the day for signing the treaty. The coincidence seemed auspicious to the Japanese, as did the fact that it stopped raining early, blue sky appeared and the sun burst forth just as Perry and escort came ashore. They entered the treaty house with all due ceremony and signed drafts of the treaty in English, Dutch and Japanese. The Shogun's delegation did likewise.

A summary of the Treaty of Kanagawa, as it was called,[1] follows: —

Article I: "Perfect, permanent and universal peace, and a sincere and cordial amity" between the United States of America and the Empire of Japan, and between their respective people, "without exception of persons or places."

Articles II, VII, VIII and X: Shimoda and Hakodate are open to American ships for supply of "wood, water, provisions and coal, and

---

[1] Yokohama, a small village in 1854, belonged to the Kanagawa prefecture. Text in *Select Documents* pp. 119-22. The day of the Feast of Dolls has since been changed.

other articles their necessities may require, as far as the Japanese have them." These may be procured only through the medium of Japanese officials and according to a tariff drawn up by subsequent agreement.

Articles III, IV and V: Shipwrecked American sailors to be taken to Shimoda or Hakodate for delivery to their countrymen. These and other American citizens to be allowed "to go where they please" within seven *ri* of the little island at Shimoda, and within limits later to be set up at Hakodate.

Article IX: Any privilege not herein specified, if granted to another nation, will be automatically extended to the United States.

Article XII: Ratifications to be exchanged within eighteen months.

"Done at Kanagawa, 31 March A.D. 1854, and of Kayei the seventh year, third month and third day." The treaty was signed by the Commodore for the United States; by Hayashi, Ido, Izawa and Udono for the Emperor.

After signing, congratulations were exchanged. Perry then presented an American flag to Hayashi, and fieldpieces to Ido and Izawa, "to evidence our intention never to oppose your country." All then sat down to a Japanese feast, which has been frequently depicted in contemporary prints, complete with lengthy menu which included an entire fish for each *convive*. It cost the Bakufu 2000 *ryo*. The Japanese found American table manners disgusting — they couldn't handle chopsticks, talked loudly and gesticulated like common people! But they did defer to Japanese custom by wrapping up the remains in paper that had been thoughtfully provided, to take back to their ships. Otherwise their hosts would have been offended.

The Japanese Commissioners knew very well that they had exceeded their instructions from the Bakufu, but in their official report did considerable covering up in order to claim a diplomatic victory over the barbarians. They had put Perry in his place by refusing to open any really important seaport to American ships, by preventing him from going to Edo or even surveying the Bay (which of course he had done), and by dissuading him "from any previous idea he had of opening hostilities" (which he never intended). They congratulated themselves on maintaining national prestige and "completing the whole affair in peace." Perry was equally pleased with the treaty. It fulfilled the two main objects of his Expedition — castaways and ports of refuge — and he rightly regarded the permission to establish an American consulate as an opening for future trade. He candidly stated in a letter of 1 April to Hayashi: that he had consented to forego insisting on trade, or free circulation of his people ashore, for the sake of peace, but "it cannot be expected that such a state of things can long exist." He assured the Lord Rector "that no injury will result to Japan . . . by the adoption of laws more congenial to the spirit of the times."

The Commissioners appear to have been offended (or at least wished the Bakufu to think they were offended) at this suggestion. It was necessary for home consumption — and to satisfy the bellicose daimyo — to insist that no real concessions had been made, and that no significant mitigation of the "ancient laws" had been permitted.

Perry entrusted his copy of the treaty to Commander Adams, who on 4 April sailed in *Saratoga*, left her at Honolulu for Panama, and reached Washington in mid-June. *Saratoga* received a fine sendoff from the squadron, the men cheering and the bands playing "Home, Sweet Home." Home was a long way off for "Sara" — she rounded Cape Horn and finally reached Boston in September 1854.

With the Japanese Commissioners' permission, Commodore and staff took long walks around Kanagawa, called on the mayor to exchange toasts in *sake*, and even were allowed to visit and compliment the ladies of his family. Fair weather brought out the full beauty of the Japanese countryside — fields and terraced gardens were in full bloom with magnificent red and white blossoms. Liberty parties were allowed to stroll around Yokohama, and several men exercised the immemorial tourist privilege of painting their names on a rock on Hachinji Hill, Honmoku. These inscriptions vastly intrigued the Japanese, who had never before seen Roman letters. One self-appointed pundit asserted that they were early Chinese characters which he proceeded to translate as an ode to the scenery.

Relations had been uniformly friendly and correct. But before leaving, the Commodore indulged a fancy which, if pursued to its logical end, might have dissipated the good will so carefully built up: a visit to Edo in his flagship. Survey boats had already approached within five miles of the forbidden city, near enough to see through a spyglass the Shogun's castle (later the imperial palace), "like a walled city or large fortress." Perry too had seen the outskirts of Edo, but that did not satisfy him. He felt a compulsion to steam near enough to view the castle at close range and honor the Emperor with a 21-gun salute. Hayashi warned him that this was absolutely inadmissible, yet Perry persisted. On 10 April the two steamers still present got under way and steamed up Edo Bay, Perry leading in *Mississippi*. Interpreter Einosuke and two other Japanese officials who had come on board to say farewell, begged him to turn back. Einosuke declared that if the proposed salute were fired off Edo he would throw himself into a cannon's mouth, and his colleague went so far as to give his cloak and long sword to the purser's son, keeping the short one with which to disembowel himself. Furthermore, if Edo were profaned, Hayashi, Ido and Izawa would be compelled to commit suicide, out of shame for not having kept the barbarians out. At that, Perry recovered his senses. When the flagship was within sight of the Haneda Pagoda, he asked Einosuke if this were part of Edo? After much circumlocution the interpreter admitted that it was. The Commodore whipped out a telescope and, looking through it, said, "How clearly Edo can be seen! Having now seen Edo, let us go," and turned his ships away. The interpreter who had prepared to die "joyfully received his property again," and lived.

Perry dismissed the Japanese very politely, according to their own account, sent his regards to Hayashi and the other Commissioners, and returned to American Anchorage. He obviously wished to leave a good impression, and did. In Edo Bay he and his men were pleasantly remembered; and the Commodore was equally determined to create good feeling at Shimoda, his next objective.

CHAPTER XXVII

Ports and Islands
18 April – 11 September 1854

This memorable success is undoubtedly due to the line of conduct adopted by Commodore Perry — a mixture of prudence, caution and inflexible determination, which led him surely, step by
step, to the end he had in view. Had he, on the one hand, submitted
to any of those Japanese usages which imply submission on the part
of a foreign embassy, and neglected to enforce all the respect due
to his position — or, on the other hand, had he assumed a hostile
attitude, or wounded the sensitive pride of the Japanese by a disregard of the courtesy and respect which they had a right to demand — the Expedition would assuredly have been a failure.

— *Editorial in New York* Tribune *14 June 1854*

Shimoda

IN order to inspect the first port opened to American ships by the Treaty
of Kanagawa, Perry in *Powhatan* left American Anchorage on 18 April
and arrived Shimoda the same day. *Vandalia* and the three storeships had
sailed ahead to select good berths. Upon entering, *Southampton* managed
to connect with a rock almost in midstream, but floated off. The obstruc-
tion was promptly buoyed and named Southampton Rock; the Japanese
have maintained a buoy there but restored the original name, Onagare Sho.

If Shimoda had been selected for scenery, the Americans could have
fared no better. It is one of the most beautiful harbors in Japan. Cupped in
the southeast point of the rugged Izu Peninsula, it has a narrow entrance
between lofty, wooded headlands of the conical type that sailors call "sugar
loaves" or, when they come in pairs, "The Paps" or "les Mamelles." As
you enter, there opens up a sheltered basin where a fleet of ships of that
era could anchor in safety. On the port hand lies the pretty town of Shimoda bearing "an air of sheltered repose and an appearance of secluded
rusticity," according to the Narrative; a description that held good for a
century. The houses, peculiar to that place, were walled with black tile,
divided in diamond pattern by strips of plaster; Buddhist shrines and temples were numerous and beautiful. The town is divided by the Inazawa

River, navigable for barge traffic and draining a fertile valley which reminded Americans of the Potomac at Harper's Ferry. Mount Fuji is visible in fair weather. The climate is warmer and more equable than that of Edo Bay. Orange orchards flourish on the slopes; cherry-tree hedges were in full bloom when the Americans arrived. They were enchanted with Shimoda; and Shimoda in the end became delighted with them; the whole town turns out for a "Black Ship Festival" every May. There is a Perry and Harris museum; hotels and shops sell Black Ship ash trays and matchboxes and a thousand different souvenirs stamped with Perry's stern countenance and Townsend Harris's bewhiskered face. An excellent bust of Perry overlooks the site of his first landing, and a monument to the Opening of Japan on the hill above records his words: "I have come here as a peace maker." Shimoda is as proud of Perry, Harris and the Black Ships as Plymouth, Massachusetts, is of the Pilgrim Fathers and the *Mayflower*.

Yet it must be admitted that the Bakufu had "put one over" in designating Shimoda as a harbor open to American ships. Nagoya or Osaka would have been far better for trade, but trade was what the Japanese did not want or intend, and Shimoda was well enough as a port of refuge. It was cut off from the rest of Japan by high mountains, and so remote from the mines that coal could be delivered only at an excessive price. There were no important industries and little trade. By way of comparison, suppose Japan, "opening" the United States, had been given Grays Harbor instead of Seattle, or Marblehead instead of Boston. Even the railroad did not reach Shimoda until after 1960.

The squadron having arrived somewhat in advance of its welcome, there were difficulties with the local authorities. On the third day after his arrival the Commodore paid an official visit to the prefect, with Einosuke as interpreter. The American officers, presuming on their treaty privilege to circulate within seven *ri* of the islet in the center of the harbor, now ran into trouble. Without explicit instructions from Edo the authorities dared not suspend laws forbidding intercourse with foreigners, hence the visitors had the same experience as at Okinawa — police shooing the populace away and shop shutters slammed down as they approached. Perry protested to the prefect, who made the wrong reply: "We do this to the Dutch at Nagasaki, so why not to you?" Perry, always nettled when Nagasaki was mentioned, pointed out that Americans had been assured better treatment by the treaty, and if the Shimoda authorities refused to raise this boycott, he would sail to Edo and see about it. This produced the desired effect. Thenceforth the people flocked about the American liberty parties, fingering the men's buttons and accoutrements and asking the English name of every article of clothing. The prefect also placed at the disposition of the Commodore the largest Buddhist temple in Shimoda, called Ryosenji; for Buddhist temples in Japan had an

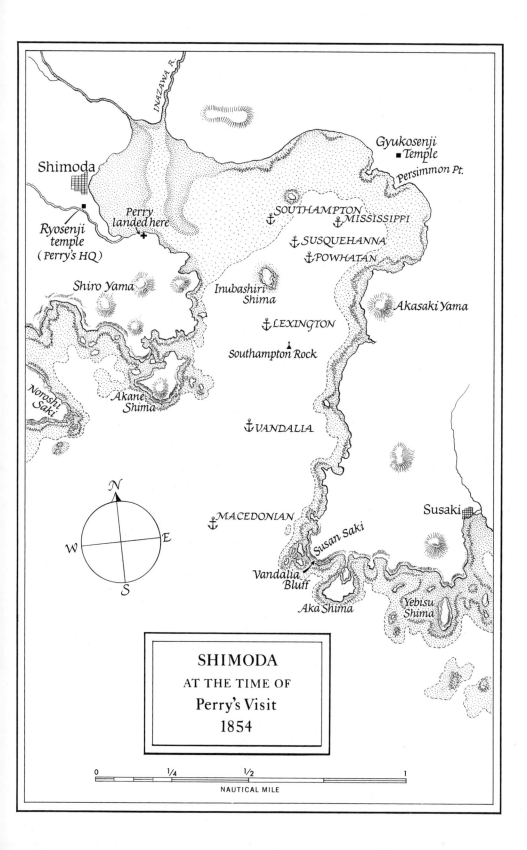

INAZAWA R.

Shimoda

Gyukosenji
■ Temple

Persimmon Pt.

Ryosenji
temple
(Perry's HQ)

Perry
landed here

⚓ SOUTHAMPTON
⚓ MISSISSIPPI

⚓ SUSQUEHANNA

⚓ POWHATAN

Shiro Yama

Inubashiri
Shima

Akasaki Yama

⚓ LEXINGTON

Southampton Rock

Noroshi
Saki

Akane
Shima

⚓ VANDALIA

N

Susaki

W   E

⚓ MACEDONIAN

Susan Saki

S

Vandalia
Bluff

Aka Shima

Yebisu
Shima

SHIMODA

AT THE TIME OF

Perry's Visit

1854

0   1/4   1/2   1

NAUTICAL MILE

annex where travelers could lodge and the townspeople hold meetings, banquets and bazaars. In another building the ships' officers were provided with mats to sleep on, servants, and local food.

One thing, however, the Commodore never could effect — to open the shops for officers and men to buy souvenirs; and as he had no treaty right to this, he did not insist. The best he could do was to persuade the prefect to let Americans enter shops and price articles, but if they chose to buy they must deposit the money with an official who paid the shopkeeper and delivered the goods. This cumbrous system required a regulation of exchange between Japanese coins, American dollars and Chinese cash. The bill of exchange, as drawn up by Einosuke, was probably based on the Dutch one at Nagasaki; in any case its principle was the same, to overvalue the Japanese *ryo* and undervalue foreign currency, in order to discourage trade.[1] This caused discontent among officers who, looking forward to obtaining silks and lacquer for their wives, found that dollars would buy very little. Captain Abbot wrote to a friend in Washington that owing to the Commodore's "terrible *faux pas*" a Mexican dollar was worth only 33⅓ cents in Japan, and that "when he found out his blundering mistake he had not the courage to rectify it. . . . One single declaration of the Movement towards Jedo would have corrected the Matter." Naturally Perry was not going to risk dissipating Japanese good will by another thrust toward the capital, to facilitate the purchase of souvenirs. At Hakodate, moreover, he so arranged matters as to reverse this ratio and there his men spent plentifully, as we shall see.

In Shimoda, owing to the relatively wide area allowed for Americans to circulate, Dr. Morrow enjoyed far better facilities for botanizing than he had in Edo Bay. Accompanied by Williams and a few other officers, he indulged in daily walks up the valley, around the harbor and over the hills, gathering seeds, specimens of wild flowers, taking notes on cultivation of crops, and observing the people.

On one of these rambles, clerk Spalding of *Mississippi* had a personal encounter with tragic consequences. Two Japanese, one a samurai, approached him and slipped within the breast of his jacket a paper which stated that the bearers wished to be taken to the United States. Before it was possible to reply, at 2 A.M. the following night, the two men rowed

---

[1] The *ryo* in 1854 was an elliptical coin, 56.7% gold and 43.3% silver, with a small diameter about that of an American double eagle. It weighed 11.2 grams, and exchanged locally for 4 silver *bu* or 4000 copper cash. According to the rate of exchange agreed to by Perry at Shimoda it took $4 U.S. to buy one *ryo*; Townsend Harris later got this down to $1.25 per *ryo*. At Hakodate, however, according to Spalding p. 300, $1 bought a *ryo*; and Preble (pp. 205, 212) confirms this, stating that a U.S. dollar bought 1400 cash in China, 1600 in Shimoda, and 4800 in Hakodate. The *ryo* is pictured in the Bank of Japan's *Brief History of Money in Japan;* and several examples are in that Bank's numismatic museum.

Dr. Morrow as
acting master's mate

The Reverend George Jones buying a vase
"His spectacles are very fine . . . He leads in funerals, and when the
sailors meet him they bow . . . He is the best of all the Americans,"
wrote Kojima.

out to *Mississippi* and cast away their boat. Taken to the flagship, the leader was found to be Yoshida (Torajiro), a young liberal who had studied Western ways and burned to overthrow the Bakufu, restore the imperial rule, and open his country to the West. As this then seemed hopeless, he wished to visit the United States and study economics. The other would-be traveler was his likeminded friend Kaneko. The Commodore would gladly have obliged them, but he knew that to do so was contrary to Japanese law, which, after signing the treaty, he felt honor-bound to respect. So, regretfully, he set them ashore at a lonely spot where it was thought they would not be noticed; but next day they were arrested and sent to Edo in iron cages, the usual method of confining prisoners. Their fate was not known until years later, when it was ascertained that Kaneko died in prison; Yoshida, released on parole, plotted the assassination of a high official and was tried and beheaded, one of the clauses in his indictment being his attempt to depart with Perry. Three of his pupils, later prominent in the Meiji Restoration, saw to it that he was inscribed as one of their martyrs.

The Americans enjoyed Shimoda. They found the Japanese married women, with their blackened teeth, hideous; but the young girls pretty, especially as they walked from their homes to the public bath house wearing almost nothing. The unselfconscious nudity of both sexes in the public baths, of which the sailors were fascinated spectators (the bathers didn't mind, asked them to "join in and take a wash"), outraged their sense of propriety. Artist Heine made an excellent sketch of this casual, uninhibited scene which was lithographed for the official Narrative. "Apart from the bathing scene," notes the same Narrative, "there was enough in the popular literature, with its obscene pictorial illustrations, to prove a licentiousness of taste and practice among a certain class of the population that was not only disgustingly intrusive, but disgracefully indicative of foul corruption." One wonders what the Japanese would have thought of the pornography current in American so-called literature of the 1960's.

Japanese artists were very active at Shimoda and recorded incidents not found elsewhere. One sketch shows two sailors taking a daguerreotype of a beautifully dressed courtesan, while a third keeps her head steady by means of one of those torturous clamps employed by early photographers. One sailor is sticking out his tongue at the courtesan as a signal that he would appreciate more intimate relations. Others who felt the same urge had their desires conveyed to the Japanese interpreter. The authorities consented, but the courtesans vetoed this extension of hospitality. Their spokeswoman declared that even though their profession was considered "ignoble," they would not sink so low as to sleep with foreigners! As the Japanese writer says, the Americans were disappointed, "like men returning empty-handed from a mountain loaded with treasure." But sailors are

Chief petty officer

Sailor in a brothel

not easily balked. Their spokesman said, "O.K. We don't have to sleep with the girls. Only let's have the pleasure of drinking with them." The girls agreed. At the first reception of this sort, when a courtesan brought in *sake* to one of the sailors, he presented her with a bolt of "fine purple woolen cloth," and woolens were rare and expensive in Japan. It then occurred to her, that if she received a present like that merely for serving him wine, what might she not get if she offered her body? "One night shortly afterward . . . she seduced the American. He, needless to say, was delighted," and had his pleasure with her nightly until the resources of whatever corresponded to a PX in his ship were exhausted. This story is inscribed on the Honolulu Black Ship Scroll on the picture of a sailor dallying with courtesans. The girls are saying, "Hey, don't pull his leg so hard when he's tight!" "Come closer to me, dear!" and "You've had too much and can't stand up!" The accounts of other officers of the squadron indicate that this enterprising fellow was not the only sailor to enjoy the favors of the Shimoda girls.

Perry left Shimoda after twenty-five days. Much of that time he spent ashore in the Ryosenji temple, negotiating with local authorities on exchange, port dues, and other practical matters. He caused the harbor to be surveyed and sounded, but had to leave unfinished business, since 19 May had been designated by the Japanese for the squadron to visit Hakodate.

After sending ahead *Macedonia, Vandalia* and *Southampton,* Perry departed in *Powhatan,* accompanied by *Mississippi.* They passed O Shima with its volcano in eruption, left Nojima Zaki (the eastern promontory of Sagami Bay) on the port hand, and ascertained the coördinates of this prominent point, which they called Cape King, fairly accurately. They hugged the coast by day to take observations of prominent capes, and stood off shore at night to study the direction and velocity of the Kuroshio current, ascertaining that it was deflected eastward by the cold Japan or North Pacific current which washes the shores of northern Honshu and Hokkaido.

On 16 May the two war steamers rounded Shiriya Zaki, the northeast promontory of Honshu, and entered Tsugaru Kaikyo, the strait between Honshu and Hokkaido.[1] There they ran into a six-knot head current and a fog. It lifted in time for them to pick up landmarks, and they came to an anchor in Hakodate harbor during the forenoon watch of 17 May.

Hakodate

Hakodate was in every way a suitable harbor to be opened to American vessels. Already an important place for trade and fisheries, it lay right on

---

[1] This strait was then called by foreigners Sangar; and Hokkaido, northernmost of the three big home islands of Japan, Yesso or Jesso.

the major thoroughfare between the North Pacific and the Sea of Japan. Hundreds of whalers and other foreign vessels passed through annually, without being allowed to land; and thousands of Japanese junks carried on trade between southern Japanese ports and the northern island. Perry reported that for extent and safety from all winds Hakodate had no superior in the world. The inner harbor is formed by a bold peaked promontory standing well out from the high land of the main, with which it is connected by a low sandy isthmus. Ohana Zaki, as it is now called, reminded old Mediterranean hands of Gibraltar; Perry called it Cape Blount to honor his friend the publisher of coast pilots.

Hokkaido is the home of the "hairy Ainus," white aborigines conquered by the ancestors of the samurai, pushed into the less desirable lands, and treated by the Japanese much as Europeans treated American Indians. The climate is so much colder than Shimoda's that Perry and his men found themselves back in early spring; it was like going from New Orleans to eastern Maine in April; all hands were "blue and shivering" according to Lieutenant Preble. And the human climate was even less hospitable. By orders of the Daimyo of Matsumae, to whom Hakodate belonged, the citizens were forbidden even to *look* at a foreign ship from windows or housetops, much less allow sailors to land. The contrast in manners and customs was even sharper. Perry's sailors remembered Shimoda as the port where women were kind but souvenirs dear and scarce; Hakodate as the place where there was plenty to buy cheap, but one never even got a look at a woman.

Vandalia, Macedonian and *Southampton* arrived 11 May and anchored off the fort at the harbor's southern entrance. Next day they moved into the inner harbor. After a few officers and men had landed, alarm gongs were beaten and a police officer rode through the city driving citizens indoors with a whip. The whole town was in a turmoil, and roads to the interior were clogged with people carrying goods and womenfolk to a place of safety. For the inhabitants, more provincial than those of Yokohama and Shimoda, really feared that foreigners were bent on plunder and rapine. That was what the crews of Russian ships had done in Hokkaido many years before; who could predict that the Americans would behave any better?

Perry in *Powhatan*, with *Mississippi*, arrived on the 17th. The steamers had been anchored but a few hours when the flagship was boarded by government officials. These, when handed a Chinese translation of the Treaty of Kanagawa and a copy of the Japanese Commissioners' letter to Perry setting a date for this visit, pretended ignorance. Endo (Matazaemon), who had galloped all the way from the Daimyo's capital at Fukayama to instruct local officials, insisted that he knew absolutely nothing about the Treaty; all requests to go ashore, etc., must be referred to his

master, and by him to the Shogun. Temporarily, however, he conceded
— doubtless after a good look at the American ships — that the Commodore might use the hotel-annex of a temple, and that his men could stroll
about this "poor little town."

A very good instance of what Perry called Japanese duplicity and prevarication. From the contemporary history by Kojima, a local official and
shopkeeper, we learn that Endo knew all about the Treaty and had been
expecting the American visit for a month. The Daimyo's prime minister
had been in Hakodate since 19 April, inspecting forts, ordering a wall
built along the waterfront and barriers set up in the streets to prevent
citizens and visitors from circulating. Moreover, the Bakufu had issued
detailed instructions for the local authorities as follows: The Americans
"will soon arrive at Hakodate. The foreigners have been ordered not to
land, but it is said that at Shimoda some of them did land and wandered
about, going to farm houses and getting food and other things. They may
land at Hakodate also. If this seems likely, shut all the houses throughout
the city, hide goods, especially rice and wine and other things that would
attract attention. . . . They are said to notice women especially, so as
much as possible send all women from parts near the sea back to relatives
or friends in the mountains and villages. Have the other women keep carefully hidden in the storehouses and do not let them go where they would
meet the foreigners while the ships are in harbor."

Besides Endo, seventy "bannermen," retainers of the Daimyo, had arrived by boat; and, in consequence of their orders, almost five hundred
women and children were evacuated before the ships arrived. Hakodate
City Hall issued additional instructions. In Shimoda the Americans "gazed
at women, petted children and stayed a long time in temples." They "like
children very much and give them candy. If they should kidnap them, it
would be terrible. . . . Deal with the Americans carefully and do not anger them, as they are short-tempered," ordered the Mayor; everyone must
hide *sake* as well as women and children. All women young and old, who
have not been evacuated, must stay at home, behind closed and locked
wooden shutters, the instructions continued; "and paste the cracks with
paper" so that sailors cannot peer in or women peek out. No musical instruments are to be played, and funerals will be postponed or held quietly
at night. Any person who breaks these regulations, and his family and associates, will be severely punished.

Naturally these regulations, had they been enforced, would have made
Hakodate a dead town. Fortunately, only the closing of shops and hiding
of women were enforced. Perry himself landed on 18 May, went to a
private residence which had been assigned as a reception center, and
talked through an interpreter with representatives both of the Daimyo
and of the Bakufu. The Commodore vigorously expressed his dissatisfac-

tion with the manner in which the town received his squadron, and threatened to sail to Matsumae and protest to the Daimyo. Caught between unenforceable orders and demonstrable naval force, the local officials were "greatly embarrassed," according to the local historian; they decided to relax all previous orders except for the removal and seclusion of women. Shops were opened to the Americans, who entered "with their boots on; their manners were bad but that seemed to be the custom of their country," noted Kojima. He even sketched a scene in one shop: the Commodore, seated, is handling a handsome lacquered box presented by "a very quick-witted person, apparently his aide" — Silas Bent. Commander Adams is sitting on a packing case, and a Negro orderly reclines on the floor in a very unmilitary attitude. "Going thus to a store to buy is not the way of a samurai, but perhaps this is the way of the American. It seems a very vulgar custom," observes Kojima. Perry was the more respected because, although he "bought a great deal," he made but this one personal visit to a shop, thereafter having an assortment of goods presented to him at the temple annex. "That was proper indeed!" It was not popular with junior officers, since it gave "Old Bruin" first choice of everything.

The American official Narrative reports that "The shopmen were at first very shy," but "showed themselves as clever at their business as any Chatham street or Bowery salesman with us. They bustled about the raised platform upon which they were perched, pulled out the drawers arranged on the walls, and displayed their goods to the greatest advantage when they thought there was a chance of catching the eye and pleasing the taste of a passing American. . . . The shopkeepers had always a fixed price for their goods, and all attempts to beat them down were useless, and generally rebuked by an expression of displeasure." In contrast to Shimoda a very favorable rate of exchange — one *ryo* to the dollar — was established. Cabin boy Allen of *Vandalia* reports that he bought 18-inch-wide silk for 13 cents a yard, and heavy crêpe for even less. In addition to opening shops, a bazaar was set up in one of the Buddhist temples by favor of the priests, who took a cut on the profits. Kojima sketches the coins used by the Americans: one-dollar goldpieces, silver three-cent pieces, and Mexican half- and quarter-dollars, indicating that they had plenty of cash besides the Chinese kind. They spent, he says, the equivalent of 1600 *ryo* and left Hakodate loaded with souvenirs.

In the meantime, Commodore Perry had Hakodate harbor sounded and surveyed, and in order to give *Southampton* something to do, sent her to sound Muroran (then called Endermo) harbor in Volcano Bay (Ochiura Wan), about seventy miles distant.

Everyone in the squadron enjoyed Hokkaido, despite being forbidden to see the women. Brown and his crew took daguerreotypes of the Daimyo's representative and the local officials, and those "magic mirrors" when developed aroused much interest. Sailors of the squadron washed themselves and their clothes in the Kamida stream which empties into the head of the bay. An entertainment was given by the Commodore on board *Mississippi* to the Daimyo's representative and his suite, and *Powhatan* laid on a minstrel show which amused the dignitaries no end. One wonders what the Japanese got out of the dialogue between "Mistah Bones" and "Mistah Tambo," but the pantomine needed no translation. Kojima states that "Berori" (Perry) tipped the boatman who brought out the guests, with six loaves of bread and a keg of meat "like pork." Such was the Commodore's custom; the Japanese watermen who brought 4500 gallons of water to *Powhatan* in Edo Bay were given 115 rations of hardtack, sugar and tea.

During the squadron's stay, a seaman of *Vandalia* died on board ship, and the authorities set aside part of a neglected burial ground for his interment. The funeral was conducted, like that of the marine at Yokohama, by Chaplain Jones. Before the squadron departed, a gravestone was selected, and on it, in English letters, was carved an epitaph composed by one of the deceased's shipmates, in the true classic mode, not unlike those in the *Greek Anthology:* —

> Sleeping on a foreign shore,
> Rest, sailor, rest! thy trials o'er
> Thy shipmates leave this token here
> That some perchance may drop a tear
> For one that braved so long the blast
> And served his country till the last.

Stone and epitaph are still there, together with the graves of other American seamen, in a quiet cemetery overlooking Hakodate harbor.

On parting the Commodore expressed his "gratification at the general kindness and courtesy of the authorities and people" of Hakodate, and the officials responded in kind. They presented a block of granite to be built into the Washington Monument, George Washington being the only American of whom most educated Japanese had heard.

"No troubles or accident whatsoever occurred between the people of the town and the Americans," states an official historian of Hakodate. This was not completely true; two sailors did break into a house just to get sight of a woman, and for that were allowed no more liberty. In no part of Japan is there today so great friendliness toward Americans as in Hokkaido. For Perry's visit was followed up by the work of several Americans, experts in their respective fields, who did great things for the economy and education of the island. Raphael Pumpelly the eminent geologist, in Hakodate as early as 1862, discovered mines of various minerals on the northern island. Horace Capron, the farming expert who attended Perry's farewell

Perry shopping: Silas Bent hands him a lacquered chest, Commander Adams looks on, Negro orderly on the floor

Marine officers, ship's boy playing fife, interpreter Williams botanizing, and his Chinese assistant

dinner in Washington, was appointed by Emperor Meiji in 1871 to modernize the primitive agriculture of Hokkaido. Under his direction dairy farming, cereals and root crops were introduced. William S. Clark, President of the University of Massachusetts, came to Sapporo (the new provincial capital laid out by an American engineer) to organize the Imperial Agricultural College. His parting admonition to the students, "Boys, be Ambitious!" is carved on a monument erected by the Japanese at the site of his residence.

These are but a few of the scores of Americans, called "Givers of Light to Hokkaido," in the commemorative tablet of 1954. And in the annual parade at Hakodate a popular feature is a float representing U.S.S. *Powhatan*, "manned" by a bevy of beautiful Japanese girls — descendants of the women who were not even permitted to peek at Perry's sailors.

Shimoda, Formosa and the Treaty of Naha

After routing *Vandalia* to Shanghai through Tsugaru Strait so that the west coast of Japan could be examined, and sending *Macedonian* ahead, Perry in *Powhatan*, with *Mississippi*, departed 3 June 1854 for Shimoda. Cherry blossoms were coming out, and the hills were crowded with people to see them depart, the prohibition against looking at the ships having been lifted. *Macedonian*, on her voyage, had a pleasant experience off the eastern headland of Sagami Bay. Japanese fishing boats avoided her until they recognized the Stars and Stripes floating at her peak. They then gave vent to a joyful shout, and boats nearest the warship broke out oars and rowed up to her, made fast, and began throwing generous portions of their catch on deck. They expected no payment, but were given in return plenty of hardtack, "of which they appear to be very fond. With mutual good wishes, unintelligible except by gesture, we separate."

The main object of this second visit to the southern Japanese port was to confer with the Shogun's Commissioners. Hakodate and Shimoda having been created imperial cities in view of their designation as ports of refuge and supply for American ships, regulations had to be drawn up. It was agreed that the principle of setting up a radius within which Americans might circulate ashore, should extend to Hakodate. Perry delegated the pursers of his two war steamers to discuss the touchy matter of currency exchange with Japanese officials, but despite the example of Hakodate, they were unable to obtain any alteration of the earlier arrangement which penalized the dollar. Regulations were agreed upon about pilotage, landing places, port dues and the like, and these were printed on the shipboard press. Coal at Shimoda was very expensive, almost $30 a ton, and the squadron's engineers pronounced it to be "of a quality so inferior that they were unable to keep up steam." Fortunately *Southampton*, arriving from Hokkaido 10 June, still had sufficient coal in her cargo to fuel *Pow-hatan* and *Mississippi* for their passage to Okinawa.

In order to procure a better source of bituminous coal, the Commodore sent two ships to investigate the mines of Formosa, then a lightly held and undeveloped part of the Chinese Empire. *Macedonian*, after speaking four or five American whaling vessels and spending a couple of weeks at Port Lloyd to lay in a supply of turtle, rendezvoused with *Supply* at the port of Keelung (Chilung) at the northern cape of Formosa (Taiwan) on 21 July. There Captain Abbot sent Chaplain Jones (who added the post of squadron geologist to his clerical function) to seek out coal mines, and he found no fewer than eight. Fair steam coal could be delivered at Keelung for only $1.50 a ton. And no objection was raised by Formosa mandarins to the American ships' buying all they wanted. From Keelung *Macedo-nian* proceeded to Manila, partly to investigate a reported murder of two Americans in a ropewalk, and partly to repatriate the Salibaboo castaways. Everything was arranged there satisfactorily between Captain Abbot and the Spanish governor general, and the ship reached Hong Kong on 26 August.

Perry, after treating the Japanese Commissioners and over one hundred of their attendants to a performance of "Ethiopian Ministrels" on board *Powhatan*, departed Shimoda with *Mississippi* on 28 June 1854. The mountains of the Izu Peninsula, dropping below the horizon, were the Commodore's last view of Japan, as they had been his first.

On 1 July the two steamers entered Naha harbor for a final visit to Okinawa. Perry's first and unpleasant duty was to investigate the murder of an American sailor belonging to *Lexington*, which had been "holding down" the island during his absence. A joint tribunal of naval officers and Okinawan officials went into the matter thoroughly. The victim, it appeared, had been the aggressor. When drunk he broke into a house in Naha and attempted to rape a young girl. Her cries attracted neighbors who stoned the sailor as he ran away, and it ended by his falling into the harbor, badly bruised and so intoxicated that he drowned. The local police delivered the leading stone thrower on board the flagship, but the Commodore refused to take jurisdiction and turned him back to the local authorities to be dealt with according to their own law, and they decided to banish him. So this unfortunate episode ended with satisfaction to both sides. Perry again demonstrated, as earlier in Africa, that Americans who abused or assaulted natives would not be protected in wrongdoing by him.

It speaks well for naval discipline during the Japan Expedition that this was the unique instance of an outrage by a sailor on a native; indeed the only serious shore incident to be recorded. That state of affairs was unusual. When the Ringgold-Rodgers Exploring Expedition (*Vincennes*, flag) lay at Hong Kong during the summer of 1854, the men became demoralized by disease and liquor. Vice Admiral Fleetwood Pellew of the British East India Squadron, after a series of waterfront brawls, stopped all liberty in Chinese ports for eighteen months, and in consequence had a mutiny on his hands. There were, of course, abuses of liberty by the American sailors. We find items in ships' logs such as ten out of fourteen men returning to *Mississippi* at Hong Kong in such an advanced state of inebriation that they were clapped in double irons; but there was remarkably little of that. The usual charge was technical desertion — a sailor wandering off to seek liquor and souvenirs, and missing the last boat from shore.

Commodore Perry must have been astonished at his success in maintaining discipline without the use of the "cat." That he did so is a tribute to his personality and those of his officers, and to his policy of keeping the men constantly occupied, as well as amusing them with minstrel shows and the like. He did not, however, know everything that went on below decks — or perhaps he did, and winked at it. Some of the petty officers and old hands were so disgusted with the few louts and shirks among the enlisted men that they licked them into shape with the "cat," regulations or no regulations.

Perry's main business at Okinawa was to obtain a treaty. In the negotiations at Yokohama he had asked for Naha as a third port of resort but was told that the Shogun had no jurisdiction — the government of Okinawa could do as it liked. Regent and Council, already having heard about the Treaty of Kanagawa, were anxious not to offend China or the Daimyo of Satsuma, but finally consented to sign up. This Treaty of Naha, of 11 July 1854, followed in general that of Kanagawa: Americans to be treated "with great courtesy and friendship" and not prohibited from circulating or buying in the shops. Ships to be supplied with wood and water in any harbor, but with provisions only in Naha. Burial ground at Tomari to be preserved — it is now the International Cemetery — and Americans will be punished if they "violently go into houses or trifle with women." Although Perry had not yet received Secretary Dobbin's dispatch of 30 May 1854 ordering him in no case to attempt to seize Okinawa, he had already given up the idea, having originally thrown it out merely as a possible alternative if Japan refused to negotiate. Nor was Perry any longer interested in the Naha coal depot, since Port Lloyd lay several hundred miles nearer to Hawaii, and he had the prospect of buying good steam coal cheap in Formosa. Accordingly, nothing was said in this Treaty of Naha about coal, and Perry carried away in his steamers all that he had left on shore.

A slight unpleasantness occurred because Perry, bent on acquiring a few Okinawan coins, was not easily persuaded that none had been minted there for centuries. But the Regent more than satisfied him by presenting a stone for the Washington Monument, and a handsome antique gong which he hoped to hang there. The Washington authorities would have none of it, so the Commodore gave the gong to the Naval Academy at Annapolis, where it may still be seen at the end of "Lovers' Lane." Perry, in return, presented a quantity of American seeds and agricultural implements to the government for the use of the people. This collection included plows, harrows, a churn, a fanning mill for threshing, a corn cracker and grinder, a cotton gin, an ox-yoke and sundry hoes, forks and chains. Williams, annoyed at being ordered by the Commodore to explain the use of each implement, sneered that these gifts were unsuitable for such primitive farmers as the Okinawans. He maliciously asked a native to tell him what he thought the churn was for. He answered, "A machine to fan people as they dined!"

The Commodore gave a parting dinner to the Okinawan "nobility" on board *Mississippi*, where the Ethiopian Minstrels put on a farewell show. The whole Bettelheim family, to their great delight — and that of the Okinawans — were given free passage to Hong Kong in *Powhatan*. Both steamers sailed on 17 July 1854; and, as *Lexington* had already departed, Naha harbor became free of American ships for the first time in over a year. *Powhatan* called at Ningpo, Foochow and Amoy "to salute the consul"; *Mississippi* sailed directly to Hong Kong, arriving after a short passage.

The *China Mail*, which had already reported the squadron's visits to Shimoda and Hakodate, declared (6 July) that Commodore Perry had been most active, "superintending and investigating everything himself, to the minutest detail." That was correct; and in so doing the Commodore exhausted himself and reached Hong Kong suffering acutely from arthritis. Believing that all principal objects of the Expedition were now attained, he wrote a report to Secretary Dobbin, of which this is the dignified conclusion: —

> Thus, sir, I have finished the work assigned to me with respect to Japan; and I trust that, on my arrival in China, I may find letters from the department authorizing my return to the United States — a relief made the more necessary to me for reason of continued ill-health, and consequent debility.

At Hong Kong he received the desired permission to turn over the squadron command to a senior captain and return home. But before he could do that, there was plenty to occupy him in China.

CHAPTER XXVIII

Conclusion of the Japan Expedition
1854–1855

The Treaty of Kanagawa

ALEXANDER VON HUMBOLDT once remarked that there were three stages in the public attitude toward a great discovery like that of Columbus: first, it isn't so; second (when the fact is confirmed), it is no good; third (when it is found to be valuable), someone else did it. Perry experienced all three, simultaneously. Some English newspapers said that Perry never got further than Okinawa; many Americans called the treaty worthless, and the Russians claimed that they got there first.

We hardly need argue that Perry visited Japan, but the Treaty of Kanagawa did look somewhat meager in comparison with Caleb Cushing's Chinese treaty. Circumstances, however, were altogether different. China had long allowed foreign trade, and Cushing found the Manchu Empire weak, beaten in war, disorganized, and in a mood to concede anything. Japan had been sealed against foreigners for two centuries and a half, her government had resolved to keep it so, and she had never been defeated in war. Thus, the main criticism of Perry respecting the Treaty — his failure to obtain the right to trade — has no justification. His instructions, and President Fillmore's letter, make it clear that the government wanted trade opened with Japan but realized that this would be very difficult and hardly expected Perry to get it. Trade requires a willingness to buy and sell on both sides, and the Bakufu was still adamant against allowing Japanese subjects to do either. It conveyed this to Perry during the treaty negotiations in no uncertain terms, and he wisely dropped the subject. But he procured one major concession — the right to appoint an American consul; and that consul, as we shall see, was the remarkable Townsend Harris, who obtained a commercial treaty. Perry correctly predicted that, once Japan had tasted foreign intercourse, she would want more; that a demand for American machinery would certainly arise, and be paid for in Japanese products. He did not even demand extraterritorial rights, as Cushing had obtained in China.

Susquehanna, departing Edo Bay 24 March, reached Hong Kong 2 April, enabling the friendly *China Mail* to score a beat on all contemporary journals by printing a full and accurate account of the negotiations in its issue of 6 April. The write-up contains this judicious tribute to the Commodore: "We feel pretty certain that the most skilfull diplomatist in Europe could not have brought matters to so speedy, pacific, and successful an issue." Ironically enough, the same Hong Kong paper reprinted a typical James Gordon Bennett editorial from the New York *Herald*, published after Perry's first visit to Japan, which said, "We expect nothing from the next visit but Commodore Perry's failure!"

On 13 June *Vandalia* brought a copy of the Treaty to Shanghai for the American minister, and he read it aloud to Admiral Sir James Stirling RN, who had relieved Admiral Pellew as commander of the British East India Squadron. Stirling wrote home, "The Commodore is said to have conducted his mission with wisdom, Temper and Firmness, and probably accomplished all that could have been done." Following in Perry's wake, Stirling negotiated a treaty at Nagasaki on 14 October 1854, a close copy of the Treaty of Kanagawa.

As for the third point in the series of denigrating discoveries — someone else did it — Russia claimed that and probably still does. This claim arose because Admiral Putiatin, after entering Shanghai emptyhanded from Nagasaki in late November 1853, gave out that two high Japanese authorities "positively announced to him (such is the language used) that they intended to 'open up' but require time to prepare." Or, as the London *Globe* put it, "They stated very candidly that the Japanese government 'has resolved to open the commerce of Japan to all nations.' " This Russian boast is palpably false; no such promise could have been given by any responsible Japanese at that time; and, as proof of its falsity, the Russian treaty with Japan in 1855 conceded no trading privileges whatsoever.[1]

---

[1] G. A. Lensen *Russia's Japan Expedition of 1852-1855* (1955) contains nothing about these rumors, but his detailed narrative shows that they were false. The chronology of Putiatin's Japan Expedition is, briefly, as follows: Oct. 1852, sails from Kronstadt (frigate *Pallada* flag, and 3 other ships), June 1853, at Canton, Putiatin first learns about Perry's Expedition. 22 Aug., arrives Nagasaki. 21 Sept., is told that the Russian foreign minister's letter to the Shogun will be delivered, "but a speedy reply is impossible." 23 Nov., the Russians, tired of waiting for the reply, depart for Shanghai, spend most of December at Saddle I and 3 Jan. 1954 return to Nagasaki. The Japanese commissioners have arrived, and conferences begin. The Japanese promise nothing. 5 Feb., Russians leave; 18 April, back at Nagasaki for 8 days. Oct. 1854, call at Hakodate; nothing doing. Nov. 1854, Putiatin tries to negotiate a treaty at Osaka, Bakufu refuses. He proceeds to Shimoda where frigate *Diana* (*Pallada's* relief) founders 16 Jan. 1855 as result of damage in earthquake. Conferences resumed with Commissioners from Edo, Treaty of Shimoda signed 7 Feb. 1855. When Putiatin first arrived at Shanghai, Perry allowed him to coal from the depot he had established there. On his second call the Russian demanded 50 tons of coal from Perry who declined, as his own supply was running short.

Whilst Perry's visit "may have expedited matters," conceded the London *Globe,* the "actual achievement is due to the Russians, not to the Americans." And on his way home the Commodore read, with mounting blood pressure, a pamphlet in German by Von Siebold who had shipped with Putiatin after being turned down by Perry. The German sneered at the Americans as crude persons so ignorant of protocol that they barged into Edo Bay, unwanted. He claimed that Russia had really opened Japan.

Perry's priority was vigorously asserted both in a circular letter to leading American newspapers from Nye, Perkins & Company of Canton dated 8 March 1854, and in one of Bayard Taylor's reports to the New York *Tribune,* written in Edo Bay just before the treaty was signed. "The Japanese Commissioners," he says, "positively deny, not only that any treaty has been made with Russia, or that they had given any assurance of establishing commercial intercourse with that country hereafter. Admiral Putiatin's report was probably of a piece with the declaration he made, on his first arrival at Hong Kong last summer, that the Government of the United States had expressed its willingness that he should co-operate with Commodore Perry. To the latter alone, belongs the glory of having broken down the barriers which, for two and a half centuries, have separated Japan from the world — and all this without the firing of a single gun, or the utterance of a single menace."

Perry and His Subordinates

When any citizen of a nation that cherishes equality sets himself apart from his fellows and insists on strict punctilio, protocol, and the like, he is certain to receive unfavorable criticism. A good example is that of General Douglas MacArthur, who exhibited many of Perry's qualities and whose imperious attitude during the Allied occupation of Japan in 1945-1951 recalls Perry. The General's dignified seclusion in office or embassy, like the Commodore's in his flag cabin, became the subject of malicious remarks and accusations of pride, arrogance, and seeking his own fame and reputation rather than that of his country.

Inevitably Perry incurred criticism of the same sort; and that he knew he would is shown in a paragraph of his letter to the Secretary of the Navy, explaining the reasons for his attitude toward Japanese subordinate officials.[1] Most of the unfavorable criticism was silenced by the Commodore's obvious success, and very little got into the American press. Some ridiculous stories are still current; for instance, that Perry spent hours before a pier glass (on a man-of-war!) brushing his hair and preening himself to impress the Japanese. There is, nevertheless, evidence of the

---

[1] Chapter XXVI above. Note Perry's own statement, "against the judgment of all about me."

Commodore's unpopularity in the confidential letters of Captain Joel Abbot of *Macedonian*, and this must be appraised since Perry had known Abbot intimately for at least twenty years. Apart from Williams's inconsequential criticisms, and a crack from Surgeon Wheelwright of *Powhatan*, who admits that he never met Perry,[1] the complaints of Captain Abbot are, to my knowledge, the only ones recorded.

On 9 September 1854 Abbot wrote from Hong Kong to Commodore Joseph Smith, chief of the navy's bureau of yards and docks, his confidential friend in Washington: —

Comdre. P. is feasted & toasted at all points here, and as I suppose he will be on his arrival home. He has worked hard & is deserving of much credit. He is rather a hard & unpleasant horse to be associated with, being very selfish & exacting & feeling but little disposition to benefit others any further than it has a direct bearing upon his own fame & interest or that of his family & connections. He therefore does not make many real warm hearted friends. And I fear he would disparage & pull down any one for a small amount of imaginary buncombe & consideration for himself or family connections. I believe I have got along with him more smoothly than most of the commanders in the Squadron, and I think there has been no one in it that he has had more confidence in and more respect & regard for, in his way, than myself.

This is most unfair, in view of Perry's many letters to the Navy Department commending the work of his officers, and his giving them abundant credit in the official Narrative.

On 18 September, one week after Perry had left for home, Captain Abbot wrote to his son John from Hong Kong, "The Comr. & myself have got along pretty well, but there has not been a very warm attachment to him in the Squadron. He has had difficulties & rather unpleasant differences with a number of his Commanders."

Williams noted in his journal that Franklin Buchanan was the only commanding officer under Perry with whom he did *not* have differences; but Captain Abbot in a letter of 18 September to Commander John Pope says, "Buchanan & Comdre. I believe separated not on good terms. I do not know the Merits of the Case." The case was this: a coal-heaver of *Susquehanna*, having beaten up the master-at-arms and defied two officers to arrest him, was tried by court-martial, found guilty of mutiny and sentenced to be hanged from the yardarm. Perry then mitigated the sentence to life imprisonment on the ground that the court did not deliberate long enough. Commander Buchanan, furious at the Commodore's lenity, took the unusual step of denouncing it before his officers and men, declaring that "the Court gave the prisoner all that justice would allow."

---

[1] "The Comdre. is as close as an oyster. I don't think he has much more sense. . . . He is as obstinate as a bull, has great energy and only wants head. At least that is his character among officers."

White-haired Joel Abbot, one year senior to Perry but his junior in the navy and looking many years older, had a good reputation as a naval officer but was noted for serious differences with superior officers. Many years earlier he had been court-martialed for accusing Commodore Isaac Hull of peculation. He had at least twice been rebuked by Perry during the Expedition, and at the time he wrote these letters he was a very sick man. We have already noted his vituperative letter home about dollar exchange at Shimoda. He may have brooded over an incident between him and Perry, who in November 1853 reproved Abbot for promoting a private of his marine guard to master's mate, since he wanted this apparently learned leatherneck to instruct midshipmen. Perry pointed out that nobody under the Navy Secretary except himself had authority to create master's mates, and he did not care to offend the marine corps by promoting one of them to a naval rating. Perry might have admonished Abbot for putting *Macedonian* on the rocks entering Edo Bay, since running a ship aground was (and is) a court-martial offense in the navy; but he tolerantly passed that off as an accident excusable under the circumstances.

A final grievance on Captain Abbot's part came over his assuming command of the squadron. The navy seems to have adopted no regulation about transferring the blue pendant when one commodore relieved another. In 1845 Perry was offended by Commodore Skinner's sailing into Porto Praia with blue pendant displayed before formally taking over command of the Africa Squadron. In 1847, as we have seen, there had been unpleasantness between Commodores Conner and Perry over the exchange of pendants off Veracruz. As next junior to Perry, Abbot became vice commodore of the East India Squadron and flew a red pendant in *Macedonian;* but in September 1854, when Perry appointed Abbot his relief upon departure for America, he refused to let him exchange the red pendant for the blue until Washington confirmed the appointment. This decision, which Abbot attributed to Perry's "supreme selfishness," forced Abbot to act as commodore without the insignia until word came from the Navy Department in January 1855. Perry might have contributed to poor Abbot's peace of mind had he stretched a point here; but it must be remembered that the blue pendant meant as much to Perry as his regimental eagles did to Napoleon; and that he was still the commodore until formally relieved by the Secretary of the Navy.

Abbot's family troubles also preyed on his mind. Not long before he sailed, his little daughter was burned to death, and a delicate son whom he took with him in *Macedonian,* in the hope that a sea voyage would restore his health, died on the passage out and was buried on Principe Island in the Gulf of Guinea. And during the period when he wrote letters complaining about Perry, Abbot himself was deathly sick. His ship's surgeon diagnosed the disease as cholera morbus (acute gastroenteritis), but

Macedonian saluting Powhatan

The former, and the small boat, wear Abbot's red vice commodore's pendant; *Powhatan* wears Perry's blue pendant

an autopsy proved it to have been severe stomach ulcers. One can trace the progress of this malignant disease in the diary of Abbot's devoted Lieutenant Preble. He refused to diet, to take leave or be invalided home, worked hard despite severe pain, and his life simply flickered out in December 1855. Under these circumstances we may discount the Captain's complaints against the Commodore who, completely unconscious of them, continued after his return home to write friendly letters to "My dear Abbot."

Williams, the chief interpreter, criticized Perry from time to time for lax observance of the Sabbath, using strong language about Japanese procrastination, attempting to enhance his own fame, and the post-treaty thrust toward Edo. Yet the most sagacious contemporary estimate of Perry's policy is found in his journal for 24 June 1854. "The appointment of a naval man as the envoy was wise, as it secured unity of purpose," said the chief interpreter. He praised "the prudence and decision" of Perry's proceedings in Japanese waters, and declared that he was the only naval officer capable of serving both as minister and squadron commander. Williams adds that Perry had little help from his captains: — "All, except Buchanan, spent their thoughts in criticising what he did and wishing they were going home. If the Commodore and the Envoy had been two persons, such a state of feeling in the officers might have crippled the firmest purposes of the latter and thwarted the whole enterprise. But such a dilemma was avoided, and Perry regarded all under him only as means and agents to serve his purpose, perhaps too often disregarding wishes and opinions of a comparatively trifling nature. But that extreme is almost unavoidable in minds of strong fibre, and bred for years to command as he has been."

This statement, by a scholar who had observed Perry closely for over a year, is worth pondering. One would like to know for sure the nature of the officers' criticisms. I infer that they related mainly to the Commodore's patience, and his stubborn insistence on certain points in the face of Japanese procrastination, which the officers, "wishing they were going home," thought prolonged their stay abroad. One can imagine wardroom comments such as "Why doesn't Old Bruin fire a few broadsides and scare the hell out of them, instead of letting them put him off with politeness and promises?"

Of all officers in the squadron, the closest to Perry was Silas Bent, his flag lieutenant and chief hydrographer, and the one he chose to accompany him home. Thirty years later, Lieutenant Bent, long since retired, wrote to Perry's biographer Griffis a statement about his personality and character which, in the present biographer's opinion, is the best: —

The Commodore was not a genial man socially. His strong characteristics were self-reliance, earnestness of purpose and untiring industry, which gave such impetus to his schemes as to attract and carry with them the support of others long after they had passed out of his own hands. It was the magnetic power of these qualities in the character of the man that enlisted the services of others in behalf of his purposes, and not any special amenities of manner or sympathies of temperament, that drew them lovingly toward him. And yet, under this austere exterior, which seemed intent only upon the performance of cold duty, as duty, he had a kind and gentle nature. . . . He was bluff, positive and stern on duty, and a terror to the ignorant and lazy, but the faithful ones who performed their duties with intelligence and zeal held him in the highest estimation, for they knew his kindness and consideration of them.

Last Days in China

On the eve of Perry's departure from China the American merchants of Canton — Russell, Wetmore, Heard, Dana and twenty others — drafted a complimentary address, thanking him for the protection he had afforded them, congratulating him on his success, and concluding with almost Oriental hyperbole: —

Whilst you have thus elevated yourself to a proud position in the eyes of the world, you have firmly reëstablished the hold which the name you bear has so long had upon the hearts of your Countrymen; and the name of *Perry*, which has so long adorned the Naval profession, will henceforth be enrolled with the highest in Diplomacy: — Columbus, Da Gama, Cook, La Pérouse, Magellan, — these inscribed their names in History, by striving with the obstacles of Nature, *you* have conquered the obstinate will of man, and by overturning the cherished policy of an Empire, have brought an estranged but cultivated people into the family of Nations; — You have done this without violence; and the World has looked on with admiration to see the barriers of prejudice fall before the Flag of our Country without the firing of a Shot.

More dear to the Commodore than the plaudits of merchants was this "humble tribute" presented to him by the enlisted men of *Mississippi:* —

U.S. Steam-Frigate *Mississippi*
July 31, 1854

Sir:

Learning, with regret, that you contemplate leaving us prior to the arrival of this ship in the United States, it is our earnest desire to express in some befitting manner the high sense of respect and esteem with which we look upon you, both as our commander and real friend. . . . We feel that we, who have had the good fortune . . . of being under your immediate notice, have a right to express to you our honest and true wishes for your future welfare and happiness.

The high and important negotiations which you have accomplished with a numerous and powerful people, we beg you to believe, are well understood by us; and at the same time . . . we have ever had the most implicit confidence that the honor of our country's flag would never be tarnished while under your command. Upon the occasion of separating from you, we desire you to accept our sincere wishes for your future happiness, and at the same time we would express to you our acknowledgments for the uniform regard which you have ever evinced for our comfort. . . . While our country stands ready to receive you with merited and appropriate honors, we beg you to accept this, our humble tribute; and while we have the honor (for it is an honor) to serve our country, we shall never feel greater confidence, or stronger pride, than while under your command.

This document was signed by a yeoman, a gunner, a carpenter, a sail-maker, a boatswain, the master-at-arms, the quartermaster, the captains of the top, the hold, the forecastle, and the afterguard; the armorer, a seaman first class, an ordinary seaman, a landsman, a sergeant on behalf of the marine guard, and a fireman on behalf of the "black gang."

Perry replied next day: —

> U.S. Steam-Frigate *Mississippi*,
> Macao, August 1, 1854.
>
> My Shipmates: I have received, and perused with much pleasure, your letter of yesterday, and am highly gratified to learn from its contents, that the feelings entertained by the crew of the *Mississippi* are so kind and friendly towards me. Those feelings I most cordially reciprocate, and shall ever look back with pride and pleasure to the several periods of time on this and other stations, where this noble and well-tried ship has borne my flag.
>
> Wishing you all prosperity, and a happy return to your families and friends at home, I subscribe myself your friend,
>
> M. C. PERRY

During the first half of 1854, when Perry was in Japanese waters and at Okinawa, things blew up in Shanghai. Sloop-of-war *Plymouth*, Commander John Kelly, there protected American interests, the Commodore having assigned him to that ungracious duty after surveying the Bonins. In the meantime converted steamer *Queen* enabled the merchants of Canton to sleep easy, and *Susquehanna*, returning early from Japan, carried Minister McLane in style from port to port.

At Shanghai the trouble was caused by the imperial forces, not the Tai-Ping rebels. In February the Manchu army encamped around the city, and the "imperial fleet" of junks and converted English steamers in the harbor commenced a series of aggressive acts toward the "foreign devils," tearing down their buildings and firing on their vessels. These hostile acts culminated in an outrage on an unarmed pilot boat with a Chinese crew, owned by American merchants and flying the American flag. She was captured by His Imperial Majesty's ship *Compton* and boarded by a gang of cutthroats who struck the ensign, dragged the crew on board *Compton*, and lashed them to the mainmast with their own pigtails. Commander Kelly, as soon as he got the word, sent Lieutenant John Guest on board in *Plymouth*'s cutter with eleven armed seamen. Guest reported that as *Compton* lay in the midst of a Chinese fleet, mounted a dozen guns and had forty men on deck, "renegadoes of all nations," he "thought the attempt to release the six prisoners who composed the crew of the captured American pilot boat, a service of some delicacy." Delicacy indeed! Boarding the warship himself but leaving his men in the cutter, the Lieutenant inquired for the Chinese commander. A Portuguese stepped forward and claimed that rank; the Lieutenant demanded release of the boat and crew *pronto;* the Portuguese refused, Guest called to his men, "Come on board!" and they soon freed the prisoners by the simple expedient of chopping off their pigtails. Members of the Chinese crew then leveled muskets at Guest, but he whipped out his pistol, pointed it at the Portuguese's head, and promised, at the first shot fired, "to blow his brains out." The captain then ordered his crew to desist, and the Lieutenant got boat and crew away "without further difficulty." Subsequently Kelly required the captain of *Compton* to raise an American ensign at the fore and salute it with 21 guns.

In early April trouble arose over imperial troops camping on the Shanghai racecourse — an abominable encroachment not to be borne! U.S.S. *Plymouth,* H.M.S. *Encounter* and H.M.S. *Grecian* organized a landing force, with civilian components, which had a sharp fight of a quarter-hour's duration with the Chinese troops and drove them off, losing three men killed and a few wounded. Horse races were then resumed.

Perry forwarded Kelly's account of these doings to the Navy Department, together with a warm commendation of his "energetic and gallant conduct." Since there was no "China lobby" in Washington or London in 1854 to denounce Kelly and his British friends for "imperialist aggression" in defending innocent people from armed ruffians, these encounters with the Chinese ended happily. Perry also wrote gracious letters to officers and others who had particularly helped the Expedition; to Williams, whom he later tried to have appointed United States minister to China, he bore "the most ample testimony to the talents zeal and fidelity" with which he conducted his duties as chief interpreter. "I declare that your services were almost indispensable to me in the successful progress of the delicate business which had been entrusted to my charge."

At last came the day of sailing, 11 September 1854, in the P. & O. steamship *Hindostan.* "Foreign devils" and Chinese alike flocked to the Hong Kong waterfront to say farewell; 13-gun salutes flashed out from *Mississippi* and *Macedonian.* Perry was glad to be on his way to see Jane and the family after two years' absence. But those who stood near him on deck while he waved goodbye to friends ashore noticed that tears were in his eyes. No wonder, for the saddest moment in a naval officer's life is the relinquishing of his last sea command; and Perry, past sixty, knew that this must be his last. Never again would he enjoy the lift of tearing along before the trades with royals and studdingsails set. No more, in the dog-watch, would he see sailors dancing heel-and-toe on the forecastle. Never again would he stand a "graveyard watch" and listen for the ship's bells and the lookout's cry of "A-a-a-all's well!" No more rosy dawns, with smell of dew on the deck while aiming his sextant at the fading stars. No more flash of great ordnance and rolling roar of broadsides. He was still Commodore Perry, with a deal of work to do compiling an official narrative of his Expedition. But the power and the glory departed when he left his last sea command.

CHAPTER XXIX

Home Port
1854–1858

I tender to you my warm congratulations on the happy success of your novel and interesting mission. You have won additional fame for yourself, reflected new honor upon the very honorable service to which you belong, and, we all hope, have secured for your country, for commerce, and for civilization, a triumph the blessings of which may be enjoyed by generations yet unborn. The Senate, very promptly, unanimously ratified the treaty.

— SECRETARY DOBBIN TO COMMODORE PERRY, *19 September 1854*

Hero's Return

BEFORE leaving Hong Kong in the P. & O. steamship *Hindostan* on 11 September 1854, Perry arranged for his notes, journals, etc. to be brought home in U.S.S. *Mississippi*. The imperial gifts, together with painted and dried specimens of fish and flora, were loaded in *Plymouth*, whilst Dr. Morrow, in *Lexington*, with the aid of a Chinese gardener boy named Oqui, nurtured on the quarterdeck some three hundred living plants, trees and ornamental shrubs of Japan and China. Officers were allowed all the space they wanted in her and *Southampton* for sending home souvenirs and bulky purchases.

Lieutenant Silas Bent and an orderly accompanied the Commodore. His secretary son Oliver, in whom he vainly tried to instill ambition for a mercantile career, remained behind. Shortly after, obviously through the influence of his uncle Senator Slidell and his brother-in-law August Belmont, Oliver was appointed United States consul at Canton. He filled that position acceptably for many years, during a troubled and uncertain period in China.

The East India Squadron now dispersed. *Mississippi* went home via Cape Horn; she is said to have been the first war steamer to cross the Pacific. Perry did not dare trust *Susquehanna* to that tempestuous route, so she returned via the Indian Ocean and the Cape of Good Hope. *Macedonian* and *Vandalia* remained in Chinese waters to look after American interests in the treaty ports, as well as *Powhatan* for Minister McLane's use. McLane left for home before the end of the year, and when Captain Adams returned to exchange ratifications of the Treaty of Kanagawa, *Powhatan* took him from Hong Kong to Japan.

Perry had hoped to visit Thailand on his way home. The Second King, who signed himself Phar Pen Clow Chow You Hou, was so impressed by the Colt revolver Perry sent him from Ceylon on the outward passage, that he persuaded his elder brother the Supreme King (Somdet Phoa Paramende) to invite the East India Squadron to pay an official visit to Bangkok. The Commodore wished to accept, and flattered himself that he could have negotiated a new treaty with Thailand; but in 1853, after his first visit to Japan, he could not spare the coal, and now he had no time. So nothing happened except an exchange of compliments by diplomatic pouch. In view of later difficulties in that part of the world, it is interesting that Perry wrote to Secretary Dobbin about the Vietnams (then Cochin China), with which England, France and the United States had unsuccessfully tried to establish friendly relations, "A favorable issue might be accomplished, provided that small steamers of light draught were employed to ascend the rivers upon which the principal cities are situated, . . . *to secure the friendship* of these singular people."

Since no canal existed, *Hindostan's* passengers had to disembark at Suez, head of navigation on the Red Sea, travel by railway to Cairo, take another train to Alexandria, and there catch another steamer for Europe. One can understand why the Commodore did not carry his notes with him. At Alexandria he took ship for Trieste, thence proceeding by rail via Vienna, Dresden and Berlin, to The Hague. His reputation preceded him. At Trieste, Archduke Charles of Austria, brother of Emperor Francis Joseph, invited Perry to a family dinner; and he wrote to Colonel Webb that in other capitals en route he "received marked attention" and high praise for his diplomacy. The Commodore reached The Hague after a ten weeks' journey from Hong Kong. This evidently gave him a much-needed rest, since upon his arrival (20 November) his daughter Caroline wrote in her diary, "Papa has arrived, in good health & spirits, he is looking uncommonly well, & seems delighted to get once more among us."

His object in visiting The Hague was to see his family, guests of August Belmont, who had been rewarded by President Pierce for long service to the Democrats by an appointment as American minister to the Netherlands. That furnished both an occasion and a setting for the long-deferred family reunion in Europe, and for the *genre* painting of it, which we have reproduced. Perry and Silas Bent were "most graciously received by the King and Queen" of the Netherlands, who wished to hear the latest news of Japan. The Dutch press annoyed August Belmont by a rather spiteful attitude toward Perry's expedition, but the government was pleased that

Belmont-Perry Reunion at The Hague, December 1854

The Commodore, right, holds his grandson August Belmont Jr; Mrs. Matthew C. Perry holds granddaughter Frederika Belmont; Mrs. August Belmont (Caroline Perry) in center. Perry Belmont snatches an engraving from his father, August Belmont; Isabella Perry seated at the left.

he had broken the ice for a treaty which they had been trying to get for years, and finally obtained in 1856.

We have a few glimpses of the Commodore's stay, in the diary of his daughter Caroline Belmont, who seems to have been perfectly at home in the diplomatic society of The Hague: —

As Papa will not be here for Christmas, we intend keeping St. Nicholas eve the 5th by having a Christmas tree for Perry. We have invited the children of the diplomats, & have received the acceptance of Lady Mary's little girl this morning. Yesterday we had a grand dinner, given to Papa. Our guests were all the different heads of missions here, & the Duke of Saxe Weimar.

Our St. Nicholas tree proved to be wonderfully successful, we had very pretty things on it, & something for every body. We had 4 children, the Spanish minister's little girl & boy, Lady Mary's little girl, & little de Kock girl. Most of the members of the diplomatic corps were here, it being early ½ past 5 in the afternoon, some could not come. We had each article numbered on tickets, & before the tree was exhibited, a plate was handed with the tickets upon it, & each person took one, & drew a prize, large or small whatever it happened to be. They all seemed to enjoy themselves, the children particularly. Augy & Perry were delighted & had a great many pretty presents. I had two things sent anonymously, one was a small basket in the shape of a fish, filled with chocolate, the other was a larger fish, filled with all sorts of miniature games, bonbons & flowers, the latter was sent by Könitz. We had been in the habit of playing games, such as backgammon, dominoes, old maid, etc. & so he tho't it was a very appropriate thing to send. I, like a goose, never thought of looking inside, seeing flowers at the top, I thought there was nothing else, but Bell having more curiosiy than I dived down to the extreme end, & found all these things. On Saturday the 9th Papa dined with Lomonosoff, he is the only person who has been polite enough to invite him.

Sergius Lomonosov was the Russian minister to The Hague. What would we not give to have overheard their conversation!

Everyone at the legation pressed the Commodore to keep Christmas there; but, as we have frequently seen, he was not one to idle when he had work to do. He must be off to England both to inspect new war steamers of the Royal Navy, and to obtain an editor for his Narrative of the Japan Expedition. "Papa left on Thursday [7 December] last," writes Caroline, "without Bell & Mamma, he decided to leave them with me, this winter, as we desired it so much provided they return home in the spring." They were probably glad to escape a winter crossing of the Atlantic.

The United States Navy had enjoyed little success with steam warships since *Mississippi* and her sister ship *Missouri* were built. Secretary Dobbin in a letter to Perry called *Princeton*, *Allegheny* and *San Jacinto* "miserable failures," and Perry described them as "abortions." Even *Susquehanna* and *Powhatan*, though serviceable, had demanded too much time and money for upkeep. Congress having recently authorized the construction of six new war steamers (including *Merrimack* and *Wabash*), Perry hoped to pick up a few hints from the British to make them more effective. Whatever information he did obtain was discreetly imparted to the Navy Department by word of mouth.

The editorial problem puzzled Perry. He wished to preserve for posterity a comprehensive account of all the Expedition's activities, scientific and cultural as well as diplomatic; one which would have enough general interest to be widely read. He had no confidence in his own literary ability, and there was a good example from the Pacific Exploring Expedition of what to avoid. Commander Wilkes wrote the narrative of that important voyage himself, but so badly and diffusely in five quarto volumes that few read it. To whom, then, should Perry turn? Of the gifted writers closest to him, Washington Irving was running a race with death to complete his biography of George Washington, and Bayard Taylor was completing his *tour du monde*. Nathaniel Hawthorne was the obvious choice. Although he had already won immortal fame with *The Scarlet Letter* and other romances, Hawthorne was always hard up, his salary as American consul at Liverpool was inadequate, and he did not despise hack work, having amiably written a campaign biography of Franklin Pierce. So to Liverpool went Perry, on the off chance that Hawthorne might "bite." The eminent author thus recorded the visit: —

Commodore Perry called to see me, this morning — a brisk, gentlemanly, off-hand (but not rough) unaffected, and sensible man, looking not so elderly as he ought, on account of a very well-made wig. . . . I seldom meet with a man who puts himself more immediately on conversible terms than the Commodore. He soon introduced his particular business with me — it being to inquire whether I could recommend some suitable person to prepare his notes and materials for the publication of an account of his voyage. He was good enough to say that he had fixed upon me, in his own mind, for this office, but that my public duties would of course prevent me from engaging in it. I spoke of Herman Melville, and one or two others; but he seems to have some acquaintance with the literature of the day, and did not grasp very cordially at any name that I could think of; nor, indeed, could I recommend anyone with full confidence. It would be a very desirable labor for a young literary man, or, for that matter, an old one; for the world can scarcely have in reserve a less hacknied theme than Japan.

Perry could not imagine the author of *White Jacket* and *Moby Dick* as his editor, nor can we. Incidentally, Perry wore no wig; his own luxuriant brown hair still grew well forward on his forehead, and never turned gray.

Shortly after this interview the Commodore, Silas Bent and the orderly took passage on the Collins liner *Baltic*, whose construction Perry had overseen. She departed Liverpool 30 December and arrived New York 11

January 1855. In the meantime, the United States Senate had asked the President to submit all correspondence relative to the Japan Expedition. Pierce delayed until he could have a talk with the Commodore; after that, on 30 January he sent the lot to the Senate, which ordered it to be printed. This came out as the 195-page *Correspondence Relative to the Naval Expedition to Japan;* valuable indeed, but not what Perry envisaged as a detailed and comprehensive narrative. He could do nothing about that except continue his search for an editor, until *Mississippi* reached New York on 23 April, carrying the literary and many of the scientific materials on which the Narrative would be based.

On the day after her arrival the Commodore experienced another sad but proud moment. From the Brooklyn Navy Yard he was rowed out to the old war steamer which had worn his blue pendant for the better part of a decade. As he boarded her for the last time, it was broken at the main truck. Officers crowded around to shake Perry's hand and the enlisted men, at a respectful distance, gave him three cheers. Then the blue pendant was struck for the last time, honored by a 13-gun salute, and Perry was rowed ashore in the courteous old fashion by his junior officers.

The navy kept Perry on the active list, and let him retain his colored orderly. On 20 June the Commodore was appointed a member of a Naval Efficiency Board lately set up by Congress to break the logjam of elderly officers. There were so many thirty-year-old passed midshipmen and forty-five-year-old lieutenants as to clog promotion for young and talented officers. Perry had complained of this situation for years, so felt obliged to serve, although frantically eager to get on with his official Narrative. After sitting for five weeks in the hot summer of 1855, the Committee of Fifteen, as it was called, recommended that 130 officers be placed on the reserved list with reduced pay. This created an uproar in the newspapers, friends of the plucked officers complained to Congress, the navy was forced to review 108 of the dismissals and reversed a majority of them. Perry, of course, came in for a share of the abuse.

But the Commodore had no complaint of the warmth of his reception. He was even "mentioned" as a presidential candidate, with Commander Duncan N. Ingraham USN. Values of that period are illustrated by the fact that Ingraham, for a single act of bravado, had become more popular than Perry. In 1853, in Smyrna Harbor, he forced an Austrian man-of-war to surrender a Hungarian confederate of Thaddeus Kossuth, not even an American citizen, whom the Austrian authorities had arrested and were about to take to Budapest for trial. Ingraham was fêted all over the United States and given a gold medal by Congress.

Congress never presented Perry with a gold medal, but gave him a vote of thanks and something far more substantial and valuable — a grant of $20,000 in consideration of his acting as diplomatic envoy in addition to his naval duty. That enabled him to pay off his debt to August Belmont for the 32nd Street house. And the merchants of Boston struck for him a gold medal, his handsome profile on the obverse, and on the reverse an inscription thanking him for negotiating the treaties of Kanagawa and Naha. Silver replicas were given to his officers, and bronze ones to the men. The New York Chamber of Commerce gave him a magnificent silver dinner service of 381 pieces, most of which now belong to the New York Historical Society. In presenting the plate the committee described the achievement of bringing "this secluded Empire into the intercourse of nations" as one of "the great events of the age; reflecting honor upon our Country, the more so as it has been accomplished, not by bloodshed and the devastations of war; but by means of a frank, energetic and determined course of negociation." To which Perry modestly replied that the treaty was "a mere commencement" in "bringing a mighty Empire into the family of nations & within the influences of our benign religion.

"It is not a commercial compact," he continued, "but one of amity and friendly intercourse; a compact indeed which has been thought worthy of imitation by four of the great powers of Europe." And he reminded his audience that Article IX automatically granted to the United States whatever privileges or advantages might in the future be extended to any other nation. This *caveat* was probably intended as an answer to James Gordon Bennett who, having sneered at the Japan Expedition from the start, was now declaiming in the columns of the New York *Herald* that it was an expensive failure.

The Commodore's most appreciated honor was a reception at Newport by the Governor and General Assembly of Rhode Island. At the same time they presented him with a huge silver salver inscribed: "In testimony of their appreciation of his services to his country, . . . in negotiating a treaty of amity and commerce with Japan; and in acknowledgment of the honor he has conferred upon his native state in ever maintaining the renown of the name he bears and adding to the triumphs of his profession, those of humanity and peace." The ceremony took place on the balcony of the Old State House at Newport on 15 June 1855; and, at Perry's request, there was no military or naval display. Deeply touched, he recalled the spring Election Day of his childhood when the incoming governor sailed to Newport from Providence in a packet sloop decorated with flags and banners. "Since then," he concluded, "I have traversed almost every part of the globe, . . . and now . . . in declining life, to be called by the representatives of my native state . . . to receive from the lips of its Chief Magistrate the commendations of my fellow citizens, is an honour I little expected."

A different sort of affair the same year, a dinner given by Mayor Fernando Wood at his New York residence, was described by an anonymous writer in *Harper's Magazine*. Among Perry's fellow guests were General Winfield Scott, Martin Van Buren and his son "Prince John," Governor Seymour of New York, Washington Irving, George Bancroft, and Ogden Hoffman. Irving cracked what the social chronicler considered a marvelous witticism by telling Scott that his biography should have "more genuine lustre than either Mr. Bancroft or I could give you; in fact you ought to be *Japanned*, and the Commodore yonder is *your* man." To this pun "the burly and bluff Commodore" replied in kind, "I prefer the Knickerbocker shines." Perry talked less than anyone; "he seemed the embodiment of a true sailor, who loved to listen to the yarns of the scholars around him." When the host brought up the Japan Expedition, "Bancroft fired off a few historical references to Japan which Perry with perfect *rapport* responded to briefly."

In June 1855 Jane and Isabella returned to New York. Caroline Perry Belmont, who remained at The Hague with her husband, wrote in her diary for 15 July, "Papa, Aunt Ann writes, has a delightful house & has furnished it beautifully for Mamma & B." This was the new house at 38 West 32nd Street, one of a brick block recently built on a corner of the old Slidell pasture, and near the then extreme northerly limit of the city. Judging by some of the articles inherited by descendants, the living rooms were furnished with a mishmash of furniture and alleged objets d'art that the Commodore had picked up in Hong Kong. At 38 West 32nd Street the Perrys lived for the rest of the Commodore's life except for excursions to Newport and Saratoga Springs. Isabella, who had already been presented at the court of the Netherlands, now made a somewhat belated debut into New York society, and her parents escorted her to the leading balls; the Commodore did so alone when Jane was indisposed. As evidence that the family now knew "everyone worth knowing" in New York, the visiting list of Mrs. Frederick De Peyster included them with the Belmonts, Stuyvesants, Winthrops, Hoffmans, Jays, Livingstons, Hones, Beekmans, Grinnells, LeRoys, Delafields, and Charles King. The Perrys were now "comfortably off"; Jane had an independent income of $7700 from the Slidell estate, according to her son-in-law, who took care that her capital did not suffer depreciation.

The Official Narrative

In the meantime, Perry's main concern was to prepare his official Narrative for the press. As editor, he was fortunate to obtain the services of the Reverend Francis L. Hawks, Rector of Calvary Church, New York, an accomplished pulpit orator, widely traveled, author of several histories and biographies, and editor of a biographical dictionary. Hawks was assisted by a literary physician, Dr. Robert Tomes, who had written several popular biographies and who, later, with Perry's permission, edited an abridgment of the Narrative.

Through Dr. Hawks's clerical connections Perry obtained two rooms in the recently built home of the American Bible Society in Astor Place at the corner of Fourth Avenue and 8th Street. ("I'm sure *you* will approve," the Commodore wrote playfully to S. Wells Williams.) There in the late spring of 1855 Perry buckled-to on the great work which would record his Japan Expedition for all time. There were many obstacles to surmount, and time-consuming trips to Washington for sessions of the Committee of Fifteen, but the work went forward at a fast pace. Dr. Tomes gave it a final polish, and Volume I was ready for the press only seven or eight months after the team started work.

The "Prefatory Note" to Volume I, written partly by Dr. Hawks and partly by the Commodore and signed by him on New Year's Day 1856, states in part: —

As the sole object on the part of the Commander was to afford to his government and countrymen the most ample account he could of what had been done by himself, his officers, and men — as in this respect he had nothing to conceal, as he wished to present truly all of interest that had been observed either by himself or others, and to do justice to the deserving officers who had so effectually sustained him in his plans for carrying out a new, delicate, and arduous work — he deemed it best to place in the hands of the compiler, without reserve, *all* the materials in his possession, whether from his own pen, or furnished by the labors of others, and to request nothing more than that the preparation of the work might be conducted in a spirit conformable to the ends and wishes just expressed.

The materials were abundant and varied. Beside the manuscript journal of the Commodore, in three large folios, and his official correspondence; the journals of his secretary and other officers, the diaries of the fleet captain and flag-lieutenants, the official reports of gentlemen detailed for special duties, and the public documents connected with the Expedition, were all placed in the hands of the writer. Of these, the Commodore's journal and official correspondence form much the larger part.

In a footnote he particularly acknowledged his debt to the journals of Commander Adams, Lieutenants Contee and Bent, Purser Harris, Bayard Taylor, Chaplain Jones, and son Oliver; to the reports of each commanding officer and of S. Wells Williams and Surgeons Green and Fahs, the services of interpreter Portman, and artists William Heine and E. Brown Jr. "In the hydrographical department he would specially acknowledge the accurate and laborious work of Lieutenants W. L. Maury and S. Bent. Nor would he pass by without notice minor contributions from any under his command; to all he would render due credit and thanks." So much for Captain Abbot's charge that Perry grabbed all the glory and left none for his subordinates. And as Hawks's name alone appeared as author on the title page, the entire work has generally been attributed to him, despite his disclaimer: "In many instances, the language of the Narrative is a *verbatim* copy from his [Perry's] journal. Wherever it was possible thus to use his manuscript, it was done, as being the course most likely to avoid error. Every word of the work was read to the Commodore in manuscript, and received his correction before it was sent back to the press."

After acknowledging the help of all and sundry — excepting, for obvious reasons, Dr. Morrow — Perry in the prefatory note declared that his "highest ambition" was to tell the story "in such manner as would not only present a true picture, but also keep alive the interest of the reader; his wish was to make a book that might furnish information without being wearisome. If in this he has succeeded, he has attained all to which he aspired. If he has not, he has only to say that he will feel more of regret than surprise."

Succeed he decidedly did. The first volume of the *Narrative of the Expedition of an American Squadron to the China seas and Japan*, announced as "nearly ready" on 5 April 1856, deserves high rank among the classics of American exploration and adventure, such as Elisha Kent Kane's *Arctic Explorations*, Washington Irving's *Captain Bonneville*, and John Wesley Powell's *Explorations of the Colorado River*. Since he could not expect a government publication, not distributed through the usual bookselling channels, to be reviewed, Perry arranged to have Volume I alone republished in a trade edition by Appleton of New York in 1856. That edition, which omitted many of the lithographs included in the official set, received a few very enthusiastic reviews: — in the *North American* by Henry T. Tuckerman, a leading critic; in the *Illustrated London News*, and a long essay review in the *Morning Courier and New York Enquirer*, probably by its editor the Commodore's old friend General Webb. About 34,000 copies of the three-volume set were printed by Congress at a cost of about $400,000. Over half were given away to members of Congress and high government officials; of the remainder, two thousand went to the Navy Department and a thousand copies to Perry. Half of these he used to compensate Hawks and the contributors.

In compiling Volume II of the Narrative, which appeared late in 1857, Perry and Hawks found out what many subsequent editors have learned to their cost, that it is often easier to write a thing yourself than to drag a promised contribution out of an eminent but reluctant specialist. Their policy was to devote about half the volume to reports by officers and enlisted members of the Expedition; e.g., Chaplain Jones on the Geology of Okinawa and Formosan Coal; Bayard Taylor and Dr. Fahs on the Botany of Okinawa and the Exploration of Chichi Jima; Joel Abbot's survey of the west coast of Japan; Silas Bent's study of the Kuro-Siwo current;

and Lieutenant Junius J. Boyle's report on Volcano Bay, Hokkaido. In addition, to enhance the value and interest of this volume, Perry persuaded several distinguished men of science to peruse the notes on various subjects made by members of the Expedition, and write the chapters on them. Among these contributors were William C. Redfield on cyclones, John Cassin on birds, James C. Brevoort on fish, and Dr. John Clarkson Jay on the shells of Japan — the last three beautifully illustrated. But S. Wells Williams, despite frequent friendly proddings by the Commodore, never finished his promised vocabulary of the Japanese language; and on botany Perry had to settle for an identification of the dried specimens by Professor Asa Gray.

Botanical Brawl and Friendly Fish

Perry had planned to devote an entire volume of the Narrative to his favorite hobby of botany, but the egotism of Dr. James Morrow thwarted him. Owing to the fact that Morrow was appointed "agriculturist" to the Expedition by the Secretary of State after Perry's departure from the United States, he received instructions from that Department. He was told, "under the direction of the Commodore and subject to his orders, to take charge of the Seeds and agricultural Implements procured for the Expedition," to "note and collect all indigenous vegetable products," to "keep a full and accurate Journal . . . which on your return, will be delivered by you to this Department." The last clause was pregnant with trouble. It enabled the thirty-two-year-old M.D., whose knowledge of botany was rudimentary, to consider himself independent of Perry and the navy, notwithstanding the fact that he had signed on as acting master's mate in *Vandalia*, wore a somewhat individualized version of the naval uniform, and accepted navy pay. Welcomed on board the flagship by Perry, and sharing a cabin with Williams, Morrow helped surgeons Fahs and Green and the interpreter to collect living plants, sketch them, and prepare dried specimens. These, together with some three hundred living plants, mostly bought by Perry in China, were sent home in storeship *Lexington* in charge of Morrow and a China-boy gardener named Oqui. With Captain Glasson's coöperation, they lined the quarterdeck with the living plants, and must have shown uncommon devotion, covering them against salt spray and hot sunshine, to keep them alive through tropic seas and across the North Atlantic.

Lexington arrived at Brooklyn 16 February 1855, with most of the plants alive. They were forwarded to Washington by another warship, and probably placed in the greenhouse behind the old Patent Office which had been built for the Wilkes Expedition plants. Congress appropriated $1500 to build a hothouse especially for Perry's plants on the Capitol grounds. Actually two greenhouses were built in 1856, and "highly approved by distinguished horticulturists," according to a report of the Commissioner of Public Buildings in 1858. The Botanic Garden at the foot of Capitol Hill, now has a dozen or more plants of the same types that were brought there by Oqui, but it is impossible to tell whether or not they are actual descendants of Perry's. In any case, the Commodore deserves credit for bringing the first living plants directly from Japan to America. His keen interest in having them introduced to American horticulture is shown by his correspondence with Francis Lieber of South Carolina. In a letter of 12 March 1856, Perry asserts that bamboo can easily be cultivated in the southern states. He modestly describes himself as "a sailor who has spent a large part of his life at sea," who knows little of horticulture but is eager to have both federal and state governments establish experimental stations for tropical and other exotic plants. Like so many of the Commodore's ideas, this was not realized until long after his death.

The dried specimens were the subject of an unfortunate controversy between the Commodore, Dr. Morrow and Asa Gray. For Morrow not only retained his Japanese journal instead of letting it be used for the official Narrative, as the Commodore had ordered; he never even reported to Perry upon his arrival in New York. Instead, he nipped off to Boston with the dried specimens, presenting them to Professor Asa Gray with the request that he identify and report on them, and return both report and specimens to himself. Perry was pleased to have Gray identify the plants — S. Wells Williams, a boyhood friend of Gray's, had doubtless recommended that the Commodore place them in Gray's hands. "I am well aware that for purposes of examination and report they could not be in better hands," Perry wrote to Gray on 21 May 1855. The Fisher Professor of Natural History at Harvard had already become the leading botanist in the New World; Gray's *Botany* was the counterpart to Bowditch's *Navigator*. But the Commodore was outraged at Morrow's presumption in claiming ownership. He begged the Professor to identify the specimens promptly and return them to him at Bible House, hoping to devote an entire volume of the Narrative to botany.

Morrow lost no time in writing to Gray that the specimens were his own property, not that of the navy, which (he claimed) had no control over him after landing; he was now subject to the orders of the State Department. Perry contended, properly, that the specimens, like everything collected by members of the Expedition, were public, not private, property. Each bombarded the Professor with requests to hurry up and send him the list. Gray stalled; he would have nothing to do with the specimens until he received an order from someone higher than the Commodore or the Doctor. Two letters of Morrow to Gray of 29 February and 7 March 1856 reveal his game. He is lobbying Congress for a grant to compensate him for his "professional" labors in Japan, and as support, desperately wants the list. "If so fortunate" as to get the appropriation, he coyly adds, "I shall not forget you." (Nor did he; when Congress voted Morrow $3,793.83, he tipped Asa Gray $100.) Morrow hoped that the State Department would issue a separate volume over his name, comprising his journal, sketches, and the list of dried specimens — but he must have the list. Won't Professor Gray "fix" his dried-plant list "as a State Department Paper" to fit in with Morrow's journal? No, Gray would not. In June 1856, after receiving a strong letter from the Commodore, the Professor promised to surrender the specimens to him if so ordered by the Navy Secretary or the Secretary of State, in order to preclude a possible lawsuit by Morrow.

In the meantime, the specimens being far too valuable for Asa Gray to ignore, he studied them carefully, drew upon the services of specialists for the algae, ferns, mosses and sedges, and compiled a full list. Still he refused to give them up without higher authority. Volumes I and III of the Narrative came out, part of Volume II was in press, and Perry, having received no botanical list from Gray, blew up about the Professor's procrastination in a letter to his former interpreter. "I have my own opinion of the conduct of this man," he wrote to S. Wells Williams on 8 January 1857, "but I shall not trouble you with a declaration of it. I had no other object than to make my report the more interesting to the scientific reader, and regret the nonappearance of that subject with plates of the many beautiful specimens and drawings collected and prepared — but as by his singular conduct he would neither describe the plants himself or allow others to do it, the chance of their publication by the government has been lost."

Not entirely lost. Within two months the logjam broke. Gray sent the list to a congressman in whom he had confidence, the congressman gave it to Secretary of State Marcy; and Marcy, thoroughly sick of Morrow's importunities, handed over both list and journal to Perry, thus thwarting the Doctor's plans for a separate volume. The Commodore received the list just in time (so he wrote Gray in April 1857) to incorporate it in Volume II; but he had no room for the Doctor's journal, which belonged in Volume I. Perry, who had already set up some rather trifling "Observations" by Morrow on Okinawan agriculture, magnanimously gave him credit for his work as a collector. And to Gray he wrote a friendly letter, asking him to retain the specimens but send duplicates to the Smithsonian. He did retain them, and they were of greatest importance in helping the Professor to compile his monograph on the botany of Japan and demolish the rival theories of Louis Agassiz.

Morrow's journal, preserved in the State Department archives, was finally published in 1947; but his sketches of Japanese plants, which he selfishly withheld from Perry, appear to have been lost. Thus the only floral paintings of the Expedition to be preserved are those that Heine and others executed on the outward passage in *Mississippi*. These still await publication, in Perry's manuscript journal.

Chaplain Jones profited from the botanical brawl by having an entire volume of the Narrative for his Report on the Zodiacal Lights. And, as Jones's name was not yet known to the scientific world, the Commodore took pains to have his Report read by leading American astronomers and mathematicians. He obtained enthusiastic encomiums from five eminent professors — Peirce and Gould of Harvard, Dana and Silliman of Yale, and Chauvenet of the Naval Academy.

Perry also corresponded with Joseph Henry, the director of the Smithsonian Institution, and with his assistant Spencer F. Baird, about the stuffed birds, the shells and the fish skins which he had deposited in that institution. To the Smithsonian he passed on almost every present that he personally had received in Japan and Okinawa, as did President Pierce. The imperial gifts, still in the Smithsonian, are not worthy examples of Japanese art. The best are a brazen gong, two gold-lacquer boxes, a lacquered writing set, and about twenty bolts of silk, spot-dyed in the weft. Many of the gifts are of the coarsest sort — wooden soup bowls, a stoneware teapot, cheap fans and tobacco pipes, an abacus, and no fewer than 68 ordinary Japanese umbrellas. The entire lot could not have cost the Bakufu more than a few hundred *ryo*. President Pierce also received two of the three imperial spaniels; but whether he kept them in the White House or gave them away we have no means of knowing.

In pleasant contrast to the unseemly floral feud were relations between the Commodore and James C. Brevoort of Bedford, New York, who identified and described the Oriental fishes for the Narrative. During the Expedition's voyage, the men took several hundred species of fish and gathered at least as many different kinds of crab and shellfish. The best of these specimens, before they died, were painted by Heine, Bayard Taylor and others, and when practicable, shells and fishes' skins were dried, preserved, and brought home. From them, two artists named H. Patterson and W. T. Peters prepared colored paintings, and these Brevoort undertook to identify and describe. Many turned out to be new to ichthyology. A beautiful salmon caught at Hakodate, of an unidentified species, Brevoort named *Salmo Perryi*; and two new sea snails he called *Helix* and *Bullia Perryi*.

All this took a great deal of time, trouble and correspondence between Washington, New York and Bedford. Owing to Congressional grumblings about the expense of publishing the Narrative, the number of colored illustrations of fish, turtles, sea-slugs and crabs for Volume II had to be drastically reduced. Brevoort's contribution to the Narrative is nevertheless a monument of American ichthyology; and the correspondence between him and Perry, bound up with the complete collection of original paintings in the New York Public Library, is a happy example of gentlemanly consideration and scientific scrupulousness.

Perry's Policies and Prophecies

The Commodore having developed positive views respecting American policy toward Oriental countries, was not backward in expressing them. He gave out his ideas in letters to General Webb's *Courier and New York Enquirer;* and in two articles and an address before the American Geographical and Statistical Society. The articles are reprinted in the second volume of the Narrative.

The first article opens with this positive statement: —

In the general increase and extension of the commerce of the world, and the necessity of employing the constantly accumulating capital which the mines of California and Australia are annually yielding, it is important that the government of the United States should turn its attention to the expediency of opening new avenues of trade, by the accomplishment of treaties of amity and commercial intercourse with those people of the East, who are, wholly or in part, independent of the control of the powers of Europe, and are looked upon as of sufficient importance to be entitled to sovereign rights.

After reviewing unsuccessful efforts of European powers to come to terms with the ancient kingdoms that comprised Indochina, he says: — "These people are too sagacious to be influenced by specious arguments or propositions of friendship, unless those professions are accompanied by corresponding acts . . . of national probity."

If this be imperialism, let us have more of it!

Following some not very intelligent remarks on the present and future of China, the Commodore waxes enthusiastic over the possibilities of the "magnificent island" of Formosa and its enormous natural wealth. The imperial government is so feeble that "an American settlement at Kelung would be looked upon with favor by the Chinese." Kelung would not only be a good base for putting down piracy, but "a port of general resort for vessels of all nations." Every country would benefit by "an American settlement, once firmly established in Formosa." Perry begs the American public not to regard "colony" as a dirty word, or object to small settlements "established merely for purposes of trade or some religious or moral object" like the trading factories of the Portuguese and Spanish discoverers; Port Lloyd and Kelung, for example. He conveniently forgot that factories developed into colonies which eventually offended the natives.

In a second article, "The Probable Future Commercial Relations with

Commodore Perry after His Return from Japan

Japan and Lew Chew," Perry states flatly that he regards the Treaty of Kanagawa as only a first step toward commercial relations. The Japanese, he predicts, will want foreign commerce if not coerced, and given time to get used to the idea. Already, he points out, the Bakufu has repealed the ancient law that all Japanese ships be constructed according to one design several centuries old, indicating that they intend to show their flag abroad. Since Japan does not raise sheep, she will need our woolens; and Americans would like to buy the beautiful silks, lacquer and porcelain made in Japan. The Ryukyus "hold out every convenience to vessels passing in their route; fertile beyond measure, as some of them are, and peopled by an inoffensive, industrious race, they could, by the practice of kind and honorable measures toward them, be brought into the most friendly intercourse." But their inveterate pacifism requires that they be protected from pirates and other aggressors.

Perry included in his "Expansion of American Commerce in the East" a prophetic paragraph which one reads today with sadness: —

The constantly ameliorating changes which have transpired in latter times in the laws and customs of war, will no longer justify those measures of coercion and cruelty which were practised in former days. The world will never again countenance rapine and murder; the wanton destruction of edifices of religion and learning, of works of art, and defenceless private property; wars will hereafter be conducted in a manner more honorable and magnanimous; and that nation will deservedly receive the execrations of all good men, who shall henceforth allow of the perpetration of those acts of barbarity which have been of common occurrence *even* in recent times.

But he also made a happier prophecy: America cannot escape the responsibilities created by her growing wealth and power. "In the developments of the future, the destinies of our nation must assume conspicuous attitudes." Assuming that "an overruling Providence" directs "our ultimate destiny" to the Far East, we had better think seriously about it, and make certain that we "act justly and honorably." We should encourage Japan, China and other Oriental nations to become strong and self-reliant; we must never enter the ignoble contest of plucking scales from the Chinese dragon.

The Commodore had more to say on 6 March 1856 before the American Geographical and Statistical Society of New York. "A large attendance of ladies and gentlemen" crowded the chapel of Columbia University. The Reverend Francis L. Hawks, Perry's editor and president of the society, presided and read the paper, after explaining that the Commodore could not do so himself; whether from innate modesty or a sore throat he does not say.

In this address the Commodore stresses the need of a United States line

of Pacific mail steamers and, for the first time in any of his published
writings, gives his views on missions. He has observed them "in different parts of the world," as a sailor. He is interested in "enlightening hea-
thenism, and imparting a knowledge of that revealed truth of God, which
. . . advances man's progress here, and gives him his only safe ground of
hope for hereafter." But "to christianize a strange people, the first important step should be to gain their confidence and respect." His paragraph
on evangelizing Japan includes a generous tribute to the Japanese character: —

With respect to Japan, . . . I am satisfied that their hatred to strangers . . .
proceeded from the abominable wrongs committed by Christians, when they
enjoyed almost unbounded influence in the country; notwithstanding, . . . I
am inclined to believe that, by just and honorable relations with the educated
classes, they will in time listen with patience and respectful attention to the
teachings of our missionaries. They are in most respects a refined and rational
people, and would on this account be more open to conviction than their
neighbors the Chinese, over whom, in almost every essential, they hold a vast
superiority. *Indeed, I have never met in any part of the world, even in
Europe, with a people of more unaffected grace and dignity,* and especially
in the bearing of the nobility.
Much time must necessarily elapse before it would be expedient to send
missionaries to Japan, or to the Lew Chew group. An honorable and friendly
understanding with these countries tending to some preliminary confidence
should, I think, precede the appearance of the Christian teacher.

In his official Narrative, Perry ventured a generalization and a prophecy
that turned out to be remarkably accurate: —

In the practical and mechanical arts, the Japanese show great dexterity,
and when the rudeness of their tools and their imperfect knowledge of machinery are considered, the perfection of their manual skill appears marvellous.
Their handicraftsmen are as expert as any in the world, and, with a freer
development of the inventive powers of the people, the Japanese would not
remain long behind the most successful manufacturing nations. Their curiosity
to learn the results of the material progress of other people, and their readiness
in adapting them to their own uses, would soon, under a less exclusive policy
of government, which isolates them from national communion, raise them to a
level with the most favored countries. Once possessed of the acquisitions of
the past and present of the civilized world, *the Japanese would enter as
powerful competitors in the race for mechanical success in the future.*

Taken together with his remarks scattered through the official Narrative, these three papers establish Perry's reputation as a social and strategic
thinker. He emphatically regarded the Pacific — not the Caribbean which
he knew even better — as America's sea of destiny. He foresaw that strategic control of the Pacific, which the United States finally asserted in

1945, would be a national necessity. He advocated the acquisition of coaling stations, naval bases and the like, for which the American government cared nothing in his day but finally came around to in the twentieth century. It is, therefore, correct to call Perry an "imperialist," but he was an imperialist with a difference, eschewing forcible annexation, punitive expeditions, or forcing religion and trade on people who desired neither. He believed that it was America's mission to bring Christianity, self-government, and a social conscience to heathen lands; but that it could not be done without American strategic control of a vast ocean which by the law of nature and of nations was free for all.

Perry was not so naïve as to expect America to assume this responsibility without opposition, at home and abroad. Before the Expedition started, he regarded England as our future rival, but during the course of it he began to think differently. In one of his papers he states that it is of little importance whether "the time-honored cross of St. George, or the more youthful emblem, the Stars and Stripes of our own country, floated over" the Bonin Islands; either country would give "an equally kind and generous welcome" to mariners of every nation. "And I cheerfully take occasion here to remark, that wherever I have found the British flag, in whatever part of the world, there have I always found a courteous and hospitable reception." But, as a result of his experience with the Russian Japan Expedition and Admiral Putiatin's unwarranted claims of priority, Perry now regarded Russia as our future rival in the Pacific. And he closed this address of 6 March 1856 with a prophetic paragraph, often quoted inaccurately: —

It requires no sage to predict events so strongly foreshadowed to us all; still "Westward" will "the course of empire take its way." But the last act of the drama is yet to be unfolded; and notwithstanding the reasoning of political empirics, Westward, Northward and Southward, to me it seems that the people of America will, in some form or other, extend their dominion and their power, until they shall have brought within their mighty embrace the Islands of the great Pacific, and placed the Saxon race upon the eastern shores of Asia. And I think too, that eastward and southward will her great rival in future aggrandizement (Russia) stretch forth her power to the coasts of China and Siam: and thus the Saxon and the Cossack will meet once more, in strife or in friendship, on another field. Will it be in friendship? I fear not! The antagonistic exponents of freedom and absolutism must meet at last, and then will be fought that mighty battle on which the world will look with breathless interest; for on its issue will depend the freedom or the slavery of the world, — despotism or rational liberty must be the fate of civilized man. I think I see in the distance the giants that are growing up for that fierce and final encounter; in the progress of events that battle must sooner or later inevitably be fought.

After the reading of Perry's paper, President King of Columbia offered a few impromptu remarks, expressing his "surprise that a man tempest-tossed from his youth as Commodore Perry has been, and living on the seas, which . . . are not generally reputed good schools for letters, should have furnished for his countrymen, such a finished memoir as this," in "which clear thoughts and suggestions of high moment are conveyed in forcible and graceful words."

Obviously, naval officers were not expected to write good English! And neither Perry nor any other naval officer received an honorary degree from an American college or university.

Perry's paper created a mild sensation, but his ideas were soon lost sight of. Events were tumbling over one another toward the Civil War. Two months later, a foretaste of it broke out in Kansas. On 19 May Senator Sumner delivered his "Crime Against Kansas" speech, for which he was beaten senseless by a fellow legislator. The recently created Republican Party polled only half a million fewer votes than James Buchanan, whom Perry supported, in the presidential election of 1856. One year to a day from the delivery of Perry's paper, the Supreme Court issued its decision in the Dred Scott case. A few months later there was a panic in the stock market. America had no wish nor could she spare the time or the energy to implement Perry's farsighted proposals. Her thoughts were turned inward, upon problems that were tearing her apart.

The End

One may wonder why Commodore Perry, after displaying remarkable skill in diplomacy, was not appointed to one of the American legations abroad. But he almost did receive the China mission. After James Buchanan had been inaugurated President, and Lewis Cass appointed Secretary of State, James Watson Webb proposed his old neighbor and friend as minister to China. Perry refused to thrust himself forward, and it took a great deal of persuasion before he would allow Webb to press his candidacy. When he did, it was too late. The President had already appointed another politician, William Bradford Reed, to succeed the ineffective McLane. If Perry was disappointed, he never showed it, and he warmly endorsed the appointment of S. Wells Williams as counsellor to the American Legation at Peking.

On 28 December 1857 the Commodore reported that his work on the Narrative was complete; Volume III was already out and Volume II in the press. Two days later he was detached from his nominal post as member of the Naval Efficiency Board and told to stand by to await orders. It was hinted that he might be asked to command the Mediterranean Squadron, which had been his highest ambition in 1851. Biographer Griffis, no doubt quoting Perry's gossipy daughter Isabella, states that "to this duty Perry looked forward with delight." The present biographer believes this to be nonsense. Perry may have relished the proposal as a compliment, but he felt far too depleted and infirm in health to accept a sea command at the "advanced age" of sixty-three. Whatever may have been the case, death intervened before any firm offer could be made.

Early in February, two months after completing his massive publication, Perry caught a severe cold. Rheumatism returned, and led to "rheumatic gout," as arthritis was then called. For weeks he lay in bed, suffering intensively. Despite a change of physicians he became worse and worse. The rheumatism mounted to his heart, and in the small hours of 4 March 1858 he died.

Among the many obituaries, that of the *Morning Courier* was the best. It ended: — "The sum of Commodore Perry's character is this. He was a model of a Naval officer, scrupulously exact in his discipline, and thoroughly American in all his views. He had the valor of a hero, and the capacity of a statesman, but both were outshone by a magnanimous heart, which beat only to the measures of generosity and justice."

For three days, flags on public buildings and on ships in New York harbor were half-masted; and the Commodore's funeral, on the afternoon of Saturday, 6 March, was a civic event. Honorary pallbearers included General Winfield Scott, Commodore John D. Sloat, and Perry's old and trusted shipmates Captains McCluney, Breese and Bigelow. The body was escorted from the Perry residence, 38 West 32nd Street, to St. Mark's Church by New York's crack 7th Regiment, two hundred militia officers, the City Common Council, the Chamber of Commerce, a marine guard, and a contingent of fifty bluejackets who had taken part in the Japan Expedition. These were no official detail but retired shipmates of the Commodore, who happened to be living in or near New York. Volunteers, marching at their own request, they were given an honorable place in the procession, immediately following the hearse. They brushed up their old uniforms or borrowed others, and made their own simple music of fife and drum; the Commodore's Negro orderly carried his beloved banner, the old blue pendant. Mastheaded in a ship, the blue pendant had indicated that "Old Bruin" was on board; displayed ashore, that he was right there, sword in hand, to fight or negotiate as the occasion demanded. This final "tribute of respect and affection to one whom they had once loved to obey," as one newspaper put it, moved spectators to tears.

As the funeral procession passed down Fifth Avenue to 14th Street, then down Second Avenue to St. Mark's at 10th Street, church bells tolled and minute guns were fired by the Brooklyn Navy Yard and by every warship in the harbor.

Within the old stone church of St. Mark's "in the Bouwerie," where

Jane and Calbraith had worshiped during their early married life, the front pews were occupied by Mrs. Perry, Isabella, and members of the Hone, Belmont, Slidell and Rodgers families. Their cousin by marriage, the Reverend Francis Vinton, and the Reverend Francis L. Hawks the editor, assisted the Rector in conducting the service according to the Book of Common Prayer. Many present must have recalled how impressively the Commodore used to read the office for the burial of the dead at sea. The choir led the congregation in singing Perry's favorite hymn by William Augustus Muhlenberg: —

> I would not live alway: I ask not to stay
> Where storm after storm rises dark o'er the way:
> I would not live alway: no — welcome the tomb,
> Since Jesus hath lain there, I dread not its gloom.

Perry had expressed the wish that his body be buried at Newport, but the weather was so boisterous — the half-masted flag on City Hall blew to shreds — that no such journey could then be contemplated for the ladies of the family. Accordingly, the coffin, with the Commodore's sword and chapeau-bras on the lid, was deposited in the Slidell family vault in St. Mark's churchyard, next that of little Anna Perry who had died in infancy. The committal service was read, marines fired three volleys of musketry over the tomb, and the mourners dispersed.

Eight years later the body was translated to Newport as the Commodore wished, and buried in the Island Cemetery near his parents. A brave sailor who had served his country skillfully and faithfully, in war and in peace for nigh half a century, had finally come home.

Epilogue

The surrender of Japan to the peaceful demands of Commodore Perry in 1854 was a more important factor in the
determination of American policy in Asia than any positive
conviction enunciated by the American Government.
— TYLER DENNETT, *Americans in Eastern Asia*

ASSUMING that the reader would like to know what became of Perry's
friends and shipmates frequently mentioned in this narrative, and what
happened in the Far East as a consequence of his Expedition, I am here
securing a number of loose lines. Thus, after a ship has anchored, the
command is "Make everything fast and coil down."

When the Civil War broke, several friends of Perry, trusted subordinates in the Mexican War and the Japan Expedition, joined the Confederacy. Franklin Buchanan became Rear Admiral CSN, Raphael Semmes captain of C.S.S. *Alabama*, Josiah Tattnall commanded coastal naval defenses,
Sidney S. Lee commanded naval defenses of the James River. Dr. Morrow, who had used his ill-deserved grant of $3793.83 to set up a physi-
cian's practice in Charleston, served as surgeon to several Confederate
centers during the war, and died in 1865. But nobody knows what became
of Oqui, the China boy who tenderly nurtured Perry's plants on the five-
month voyage from Hong Kong to Brooklyn and got most of them alive
to Washington. He is the unsung hero of the Japan Expedition. Reverend
Francis Hawks, editor of the official Narrative and a Southerner by birth,
left New York for a Baltimore parish in order to live in a congenial atmosphere, but had to go into hiding to avoid the attentions of the Union
provost marshal. He returned to New York after the war and died in
1866.

All Perry's sons and Rodgers nephews remained loyal to the old flag, as
did the two Sands, Benjamin F. and Joshua R., who rose to be rear admi-

rals after the war. Henry A. Adams, the Commodore's trusted chief of
staff, returned to Japan to exchange ratifications of the Treaty of Kanagawa, and commanded a frigate early in the Civil War. Only a year or
two younger than Perry, he retired as commodore in 1862, but served
through the war as superintendent of coal shipments for the navy. Lieutenant Walke, the naval artist, served with great distinction in the Civil
War, rose to flag rank, retired in 1871 and died in 1896.

Eliphalet Brown Jr., the daguerreotypist, liked the navy so much that
he stayed with it, and during the Civil War earned an ensign's commission. After that he became flag secretary to a commodore of the Mediterranean Squadron, retired in 1875 and died eleven years later. William
Heine returned to Germany in 1859, having already published a partial
German translation of the official Narrative, with some illustrations that
do not appear elsewhere. He also wrote a brief history of Japan in German, and became a private teacher of landscape painting; he died in 1885.

Of the younger officers who wrote entertainingly about the Japan Expedition, Lieutenant Preble had a checkered career in the Civil War but
came through well enough and held various commands thereafter; he retired as rear admiral in 1878 and devoted himself to literature. His *Macedonian* shipmate John G. Sproston, after commanding several small
United States ships, fell in action when leading a landing operation in
1862. Major Jacob Zeilin in 1864 became Colonel Commandant of the marine corps and retired as brigadier general in 1876 after serving for forty-
five years. Acting Master Edward Y. McCauley fought through the war,
rose to flag rank in 1881, and after retirement studied Egyptology, became
a member of several learned societies, and died in 1894. Seaman Hardy,
apparently the last survivor of the Japan Expedition, visited Yokohama in
1917 and, dressed in an old blue uniform, posed for his photograph with
several Japanese friends whom he had met in 1854.

The versatile chaplain George Jones took leave of absence in 1856 and
spent a year in Quito, to continue his studies of zodiacal light. In the following spring he became for a second time chaplain of the Naval Academy. After a short tour of duty in U.S.S. *Minnesota* during the Civil War
he retired, but continued to serve in Union hospitals, and died in 1870.
Commander John Kelly of *Plymouth* received another stripe as a reward
for his gallant action at Shanghai, and retired as commodore in 1862,
shortly before his death. Captain McCluney of *Powhatan* retired in 1861
and died three years later. Silas Bent resigned from the navy in 1856 to
take a job on the Illinois Central Railroad.

Williams and Bettelheim, the rival interpreters whom Perry tactfully
sent to Hong Kong in different ships, had widely divergent careers. Williams served for ten years as secretary and interpreter of the American
legation at Peking; then, at the age of sixty-five, received an appointment

"Auld Lang Syne" at Tokyo, 1917
Seamen Hardy, who had been with Perry, poses under a portrait of the Commodore with five Japanese whom he had met at Yokohama in 1854.

Reunion at Hikone, 1966
Captain Roger Pineau, Mayor Ii of Hikone, statue of Daimyo Ii (Nao-suke) Tairo no kami, and S. E. Morison

to the new chair of Chinese Language and Literature at Yale. He died at New Haven in 1884. Dr. Bettelheim took passage from Hong Kong for England in a ship which put in for repairs at Bermuda, visited the United States, and liked it so much that he bought a farm in Illinois. During the Civil War he served as surgeon in a volunteer regiment. After the war he moved to Brookfield, Missouri, bought a drugstore, and died in 1870. Okinawa eventually did justice to his fruitless efforts to evangelize the Ryukyus by erecting a monument to his memory.

Most of the Japanese with whom Perry dealt did not live long. Ido died in 1854, Hayashi in 1858, Toda the same year, after being promoted Governor of Osaka. Abe died in 1857. Ii (Neasuke), who became the Shogun's prime minister in 1858, was assassinated two years later by retainers of Mito as punishment for favoring foreigners.[1] Kayama, the genial Uraga chief of police whose shipboard conferences helped to smooth the negotiations, was relegated to an inferior post at Edo as punishment for being too intimate with the Americans, and disappears from history.

Perry's plans for coaling stations at Port Lloyd and Naha were not accepted by his government. In view of what happened in World War II, one is tempted to regard this decision as shortsighted; but the probable result of American determination to hold either place would have been an earlier conflict with Japan, which had a legitimate claim to the Bonins and Ryukyus. Nathaniel Savory died in 1874, and the following year Japan formally annexed the Bonins, brought in colonists and renamed Peel and Coffin Islands Chichi and Haha Jima. Sugar cane was introduced, and the entire group denuded of trees. During the Second World War the civilian population was evacuated to Japan because the Bonins became an important Japanese air and naval base, with a garrison of some forty thousand men. They surrendered to Commodore John H. Magruder USN on 3 September 1945. Through Frederick Savory, a descendant of Nathaniel and of Horace Perry Savory, the Commodore obtained evidence that American prisoners had been beheaded, and gobbets of their flesh incorporated by the island commander in his *sukiyaki*. This monster was tried for war crimes at Guam and executed.

In the Japanese-American treaty of 1951 the Bonins were placed under the administration of the United States. The Savory group of settlers, now numbering some two hundred people, have been repatriated, but no Japanese. Consequently, except for the shores of Port Lloyd, these islands have reverted to jungle. When we visited Chichi Jima in 1966, the Savory col-

---

[1] In 1966 we had the pleasure of presenting, on behalf of the Smithsonian Institution, a contemporary statue of Ii to the city of Hikone, of which the elder statesman's great-grandson Dr. Ii (Naoyoshi), had been elected mayor.

ony appeared to be flourishing. Wilson Savory, almost eighty years old, looked the part of an intelligent and energetic Yankee, and his son Nathaniel was carrying on the name and tradition. But the great "character" of the place proved to be eighty-five-year-old "Uncle Charlie" Washington, the son of a native of Madagascar who signed on in an American whaler, jumped ship at Port Lloyd, changed his unpronounceable Malgache name for that of George Washington, and married a daughter of the pioneer Savory. Uncle Charlie's standing joke is that members of the United States Naval Facility at Chichi Jima celebrate annually the birthday of his "adopted great-grandfather."

In Okinawa, Perry's proposals to establish American influence (which he called "surveillance") were never implemented; the Pierce administration washed its hands of "Lew Chew," and the Treaty of Naha, although duly ratified, became dead letter. When Commander John Rodgers, son of Perry's old Commodore, called at Naha within six months of Perry's last visit, he had to set up another formal procession to Shuri to obtain supplies. Okinawa was too far off the beaten track to be of much use to American whalers, or merchant ships. And although Perry's visits aroused the interest of Japan in the Ryukyus, the government hesitated for eighteen years to assert sovereignty. It finally did so as the result of a shipwreck. An Okinawan junk, cast away on a part of the Formosan coast controlled by aborigines, lost her entire crew by murder. China not only refused to accept responsibility for the wild men of Formosa, but claimed that the Ryukyus belonged to her. So, in 1872, Emperor Meiji formally annexed the Ryukyus, allowing the king to remain as governor but ordering him to cease sending tribute to China. The United States, officially informed, raised no objection.

Peaceful Okinawa now for the first time had an army garrison, efficient administrative methods and other reforms which caused much anguish among the population. China protested, claiming her ancient sovereign rights. In 1879 the Japanese government, fearing that ex-president Ulysses S. Grant, then on his world tour, might intervene in this dispute, deposed the king, created the Ryukyus a prefecture of Japan, and strengthened Japanese control over the entire Nansei Shoto, as the Ryukyus were renamed. This was not to the liking of the inhabitants; Japan broke the old pattern of life that Perry's Expedition had observed. The islanders, despised by the Japanese for their pacifism and lack of culture, had the benefit of Japanese schools but otherwise were treated as an inferior race, and not allowed to occupy any of the well-paid positions in government. They continued to speak their own language and to observe their ancient rites and customs. Thousands of Okinawans emigrated to Hawaii, where they became completely loyal to the United States. In 1940, with a population of 839,000, the Ryukyus were one of the most thickly populated parts of the world.

During World War II, in 1945, the Japanese used Okinawa in a desperate defensive campaign, "The Iron Typhoon" as it is called locally. Shuri castle and other ancient monuments were destroyed, and many thousand Okinawan civilians were killed or wounded; but the sharing of this calamity with Japan made the Okinawans for the first time feel that they were fundamentally Japanese. After the war the Ryukyus, according to the Treaty of 1951, remained under United States administration and Okinawa has become an immense American military base. As Perry prophesied, and in an air age of which he had no conception, the strategic situation of this group made it the key to the South China coast, the China Seas, and the Yellow Sea. Land-taking for missile and other sites, as well as the inevitable friction between an occupying force and natives, had caused a certain amount of discontent in this heavily populated island (now 1200 to the square mile), but friendliness between Okinawans and Americans, which Perry proclaimed in 1853, has endured. As an indication of this, the Okinawans themselves celebrate "Perry Day" every June, anniversary of the Commodore's formal landing at Tomari, and put on a procession to Shuri in costume. Americans have reciprocated by returning historical manuscripts and other treasures which the GIs carried away as "souvenirs," and by contributing largely to building a new University of the Ryukyus on the old royal palace grounds. Moreover, under American rule, the Ryukyus have an autonomous government with a freely elected legislature, a municipal government, and a civilian executive. Nevertheless the local politicians are agitating for reunion with Japan. At the inauguration of a new United States high commissioner in November 1966, Reverend Osamu Tairo prayed that he would be the last of his line and that "Okinawa will be returned to what it once was."

Of Perry's proposed three-pronged insular empire there remains Formosa. Over this "Beautiful Isle" he proposed, with Chinese consent, to establish a protectorate in order to control the coal-bearing northern end, and suppress the piratical activities of the east-coast aborigines. The Reverend Dr. Peter Parker, the medical missionary whom President Pierce appointed minister to China in 1855, strongly urged this on his government; but the Pierce administration instructed both the ambitious doctor and his successor to keep hands off Formosa. In the meantime, with Parker's encouragement, two American "China hands" at Hong Kong obtained from local mandarins a camphor-exporting concession at Takao (now Kaohsiung) on the southwest coast of Formosa, and ran up the Stars and Stripes at the harbor entrance. After two years' profitable trade they sold out to an English firm. That was the end of the "American colony" in Formosa.

China's failure to exercise control over the wild coast of Formosa stimulated Japan to acquire the island; at the end of her war with China in 1895, she secured it for fifty years. Reoccupied by China in 1945, Taiwan (Formosa) became the seat of Chiang Kai-Shek's Nationalist Chinese government. Hence, by another unpredictable overturn, Chiang's dependence on subsidies has made Formosa a fulcrum of American strategic power in the Orient.

Thus, by devious ways and through strange chances, Perry's ambition for his country to control the Western Pacific through naval bases in the Bonins, Okinawa, and Formosa, reached fruition about a century after his death.

In Japan, Perry started something, the consequences of which "no one can at present foretell," as he himself said in 1855; nor can anyone now predict the end. The uneasy epoch of fifteen years that followed his second visit was filled with episodes that have the unearthly logic of a dream. As Sir George Sansom put it, "From the highest sources issue proclamations which do not say what they mean or mean what they say. The Throne rebukes great officers for doing what it has already approved, or enjoins them not to do what it knows they have already done. . . . Patriots assassinate other patriots for views they have never held or professed, and statesmen declare intentions which everybody knows to be contrary to their real purpose." Confusion incident to changing abruptly from a medieval hermit state to a modern nation explains a good deal of this. The basic issue was what to do about these importunate "outer barbarians," American and European, who insisted on breaking Japan's exclusion laws. There is no doubt that "throw 'em out!" was the wish of the samurai. And the dismay with which conservative Japanese saw barbarians breaking into their beloved country was accented by disasters of nature. The imperial palaces at Kyoto burned down shortly after Perry's second visit. There were three big earthquakes, one of which destroyed the castle and ten thousand houses in Edo. A conflagration in which more than a hundred thousand lives were lost followed. According to a Japanese historian, "These constantly occurring signs and wonders were attributed by the people to the anger of the gods at the continual pollution of our country by the visits of the outer barbarians."

One of these disastrous portents heralded Captain Henry A. Adams's return to Japan to exchange ratifications of the Treaty of Kanagawa. He arrived off Shimoda in U.S.S. *Powhatan* on 25 January 1855. About a month earlier, as a result of an underwater earthquake, Shimoda harbor had been sucked dry to a depth of five or six fathom, then submerged by an enormous wave which overflowed the town to its rooftops, and this happened five times in succession. Admiral Putiatin's flagship *Diana*, lying there at the time, crashed on the harbor bottom, whirled helplessly round and round the harbor islet, and foundered in the open sea; her ship-wrecked crew had to be fed from *Powhatan's* stores.

Captain Adams's exchange of ratifications encountered evasions similar to those of the treaty negotiation. Having no senate to "advise and consent," the Japanese officials could not understand why ratification was necessary, after the Emperor had given his word; and when convinced that it must be done, they engaged in a long hassle over who would sign the instrument. Adams, following the Perry pattern of patient firmness, insisted that the Emperor sign, since President Pierce had signed the corresponding American document; but he was told that the Emperor never signed anything! After almost a month spent in argument, he compromised on having the Shogun affix his seal, and in a Shimoda temple which the earthquake had spared, ratifications were exchanged on 21 February 1855. "I found the Japanese during my visit much more disposed to be friendly and sociable than formerly," reported Adams. *Powhatan's* officers roamed about town and country with no police escort, were welcomed everywhere, bought souvenirs freely, and High Commissioner Izawa Mimasaka no kami declared he would not only welcome trading vessels from America, but be pleased to have an American consul reside there. Obviously the Bakufu was softening up.

But not altogether. The first American consul had a very cold reception. This was Townsend Harris, a public-spirited merchant of New York trading with the Far East, who had met Perry in Hong Kong. President Pierce in August 1855 appointed Harris consul-general to Japan and special agent to obtain a commercial treaty. Commodore Perry warmly approved the appointment, although he had hoped Bayard Taylor would get the job. When Harris arrived off Shimoda in steam frigate *San Jacinto*, the anti-foreign daimyo were in the ascendant at Edo. The Bakufu protested that we had no right to send a consul until and unless they asked for one; but Harris persisted, obtained the Gyukosenji temple for his residence, and raised an American flag to emphasize his official character. For eighteen months he remained on his own, with no word from his government, snubbed by the Japanese and having as sole male companion a Dutch interpreter. According to local tradition, he enjoyed a form of consolation that Perry never had — the company of a beautiful young girl named Okichi.[1] With no naval support such as Perry enjoyed, Harris by

---

[1] This possibly mythical romance of the Consul and the Geisha is a favorite subject in Japanese popular literature and theatre; Okichi therein becomes a key figure, as important as Perry or Harris, in establishing Nippon-American friendship.

tact and persistence managed to negotiate a convention on 17 June 1857. It gave the United States the right to appoint consuls at Shimoda and Hakodate, each to enjoy extra-territorial rights; and established an exchange rate reversing the earlier unfavorable one.

Since this was not the commercial treaty which he had been sent to obtain, Harris insisted on calling personally on the Shogun at Edo, both to present a letter from the President to the Emperor, and to negotiate a treaty. By patiently waiting until the "get tough" boys had lost influence and Ii Kamon no kami had become the Shogun's prime minister, he got away with it. And, having learned from Perry the value that the Japanese attached to ceremonial, he did the thing in style by a regular daimyo procession such as Hiroshige depicts in his *Fifty-three Stages of Tokkaido*. Over 350 persons, horse and foot, escorted the first diplomatic official of a foreign power ever to be received by a Shogun, from Shimoda to Edo. Harris had built for himself an oversize palanquin, which required twelve bearers, but rode mostly on horseback, especially when crossing the high mountains of the Izu peninsula. An American flag on a staff headed the procession, arms of the United States were embroidered on dark blue gowns worn by bearers and retainers, and boy heralds ran ahead crying *shitaniro* (get down!) to the populace. And down they got — the common people averting their eyes as token of respect, the gentry knocking their foreheads on the ground. After seven nights en route, spent at official inns, the cavalcade entered Edo on 30 November 1857 and crossed the moat to the castle, within which Harris received quarters. Eight commissioners, including Hayashi and Udono who had served in 1854, were appointed to treat with him. Received in audience by the Shogun, Harris presented the President's letter to his "Great and Good Friend" the Emperor, and received a courteous reply which concluded, "Intercourse shall be continued forever."

Seemingly interminable negotiations followed, and a plot to assassinate Harris was frustrated. Finally on 2 March 1858, two days before the death of Commodore Perry, the Shogun's Council accepted in principle the draft of a commercial treaty which, as Dennett wrote, became "the basis of Japan's foreign relations until near the close of the century." Americans in Japan were even permitted the exercise of the Christian religion within their own dwellings, a concession that would have been unthinkable at the time of Perry's visit. This treaty was signed on 29 July, after a visit of U.S.S. *Mississippi* and *Powhatan* to Edo, and, appropriately, on board Perry's old flagship. President Buchanan then rewarded Harris by promotion to the rank of minister resident to Japan. In 1860 the Japanese sent a mission to Washington to exchange ratifications of Harris's treaty — their first foreign mission since 1600. Thus Harris proved to be a worthy successor to Perry. But it should not be forgotten that the Commodore set the pattern to which the Consul General conformed; or that Harris, in building on bases established by Perry, virtually completed his work. Moreover, owing to Perry's pioneer work, England, France, Russia and other European powers were able to obtain treaties similar to his. By 1859 Yokohama, opened to foreign trade and foreign merchants, began growing from a little village to a great commercial city, and the coal depot established there became far more valuable to American steamship lines than Port Lloyd or Naha could ever have been.

There were several ups and downs in American-Japanese relations during the following years, during most of which civil war raged in Japan as in America: anti-foreign forces battling liberals. The Daimyo of Chosu, an especially vehement isolationist, ordered his forts on Shimonoseki Strait to fire on all black ships, including one flying the Stars and Stripes. U.S.S. *Wyoming* replied on 16 July 1863, and a French landing force destroyed the batteries; but the strait remained closed to foreign shipping until September 1864 when a combined expedition of the Royal British, Imperial French and Royal Netherlands Navies bombarded Shimonoseki and removed the cannon.

Finally, in 1868, the Bakufu was overthrown by determined anti-foreign daimyo and other aristocratic leaders, the last Shogun banished, and the young Emperor Meiji brought to Edo, the name of which was changed to Tokyo. Then, by the most stupendous paradox in a history full of paradoxes, Emperor Meiji repudiated his following, adopted harmonious relations with all foreign powers, and brought his country into line with modern technology.

In 1901, on the site of the reception hall at Kurihama where Perry delivered President Fillmore's letter to the Emperor, a granite shaft was erected to the memory of the Commodore. It was unveiled by Rear Admiral Frederick Rodgers, a great-nephew of Commodore Perry, and the Japanese premier Viscount Katsura delivered a memorial address. This monument was thrown down by superpatriots in 1944; but during the peace which followed, when friendly relations between the two countries were restored, it was reërected, and a centenary celebration took place there in 1953. Annual Black Ship Festivals are also held at Shimoda, Hakodate and Naha.

The attitudes of Japanese historians toward Perry have varied according to the temper of the time and the writers' basic ideas; those wedded to the Marxian dialectic, as many are, feel obliged to denigrate the Commodore as an "imperialist" harboring territorial designs on Japan; but even they are forced to admit that he unwittingly served their country well by helping her to get rid of "feudalism." On the other hand, a recent work on Japan's Representative Men (1961) by Itchimura praises Perry's restraint, denies that he was in any sense an imperialist, and goes so far as to call his

Japanese mission "sublime." During my stay in Tokyo in 1966, a charming young Japanese matron who holds a doctoral degree from Columbia University, put it this way: "I'm for Perry, of course. But for him I would be doing nothing but pouring tea and arranging flowers!"

So, let us leave the subject there. The cordial relations initiated by Perry, although broken during a bitter war, were welded again by the good will of both peoples, under the leadership of President Truman, Emperor Hirohito and General Douglas MacArthur. May they endure forever!

Appendix

Appendix

CHILDREN OF MATTHEW CALBAITH and
JANE (SLIDELL) PERRY
married 24 December 1814 at Grace Church, New York
Commodore Perry died in New York City, 4 March 1858, aged 64.
Mrs. Perry died 14 June 1879, aged 82.

1. John Slidell Perry, b. New York 29 Feb. 1816, d. 24 March 1817.

2. Sarah Perry, b. New York 8 Jan. 1818; m. at Commandant's quarters, Brooklyn Navy Yard, 15 Dec. 1841, Robert S. Rodgers, son of Commodore John Rodgers and nephew to her uncle by marriage, Lieutenant George W. Rodgers. All their sons and sons-in-law served in the U.S.N. or U.S.A. Their grandson John Rodgers (1881-1926), a pioneer naval aviator, chief of the Bureau of Naval Aeronautics, was killed in an airplane crash.

3. Jane Oliver Hazard Perry, b. New York 31 Oct. 1819; m. 20 Oct. 1841, at Commandant's quarters, Brooklyn Navy Yard, John Hone, son of John Hone II and Maria de Peyster and great-nephew of Philip Hone the social leader and diarist. Jane d. 24 Dec. 1882.

4. Matthew C. Perry, Jr., b. New York 6 Oct. 1821; warranted midshipman 1835, passed midshipman 1841. Served in U.S.S. *Potomac* and *Missouri*, and in *Somers* during the mutiny. Served under his father during the Mexican War and continuously thereafter in the navy, rising to be Captain usn. He m. 26 April 1853 Harriet E. Taylor of Brooklyn. She d. 2 June 1859, aged 24; he d. 16 Nov. 1873.

5. Susan M. Perry, b. New York 24 May 1824, d. 15 Aug. 1825.

6. Oliver Hazard Perry II, b. New York 9 Aug. 1825, never married. Captain's clerk and acting midshipman in U.S.S. *Somers* during the mutiny; studied law in New Orleans; went to California with the forty-niners, served as his father's clerk in the Japan Expedition, and afterwards was appointed U.S. consul at Hong Kong; d. London 17 Nov. 1870.

7. William Frederick Perry, b. New London 20 May 1828; 2nd Lieutenant usmc in the Mexican War, attached to U.S.S. *Mississippi* commanded by his father. He did not amount to much and d. unmarried, 18 March 1884.

8. Caroline Slidell Mackenzie Perry, b. Charlestown Navy Yard 23 Aug. 1829; m. 7 Nov. 1849 in Church of the Ascension, New York, August Belmont,

financier, sportsman and diplomat. He d. 24 Nov. 1890; she, 20 Nov. 1892.[1]

9. Isabella Bolton Perry, b. New York 1 Sept. 1834, m. at New York, 17 Aug. 1864, George Tiffany of Baltimore. She d. 5 Jan. 1912, last of her generation.

10. Anna Rodgers Perry, b. New York 30 March 1838, d. 9 March 1839.

CHILDREN OF CHRISTOPHER RAYMOND PERRY and SARAH WALLACE (ALEXANDER) PERRY
Christopher, 1761-1818; Sarah, 1768-1830

1. Oliver Hazard Perry, b. 20 Aug. 1785, m. 1811 Elizabeth Champlin Mason, d. 23 Aug. 1819. Victor of Battle of Lake Erie, Captain usn. Mrs. Perry d. 1858. Their son Oliver Hazard Perry Jr., b. 1815, warranted midshipman 1829, Lieutenant usn 1841, who resigned from the service after the Mexican War in 1849 and d. 1878, is often confused with his first cousin O. H. Perry II. Another son, Christopher Grant Perry, m. Frances Sergeant of Philadelphia; Thomas Sergeant Perry (1845-1925) was their son. The fifth child, Elizabeth Mason Perry, born 1819 after the Commodore's death, m. 1841 the Reverend Francis Vinton.

2. Raymond Henry Jones Perry, b. 1789, m. 1814 Mary Ann (or Marianne) D'Wolf of Bristol, Rhode Island, daughter of Senator James D'Wolf. He entered U. S. Navy, commanded a vessel under Commodore Macdonough in Battle of Plattsburg, d. 12 March 1826. She then m. Gen. William H. Sumner and d. 1834. Raymond's children were James DeWolf Perry of Bristol, R. I., J. Alexander Perry, and Nancy B. Perry. Raymond's great-grandson James De-Wolf Perry, became Bishop of the Episcopal diocese of Rhode Island.

3. Sarah Wallace Perry, b. 1791, d. 1851 unmarried.

4. Matthew Calbraith Perry, b. 10 April 1794, m. Jane Slidell 24 Dec. 1814, d. 4 March 1858. The subject of this biography.

5. Anna Maria Perry, b. 1797, m. July 1815 Lieutenant George Washington Rodgers usn (1787-1832), younger brother of Commodore John Rodgers and veteran of the War of 1812. He d. Buenos Aires 1832 when in command of the Brazil Squadron U.S.N. Anna Maria d. 1856. Their son Christopher Raymond Perry Rodgers (1819-1892) entered the navy, sailed with his uncle Matthew C. Perry in the Africa Squadron, m. Julia Slidell, a younger sister of John Slidell and of Mrs. M. C. Perry. After a notable naval career, he became Superintendent of the Naval Academy 1874-1878.

The third son of Christopher R. P. and Julia Rodgers, George Washington Rodgers (b. 1822), entered the navy and as Commander was killed in the attack on Charleston in 1863. The fourth son, Alexander Perry Rodgers (1825-1847), 1st Lieutenant 4th U. S. Infantry, was killed in the attack on Chapultepec.

---

[1] Their children were Perry Belmont, b. 1850; August Belmont Jr., organizer of the Triborough Subway and the Cape Cod Canal, and sportsman, b. 1853, m. (1) 1881 Bessie Morgan; (2) 1910 Eleanor Robson, the Mrs. Belmont who has been of great help to this writer; Fredericka Belmont, b. 1859, m. 1877 Samuel Shaw Howland; Oliver H. Perry Belmont, b. 1858, member of Congress; Raymond Rodgers Belmont, b. 1863.

The fifth son, John Frederic Rodgers, was Captain U. S. Army in the Civil War. Two more sons of C. R. P. Rodgers entered the navy and rose to be rear admirals; Frederick Rodgers and John A. Rodgers, and another, Calbraith Perry Rodgers became Captain usn. His son C. P. Rodgers Jr., a pioneer aviator, was killed in an airplane crash in 1912.

6. Jane Tweedy Perry, b. 1799, m. 1819 Dr. William Butler, naval surgeon. They had seven daughters and ten sons, including Christopher R. Perry Butler whom his uncle the Commodore offered to make captain's clerk in the Mexican War, and Matthew Calbraith Butler (1836-1909), general C.S.A. and U. S. Senator from South Carolina.

7. James Alexander Perry (1801-1822), midshipman in brother Oliver's flagship at Lake Erie, later Lieutenant usn. Drowned at Valparaiso while trying to save a shipmate.

8. Nathaniel Hazard Perry (1802-1832), purser in the navy; m. 1828 Lucretia M. Thatcher of New London. Their son Alexander James Perry graduated from the Military Academy in 1847 and at the end of the Civil War was breveted brigadier general "for faithful and meritorious service."

Bibliography

Bibliography

LIST OF ABBREVIATIONS

DAB	*Dictionary of American Biography*
FDRL	Franklin D. Roosevelt Library, Hyde Park, N.Y.
Griffis	William E. Griffis *Matthew C. Perry* (1887)
HCL	Harvard College Library, including Houghton and Gray Herbarium
HEHL	Henry E. Huntington Library, San Marino, California
HI Tokyo	Historiographical Institute, University of Tokyo
HS Pa.	Historical Society of Pennsylvania, Philadelphia
LC	Library of Congress
MHS	Massachusetts Historical Society, Boston
NA	National Archives, Washington, D.C.
NAM	Naval Academy Museum, Annapolis
NYHS	New York Historical Society
NYPL	New York Public Library
PRO	Public Records Office, London
USNI	U. S. Naval Institute *Proceedings*
Yale	Sterling or Beinecke Library, Yale University

GENERAL

There is no corpus of M. C. Perry manuscripts, as his heirs dispersed most of his files, keeping only a few letters and documents. The most important collections of scattered letters in the hands of descendants are the Belmont mss. (Mrs. August Belmont, New York), Phelps mss. (Mrs. Gouverneur Phelps, South Ashfield, Mass.), and Tilton mss. (Mrs. Theodora Tilton, Littleton, N.H.). All three kindly lent me what they had. Many of Perry's letters, sea journals, etc., went to his Rodgers nephews and descendants and are now included in the Rodgers mss., HS Pa. Almost every historical society in the United States, and many libraries too, have a few original letters which will be mentioned in due course.

The United States Navy Department files in NA (National Archives, Washington) contain Perry's official correspondence, and many of his sea journals and letter books. Others are in LC, Ms. Division.

The only biography of Perry worthy of the name is William Elliot Griffis *Matthew Calbraith Perry: A Typical American Naval Officer* (1887). The title is unfortunate, as Perry was anything but typical, but Griffis visited Japan in the 1870's, knew Perry's background, and obtained anecdotes from his surviving children and former shipmates. C. O. Paullin's sketch in DAB is good as far as it goes. General naval histories, of which the best is Dudley W. Knox *A History of the United States Navy*, have considerable data about Perry. Griffis's mss. are in Rutgers Univ. Library.

I and II: PEACEFUL PERRYS AND CAPTAIN CHRISTOPHER

FAMILY: Calbraith B. Perry *The Perrys of Rhode Island* (1913), the best of the Perry genealogies, states that Edward Perry circulated a tract called *A Warning to New England*, in which he denounced the degeneracy of that part of the world, and for which he was fined £50. No such tract, or any publication by that Perry, can be found in any catalogue of colonial or contemporary English imprints. The statements about his fines are in *Records of the Colony of New Plymouth*. Other important genealogies are Caroline E. Robinson *The Hazard Family of Rhode Island* (1895), Dorcas W. Matteson *Record of the Ancestry and Descendants of Edward Barber* (1892), and Samuel Raymond *Genealogies of the Raymond Families of New England* (1886). Caroline Hazard *The Narragansett Friends' Meeting* (1899); Esther B. Carpenter *South County Studies* (1924) pp. 175-94; W. D. Miller "The Narragansett Planters," American Antiquarian Society *Proceedings* XLIII (1933) 49-115.

WAR OF INDEPENDENCE: Sketch of C. R. Perry by Paullin in DAB. Details on R.I. privateers in William P. Sheffield *Address Before the Rhode Island Historical Society* (1883). For Nicholson, G. W. Allen *Naval History of Am. Rev.* II 499-506 and Almon's *Remembrancer* X 142-43, 225-27. *Favorite's* arrival is noted in *Pennsylvania Packet* 3 Aug. 1784.

The Newport birthplace of M. C. Perry is proved by the fact that his mother was attended by Dr. Isaac Senter, who did not practise on the other side of the Bay. His account book is in the R. I. Hist. Soc. The baptismal record of Trinity Church shows that our hero was christened Matthew James Calbreth; but he never used the James, and spelled his middle name Calbraith, as did his namesake.

III: NEWPORT AND THE *GENERAL GREENE*

Antoinette F. Downing and Vincent J. Scully Jr. *The Architectural Heritage of Newport* (1952); Carl Bridenbaugh "Colonial Newport as a Summer Resort," R. I. Hist. Soc. *Collections* XXVI (1933); George G. Channing *Early Recollections of Newport* (1868); Records of Trinity Church; files of *The Newport Mercury*. For the Frazer school and the Perry brothers' zeal for improving the minds of their officers, Alexander S. Mackenzie *Life of Oliver H. Perry* (1840) I 28-30, II 140-41.

NAVAL WAR WITH FRANCE: C. R. Perry's letters to and from Toussaint and General Wilkinson, Belmont mss. Dudley W. Knox ed. *Naval Documents Related to the Quasi-War Between the United States and France* (6 vols., 1935-38). Appendix B of H. P. Sannon *Histoire de Toussaint Louverture* II (Port-au-Prince 1933). Record of court of inquiry on Capt. Perry, NA "Court Martial Records" I No. 6. G. W. Allen *Our Naval War with France* (1909).

IV and V: WAR OF 1812

Christopher Perry's letter to Senator Foster and Calbraith's boyish letter to Breese belong to Mrs. Henry W. Hitzrot of Westport, Conn. Oliver H. Perry's letter of 15 Dec. 1812 in HEHL. M. C. Perry's Journal kept on board *President*, Rodgers mss. LC.

Debates about the Navy in *Annals of Congress*, 11 Cong. Documents of *Little Belt* inquiry, *Am. State Pap., Foreign Relations* III 471-99, *Wait's State Papers* VII (1815) 404-19. *Highflyer* episode, B. J. Lossing *Pictorial Field Book of the War of 1812* (1868). C. O. Paullin *Commodore John Rodgers* (1910); Mahan *Sea Power . . . War of 1812* Vol. I; Henry Adams *United States* Vol. VI.

BATTLE OF LAKE ERIE: Mahan, Adams and Lossing have excellent secondary accounts;

they and George Bancroft *History of the Battle of Lake Erie* (1891) decidedly favor Perry. Sources and statistics in Paullin ed. *The Battle of Lake Erie . . . Documents* (1918), and William Wood ed. *British Documents . . . War of 1812* (1920).

VI *and* VII: NEW YORK AND LIBERIA, 1814-1822

New York City directories, NYPL. Genealogies mentioned under Chapter I. Life at Bristol when *Chippewa* was building, and O. H. Perry's last cruise, Mackenzie's *O. H. Perry* Vol. II and Thomas Harris *Life of William Bainbridge* (1837).

FOUNDING OF LIBERIA: Jehudi Ashmun *History of the American Colony in Liberia* (1826) and Ralph R. Gurley *Life of Jehudi Ashmun* (1839). Early L. Fox *The American Colonization Society 1817-1840* (1919). For Perry's part (1) his ms. *Cyane* journal, NAM (extracts and letters in *Maryland Colonization Journal* II, 1843, 328-30); (2) his private Journal in *Shark*, of which the ms. to 10 Oct. 1821 is in FDRL and extracts from the whole were printed (very inaccurately) in *Life in Letters*, "American Autograph Journal" VII (1941) 50-64; (3) Official logs of *Cyane* and *Shark*, NA, and part of *Shark's* printed in 27 Cong. 3 Sess. Ho. Rep. III No. 283 p. 821. List of the first colonists in 28 Cong. 2 Sess. Pub. Docs. IX No. 150 pp. 152-54. Perry's letter of 1819 to his brother Raymond, C. B. Perry *The Perrys of Rhode Island;* letter of 24 July 1821 to Rodgers, Perry Letter Book I, NA.

Other contemporary accounts: Midshipman William F. Lynch *Naval Life; or, Observations Afloat and On Shore* (1851); Edgar S. Maclay *Reminiscences of the Old Navy* (1898) of which chap. i is based on Capt. Trenchard's mss.; the anon. *Sketch of the Life of Com. Robert F. Stockton* (1856) chap. iv.

SEAMEN'S HEALTH: Blane's *Select Dissertations* (1822) reprints his 1815 article; also reprinted in Christopher L. Loyd *The Health of Seamen* (Navy Records Society, 1965) pp. 133, 185 and ff, and (with J. L. S. Coulter) *Medicine and the Navy* IV (London: 1963) 173-93. Prof. Loyd suggests that Perry may have read William Turnbull *The Naval Surgeon* (1806) and T. Winterbottom *Medical Directions for the Use of Navigators* (1807).

VIII: HUNTING PIRATES IN WEST INDIES

Perry's log of *Shark* in West Indies waters, letter to Commo. Rodgers and letter to Commo. Porter, in Rodgers mss. and Gratz coll., HS Pa.; Perry's own Letter Book in NA. His correspondence with Commo. Porter, and Porter's with Secnav, in *Am. State Pap. Naval Aff.* I 1109 and II 222-41; Commo. Biddle's in same, 191-203. Contemporary copies of Perry's letters to Porter in HEHL.

Caspar F. Goodrich "Our Navy and the West Indian Pirates, a Documentary History," a series of articles in USNI July 1916 to Sept. 1917. Francis B. C. Bradlee *Piracy in the West Indies and Its Suppression* (1923) adds data from newspapers. G. W. Allen boils down Goodrich in *Our Navy and the West Indian Pirates* (1929). For Midshipman Lynch, see previous chapter. Nicholas B. Wainwright "Commo. James Biddle" in *Penn. Mag. Hist.* XC (1966) 19-21. The 1824 invitation from Perry to J. Fenimore Cooper, Yale. Perry's letter to Breese belongs to Mr. W. Breese Welling of New York.

IX: FIRST LIEUTENANT OF *NORTH CAROLINA*

Commodore Rodgers's ms. Journal of *North Carolina* and Letter Book 1825-27, LC. The following are in NA: official log of *North Carolina;* photostat of Midshipman W. L. Rodgers's log; Midshipman Goldsborough's and William J. Slidell's ms. Journals, 1825-27. Chaplain C. H. Alden's ms. Journal of a cruise in U.S.S. *Delaware*, 1841-42, illustrated by himself, is most illuminating; this is in private hands. Perry's views on the duties of "1st Luff," 3 Oct. 1835 to Lt. W. C. Nicholson, at back of *Concord* Letter Book (Rodgers mss. HS Pa.). Perry's letters on recruiting, and little Sarah's letter to cousin Oliver, HS Pa. Letter of 5 Jan. 1824 in *The Army and Navy Chronicle* 2 April 1840. Conner mss. FDRL for gossip about Commo. Patterson.

Several young men with literary talent enlisted in the navy at this period and recorded their impressions. Herman Melville, the most noted, wrote *White Jacket* (1850) and his diary on board, ed. by Charles R. Anderson, is printed as *Journal of a Cruise to the Pacific Ocean, 1842-1844, in the Frigate United States* (1937). S. R. Franklin *Memoirs of a Rear Admiral* (1898) tells about the same cruise. Walter McJ. Merrill edited the untrustworthy *Behold Me Once More, the Confessions of James Holley Garrison* (1934). Other seamen's narratives are Nathaniel Ames *A Mariner's Sketches* (1830); William McNally *Evils and Abuses in the Naval and Merchant Service Exposed* (1839); Charles Nordhoff *Man-of-War Life* (1856), reprinted in *Nine Years a Sailor* (1857) and again as *Life on the Ocean* (1874).

K. Jack Bauer "Naval Building Programs," *Military Affairs* XXIX (1965) 30-36; James C. Tily *The Uniforms of the United States Navy* (1964) pp. 94-96; Charles Morris *Autobiography* (1880); E. A. Sherman *Life of Rear Admiral John D. Sloat* (1902). For Flogging, see next chapter.

X: *CONCORD* TO RUSSIA AND MEDITERRANEAN

Sea Journal of *Concord* and her log, in several volumes, are in NA; Perry's Letter Book and letter to John Rodgers, HS Pa; other letters in Alderman Lib., Univ. of Va., *The American Clipper* (organ of American Autograph Shop) Aug. 1936 p. 435; Jackson mss. and Van Buren mss., LC; Belmont mss., Tilton mss., J. S. Bassett ed. *Correspondence of Andrew Jackson* IV 363-64, and William C. Bruce *John Randolph* (1922) I 644-45. Clerk Jenckes's narrative, reported in Griffis, is not now to be found. Secnav's orders to Perry of 1 June 1830 in Tilton mss., those of 14 June in NA. Several myths have sprung up about this cruise to Russia: — (1) John Randolph fell on his knees, or his face, when he first met the Emperor; that was denied by him and by others who were present. (2) Perry dined with the Emperor; no record of any meeting between the two except the stand-up one at the palace. (3) Emperor visited and inspected *Concord;* no mention of it in her log.

NAPLES MISSION: State Dept. Archives "Italy and Naples" Vol. I Nelson to Sec. Livingston 12 July and 3 Sept. 1832. Griffis's account is based allegedly on an article by Rear Adm. Almy in *Washington Republican* 13 March 1884, which does not exist, at least not there. Commo. Biddle's trip in *Concord, Penna. Mag. Hist.* XC (Jan. 1966) 31. The goblets were owned by the late Sarah L. Merrell.

ABOLITION OF FLOGGING: Leo F. S. Horan, "Flogging in the U. S. Navy," USNI LXXVI (1950) 969-75. Master Commandants' Letters, Jan.-June 1832, NA; Letter of Secnav 8 Feb. 1849 with enclosures 30 Cong. 2 Sess. Ho. Exec. Doc. 51. Perry's letters to William Sinclair, NAM; his official "Report in respect to Corporal Punishment," 4 July 1850, in Letter Book 1849-51, Yale. *An Essay on Flogging in the Navy* (1849). *Corporal Punishment in the Navy. Speech of Mr. Mallory of Florida . . . 14-15 Jan. 1852,* against abolition. USNI LV (1929) 271 presents claims of Ulrich P. Levy to have been the abolisher.

BOTANY: Letter of H. A. S. Dearborn to Perry, 14 Dec. 1832, Tilton mss. I have sought in vain for further correspondence between Perry and Dearborn — the Mass. Hort. Soc. appears to have destroyed all records as well as the specimens.

INCREASE OF PAY: Perry's leaflet urging increase, HEHL. Perry's special grant of $1500 attested in NA, Fiscal Div. Treas. Dept., Navy Pay Warrant No. 6311.

XI: NAVY REFORMER

BROOKLYN NAVY YARD, STEAM NAVY AND ORDNANCE: *Diary of Philip Hone* (Tuckerman or Nevins ed.), and the ms. in NYHS. Letter Book of 4th Auditor of Treas., 27 Dec. 1833, NA. Perry to Conner, 24 Nov. 1841, Anthony Collection, NYPL. Perry to Lt. W. L. Hudson 30 Jan. 1835, and to Navy Commissioners 7 Sept. 1835, HS Pa. "Report of Gun Practice by Capt. M. C. Perry, 12 Oct. 1839," with panorama of the

Staten Island range and covering letter to Sec. Paulding, NAM. Annual Report of
Secnav for 1841, 27 Cong. 2 Sess. Sen. Docs. I 367-80; Perry to Sec. Paulding 20 Feb.
1841, "Navy Box" at Ms. Div. NYPL, and an earlier report quoted by Griffis p. 115;
Perry to Aspinwall 31 Jan. and 18 April 1842, NYHS; Chauncey to Perry 23 May
1839, Tilton mss. Perry's letters to W. L. Redfield, Redfield mss., Yale.

Article "Thoughts on the Navy," *The Naval Magazine* II (1837) 1-42, is signed
"A.S." — Perry's brother-in-law Alexander Slidell, an associate editor, who had not
yet added Mackenzie to his name. He wrote it in close collaboration with Perry and
expressed his ideas. James P. Baxter *Introduction of Ironclad Warship* (1933) for
Paixhans guns and ramming; H. I. Chapelle *History of the American Sailing Navy;*
Frank M. Bennett *Steam Navy of the United States* (1896).

EDUCATION, SCIENCE, AND THE LYCEUM: *Naval Magazine* II (1837) 23-25. Perry's rec-
ommendation of 5 Jan. 1824 printed in *Army and Navy Chronicle* 2 April 1840; 27
Cong. 2 Sess. Sen. Doc. I, No. 1 p. 373; *U. S. Statutes at Large* V (1836-45) 153.
Rates of pay from estimates in Secnav's 1837 report in 25 Cong. 2 Sess. Ho. Exec.
Docs. I No. 3 pp. 775-92. See III, above, for Perry's efforts to educate officers in the
Mediterranean. Perry's letter to Usher Parsons, William L. Clements Library, Ann
Arbor. James Russell Soley *Historical Sketch of the U. S. Naval Academy* (1876);
M. A. DeWolfe Howe *Life and Letters of George Bancroft* (1908) I 276-7; Michael
Lewis *England's Sea Officers* p. 88; F. M. Brown "A Half Century of Frustration,"
USNI LXXX (1954) 631 ff. *Report of a Special Committee of the U. S. Naval
Lyceum, on the Progress and Condition of the Institution* (1839). Lt. Cdr. S. de Chris-
tofaro's brief account of the Lyceum in USNI LXXVII (1951) 869-73. The "Book of
Donations" and an inventory of the Lyceum when broken up in 1892 are in NAM. In
Concord Letter Book (Rodgers mss. HS Pa.) pp. 60-61, Perry writes to Master John
Bates RN, offering to exchange shells of the Mediterranean for those of the British Isles.

LIGHTHOUSE MISSION: Perry's Letter Book of the 1837 commission, FDRL. His Report of 9 Dec. 1837, 25 Cong. 2 Sess. Sen. Doc. 375; later report, submitted to Congress
25 July 1840 by President Van Buren, 26 Cong. 1 Sess. Sen. Doc. 619 (1840). Perry's
letters to Andrew Stevenson 16 Feb. 1839, and "Notes" dated 8 Dec. 1838 on lighthouse situation, Stevenson mss., LC. Report of Lighthouse Board 15 Jan. 1853 carrying
out most of Perry's recommendations, 32 Cong. 2 Sess. Sen. Exec. Docs. V No. 22)
pp. 70-179. Arnold B. Johnson *The Modern Light-House Service* (1889). G. R. Put-
nam *Lighthouses and Lightships* (1917) says that there were only 59 in the entire
United States (Atlantic, Gulf and Lakes) in 1820. Francis F. Wayland *Andrew Stevenson, Democrat and Diplomat* (1949).

ELLIOTT-PERRY CONTROVERSY: Edward Channing includes a bibliography in his
History of the U. S. IV (1917) 521-22; another is in Charles J. Dutton *Oliver H. Perry*
(1935). Perry's letter of 13 March 1839 to Cooper, printed in Cooper ed. *Correspondence of James Fenimore Cooper* (1922) II 386-87; his letter of 18 May and other
correspondence, in Cooper mss., Yale. Elliott said his last word in *Address . . . to his
Early Companions* (1843).

XII: *SOMERS* MUTINY

CONTEMPORARY SOURCES: *Inquiry into the Somers Mutiny. Proceedings of the Court
of Inquiry, with a Full Account of the Execution of Spencer, Cromwell and Small*
(1843); *Proceedings of the Naval Court Martial in the Case of A. S. Mackenzie . . .
to which is added . . . Review by James Fenimore Cooper,* 342 pp. (1844). This includes (pp. 194-211) Mackenzie's Report to Secnav dated 19 Dec. 1842 and (pp. 228-
42) George Griffin *Case of the Somers' Mutiny. Defence of A. S. Mackenzie before
the Court Martial,* printed separately in 1843. Harrison Hayford *The Somers Mutiny
Affair* (1959) contains extracts from the above, and other important sources. Perry's
correspondence with Aaron Ward, Ward mss., Boston Pub. Library.

*Cruise of the Somers: Illustrative of the Despotism of the Quarter Deck; and the
Unmanly Conduct of Commander Mackenzie* (102 pp., 1844); Cooper's *Review of the
Proceedings of the Naval Court Martial* (81 pp. 1844); Cooper ed. *Correspondence*

of J. Fenimore Cooper (1922) II 487-88, 494-98, 519-20; Charles Sumner in *North Am. Rev.* LVII (1843) 195-241; Richard Henry Dana's three Letters (Boston *Atlas* 17 Jan., Boston *Courier* 18 Aug., *Semi-Weekly Courier* 21 Aug. 1843) partly reprinted in C. F. Adams *R. H. Dana I* (1891), where Craney's story will be found. Capt. William Sturgis's Letters, Boston *Courier* 4 and 18 Aug. 1843.

LATER DISCUSSIONS: Livingston Hunt "The Attempted Mutiny on the U. S. Brig *Somers*" USNI Vol. LI (1925) 2062-99; Hanson Baldwin *Sea Fights and Shipwrecks* (1955); Frederic F. Van de Water *The Captain Called It Mutiny* (1954). Admiral Nimitz's Pacific Fleet Letter of 13 Feb. 1945 in S. E. Morison *Liberation of the Philippines* pp. 84-86.

A myth about the affair is that Gansevoort told his cousin Herman Melville the "real truth" about it, which inspired *Billy Budd*. But Melville in his poem "Bridegroom Dick" calls Gansevoort "Tom Tight" because he refused to talk about the *Somers* case! And the character of Billy Budd is completely different from that of Spencer. Billy's case resembles that of Samuel Jackson who was hanged for mutiny in U.S.S. *St. Mary's* in 1847 (see Chap. XV); and Gansevoort, who witnessed that hanging, may well have told Melville about it.

XIII: AFRICA SQUADRON

Perry's ms. Letter Book, including letters to Slidell and McLane, Rodgers mss., HS Pa. His official letters are bound together as "Squadron Coast of Africa under Commo. M. C. Perry" in NA. Many of his letters are printed as 28 Cong. 1 Sess. Ho. Doc. No. 244 under title *Colonial Correspondence from Commodore M. C. Perry, May 4, 1844*. Horatio Bridge *Journal of an African Cruiser . . . on the West Coast of Africa*, Nathaniel Hawthorne ed. (N.Y. 1845, 2nd ed. 1853) gives a lively account of this cruise in which Bridge served as purser in U.S.S. *Saratoga. The African Repository*, organ of the American Colonization Society (file at NYPL) XX (Feb.-May 1844) 133-44, contains a sprightly Report, 28 Dec. 1843, to the A.C.S. by Governor Roberts of the palaver proceedings. Other important docs. are in President Tyler's Message of 20 Feb. 1845, communicating "Information . . . on the West Coast of Africa," 28 Cong. 2 Sess. Sen. Doc. 150.

Letter of O. H. Perry II to his sister, Rodgers mss., HS Pa. Griffis gives a summary of Perry's sanitary regulations, incorporated in a Perry report (now unfindable) which he made to the Department around 1840. Washington Irving's letter, Belmont mss. Correspondence about Madeira wine, DePeyster mss., NYHS. For the Catesby Jones and Gregory rows, Perry to Navy Commissioners 7 Sept. 1836, HS Pa., and Sec. Paulding to Perry 24 Sept. 1840, Tilton mss. Joel Abbot's Journal, owned by Mrs. Grace Abbot Fletcher of Bristol, R. I. The letter of the C.O. of H.M.S. *Iris* 22 May 1842, and Perry's order of 11 Feb. 1844 to Tattnall, in "Squadron Coast of Africa" Letters, NA. Andrew H. Foote *Africa and the American Flag* (1854). R. H. Nassau *The Gaboon and Corisco Mission* (1873).

XIV-XVIII: THE MEXICAN WAR

General

PRINTED SOURCES: Perry's and Sec. Mason's reports, including both Tabasco expeditions and Veracruz, 29 Cong. 2 Sess. Sen. Doc. I 377-678, 30 Cong. 1 Sess. Sen. Exec. Docs. I 945-1310, and 2 Sess. Ho. Exec. Docs. I 1165-70, 1204-37. Sec. Mason's *Reports and Despatches Exhibiting the Operations of the United States Naval Forces During the War with Mexico* which occupies pp. 1006-1275 of same volume, contains many letters from Perry and references to him.

Milo M. Quaife ed. *Diary of James K. Polk* (1900) has little on naval matters, but records his two interviews with Perry (II 392-93) and his excitement over young Rodgers. Valuable contemporary narratives, memoirs and biographies of naval officers containing letters are: Charles L. Lewis *Admiral Franklin Buchanan* (1929); John M. Ellicott *Life of John Ancrum Winslow* (1902); Raphael Semmes *Service Afloat and*

Ashore During the Mexican War (1851); William Harwar Parker *Recollections of a Naval Officer 1841-1865* (1883); Benjamin F. Sands *From Reefer to Rear Admiral* (1899); Charles C. Jones Jr. *Life and Services of Commodore Josiah Tattnall* (1878); Reverend Fitch W. Taylor *The Broad Pennant: a Cruise in the United States Flag Ship of the Gulf Squadron* (1848). For below decks: James D. Bruell *Sea Memories — Personal Experiences in the U.S.N. in Peace and War, by an Old Salt* (1886), unique copy in FDRL. The weekly *Niles' National Register* LXX-LXXI (1846-48) contains many letters and reports of the war.

Lieutenant Henry Walke's paintings of naval events in the war, from his own observations as exec. of *Vesuvius*, were lithographed and reproduced as *A Naval Portfolio;* set in FDRL.

MANUSCRIPT SOURCES: Perry's instructions from Secnav in "Confidential Letters," NA. His letters, with many enclosures, are bound in three volumes called "Home Squadron Letters, Commo. Perry's Cruise" (followed by inclusive dates), also NA. His letters to Jane, Isabella, and John Hone, Belmont, Tilton and Phelps mss. Letter to Dr. Butler in NAM. Polk's note to Mason 26 Feb. 1847 to bring Perry to the White House, Tilton mss. Perry's correspondence with James Watson Webb, Yale. Commo. Conner's mss. were sold at auction by Stan V. Henkels in 1914 and calendared in his catalogues 1113 and 1120. Four large lots are now in public institutions: FDRL, NYPL, LC and NA. Philip S. P. Conner, the Commodore's son, published some of these as *The Home Squadron under Commodore Conner* (1896). George Bancroft mss., MHS, contain a few letters on early part of the war. Perry's Letter Book for 1848, Rodgers mss., HS Pa. Anthony Collection, NYPL, contains Perry's letters thanking foreign ships for rescuing men from *Somers*.

SECONDARY AUTHORITIES: K. Jack Bauer Ph.D. "A History of U. S. Naval Operations During the Mexican War," unpublished doctoral dissertation at Indiana University, is the most careful, detailed and well-documented work on this subject. Justin H. Smith *The War with Mexico* (1919) II 188-209, 438-49; Bennett *Steam Navy*. Best Mexican history of the naval war is in J. M. Roa Barcena *Recuerdos de la Invasión Norte Americana* (3 vols., 1883).

Individual Operations and Incidents

ALVARADO: C. F. Goodrich "Alvarado Hunter," USNI XLIV (1918) 495-514; Parker *Recollections* pp. 103-05; docs. of court-martial in Taylor *Broad Pennant* 381-92; 30 Cong. 2 Sess. Ho. Exec. Docs. I 1190, 1200-02; more details in "Com. Perry's Cruise March-July 1847," f. 38, NA; Perry's Letter Book of 1840-45, and correspondence in Webb mss., Yale.

COMMAND QUESTION: Cdr. Franklin Buchanan's letter of 9 Feb. 1849 on Bancroft offering Perry Gulf Squadron command in Sept. 1845, NAM. Letters in Conner mss., FDRL, NYPL, and Conner's Letter Book E-21, NA. Bancroft's letter of 12 Aug. 1846 to Perry in NA, "Officers Ships of War No. 39" p. 431. Upshur's account of Perry's assuming command in Griffis pp. 222-23.

TABASCO: Perry's Report (see Sources above), and letters in "Perry Cruise March-July 1847," NA. Letter to Secnav 28 July 1847 Buchanan mss., HS Pa.; Conner's orders of 16 Oct. 1845, Letter Book E-21 IV, NA; Perry's reports to Conner and Mason, Conner mss. NYPL, and "Com. Conner's Cruise 1846-47" f. 66, NA. Manuel Mestre Ghigliazza *Invasión Norteamericana en Tabasco 1846-1847* (Mexico: 1848), a valuable collection of contemporary documents. Taylor, Ellicott, Buchanan and Semmes biographies, as above. For underwater obstacles, *Niles Register* LXXII (1847) 322 and ms. letters of Mason to bureaus, I 379-416, NA. A newspaper published by the army at Veracruz, *The Sun of Anahuac* I No. 14 (2 July 1847), copy in Phelps mss., has a long account of Second Tabasco by "a well informed gentleman" who was present, and the order of battle. Perry's letter to Gen. Pierce in Amer. Antiq. Soc., Worcester. The chart here reproduced was the work of Lt. B. F. Sands, exec. of U.S.S. *Washington*. See his *From Reefer to Rear Admiral* pp. 185-86.

TUXPAN: Semmes describes this operation in detail, quotes Perry's official report of 24 April to Mason, also printed in Taylor p. 393 and 30 Cong. 2 Sess. Ho. Exec. Docs.

I 1192-96. Order of battle in "Com. Perry's Cruise March-July 1847" f. 3, NA. Conner mss. in FDRL; letters of Buchanan and Tattnall in their biographies. "Com. Perry's Cruise March-July 1847," NA.

YELLOW FEVER: Rear Adm. Lucius W. Johnson USN "Yellow Jack, Master of Strategy," USNI LXXVI (1950) 1077; Perry's letters to John Hone, 25 and 29 July 1847, Phelps mss. Perry to Secnav 30 Sept. 1847, Home Squadron Letters, NA. Perry to Webb, 16 Aug. 1847, Yale.

Teviot AFFAIR: Farragut to William Loyall 19 Sept. and 16 Dec. 1847, HEHL; Loyal Farragut *Life of Farragut* pp. 159-64; C. L. Lewis *Farragut* p. 247. Official correspondence in "Commo. Perry Cruise July-Dec. 1847," NA, and 30 Cong. 1 Sess. Ho. Exec. Docs. VII 787-98. *Messages of the President of the United States on the Subject of the Mexican War* (1848) pp. 788-98.

VERACRUZ: Manuel B. Trens *Historia de Veracruz* (Mexico: 1950) IV Part 2 ch. viii, and Juan Zilli *Historia Sucinta de Veracruz* (Tacubaya 1962). K. Jack Bauer "The Veracruz Expedition of 1847," *Military Affairs* XX (1956) 162-69. "Capture of Vera Cruz, by an Eye Witness," *The Knickerbocker* XXX 1-8 (July 1847); Lt. William G. Temple "Memoir of the Landing of the U. S. Troops at Vera Cruz" in P. S. P. Conner *Home Squadron.* Perry on the naval battery in letter of 25 March, "Commo. Perry Cruise March-July 1847," NA. His general order of 29 March, 29 Cong. 1 Sess. Ho. Exec. Docs. I 1185, 1189. Casualties in Justin H. Smith II 33, 341, Trens IV 429, and dispatches from British officers in PRO, London.

YUCATÁN: Bancroft to John L. Stephens 20 May 1846, Bancroft mss. MHS. Conner's Letter Book E-21 IV and V, NA. Perry's orders to Sands and Parker, 21 Dec. 1846, in Conner mss., NYPL; his report of 27 Dec. 1846 to Conner, 30 Cong. 2 Sess. Ho. Exec. Docs. I 1176-77. Arthur Winslow *Francis Winslow, his Forbears* (1935) for blockade of Carmen. Frederick Merk *Manifest Destiny and Mission in American History* (1963), and *Monroe Doctrine and American Expansionism* (1966). Francis J. Manno "Yucatán en la Guerra entre México y Estados Unidos," *Revista de la Universidad de Yucatán* V (1963) 50-72; Mary W. Williams "Secessionist Diplomacy of Yucatán," *Hisp. Am. Hist. Rev.* IX (1929) 132-43; Dexter Perkins *Hands Off, a History of the Monroe Doctrine* (1941) chap. iii. Martinez ed. Justo Sierra O'Reilly *Diario de Nuestro Viaje a los Estados Unidos* (1938), and M. R. Gomez ed. Sierra's *Segundo Libro del Diario* (1949). Perry's Manifest Destiny letter, of which the original is in "Perry's Cruise March-July 1847" f. 35, NA, is printed in Merk *Manifest Destiny* p. 141; contemporary copy in HEHL. Benj. F. Sands *From Reefer to Rear Admiral* (1899). Semmes *Service Afloat* prints the Carmen appeal.

FLAGSHIP'S BOILERS: Perry to Conner, 11 Nov. and 14 Dec. 1846, with engineers' reports, Conner mss. NYPL. The three "Commo. Perry Cruise" books in NA contain many interesting letters from his subordinates. Perry's reproof by Mason, NA, "Confidential Letters 1843-49" p. 358.

PERRY'S COLLECTING: Redfield mss., Yale; Letter to unknown addressee of 25 July 1848, Morgan Lib., N.Y.; Lt. W. M. Bagley to Perry 22 Feb. 1848, NYHS; Griffis p. 259.

XIX: SHORE DUTIES 1848-1852

FAMILY LIFE AND THE MOORINGS: Letters and documents in Belmont and Phelps mss. "Freedom of the City" in NYHS. Printed sheet containing Perry's testimonials to Buchanan and Pinkney, Belmont mss. Perry's letter to Duer of 20 Apr. 1850 on Hunter's blackguardism, Hitzrot mss. Mrs. John K. Van Rensselaer *The Social Ladder* (1924) pp. 172, 230; Mary E. Wilson Sherwood *Epistle to Posterity* (1897).

STEAMSHIPS: Perry's Letter Book for this period, Yale, contains many letters about the new ships. The enabling act of 3 March 1847, *Statutes at Large* IX 187. Perry's reports to Secnav and attached documents are scattered through 31 Cong. 1 Sess. Sen. Report No. 202, and 32 Cong. 1 Sess. Ho. Exec. Docs. IX No. 91. Perry to Secretary Preston 14 June 1849, NA "Captains' Letters Jan.-June 1849," other reports by Perry are indexed in same volume. Mason to Perry 20 Nov. 1848 in NA, "Officers Ships of

War No. 42" p. 296. The Collins contract, Charles B. Stuart *Naval and Mail Steamers of the U.S.* (1853) pp. 199-208. Perry's letter on Safety at Sea, *De Bow's Review* XVIII (1855) pp. 199-208. Alexander Crosby Brown *Women and Children Last: The Loss of the Steamship Arctic* (1961), best history of the Collins Line. Legislative battles in David B. Tyler *Steam Conquers the Atlantic* (1939).

XX *and* XXI: JAPAN EXPEDITION, BACKGROUND AND PREPARATION

JAPANESE HISTORY AND EARLY WESTERN CONTACTS: Principal secondary works: Sir George B. Sansom *The Western World and Japan* (1950) and *A History of Japan 1615-1861* (1963); Foster Rhea Dulles *Yankees and Samurai* (1965); I. Nitobe *Intercourse Between the United States and Japan* (1891). C. O. Paullin "Early Voyages of American Naval Vessels to the Orient," USNI XXXVI (1910) 429-63, 707-34; E. K. Haviland "Early Steam Navigation to China," *American Neptune* XXVI (1966) 5-32, 109-33. Charles W. King *The Claims of Japan and Malaysia upon Christendom* (1839). Aaron Haight Palmer's printed letters and petitions reprinted in his *Documents and Facts Illustrating the Origin of the Mission to Japan* (1857). Dulles and Sansom have best accounts of early Japanese knowledge of America. There are several biographies of Manjiro (also called Nakahama), best by Hisakazu Kaneko (1956).

PREPARATION FOR THE EXPEDITION: For the official *Narrative* and *Correspondence*, see next section. Perry's letters to William Sinclair, NAM. His Letter Book of 1849-51 and letters to James W. Webb, Yale. His letter to Joel Abbot, Fletcher mss., Bristol, R.I. His correspondence with Delano, owned by Mr. J. Delano Hitch, Jr. Perry's Instructions, Nov. 1852 and Feb. 1853, in State Dept. mss., NA, "Official Missions 1852-86." The first is in the form of a letter from State to Navy Department printed in 33 Cong. 2 Sess. Sen. Exec. Doc. No. 34 pp. 4-9.

President Fillmore's letter to the Emperor, F. H. Severance ed. *Millard Fillmore Papers* I 395-96; Letter of Credence in same and official *Narrative* I 259. Original presidential order to affix Great Seal in NAM, Annapolis.

Complete list of vessels and officers in official *Narrative* II 410-14. For trip to New Bedford, *Whalemen's Shipping List and Merchants' Transcript* in Old Dartmouth Historical Society, New Bedford. Perry's letter from Funchal about Okinawa in *Narrative* I 85. Perry's letters to Cdrs. F. Buchanan and J. R. Sands in Rutgers Univ. Library.

DOWN EAST INTERLUDE: Lorenzo Sabine "Report on the Principal Fisheries of the American Seas," 1852, 32 Cong. 2 Sess. Sen. Exec. Docs. V 435-46. President's message of 3 Aug. 1852 transmitting documents, *ibid.* X No. 100. *Fillmore Papers* I, Daniel Webster *Writings* (1903) XIV. Perry's report to Secnav, 26 Aug. 1852, in NA "Consular Letters St. John, N.B. 1851-1858." Official log of *Mississippi* in NA. Archbishop Hughes's letter to Perry in Tilton mss.; Perry's letter to Jane, Belmont mss.

XXII-XXVIII: THE JAPAN EXPEDITION

AMERICAN SOURCES (PRINTED): The official *Correspondence Relative to the Naval Expedition to Japan*, printed as 33 Cong. 2 Sess. Sen. Exec. Doc. 34, was reprinted separately with title on spine JAPAN/PERRY (1855).

What I refer to as the official *Narrative* is the following: *Narrative of the Expedition of an American Squadron to the China Seas and Japan, performed in the years 1852, 1853, and 1854, under the Command of Commodore M. C. Perry, United States Navy, by Order of the Government of the United States. Compiled from the Original Notes and Journals of Commodore Perry and his Officers, at his request, and under his supervision, by Francis L. Hawks, D.D., L.L.D.* Published by Order of the Congress of the United States. 3 vols. 4to. Washington: Beverley Tucker, Senate Printer, 1856. (Vols. II and III actually appeared in 1857-58). Lavishly illustrated with lithographs and woodcuts. The one-volume trade edition, published by D. Appleton Co. (1856) carries the same title, with few illustrations. Abridgments: Sidney Wallach ed.

Narrative of the Expedition, with foreword by Rear Adm. John B. Heffernan (1954); Robert Tomes *The Americans in Japan* (1857), and an anonymous *Japan Opened* (London: Religious Tract Soc. 1858).

Contemporary works by participants: J. W. Spalding (captain's clerk in *Mississippi*) *The Japan Expedition: Japan and Around the World* (1855) and Bayard Taylor *A Visit to India, China and Japan* (1855, 1872) record incidents not in the official *Narrative*. Journals and diaries which (despite Perry's orders to the contrary) were not available to Hawks, have appeared from time to time. The most informative are S. Wells Williams "Journal of the Perry Expedition to Japan," Asiatic Society of Japan *Transactions* XXXVII (1910); Boleslaw Szczesniak ed. *The Opening of Japan, a Diary of Discovery in the Far East*, being the diary of Lt. George Henry Preble of *Macedonian* (1962) from the ms. in MHS (carelessly edited and not including illustrations); and Dr. Sakanishi (Shio) ed. *A Private Journal of John Glendy Sproston*, midshipman in *Macedonian* (1940). Dr. Bettelheim's Diary appeared as "Commodore Perry at Okinawa. From the Unpublished Diary of a British Missionary," W. L. Schwartz ed., *Am. Hist. Rev.* LI (1946) 262-76. Also Henry F. Graff ed. *Bluejackets with Perry in Japan* (1952), the diaries of Master's Mate J. R. C. Lewis of *Macedonian* and cabin boy W. B. Allen of *Vandalia;* Allan B. Cole ed. *With Perry in Japan: The Diary of Edward Yorke McCauley*, acting master's mate in *Powhatan* (1942); same ed., *A Scientist with Perry in Japan: The Journal of Dr. James Morrow* (1947); Hildegarde B. Forbes ed. *Correspondence of Dr. Charles H. Wheelwright* (1958), assistant surgeon of *Powhatan;* John S. Sewall *Logbook of the Captain's Clerk* (1905). Best newspaper coverage was by Bayard Taylor in letters to the New York *Tribune*. These, with other Taylor letters, were reprinted in the New Bedford *Whalemen's Shipping List*, 1853-54.

AMERICAN SOURCES (MANUSCRIPT): Perry's own Journals, one with colored illustrations of scenes, fruits and flowers, Belmont mss; continuation in two parts through 1854, in NA, which also has in Record Group No. 45 Area 90, Box 1853-57, Perry's official report and letters of other members of Expedition. Contemporary copies of several journals, such as Silas Bent's, Taylor's, and Oliver H. Perry II's, are privately owned. Logs of Perry's flagships and other vessels of the Squadron in NA; that of *Macedonian* in NYPL. *Lexington*'s in NA has the data about mutiny in *Susquehanna*.

Twelve letters of Perry to his wife, two to daughter Isabella, nine to the Belmonts and two from Bayard Taylor to Perry, Belmont mss. That of 15 May 1853, Norfolk museum. Letters of Perry to William Sinclair, and Address of Canton Merchants to Perry, NAM. His correspondence with King of Siam, Maritime Museum, Mystic. His letters to J. Watson Webb and S. Wells Williams, Yale. His letter of 5 Sept. 1853 on Japanese gifts to President Pierce, HEHL. Savory's original deed to land at Chichi Jima, Phelps mss. Joel Abbot mss., owned by Mrs. Grace A. Fletcher, Bristol, R. I. Letters of Asst. Engineer William H. Rutherford to his sweetheart, LC; diary of marine drummer Philip C. Van Buskirk, Univ. of Wash. Lib., Seattle; diary of Mid. R. D. Minor, Va. Hist. Soc., Richmond.

HONG KONG: Files of *The China Mail* and *The Friend of China* and *Hongkong Gazette* in Univ. of Hong Kong Library. Naval dispatches from Hong Kong and Shanghai in PRO London Admiralty 5618; Sir George Bonham's dispatches in same, C.O. 129/43-46.

JAPANESE SOURCES (PRINTED): W. G. Beasley ed. and tr. *Selected Documents on Japanese Foreign Policy 1853-1868* (1955) with useful glossary, biographical notes and authoritative text of Treaty of Kanagawa. "Diary of an Official of the Bakufu," Asiatic Society of Japan *Transactions* 2nd ser. VII (1930) 98-119; notes from Sakamaki (Shunzo) *Japan and the U. S. 1790-1853* in same series XVIII (1939). Kojima (Matajiro) *Commodore Perry's Expedition to Hakodate May 1854, a Private Account with Illustrations* (Hakodate 1953); Sir Ernest Satow tr. of Baba (Bun'ei) *Genji yume monogatari* or *Japan 1853-1864* (Tokyo 1905), and Kinsé Shiriaku *A Recent History of Japan 1853-1869* (Tokyo 1906), both contemporary histories; Oliver Statler *The Black Ship Scroll* (1964) reproduces colored illustrations from scrolls with texts tr. by

Richard Lane; Joseph H. Neesima *My Younger Days* (Doshisha Univ. Kyoto). *Mikan Yokohama Kaiko Shiryo* (*Historical Materials on the Opening of Yokohama Harbor*) 1960. *Izu Shimoda*, organ of the Shimoda Historical Society, beginning 1964.

JAPANESE SOURCES (MANUSCRIPT): (1) The National Archives, which, pending the erection of an archives building, are in Shiryo Hensanjo, the Historiographical Institute of the University of Tokyo (brief inventory in pamphlet dated March 1964). (2) The Nabeshima Archives in Saga Prefecture Library, Kyushu. Through the kindness of Mr. Edgar Noël, Director of U. S. Cultural Center at Fukuoka, translations of these by Prof. Muto (Kiyoshi) of Univ. of Kyushu have been sent to me. They include Memo. by Kayama (Eizaemon) on his contacts with Perry in 1853, Kobayashi (Tetsujiro) "Assorted News on the Visit of Foreign Ships," Takeda (Ayasaburo) "Notes on the Barbarian Vessels" by a student of military science; Ito (Genboku) "A Doctor's Memorandum," diary of a court physician; and "Reception of the Embassy of America" — a list and description of principal officers on both sides and of the gifts. Other documents in this series have been printed in *Bakumatsu Gaiko Kankei Bunsho* (Docs. on Foreign Relations at close of Shogunate 1853-68) I (1910), and IV, for the 1854 visit, pub. by Univ. of Tokyo. (3) Many documents on the 1854 negotiation are in the prefectural and municipal libraries of Yokohama, the Kanagawa Library, and the Hakodate City Library.

GRAPHIC SOURCES (WESTERN): The official *Narrative* is richly illustrated, and William Heine's folio volume *Graphic Scenes of the Japan Expedition* (1856) contains nine scenes at Macao, Whampoa, Canton, Okinawa, Yokohama, and four at Shimoda.

The big 25- by 36-inch lithographs by Sarony, after paintings by Heine and Brown, are to be found mostly in public collections such as the Mystic Marine Museum, Phila. Maritime Museum, and the L.C. No one has a complete set, which comprises: *Return of Commodore Perry, Officers and Men of the Squadron from an Official Visit to the Prince Regent at Shui*, June 6th 1853; *Passing the Rubicon. Lieut. S. Bent in Mississippi's First Cutter forcing his way through a Fleet of Japanese boats while surveying the Bay of Yedo, Japan*, July 11th 1853; *First Landing of Americans in Japan, under Commodore M. C. Perry at Gore-Hama* July 14th 1853; *Landing of Commodore Perry, officers and men of the Squadron to Meet the Imperial Commissioners at Yoku-Hama, Japan*, March 8th 1854; *Landing of Commodore Perry, Officers and Men of the Squadron, to meet the Imperial Commissioners at Simoda*, June 8th 1854; *Exercise of Troops in Temple Grounds, Simoda, Japan, in presence of the Imperial Commissioners*, June 8th 1854. *Commodore Perry in Japan*, by editors of *American Heritage* (1963) draws on above and Japanese sources too.

GRAPHIC SOURCES (JAPANESE): Japanese scrolls (*makimono*) depicting Perry and his men, ships, etc. (see Chap. XXVIII) are in Prints Division of LC, by Hibata (Osuke) and Takagawa (Bunsen); Honolulu Academy of Art; Japan Society San Francisco; Norfolk Museum; Print Dept. NYPL; Stillman collection H.C.L. Dawson's Book Shop, Los Angeles, illustrates several in his catalogues Nos. 343, 354 and 363, and most of these are now in private hands. A second form of illustration was the woodblock; and a third, the *kawaraban* or news sheet by which illustrations, ballads and caricatures of the Americans were circulated. The Smithsonian Inst., Washington, has a representative lot of these. In Japan itself, graphic materials are very numerous. The Shiryo Hensanjo, Univ. of Tokyo, has a rich collection of all three, including copies of material in private hands, since destroyed. So have the Mori Museum at the Shirahama Hotel, Shimoda, and the Hakodate City Library. Among the private collections are those of Mr. Iwasaki (Yoshio) at Yokosuka, Mr. Yoshida (Shotaro) at Kashiwazaki (where a centennial catalogue was published, 1953); Mr. Tamba (Tsuneo) of Yokohama, who has published two catalogues of his collection in color; Mr. Carl H. Boehringer and Mr. Paul C. Blum, both of Tokyo.

Contemporary illustrated books in Japanese: *Ingarudo Ochiba Kusa* (*Foreign Episodes*), copy in Hakodate City Lib.; *Ikoku Ochiba Kago* (*Basket of Fallen Leaves from Foreign Lands*), and others in Boehringer collection; *Hinawa Sen No Za* (1853), copy in Mori Museum, Shimoda. Later printed books: *Yokohama Shiryo* (*Historical*

Materials Relating to Yokohama), collection, 1928; *Shinsei Nippon Gaiko Hyakunen-shi (Newly Compiled One-Hundred-Year History of Japanese Diplomacy)*, supervised by Foreign Office, Tokyo 1952), lavishly illustrated; *Hyaku Nen Shi* (History of 100 years, 1850-1863), a serial publication: Vol. I (1956) is devoted to the Perry-Harris period; S. Yamada *Commodore Perry Centennial Issue "Okinawa" 1853-1953* (Univ. of Ryukyus, Shuri, 1953), a very beautiful publication.

SECONDARY AUTHORITIES (WESTERN): For background, and the power struggle within Japan, Sir George B. Sansom *The Western World and Japan* (1950) and Albert M. Craig *Choshu in the Meiji Restoration* (1961). Foster Rhea Dulles *Yankees and Samurai, America's Role in the Emergence of Modern Japan: 1791-1900* (1965) places Perry in the continuum of Japanese-American relations. Arthur C. Walworth *Black Ships Off Japan* (1946) is a good popular account of the Expedition.

Monographs covering parts of the Expedition: Lionel B. Cholmondeley *The History of the Bonin Islands 1827-1876* (1915); Eldon Griffin *Clippers and Consuls. American Consular and Commercial Relations with Eastern Asia 1845-1860* (1938); A. B. Cole ed. *Yankee Surveyors in the Shogun's Seas* (1947). For Okinawa: Basil Hall *Voyage to Loo Choo* (Edinburgh 1826); Earl R. Bull *Okinawa or Ryukyu: the Floating Dragon* (1958), and "Life of B. J. Bettelheim" in *The Japan Evangelist* (Feb.-May 1925); S. Hokama *Commodore Perry's Visit to Okinawa* (Tokyo 1962), extracts from the official *Narrative* with Japanese trans. and notes. For Admiral Putiatin's efforts, G. A. Lensen *Russia's Japan Expedition of 1852-1855* (1955). Von Siebold's pamphlet which aroused Perry's ire is *Urkundliche Darstellung der Bestrebungen von Niederland und Russland zur Eröffnung Japan's für die Schifffahrt und den Seehandel aller Nationen* (Bonn 1854).

CURRENCY AND EXCHANGE: Perry's letters to Jane, Belmont mss.; Preble *Diary* p. 51; files of *China Mail* of Hong Kong; pamphlet "A Brief History of Money in Japan," issued by the Bank of Japan, and that bank's numismatic museum; New York Spectator 4 Sept. 1852 quoting U.S.-Mex. exchange; Report of U. S. Consul, Shanghai, 1855 in 34 Cong. 1 Sess. Ho. Exec. Doc. No. 2 pp. 166ff, and part 3 pp. 376-78; Report of U. S. Consul, Hong Kong, 14 Apr. 1855, NA, "Consular Despatches Hong Kong" II No. 7; Admiral Pellew to Admiralty, 26 Sept. 1853, PRO Admiralty 5618, and Sir George Bonham to Colonial Office 10 March 1853 in same, C.O. 129/45.

SECONDARY AUTHORITIES (JAPANESE): The best of the many that Captain Ohmae has translated and abstracted for me are Konishi (Shiro) *Nippon no rekishi (A History of Japan)* Tokyo 1966, of which Vol. XIX covers Perry and Harris in some detail; Sasama (Yoshihiko) *Edo Bakufu yakushoku shusei (Organization of the Edo Bakufu)* Tokyo 1965; *Taiheiyo nisen roppyaku nen shi (2600-Year History of the Pacific Ocean)* pub. by Kaigun Yushukai (1940); Matsudaira (Shungaku) *Gokohaku myoso hiki (Secret Story of American Ships at Uraga)* in his *Works* II (1941). *Kurobune Dangi (Black Ship Essays)*, Shimoda 1944, contains reprints from the magazine published by Mr. Mori at Shimoda, 1921-1944. Motoki (Seigo) *Hoppo torai*, for the northern visit, and Vols. XXX, XXXI and XXXII of Tokutomi (Soho) *History of the Japanese Nation* — the monumental hundred-volume work, a ten-volume edition of which is in course of publication.

XXIX: HOME PORT 1854-1858

Caroline (Perry) Belmont's Diary at The Hague, owned by Mrs. Frank L. Lineberry of Hingham, Mass.; Perry's letters to and from J. Watson Webb and S. Wells Williams, Yale. Hawthorne's diary in Randall Stewart ed. *The English Notebooks* (1962) p. 98; Perry's "mention" for the presidency, Abbot mss. Book No. 13, Personal Letters p. 93. N. Y. Chamber of Commerce presentation of plate, NYHS *Quart. Bulletin* XX (Jan. 1936) 80-83; Perry's speech at Newport and August Belmont's letters, Belmont mss. DePeyster visiting list, DePeyster mss., NYHS. Two Perry articles are in *Narrative* II 171-87; the third was published as *A Paper by Commodore M. C. Perry, U.S.N., Read Before the American Geographical and Statistical Society, at a Meeting held March 6th, 1856.*

The Morrow-Perry-Gray controversy over botany may be pieced together from the Asa Gray mss. in the Arnold Arboretum-Gray Herbarium Library HCL, Williams mss. Yale, and Morrow mss., Univ. of So. Carolina Library, Columbia. A. Hunter Dupree "Science vs. the Military, Dr. James Morrow and the Perry Expedition," *Pacific Hist. Rev.* XXII (1953) 29-37 used these sources but reaches conclusions opposite to mine. A partial list of the plants he brought home is in A. B. Cole ed. *A Scientist with Perry*. John B. Blake's report on the greenhouses, 11 Oct. 1856, 34 Cong. 3 Sess. Ho. Exec. Docs. No. 1. The congressional debate on Morrow's bonus, Washington *Globe* 17 Feb. 1857, supplement. Perry's letter about bamboo to Francis Lieber, 12 March 1856, HEHL. Morrow's and Perry's letters to Spencer F. Baird and Joseph Henry, Smithsonian Inst. mss. "Incoming Correspondence — U. S. Explorations and Government Reports 1852-60." Perry's correspondence with Brevoort about fishes, and the complete collection of his fish paintings, in a bound volume in Ms. Div. NYPL; some letters from Cassin on the birds are included. Reports and papers on Morrow's, Heine's, Brown's and Portman's bonuses are in Treasurer's accounts 35 Cong. 1 Sess., and Report of 1st Auditor T. L. Smith 14 Oct. 1857, NA, Senate Papers NA, 34A-H7, 35A-H10, 36A-B 1&2, 36A-H10, and 40A-H3.

Mr. H. B. Fant and Mr. Mark G. Eckhoff of the NA, who have been my guides through the maze of congressional documents, deduced the number of sets of the *Narrative* printed, and their cost, from successive Reports of the Superintendent of Public Printing in 34 and 35 Cong. papers.

Obituaries and accounts of Perry's funeral: New York *Morning Courier* 5 and 8 March, *Herald* 5 and 7 March, *Frank Leslie's Illustrated* and *Harper's Weekly* 13 March 1858. Public belief in the location of Perry's final resting place was upset by his 1935 biographer E. M. Barrows (*The Great Commodore* p. 354n) declaring that no permit for removal of body from N.Y. to Newport was ever issued, so it must still be in the Slidell vault. This is false. An official copy of the permit to remove the bodies of Matthew C. and Anna Perry, dated 21 March 1866, authenticated by Mayor V. R. Impellitteri in 1953, is in the Newport Historical Society; and in 1954 August Belmont III inspected the Slidell vault and verified the fact that the remains of the Commodore and his daughter were not there.

Index